The American Economic History Reader

This is an extremely useful reader in American economic history. The well-picked selections include many contemporary documents and important recent journal articles, as well as excellent introductory material. Particularly useful is that about one-half of the volume is devoted to twentieth-century monetary and fiscal issues.

Stanley L. Engerman, editor of *Finance, Intermediaries,*
and Economic Development

Spanning three centuries, this fine collection of primary and secondary writings spurns the trendy and ephemeral in favor of documents and essays of enduring value that engage the major issues and actors. An excellent sourcebook for courses in American economic history and historiography."

David B. Sicilia, co-author of *Constructing Corporate America:*
History, Politics, Culture

The American economy has developed through war, slavery, industrialization, and globalization. *The American Economic History Reader* explores the economy's evolution from colonial times to the post-industrial state of the twenty-first century.

Through a judicious selection of primary documents and essays, supplemented by detailed chapter introductions, the major issues in American economic history and the frequently lively scholarly debate they provoked are brought to life by editors John W. Malsberger and James N. Marshall. They succeed in blending the most important economic ideas and theories from each era with the unfolding history of America's economic development. From colonial farming to slave labor in the antebellum south, and from the New Deal to Clintonomics and beyond, *The American Economic History Reader* will prove invaluable for those interested in the economic development of the United States and its role in shaping a nation.

John W. Malsberger is Professor of History at Muhlenberg College. He is the author of *From Obstruction to Moderation: The Transformation of Senate Conservatism, 1938–1945.*

James N. Marshall is Professor of Economics at Muhlenberg College. He is the author of *William J. Fellner: A Bio-Bibliography.*

The American Economic History Reader

Documents and Readings

Edited by
John W. Malsberger
James N. Marshall

Routledge
Taylor & Francis Group

NEW YORK AND LONDON

First published 2009
by Routledge
270 Madison Ave, New York, NY 10016

Simultaneously published in the UK
by Routledge
2 Park Square, Milton Park, Abingdon, Oxon OX14 4RN

Routledge is an imprint of Taylor & Francis Group, an informa business

© 2009 Taylor & Francis

Typeset in Sabon by
HWA Text and Data Management Ltd, London

Printed and in the United States of America on acid-free paper by
Sheridan Books, Inc.

Library of Congress Cataloging-in-Publication Data
American economic history reader / editors, John W.
Malsberger and James N. Marshall.
    p. cm.
    Includes bibliographical references and index.
    1. United States—Economic conditions. 2. United States—
Economic policy. 3. Economics--United States--History.
I. Malsberger, John W. (John William) II. Marshall, James N.
HC103.A453 2008
330.973–dc22   2008005438

ISBN 10: 0-415-96266-8 (hbk)
ISBN 10: 0-415-96267-6 (pbk)

ISBN 13: 978-0-415-96266-7 (hbk)
ISBN 13: 978-0-415-96267-4 (pbk)

To our wives and daughters, we dedicate this book

Jill and Heidi

Helene and Kit

CONTENTS

CHAPTER 11   The Collapse of the Keynesian Consensus, 1969–1980   427

Documents

Essays

CHAPTER 12   Reaganomics   476

Documents

Essays

PREFACE

Many students might approach the study of American economic history with some trepidation. It is, of course, a hybrid of economics and history, two disciplines that unfortunately suffer sometimes from unfair public perceptions. Because of its reliance on abstract theories and mathematical formulae, economics is sometimes regarded as an arcane discipline with little practical application to the lives of average Americans. Similarly, history is often perceived as a dry, dull collection of names, dates, and events that have no relevance to today's life. President George H. W. Bush famously summarized this attitude when he dismissed a question in a 1989 press conference about the Senate's rejection of his nominee for Secretary of Defense with: "But look, that's history. We're moving forward with a new nominee." We hope that the readings in this volume will demonstrate that economic history is neither dull nor irrelevant, but is, rather, a dynamic discipline often marked by lively debate and disagreement.

This volume is divided into thirteen chapters that survey the development of the American economy from colonial times through the presidency of George W. Bush. Each chapter focuses on a major issue in American economic history and includes several primary source documents that allow readers to view the problem from the perspective of contemporaries. In addition, each chapter also contains two or more essays written by experts that provide different interpretations of that problem. In reading these essays we encourage students to take particular note of how economic historians have defined questions to be explored and the often unique ways they have developed to answer those questions. Note too, how interpretations have changed over time, how our understanding of American economic history is constantly evolving. This volume, then, is designed not to provide answers but to pose questions and thereby encourage readers to engage with the professional scholarly discourse to determine for themselves the most logical explanation of important issues in American economic history.

We hope that the readings in this volume will provide the basis for lively classroom discussion and encourage students to be active learners. We also hope that readers of this volume come away with a fuller and deeper appreciation of the economic history of the United States and for the lively state of the ongoing discourse among economic historians. But in the final analysis we also believe that students can profitably use the readings in this volume to hone their analytical thinking abilities. By carefully evaluating the interpretations of economic historians, weighing their use of evidence, exposing their implicit assumptions, testing the soundness of their logic, readers of this volume can develop skills that will last a lifetime.

ACKNOWLEDGMENTS

In preparing this volume we have benefited greatly from the kindness and assistance of many individuals. We are, of course, grateful to the authors and publishers that have granted us permission to reproduce portions of their works. They are individually acknowledged in the "Permissions and Citation Information" section of this volume. But here we would like to thank those individuals who provided indispensable assistance to the completion of this book. We are deeply grateful to Mrs. Catherine L. Ramella, faculty secretary for History & Economics, for her unstinting efforts to convert into Word files many of the readings in this volume. Without her timely help our job of editing the readings for this book would have been nearly impossible. We are also grateful to the staff of Muhlenberg College's Trexler Library who helped us to locate many of the readings that appear in this book. Finally, we are grateful to our colleagues, Dan and Carol Wilson. An award from the Wilson Book Fund, established by them at Muhlenberg, helped to defray the cost of the permissions.

CHAPTER 1

Mercantilism and the Colonial Economy

INTRODUCTION

The colonies established by western European nations in the New World in the 16th and 17th Centuries were part of a larger effort made by those nations to expand their wealth and power. Prior to colonization each of the western European nations was to a degree dependent on its neighbors as a source of the raw materials it could not produce for itself and as a market for the finished products its national economy could not absorb. This economic dependence was troublesome for it often led to an unfavorable balance of trade which drained a country's stock of gold and silver. It also created economic uncertainty because a shift in national alliances which was not at all uncommon in this era could cut off vital raw materials or markets. Colonies were thus seen as a means to economic independence for the mother country. With colonies providing raw materials and serving as markets for finished products, the mother country would be more apt to maintain a favorable balance of trade with its European rivals, thereby increasing its stock of gold and silver. Increased stocks of gold and silver, in turn, could be used to expand the mother country's army and navy. This was the essence of the mercantilistic system that guided the western European colonization of the New World.

Although Great Britain was a relative latecomer in the European colonization of the New World, it ultimately emerged as the dominant power in North America. This was due in no small part to the bountiful output of the colonial American economy. In the decades after Jamestown was established in 1607 the economies of the British colonies in North America developed rapidly. The southern colonies produced increasingly large crops of tobacco, rice, and indigo, all of which were in great demand on the European continent. The New England forests supplied the mother country with vast quantities of naval stores (resin, turpentine, and lumber), and its waters yielded plentiful harvests of fish that were shipped to British sugar colonies in the Caribbean. And the Middle Atlantic colonies produced ever larger amounts of grains and fruits.

To ensure that it reaped the full rewards of the colonies' rapid economic development Britain took a number of actions to integrate them more firmly into the mercantilistic system. Beginning in 1651 Parliament enacted a series of Navigation Acts which stipulated that all trade between England and the American colonies had to be carried in British ships whose crews were predominantly English, required all colonial imports to be routed through England, and established a list of "enumerated" goods that could only be shipped to England or her colonies. The list of "enumerated" goods was subsequently expanded by a series of acts adopted by Parliament beginning with the 1699 Hat Act which prohibited the exportation of hats manufactured in the colonies and culminating with the 1750 Iron Act which prevented the colonists from establishing new iron mills that manufactured finished products. Britain soon learned, however, that it was one thing to enact such regulations but it was quite another matter to enforce them.

The American colonists were from the start an enterprising lot. To them the New World represented the chance for a better life and most defined that better life in economic terms. Consequently, they soon came to chafe under the trade restrictions imposed by British mercantilism, seeing them as a barrier to economic opportunity. As a result, almost from the beginning Americans took advantage of their geographic isolation from the Mother Country to find ways to evade the Navigation Acts. For example, New England merchants opened up trade routes with Holland and France and textiles imported from both those countries were sold openly throughout the colonies. Similarly, although the colonies were required to ship all their tobacco to England, much of it never made it to the Mother Country.

British attempts to enforce the mercantilistic restrictions on American trade aroused the ire of the colonists. Initially, the Crown sent customs agents to the colonies to enforce the Navigation Acts but then, as now, tax collectors were not viewed kindly by the Americans. Subsequent efforts employed by the British to enforce the Navigation Acts included writs of assistance which gave sweeping authority to customs officials to search properties for contraband, and Admiralty Courts where those accused of violating the trade laws could be tried in the absence of a jury. In this way, then, when Americans began to protest such British measures as the Stamp Act and the Townsend Acts with cries of "no taxation without representation," the long British attempt to draw the colonies more completely into their mercantilistic system added powerful evidence to the colonists' growing perception that their rights as Englishmen were under assault.

Because the issues and rhetoric in the colonial resistance to mercantilism resonated throughout the protests and petitions that led to American independence historians initially argued that the British trade restrictions were a leading cause of the American Revolution. By impeding their economic opportunity, or as Jefferson styled it, "the pursuit of happiness," British mercantilism, they claimed, imposed a substantial burden on the colonial economy. Because they were required to export their goods to England or her colonies, British mercantilism denied colonists the opportunity to sell their wares in a competitive marketplace. Similarly, because Americans were prohibited from manufacturing a wide variety of products, mercantilism both stifled an individual's economic opportunity and raised his cost of living. And because the aim of the mercantilistic system was to enrich the mother country it ensured that the American economy remained a colonial, extractive economy during the 169 years it was part of the British Empire.

Some economic historians have pointed out, however, that the American colonies derived distinct economic benefits from British mercantilism. The British, for example, paid bounties on a variety of colonial products such as naval stores, rice, and indigo to encourage the production of adequate supplies to meet the mother country's demands. Enumerated colonial good imported into Britain were subject to lower duties than similar products originating outside of the empire, thereby giving a price advantage to American producers. The American economy was able to grow over the long colonial period, moreover, under the protection of the British military, providing another advantage.

The impact of British mercantilism on the colonial American economy thus challenges students of economic history. Did the costs and lost opportunities outweigh the benefits the Americans may have received from the British economic system? If mercantilism imposed economic burdens on the colonies, how great were those burdens? Were they sufficient to act as a cause of the American Revolution? In their analysis of the Americans' protests against mercantilism have economic historians always separated its economic impact from its legal/constitutional impact?

DOCUMENTS

The English civil war (1640–1649) which culminated in Oliver Cromwell's rule as Lord Protector (1653–1658) distracted British attention from the colonies in North America. By the time Charles II was restored to the throne in 1660 the American colonies had grown substantially and the new monarch was determined to revive and expand mercantilistic control of them. The first two documents are examples of Charles' efforts. Document 1–1 is the Navigation Act of 1660 which expanded the trade regulations originally adopted by Parliament in 1651. In Document 1–2, the charter granted to the proprietors of the Carolina colony in 1663, King Charles specified thoroughly how the colony was to be used to enrich the empire.

As long as France remained an active colonizer of North America British mercantilistic regulations were enforced loosely for fear that a vigorous enforcement of them would alienate the loyalties of the Americans. But when Britain triumphed over France in the Seven Years' War the period of salutary neglect ended. Beginning in 1763 Parliament enacted a series of laws to compel the colonies to contribute to the defense of the Empire, actions which ultimately led to the American Revolution. In Document 1–3 Thomas Whately, a member of the Board of Trade that oversaw the mercantilistic system, defended the recently adopted Stamp Act.

The final document is an excerpt from Adam Smith's classic 1776 work, *The Wealth of Nations*. Smith was especially critical of the extensive government regulation of the economy occasioned by the mercantilistic system. In this excerpt Smith maintained that although British mercantilism was more liberal than the trade policies of other European powers, it nonetheless harmed the economy of both the colonies and the mother country.

1–1. NAVIGATION ACT OF 1660

AN ACT for the Encourageing and Increasing of Shipping and Navigation.

I. For the increase of Shiping and incouragement of the Navigation of this Nation, wherin under the good providence and protection of God the Wealth Safety and Strength of this Kingdome is soe much concerned Bee it Enacted by the King's most excellent majesty, and by the lords and commons in this present parliament assembled, and by the authority thereof, That from and after the first day of December 1660, and from thence forward noe Goods or Commodities whatsoever shall be Imported into or Exported out of any Lands Islelands Plantations or Territories to his Majesty belonging or in his possession or which may hereafter belong unto or be in the possession of His Majesty His Heires and Successors in Asia Africa or America in any other Ship or Ships Vessell or Vessells whatsoever but in such Ships or Vessells as doe truely and without fraude belong onely to the people of England or Ireland Dominion of Wales or Towne of Berwicke upon Tweede, or are of the built of, and belonging to any of the said Lands Islands Plantations or Territories as the Proprietors and right Owners therof and wherof the Master and three fourthes of the Marriners at least are English under the penalty of the Forfeiture and Losse of all the goods and commodities which shall be imported into or exported out of any of the aforesaid places in any other ship or vessel....

II. And be it enacted, That no alien or person not born within the allegiance of our sovereign lord the King, his heirs and successors ... shall from and after the first day of February, 1661, exercise the trade of a merchant or factor in any of the said places; upon the pain of forfeiture and loss of all his goods and chattels....

III. And it is further Enacted, That noe Goods or Commodityes whatsoever of the growth production or manufacture of Africa Asia or America or of any part thereof... be Imported into England Ireland or Wales Islands of Guernsey or Jersey or Towne of Berwicke upon Tweede in any other Ship or Ships Vessell or Vessels whatsoever, but in such as doe truely and without fraude belong onely to the people of England or Ireland, Dominion of Wales or Towne of Berwicke upon Tweede or of the Lands Islands Plantations or Territories in Asia Africa or America to his Majesty belonging as the proprietors and right owners therof, and wherof the Master and three fourthes at least of the Mariners are English under the penalty of the forfeiture of all such Goods and Commodityes, and of the Ship or Vessell in which they here Imported with all her Guns Tackle Furniture Ammunition and Apparell....

IV. And it is further Enacted... that noe Goods or Commodityes that are of forraigne growth production or manufacture and which are to be brought into England Ireland Wales, the Islands of Guernsey & Jersey or Towne of Berwicke upon Tweede in English built shiping, or other shiping belonging to some of the aforesaid places, and navigated by English Mariners as abovesaid shall be shiped or brought from any other place or Places, Country or Countries but onely from those of their said Growth Production or Manufacture, or from those Ports where the said Goods and Commodityes can onely or are or usually have beene first shiped for transportation and from none other Places or Countryes under the penalty of the forfeiture of all such of the aforesaid Goods as shall be Imported from any other place next ensuing and expresly named in the said List shall enjoye the priviledge of a Ship belonging to England or Ireland although owned or manned by English (except such Ships only as shall be taken at Sea by Letters of Mark or Reprizal and Condemnation made in the Court of Admiralty as lawfull Prize) but all such Ships shall be deemed as Aliens Ships....

VIII. And it is further Enacted... That noe Goods or Commodityes of the Growth Production or Manufacture of Muscovy or of any the Countryes... to the Great Duke or Emporer of Muscovia or Russia belonging, As alsoe that noe sorts of Masts Timber or boards noe forraigne Salt Pitch Tar Rozin Hempe or Flax Raizins Figs Prunes Olive Oyles noe... Corne or Graine Sugar Pot-ashes Wines Vinegar or Spirits called Aqua-vite or Brandy Wine shall from and after... April 1, 1661... be imported into England Ireland Wales or Towne of Berwicke upon Tweede in any Ship or Ships Vessel or Vessels whatsoever but in such as doe truely and without fraude belong to the people therof or of some of them as the true Owners and proprietors therof, and wherof the Master and Three Fourths of the Mariners at least are English, and that noe Currants, nor Commodityes of the growth production or Manufacture of any the Countryes... to the Othoman or Turkish Empire belonging shall from and after... September 1, 1661... be imported into any the forementioned places in any Ship or Vessel, but which is of English built and navigated as aforesaid and in noe other, except onely such forraigne ships and vessels as are of the built of that Country or place of which the said Goods are the growth production or Manufacture respectively, or of such Port where the said Goods can onely be or most usually are first shiped for transportation, and wherof the Master and three Fourths of the Mariners at least are of the said Country... under the penalty and forfeiture of Ship and Goods....

XVIII. And it is further Enacted, That from and after the first day of April, 1661, noe Sugars Tobaccho Cotton-Wool Indicoes Ginger Fustick or other dyeing wood of the Growth Production or Manufacture of any English Plantations in America Asia or Africa shall be shiped carryed conveyed or transported from any of the said English Plantations to any Land Island Territory Dominion Port or place whatsoever other then to such English

Plantations as doe belong to His Majesty... or to the Kingdome of England or Ireland or Principallity of Wales or Towne of Berwicke upon Tweede there to be laid on shore under the penalty of the Forfeiture of the said Goods or the full value thereof, as alsoe of the Ship with all her Guns Tackle Apparel Ammunition and Furniture....

XIX. And be it further Enacted, That for every Ship or Vessel which from and after ... December 25, 1660... shall set saile out of, or from England Ireland Wales or Towne of Berwicke upon Tweede for any English Plantation in America Asia Africa sufficient bond shall be given with one surety to the cheife Officers of the Custome house, of such Port or place from whence the said Ship shall set saile.... That in case the said Ship or Vessel shall loade any of the said Commodityes at any of the said English Plantations, that the same Commodityes shall be by the said ship brought to some Port of England Ireland Wales, or to the Port or Towne of Berwicke upon Tweede and shall there unload and put on shore the same, the danger of the Seas onely excepted, And for all ships coming from any other Port or Place to any of the aforesaid plantations who by this Act are permited to trade there, that the Governour of such English plantation shall before the said Ship or Vessel be permited to loade on board any of the said Commodityes take Bond in manner and to the value aforesaid for each respective Ship or Vessel, That such Ship or Vessell shall carry all the aforesaid Goods that shall be laden on board in the said ship to some other of His Majestyes English Plantations, or to England Ireland Wales or Towne of Berwicke upon Tweede... under penalty of forfeiture of the vessel, &c.

1–2. CHARTER OF CAROLINA - MARCH 24, 1663

CHARLES the Second, by the grace of God, king of England, Scotland, France, and Ireland, Defender of the Faith, &c., To all to whom these present shall come Greeting:

1st. Whereas our right trusty, and right well beloved cousins and counsellors, Edward Earl of Clarendon, our high chancellor of England, and George Duke of Albemarle, master of our horse and captain general of all our forces, our right trusty and well beloved William Lord Craven, John Lord Berkley, our right trusty and well beloved counsellor, Anthony Lord Ashley, chancellor of our exchequer, Sir George Carteret, knight and baronet, vice chamberlain of our household, and our trusty and well beloved Sir William Berkley, knight, and Sir John Colleton, knight and baronet, being excited with a laudable and pious zeal for the propagation of the Christian faith, and the enlargement of our empire and dominions, have humbly besought leave of us, by their industry and charge, to transport and make an ample colony of our subjects, natives of our kingdom of England, and elsewhere within our dominions, unto a certain country hereafter described, in the parts of America not yet cultivated or planted, and only inhabited by some barbarous people, who have no knowledge of Almighty God.

2d. And whereas [they]... have humbly besought us to give, grant and confirm unto them and their heirs, the said country, with priviledges and jurisdictions requisite for the good government and safety thereof: Know ye, therefore, that we, favouring [their]... pious and noble purpose... have given, granted, confirmed, and by this our present charter, for us, our heirs and successors, do give, grant and confirm unto the said Edward Earl of Clarendon, George Duke of Albemarle, William Lord Craven, John Lord Berkley, Anthony Lord Ashley, Sir George Carteret, Sir William Berkley, and Sir John Colleton, their heirs and assigns, all that territory or tract of ground, scituate, lying and being within our dominions of America, extending from the north end of the island called Lucke island, which lieth in the southern Virginia seas, and within six and thirty degrees of the northern latitude, and to the west as far as the south seas, and so southerly as far as the river St. Matthias, which bordereth upon the coast of Florida, and within one and thirty degrees of northern latitude, and so west in a direct line as far as the south seas aforesaid; together with all and singular ports, harbours, bays, rivers, isles and islets belonging to the country aforesaid; and also all the soil, lands, fields, woods, mounthills, fields, lakes, rivers, bays and islets, scituate or being within the bounds or limits aforesaid, with the fishing of all sorts of fish, whales, sturgeons and all other royal fishes in the sea, bays, islets and rivers within the premises, and the fish therein taken; and moreover all veins, mines, quarries, as well discovered as not discovered, of gold, silver, gems, precious stones, and all other whatsoever, be it of stones, metals, or any other thing whatsoever, found or to be found within the countries, isles and limits aforesaid....

5th. And that the country, thus by us granted and described... we do, for us, our heirs and successors, erect, incorporate and ordain the same into a province, and call it the Province of Carolina, and so from henceforth will have it called; and... do grant full and absolute power, by virtue of these presents, to them the said Edward Earl of Clarendon, George Duke of Albemarle, William Lord Craven, John Lord Berkley, Anthony Lord Ashley, Sir George Carteret, Sir William Berkley, and Sir John Colleton, and their heirs, for the good and happy government of the said province, to ordain, make, enact, and under their seals to publish any laws whatsoever....

6th. And... we do... by these presents, give and grant unto the said Edward Earl of Clarendon, George Duke of Albemarle, William Lord Craven, John Lord Berkley, Anthony Lord Ashley, Sir George Carteret, Sir William Berkley, and Sir John Colleton, their heirs and assigns, by themselves or their magistrates, in that behalf lawfully authorized full power and authority from time to time to make and ordain fit and wholesome orders and ordinances, within the province aforesaid to be kept and observed as well for the keeping of the peace, as for the better government of the people there abiding, and to publish the same to all to whom it may concern; which ordinances, we do by these presents straightly charge and command to be inviolably observed within the said province, under the penalties therein expressed, so as such ordinances be reasonable, and not repugnant or contrary, but as near as may be, agreeable to the laws and statutes of this our kingdom of England, and so as the same ordinances do not extend to the binding, charging, or taking away of the right or interest of any person or persons, in their freehold, goods or chattels whatsoever.

7th. And to the end the said province may be more happily increased, by the multitude of people resorting thither, and may likewise be the more strongly defended from the incursions of salvages and other enemies, pirates and robbers, therefore we... do give and grant by these presents, power, license and liberty unto all the liege people of us, our heirs and successors in our kingdom of England or elsewhere, within any other our dominions, islands, colonies or plantations... to transport themselves and families unto the said province, with convenient shipping and fitting provisions, and there to settle themselves, dwell and inhabit.... And we... do straightly enjoin, ordain, constitute and command, that the said province of Carolina, shall be of our allegiance, and that all and singular the subjects and liege people of us, our heirs and successors, transported or to be transported into the said province, and the children of them and of such as shall descend from them, there born or hereafter to be born, be and shall be denizens and lieges of us, our heirs and successors of this our kingdom of England....

8th. And furthermore, that our subjects of this our said kingdom of England, and other our dominions, may be the rather encouraged to undertake this expedition with ready and cheerful minds, know ye, that we... do give and grant... to the said Edward Earl of Clarendon, George Duke of Albemarle, William Lord Craven, John Lord Berkley, Anthony Lord Ashley, Sir George Carteret, Sir William Berkley, and Sir John Colleton, and their heirs, as unto all others as shall from time to time repair unto the said province, with a purpose to inhabit there, or to trade with the natives of the said province, full liberty and license to lade and freight in any port whatsoever, of us, our heirs and successors, and into the said province of Carolina, by them, their servants or assigns, to transport all and singular their goods, wares and merchandises, as likewise all sorts of grain whatsoever, and any other things whatsoever, necessary for the food and clothing, not prohibited by the laws and statutes of our kingdoms and dominions,... the customs and other duties and payments, due for the said wares and merchandises, according to the several rates of the places from whence the same shall be transported. We... also... do give and grant license by this our charter, full power and absolute authority to import or unlade by themselves or their servants, factors or assigns, all merchandises and goods whatsoever, that shall arise of the fruits and commodities of the said province, either by land or by sea, into any of the ports of... our kingdom of England, Scotland or Ireland, or otherwise to dispose of the said goods, in the said ports; and if need be, within one year next after the unlading, to lade the said merchandises and goods again into the same or other ships, and to export the same into any other countries either of our dominions, or foreign being in amity with us, our heirs and successors, so as they pay such customs, subsidies, and other duties for the same, to us, our heirs and successors, as the rest of our subjects of this our kingdom, for the time being, shall be bound to pay, beyond which we will not, that the inhabitants of the said province of Carolina, shall be any ways charged.

9th. ...[B]y these presents... [we] do give and grant... full and free license, liberty and authority, at any time or times, from and after the feast of St. Michael the archangel, which shall be in the year of our Lord Christ, one thousand six hundred sixty and seven, as well to import, and bring into any of our dominions from the said province of Carolina, or any part thereof, the several goods and commodities, hereinafter mentioned, that is to say, silks, wines, currants, raisins, capers, wax, almonds, oyl and olives, without paying or answering to us, our heirs or successors, any custom, import, or other duty, for and in respect thereof, for and during the term and space of seven years, to commence and be accompted, from and after the first importation of four tons of any the said goods, in any one bottom, ship or vessel from the said province, into any of our dominions, as also to export and carry out of any of our dominions, into the said province of Carolina, custom free, all sorts of tools which shall be usefull or necessary for the planters there, in the accommodation and improvement of the premises, any thing before, in these presents contained, or any law, act, statute, prohibition or other matter, or anything heretofore had, made, enacted or provided, or hereafter to be had, made, enacted or provided, to the contrary, in any wise notwithstanding.

10th. And furthermore... we... grant... full and absolute power and authority to make erect and constitute, within the said province of Carolina, and the isles and islets aforesaid, such and so many seaports, harbours, creeks and other places, for discharge and unlading of goods and merchandises, out of ships, boats and other vessels, and for lading of them, in such and so many places, and with such jurisdiction, priviledges and franchises unto the said ports belonging, as to them shall seem most expedient, and that all and singular the ships, boats and other vessels, which shall come for merchandises and trade into the said province, or shall depart out of the same, shall be laden and unladen at such ports only, as shall be erected and constituted by the said Edward Earl of Clarendon, George Duke of Albemarle, William Lord Craven, John Lord Berkley, Anthony Lord Ashley, Sir George Carteret, Sir William Berkley, and Sir John Colleton, their heirs and assigns, and not elsewhere, any use, custom or any other thing to the contrary, in any wise notwithstanding....

15th. And because that in so remote a country, and scituate among so many barbarous nations, and the invasions as well of salvages as of other enemies, pirates and robbers, may probably be feared; therefore we... do give power... unto the said Edward Earl of Clarendon, George Duke of Albemarle, William Lord Craven, John Lord Berkley, Anthony Lord Ashley, Sir George Carteret, Sir William Berkley, and Sir John Colleton, their heirs and assigns, by themselves, or their captains, or other their officers, to levy, muster and train all sorts of men, of what condition or wheresoever born, in the said province for the time being, and to make war and pursue the enemies aforesaid, as well by sea as by land, yea, even without the limits of the said province, and by God's assistance to vanquish and take them, and being taken to put them to death by the law of war, or to save them at their pleasure; and to do all and every other thing, which unto the charge of a captain general of an army belongeth, or hath accustomed to belong, as fully and freely as any captain general of an army hath or ever had the same.

16th. Also our will and pleasure is, and by this our charter... we do give and grant... full power and authority, to exercise martial law against mutinous and seditious persons of those parts, such as shall refuse to submit themselves to their government, or shall refuse to serve in the wars, or shall fly to the enemy, or forsake their colours or ensigns, or be loyterers or straglers, or otherwise howsoever offending against law, custom or discipline military, as freely and in as ample manner and form as any captain general of an army by vertue of his office, might or hath accustomed to use the same....

1–3. THOMAS WHATELY, *THE REGULATIONS LATELY MADE*

Source: Thomas Whately, *The Regulations Lately Made Concerning the Colonies, and the Taxes Imposed Upon Them, Considered*. London: J. Willkie, 1775.

...The Revenue that may be raised by the Duties which have been already, or by these [stamp duties] if they should be hereafter imposed, are all equally applied by Parliament, towards defraying the necessary Expences of defending, protecting, and securing, the British Colonies and Plantations in America.... The very Words of the Act of Parliament and of the Resolution of the House of Commons imply, that the whole of the Expence is not to be charged upon the Colonies: They are under no Obligation to provide for this or any other particular national Expence; neither can they claim any Exemption from general Burthens; but being a part of the British Dominions, are to share all necessary Services with the rest. This in America does indeed first claim their Attention: They are immediately, they are principally concerned in it; and the Inhabitants of their Mother Country would justly and loudly complain, if after all their Efforts for the Benefit of the Colonies, when every Point is gained, and every wish accomplished, they, and they alone should be called upon still to answer every additional Demand, that the Preservation of these Advantages, and the Protection of the Colonies from future Dangers, may occasion: Great Britain has a Right at all Times, she is under a Necessity, upon this Occasion, to demand their Assistance; but still she requires it in the Manner most suitable to their Circumstances; for by appropriating this Revenue towards the Defence and Security of the Provinces where it is raised, the Produce of it is kept in the Country, the People are not deprived of the Circulation of what Cash they have amongst themselves, and thereby the severest Oppression of an American Tax, that of draining the Plantations of Money which they can so ill spare, is avoided. What Part they ought to bear of the national Expence, that is necessary for their Protection, must depend upon their Ability, which is not yet sufficiently known: to the whole they are certainly unequal, that would include all the military and all the naval Establishment, all Fortifications which it may be thought proper to erect, the Ordnance and Stores that must be furnished, and the Provisions which it is necessary to supply; but surely a Part of this great Disbursement, a large Proportion at least of some particular Branches of it, cannot be an intolerable Burthen upon such a Number of Subjects, upon a Territory so extensive, and upon the Wealth which they collectively possess. As to the Quota which each Individual must pay, it will be difficult to persuade the Inhabitants of this Country, where the neediest Cottager pays out of his Pittance, however scanty, and how hardly soever earned, our high Duties and Customs and Excise in the Price of all his Consumption; it will be difficult I say, to persuade those who see, who suffer, or who relieve such Oppression; that the West Indian [sugar planter] out of his Opulence, and the North American out of his Competency, can contribute no more than it is now pretended they can afford towards the Expence of Services, the Benefit of which, as a Part of this Nation they share, and as Colonists they peculiarly enjoy. They have indeed their own civil Governments besides to support; but Great Britain has her civil Government too; she has also a large Peace Establishment to maintain; and the national Debt, tho' so great a Part, and that the heaviest Part of it has been incurred by a War undertaken for the Protection of the Colonies, lies solely still upon her.

The Reasonableness, and even the Necessity of requiring an American Revenue being admitted, the Right of the Mother Country to impose such a Duty upon her Colonies, if duly considered, cannot be questioned: they claim it is true the Privilege, which is common to all British Subjects, of being taxed only with their own Consent, given by their Representatives; and may they ever enjoy the Privilege in all its Extent: May this sacred Pledge of Liberty be preserved inviolate, to the utmost Verge of our Dominions, and to the latest Page of our History! but let us not limit the legislative Rights of the British People to Subjects of Taxation only: No new Law whatever can bind us that is made without the Concurrence of our Representatives. The Acts of Trade and Navigation, and all other Acts that relate either to ourselves or to the Colonies, are founded up on no other Authority; they are not obligatory if a Stamp Act is not and every Argument in support of an Exemption from the Superintendance of the British Parliament in the one Case, is equally applicable to the others....

The Instances that have been mentioned prove, that the Right of the Parliament of Great Britain to impose Taxes of every Kind on the Colonies, has been always admitted; but... the Fact is, that the Inhabitants of the Colonies are represented in Parliament: they do not indeed chuse the Members of that Assembly; neither are Nine Tenths of the People of Britain Electors; for the Right of Election is annexed to certain Species of Property, to peculiar Franchises, and to Inhabitancy in some particular Places; but these Descriptions comprehend only a very small Part of the Land, the Property, and the People of this Island: all Copyhold, all Leasehold Estates, under the Crown, under the Church, or under private Persons, those for Terms ever so long; all landed Property in short, that is not Freehold, and all monied Property whatsoever are excluded: the Possessors of these have no Votes in the Election of Members of Parliament; Women and Persons under Age be their Property ever so large, and all of it Freehold, have none. The Merchants of London, a numerous and respectable Body of Men, whose Opulence exceeds all that America could collect; the Proprietors of that vast Accumulation of Wealth, the public Funds; the Inhabitants of Leeds, of Halifax, of Birmingham, and of Manchester, Towns that are each of them larger than the Largest in the Plantations; many of less Note that are yet incorporated;

and that great Corporation the East India Company, whose Rights over the Countries they possess, fall little short of Sovereignty, and whose Trade and whose Fleets are sufficient to constitute them a maritime Power, are all in the same Circumstances; none of them chuse their Representatives; and yet are they not represented in Parliament? Is their vast Property subject to Taxes without their Consent? Are they all arbitrarily bound by Laws to which they have not agreed? The Colonies are in exactly the same Situation: All British Subjects are really in the same; none are actually, all are virtually represented in Parliament; for every Member of Parliament sits in the House, not as Representative of his own Constituents, but as one of that august Assembly by which all the Commons of Great Britain are represented. Their Rights and their Interests, however his own Borough may be affected by general Dispositions, ought to be the great Objects of his Attention, and the only Rules for his Conduct; and to sacrifice these to a partial Advantage in favour of the Place where he was chosen, would be a Departure from his Duty.... [T]he Colonies and all British Subjects whatever, have an equal Share in the general Representation of the Commons of Great Britain, and are bound by the Consent of the Majority of that House, whether their own particular Representatives consented to or opposed the Measures there taken, or whether they had or had not particular Representatives there.

The Inhabitants of the Colonies however have by some been supposed to be excepted, because they are represented in their respective Assemblies. So are the Citizens of London in their Common Council; and yet so far from excluding them from the national Representation, it does not impeach their Right to chuse Members of Parliament: it is true, that the Powers vested in the Common Council of London, are not equal to those which the Assemblies in the Plantations enjoy; but still they are legislative Powers, to be exercised within their District, and over their Citizens; yet not exclusively of the general Superintendance of the great Council of the Nation....

[The colonies are] a Part, and an important Part of the Commons of Great Britain: they are represented in Parliament, in the same Manner as those Inhabitants of Britain are, who have not Voices in Elections; and they enjoy, with the Rest of their Fellow subjects the inestimable Privilege of not being bound by any Laws, or subject to any Taxes, to which the Majority of the Representatives of the Commons have not consented....

The Parliament will not often have occasion to exercise its Power over the Colonies, except for those Purposes, which the Assemblies cannot provide for. A general Tax is of this Kind; the Necessity for it, the Extent, the Application of it, are Matters which Councils limited in their Views and in their Operations cannot properly judge of; and when therefore the national Council determine these Particulars, it does not encroach on the other, it only exercises a Power which that other does not pretend to, never claimed, or wished, nor can ever be vested with: The latter remains in exactly the same State as it was before, providing for the same Services, by the same Means, and on the same Subjects; but conscious of its own Inability to answer greater Purposes than those for which it was instituted, it leaves the care of more general Concerns to that higher Legislature, in whose Province alone the Direction of them always was, is, and will be. The Exertion of that Authority which belongs to its universal Superintendance, neither lowers the Dignity, nor deprecates the Usefulness of more limited Powers: They retain all that they ever had, and are really incapable of more.

The Concurrence therefore of the provincial Representatives cannot be necessary in great public Measures to which none but the national Representatives are equal: The Parliament of Great Britain not only may but must tax the Colonies, when the public Occasions require a Revenue there: The present Circumstances of the Nation require one now; and a Stamp Act, of which we have had so long an Experience in this, and which is not unknown in that Country, seems an eligible Mode of Taxation. From all these Considerations, and from many others which will occur upon Reflexion and need not be suggested, it must appear proper to charge certain Stamp Duties in the Plantations to be applied towards defraying the necessary Expences of defending, protecting, and securing the British Colonies and Plantations in America....

1–4. ADAM SMITH, "OF COLONIES"

...Every European nation has endeavored more or less to monopolize to itself the commerce of its colonies, and, upon that account, has prohibited the ships of foreign nations from trading to them, and has prohibited them from importing European goods from any foreign nation. But the manner in which this monopoly has been exercised in different nations has been very different.

... In the exportation of their own surplus produce... it is only with regard to certain commodities that the colonies of Great Britain are confined to the market of the mother country. These commodities having been enumerated in the act of navigation and in some other subsequent acts, have upon that account been called enumerated commodities. The rest are called non-enumerated, and may be exported directly to other countries provided it is in British or Plantation ships, of which the owners and three-fourths of the mariners are British subjects.

Among the non-enumerated commodities are some of the most important productions of America and the West Indies; grain of all sorts, lumber, salt provisions, fish, sugar and rum.

Grain is naturally the first and principal object of the culture of all new colonies. By allowing them a very extensive market for it, the law encourages them to extend this culture much beyond the consumption of a thinly inhabited country, and thus to provide beforehand an ample subsistence for a continually increasing population.

In a country quite covered with wood, where timber consequently is of little or no value, the expense of clearing the ground is the principal obstacle to improvement. By allowing the colonies a very extensive market for their lumber, the law endeavors to facilitate improvement by raising the price of a commodity which would otherwise be of little value, and thereby enabling them to make some profit of what would otherwise be a mere expense.

In a country neither half-peopled nor half-cultivated, cattle naturally multiply beyond the consumption of the inhabitants, and are often upon that account of little or no value. But it is necessary... that the price of cattle should bear a certain proportion to that of corn before the greater part of the lands of any country can be improved. By allowing to American cattle, in all shapes, dead or alive, a very extensive market, the law endeavors to raise the value of a commodity of which the high price is so very essential to improvement....

To increase the shipping and naval power of Great Britain, by the extension of the fisheries of our colonies, is an object which the legislature seems to have had almost constantly in view. Those fisheries, upon this account, have had all the encouragement which freedom can give them, and they have flourished accordingly. The New England fishery in particular was, before the late disturbances [the Seven Years' War], one of the most important, perhaps, in the world. The whale-fishery which, notwithstanding an extravagant bounty, is in Great Britain carried on to so little purpose that in the opinion of many people... the whole produce does not much exceed the value of the bounties which are annually paid for it, is in New England carried on without any bounty to a very great extent. Fish is one of the principal articles with which the North Americans trade to Spain, Portugal, and the Mediterranean.

Sugar was originally an enumerated commodity which could be exported only to Great Britain. But in 1731, upon a representation of the sugar planters, its exportation was permitted to all parts of the world. The restrictions, however, with which this liberty was granted, joined to the high price of sugar in Great Britain, have rendered it, in a great measure, ineffectual. Great Britain and her colonies still continue to be almost the sole market for all the sugar produced in the British plantations. Their consumption increases so fast that though... the importation of sugar has increased very greatly within these twenty years, the exportation to foreign countries is said to be not much greater than before.

Rum is a very important article in the trade which the Americans carry on to the coast of Africa, from which they bring back negro slaves in return.

If the whole surplus produce of America in grain of all sorts, in salt provisions and in fish, had been put into the enumeration, and thereby forced into the market of Great Britain, it would have interfered too much with the produce of the industry of our own people. It was probably not so much from any regard to the interest of America as from a jealousy of this interference that those important commodities have not only been kept out of the enumeration, but that the importation into Great Britain of all grain, except rice, and of salt provisions, has, in the ordinary state of the law, been prohibited.

... The enumerated commodities are of two sorts: first, such as are either the peculiar produce of America, or as cannot be produced, or at least are not produced, in the mother country. Of this kind are molasses, coffee, cacao-nuts, tobacco, pimento, ginger, whale fins, raw silk, cotton wool, beaver, and other peltry of America, indigo, fustic, and other dyeing woods; secondly, such as are not the peculiar produce of America, but which are and may be produced in the mother country, though not in such quantities as to supply the greater part of her demand, which is principally supplied from foreign countries. Of this kind are all naval stores, masts, yards, and bowsprits, tar, pitch, and turpentine, pig and bar iron, copper ore, hides and skins, pot and pearl ashes. The largest importation of commodities of the first kind could not discourage the growth or interfere with the sale of any part of the produce of the mother country. By confining them to the home market, our merchants, it was expected, would not only be enabled to buy them cheaper in the Plantations, and consequently to sell them with a better profit at home, but to establish between the Plantations and foreign countries an advantageous carrying trade, of which Great Britain was necessarily to be the center or emporium, as the European country into which those commodities were first to be imported. The importation of commodities of the second kind might be so managed too, it was supposed, as to interfere, not with the sale of those of the same kind which were produced at home, but with that of those which were imported from foreign countries; because, by means of proper duties, they might be rendered always somewhat dearer than the former, and yet a good deal cheaper than the latter. By confining such commodities to the home market, therefore, it was proposed to discourage the produce, not of Great Britain, but of some foreign countries with which the balance of trade was believed to be unfavorable to Great Britain.

The prohibition of exporting from the colonies, to any other country but Great Britain, masts, yards, and bowsprits, tar, pitch, and turpentine, naturally tended to lower the price of timber in the colonies, and consequently to increase the expense of clearing their lands, the principal obstacle to their improvement. But about the beginning of the present century, in 1703, the pitch and tar company of Sweden endeavored to raise the price of their commodities to Great Britain, by prohibiting their exportation, except in their own ships, at their own price, and in such quantities as they thought proper. In order to counteract this notable piece of mercantile policy, and to render herself as much as possible independent, not only of Sweden, but of all the other northern powers, Great Britain gave a bounty upon the importation of naval stores from America and the effect of this bounty was to raise the price of timber in America, much more than the confinement to the home market could lower it; and as both regulations were enacted at the same time, their joint effect was rather to encourage than to discourage the clearing of land in America

Though pig and bar iron too have been put among the enumerated commodities, yet as, when imported from America, they were exempted from considerable duties to which they are subject when imported from any other country, the one part of the regulation contributes more to encourage the erection of furnaces in America than the other to discourage it. There is no manufacture which occasions so great a consumption of wood as a furnace, or which can contribute so much to the clearing of a country over grown with it.

The tendency of some of these regulations to raise the value of timber in America, and thereby to facilitate the clearing of the land, was neither, perhaps, intended nor understood by the legislature. Though their beneficial effects, however, have been in this respect accidental, they have not upon that account been less real.

The most perfect freedom of trade is permitted between the British colonies of America and the West Indies, both in the enumerated and in the non-enumerated commodities. Those colonies are now become so populous and thriving that each of them finds in some of the others a great and extensive market for every part of its produce. All of them taken together, they make a great internal market for the produce of one another.

The liberality of England, however, towards the trade of her colonies has been confined chiefly to what concerns the market for their produce, either in its rude state, or in what may be called the very first stage of manufacture. The more advanced or more refined manufactures even of the colony produce, the merchants and manufacturers of Great Britain choose to reserve to themselves, and have prevailed upon the legislature to prevent their establishment in the colonies, sometimes by high duties, and sometimes by absolute prohibitions.

… While Great Britain encourages in America the manufactures of pig and bar iron, by exempting them from duties to which the like commodities are subject when imported from any other country, she imposes an absolute prohibition upon the erection of steel furnaces and slitmills in any of her American plantations. She will not suffer her colonists to work in those more refined manufactures even for their own consumption; but insists upon their purchasing of her merchants and manufacturers all goods of this kind which they have occasion for.

She prohibits the exportation from one province to another by water, and even the carriage by land upon horseback or in a cart, of hats, of wools and woolen goods, of the produce of America; a regulation which effectually prevents the establishment of any manufacture of such commodities for distant sale, and confines the industry of her colonists in this way to such coarse and household manufactures as a private family commonly makes for its own use or for that of some of its neighbors in the same province.

To prohibit a great people, however, from making all that they can of every part of their own produce, or from employing their stock and industry in the way that they judge most advantageous to themselves, is a manifest violation of the most sacred rights of mankind. Unjust, however, as such prohibitions may be, they have not hitherto been very hurtful to the colonies. Land is still so cheap, and, consequently, labor so dear among them, that they can import from the mother country almost all the more refined or more advanced manufactures cheaper than they could make for themselves. Though they had not, therefore, been prohibited from establishing such manufactures, yet in their present state of improvement a regard to their own interest would, probably, have prevented them from doing so. In their present state of improvement those prohibitions, perhaps, without cramping their industry, or restraining it from any employment to which it would have gone of its own accord, are only impertinent badges of slavery imposed upon them, without any sufficient reason, by the groundless jealousy of the merchants and manufacturers of the mother country. In a more advanced state they might be really oppressive and insupportable.

Great Britain too, as she confines to her own market some of the most important productions of the colonies, so in compensation she gives to some of them an advantage in that market, sometimes by imposing higher duties upon the like productions when imported from other countries, and sometimes by giving bounties upon their importation from the colonies. In the first way she gives an advantage in the home market to the sugar, tobacco, and iron of her own colonies, and in the second to their raw silk, to their hemp and flax, to their indigo, to their naval stores, and to their building timber. This second way of encouraging the colony produce by bounties upon importation, is, so far as I have been able to learn, peculiar to Great Britain. The first is not. Portugal does not content herself with imposing higher duties upon the importation of tobacco from any other country, but prohibits it under the severest penalties.

With regard to the importation of goods from Europe, England has likewise dealt more liberally with her colonies than any other nation.

Great Britain allows a part, almost always the half, generally a larger portion, and sometimes the whole of the duty which is paid upon the importation of foreign goods, to be drawn back upon their exportation to any foreign country. No independent foreign country… would receive them if they came to it loaded with the heavy duties to which almost all foreign goods are subjected on their importation into Great Britain. Unless, therefore, some part of those duties was drawn back upon exportation, there was an end of the carrying trade; a trade so much favored by the mercantile system.

Our colonies, however, are by no means independent foreign countries; and Great Britain having assumed to herself the exclusive right of supplying them with all goods from Europe, might have forced them… to receive such goods, loaded with all the same duties which they paid in the mother country. But, on the contrary, till 1763, the same drawbacks were paid upon the exportation of the greater part of foreign goods to our colonies as to any independent foreign country….

Of the greater part of the regulations concerning the colony trade, the merchants who carry it on… have been the principal advisers. We must not wonder, therefore, if, in the greater part of them, their interest has been more considered than either that of the colonies or that of the mother country. In their exclusive privilege of supplying the colonies with all the goods which they wanted from Europe, and of purchasing all such parts of their surplus produce as could not interfere with any of the trades which they themselves carried on at home, the interest of the colonies was sacrificed to the interest of those merchants. In allowing the same drawbacks upon the re-exportation of the greater part of European and East India goods to the colonies as upon their re-exportation to any independent country, the interest of the mother country was sacrificed to it, even according to the mercantile ideas of that interest. It was for the interest of the merchants to pay as little as possible for the foreign which they sent to the colonies, and, consequently, to get back as much as possible of the duties which they advanced upon their importation into Great Britain. They might thereby be enabled to sell in the colonies either the same quantity of goods with a greater profit, or a greater quantity with the same profit, and, consequently, to gain something either in the one way or the other. It was likewise for the interest of the colonies to get all such goods as cheap and in as great abundance as possible. But this might not always be for the interest of the mother country. She might frequently suffer both in her revenue, by giving back a great part of the duties which had been paid upon the importation of such goods; and in her manufactures, by being undersold in the colony market, in consequence of the easy terms upon which foreign manufactures could be carried thither by means of those drawbacks….

In what way, therefore, has the policy of Europe contributed either to the first establishment, or to the present grandeur of the colonies of America? In one way, and in one way only, it has contributed a good deal. *Magna virum Mater*! It bred and formed the men who were capable of achieving such great actions, and of laying the foundation of so great an empire; and there is no other quarter of the world of which the policy is capable of forming, or has ever actually and in fact formed such men. The colonies owe to the policy of Europe the education and great views of their active and enterprising founders; and some of the greatest and most important of them… owe to it scarce anything else.

… [Mercantilistic policy] tends to diminish, or, at least, to keep down below what they would otherwise rise to, both the enjoyments and industry of all… nations in general, and of the American colonies in particular. It is a dead weight upon the action of one of the great springs which puts into motion a great part of the business of mankind. By rendering the colony produce dearer in all other countries, it lessens its consumption, and thereby cramps the industry of the colonies, and both the enjoyments and the industry of all other countries, which both enjoy less when they pay more for what they enjoy, and produce less when they get less for what they produce. By rendering the produce of all other countries dearer in the colonies, it cramps, in the same manner the industry of all other countries, and both the enjoyments and the industry of the colonies. It is a clog which, for the supposed benefit of some particular countries, embarrasses the pleasures and encumbers the industry of all other countries; but of the colonies more than of any other. It not only excludes, as much as possible, all other countries from one particular market; but it confines, as much as possible, the colonies to one particular market; and the difference is very great between being excluded from one particular market, when all others are open, and being confined to one particular market, when all others are shut up. The surplus produce of the colonies, however, is the original source of all that increase of enjoyments and industry which Europe derives from the discovery and colonization of America; and the exclusive trade of the mother countries tends to render this source much less abundant than it otherwise would be.

… The tobacco of Maryland and Virginia, for example, by means of the monopoly which England enjoys of it, certainly comes cheaper to England than it can do to France, to whom England commonly sells a considerable part of it. But had France, and all other European countries been, at all times, allowed a free trade to Maryland and Virginia, the tobacco of those colonies might, by this time, have come cheaper than it actually does, not only to all those other countries, but likewise to England. The produce of tobacco, in consequence of a market so much more extensive than any which it has hitherto enjoyed, might, and probably would, by this time, have been so much increased as to reduce the profits of a tobacco plantation to their natural level with those of a corn plantation, which, it is supposed, they are still somewhat above. The price of tobacco might, and probably would, by this time, have fallen somewhat lower than it is at present. An equal quantity of the commodities either of England or of those other countries might have purchased in Maryland and Virginia a greater quantity of tobacco than it can do at present, and consequently have been sold there for so much a better price. So far as that weed, therefore, can, by its cheapness and abundance, increase the enjoyments or augment the industry either of England or of any other country, it would, probably, in the case of a free trade, have produced both these effects in somewhat a greater degree than it can do at present.…

In order, however, to obtain this relative advantage in the colony trade, in order to execute the invidious and malignant project of excluding as much as possible other nations from any share in it, England… has not only sacrificed a part of the absolute advantage which she, as well as every other nation, might have derived from that trade, but has subjected herself both to an absolute and to a relative disadvantage in almost every other branch of trade.

... The effect of the colony trade in its natural and free state is to open a great, though distant, market for such parts of the produce of British industry as may exceed the demand of the markets nearer home, of those of Europe, and of the countries which lie round the Mediterranean Sea. In its natural and free state, the colony trade, without drawing from those markets any part of the produce which had ever been sent to them, encourages Great Britain to increase the surplus continually by continually presenting new equivalents to be exchanged for it. In its natural and free state, the colony trade tends to increase the quantity of productive labor in Great Britain, but without altering in any respect the direction of that which had been employed there before. In the natural and free state of the colony trade, the competition of all other nations would hinder the rate of profit from rising above the common level either in the new market or in the new employment. The new market, without drawing anything from the old one, would create, if one may say so, a new produce for its own supply; and that new produce would constitute a new capital for carrying on the new employment, which in the same manner would draw nothing from the old one.

... [Thus] the monopoly of the colony trade... like all the other mean and malignant expedients of the mercantile system, depresses the industry of all other countries, but chiefly that of the colonies, without in the least increasing, but on the contrary diminishing that of the country in whose favor it is established.

The monopoly hinders the capital of that country... from maintaining so great a quantity of productive labor as it would otherwise maintain, and from affording so great a revenue to the industrious inhabitants as it would otherwise afford. But as capital can be increased only by savings from revenue, the monopoly, by hindering it from affording so great a revenue as it would otherwise afford, necessarily hinders it from increasing so fast as it would otherwise increase, and consequently from maintaining a still greater quantity of productive labor, and affording a still greater revenue to the industrious inhabitants of that country. One great original source of revenue, therefore, the wages of labor, the monopoly must necessarily have rendered at all times less abundant than it otherwise would have been.

...The monopoly indeed raises the rate of mercantile profit, and thereby augments somewhat the gain of our merchants. But as it obstructs the natural increase of capital, it tends rather to diminish than to increase the sum total of the revenue which the inhabitants of the country derive from the profits of stock; a small profit upon a great capital generally affording a greater revenue than a great profit upon a small one. The monopoly raises the rate of profit, but it hinders the sum of profit from rising so high as it otherwise would do.

...To found a great empire for the sole purpose of raising up a people of customers may at first sight appear a project fit only for a nation of shopkeepers. It is, however, a project altogether unfit for a nation of shopkeepers; but extremely fit for a nation whose government is influenced by shopkeepers. Such statesmen, and such statesmen only, are capable of fancying that they will find some advantage in employing the blood and treasure of their fellow citizens to found and maintain such an empire. Say to a shopkeeper, Buy me a good estate, and I shall always buy my clothes at your shop, even though I should pay somewhat dearer than what I can have them for at other shops; and you will not find him very forward to embrace your proposal. But should any other person buy you such an estate, the shopkeeper would be much obliged to your benefactor if he would enjoin you to buy all your clothes at his shop. England purchased for some of her subjects, who found themselves uneasy at home, a great estate in a distant country. The price, indeed, was very small... and it amounted to little more than the expense of the different equipments which made the first discovery, reconnoitered the coast, and took a fictitious possession of the country. The land was good and of great extent, and the cultivators having plenty of good ground to work upon, and being for some time at liberty to sell their produce where they pleased, became in the course of little more than thirty or forty years (between 1620 and 1660) so numerous and thriving a people that the shopkeepers and other traders of England wished to secure to themselves the monopoly of their custom. Without pretending, therefore, that they had paid any part, either of the original purchase money, or of the subsequent expense of improvement, they petitioned the parliament that the cultivators of America might for the future be confined to their shop; first, for buying all the goods which they wanted from Europe; and, secondly, for selling all such parts of their own produce as those traders might find it convenient to buy. For they did not find it convenient to buy every part of it. Some parts of it imported into England might have interfered with some of the trades which they themselves carried on at home. Those particular parts of it, therefore, they were willing that the colonists should sell where they could; the farther off the better; and upon that account purposed that their market should be confined to the countries south of Cape Finisterre. A clause in the famous act of navigation established this truly shopkeeper proposal into a law.

The maintenance of this monopoly has hitherto been the principal, or more properly perhaps the sole end and purpose of the dominion which Great Britain assumes over her colonies. In the exclusive trade, it is supposed, consists the great advantage of provinces, which have never yet afforded either revenue or military force for the support of the civil government, or the defense of the mother country. The monopoly is the principal badge of their dependency, and it is the sole fruit which has hitherto been gathered from that dependency. Whatever expense Great Britain has hitherto laid out in maintaining this dependency has really been laid out in order to support this monopoly. The expense of the ordinary peace establishment of the colonies amounted, before the commencement of the present disturbances [the American Revolution], to the pay of twenty regiments of foot; to the expense of the artillery, stores, and extraordinary provisions with which it was necessary to supply them; and to the expense of a very considerable naval force which was constantly kept up, in order to guard, from the smuggling vessels of other nations, the immense coast of North America, and that of our West Indian islands. The whole expense of this peace establishment was a charge upon the revenue of Great Britain, and was, at the same time, the smallest part of what the dominion of the colonies has cost the mother country. If we would know the amount of the whole, we must add to the annual expense of this peace establishment the interest of the sums which, in consequence of her considering her colonies as provinces subject to her dominion, Great Britain has upon different occasions laid out upon their defense. We must add to it, in particular, the whole expense of the late war [the Seven Years' War], and a great part of that of the war which preceded it [the Anglo-Spanish War, 1739–1748]. The late war was altogether a colony quarrel, and the whole expense of it, in whatever part of the world it may have been laid out, whether in Germany or the East Indies, ought justly to be stated to the account of the colonies. It amounted to more than ninety millions sterling, including not only the new debt which was contracted, but the two shillings in the pound additional land tax, and the sums which were every year borrowed from the sinking fund. The Spanish war, which began in 1739, was principally a colony quarrel. Its principal object was to prevent the search of the colony ships which carried on a contraband trade with the Spanish Main. This whole expense is, in reality, a bounty which has been given in order to support a monopoly. The pretended purpose of it was to encourage the manufactures, and to increase the commerce of Great Britain. But its real effect has been to raise the rate of mercantile profit, and to enable our merchants to turn into a branch of trade, of which the returns are more slow and distant than those of the greater part of other trades, a greater proportion of their capital than they otherwise would have done; two events which, if a bounty could have prevented, it might perhaps have been very well worth while to give such a bounty.

Under the present system of management, therefore, Great Britain derives nothing but loss from the dominion which she assumes over her colonies.

ESSAYS

Historians have long debated the economic impact British mercantilism had on the colonial American economy. While many have concluded that the complaints of the colonists were justified, others have contended that mercantilism actually benefited the Americans. In the first essay, Robert Paul Thomas, Associate Professor of Economics Emeritus at the University of Washington, used a quantitative analysis to address this debate directly. He concluded that mercantilism imposed only a slight economic burden on the colonists, not more than $1.24 per capita in 1770, and therefore was not a major factor leading to independence.

Writing twenty-seven years after Thomas's article re-shaped the historical interpretation of mercantilism's impact, Larry Sawers, Professor of Economics at American University, challenged the ruling paradigm. Those claims which held that British trade restrictions imposed only a slight economic burden on the colonies, he maintained, were based on faulty logic. If one examined the economic burden mercantilism would have had after 1776 as well as its impact on the leading Revolutionaries it was clear that the British system exacted a heavy price on the colonies. Viewed in this sense, then, Professor Sawers argued that British mercantilism should indeed be regarded as an important factor leading to independence.

1–1. ROBERT PAUL THOMAS, "A QUANTITATIVE APPROACH TO THE STUDY OF THE EFFECTS OF BRITISH IMPERIAL POLICY UPON COLONIAL WELFARE"

Historians have long debated whether the American colonies on balance benefited or were hindered by British imperial regulation. George Bancroft thought the regulations worked a definite hardship on the colonies. George L. Beer believed these regulations nicely balanced and that the colonies shared in the general advantages. Lawrence Harper, in a now classic article, actually attempted to calculate the cost and found that British policies "placed a heavy burden upon the colonies." Oliver Dickerson wrote that "no case can be made ... that such laws were economically oppressive," while Curtis P. Nettels, writing at the same time to the same point, stated: "British policy as it affected the colonies after 1763 was restrictive, injurious, negative." It is quite evident that a difference of opinion exists among reputable colonial historians over this important historical issue.

In this paper an effort is made to meet this issue head on. I shall attempt to measure, relative to a hypothetical alternative, the extent of the burdens and benefits stemming from imperial regulation of the foreign commerce of the thirteen colonies. The main instruments of this regulation were the Navigation Acts, and we shall confine our attention to evaluating the effect of these Acts upon colonial welfare....

The hypothesis of this paper is that membership in the British Empire, after 1763, did not impose a significant hardship upon the American colonies. To test this hypothesis I shall endeavor to bias the estimates against the hypothesis, thus not attempting to state what actually would have happened but only that it would not have amounted to as much as my estimate. The end result will, therefore, err on the side of overstating the real costs of the Navigation Acts to the thirteen colonies.

The traditional tools of economic theory will guide the preparation of these estimates. Two series of estimates will be prepared where possible: one, an annual average for the period 1763–1772, based upon official values; the other, for the single year 1770. The official trade statistics for the year 1770 have been adjusted to make them more accurate.

…All attempts at measurement require a standard to which the object being measured is made relative or compared. In the case of this paper, the colonies either on balance benefited or were burdened by British imperialism, relative to how they would have fared under some alternative political situation. The problem is to pick the most probable alternative situation….

The alternative situation that I shall employ to calculate the economic effects of the Navigation Acts after 1763 is that of a free and independent thirteen colonies outside the British Empire. This new nation would, therefore, be subject to most of the same restrictions hindering foreign nations attempting to carry on commerce with the eighteenth-century British Empire.

…The American colonies by 1763 formed the foundation of Great Britain's Atlantic empire and had become, as a group, England's most important commercial ally. The basis of this commerce was a vigorous colonial export trade. The total exports in 1770 amounted to £3,165,225. Trade with Great Britain and Ireland accounted for 50 per cent of colonial exports. The West Indies trade constituted another 30 per cent, and commerce with southern Europe and the Wine Islands, another 17 per cent. Trade with Africa and South America accounted for most of the residual.

The colonists, of course, used their exports to purchase imports. They were Great Britain's most important customer and Great Britain their most important supplier. The British Isles shipped to the American colonies in 1768 (a year for which a detailed breakdown is available) £2,157,000 worth of goods, or nearly 75 per cent of all colonial imports, which totaled £2,890,000. Of this, £421,000 were British re-exports from northern Europe. The West Indies, the other important source of imports, accounted for 20.5 per cent of the colonial imports; southern Europe and the Wine Islands, 2.9 per cent; and Africa, a little less than 2.0 per cent.

The thirteen American colonies carried on this foreign commerce subject to the constraints of a series of laws designed to alter the trade of the British Empire in the interests of the mother country. This commercial system can be viewed as being made up of four types of laws: (1) laws regulating the nationality, crews, and ownership of the vessels in which goods could be shipped; (2) statutes regulating the destination to which certain goods could be shipped; (3) laws designed to encourage specific primary industries via an elaborate system of rebates, drawbacks, import and export bounties, and export taxes; (4) direct prohibition of colonial industries and practices that tended to compete with English industries or to harm a prominent sector of the British economy or even, occasionally, the economy of a British colony. These laws, it should be stressed, did not regulate the American colonies alone, but with occasional local modifications applied equally to the entire British Empire.

The laws regulating the nationality of vessels were designed to insure a monopoly of the carrying trade of the empire to ships of the empire. In the seventeenth and eighteenth centuries the freight factor on goods traded internationally probably averaged at least 20 per cent, and these laws were designed to insure that this revenue stayed within the empire. The Navigation Acts also insured, to the extent that they were effective, that England would be the entrepôt of the empire and that the distributing trade would be centered in the British Isles.

The commodity clauses of these various regulatory Acts controlled the destination to which certain goods could be shipped. These enumerated commodities generally could be shipped only to England. The original list contained tobacco, sugar, indigo, cotton-wool, ginger, fustic and other dyewoods. Later, naval stores, hemp, rice, molasses, beaver skins, furs, and copper ore were added. The Sugar Act of 1764 added coffee, pimiento, coconuts, whale fins, raw silk, hides and skins, potash and pearl ash to the list. In 1766, the law was amended to prohibit the direct export of any colonial product north of Cape Finisterre.

There were exceptions and compensations to these commodity clauses which benefited the American colonies. Rice, after 1730, could be directly exported south of Cape Finisterre and, after 1764, to South America. Tobacco was given a monopoly in Great Britain, as its local cultivation was prohibited. While the list appears extensive, of the enumerated commodities only tobacco, indigo, copper ore, naval stores, hemp, furs and skins, whale fins, raw silk, and potash and pearl ash were products of the thirteen colonies, and only tobacco, rice, and perhaps indigo and naval stores could be considered major exports of the colonies that later became the United States.

An elaborate series of laws was enacted by the English Parliament to encourage specific industries in the interest of a self-sufficient empire. These included preferential tariffs for certain goods of colonial origin. A distinctive feature of these laws was an elaborate system of rebates and drawbacks to encourage the exports of certain commodities from England and extensive bounties to encourage the production of specific goods for export to Great Britain.

Most enumerated goods benefited from a preferential duty. These goods were thus given a substantial advantage in the markets of the mother country. Goods receiving preferential treatment included cotton-wool, ginger, sugar, molasses, coffee, tobacco, rice, naval stores, pitch, rosin, hemp, masts, whale fins, raw silk, potash and pearl ash, bar and pig iron, and various types of lumber. Certain of these goods also received drawbacks of various amounts upon their re-export from Great Britain. Foreign goods competing in the English market with enumerated colonial commodities were thus subject to a disadvantage from these preferential duties.

A system of bounties was also implemented to encourage the production of specific commodities in the colonies or to allow the British manufacturers to compete with foreign exports in the colonial markets. The production of naval stores, silk, lumber, indigo, and hemp was encouraged in the colonies with bounties. In the mother country the manufacture of linen, gunpowder, silks, and many non-woolen textiles was encouraged by a bounty to allow these products to compete with similar foreign manufactures in the colonial markets.

Certain of the colonial commodities favored by legislation were given what amounted to a monopoly of the home market of the mother country. The colonial production of tobacco, naval stores, sugar and sugar products was so favored. In the case of tobacco, the major share of total imports was re-exported, so the local monopoly proved not a great boon.

In economic terms, the Navigation Acts were designed to insure that the vast bulk of the empire's carrying trade was in ships owned by Englishmen. The design of the commodity clauses was to alter the terms of trade to the disadvantage of the colonists, by making all foreign imports into the colonies, and many colonial exports whose final destination was the Continent, pass through England. The effect was to make colonial imports more expensive and colonial exports less remunerative by increasing the transportation costs of both. Finally, through tariff preferences, bounties, and outright prohibitions, resources were allocated from more efficient uses to less.

I shall approach the problem of assessing the overall effect of the various British regulations of trade by considering their effect on the following aspects of the colonial economy:

(1) exports of colonial products; (2) imports into the colonies; (3) colonial foreign commerce; and (4) colonial shipping earnings. An assessment will then be undertaken of compensating benefits arising from membership in the British Empire. Finally, an attempt will be made to strike a balance on the total impact of British imperial policy upon the colonial economy.

...The export trade between the colonies and the mother country was subjected to regulations which significantly altered its value and composition over what it would have been if the colonies had been independent. The total adjusted value of exports from the American colonies to Great Britain in 1770 was £1,458,000, of which £1,107,000, or 76 per cent, were enumerated goods. Such goods were required to be shipped directly to Great Britain. The largest part, 85.4 per cent, of the enumerated goods was subsequently re-exported to northern Europe and thus when competing in these markets bore the burden of an artificial, indirect routing through England to the Continent. The costs of this indirect route took the form of an added transshipment, with the consequent port charges and fees, middlemen's commissions, and what import duties were retained upon re-export. The enumerated goods consumed in England benefited from preferential duties relative to goods of foreign production. A few of these enumerated commodities also were favored with import bounties.

The additional transport costs borne by enumerated goods upon their re-export had the effect of lowering the prices received by the colonial producer and depressing the quantity exported....

In order to calculate the direct burden borne by the colonial producers of enumerated goods that were re-exported from England, we need to know three separate time series. In the case of tobacco, we need to know the world market price in a European port, the price actually received in the colonies, and the actual re-exports of tobacco from England—all three of which are readily available.

The price that would have existed in the colonies in the absence of enumeration... was estimated by dividing the observed Amsterdam price of Virginia tobacco before the Revolution by the ratio of Amsterdam to Philadelphia tobacco prices after the Revolution. The postwar ratio of prices reflects the advantages received by the colonists by shipping directly to northern Europe rather than indirectly through England....

Calculated in this manner, the price of tobacco in 1770 colonial America, had the colonies been independent, would have been over 49 per cent higher than it actually was. The average price for the decade 1763–1772 would have been 34 per cent higher than was actually recorded. These higher prices indicate that tobacco planters suffered a burden on the tobacco they actually grew in 1770 of £262,000 and, for the decade, an average annual burden of £177,000.

The direct burden is only a portion of the total colonial loss due to enumeration. The hypothetical higher tobacco prices would certainly have stimulated an increase in the supply of tobacco. Assuming that a 1 per cent increase in price would generate a 1 per cent increase in supply, the resulting increase in supply would have been about 39,000,000 pounds in 1770, or an annual average of 29,000,000, pounds for the decade. The loss to the colonies of this foregone output [was]... £64,000 for 1770, or an average of £30,000 for the decade. Thus, the total burden on tobacco amounts to £326,000 for the year 1770, or an average of £207,000 for the period 1763–1772.

The calculation of the encumbrance suffered by rice proceeded in the same manner as the calculation of the burden on tobacco, except that Charleston prices were used instead of Philadelphia prices since South Carolina was the center of colonial rice production. The burden on the price of rice re-exports was calculated to be an appreciable 105 per cent. This amounted to £95,000 in 1770, or £110,000 average for the decade 1763–1772.

The indirect loss attributable to the expected increase in rice exports with the increase in price amounted to £25,000 for 1770, or an average of £29,000 for the longer period.

In the case of rice, an elasticity of supply of .5 was assumed, due to the limited area of southern marshlands suitable to the cultivation of rice. The whole burden on rice products totaled £120,000 for 1770, or an average of £139,000 for the period 1763–1772.

Tobacco and rice together accounted for the vast bulk of the enumerated products that were re-exported and therefore bore most of the burden. If we apply the weighted average of the tobacco and rice burden to the remainder of enumerated re-exports, and adjust for the expected increase in supply, we obtain an estimated additional burden of £53,000 for 1770, or an annual average of £35,000 for the ten-year period.

However, to arrive at the total burden on enumerated exports we must allow for the benefits that colonial exports received from preferential duties or bounties. Most enumerated commodities benefited from one or the other: beaver skins, furs, and copper ore appear to be the only exceptions. Enumerated goods consumed in Great Britain amounted to £161,570 in 1770, or an average of £126,716 for the decade. The average preference amounted to 38 per cent of the price of enumerated products consumed in the mother country. Again, assuming an elasticity of supply of one, we find that in the absence of these preferential duties the first-order effects would result in a decline in the amount of these enumerated commodities consumed in England of about £61,000 for 1770, or an average of £48,000 for the decade. The benefit of preferential duties to the colonists is the gain enjoyed by those exports that would have been sent to England in the absence of preferential duties had the colonies been independent (or £38,000 in 1770 and £30,000 average for the decade) plus the gain on the commodities actually sent that would not have been sent to England had the colonies been free. This amounted to £17,000 in 1770, or £9,000 as the annual average between 1763 and 1772. The benefit accruing to the colonies from preferential duties thus totals £55,000 for 1770, or £39,000 for the decade average.

In addition to preferential duties, the Crown annually spent large sums in the form of bounties to promote certain industries. The recorded bounties for the year 1770, for instance, totaled £47,344. These payments were designed to divert resources from more efficient uses into industries where they were employed less efficiently but where, for political purposes, they were thought better occupied....

The export of colonial naval stores was stimulated by bounty payments in significant amounts. The average for the decade 1763–1772 totaled £33,000, and for the year 1770

Table 1.1 Net Burden on Colonial Foreign Commerce

	1770	1763–1772
Exports		
Tobacco	£ 326,000	£ 207,000
Rice	120,000	139,000
Other	53,000	35,000
Burden	499,000	381,000
Preference	55,000	39,000
Bounty	33,000	35,000
Benefit	88,000	74,000
Imports		
Burden	121,000	144,000
Net burden on foreign commerce	£ 532,000 or $ 2,660,000	£ 451,000 or $ 2,255,000

the payment amounted to £29,803. The average bounty amounted to about 28 per cent of the price; therefore, assuming an elasticity of supply of one, the bounty was responsible for roughly 28 per cent of the exports of naval stores to Great Britain. Figured on this basis, the net gain to the colonists from the bounty on naval stores was 86 per cent of the payment. This amounted to an average of £28,000 for the decade, or £26,000 for the single year 1770.

The second largest bounty payments were for the production of indigo; in 1770 this amounted to £8,732 and for the decade an average of £8,065. Evidently, the indigo bounty not only stimulated increased output but was responsible for the entire output, since the production of indigo in the colonies disappeared after independence.... The net gain to the colonists from the indigo bounty at best is equal to, and is probably something less than, one half the amount of the bounty. We estimated that 50 per cent of the bounty payment for indigo was gain for indigo producers — gain they would not have enjoyed if the colonies had been independent. This totaled £4,400 in 1770, or £4,000 as the annual average for the decade. The importation of colonial lumber into Great Britain also received a bounty which... totaled £6,557 in 1769.

Sufficient data are not available to allow a calculation of the gain to the colonists from this payment, but it appears that the bounty was just sufficient to pay the added cost of shipping lumber to England. This payment was necessary to divert lumber from the West Indies, which was the colonies' natural market, and to attract it to England. It appears justifiable to assign the entire payment as the cost of a less efficient use of resources. Nevertheless we shall include 50 per cent as a net gain to the colonists, which amounts to £3,300.

The total net gain to the colonies from the bounties paid for colonial products was, therefore, £33,000 in 1770 and an average of £35,000 for the decade. Our analysis of the effect of the Navigation Acts on colonial exports has included the burden on exports, the benefit of the preferential duties, and the net gain from bounty payments. The sum total of these burdens and benefits is a net burden upon exports of £411,000 for 1770. The average annual burden for the decade 1763–1772 was calculated to be £307,000.

...British law required that the colonies purchase their East Indian and European goods in England. The colonies actually purchased three-quarters of their imports from the mother country, of which about 20 per cent were goods originally manufactured in Europe or Asia. These imported goods also bore the burden of an indirect route to the colonies, analogous to that borne by tobacco destined to be consumed in Europe. This burden was reflected in higher prices for goods of foreign manufacture in the colonies than otherwise would have been the case.

Our method for calculating the burden borne by colonial imports of foreign manufactures is similar to the method used to calculate the cost of enumeration on colonial goods re-exported to Europe. Two commodities, tea and pepper, for which both colonial and Amsterdam prices are available, were selected as our sample. Tea and pepper accounted for about 16 per cent of the value of foreign goods imported into the colonies through England. The price that would have obtained in the colonies had they been independent was calculated for these goods exactly as in the case of tobacco. The alternative prices of these commodities, according to our estimates, would have averaged 16 per cent lower than they in fact were. Thus, the colonists paid more for their imports of foreign origin than they would have paid had they been independent.

The colonies actually imported foreign goods to the average value of £412,000 for the decade 1763–1772 and of £346,000 for the single year 1770. The burden on the goods, according to our measurement, averaged £66,000 for the decade, or £55,000 for 1770. However, the burden on imports should not be calculated on the basis of foreign goods alone. The burden should also be calculated on goods of English manufacture which were made competitive in the colonial markets by virtue of the artificially increased cost of foreign goods forced to travel an indirect route to the colonies.

The bounty laws benefiting English manufactures which were designed to make English goods competitive with those of foreign manufacture give us a clue to the identity of these English manufactures. If goods of English manufacture required a bounty to compete with similar foreign goods suffering the handicap of an indirect shipment, then the colonists, if independent, would have purchased foreign instead of English goods. Thus, some English goods actually purchased by the colonists would not have been purchased if the colonies had been independent.

Linen was the most important of these goods; the list also included cottons and silks. The colonies thus paid more for most non-woolen textiles than they would have if they had existed outside the British Empire. The additional monetary loss resulting from the purchase of English rather than foreign goods was calculated to average £73,000 for the decade or £61,000 for 1770 alone. The colonists thus paid a total of £116,000 more in 1770 or £139,000 average for the decade for their imports than they would have if independent. If we assume, for convenience, a price elasticity of demand for imports of one, the colonists would have spent the same amount on imports but they would have received more goods for their money.

The results of this preliminary investigation into the effects of the Navigation Acts upon the foreign commerce of the American colonies are found in Table 1.1. The result is an overall burden for the year 1770 of £532,000, and an average of £451,000 for the decade.

... The main obligation of the mother country to its colonies in a mercantilist world was to provide protection. In this area lies the significant benefit to the colonies from membership in an empire. The empire of course also performed certain administrative functions for the colonies from which they benefited.

Great Britain in the defense of the empire could provide for the protection of the American colonies at very little additional expense to itself. That is to say that the colonies, if independent, would have had to expend more resources in their own defense than did England, just to maintain the same level of protection. Our estimate of the value of military and naval protection provided by the British to the colonists, since it is based in part upon actual British expenditures, is therefore too low.

The value of British military protection was estimated as follows. Great Britain, before 1762, maintained a standing army in America of 3,000 officers and men. After 1762, the size of this troop complement was increased to 7,500 men. These troops were garrisoned throughout the colonies, including the frontiers where they served as a defensive force against the incursions of hostile Indians. Each man stationed in America cost the mother country an average of £29 a year, or annually a total expense of at least £217,500.

The colonists constantly complained about the quality of the "redcoats" as Indian fighters. Furthermore, they believed the larger standing army in the colonies after 1762 was there not primarily to protect them but for other reasons. However, they found after independence that a standing army of at least 5,000 men was required to replace the British. Thus the benefit to the colonies from the British army stationed in America was conservatively worth at least the cost of 5,000 troops, or £145,000.

Another large colonial benefit stemmed from the protection offered colonial shipping by the British navy, which included the Crown's annual tribute to the Barbary powers. The ability of the British navy to protect its merchant ships from the ravages of pirates far surpassed anything a small independent country could provide. This the colonies learned to their sorrow following the Revolution....

The colonists upon obtaining their independence lost the protection of the British fleet. Insurance rates, as a result, must have increased over the pre-revolutionary levels.

To estimate the approximate rise in insurance rates, we calculated the percentage decline in insurance rates for American merchant vessels following the launching in 1797 of three frigates which formed the foundation of the small, eighteenth-century American navy.

The percentage difference between the rates on an unprotected merchant marine and those charged on the merchant fleet safeguarded by our small navy was applied to the insurance rates prevailing before the Revolution. The weighted difference in rates between a barely protected merchant marine and a totally unprotected one was slightly over 50 per cent.

Applying this percentage to existing pre-revolutionary rates, it appears that the average cargo insurance rate, if the colonies had been independent, would have been at least 8.7 per cent of the value of the cargo instead of 5.4 per cent, a difference in rates of 2.7 per cent. Figuring this increase in insurance charges on the value of colonial cargoes in 1770 gives a low estimate of the value derived from British naval protection of £103,000. Three ships were not the British navy and could not be expected to provide equal protection. Marine insurance rates thus probably increased more than 2.7 per cent. An estimate that rates doubled does not seem unreasonable and would raise the annual value of naval protection to £206,000.

The estimate of the value of British protection for the American colonies is thus made up of the adjusted cost of the army in the colonies, £145,000, plus the estimated value of naval protection for the merchant marine of £206,000. The estimated total value of the protection afforded the colonies by their membership in the British Empire was thus calculated to be at least £351,000.

By way of a check upon this estimate, the Government of the United States, during its first nine years under the Constitution, found it necessary to spend annually an average of $2,133,000, or £426,600, for national defense. This included the purchase of arms and stores, the fortification of forts and harbors, and the building and manning of a small navy. In addition, an independent America had to bear the expense of conducting an independent foreign policy. The support of ministers to foreign nations, the cost of negotiating and implementing treaties, the payment of tribute to the Barbary nations, all previously provided for by Great Britain, now had to be borne by the independent colonies. These expenses alone cost the United States, during the last decade of the eighteenth century, annually over £60,000.

After achieving independence, the United States found it necessary to spend annually about £487,000 to provide certain functions of government formerly provided by Great Britain. This suggests that our estimate of £351,000 for the value of British protection to the American colonists is too low. It is doubtful, in the light of history, whether the new nation was able to provide this type of governmental services of equal quality to those furnished by the British. If not, even the £487,000 a year understates the value of governmental services supplied by Great Britain to her American colonies.

... My findings with reference to the effect of the Navigation Acts upon the economy of the thirteen colonies indicate a net burden of £532,000, or $2,660,000, in 1770. The average burden for the decade 1763–1772, based upon official values, was somewhat lower — £451,000, or $2,255,000.... Considering for a moment only the value of the losses on colonial exports and imports, the per capita annual cost to the colonist of being an Englishman instead of an American was $1.24 in 1770. The average per capita cost for the decade based upon official values was a somewhat lower $1.20. The benefits per capita in 1770 were figured to be 82 cents, and for the decade 94 cents.

Subtracting the benefits from the burdens for 1770 shows a per capita loss of 42 cents. The estimate for the decade shows a smaller loss of 26 cents a person. It is unlikely, because of the nature of the estimating procedures employed, that these losses are too low.

Table 1.2 SUMMARY OF THE RESULTS

	1763–1772	1770
Burdens		
Burden on colonial foreign commerce	£451,000 or $2,255,000	£532,000 or $2,660,000
Burden per capita	$1.20	$1.24
Benefits		
Benefit of British protection	£351,000 or $1,775,000	£351,000 or $1,775,000
Benefit per capita	$0.94	$0.82
Balance		
Estimate 1	$–0.26	$ –0.42

Conversely it is not at all improbable, and for the same reasons, that the estimated losses are too high.

Suppose that these findings reflect the true magnitude of the cost of the Navigation Acts to the thirteen colonies. The relevant question becomes: How important were these losses? Albert Fishlow stated... that he believed that the average per capita income in the 1780's "could not have been much less than $100." George Rogers Taylor... hazarded a guess that per capita income did not grow very rapidly, if at all, between 1775 and 1840. Therefore, assuming that average per capita income hovered about $100 between 1763 and 1772, what would it have been had the colonies been independent?

The answer is obvious from Table 1.2: it would not have been much different. The largest estimated loss on this basis is .54 of 1 per cent of per capita income, or 54 cents on a hundred dollars. Suppose for a moment that my estimates are off by 100 per cent; then, in that case the largest burden would be slightly more than 1 per cent of national income. It is difficult to make a convincing case for exploitation out of these results.

1–2. LARRY SAWERS, "THE NAVIGATION ACTS REVISITED"

...Before the outbreak of the civil war in England in 1642, the primary issue facing settlers in America was simply physical survival. Dependence on Britain was literally a life and death necessity. But the civil strife in England cut the colonies adrift and commercial relations with other Europeans, especially the Dutch and the French, grew rapidly. In an attempt to reimpose control over the wayward colonies after the war, and to keep other nations out of the colonies, the first of a series of laws which came to be known as the Navigation Acts was passed by Parliament. These laws were repeatedly extended and revised between the 1650s and the 1770s, but their essential thrust remained unchanged.

The Navigation Acts reserved all commerce between the colonies and Europe to British citizens (which included therefore the colonists themselves). Certain 'enumerated' goods bound for Europe from the colonies had first to be landed in a British port and then re-exported. Similarly, 'enumerated' imports from Europe had to be routed through England. The Navigation Acts also mandated the subsidy of certain commodities in the colonies such as naval stores and indigo, and forbade the manufacture of other goods such as fur hats.

Over the years, historians have taken sharply different positions with regard to the impact of the Navigation Acts. During the nineteenth century, historians generally accepted the interpretation of the Revolution that the patriots, or Whigs, as they were called at the time of the war, had formulated. The war was fought to end the oppression by the British and to bring liberty and justice to the American people.

Early in this century, two different groups of historians argued, instead, that the participants in the Revolution had economic, rather than merely political motivations. The Imperial School, led by [G.L.] Beer and [Charles M.] Andrews, viewed British mercantilism as essentially benign. Nevertheless, British mismanagement of the crisis which began in 1763 at the end of the Seven Years War (or French and Indian War) imposed economic hardships upon the colonies which encouraged them to rebel. The Progressive School, led by [Louis] Hacker and Charles and Mary Beard, viewed the relationship between Britain and America as essentially exploitative. Their analysis of the economic burdens of British mercantilism focused on the restrictions that the Navigation Acts placed on Northern merchants and on the debts which encumbered the Southern planter.

In the first quarter-century after World War II a new orthodoxy emerged. The political climate had changed in a sharply conservative direction and the notion that the founding fathers were avaricious, and dead beats besides, did not sit well. The neo-Whig School revived the nineteenth-century version of the events leading up to the war and focused on the struggle for democracy and liberty. For neo-Whigs, the ideals for which the patriots fought were the key. Their scholarship has traced out the intricate evolution of patriot political thinking in the century before 1776.

The neo-Whigs spent considerable effort in disproving the central tenets of the Progressive School, now largely considered discredited. Most scholars, following [Robert Paul] Thomas, agreed that the Navigation Acts imposed only an insignificant burden on the colonies. [E.G.] Evans demonstrated, to the satisfaction of most historians, that the external debt owed by the colonists, and especially by the tobacco planters, was not a grievance, or at least not so until the early 1770s. The twin pillars of the Progressives' argument were thus rejected.

In 1942 [Lawrence] Harper had changed the nature of the debate over the impact of the Navigation Acts on the colonial economy and their role in provoking the American Revolution by quantifying, rather than merely describing, the burden of British mercantilism on the colonies. Twenty years later Thomas refined Harper's analysis with a carefully constructed counterfactual, estimating the burdens of the Navigation Acts on the individual to be less than 0.5 per cent of the average colonist's income. A flurry of articles between 1968 and 1973 further clarified the analysis, but Thomas's conclusion that the Navigation Acts were an insignificant burden survived scrutiny.

Thomas proceeded along the following lines: the colonial economy was compared with an imaginary economy independent of Britain—the counterfactual—in order to measure the impact of British mercantilism. The various effects that British mercantilism had on the colonies in the decade or so before 1776 were individually assessed on an annual basis and then added to find the net annual burden. In order to decide whether this burden was 'heavy' (that is, sufficient to justify a war of independence) or 'not heavy' (insufficient to justify war), something with which to compare the annual burden was needed; Thomas chose GNP per caput. Estimates of the burden of the Navigation Acts range from less than 1 per cent to 3 per cent of gross colonial product, too small it was believed to have sparked the War of Independence.

Before examining in detail the burdens of the Navigation Acts, it is necessary to point out important errors of methodology and approach committed by Harper, Thomas, and their followers that encourage an underestimation of the burden of the Navigation Acts and reinforce the neo-Whig dismissal of economic grievances of the colonists.

First, Harper and Thomas chose the wrong counterfactual. They set out to measure the burden of the Navigation Acts on the colonies by comparing the actual pre-1776 colonial economy with an imaginary or counterfactual pre-1776 economy independent from Britain. But a rational colonist in 1776 trying to decide whether to join the patriot cause would have been concerned about the *future*, not the *past* burdens of British mercantilism. The appropriate counterfactual for the rational colonist was a post-1776 one. The past burdens were sunk costs and thus important only as indicators of future burdens....

If... the colonists were indeed thinking of the future gains of independence rather than smarting over prior insults, the appropriate methodology would compare actual, independent America after 1776 with a counterfactual colonial America after 1776. This is the appropriate comparison because it captures what was going on in the minds of American colonists, perhaps not perfectly, but better than the Harper/Thomas counterfactual....

My aim is to show that the various burdens of the pre-1776 period were typically less, often much less, than the future burdens that the colonists could and did expect to bear if independence had not been gained. Thus, the pre-1776 counterfactual seriously underestimates the burden of the Navigation Acts. The extent of this underestimate, however, is impossible to determine.

The post-1776 counterfactual is very different from the pre-1776 one. Harper and Thomas found that their task amounted to not much more than showing how a few key prices might have differed without the enumeration provisions of the Navigation Acts, and even this effort stirred considerable controversy. But if a counterfactual diverges substantially from the historical record, then its empirical estimation becomes more problematic. Too many relative prices change too drastically for accurate estimation. We know that the Revolution profoundly reshaped the American, and even the global, economy. Accordingly, one can speak qualitatively about the post-1776 counterfactual, but measuring the net burden of the costs of membership in the British empire in the post-1776 period is a hopeless task.

A second methodological criticism concerns the distribution of the burden of the Navigation Acts. Thomas and his followers have ignored distributional issues, dismissing the Navigation Acts because their burden was only a minute fraction of gross colonial income. Nevertheless, until hostilities broke out in 1775, and perhaps for several years after, the great majority of colonists wanted neither war nor independence. Before 1776 there were about as many loyalists as patriots. Even among those who supported the war, there were very different levels of commitment. In order to determine whether the burdens of the Navigation Acts sparked the Revolution, we must know the burdens on the revolutionaries, not on all the colonists. Conversely, in order to understand the motivation of those who opposed the Revolution, we must examine the benefits of the Acts that they received. Both the gross burden and the gross benefit of the Acts far exceeded the net burden. Thomas divided the net burden by the number of colonists, a statistic that cannot illuminate the impact of the Navigation Acts.

Those who played a leading role in supporting the Revolution could expect to bear substantial burdens if the Navigation Acts were not repealed. The most prominent leaders were, for the most part, merchants who dominated the Atlantic trade like John Hancock, and tobacco planters such as Thomas Jefferson or George Washington. Carolina rice planters such as Henry Laurens tended to support the Revolution, though without the same vigor as the Chesapeake tobacco planters. Urban artisans such as Benjamin Franklin or Paul Revere, as well as the journeymen in their employ, such as Thomas Paine, were generally patriots. These groups bore important costs imposed by the Navigation Acts. Other groups in colonial society, such as yeoman farmers outside Massachusetts, slaves, factors (commercial agents for merchants), and merchants with close ties to Britain, tended to be Loyalist. These groups were largely untouched by the Navigation Acts or actually benefited from them.

The traditional approach includes another major error by utilizing an inappropriately narrow conceptualization of the Navigation Acts. The Acts brought the colonists into head-to-head competition with the British. This imposed important costs in foregone profits on the colonists who were the underdogs in the struggle, and served as an important grievance leading up to the Declaration of Independence.

Taken together, the provisions of the Navigation Acts defined what amounted to a common market between Britain and its colonies in North America. There were few internal tariffs (Parliament disallowed most of the colonial attempts to impose protective tariffs on British goods) and a common external tariff. Within this common market, colonists and Britons competed with each other. From the British point of view, however, the Americans were supposed to be the junior member....

In the modern world, it is nearly universal practice for a nation's government to protect and assist that nation's commerce. Americans for the most part were not permitted to use the instruments of government to protect the American economy from the competition with the British that was forced on them by the Navigation Acts. The British, on the other hand, had a government which was willing and able to use governmental powers to maintain the economic supremacy of the mother country. It was not a level playing field. Over the course of the eighteenth century, American merchants in their commercial as well as industrial pursuits, tobacco planters acting as merchants, and artisans and journeymen in import substitution industries, were all under increasing pressure from British competition. This competition, unrecognized in the conventional analysis of the Navigation Acts, imposed substantial costs upon most of those groups in colonial society that took a leading role in the Revolution.

While most writers have noted the burden of re-export on the tobacco and rice planters, the impact of the re-exportation provisions of the Navigation Acts on colonial merchants has been largely ignored. Enumeration almost completely excluded colonial merchants from the lucrative tobacco trade. A bond had to be posted for a vessel bound from England to Virginia which could not be cancelled until the vessel returned to England with the enumerated goods. An unbonded ship leaving Virginia for England with a cargo of tobacco had to pay high duties. Only after transshipment in England could drawbacks on the tariffs be remitted. These procedures tied up a substantial amount of working capital and few colonial merchants had the financial resources to expedite the transactions. The colonial merchant believed that an end to the Navigation Acts would lead to American commercial dominance of the nation's commodity exports. The burden of the Acts on the colonial merchants was thus considerable.

Scottish and English dominance of the Atlantic tobacco trade affected the tobacco planter as well as the colonial merchant. By the mid-eighteenth century, and far more so by the depression of the 1760s, the Virginia planter had come to regard the English merchant as an enemy. Indeed, the notion that the British merchants had entered a deliberate conspiracy to bankrupt the planters and seize their possessions had achieved widespread currency among Tidewater planters. Even such a model of calm and enlightened reason as Thomas Jefferson subscribed to this conspiracy theory. The planters complained bitterly of the low price they received for their tobacco and were terrified by the rapidly growing number of prominent planters who lost their fortunes to British merchants in the turbulent 1760s and 1770s. During the 1760s, many tobacco planters (for example, George Washington) became wheat farmers. Unlike tobacco, wheat was largely excluded from export to Britain by the Corn Laws; it was thus marketed, to colonial merchants, thereby eluding the grasp of the British merchant.

...Thomas's own data show that tobacco planters' cash income would have been about one-third higher on average between 1763 and 1772 if tobacco had not been enumerated.... A number of authors have attempted to refine Thomas's estimation procedures, but all argue that enumeration produced substantially lower farm-gate tobacco prices. Furthermore, the phrase 'tobacco planter' obscures the issue in yet another way. There were several tens of thousands of tobacco planters in colonial America, but most were back-country farmers who sold only a few hogsheads of tobacco each year and who were otherwise subsistence farmers. Therefore, the Navigation Acts reduced their total income—which was largely income in kind—far less than their cash income. A handful of Tidewater planters grew most of the tobacco and the re-exportation provisions of the Navigation Acts fell principally on them.

The rice planters of the deep South, often neglected in discussions of the Revolution and its economic origins, faced a somewhat different situation. Rice was first enumerated in 1705, soon after commercially important quantities were produced in the colonies. While the bulk of colonial rice was shipped to England and then re-exported elsewhere, exemptions provided substantial relief from the burdens of the Navigation Acts. In 1731, rice export to southern Europe was taken off the enumeration list; then in 1763, to the French West Indies; and in 1764, to South America. Export of rice to the British Caribbean was never enumerated and a significant amount of rice was shipped to Northern colonies where it managed to escape the re-export requirements. Because of the partial exemption of rice from the re-export provisions of the Navigation Acts, the burdens of enumeration were proportionately lower. The lower level of patriotic enthusiasm among the Carolina rice planters compared with the Chesapeake tobacco planters is consistent with their lesser burden.

In summary, the enumeration provisions of the Navigation Acts imposed substantial burdens on certain segments of the colonial elite which formed the core of the patriot leadership. These provisions excluded the Northern merchants from the lucrative tobacco trade, reduced the cash incomes of the Southern planters, and forced them into a humiliating and precarious dependence on British merchants....

The merchants were [also] increasingly threatened by English and Scottish merchants in the years before the Revolution. After 1745 British merchants waged an aggressive campaign to seize control of the import of British manufactured goods into the colonies. English merchants engaged in two tactics to muscle their way into colonial commerce. First, they began selling directly to shopkeepers in the colonies with liberal extensions of credit, thus cutting the larger merchants out. Second, they engaged increasingly in auction sales, selling large quantities of goods with a very low mark-up, Furthermore, the Scottish factors in the Chesapeake region set up stores in the backcountry and sold British goods directly to farmers, thereby displacing the indigenous merchant.

From the early 1740s to the early 1750s, imports from Britain to the northern colonies increased by 40 per cent per caput, producing a depression of unprecedented proportions as unsold imported goods piled up on the shelves. The war with France yielded a temporary respite, but at the war's end in 1763, depression returned. A wave of bankruptcies brought down some of the most prominent colonial merchants, and throughout the colonies commerce retrenched.

The merchants' solution was a series of non-importation agreements. The first boycott of British imports occurred during 1765 and 1766. The inventory overhang abated as a result, but the boycott's end brought an even greater mercantile crisis. A second period of non-importation in 1769 and 1770 reproduced the cycle....

The colonial merchants repeatedly sought legal redress in their struggles with British merchants before 1776, but were just as often frustrated. The legal restrictions on auction sales, for example, proved ineffective or were overturned by British authorities; colonial efforts to achieve control over the money supply came to naught. Colonial merchants thus resorted to the extra-legal non-importation movement....

Whereas the Navigation Acts forced the colonial merchants into competition with the British, they actually protected the merchants from competition with merchants in other countries by reserving all trade with the colonies to British citizens. The Dutch were potentially the most threatening in this regard, followed by the French. Furthermore, shipping to and from the colonies had to be carried in British vessels, thus also providing protection from foreign competition to the many colonial merchants who were owners or insurers of vessels.

Indeed, it has sometimes been thought surprising that merchants typically supported a struggle for independence since the Navigation Acts provided such valuable protection. But the value to the colonists of protection from Dutch and French competition declined sharply in the second half of the eighteenth century. The Dutch had long since been forced out of their colony in North America. Throughout the world, from the Caribbean to the Spice Islands, Dutch commercial and military power had been checked by the British. Indeed British dominance over the Dutch had been clear since 1675, and their power had continued to decline since that date. The French had lost a long series of wars with Britain and the colonies in the eighteenth century, culminating in 1763 with the Treaty of Paris which sealed British hegemony in North America. When the Navigation Acts were first imposed in the seventeenth century, colonial merchants had little capital or expertise; protection from foreign competition was pivotal to their success. By 1776, however, the value of this protection had depreciated. The colonial merchants felt little threat from the Dutch and expected (correctly as it turned out) that the French would assist, not oppose, their quest for sovereignty.

Independence from Britain, however, would not abrogate the Navigation Acts in the British empire generally, but only in the newly independent country. It would mean that the Americans would be outside the empire and thus excluded from the British mercantilist system. Trade with Britain, Canada, Newfoundland, and the West Indies would be at a substantial disadvantage. The patriots, however, were sanguine on this score, believing that Britain's need for trade with the former colonies was so great that they could not be excluded, and that a neutral America would prosper through trade with the belligerents in future wars in Europe.

The fact that the Navigation Acts provided benefits to the merchants, as well as imposing costs on them, led to initial confusion and equivocation. Until the 1760s merchants were generally willing to accept the *status quo*. The gains from the Acts (protection from foreign competition) were significant, although diminishing. The costs imposed by enumeration were partially evaded by smuggling. The costs imposed by competition with the British, although growing rapidly, were still of manageable proportions. The balance of advantage swung after 1760 due to the vigorous attempt by the British to impose a strict and orthodox mercantilist policy, the defeat of the French in 1763, and the economic crisis in the colonies that dramatically increased the competitive disadvantage of the colonial merchant.

At issue is not whether independence from Britain did in fact allow American merchants to gain control of American commerce from English and Scottish merchants and at the same time continue to keep the Dutch and French merchants out of the picture (it did both eventually), but whether the colonial merchants expected independence to do so. There is considerable evidence that they did.

A central theme of the neo-Whigs' analysis of the Revolution was the ever-growing desire of Americans for sovereignty. The error of the neo-Whigs is in treating sovereignty as a purely political issue. For the colonial merchants, especially after 1760, political sovereignty was seen as an indispensable means to establish American economic independence, prosperity, and ultimately hegemony.

As soon as the new nation's legal structure allowed, political sovereignty was used to afford the economic protection to American commerce that the colonial governments had not been permitted to provide. Two of the first laws passed by Congress under the constitution of 1787 protected American merchants from foreign competition. Certain tariffs were lower on goods carried in American vessels and a tonnage duty on imported merchandise was lower if shipped in American vessels than in foreign ones. It was widely expected that this legislation would emancipate the country from its commercial subordination to England.

Not only were the merchants facing growing and costly competition from their counterparts in Britain, but the tobacco planter faced a similar challenge. Economic historians have often spoken admiringly of the Scottish merchants and factors who in the mid-eighteenth century rationalized Southern commerce and lowered transactions costs. But from the planters' point of view, the Scottish rationalization of commerce was more like an invasion in an economic war which they were losing. Before the Scottish challenge, the Southern planters themselves, many of whom acted as merchants on their own account, dominated the region's commerce. The growing Scottish influence over Southern commerce threatened the planters' hold over the smaller farmers who had formerly sold their tobacco to them on consignment. By the 1760s most of the small planters sold their tobacco directly to the Scottish factors for cash. The Scottish merchants were seen not only to exercise inordinate economic control, but to wield political power directly by intervening in the Virginia House of Burgesses to block unfavorable legislation. The tobacco planters faced a sharp economic and political challenge from Scottish factors and merchants. The real issue was who was going to run the South....

In summary, the Navigation Acts protected colonial commerce from competition from foreign merchants but encouraged competition with the British. The value of protection from foreign competition diminished steadily in the years before the Revolution while the intensity of competition with the British grew.

The Navigation Acts [also] prohibited the manufacture of a variety of products in the colonies. This affected the merchants as well as the manufacturers themselves. Harper argued that British restrictions against colonial manufacturing had little effect. Later, neo-Whigs did not challenge his assertion which, of course, supports their view that economics played little role in the coming of the Revolution. In my view, however, British obstruction of colonial manufacture was an important issue for merchants, artisans, and journeymen, most of whom supported independence from Britain.

...British mercantilism would have had a very different impact after 1776 than before. The most striking and ultimately profound economic change in the immediate post-revolutionary economy was the spread of the factory system. The advent of the mechanized factory in England in the early 1770s radically altered the possibilities of American industrialization. In less than a decade after the end of the Revolutionary War, the factory movement had spread to America despite vigorous British attempts to prevent this from happening.

If America had still been a British colony after 1776 and if the colonists had become successful in expanding manufacturing, the Navigation Acts would undoubtedly have been amended and enforced more strictly to obstruct American industrialization. Parliament had shown itself ready on several occasions to protect English enterprises at the expense of colonial ones. The prohibition against the manufacture of hats at the request of English hatters is one example and the Tea Act to shore up the East India Company is another. Furthermore, the mere possibility of British intervention in colonial America raised the risk, and thus the cost, of doing business, even if the intervention never came about.

There is a second aspect of the Navigation Acts that imposed substantial costs upon colonial manufacture. Since the Navigation Acts created a common market which included the colonies and the mother country, American manufactures competed directly with British manufactures in both American and British markets. Only transportation costs protected American manufactures from British competition. And as the costs of Atlantic transportation fell steadily over the eighteenth century, American manufactures were increasingly exposed to British competition. On many occasions the colonies attempted to impose protective tariffs, but most of these attempts were disallowed.

Political independence allowed the United States to give tariff protection to American industry that was largely denied the colonies. The second law passed by the US Congress under the 1787 constitution was a protectionist tariff, and protectionism continued as a guiding principle of US tariff policy. Without a protective tariff, America's industrialization undoubtedly would have been slowed. In sum, the burden of British mercantilism on colonial manufactures would have been substantial if independence had not been achieved and far larger than the Harper/Thomas-type counterfactual would suggest.

There were two groups within colonial society that had an important stake in the development of manufacturing in America, merchants and manufacturers themselves. Merchants, as a group, were playing a leading role in the transition from commercial to industrial capitalism in England at the time, and colonial merchants had already begun to play that role in the US, long before the Revolutionary War. The Northern merchants were well aware of the possibilities of import substitution manufacturing as one part of a strategy of achieving greater economic sovereignty.

Artisans produced a broad range of goods for domestic consumption and for export and were, like the merchants, threatened by competition from British manufacturers. As the volume of British imports mushroomed in the quarter-century before the Revolution, they increasingly felt the pinch of competition from the British. Because of lower wage costs and higher productivity, the British were able to undersell colonial manufacturers despite the high cost of Atlantic transport. The economic roller coaster in the last few decades before 1776 produced distress not just for the merchants, but also for domestic manufacturers. This makes understandable the enthusiastic participation of the artisans and mechanics—who formed the bulk of the urban 'lower orders'—in the revolutionary process. They made up the majority of the Sons of Liberty whose heavy-handed and violent enforcement of the non-importation agreements ensured their success. Furthermore, their interest in limiting competition with the British imports explains their bitter disputes with the merchants who ended each of the first two nonimportations after only a year. With the inventory overhang worked down by non-importation, the merchants were eager to quit. But non-importation had stimulated import substitution manufacturing and the artisans and mechanics wanted to continue. Indeed, interest in non-importation began as early as the 1750s among the urban lower classes.

…[T]he Navigation Acts [thus] established a legal framework which would have permitted substantial expansion of restrictions on colonial manufacture should the need arise, and which for the most part prohibited the colonists from using the instruments of government to protect domestic industry. Furthermore, the Acts taken as a whole established the legal framework of a common market between Britain, and its American colonies which imposed substantial costs on colonial artisans and mechanics who had to compete with British workers, and on colonial merchants who hoped to play a guiding and profitable role in American industrial growth.

The Tidewater tobacco planters and the colonial merchants were the most vigorous proponents of independence. The rice planters, artisans, and mechanics played a secondary but still vital role in the Revolution. The economic circumstances in which they found themselves were such that independence from Britain and the abrogation of the Navigation Acts could have been expected to produce substantial economic gain. The belief of neo-Whig historians that the patriots had little economic stake in seeking independence has been shown to be unfounded. But to have shown the existence of important economic burdens on key players in the revolutionary drama is not the same thing as showing that these burdens motivated the patriots. The appropriate counterfactual is that of the colonists, not of the historian.

The neo-Whigs have searched the speeches, memoirs, letters, and pamphlets of the patriots and found that the Navigation Acts, while often mentioned, do not head the patriots' list of grievances. For example, the Declaration of Independence, which presumably sums up the patriots' case for independence, lists about two dozen grievances against the British. Only two of these are narrowly economic in nature, and only one refers directly to the economic burdens of the Navigation Acts (that they prevented trade with non-British ports). Several other of the grievances listed in the Declaration of Independence make reference to the increasing rigor of the administration of the Navigation Acts in the last years before 1776. The 'swarms of officials' who came to harass the colonists is one such reference and the mention of trial without jury (the Admiralty courts used to enforce the Navigation system did not use juries) is another. But the Navigation Acts, narrowly construed, or economic grievances in general, are only a small part of the thrust of the Declaration of Independence. What then is the role of the Acts in sparking revolution?

The Acts imposed heavy costs upon some colonists who, not coincidentally, led the struggle that would end those Acts. Others received benefits from the Acts, but the vast majority was untouched. Most colonists consumed, either directly or indirectly, few imported goods and sold little or nothing in export markets. Tea, for example, was a luxury that most colonists could not afford; the Tea Act for them was not a great grievance. The Navigation Acts thus had little impact on their lives. Indeed, the Acts actually produced benefits for most colonists. Enumeration lowered the price of tobacco and rice in the colonies. Competition from English and Scottish merchants and factors helped the colonial consumer by lowering prices. The Navigation Acts mandated subsidies to the producers of more than two dozen different goods. The patriot leaders, in their effort to arouse the politically inert majority, could hardly make the Navigation Acts the centerpiece of their case for independence if the majority was unaffected by them or even benefited from them.

…The patriots formulated their arguments in favor of independence largely in political, not economic terms. This fact has encouraged the neo-Whigs in their effort to depict the Revolution as a struggle over ideas, not over pocketbooks. But in recruiting supporters to one's position, it may simply be impolitic to emphasize one's economic stake in a particular course of action since appeals to higher ideals than greed may win more support. Furthermore, an exclusive focus on the world of ideas cannot explain why certain people held those ideas and others did not. Only a minority of colonial society was patriot and a substantial majority, at least before 1776, was opposed to independence. Why did only certain colonists espouse the ideals of freedom and liberty? Perhaps these ideals were much more salient to the planters, merchants, and artisans who were paying dearly for their dependence on the British. Those who were unaffected by or gained from that dependence could not be expected to see so vividly the virtue of liberty.

At this juncture, most would agree that in the long run, perhaps the very long run, independence was better than dependence for most Americans. If this is so, then by couching their argument in mostly political terms, the elite was speaking directly to the (very) long-term interests of the American colonist while avoiding discussion of the shorter-term costs. But if we seek a full understanding of the roots of the American Revolution the fact that much of the revolutionary rhetoric was couched in political and not economic terms does not mean that we can safely ignore, as have the neo-Whigs, the narrowly economic burdens imposed on the colonial elite by dependence on Britain.

One can never know why the patriots supported the Revolutionary War since motivation can never be directly observed. Deeds and words are often a matter of record; motives can only be inferred. But it has been demonstrated that, contrary to the contemporary consensus, the Navigation Acts imposed substantial burdens on the leaders of the patriot cause; that these patriots were aware of those burdens; and that the burdens played a role in motivating the patriots to support the Revolution. It can also be shown that these patriots had good cause to downplay or conceal the extent of their concern over the Acts.

SUGGESTIONS FOR FURTHER READING

Charles M. Andrews, *The Colonial Period of American History. Volume 4 of England's Commercial and Colonial Policy* (1938).

T.C. Barrow, *Trade and Empire: the British Customs Service in Colonial America, 1600–1775* (1967).

George L. Beer, *British Colonial Policy, 1754–1765* (1958).

A. Bezanson, *et. al., Prices and Inflation During the American Revolution* (1951).

G.C. Bjork, "The Weaning of the American Economy: Independence, Market Changes, and Economic Development," *Journal of Economic History*, XXIV(1964), 541–560.

Timothy H. Breen, Tobacco Culture: *The Mentality of the Great Tidewater Planters on the Eve of the Revolution* (1985).

F. Broeze, The New Economic History, the Navigation Acts, and the Continental Tobacco Market, 1770–1790," *Economic History Review*, XXVI(1973), 668–678.

Oliver M. Dickerson, *The Navigation Acts and the American Revolution* (1951).

M. Egnal and J.A. Ernst, "An Economic Interpretation of the American Revolution," *William & Mary Quarterly*, 29(1972), 3–32.

Lawrence A. Harper, "Mercantilism and the American Revolution," *Canadian Historical Review*, 22(1942), 1–15.

James A. Henretta, "The War for Independence and American Economic Development," in R. Hoffman, *et. al., The Economy of Early America: The Revolutionary Period: 1763–1790* (1988).

D. Loschky, "Studies of the Navigation Acts: New Economic Non-History," *Economic History Review*, XXVI(1973), 689–691.

Peter McClelland, "The Cost to America of British Imperial Policy," *American Economic Review*, 59(1969), 370–381.

John J. McCusker, "British Mercantilist Policies and the American Colonies," in Stanley L. Engerman and Robert E. Gallman, eds., *The Cambridge Economic History of the United States*, vol. 1 (1996).

Roger Ransom, "British Policy and Colonial Growth: Some Implications of the Burden from the Navigation Acts," *Journal of Economic History*, XXVII(1968), 427–435.

James F. Shepherd and Gary M. Walton, *Shipping, Maritime Trade and the Economic Development of Colonial North America* (1972).

J. Reid, "Economic Burden: Spark to the Revolution?" *Journal of Economic History*, XXXVIII(1978), 81–100.

CHAPTER 2

The Economy of the New Nation

INTRODUCTION

When the Americans declared their independence in July, 1776 they also severed the economic umbilical cord that had connected them to Great Britain for 169 years. However much they had complained about Britain's mercantilistic restrictions and notwithstanding the rather robust smuggling trade in which they engaged, Britain remained the most important trading partner for the Americans throughout the entire colonial period. Loss of that trade threatened to devastate the economy of the new nation.

The Continental Congress was deeply aware of the economic implications of independence. Indeed, on the day that Congress formed a committee to draft the Declaration of Independence it also created another committee consisting of John Adams, Benjamin Franklin, and John Dickinson to draft a "Model Treaty" that could be used by the new nation to negotiate trade treaties with foreign powers. After independence was won in 1783 how best to structure the economy to promote growth and prosperity was central to the national discourse.

Economic considerations were a significant aspect of the effort to form a national government. Many of the difficulties the nation experienced in the 1780s arose because its first national government, the Articles of Confederation, lacked the power to tax, to regulate trade, and to coin money. The adoption of the U.S. Constitution in 1787 signaled in turn that a majority of the framers had come to believe that more centralized government control over the economy was vital to the new nation's success. But the Constitution created only a general framework for a national government and fleshing it out during George Washington's presidency proved to be an extremely divisive proposition. While members of the Revolutionary generation generally agreed that economic growth and prosperity were integral to the success of America's republican experiment, events soon demonstrated that they had vastly different concepts of how the new nation's economy should be structured.

Alexander Hamilton, the first Secretary of the Treasury, believed that the United States's best chance for survival in the dangerous international environment of the late 18th Century was to develop as quickly as possible into an economic and military power. During his tenure in Washington's cabinet he made several proposals to stimulate the development of the manufacturing sector of the economy and to centralize economic power in the new national government. One of Hamilton's proposals was to establish a national bank which was in a sense an early version of today's Federal Reserve System. Hamilton's proposals were among the issues that quickly divided the Revolutionary generation in the 1790s. Thomas Jefferson and his followers believed that Hamilton's economic plans, by stimulating commercial development, would lead to economic inequality in the new nation, thereby corrupting America's revolutionary idealism. They also feared that Hamilton's intention to centralize economic power in the national government would crush individual liberty. To the Jeffersonians, America's best hope for survival lay in encouraging the development of small, self-sufficient farming. They reasoned that this path would preserve economic equality and postpone the commercial development of the United States as long as possible. This disagreement between the Hamiltonians and the Jeffersonians over the new nation's economic future did much to contribute to the bitter divisions that split asunder the Revolutionary generation in the 1790s and led to the formation of the nation's first political parties.

Jefferson's election to the presidency in 1800 and the subsequent decline of Washington's Federalist Party settled the debate over the structure of the new nation's economy for a generation. As president, Jefferson moved quickly to dismantle much of Hamilton's economic system and through his 1803 Louisiana Purchase and his trade policies that ultimately led to a second war with Britain in 1812, the Virginian tried to realize his economic vision of the agrarian republic.

In the decades after the War of 1812 the American economy developed rapidly. Although agriculture continued to be the chief economic activity of most Americans, business and industry grew substantially after 1815. This economic growth and diversification raised a series of questions that rekindled a national debate over economic policy similar to that which had earlier divided the Jeffersonians and the Federalists. By the late 1820s, for example, the territorial expansion of the United States had created a demand for improved forms of internal transportation and many argued that the national government should help to pay for those improvements. Similarly, the growth of manufacturing in this era led to calls for high tariffs to protect American industry from foreign competition. And the rapid economic growth also convinced many Americans that the nation's financial needs could be met best through a new national bank.

Andrew Jackson's Democratic Party, the ideological descendent of the Jeffersonians, was the party in the antebellum decades that spoke mainly for the interests of farmers and small business. Jacksonian Democrats tended to believe that the nation's economic interests were best promoted with a minimum of interference from the national government and so generally opposed federally-funded internal improvements, high protective tariffs, and a national bank. As president Andrew Jackson wielded his veto power regularly to promote his party's vision for the United States's economic future, most famously with his 1830 veto of the Maysville Road Bill and his 1832 veto of the bill re-chartering the Second Bank of the United States. The Whig Party, led by Henry Clay and Daniel Webster, took form in the 1830s and for the remainder of the antebellum era promoted an alternative vision of the economic future. The Whigs, a party that mainly spoke for the emerging commercial and manufacturing interests, believed that active involvement by the national government in economic affairs was the best way to promote and sustain growth. They were strong advocates of protective tariffs, federally-funded internal improvements, and a national bank. The Whigs' most famous economic policy, Henry Clay's American System, proposed to use revenue from high tariffs to improve internal transportation throughout the nation.

The development of the economy from the end of the Revolution until the Civil War poses one of the most interesting and important questions of early American economic history. While economic historians generally agree that the colonial patterns of the economy remained intact until at least 1815 and that by 1860 a national, increasingly self-sufficient economy had emerged, they disagree over the factors that account for this transformation. How did the patterns of trade change between 1787 and 1860? What contributions did improvements in internal transportation make to the development of a national economy?

Did the cotton produced on southern plantations help to promote a national economy? What contribution did the policies of the federal government from the U.S. Constitution to the protective tariffs make to the transformation of the economy in this period? Shall we regard the era's rapid population growth and its improvements in public education as contributing factors to the emergence of a national economy? What role did technological innovation play in the economic growth? How similar are these early American debates over economic policy to today's debates?

DOCUMENTS

Document 2–1 is the U.S. Constitution, a document with which all Americans are familiar because of the national government it established. But it was also an attempt to resolve the serious economic problems that threatened to undermine the nation's experiment in independence in the 1780s. Consider, then, how this document attempted to solve those problems and what it reveals about early American ideas of political economy. Documents 2–2 and 2–3 are two of the important efforts Alexander Hamilton made as Treasury Secretary to promote the development of a national economy. The first of these, his 1790 "Report on Public Credit," was his attempt to resolve the nation's serious debt problem; his 1791 "Report of Manufactures" was his effort to encourage the development of the manufacturing sector of the economy.

Documents 2–4 and 2–5 reflect the competing philosophies that formed the national economic discourse in the antebellum decades. Henry Clay of Kentucky, a three-time presidential candidate of the Whig Party, was a forceful advocate of his party's belief in using the power of the national government to promote economic growth. His 1832 "Defense of the American System" summarizes the economic program of high tariffs and internal improvements that he sponsored for most of his political career. The Democratic Party's Andrew Jackson was the great nemesis of Clay and the Whig Party. Elected president in 1828, the Tennessee planter and hero of the Battle of New Orleans used his forceful personality to shape a political economy that was consistently at odds with that of the Whigs'. Document 2–5, Jackson's famous veto of the Whigs' 1832 bill to re-charter the Second Bank of the United States, offers a vigorous statement of that philosophy.

The final two documents provide interesting contemporary accounts of the evolving national economy. In 1843 John Finch, a British disciple of utopian socialist Robert Owen, traveled throughout the United States to observe the nature of economic life. Document 2–6 provides excerpts from the published account of his travels. Thomas Mooney was an Irishman who toured the United States during the 1840s. In letters he sent to his cousin Patrick, an Irish farmer, Mooney described the abundant economic opportunity the United States offered to the countless immigrants who were drawn to the United States in the 19th Century. Excerpts from Mooney's letters to his cousin form Document 2–7.

2–1. CONSTITUTION OF THE UNITED STATES

We the People of the United States, in Order to form a more perfect Union, establish Justice, insure domestic Tranquility, provide for the common defense, promote the general Welfare, and secure the Blessings of Liberty to ourselves and our Posterity, do ordain and establish this Constitution for the United States of America.

Article. I.

Section. 1.

All legislative Powers herein granted shall be vested in a Congress of the United States, which shall consist of a Senate and House of Representatives.

Section. 2.

The House of Representatives shall be composed of Members chosen every second Year by the People of the several States, and the Electors in each State shall have the Qualifications requisite for Electors of the most numerous Branch of the State Legislature.

No Person shall be a Representative who shall not have attained to the Age of twenty five Years, and been seven Years a Citizen of the United States, and who shall not, when elected, be an Inhabitant of that State in which he shall be chosen.

Representatives and direct Taxes shall be apportioned among the several States which may be included within this Union, according to their respective Numbers, which shall be determined by adding to the whole Number of free Persons, including those bound to Service for a Term of Years, and excluding Indians not taxed, three fifths of all other Persons. The actual Enumeration shall be made within three Years after the first Meeting of the Congress of the United States, and within every subsequent Term of ten Years, in such Manner as they shall by Law direct. The Number of Representatives shall not exceed one for every thirty Thousand, but each State shall have at Least one Representative; and until such enumeration shall be made, the State of New Hampshire shall be entitled to choose three, Massachusetts eight, Rhode-Island and Providence Plantations one, Connecticut five, New-York six, New Jersey four, Pennsylvania eight, Delaware one, Maryland six, Virginia ten, North Carolina five, South Carolina five, and Georgia three.

When vacancies happen in the Representation from any State, the Executive Authority thereof shall issue Writs of Election to fill such Vacancies.

The House of Representatives shall choose their Speaker and other Officers; and shall have the sole Power of Impeachment.

Section. 3.

The Senate of the United States shall be composed of two Senators from each State, chosen by the Legislature thereof for six Years; and each Senator shall have one Vote.

Immediately after they shall be assembled in Consequence of the first Election, they shall be divided as equally as may be into three Classes. The Seats of the Senators of the first Class shall be vacated at the Expiration of the second Year, of the second Class at the Expiration of the fourth Year, and of the third Class at the Expiration of the sixth Year, so that one third may be chosen every second Year; and if Vacancies happen by Resignation, or otherwise, during the Recess of the Legislature of any State, the Executive thereof may make temporary Appointments until the next Meeting of the Legislature, which shall then fill such Vacancies.

No Person shall be a Senator who shall not have attained to the Age of thirty Years, and been nine Years a Citizen of the United States, and who shall not, when elected, be an Inhabitant of that State for which he shall be chosen.

The Vice President of the United States shall be President of the Senate, but shall have no Vote, unless they be equally divided.

The Senate shall choose their other Officers, and also a President pro tempore, in the Absence of the Vice President, or when he shall exercise the Office of President of the United States.

The Senate shall have the sole Power to try all Impeachments. When sitting for that Purpose, they shall be on Oath or Affirmation. When the President of the United States is tried, the Chief Justice shall preside: And no Person shall be convicted without the Concurrence of two thirds of the Members present.

Judgment in Cases of Impeachment shall not extend further than to removal from Office, and disqualification to hold and enjoy any Office of honor, Trust or Profit under the United States: but the Party convicted shall nevertheless be liable and subject to Indictment, Trial, Judgment and Punishment, according to Law.

Section. 4.

The Times, Places and Manner of holding Elections for Senators and Representatives, shall be prescribed in each State by the Legislature thereof; but the Congress may at any time by Law make or alter such Regulations, except as to the Places of choosing Senators.

The Congress shall assemble at least once in every Year, and such Meeting shall be on the first Monday in December, unless they shall by Law appoint a different Day.

Section. 5.

Each House shall be the Judge of the Elections, Returns and Qualifications of its own Members, and a Majority of each shall constitute a Quorum to do Business; but a smaller Number may adjourn from day to day, and may be authorized to compel the Attendance of absent Members, in such Manner, and under such Penalties as each House may provide.

Each House may determine the Rules of its Proceedings, punish its Members for disorderly Behavior, and, with the Concurrence of two thirds, expel a Member.

Each House shall keep a Journal of its Proceedings, and from time to time publish the same, excepting such Parts as may in their Judgment require Secrecy; and the Yeas and Nays of the Members of either House on any question shall, at the Desire of one fifth of those Present, be entered on the Journal.

Neither House, during the Session of Congress, shall, without the Consent of the other, adjourn for more than three days, nor to any other Place than that in which the two Houses shall be sitting.

Section. 6.

The Senators and Representatives shall receive a Compensation for their Services, to be ascertained by Law, and paid out of the Treasury of the United States. They shall in all Cases, except Treason, Felony and Breach of the Peace, be privileged from Arrest during their Attendance at the Session of their respective Houses, and in going to and returning from the same; and for any Speech or Debate in either House, they shall not be questioned in any other Place.

No Senator or Representative shall, during the Time for which he was elected, be appointed to any civil Office under the Authority of the United States, which shall have been created, or the Emoluments whereof shall have been increased during such time; and no Person holding any Office under the United States, shall be a Member of either House during his Continuance in Office.

Section. 7.

All Bills for raising Revenue shall originate in the House of Representatives; but the Senate may propose or concur with Amendments as on other Bills.

Every Bill which shall have passed the House of Representatives and the Senate, shall, before it become a Law, be presented to the President of the United States: If he approve he shall sign it, but if not he shall return it, with his Objections to that House in which it shall have originated, who shall enter the Objections at large on their Journal, and proceed to reconsider it. If after such Reconsideration two thirds of that House shall agree to pass the Bill, it shall be sent, together with the Objections, to the other House, by which it shall likewise be reconsidered, and if approved by two thirds of that House, it shall become a Law. But in all such Cases the Votes of both Houses shall be determined by yeas and Nays, and the Names of the Persons voting for and against the Bill shall be entered on the Journal of each House respectively. If any Bill shall not be returned by the President within ten Days (Sundays excepted) after it shall have been presented to him, the Same shall be a Law, in like Manner as if he had signed it, unless the Congress by their Adjournment prevent its Return, in which Case it shall not be a Law.

Every Order, Resolution, or Vote to which the Concurrence of the Senate and House of Representatives may be necessary (except on a question of Adjournment) shall be presented to the President of the United States; and before the Same shall take Effect, shall be approved by him, or being disapproved by him, shall be repassed by two thirds of the Senate and House of Representatives, according to the Rules and Limitations prescribed in the Case of a Bill.

Section. 8.

The Congress shall have Power To lay and collect Taxes, Duties, Imposts and Excises, to pay the Debts and provide for the common Defense and general Welfare of the United States; but all Duties, Imposts and Excises shall be uniform throughout the United States;

To borrow Money on the credit of the United States;

To regulate Commerce with foreign Nations, and among the several States, and with the Indian Tribes;

To establish an uniform Rule of Naturalization, and uniform Laws on the subject of Bankruptcies throughout the United States;

To coin Money, regulate the Value thereof, and of foreign Coin, and fix the Standard of Weights and Measures;

To provide for the Punishment of counterfeiting the Securities and current Coin of the United States;

To establish Post Offices and post Roads;

To promote the Progress of Science and useful Arts, by securing for limited Times to Authors and Inventors the exclusive Right to their respective Writings and Discoveries;

To constitute Tribunals inferior to the supreme Court;

To define and punish Piracies and Felonies committed on the high Seas, and Offences against the Law of Nations;

To declare War, grant Letters of Marque and Reprisal, and make Rules concerning Captures on Land and Water;

To raise and support Armies, but no Appropriation of Money to that Use shall be for a longer Term than two Years;

To provide and maintain a Navy;

To make Rules for the Government and Regulation of the land and naval Forces;

To provide for calling forth the Militia to execute the Laws of the Union, suppress Insurrections and repel Invasions;

To provide for organizing, arming, and disciplining, the Militia, and for governing such Part of them as may be employed in the Service of the United States, reserving to the States respectively, the Appointment of the Officers, and the Authority of training the Militia according to the discipline prescribed by Congress;

To exercise exclusive Legislation in all Cases whatsoever, over such District (not exceeding ten Miles square) as may, by Cession of particular States, and the Acceptance of Congress, become the Seat of the Government of the United States, and to exercise like Authority over all Places purchased by the Consent of the Legislature of the State in which the Same shall be, for the Erection of Forts, Magazines, Arsenals, dock-Yards, and other needful Buildings;—And

To make all Laws which shall be necessary and proper for carrying into Execution the foregoing Powers, and all other Powers vested by this Constitution in the Government of the United States, or in any Department or Officer thereof.

Section. 9.

The Migration or Importation of such Persons as any of the States now existing shall think proper to admit, shall not be prohibited by the Congress prior to the Year one thousand eight hundred and eight, but a Tax or duty may be imposed on such Importation, not exceeding ten dollars for each Person.

The Privilege of the Writ of Habeas Corpus shall not be suspended, unless when in Cases of Rebellion or Invasion the public Safety may require it.

No Bill of Attainder or ex post facto Law shall be passed.

No Capitation, or other direct, Tax shall be laid, unless in Proportion to the Census or enumeration herein before directed to be taken.

No Tax or Duty shall be laid on Articles exported from any State.

No Preference shall be given by any Regulation of Commerce or Revenue to the Ports of one State over those of another; nor shall Vessels bound to, or from, one State, be obliged to enter, clear, or pay Duties in another.

No Money shall be drawn from the Treasury, but in Consequence of Appropriations made by Law; and a regular Statement and Account of the Receipts and Expenditures of all public Money shall be published from time to time.

No Title of Nobility shall be granted by the United States: And no Person holding any Office of Profit or Trust under them, shall, without the Consent of the Congress, accept of any present, Emolument, Office, or Title, of any kind whatever, from any King, Prince, or foreign State.

Section. 10.

No State shall enter into any Treaty, Alliance, or Confederation; grant Letters of Marque and Reprisal; coin Money; emit Bills of Credit; make any Thing but gold and silver Coin a Tender in Payment of Debts; pass any Bill of Attainder, ex post facto Law, or Law impairing the Obligation of Contracts, or grant any Title of Nobility.

No State shall, without the Consent of the Congress, lay any Imposts or Duties on Imports or Exports, except what may be absolutely necessary for executing it's inspection Laws: and the net Produce of all Duties and Imposts, laid by any State on Imports or Exports, shall be for the Use of the Treasury of the United States; and all such Laws shall be subject to the Revision and Control of the Congress.

No State shall, without the Consent of Congress, lay any Duty of Tonnage, keep Troops, or Ships of War in time of Peace, enter into any Agreement or Compact with another State, or with a foreign Power, or engage in War, unless actually invaded, or in such imminent Danger as will not admit of delay.

Article. II.

Section. 1.

The executive Power shall be vested in a President of the United States of America. He shall hold his Office during the Term of four Years, and, together with the Vice President, chosen for the same Term, be elected, as follows:

Each State shall appoint, in such Manner as the Legislature thereof may direct, a Number of Electors, equal to the whole Number of Senators and Representatives to which the State may be entitled in the Congress: but no Senator or Representative, or Person holding an Office of Trust or Profit under the United States, shall be appointed an Elector.

The Electors shall meet in their respective States, and vote by Ballot for two Persons, of whom one at least shall not be an Inhabitant of the same State with themselves. And they shall make a List of all the Persons voted for, and of the Number of Votes for each; which List they shall sign and certify, and transmit sealed to the Seat of the Government of the United States, directed to the President of the Senate. The President of the Senate shall, in the Presence of the Senate and House of Representatives, open all the Certificates, and the Votes shall then be counted. The Person having the greatest Number of Votes shall be the President, if such Number be a Majority of the whole Number of Electors appointed; and if there be more than one who have such Majority, and have an equal Number of Votes, then the House of Representatives shall immediately choose by Ballot one of them for President; and if no Person have a Majority, then from the five highest on the List the said House shall in like Manner choose the President. But in choosing the President, the Votes shall be taken by States, the Representation from each State having one Vote; A quorum for this purpose shall consist of a Member or Members from two thirds of the States, and a Majority of all the States shall be necessary to a Choice. In every Case, after the Choice of the President, the Person having the greatest Number of Votes of the Electors shall be the Vice President. But if there should remain two or more who have equal Votes, the Senate shall choose from them by Ballot the Vice President.

The Congress may determine the Time of choosing the Electors, and the Day on which they shall give their Votes; which Day shall be the same throughout the United States.

No Person except a natural born Citizen, or a Citizen of the United States, at the time of the Adoption of this Constitution, shall be eligible to the Office of President; neither shall any Person be eligible to that Office who shall not have attained to the Age of thirty five Years, and been fourteen Years a Resident within the United States.

In Case of the Removal of the President from Office, or of his Death, Resignation, or Inability to discharge the Powers and Duties of the said Office, the Same shall devolve on the Vice President, and the Congress may by Law provide for the Case of Removal, Death, Resignation or Inability, both of the President and Vice President, declaring what Officer shall then act as President, and such Officer shall act accordingly, until the Disability be removed, or a President shall be elected.

The President shall, at stated Times, receive for his Services, a Compensation, which shall neither be increased nor diminished during the Period for which he shall have been elected, and he shall not receive within that Period any other Emolument from the United States, or any of them.

Before he enter on the Execution of his Office, he shall take the following Oath or Affirmation:—"I do solemnly swear (or affirm) that I will faithfully execute the Office of President of the United States, and will to the best of my Ability, preserve, protect and defend the Constitution of the United States."

Section. 2.

The President shall be Commander in Chief of the Army and Navy of the United States, and of the Militia of the several States, when called into the actual Service of the United States; he may require the Opinion, in writing, of the principal Officer in each of the executive Departments, upon any Subject relating to the Duties of their respective Offices, and he shall have Power to grant Reprieves and Pardons for Offences against the United States, except in Cases of Impeachment.

He shall have Power, by and with the Advice and Consent of the Senate, to make Treaties, provided two thirds of the Senators present concur; and he shall nominate, and by and with the Advice and Consent of the Senate, shall appoint Ambassadors, other public Ministers and Consuls, Judges of the supreme Court, and all other Officers of the United States, whose Appointments are not herein otherwise provided for, and which shall be established by Law: but the Congress may by Law vest the Appointment of such inferior Officers, as they think proper, in the President alone, in the Courts of Law, or in the Heads of Departments.

The President shall have Power to fill up all Vacancies that may happen during the Recess of the Senate, by granting Commissions which shall expire at the End of their next Session.

Section. 3.

He shall from time to time give to the Congress Information of the State of the Union, and recommend to their Consideration such Measures as he shall judge necessary and expedient; he may, on extraordinary Occasions, convene both Houses, or either of them, and in Case of Disagreement between them, with Respect to the Time of Adjournment, he may adjourn them to such Time as he shall think proper; he shall receive Ambassadors and other public Ministers; he shall take Care that the Laws be faithfully executed, and shall Commission all the Officers of the United States.

Section. 4.

The President, Vice President and all civil Officers of the United States, shall be removed from Office on Impeachment for, and Conviction of, Treason, Bribery, or other high Crimes and Misdemeanors.

Article III.

Section. 1.

The judicial Power of the United States shall be vested in one supreme Court, and in such inferior Courts as the Congress may from time to time ordain and establish. The Judges, both of the supreme and inferior Courts, shall hold their Offices during good Behavior, and shall, at stated Times, receive for their Services a Compensation, which shall not be diminished during their Continuance in Office.

Section. 2.

The judicial Power shall extend to all Cases, in Law and Equity, arising under this Constitution, the Laws of the United States, and Treaties made, or which shall be made, under their Authority;—to all Cases affecting Ambassadors, other public Ministers and Consuls;—to all Cases of admiralty and maritime Jurisdiction;—to Controversies to which the United States shall be a Party;—to Controversies between two or more States;—between a State and Citizens of another State;—between Citizens of different States;—between Citizens of the same State claiming Lands under Grants of different States, and between a State, or the Citizens thereof, and foreign States, Citizens or Subjects.

In all Cases affecting Ambassadors, other public Ministers and Consuls, and those in which a State shall be Party, the supreme Court shall have original Jurisdiction. In all the other Cases before mentioned, the supreme Court shall have appellate Jurisdiction, both as to Law and Fact, with such Exceptions, and under such Regulations as the Congress shall make.

The Trial of all Crimes, except in Cases of Impeachment, shall be by Jury; and such Trial shall be held in the State where the said Crimes shall have been committed; but when not committed within any State, the Trial shall be at such Place or Places as the Congress may by Law have directed.

Section. 3.

Treason against the United States, shall consist only in levying War against them, or in adhering to their Enemies, giving them Aid and Comfort. No Person shall be convicted of Treason unless on the Testimony of two Witnesses to the same overt Act, or on Confession in open Court.

The Congress shall have Power to declare the Punishment of Treason, but no Attainder of Treason shall work Corruption of Blood, or Forfeiture except during the Life of the Person attainted.

Article. IV.

Section. 1.

Full Faith and Credit shall be given in each State to the public Acts, Records, and judicial Proceedings of every other State. And the Congress may by general Laws prescribe the Manner in which such Acts, Records and Proceedings shall be proved, and the Effect thereof.

Section. 2.

The Citizens of each State shall be entitled to all Privileges and Immunities of Citizens in the several States.

A Person charged in any State with Treason, Felony, or other Crime, who shall flee from Justice, and be found in another State, shall on Demand of the executive Authority of the State from which he fled, be delivered up, to be removed to the State having Jurisdiction of the Crime.

No Person held to Service or Labor in one State, under the Laws thereof, escaping into another, shall, in Consequence of any Law or Regulation therein, be discharged from such Service or Labor, but shall be delivered up on Claim of the Party to whom such Service or Labor may be due.

Section. 3.

New States may be admitted by the Congress into this Union; but no new State shall be formed or erected within the Jurisdiction of any other State; nor any State be formed by the Junction of two or more States, or Parts of States, without the Consent of the Legislatures of the States concerned as well as of the Congress.

The Congress shall have Power to dispose of and make all needful Rules and Regulations respecting the Territory or other Property belonging to the United States; and nothing in this Constitution shall be so construed as to Prejudice any Claims of the United States, or of any particular State.

Section. 4.

The United States shall guarantee to every State in this Union a Republican Form of Government, and shall protect each of them against Invasion; and on Application of the Legislature, or of the Executive (when the Legislature cannot be convened), against domestic Violence.

Article. V.

The Congress, whenever two thirds of both Houses shall deem it necessary, shall propose Amendments to this Constitution, or, on the Application of the Legislatures of two thirds of the several States, shall call a Convention for proposing Amendments, which, in either Case, shall be valid to all Intents and Purposes, as Part of this Constitution, when ratified by the Legislatures of three fourths of the several States, or by Conventions in three fourths thereof, as the one or the other Mode of Ratification may be proposed by the Congress; Provided that no Amendment which may be made prior to the Year One thousand eight hundred and eight shall in any Manner affect the first and fourth Clauses in the Ninth Section of the first Article; and that no State, without its Consent, shall be deprived of its equal Suffrage in the Senate.

Article. VI.

All Debts contracted and Engagements entered into, before the Adoption of this Constitution, shall be as valid against the United States under this Constitution, as under the Confederation.

This Constitution, and the Laws of the United States which shall be made in Pursuance thereof; and all Treaties made, or which shall be made, under the Authority of the United States, shall be the supreme Law of the Land; and the Judges in every State shall be bound thereby, any Thing in the Constitution or Laws of any State to the Contrary notwithstanding.

The Senators and Representatives before mentioned, and the Members of the several State Legislatures, and all executive and judicial Officers, both of the United States and of the several States, shall be bound by Oath or Affirmation, to support this Constitution; but no religious Test shall ever be required as a Qualification to any Office or public Trust under the United States.

Article. VII.

The Ratification of the Conventions of nine States, shall be sufficient for the Establishment of this Constitution between the States so ratifying the Same.

The Word, "the," being interlined between the seventh and eighth Lines of the first Page, the Word "Thirty" being partly written on an Erasure in the fifteenth Line of the first Page, The Words "is tried" being interlined between the thirty second and thirty third Lines of the first Page and the Word "the" being interlined between the forty third and forty fourth Lines of the second Page.

Attest William Jackson Secretary

Done in Convention by the Unanimous Consent of the States present the Seventeenth Day of September in the Year of our Lord one thousand seven hundred and Eighty seven and of the Independence of the United States of America the Twelfth In witness whereof We have hereunto subscribed our Names,

G°. Washington
Presidt and deputy from Virginia

Delaware
Geo: Read
Gunning Bedford jun
John Dickinson
Richard Bassett
Jaco: Broom

Maryland
James McHenry
Dan of St Thos. Jenifer
Danl. Carroll

Virginia
John Blair
James Madison Jr.

North Carolina
Wm. Blount
Richd. Dobbs Spaight
Hu Williamson

South Carolina
J. Rutledge
Charles Cotesworth Pinckney
Charles Pinckney
Pierce Butler

Georgia
William Few
Abr Baldwin

New Hampshire
John Langdon
Nicholas Gilman

Massachoosetts
Nathaniel Gorham
Rufus King

Connecticut
Wm. Saml. Johnson
Roger Sherman

New York
Alexander Hamilton

New Jersey
Wil: Livingston
David Brearley
Wm. Paterson
Jona: Dayton

Pennsylvania
B Franklin
Thomas Mifflin
Robt. Morris
Geo. Clymer
Thos. FitzSimons
Jared Ingersoll
James Wilson
Gouv Morris

2–2. ALEXANDER HAMILTON, JANUARY 9, 1790, "REPORT OF THE SECRETARY OF THE TREASURY, WITH HIS PLAN FOR SUPPORTING PUBLIC CREDIT"

The Secretary of the Treasury, in obedience to the resolution of the House of Representatives, of the twenty-first day of September last, has, during the recess of Congress, applied himself to the consideration of a proper plan for the support of public credit, with all the attention which was due to the authority of the House and to the magnitude of the object.

In the discharge of this duty, he has felt…a deep and solemn conviction of the momentous nature of the truth contained in the resolution under which his investigation had been conducted: "That an adequate provision for the support of the public credit is a matter of high importance to the honor and prosperity of the United States."

…In the opinion of the Secretary, the wisdom of the House, in giving their explicit sanction to the proposition…cannot but be applauded by all, who will seriously consider… these plain and undeniable truths.

That exigencies are to be expected to occur, in the affairs of nations, in which there will be a necessity for borrowing.

That loans in times of public danger, especially from foreign war, are found an indispensable resource, even to the wealthiest of them.

And that in a country, which, like this, is possessed of little active wealth, or in other words, little moneyed capital, the necessity for that resource, must, in such emergencies, be proportionably [sic.] urgent.

And as on the one hand, the necessity for borrowing in particular emergencies cannot be doubted, so on the other, it is equally evident, that to be able to borrow upon good terms, it is essential that the credit of a nation should be well established.

For when the credit of a country is in any degree questionable, it never fails to give an extravagant premium, in one shape or another, upon all the loans it has occasion to make. Nor does the evil end here; the same disadvantage must be sustained upon whatever is to be bought on terms of future payment.

From this constant necessity of borrowing and buying dear, it is easy to conceive how immensely the expenses of a nation, in a course of time, will be augmented by an unsound state of the public credit.

To attempt to enumerate the complicated variety of mischiefs in the whole system of the social economy, which proceed from a neglect of the maxims that uphold public credit, and justify the solicitude manifested by the House on this point, would be an improper intrusion on their time and patience.

In so strong a light nevertheless do they appear to the Secretary, that on their due observance at the present critical juncture, materially depends, in his judgment, the individual and aggregate prosperity of the citizens of the United States; their relief from the embarrassments they now experience; their character as a People; the cause of good government.

If the maintenance of public credit, then, be truly so important, the next enquiry which suggests itself is, by what means it is to be effected? The ready answer to which question is, by good faith, by a punctual performance of contracts. States, like individuals, who observe their engagements, are respected and trusted: while the reverse is the fate of those, who pursue an opposite conduct….

While the observance of that good faith, which is the basis of public credit, is recommended by the strongest inducements of political expediency, it is enforced by considerations of still greater authority. There are arguments for it, which rest on the immutable principles of moral obligation. And in proportion as the mind is disposed to contemplate, in the order of Providence, an intimate connection between public virtue and public happiness, will be its repugnancy to a violation of those principles.

This reflection derives additional strength from the nature of the debt of the United States. It was the price of liberty. The faith of America has been repeatedly pledged for it, and with solemnities, that give peculiar force to the obligation. There is indeed reason to regret that it has not hitherto been kept; that the necessities of the war, conspiring with inexperience in the subjects of finance, produced direct infractions; and that the subsequent period has been a continued scene of negative violation, or non-compliance. But a diminution of this regret arises from the reflection, that the last seven years have exhibited an earnest and uniform effort, on the part of the government of the union, to retrieve the national credit, by doing justice to the creditors of the nation; and that the embarrassments of a defective constitution, which defeated this laudable effort, have ceased.

From this evidence of a favorable disposition, given by the former government, the institution of a new one, clothed with powers competent to calling forth the resources of the community, has excited correspondent expectations. A general belief, accordingly, prevails, that the credit of the United States will quickly be established on the firm foundation of an effectual provision for the existing debt. The influence, which this has had at home, is witnessed by the rapid increase, that has taken place in the market value of the public securities. From January to November, they rose thirty-three and a third per cent, and from that period to this time, they have risen fifty per cent more. And the intelligence from abroad announces effects proportionably [sic.] favorable to our national credit and consequence....

The advantage to the public creditors from the increased value of that part of their property which constitutes the public debt, needs no explanation.

But there is a consequence of this, less obvious, though not less true, in which every other citizen is interested. It is a well known fact, that in countries in which the national debt is properly funded, and an object of established confidence, it answers most of the purposes of money. Transfers of stock or public debt are there equivalent to payments in specie; or in other words, stock, in the principal transactions of business, passes current as specie. The same thing would, in all probability happen here, under the like circumstances.

The benefits of this are various and obvious.

First. Trade is extended by it; because there is a larger capital to carry it on, and the merchant can at the same time, afford to trade for smaller profits; as his stock, which, when unemployed, brings him in an interest from the government, serves him also as money, when he has a call for it in his commercial operations.

Secondly. Agriculture and manufactures are also promoted by it: For the like reason, that more capital can be commanded to be employed in both; and because the merchant, whose enterprise in foreign trade, gives to them activity and extension, has greater means for enterprise.

Thirdly. The interest of money will be lowered by it; for this is always in a ratio, to the quantity of money, and to the quickness of circulation. This circumstance will enable both the public and individuals to borrow on easier and cheaper terms.

And from the combination of these effects, additional aids will be furnished to labor, to industry, and to arts of every kind.

But these good effects of a public debt are only to be looked for, when, by being well funded, it has acquired an adequate and stable value. Till then, it has rather a contrary tendency. The fluctuation and insecurity incident to it in an unfunded state, render it a mere commodity, and a precarious one. As such, being only an object of occasional and particular speculation, all the money applied to it is so much diverted from the more useful channels of circulation, for which the thing itself affords no substitute: So that, in fact, one serious inconvenience of an unfunded debt is, that it contributes to the scarcity of money.

This distinction which has been little if at all attended to, is of the greatest moment. It involves a question immediately interesting to every part of the community; which is no other than this—Whether the public debt, by a provision for it on true principles, shall be rendered a substitute for money; or whether, by being left as it is, or by being provided for in such a manner as will wound those principles, and destroy confidence, it shall be suffered to continue, as it is, a pernicious drain of our cash from the channels of productive industry.

The effect, which the funding of the public debt, on right principles, would have upon landed property, is one of the circumstances attending such an arrangement, which has been least adverted to, though it deserves the most particular attention. The present depreciated state of that species of property is a serious calamity. The value of cultivated lands, in most of the states, has fallen since the revolution from 25 to 50 per cent. In those farthest south, the decrease is still more considerable. Indeed, if the representations, continually received from that quarter, may be credited, lands there will command no price, which may not be deemed an almost total sacrifice.

This decrease, in the value of lands, ought, in a great measure, to be attributed to the scarcity of money. Consequently whatever produces an augmentation of the moneyed capital of the country, must have a proportional effect in raising that value. The beneficial tendency of a funded debt, in this respect, has been manifested by the most decisive experience in Great Britain.

The proprietors of lands would not only feel the benefit of this increase in the value of their property, and of a more prompt and better sale, when they had occasion to sell; but the necessity of selling would be, itself, greatly diminished. As the same cause would contribute to the facility of loans, there is reason to believe, that such of them as are indebted, would be able through that resource, to satisfy their more urgent creditors.

It ought not however to be expected, that the advantages, described as likely to result from funding the public debt, would be instantaneous. It might require some time to bring the value of stock to its natural level, and to attach to it that fixed confidence, which is necessary to its quality as money. Yet the late rapid rise of the public securities encourages an expectation, that the progress of stock to the desireable point, will be much more expeditious than could have been foreseen. And as in the mean time it will be increasing in value, there is room to conclude, that it will, from the outset, answer many of the purposes in contemplation. Particularly it seems to be probable, that from creditors, who are not themselves necessitous, it will early meet with a ready reception in payment of debts, at its price current.

Having now taken a concise view of the inducements to a proper provision for the public debt, the next inquiry which presents itself is, what ought to be the nature of such a provision? This requires some preliminary discussion.

It is agreed on all hands, that that part of the debt which has been contracted abroad, and is denominated the foreign debt, ought to be provided for, according to the precise terms of the contracts relating to it. The discussions, which can arise, therefore, will have reference essentially to the domestic part of it, or to that which has been contracted at home. It is to be regretted, that there is not the same unanimity of sentiment on this part, as on the other.

The Secretary has too much deference for the opinions of every part of the community, not to have observed one, which has, more than once, made its appearance in the public prints, and which is occasionally to be met with in conversation. It involves this question, whether a discrimination ought not to be made between original holders of the public securities, and present possessors, by purchase. Those who advocate a discrimination are for making a full provision for the securities of the former, at their nominal value; but contend, that the latter ought to receive no more than the cost to them, and the interest: And the idea is sometimes suggested of making good the difference to the primitive possessor.

In favor of this scheme, it is alleged, that it would be unreasonable to pay twenty shillings in the pound, to one who had not given more for it than three or four. And it is added, that it would be hard to aggravate the misfortune of the first owner, who, probably through necessity, parted with his property at so great a loss, by obliging him to contribute to the profit of the person, who had speculated on his distresses.

The Secretary, after the most mature reflection on the force of this argument, is induced to reject the doctrine it contains, as equally unjust and impolitic, as highly injurious, even to the original holders of public securities; as ruinous to public credit.

It is inconsistent with justice, because in the first place, it is a breach of contract; in violation of the rights of a fair purchaser.

The nature of the contract in its origin, is, that the public will pay the sum expressed in the security, to the first holder, or his assignee. The intent, in making the security assignable, is, that the proprietor may be able to make use of his property, by selling it for as much as it may be worth in the market, and that the buyer may be safe in the purchase.

Every buyer, therefore, stands exactly in the place of the seller, has the same right with him to the identical sum expressed in the security, and having acquired that right, by fair purchase and in conformity to the original agreement and intention of the Government, his claim cannot be disputed without manifest injustice....

...[T]hough many of the original holders sold from necessity, it does not follow that this was the case with all of them. It may well be supposed that some of them did it either through want of confidence in an eventual provision, or from the allurement of some profitable speculation. How shall these different classes be discriminated from each other? How shall it be ascertained...that the money which the original holder obtained for his securities was not more beneficial to him than if he had held to the present time to avail himself of the provision which shall be made? How shall it be known if the purchaser had employed his money in some other way, he would not be in a better situation than by having applied it in the purchase of securities, though he should now receive the full amount? And if neither of these things can be known, how shall it be determined if a discrimination... would not do a real injury to the purchasers; and if it included a compensation to the primitive proprietors, would not give them an advantage to which they had no equitable pretensions....

The impolicy of a discrimination results from two considerations; one, that it proceeds upon a principle destructive of that quality of the public debt, or the stock of the nation, which is essential to its capacity for answering the purposes of money—that is the security of transfer; the other, that as well on this account, as because it includes a breach of faith, it renders property in the funds less valuable; consequently induces lenders to demand a higher premium for what they lend, and produces every other inconvenience of a bad state of public credit.

It will be perceived at first sight, that the transferable quality of stock is essential to its operation as money, and that this depends on the idea of complete security to the transferree, and a firm persuasion, that no distinction can in any circumstances be made between him and the original proprietor....

But there is still a point in view in which it will appear perhaps even more exceptionable, than in either of the former. It would be repugnant to an express provision of the Constitution of the United States. This provision is, that "all debts contracted and engagements entered into before the adoption of that Constitution shall be as valid against the United States under it, as under the confederation," which amounts to a constitutional ratification of the contracts respecting the debt, in the state in which they existed under the confederation. And resorting to that standard, there can be no doubt, that the rights of assignees and original holders, must be considered as equal....

The Secretary concluding, that a discrimination, between the different classes of creditors of the United States, cannot with propriety be made, proceeds to examine whether a difference ought to be permitted to remain between them, and another description of public creditors—Those of the states individually.

The Secretary, after mature reflection on this point, entertains a full conviction, that an assumption of the debts of the particular states by the union, and a like provision for them, as for those of the union, will be a measure of sound policy and substantial justice.

It would… contribute… to an orderly, stable and satisfactory arrangement of the national finances. Admitting, as ought to be the case, that a provision must be made in some way or other, for the entire debt; it will follow, that no greater revenues will be required, whether that provision be made wholly by the United States, or partly by them, and partly by the states separately.

The principal question then must be, whether such a provision cannot be more conveniently and effectually made, by one general plan issuing from one authority, than by different plans originating in different authorities....

The difficulty of an effectual command of the public resources, in case of separate provisions for the debt, may be seen in… a more striking light. It would naturally happen that different states, from local considerations, would…have recourse to different objects, in others to the same objects in different degrees for procuring the funds of which they stood in need. It is easy to see how this diversity would affect the aggregate revenue of the country.... [A]rticles which yielded a full supply in some states, would yield nothing or an insufficient product in others. And hence the public revenue would not derive the full benefit of those articles from state regulations....

If all the public creditors receive their dues from one source, distributed with an equal hand, their interest will be the same. And having the same interests, they will unite in the support of the fiscal arrangements of the government....

If this view of the subject be a just one, the capital debt of the United States may be considered in the light of an annuity, at the rate of six percent per annum, redeemable at the pleasure of the government, by payment of the principal.... Wherefore, as long as the United States should pay the interest of their debt… their creditors would have no right to demand the principal....

The result of the foregoing discussions is this: That there ought to be no discrimination between the original holders of the debt and present possessors by purchase; that it is expedient there should be an assumption of state debts by the Union, and the arrears of interest should be provided for on an equal footing with the principal....

Persuaded as the Secretary is, that the proper funding of the present debt, will render it a national blessing: Yet he is so far from acceding to the position, in the latitude in which it is sometimes laid down, that "public debts are public benefits," a position inviting to prodigality, and liable to dangerous abuse,—that he ardently wishes to see it incorporated, as a fundamental maxim, in the system of public credit of the United States, that the creation of debt should always be accompanied with the means of extinguishment. This he regards as the true secret for rendering public credit immortal. And he presumes, that it is difficult to conceive a situation, in which there may not be an adherence to the maxim....

Deeply impressed as the Secretary is… that the establishment of public credit, upon the basis for a satisfactory provision for the public debt…is the true desideratum towards relief from individual and national embarrassments…he cannot but indulge an anxious wish that an effectual plan…may…be the result of the united wisdom of the legislature.

He is fully convinced that it is of the greatest importance that no further delay should attend the making of the requisite provision; not only because it will give a better impression of the good faith of the country, and will bring earlier relief to the creditors; both which circumstances are of great moment to public credit....

2–3. ALEXANDER HAMILTON, DECEMBER 5, 1791, "REPORT ON MANUFACTURES"

The Secretary of the Treasury, in obedience to the order of the House of Representatives, of the 15th day of January, 1790, has applied his attention… to the subject of Manufactures, and particularly to the means of promoting such as will tend to render the United States independent of foreign nations for military and other essential supplies; and he thereupon respectfully submits the following report:

The expediency of encouraging manufactures in the United States, which was not long since deemed very questionable, appears at this time to be pretty generally admitted. The embarrassments which have obstructed the progress of our external trade, have led to serious reflections on the necessity of enlarging the sphere of our domestic commerce. The restrictive regulations, which, in foreign markets, abridge the vent of the increasing surplus of our agricultural produce, serve to beget an earnest desire that a more extensive demand for that surplus may be created at home; and the complete success which has rewarded manufacturing enterprise in some valuable branches, conspiring with the promising symptoms which attend some less mature essays in others, justify a hope that the obstacles to the growth of this species of industry are less formidable than they were apprehended to be….

There still are, nevertheless, respectable patrons of opinions unfriendly to the encouragement of manufactures. The following are, substantially, the arguments by which these opinions are defended.

"In every country (say those who entertain them) agriculture is the most beneficial and productive object of human industry. This position, generally if not universally true, applies with peculiar emphasis to the United States on account of their immense tracts of fertile territory, uninhabited and unimproved. Nothing can afford so advantageous an employment for capital and labor as the conversion of this extensive wilderness into cultivated farms. Nothing, equally with this, can contribute to the population, strength and real riches of the country."

"To endeavor by the extraordinary patronage of Government to accelerate the growth of manufactures is, in fact, to endeavor by force and art to transfer the natural current of industry from a more to a less beneficial channel. Whatever has such a tendency must necessarily be unwise. Indeed it can hardly ever be wise in a government, to attempt to give a direction to the industry of its citizens. This, under the quick sighted guidance of private interest, will, if left to itself, infallibly find its own way to the most profitable employment; and 'tis by such employment that the public prosperity will be most effectually promoted. To leave industry to itself, therefore, is, in almost every case, the soundest as well as the simplest policy."

"This policy is not only recommended to the United States by considerations which affect all nations, it is, in a manner, dictated to them by the imperious force of a very peculiar situation. The smallness of their population compared with their territory—the constant allurements to emigration from the settled to the unsettled parts of the country—the facility with which the less independent condition of an artisan can be exchanged for the more independent condition of a farmer, these and similar causes conspire to produce, and for a length of time must continue to occasion, a scarcity of hands for manufacturing occupation, and dearness of labor generally. To these disadvantages for the prosecution of manufactures, a deficiency of pecuniary capital being added, the prospect of a successful competition with the manufactures of Europe must be regarded as little less than desperate. Extensive manufactures can only be the offspring of a redundant, at least of a full, population. Till the latter shall characterize the situation of this country, 'tis vain to hope for the former."

"If, contrary to the natural course of things, an unseasonable and premature spring can be given to certain fabrics by heavy duties, prohibitions, bounties, or by other forced expedients, this will only be to sacrifice the interests of the community to those of particular classes. Besides the misdirection of labor, a virtual monopoly will be given to the persons employed on such fabrics; and an enhancement of price, the inevitable consequence of every monopoly, must be defrayed at the expense of the other parts of the society. It is far preferable that those persons should be engaged in the cultivation of the earth and that we should procure, in exchange for its productions, the commodities with which foreigners are able to supply us in greater perfection and upon better terms."

It ought readily be conceded that the cultivation of the earth, as the primary and most certain source of national supply, as the immediate and chief source of subsistence to a man, as the principal source of those materials which constitute the nutriment of other kinds of labor, as including a state most favorable to the freedom and independence of the human mind—one, perhaps, most conducive to the multiplication of the human species, has intrinsically a strong claim to preeminence over every other kind of industry.

But that it has a title to any thing like an exclusive predilection, in any country, ought to be admitted with great caution; that it is even more productive than every other branch of industry, requires more evidence than has yet been given in support of the position. That its real interests, precious and important as... they truly are, will be advanced, rather than injured, by the due encouragement of manufactures, may it is believed, be satisfactorily demonstrated. And it is also believed that the expediency of such encouragement... may be shown to be recommended by the most cogent and persuasive motives of national policy.

It has been maintained that agriculture is not only the most productive, but the only productive species of industry. The reality of this suggestion... has, however, not been verified by any accurate detail of facts and calculations and the general arguments, which are adduced to prove it, are rather subtle and paradoxical than solid and convincing....

To affirm that the labor of the manufacturer is unproductive, because he consumes as much of the produce of land as he adds value to the raw material, which he manufactures, is not better founded than it would be to affirm that the labor of the farmer, which furnishes materials to the manufacturer, is unproductive, because he consumes an equal value of manufactured articles. Each furnishes a certain portion of the produce of his labor to the other, and each destroys a corresponding portion of the produce of the labor of the other. In the mean time, the maintenance of two citizens, instead of one, is going on; the State has two members instead of one; and they, together, consume twice the value of what is produced from the land. If, instead of a farmer and an artificer [manufacturer], there were a farmer only, he would be under the necessity of devoting a part of his labor to the fabrication of clothing and other articles... and of course he would be able to devote less labor to the cultivation of his farm, and would draw from it proportionably less product.... Again: if there were both an artificer and a farmer, the latter would be left to pursue exclusively the cultivation of his farm.... The artificer, at the same time, would be going on in the production of manufactured commodities to an amount sufficient not only to repay the farmer in those commodities for the provisions and materials which were procured from him, but to furnish the artificer with a supply of similar commodities for his own use. Thus... there would be two quantities or values in existence, instead of one; and the revenue and consumption would be double in one case what it would be in the other....

The produce of the labor of the artificer, consequently, may be regarded as composed of three parts; one by which the provisions for his subsistence and the materials for his work are purchased of the farmer, one by which he supplies himself with manufactured necessaries, and a third which constitutes the profit on the stock employed. The last two portions seem to have been overlooked in the system which represents manufacturing industry as barren and unproductive....

It is now proper to proceed a step further, and to enumerate the principal circumstances from which it may be inferred that manufacturing establishments not only occasion a positive augmentation of the produce and revenue of society, but that they contribute essentially to rendering them greater than they could possibly without such establishments.

These circumstances are—

1. The division of labor.
2. An extension of the use of machinery.
3. Additional employment to classes of the community not ordinarily engaged in business.
4. The promoting of emigration from foreign countries.
5. The furnishing greater scope for the diversity of talents and dispositions, which discriminate men from each other.
6. The affording a more ample and various field for enterprise.
7. The creating, in some instances, a new, and securing, in all, a more certain and steady demand for the surplus produce of the soil.

Each of these circumstances has a considerable influence upon the total mass of industrious effort in a community; together, they add to it a degree of energy and effort which is not easily conceived. Some comments on each of them…may serve to explain their importance.

I. As to the division of labor

It has justly been observed, that there is scarcely any thing of greater moment in the economy of a nation than the proper division of labor. The separation of occupations causes each to be carried to a much greater perfection than it could possibly acquire if they were blended….

II. As to an extension of the use of machinery…

The employment of machinery forms an item of great importance in the general mass of national industry. It is an artificial force brought in aid of the natural force of man; and, to all the purposes of labor, is an increase of hands, an accession of strength, unencumbered too by the expense of maintaining the laborer. May it not, therefore, be fairly inferred, that those occupations which give greatest scope to the use of this auxiliary, contribute most to the general stock of industrious effort, and, in consequence, to the general product of industry?

It shall be taken for granted, and the truth of the position referred to observation, that manufacturing pursuits are susceptible, in a greater degree, of the application of machinery, than those of agriculture. If so, all the difference is lost to a community which, instead of manufacturing for itself, procures the fabrics requisite to its supply from other countries. The substitution of foreign for domestic manufactures is a transfer to foreign nations of the advantages accruing from the employment of machinery, in the modes in which it is capable of being employed with most utility and to the greatest extent.

The cotton mill, invented in England, within the last twenty years, is a signal illustration of the general proposition which has been just advanced. In consequence of it, all the different processes for spinning cotton are performed by means of machines, which are put in motion by water, and attended chiefly by women and children and by a smaller number of persons, in the whole, than are requisite in the ordinary mode of spinning. And it is an advantage of great moment, that the operations of this mill continue with convenience during the night as well as through the day. The prodigious effect of such a machine is easily conceived. To this invention is to be attributed, essentially, the immense progress which has been so suddenly made in Great Britain, in the various fabrics of cotton.

III. As to the additional employment of classes of the community not originally engaged in the particular business

This is not among the least valuable of the means by which manufacturing institutions contribute to augment the general stock of industry and production. In places where those institutions prevail, besides the persons regularly engaged in them, they afford occasional and extra employment to industrious who are willing to devote the leisure resulting from the intermissions of their ordinary pursuits, to collateral labors, as a resource for multiplying their acquisitions or their enjoyments. The husbandman himself experiences a new source of profit and support from the increased industry of his wife and daughters, invited and stimulated by the demands of the neighboring manufactories.

Besides this advantage of occasional employment to classes having different occupations, there is another, of a nature allied to it, and of a similar tendency. This is the employment of persons who would other wise be idle, and in many cases a burthen on the community, either from the bias of temper, habit, infirmity of body, or some other cause, indisposing or disqualifying them for the toils of the country. It is worthy of particular remark that, in general, women and children are rendered more useful, and the latter more early useful, by manufacturing establishments, than they would otherwise be. Of the number of persons employed in the cotton manufactories of Great Britain, it is computed that four sevenths nearly are women and children, of whom the greatest proportion are children, and many of them of a tender age.

IV. As to the promoting of emigration from foreign countries

Men reluctantly quit one course of occupation and livelihood for another, unless invited to it by very apparent and proximate advantages. Many who would go from one country to another, if they had a prospect of continuing with more benefit the callings to which they have been educated, will often not be tempted to change their situation by the hope of doing better in some other way. Manufacturers who, listening to the powerful invitations of a better price for their fabrics or their labor, of greater cheapness of provisions and raw materials, of an exemption from the chief part of the taxes, burdens, and restraints which they endure in the Old World, of greater personal independence and consequence, under the operation of a more equal government, and of what is far more precious than mere religious toleration, a perfect equality of religious privileges, would probably flock from Europe to the United States, to pursue their own trades or professions.... Here is perceived an important resource, not only for extending the population, and with it the useful and productive labor of the country, but likewise for the prosecution of manufactures, without deducting from the number of hands which might otherwise be drawn to tillage....

V. As to the furnishing greater scope for the diversity of talents and dispositions, which discriminate men from each other

This is a much more powerful means of augmenting the fund of national industry, than may at first sight appear. It is a just observation, that minds of the strongest and most active powers for their proper objects, fall below mediocrity, and labor without effect, if confined to uncongenial pursuits. And it is thence to be inferred, that the results of human exertion may be immensely increased by diversifying its objects. When all the different kinds of industry obtain in a community, each individual can find his proper element, and can call into activity the whole vigor of his nature. And the community is benefited by the services of its respective members, in the manner in which each can serve it with most effect.

VI. As to the affording a more ample and various field for enterprise

The spirit of enterprise, useful and prolific as it is, must necessarily be contracted or expanded, in proportion to the simplicity or variety of the occupations and productions which are to be found in a society. It must be less in a nation of mere cultivators, than in a nation of cultivators and merchants; less in a nation of cultivators and merchants, than in a nation of cultivators, artificers, and merchants.

VII. As to the creating, in some instances, a new, and securing, in all, a more certain and steady demand for the surplus produce of the soil

It is evident that the exertions of the husbandman will be steady or fluctuating, vigorous or feeble, in proportion to the steadiness or fluctuation, adequateness or inadequateness, of the markets on which he must depend for the vent of the surplus which may be produced by his labor; and that such surplus, in the ordinary course of things, will be greater or less in the same proportion.

It is a primary object of the policy of nations to be able to supply themselves with subsistence from their own soils; and manufacturing nations, as far as circumstances permit, endeavor to procure from the same source the raw materials necessary for their own fabrics. This disposition, urged by the spirit of monopoly, is sometimes even carried to an injudicious extreme. It seems not always to be recollected that nations who have neither mines nor manufactures can only obtain the manufactured articles of which they stand in need by an exchange of the products of their soils; and that, if those who can best furnish them with such articles are unwilling to give a due course to this exchange, they must of necessity make every possible effort to manufacture for themselves, the effect of which is that the manufacturing nations abridge the natural advantages of their situation through an unwillingness to permit the agricultural countries to enjoy the advantages of theirs, and sacrifice the interests of a mutually beneficial intercourse to the vain project of selling every thing and buying nothing.

But it is also a consequence of the policy which has been noted that the foreign demand for the products of agricultural countries is, in a great degree, rather casual and occasional than certain or constant. To what extent injurious interruptions of the demand for some of the staple commodities of the United States may have been experienced from that cause must be referred to the judgment of those who are engaged in carrying on the commerce of the country, but it may be safely assumed that such interruptions are at times very inconveniently felt, and that cases not unfrequently occur in which markets are so confined and restricted as to render the demand very unequal to the supply.

Independently likewise of the artificial impediments which are created by the policy in question, there are natural causes tending to render the external demand for the surplus of agricultural nations a precarious reliance. The differences of seasons in the countries which are the consumers make immense differences in the produce of their own soils, in different years; and consequently in the degrees of their necessity for foreign supply. Plentiful harvests with them, especially if similar ones occur at the same time in the countries which are the furnishers, occasion of course a glut in the markets of the latter.

Considering how fast and how much the progress of new settlements in the United States must increase the surplus produce of the soil, and weighing seriously the tendency of the system which prevails among most of the commercial nations of Europe, whatever dependence may be placed on the force of natural circumstances to counteract the effects of an artificial policy, there appear strong reasons to regard the foreign demand for that surplus as too uncertain a reliance, and to desire a substitute for it in an extensive domestic market.

To secure such a market, there is no other expedient than to promote manufacturing establishments. Manufacturers, who constitute the most numerous class after the cultivators of land, are for that reason the principal consumers of the surplus of their labor.

This idea of an extensive domestic market for the surplus produce of the soil, is of the first consequence. It is, of all things, that which most effectually conduces to a flourishing state of agriculture. If the effect of manufactories should be to detach a portion of the hands which would otherwise be engaged in tillage, it might possibly cause a smaller quantity of lands to be under cultivation; but, by their tendency to procure a more certain demand for the surplus produce of the soil, they would, at the same time, cause the lands which were in cultivation to be better improved and more productive. And while by their influence, the condition of each individual farmer would be meliorated, the total mass of agricultural production would probably be increased. For this must evidently depend as much upon the degree of improvement, if not more, than upon the number of acres under culture.

The foregoing considerations seem sufficient to establish, as general propositions, that it is the interest of nations to diversify the industrious pursuits of the individuals who compose them—that the establishment of manufactures is calculated not only to increase the general stock of useful and productive labor, but even to improve the state of agriculture in particular; certainly to advance the interests of those who are engaged in it....

A full view having now been taken of the inducements to the promotion of manufactures in the United States... it is proper, in the next place, to consider the means by which it may be effected....

In order to a better judgment of the means proper to be resorted to by the United States, it will be of use to advert to those which have been employed with success in other countries. The principal of these are:

I. Protecting duties, or duties on those articles which are the rivals of the domestic ones to be encouraged....

II. Prohibitions on rival articles, or duties equivalent to prohibitions....

III. Prohibitions of the exportation of materials of manufactures....

IV. Pecuniary bounties....

It cannot escape notice, that a duty upon the importation of an article can no otherwise aid the domestic production of it, than by giving the latter greater advantages in the home market. It can have no influence upon the advantageous sale of the article produced, in foreign markets,—no tendency, therefore, to promote its exportation.

The true way to conciliate these two interests, is to lay a duty on foreign manufactures of the material, the growth of which is desired to be encouraged, and to apply the produce of that duty by way of bounty, either upon the production of the material itself, or upon its manufacture at home, or upon both. In this disposition... the manufacturer commences his enterprise under every advantage which is attainable as to quantity or price of the raw material. And the farmer, if the bounty be immediately to him, is enabled by it to enter into a successful competition with the foreign material....

Except the simple and ordinary kinds of household manufacture, or those for which there are very commanding local advantages, pecuniary bounties are in most cases indispensable to the introduction of a new branch [of economic activity]. A stimulus... is... essential to the overcoming of the obstacles which arise from the competitions of superior skill and maturity elsewhere....

In countries where there is great private wealth, much may be effected by voluntary contributions of patriotic individuals; but in a community situated like that of the United States, the public purse must supply the deficiency of private resource. In what can it be so useful, as in promoting and improving the efforts of industry?

2–4. HENRY CLAY, FEBRUARY 2, 3, AND 6, 1832
"IN DEFENSE OF THE AMERICAN SYSTEM"

In one sentiment, Mr. President, expressed by the honorable gentleman from South Carolina [Mr. Hayne]... I entirely concur. I agree with him that the decision on the system of policy embraced in this debate, involves the future destiny of this growing country. One way... would lead to deep and general distress; general bankruptcy and national ruin without benefit to any part of the Union. The other, the existing prosperity will be preserved and augmented, and the nation will continue rapidly to advance in wealth, power and greatness without prejudice to any section of the confederacy....

Eight years ago, it was my painful duty to present to the other House of Congress, an unexaggerated picture of the general distress pervading the whole land. We must all yet remember some of its frightful features. We all know that the people were then oppressed and borne down by an enormous load of debt; that the value of property was at the lowest point of depression; that ruinous sales and sacrifices were everywhere made of real estate; that stop laws and relief laws and paper money were adopted to save the people from impending destruction; that a deficit in the public revenue existed, which compelled Government to seize upon, and divert from its legitimate object, the appropriation to the sinking fund to redeem the national debt and that our commerce and navigation were threatened with complete paralysis. In short, sir, if I were to select any term of seven years since the adoption of the present constitution, which exhibited a scene of the most widespread dismay and desolation, it would be exactly the term of seven years which immediately preceded the adoption of the Tariff of 1824.

I have now to perform the more pleasing task of exhibiting an imperfect sketch of the existing state of unparalleled prosperity of the country. On a general survey, we behold cultivation extended, the arts flourishing, the face of the country improved, our people fully and profitably employed and the public countenance exhibiting tranquility, contentment, and happiness.... [W]e have the agreeable contemplation of a people out of debt; land rising slowly in value, but in a secure and salutary degree; a ready, though not extravagant market for all the surplus productions of our industry; innumerable flocks and herds browsing and gamboling on ten thousand hills and plains, covered with rich and verdant grasses; our cities expanded, and whole villages springing up, as it were, by enchantment; our exports and imports increased and increasing; our [shipping] tonnage, foreign and coastwise, swelling and fully occupied; the rivers of our interior animated by the perpetual thunder and lightning of countless steam boats; the currency sound and abundant; the public debt of two wars nearly redeemed; and, to crown all, the public treasury overflowing.... If the term of seven years were to be selected of the greatest prosperity... since the establishment of the present constitution, it would be exactly that period of seven years which immediately followed the passage of the Tariff of 1824.

This transformation of the condition of the country from gloom and distress to brightness and prosperity has been mainly the work of American legislation, fostering American industry.... The foes of the American system in 1824... predicted, 1st the ruin of the public revenue, and the creation of the necessity to resort to direct taxation.... 2nd the destruction of our navigation. 3rd the desolation of our commercial cities. And 4th the augmentation of the price of objects of consumption, and further decline in that of the articles of our exports. Every prediction which they made has failed—utterly failed....

The question we are now called upon to determine... is whether we shall break down and destroy a long established system.... And are we not bound deliberately to consider whether we can proceed to this work of destruction without a violation of the public faith? The people of the United States have justly supposed that the policy of protecting *their* industry against *foreign* legislation and *foreign* industry was fully settled.... In full confidence that the policy was firmly... fixed, thousands upon thousands have invested their capital, purchased a vast amount of real and other estate, made permanent establishments, and accommodated their industry. Can we expose to utter and irretrievable ruin this countless multitude...?

When gentlemen have succeeded in their design of an immediate or gradual destruction of the American system, what is their substitute? Free trade! Free trade! The call for free trade is as unavailing as the cry of a spoiled child... for the moon or the stars.... It never has existed; it never will exist. Trade implies at least two parties. To be free it should be fair and reciprocal. But if we throw our ports wide open to the admission of foreign productions, free of all duty, what ports of any foreign nation shall we find open to the free admission of our surplus produce...?

Gentlemen deceive themselves. It is not free trade that they are recommending to our acceptance. It is, in effect, the British colonial system that we are invited to adopt; and, if their policy prevail, it will lead, substantially, to the recolonization of these States, under the commercial dominion of Great Britain....

I conclude... with the hope that my humble exertions have not been altogether unsuccessful in showing –

1. That the [tariff] policy which we have been considering ought to continue to be regarded as the genuine American system.
2. That the free trade system... ought really to be considered as the British colonial system.
3. That the American system is beneficial to all parts of the Union, and absolutely necessary to much the larger portion of it.
4. That the price of the great staple of cotton, and of all our chief productions of agriculture, has been sustained and upheld and a decline averted by the protective system.
5. That, if the foreign demand for cotton has been at all diminished by the operation of that system, the diminution has been more than compensated in the additional demand created at home.

6. That the constant tendency of the system, by creating competition among ourselves, and between American and European industry, acting reciprocally on each other, is to reduce prices of manufactured objects.
7. That…objects within the scope of the policy of protection have greatly fallen in price.
8. That if… these benefits are experienced in a season of war, when the foreign supply might be cut off, they would be much more extensively felt.
9. And finally, that the substitution of the British colonial system for the American system… would lead to the prostration of manufactures, general impoverishment, and general ruin…

2–5. ANDREW JACKSON, JULY 10, 1832, MESSAGE FROM THE PRESIDENT OF THE UNITED STATES RETURNING THE BANK BILL TO THE SENATE WITH HIS OBJECTIONS

To the Senate:

The bill "to modify and continue" the act entitled "An act to incorporate the subscribers to the Bank of the United States" was presented to me on the 4th July instant. Having considered it with that solemn regard to the principles of the Constitution which the day was calculated to inspire, and come to the conclusion that it ought not to become a law, I herewith return it to the Senate, in which it originated, with my objections.

A bank of the United States is in many respects convenient for the Government and useful to the people. Entertaining this opinion, and deeply impressed with the belief that some of the powers and privileges possessed by the existing bank are unauthorized by the Constitution, subversive of the rights of the States, and dangerous to the liberties of the people, I felt it my duty at an early period of my Administration to call the attention of Congress to the practicability of organizing an institution combining all its advantages and obviating these objections. I sincerely regret that in the act before me I can perceive none of those modifications of the bank charter which are necessary, in my opinion, to make it compatible with justice, with sound policy, or with the Constitution of our country.

The present corporate body, denominated the president, directors, and company of the Bank of the United States, will have existed at the time this act is intended to take effect twenty years. It enjoys an exclusive privilege of banking under the authority of the General Government, a monopoly of its favor and support, and, as a necessary consequence, almost a monopoly of the foreign and domestic exchange. The powers, privileges, and favors bestowed upon it in the original charter, by increasing the value of the stock far above its par value, operated as a gratuity of many millions to the stockholders….

It is not conceivable how the present stockholders can have any claim to the special favor of the Government. The present corporation has enjoyed its monopoly during the period stipulated in the original contract. If we must have such a corporation, why should not the Government sell out the whole stock and thus secure to the people the full market value of the privileges granted? Why should not Congress create and sell twenty-eight millions of stock, incorporating the purchasers with all the powers and privileges secured in this act and putting the premium upon the sales into the Treasury?

But this act does not permit competition in the purchase of this monopoly. It seems to be predicated on the erroneous idea that the present stockholders have a prescriptive right not only to the favor but to the bounty of Government. It appears that more than a fourth part of the stock is held by foreigners and the residue is held by a few hundred of our own citizens, chiefly of the richest class. For their benefit does this act exclude the whole American people from competition in the purchase of this monopoly and dispose of it for many millions less than it is worth. This seems the less excusable because some of our citizens not now stockholders petitioned that the door of competition might be opened, and offered to take a charter on terms much more favorable to the Government and country.

But this proposition, although made by men whose aggregate wealth is believed to be equal to all the private stock in the existing bank, has been set aside, and the bounty of our Government is proposed to be again bestowed on the few who have been fortunate enough to secure the stock and at this moment wield the power of the existing institution. I can not perceive the justice or policy of this course. If our Government must sell monopolies, it would seem to be its duty to take nothing less than their full value, and if gratuities must be made once in fifteen or twenty years let them not be bestowed on the subjects of a foreign government nor upon a designated and favored class of men in our own country. It is but justice and good policy, as far as the nature of the case will admit, to confine our favors to our own fellow-citizens, and let each in his turn enjoy an opportunity to profit by our bounty. In the bearings of the act before me upon these points I find ample reasons why it should not become a law....

The fourth section provides " that the notes or bills of the said corporation, although the same be, on the faces thereof, respectively made payable at one place only, shall nevertheless be received by the said corporation at the bank or at any of the offices of discount and deposit thereof if tendered in liquidation or payment of any balance or balances due to said corporation or to such office of discount and deposit from any other incorporated bank." This provision secures to the State banks a legal privilege in the Bank of the United States which is withheld from all private citizens. If a State bank in Philadelphia owe the Bank of the United States and have notes issued by the St. Louis branch, it can pay the debt with those notes, but if a merchant, mechanic, or other private citizen be in like circumstances he can not by law pay his debt with those notes, but must sell them at a discount or send them to St. Louis to be cashed. This boon conceded to the State banks, though not unjust in itself, is most odious because it does not measure out equal justice to the high and the low, the rich and the poor. To the extent of its practical effect it is a bond of union among the banking establishments of the nation, erecting them into an interest separate from that of the people, and its necessary tendency is to unite the Bank of the United States and the State banks in any measure which may be thought conducive to their common interest...

In another of its bearings this provision is fraught with danger. Of the twenty-five directors of this bank five are chosen by the Government and twenty by the citizen stockholders. From all voice in these elections the foreign stockholders are excluded by the charter. In proportion, therefore, as the stock is transferred to foreign holders the extent of suffrage in the choice of directors is curtailed. Already is almost a third of the stock in foreign hands and not represented in elections. It is constantly passing out of the country, and this act will accelerate its departure. The entire control of the institution would necessarily fall into the hands of a few citizen stockholders, and the ease with which the object would be accomplished would be a temptation to designing men to secure that control in their own hands by monopolizing the remaining stock. There is danger that a president and directors would then be able to elect themselves from year to year, and without responsibility or control manage the whole concerns of the bank during the existence of its charter. It is easy to conceive that great evils to our country and its institutions might flow from such a concentration of power in the hands of a few men irresponsible to the people.

Is there no danger to our liberty and independence in a bank that in its nature has so little to bind it to our country? The president of the bank has told us that most of the State banks exist by its forbearance. Should its influence become concentered, as it may under the operation of such an act as this, in the hands of a self-elected directory whose interests are identified with those of the foreign stockholders, will there not be cause to tremble for the purity of our elections in peace and for the independence of our country in war? Their power would be great whenever they might choose to exert it; but if this monopoly were regularly renewed every fifteen or twenty years on terms proposed by themselves, they might seldom in peace put forth their strength to influence elections or control the affairs of the nation. But if any private citizen or public functionary should interpose to curtail its powers or prevent a renewal of its privileges, it can not be doubted that he would be made to feel its influence....

It is to be regretted that the rich and powerful too often bend the acts of government to their selfish purposes. Distinctions in society will always exist under every just government. Equality of talents, of education, or of wealth can not be produced by human institutions. In the full enjoyment of the gifts of Heaven and the fruits of superior industry, economy, and virtue, every man is equally entitled to protection by law. But when the laws undertake to add to these natural and just advantages artificial distinctions—to grant titles, gratuities, and exclusive privileges—to make the rich richer and the potent more powerful—the humble members of society, the farmers, mechanics, and laborers, who have neither the time nor the means of securing like favors to themselves, have a right to complain of the injustice of their Government. There are no necessary evils in government. Its evils exist only in its abuses. If it would confine itself to equal protection, and, as Heaven does its rains, shower its favors alike on the high and the low, the rich and the poor, it would be an unqualified blessing. In the act before me there seems to be a wide and unnecessary departure from these just principles.

Nor is our Government to be maintained or our Union preserved by invasions of the rights and powers of the several States. In thus attempting to make our General Government strong we make it weak. Its true strength consists in leaving individuals and States as much as possible to themselves; in making itself felt, not in its power, but in its beneficence—not in its control, but in its protection—not in binding the States more closely to the center, but leaving each to move unobstructed in its proper orbit.

Experience should teach us wisdom. Most of the difficulties our Government now encounters and most of the dangers which impend over our Union have sprung from an abandonment of the legitimate objects of Government by our national legislation, and the adoption of such principles as are embodied in this act. Many of our rich men have not been content with equal protection and equal benefits, but have besought us to make them richer by act of Congress. By attempting to gratify their desires we have in the results of our legislation arrayed section against section, interest against interest, and man against man, in a fearful commotion which threatens to shake the foundations of our Union. It is time to pause in our career to review our principles, and if possible revive that devoted patriotism and spirit of compromise which distinguished the sages of the Revolution and the fathers of our Union. If we can not at once, in justice to interests vested under improvident legislation, make our Government what it ought to be, we can at least take a stand against all new grants of monopolies and exclusive privileges, against any prostitution of our Government to the advancement of the few at the expense of the many, and in favor of compromise and gradual reform in our code of laws and system of political economy.

I have now done my duty to my country. If sustained by my fellow citizens, I shall be grateful and happy; if not, I shall find in the motives which impel me ample grounds for contentment and peace. In the difficulties which surround us and the dangers which threaten our institutions there is cause for neither dismay nor alarm. For relief and deliverance let us firmly rely on that kind Providence which I am sure watches with peculiar care over the destinies of our Republic, and on the intelligence and wisdom of our countrymen. Through His abundant goodness and their patriotic devotion our liberty and Union will be preserved.

Andrew Jackson

2–6. JOHN FINCH, "NOTES OF TRAVEL IN THE UNITED STATES"

It is much easier to obtain employment, at present, in the United States than in England; but in this respect they are getting into a worse and worse condition. The manufacturers, in the East, have introduced all our improvements in machinery, (and the effects are the same as in this country) they are making very large quantities of goods; competition is increasing, prices are very much reduced, and the wages of labor, generally, throughout the States and Canada, have been reduced from thirty to fifty per cent within the last four years, and wages are still reducing in some parts of the country, in spite of their trades' unions and democratic institutions; and, if competition continue, no parties can prevent wages from falling as low there as they are in England, and this within a comparatively short period. Wages in America are not much higher, even now, than they are with us. Agricultural laborers can be hired, in Illinois and other states, for from eight to twelve dollars per month. Smiths and mechanics for from twelve to eighteen dollars per month, with board. The boarding of laborers of all kinds is almost universal in the small towns and villages in the agricultural districts. They think nothing of board and lodging in the west; it can be found them well for from $1 to $1.50, or 4.s. to 6s. per week. At Baltimore iron works the laborers earn about 2s. 8d. per day, and the head men, at the furnaces, get about $1, or 4s. per day. In Pittsburg the wages of the laborers, at the iron works, is about the same. A few of the principal workmen, at the iron works, earn as much as $2 per day. At the foundries and engineering establishments, at Paterson, near New York, the average wages of labor throughout the works is only about 4s. 6d. per day now; and this may be taken as a fair average of the wages of engineers [machinists] and founders, in the eastern cities; great numbers were out of employ when I landed, in May last; but the trade is much better, and very few are out of work now. In the great lead district of Galena there are about 40 smelt works, and first-rate smelters earn 25s. per week; second-rate smelters, 18s. per week; laborers at the smelt works, 16s. per week, and carters, 15s. per week, all without board; but wages are paid in Galena with cash, not in truck, as in most places. The miners were getting 5s. 8d. per 112 lbs. for their lead ore, and pig lead was selling at 9s. 6d. per cwt., 112 lbs. The wages of labor was double what it is now, in Galena, in 1838. Great quantities of sale shoes and boots are made in and about Salem, in Massachusetts; the workmen can earn only about 16s. per week; and the shoes are sold as cheap as sale shoes are sold in England. Tailors generally get good wages, but they are not usually well employed; their wages are about 6s. per day. Bricklayers, stonemasons, and plasterers earn as much as tailors. This will give some idea of the rate of wages. The price of fuel, and the rents of houses for laborers are very high in all the eastern states; food is also much higher there than in the west. It is highest at Boston and New York, but even there, food is from 25 to 50 per cent cheaper than in Liverpool. Rents are high in all parts of the Union, and clothing is higher than it is with us. Wood fuel can be had for merely the expense of cutting and preparing in most parts of the west. On the banks of the Ohio and Mississippi the steam-boats are supplied at from 4s. to 6s. per cord of 8 feet by 4 feet, and 4 feet high, and coals can be had at Pittsburg, and on the Ohio, for less than 5s. per ton. Pork, beef, and mutton are bought in Indiana, Illinois, and other western states, at from 1d. to 1.5d. per lb. Our friend C. F. Green, killed a cow in New Harmony while we were there, and he could scarcely sell it at that price, on credit. A whole carcass of good mutton sells there for a dollar, eggs are sold at 2d. per dozen, good fowls at 4s. per dozen, butter at 3d. to 4d. per lb., Indian corn 7d. to 10d. per bushel, wheat at $.50 to $.60 or 2s. to 2s. 6d. per bushel. Most of these articles are more than double these prices in the eastern states, owing to their not growing enough for themselves, and the expense of carriage from the far west. Apples, pears, peaches, &c., are very plentiful and very cheap in the west. We saw whole orchards of fine apples in Indiana and Kentucky rotting on the trees, not being considered worth the expense of gathering. The same evil exists in the western states of America, as respects agricultural produce, as we find in England as to manufactured goods; excessive competition, and consequent reductions in wages, have driven so many from the eastern states, to cultivate land in the west, added to the shoals of emigrants daily arriving from other countries, that the produce is so abundant, it can scarcely be sold for the expense of taking it fifty miles to a market, and prices will still go lower and lower as more and more land is brought into cultivation, till the man who cultivates his own land will not be able to get a living, as is now the case with our friend C. F. Green, with a most beautiful and fertile farm of 140 acres freehold....

In judging of their condition, you must take into account the length and severity of their winters, and the excessive heat of their summers, in the northern states and in Canada. Their winters commence in November, and continue till the end of April-about six months in the year-during which period all building operations, and all agricultural employments, except the felling of timber and preparing fuel, are suspended; and, being all frozen up, navigation on their rivers and canals, and all employments dependent on these, are stopped, and many other employments, depending on water power, are also stopped....

In the middle of summer, on the contrary, the weather is so excessively hot, (frequently ninety to a hundred degrees), that it is very difficult to do a day's work at hard labor, beside which, in the western states, you are much annoyed by the bite of mosquitoes, and, in those parts, fever and ague are very prevalent in summer. Imagine a settler, in the west, on his own farm of one hundred acres, situated four miles distant from any other dwelling, and fifty miles from a market for his produce, living in the middle of a forest, in a log cabin of his own construction, and with the exception of a few acres, which he has prepared for Indian corn and wheat, for the support of himself and family and cattle, all around him impenetrable thicket and lumber. His land is very fertile without the use of manure, and he has had good crops this year, he has provided all the food he requires for his cattle and his family, and he has 30 bushels of wheat and 70 lbs. of butter, surplus, to dispose of, to buy iron for his ploughs, and clothing and other articles for his family, consisting of himself his wife and three children. He lives in Illinois, and sets out for Chicago with his wagon, yoke of oxen, and his load of produce, over a bad road, and the journey, sale, and purchase, takes him eight days; he takes with him food for himself and oxen, which reduces his expenses to $.50 per day, which is $4; his wages are worth $4 more; he has the good fortune to sell his wheat at $.50 per bushel, cash, which is $15, and the butter for $.08 per lb., which is $5.60; the whole is $20.60, for all his year's surplus produce, or £4.5s.6d. English; take from this 16s. 8d., expenses, and 20s. for 1 cwt. assorted iron, he has no poor-rates, tithes, taxes, church-rates, or rent, to pay, except about 2s. 6d. for land tax, and yet he has only £2 6s. 4d. left to buy clothing for himself and family, for the rigors of an American winter, and for all other family expenses....

Now I put to the smallest grain of wit that may be contained in the cranium of the most thick-headed dunce in existence, whether there is the least probability, that an educated, intelligent, enterprising, and industrious people, (as the Americans undeniably are,) will, any longer than they can possibly help it, suffer this incalculable amount of wealth to be buried in the earth, and supply themselves with the same articles from a country that altogether excludes their principal surplus article -corn; that taxes their tobacco from the south 1000 per cent, their mutton, beef, and pork of the Western States 100, and butter and cheese 50 per cent.

These restrictions upon their trade in England, have produced in every part of the United States (even at a present sacrifice to themselves in price) a fixed determination to do without British goods of every kind as soon as possible, and in the mean time, by laying a heavy duty upon all imported articles, to give every encouragement to their own mining and manufacturing operations. They already make two-thirds as much lead as is made in Great Britain, in the neighborhoods of Galena, Dubuque, and St. Genevieve on the Mississippi alone, and they have lead mines in other States to some extent-and they can now produce lead at least 10 to 20 per cent cheaper than it can be made for in this country. Their anthracite coal mines produce one million tons, and their bituminous coal mines considerably more than one million tons of coals annually. Their copper mines are fast extending, but at present the quantity produced is inadequate to the demand. The quantity of iron now made in the United States is not much less than 500,000 tons annually, and is continually increasing; it is made principally by the use of charcoal fuel, which greatly improves its quality. In a very few years they will not only make all they require, but have a large surplus. Salt is made in very large quantities in New York, Pennsylvania, Virginia, and other States; this manufacture will also soon supersede the use of the foreign article. Machine making is carried on on a very extensive scale in Massachusetts, Rhode Island, and other States in that part of the Union, and also in Pittsburg and other places, for the use of the factories. The manufacture of steam engines, water wheels, and machinery for saw mills and other purposes, is very extensive in and near Boston, New York, Philadelphia, and Pittsburg, and there are large establishments of these kinds in many other places that I visited. American boiler plates are used, exclusive of all other, for making their engine boilers, &c., and are superior in quality to most, and inferior to none, that are made in England. The quantity of cut nails made there exceeds anything I could have supposed; most of their buildings, even their churches, being of wood. Many of the iron manufacturers work up the whole of what they produce into cut nails on the spot. A rolling mill at Boston, another at Reading in Pennsylvania, and a third at Cincinnati, which I saw, each makes from fifty to sixty tons of cut nails weekly, besides many others that I heard of. Till within the last three years, a large quantity of Swedish iron was imported for cut nail making; this trade is now at an end, as they use none but their own iron. Some idea may be formed of the extent of their engineering business, from the fact of their having about 400 steam boats on the waters of the Mississippi, and more than 60 on the large lakes alone. These steam boats wear out every four years, and their double engines in eight years, so that it requires 100 steam boats and 100 engines to be made every year to meet the demand, which is every year increasing; besides which, there are great numbers of steamers employed in the coasting trade, and on the Hudson and other rivers. Locomotive engines are made there for their 7,000 miles of railroad, and steam engines are used for a hundred other purposes. All their superior kind of locks are made at home. Their axes for cutting down timber, joiners' edge tools, wood screws, scythes, and many other articles in the cutlery trade, are superior to any that are made in England. All these articles are made there in very large quantities, and are bought by workmen in preference to English, at 50 per cent higher prices, both in the States and in Canada. I saw some beautiful articles of these kinds in various places, and compared them with the best they can get from England, which were much inferior....

In England, capital is superabundant among the wealthy classes, and yet, both in and out of parliament, the general cause of distress and want of work is stated to be over-population, and the great panacea recommended is emigration. In Nova Scotia, New Brunswick, Upper Canada, Lower Canada, and the United States, on the contrary, the cause of their difficulties, and the want of greater prosperity, is attributed to deficiency of capital and want of population. Converse with whom you will in America, they will tell you of the great resources and numerous means of acquiring wealth these countries afford: "Only," say they, "send us any number you please of good workmen, sober, steady, with a little capital, prudent, and industrious, and we will engage them and they will soon become rich in this country; but these are not the sort of persons you generally send us; instead of these, there come out a set of ragged, penniless, shiftless, helpless, drunken creatures, that know how to do scarcely anything, and consequently cannot get employed, and become paupers; and these are almost the only paupers we have, and almost the only drunkards; for you will scarcely ever see a native American that is either a pauper or a drunkard."

... For persons well skilled in agriculture, with a little capital, (and much less will do in America than in England), men who are not prejudiced, but willing to learn, and to follow the modes of culture there adopted, which are altogether different from English farming, will succeed much better either in Canada or the United States than they can possibly do in England. Good workmen at any handicraft, mechanical or manufacturing operations, particularly if they can turn their hands to a variety of operations connected with their business, with good moral character and sober habits, will be sure to meet with encouragement as soon as they are known....

Though land of the very best quality may be obtained in Virginia, Kentucky, and Tennessee much cheaper indeed than in any of the free States-though the climate is milder, more pleasant, and more healthy than in the northern States-and though the Virginians, Kentuckians, and Tennesseans are very desirous of a grand accession of white settlers in these States, where large quantities of good land may be had for from two shillings to four shillings per acre, and their mineral wealth is inexhaustible-still I cannot recommend Englishmen to go there, because labor being generally performed by slaves, labor there, as in our own country, is considered degrading, and wealthy idleness honorable....

There are large tracts of good land to be had in New York, New Jersey, Pennsylvania, and other eastern States. The Yankees are leaving these States and these lands in shoals, and stretching themselves out to the farthest west, to Wisconsin, Iowa, and even the Oregon territory; let them go, they are the best pioneers for settling that country. English farmers will thrive best in the eastern States, and will feel themselves more at home there.

Factory machine makers will find most employment in the States of Massachusetts, Rhode Island, New York, at Pittsburg, and in the State of Ohio. Engineers and locomotive engineers will do best in the same States, and also at Philadelphia, Baltimore, Cincinnati, Louisville, and St. Louis. Workmen in factories will also get employment in these places more readily than in any other part of the States. Canada is engaged almost entirely in agriculture and the timber trade ... A great number of ship and boat-builders are employed on the Ohio River, at Pittsburg, Cincinnati, and Louisville, and many are employed at St. Louis, Boston, New York, and Philadelphia. Colliers will find most employment in the neighborhoods of Pittsville, Cumberland, and Pittsburg, in Pennsylvania. Furnace-men, puddlers, and rollers at iron works, will find most work in Pittsburg, and other parts of Pennsylvania. Edge-tool makers in the neighborhoods of Boston and New York, and in the country lying between these two places. Tanners, curriers, and leather-cutters will find more employment in the State of Massachusetts than in any other. Large quantities of leather are also made in New York State, New Hampshire, and Pennsylvania. Sale shoe-makers will find most employment in Massachusetts; large numbers are also employed in New Hampshire, New York, Pennsylvania, and Ohio States....

The... government land agents, in Boston, New York, Philadelphia, and in every State in the Union, will willingly and cheerfully give every information and assistance, and the best advice to all respectable emigrants that are able to purchase land and support themselves till they can get their first crop from the land; and these are the parties both you and your pioneers should first apply to on arriving there, because they will be able to inform you what land the governments have to dispose of, and probably can in form you of eligible estates to be sold by private individuals.... The government of Michigan, United States, had five hundred thousand acres of land to sell when I was there. I saw the agent, the price was one dollar and a quarter per acre, payable (if the purchaser choose) in government bonds, reckoned at par, which might then be had at less than fifty per cent, which would reduce the price of the land to about two shillings and sixpence per acre. There is very good land there: apply to the government land agent, at Jacksonville, on the railroad,

Michigan, about fifty miles from Detroit. There is a large quantity of land to be sold in Illinois; and there are also large tracts of land to be sold in many of the States, that were bought by speculators during the speculative mania a few years since, and are now being sold for the payment of the arrears of state taxes upon them. The only internal taxes they have to pay, are the municipal taxes in the towns and cities, and a tax upon land amounting to from about thirty-five to seventy cents upon every hundred dollars' value of the land per annum: this pays the expenses of the state governments and the education of the people. The federal government is supported by the customs duties....

The Americans are a restless people, always on the move; they cannot endure to remain long in one place, and are always traveling west: there is just as great a rage for the west on the borders of the Mississippi as there is in New York and Boston. I found numbers of Yankees from the eastern States living in wretched log cabins in Illinois, that were doing well and saving money fast in Massachusetts, Rhode Island, &c. In traveling by stage coach from St. Louis to St. Charles, whilst stopping at an inn in a little village to water the horses, I inquired of a farmer the price of land there, and whether there was any to be sold. "Yes," he replied, "there is plenty to be had here: I have about one hundred and seventy acres, half of it under cultivation." "What will you take for it?" "I will sell it for ten dollars per acre, including the buildings, consisting of a log cabin, stables, &c." "How long have you been here?" "About eleven years." "Why do you wish to leave?" "I wish to purchase a larger lot farther west: I have a large family, and this will not be land enough for a farm for each of them, besides which, my lads are getting into an idle way, hunting and shooting a great part of their time, because I have not work enough for them. The fact is we get our living too easily; but if I can get a large farm of new land, they will be obliged to work to clear it, and bring it into cultivation."

2–7. THOMAS MOONEY, *NINE YEARS IN AMERICA*

... The necessity imposed upon every one to obtain by his or her own exertions a living, begets that industry which pervades every American family. Every member of the family will do something to contribute to the family commonwealth: though the father may hold a public office, the boys are ready and willing to do any work which they know how to do to obtain money. I have frequently had the advertisements for my lectures posted on the walls of a town, by the sons of printers of newspapers, or by sons of sheriffs, jailors, or other public men. Butchers serve out their meats—bakers their bread—dairymen their milk—grocers their various wares. On the other hand, the wealthiest men may be seen returning from the public markets with various articles of food, such as turkeys, legs of lamb, pieces of pork or beef, or baskets of vegetables, in their hands. A great share of the light manufacture of America, is done by women in the farm houses, especially in the New England states. For instance, straw bonnets. There are large straw bonnet establishments in New York and Boston, which have their agents continually traveling among the farm houses. This agent drives a sort of van or omnibus, and brings round bunches of straw plait, and models of bonnets of the newest fashion. These he leaves with the farmers' wives and daughters, all round the country, who work up into bonnets, according to the peculiar model, the plait so left. In due season the agent returns with some more plait, and distributes it to the straw sewers as before, and receives up the bonnets, for the making of which he pays. All the females of an entire district, including the doctors' and ministers' wives, are engaged in this work. In another district, where boot and shoemaking is carried on upon a large scale, the upper parts of boots and shoes are sent in bound into the farmhouses, where they are closed, bound, and otherwise prepared by female labor, and sent back in the same box by the stage coach, the wagon, or the railway. In the getting up of clothing, shirts, stocks, hosiery, suspenders, carriage trimmings, buttons, and a hundred other light things, the cheap labor of the farm house is brought to the aid of manufactures: every district has in it some peculiar branch which is there successfully cultivated. The readiness, too, with which females enter into the factories, into the great book binding and tailoring establishments, contributes to make industry the leading idea of every one, for the females of a nation form the nation....

The American farmer, Patrick, never pays any rent. When he takes a farm he buys it forever. If it be what is called "wild land," he pays the government about five British shillings an acre; and if he has no money on his first settling, it makes little matter, provided the land be not taken up, or "entered" by another. He goes on cultivating in perfect confidence, giving notice to the nearest government office. Two, three, or possibly seven years may pass over before he is called upon to pay the purchase money. Even then, if he should be so unfortunate as not to be able to discharge the claim, he still has a "squatter's right;" and if another man has the hardihood, in face of public opinion, to buy his farm over his head, then the buyer must allow him for his "improvements," according to the valuation of twelve sworn men....

I will first suppose you are unmarried; if so you can get on right well in the new world. If you don't fall into work which you like, or are accustomed to, you will get work of some sort. The lowest wages going in the United States for a laborer's day's work, is seventy cents, or about three shillings British money. This would be eighteen shillings for a week; and you can obtain good board, lodging, and washing for a little less than ten British shillings, or two and a half dollars a week. So that you will be able to save seven or eight shillings a week to buy the farm, which farm you can buy for five shillings an acre, and about which I shall fully inform you as we go along. Remember that, if you please, you can, as soon as you get into a regular employment, save the price of an acre and a half of the finest land in the world every week! and in less than a year you will have money enough to start to the west, and take up an eighty acre farm, which will be your own for ever. When you are in America six months, you will become so accustomed to their work, and generally so handy, that you will get a dollar a day, or even something more, if you mind well your character and business.

Let me next suppose you are married, but as yet without children. In this case your chance is still better. A "man and wife" will soon get employment in the same family: the man in the laborious duties belonging to his class, and his wife as an indoor help-not "servant," as such are styled at home. A female house servant is worth four to five dollars a month and board, in any part of the United States; and if she has any good idea of cooking, or washing, and "doing up" fine washing, or will learn to do these things from her American mistress, she will readily get six or seven dollars a month and board. In all the British provinces of North America, the wages of common laborers and females is, as a general rule, one third less than it is in the United States. There are some classes of mechanics, however, who get as good wages in the British provinces as the same kind get in the States....

Here then we will suppose your wife is putting up at least four dollars a month, or about fifty dollars in the year, which will stock the farm; and in one year, or thereabouts, though you land here without a penny, you and she will have enough wherewith to start off to the west, where the land is good and cheap....

I will next suppose you have a wife and children, large and small. In this case I confess I feel great difficulty in giving advice. The cost of getting a family over to the United States is nothing to the supporting of them here. I speak now of young children from ten or twelve years of age downwards. All healthy active children above these ages can provide for themselves; the girls as well as the boys can readily obtain employment either in families or in factories; but the smaller children will be a dead weight on you, like a millstone round your neck, as long as you are earning wages from week to week: but when you get the farm, Patrick, the more children you have the happier you will be. However, in the beginning the smaller children will be a very serious pull-back on your progress; for if you bring them out with you before you get the farm, your wife will have to stay at home in some expensive lodging to mind them; and then all the money you can earn will be required to support your idle wife and idle little children, and you will hardly ever get one dollar to overtake another; and there you will remain an unfortunate town drudge all the days of your life, not much better than you have been in Ireland. Thousands of our countrymen, who were reared all their lives on farms, and who never were acquainted with the vicious life of cities, have, on arriving in America, nestled in the filthy cellars and garrets, and have worked in the nasty labor which is alone open to friendless strangers; and when they have earned a little money in this way, instead of moving out in quest of a wholesome farm, have married, and commenced a family in the midst of poverty, vice, and sin, which family are subject to the thousand evil influences of city life, and too frequently disgrace the parent and the fatherland which gave the parents birth. Remember then, that the American cities are not the homes you seek for. Get out of them as fast as you can, either on foot or otherwise. Face towards the setting sun; take any work or job that offers as you travel; do this, and you will find at last the true home you seek....

ESSAYS

How and why the American economy was transformed into a national economy by 1860 has long intrigued economic historians. One of the leading interpretations was offered by the late George Rogers Taylor, a professor of economics at Amherst College. In *The Transportation Revolution, 1815–1860*, Professor Taylor argued that improvements made to internal transportation in the decades after 1815, especially the advent of canals, steamboats, and railroads, made possible a regional economic specialization that produced a large degree of national self-sufficiency by the eve of the Civil War. Professor Taylor's classic work is excerpted in Essay 2–1. Douglass C. North, the Spencer T. Olin Professor in Arts and Sciences at Washington University in St. Louis and a 1993 Nobel Laureate in Economics, offered a different explanation for the transformation of the United States economy. Essay 2–2 is excerpted from his important work, *The Economic Growth of the United States, 1790–1860*. In it Professor North, while not discounting the contributions of improved internal transportation, maintained that interregional cash flows made possible by the earnings of southern cotton plantations was the stimulus for growth and regional specialization.

2–1. GEORGE ROGERS TAYLOR, *THE TRANSPORTATION REVOLUTION, 1815–1860*

From the "cutting edge" of the frontier, which already reached far into the Ohio River Valley, to the outskirts of its seaboard cities the United States was in 1815 chiefly an agricultural country. Commerce, largely sea- and river-borne, was organized and directed by the merchant capitalists residing in a few cities along the Atlantic coast. This American economy of the early nineteenth century might best be described as extractive-commercial in character. It is true that the beginnings of industrial growth were already discernable. But in this land of continental expanses only revolutionary developments in the techniques of transportation and communication would make possible that almost explosive rush of industrial expansion which characterized the later decades of the century....

The United States of 1815 possessed vast but largely untapped natural resources. Wherever arable lands lay close to the ocean or along easily navigable rivers flowing into it, they yielded a rich agricultural output which constituted by far the most important product of the country. From roughly the same area came such products of the forest as lumber and masts, and tar, pitch, and turpentine. Vast areas of fertile lands and primeval forests stretched to the westward awaiting the development of transportation before they could be economically utilized....

The long Atlantic coast line, with its hundreds of harbors suitable for the small sailing craft of the period, provided the chief highway for travel and transportation by methods surprisingly little changed from the days of the Phoenicians. And the unexcelled fishing grounds off the coast of New England and Newfoundland, utilized by European fisherman even before the shores were settled, continued to provide a rich harvest of cod and mackerel for successive generations of American fisherman. From one end of the country to the other the larger rivers were used for the movement of goods to market and the smaller streams to turn the water wheels for gristmills, sawmills, and bloomeries. But techniques were still lacking to make possible utilization of the tremendous power potentialities of the larger rivers such as the Connecticut, the Susquehanna, and the Potomac....

The United States was still predominantly a rural country in 1815. According to the census returns, the proportion of the total population living in cities of 2,500 or more increased from 5.1 in 1790 to 7.3 per cent in 1810, then declined to 7.2 per cent in 1820, and rose in subsequent decades to 19.8 in 1860 [and] ... more than half of the total urban population was concentrated in the six largest cities: New York, Philadelphia, Baltimore, Boston, New Orleans, and Charleston....

The chief business of the cities was commerce, and their leading citizens were merchants. Wharves, warehouses, and stores characterized their physical appearance, and everything was tied together and directed from their nerve centers, the counting rooms. The streets of every large city led down past the warehouses to the piers. From the farms by river or road came products for export, but this was the *back country*; in 1815 every city seemed to face the sea, the direction from which came not only the needed products of every land but the news of distant nations and markets.....

...The leading citizens of the cities and the men who organized and directed the commerce of the country were the merchants... [who] typically owned their own ships and were engaged on their own account in the coastwise and foreign trade. Their activities comprehended almost every aspect of business. They bought and sold goods at wholesale and retail. They owned and sometimes built their own ships, which they operated as ocean carriers for others. In addition to trading on their own capital they often acted as commission agents or factors for others, assumed marine insurance risks, and performed numerous banking functions. In many cases, they also had manufacturing interests, perhaps a distillery or a ropewalk in New England or a flour mill or a tannery in Pennsylvania or Maryland....

Even before the War of 1812 considerable progress had been made in the Middle Atlantic and New England states toward linking together the chief commercial centers by means of turnpikes, a term used to designate a road upon which tolls were charged. These roads were typically built by private stock companies, which were chartered by the state governments, and were erected over the most important routes of travel. The best ones, like the early Lancaster Turnpike in Pennsylvania or the Cumberland Road, were built on a solid stone foundation with a gravel dressing. Others consisted of merely a layer of loose gravel with drainage ditches on each side. Usually some attempt was made to reduce the steeper grades by cuts or fills. The poorest were little more than country roads kept in barely passable condition by the turnpike company....

Intensified and almost unanimous enthusiasm for improved routes of land transportation followed the War of 1812. In part this was an outgrowth of the war experience. The extreme difficulty of moving troops on the Canadian frontier as well as on the southern boundary, due to the almost complete absence of highways, demonstrated that through roads in those areas were essential for effective national defense. Moreover, the British blockade of the Atlantic coast had compelled an unprecedented amount of land carriage and had emphasized the unsatisfactory character of the highways. Wagons carrying butter had made the long trip from New York to Charleston, South Carolina, and merchandise had been shipped in similar fashion from Boston to Philadelphia. A wagon loaded with cotton cards and drawn by four horses had actually been sent from Worcester, Massachusetts, to Charleston, South Carolina. This trip took seventy-five days! But the agitation for better roads also arose from the generally improved commercial conditions following the war. Farmers needed to get their war-accumulated surpluses to the seaports, merchants and manufacturers to sell their products in the interior. Especially were roads necessary to make contact with the rapidly expanding West, roads which must be built for long distances across unsettled portions of the Appalachians where no local government existed....

[The demand for roads was first met by the construction of turnpikes.] Where well built and kept in good repair, the turnpikes provided fine hard-surfaced roads.... To travelers, whether by carriage or stage coach, they were an unquestioned blessing. For immigrants pressing westward they literally smoothed the way, greatly reducing the hardships of that difficult trek. For local transportation with the heavy, clumsy wagons of the day they offered real advantages, though even low tolls discouraged traffic when freight was large in bulk or weight but small in value. But for long freight hauls the value of turnpikes was sharply limited. Even where tolls were very low or nonexistent, transportation by heavy wagons with four- to eight-horse teams proved profitable only to a very limited extent. As a result, though a boon to travelers, turnpikes generally did not cheapen and stimulate land transportation sufficiently to provide satisfactory earnings from tolls....

When, at the close of the War of 1812, the nation turned enthusiastically to developing more effective means of internal transportation, attention was directed to canals as well as turnpikes... [and] the success of the Erie Canal provided the spark which set off a nation-wide craze for canal building. With the need for improved transportation so great and the financial and economic benefits to be secured from artificial waterways now apparently assured, a veritable canal-building fury gripped the country from Maine to Virginia and from New Jersey to Illinois....

On the wave of enthusiasm...which arose out of the success of the Erie, three types of major canals were built: (1) those designed to improved transportation between the upcountry and tidewater in states bordering on the Atlantic from Maine to Virginia; (2) those, like the Erie, designed to link the Atlantic states with the Ohio River Valley; and (3) those in the West which were planned to connect the Ohio-Mississippi system with the Great Lakes....

By 1840 the people of the United States had constructed canals totaling 3,326 miles, a distance greater than that across the continent from New York to Seattle. All but approximately 100 miles had been built since 1816, mostly between 1824 and 1840. The total canal mileage, 1,277 in 1830, increased by over 2,000 miles in the decade following....

With its continental expanse and vast inland distances the United States was from the beginning peculiarly dependent upon river transportation. Sale crops were of little value unless they could be taken to market without great expense. As but few products could bear the cost of land carriage over appreciable distances, the rivers proved the only economical routes of commerce for early inland settlements. It was said in 1818 that two thirds of the market crops of South Carolina were raised within five miles of a river and that the other third not more than ten miles from navigable water....

On ocean bays and the lower reaches of broad rivers, the small seagoing sailing ships of the time might tack their way under favorable conditions. Such vessels sailed up the Mississippi above New Orleans as far as Natchez and were at home on the lower James, Potomac, Delaware, Hudson, Connecticut, and a few other Atlantic rivers. Elsewhere swift currents, shallow water, narrow, winding channels or high banks and forests which broke the wind rendered such navigation impracticable. As a consequence, the great bulk of the products of the country was floated down the streams and rivers on crude rafts and flatboats. Too clumsy for upriver navigation, they were usually broken up for lumber at the end of the journey. Transportation up the rivers proved extremely time consuming and costly. Narrow keelboats provided a limited service but their capacity was small and the labor of propelling them often so great that only small quantities of the most needed items would bear the cost of upriver shipment....

That the solution of this problem lay in the application of steam power to water transportation had been clearly recognized toward the end of the eighteenth century.... [T]he technique of steam engine construction advanced rapidly and, shortly before the War of 1812, the commercial feasibility of the steamboat was demonstrated by Robert Fulton in 1807 on the Hudson and, two years later, by John Stevens on the Delaware. With the return of peace in 1815 the stage was set for a great expansion in the use of steamboats....

The years from 1815 to 1860 mark the golden age of the river steamboat. By 1830 it dominated American river transportation and for two decades thereafter was the most important agency of internal transportation in the country. For the most part turnpikes and canals proved feeders rather than effective competitors and not until the fifties did railroads become a serious threat....

Wherever inland waters were suitable for steam navigation, the steamboat quickly demonstrated its competitive superiority over earlier means of transportation for travelers and on many routes for freight as well. For speed and for comfort of passengers neither canals nor turnpikes could compete, and even on the basis of cost, the steamboat had an advantage over most routes....

[The 1850s] marked the peak of the steamboat's development. At first railroads often stimulated water transportation. Thus, completion of rail lines from New York to Buffalo and across southern Michigan greatly added to the demand for steamboats on Lakes Erie and Michigan. Steamboats on Long Island Sound increased their business when they were able to connect with railroads leading to Boston from Providence, Fall River, and Stonington. But when through rail routes were completed, the steamboats found their erstwhile helper their deadly enemy....

Improved roads, canals, and steamboats made their contribution, but they were not entirely effective in loosening the bonds which fettered the agrarian, merchant-capitalist economy of the early nineteenth century. The United States encompassed vast distances, difficult mountain barriers, virgin forests, and great unsettled plains. Only a method of transportation by land – cheap, fast, and flexible – could meet the pressing needs of agriculture and industry. The steam railroad...provided the solution.... The railroad was essentially a simple device consisting of smooth fixed track upon which vehicles were moved by steam power. Before it could become an efficient agent of transportation many technical problems of track building, steam-engine construction, and practical railroad operation had to be solved. These came so rapidly that most of the major difficulties had been overcome by 1860. Of course, many improvements continued to be made: steel rails, the safety coupler, the automatic air brake, larger cars of steel construction, and heavier, faster, and more efficient locomotives. Important as were these improvements of the future, it was nonetheless true that by 1860 the railroad as a major instrument of transportation had come of age. Already it had built great cities, hastened the settlement of the West, made farming practicable on the prairies, and greatly stimulated the flow of internal commerce....

Wherever traffic was dense or distances were great the railroad could transport goods so much more cheaply than could be done by turnpikes that its superiority was easily established. The railroads won an easy victory over the smaller and weaker canals for the same reason. But some of the larger canals could easily meet or even better the lowest rates which the railroad could offer. Nevertheless, the railroads proved to have decisive advantage which assured their ultimate victory. In part, this superiority arose from greater dependability and flexibility. Closed by ice during at least a portion of the year and frequently subject to serious interruptions of traffic from either too little or too much water, the canal could not rival the railroad in either regularity or dependability of service....

Turnpikes, canals, steamboats, railroads – these were the technical devices by which Americans in the forty-five years preceding the Civil War solved the problem of moving goods and persons quickly and cheaply in the interior of their vast country....

Fundamental as is the story of the rise of the new agencies of transportation to an understanding of American economic development, it must be emphasized that the foregoing account...is but one important aspect of the transportation revolution. The impact of these developments on commerce and industry still remains to be examined....

At the close of the War of 1812, heavy wagons drawn along common roads or turnpikes by four-and six-house teams provided the only means of moving bulky goods over appreciable distances by land. It is hard to realize how prohibitively expensive was such transportation.... [A] United States Senate Committee Report written in 1816 gives concrete illustration of the obstacles to the development of inland industry. "A coal mine," says the report, "may exist in the United States not more than ten miles from valuable ores of iron and other materials, and both of them be useless until a canal is established between them, as the price of land carriage is too great to be borne by either." The same report points out that a ton of goods could be brought 3,000 miles from Europe to America for about nine dollars, but that for the same sum it could be moved only 30 miles overland in this country. Little wonder that under such conditions foreign trade flourished while domestic commerce developed only very slowly....

Between 1819 and 1822 rates for hauling goods by wagon fell drastically. Before 1819 westward from Philadelphia and Baltimore they had ranged from 30 cents a ton-mile to more than double that figure. During 1822 they were quoted as low as 12 cents. Thereafter charges ranged down to 7 and as high as 20 cents a ton-mile, although charges between about 12 and 17 cents were most common.... The spread of the turnpikes during this period may possibly have helped to reduce the rates. Some have held that these new toll roads lowered costs by as much as 50 per cent....

On even the earliest railroads rates were appreciably lower than those charged for wagon transportation. When the railroad from Boston to Worcester began operation in 1833, its charge between the two terminals was 6.25 cents a ton-mile as compared to 17.5 cents on the turnpike. As railroads improved and iron rails linked the chief commercial centers of the country, land transportation became so cheap as to permit long-distance shipment of bulky products.... When these [1860] rates... are compared with those for 1815–1820 it will be seen that for shipments by land of bulky products over appreciable distances freight charges had been reduced by approximately 95 per cent. Less than half of this decline merely reflects a decline in the general level of prices; the remainder represents a real reduction in the cost of land transport.

During the period covered by this study, steamboats [also] facilitated and cheapened the carriage of freight, especially upstream, and canals created new routes over which low water rates replaced the high cost of land carriage.... The canals made their contribution by permitting relatively cheap water transportation to be substituted for high-cost movement by land....

The most successful artificial waterways greatly stimulated trade by their ability to offer extremely low-cost transportation. In 1853, ton-mile rates on the Ohio Canal were 1.00 cents; on the Illinois, 1.40 cents. During the [1850s], rates on the Chesapeake and Ohio Canal varied from 2 cents a ton-mile for valuable commodities shipped relatively short distances to .25 cents a ton-mile for coal. Before construction of the Erie Canal the expense of transportation from Buffalo to New York City was $100 a ton, but rates fell sharply with the completion of the canal. From 1830 to 1850 they averaged only $8.81 a ton, and in 1852 ranged from $3.00 to $7.00, depending on the character of the shipments.... The Erie Canal ton-mile average for 1857–1860 was .8155 cents, a reduction of more than 95 per cent from rates a ton-mile charged in 1817 from Buffalo to New York. Ton-mile charges for the canal trip from Albany to Buffalo fell from 5.51 cents in 1830 to .66 cents in 1860, and from Buffalo to Albany from 2.50 cents to 1.07 cents in the same period. The average cost of transporting a barrel of flour from Buffalo to Albany fell from 71 cents in 1841 to 34 cents in 1853....

The prosperity of the western states depended upon their ability to exchange the products of their farms for needed manufactures and other outside products like salt, sugar, and coffee. At the beginning of this period the high cost of transportation erected a wall around the states west of the Alleghenies which seriously blocked the economic development of that area.... Three great developments in the technique of transportation – steamboats, canals, and steam railroads – helped to raze this wall....

By making possible upriver trade and greatly reducing transport costs both up and down the river, the steamboat gave the first great impetus to western growth. An increasing flood of western products came down the rivers, while northward from New Orleans there began to move a growing stream of eastern and European merchandise – salt, sugar, coffee, and a hundred other needed items – which frontiersmen could now afford to purchase....

No sooner had trade adjusted itself to changes wrought by the river steamboat, than canals, penetrating the barriers on the short Appalachian route, further stimulated western commerce and influenced the direction of its flow. It will be remembered that the Erie Canal was opened for through traffic in 1825, the Pennsylvania Main Line in 1834, the two canals across Ohio respectively in 1833 and 1845, and the Illinois and Michigan Canal in 1848. The first effect of these new waterways was greatly to stimulate traffic from the land-locked areas through which they passed, although before long the commerce of the whole Great Lakes area and the Ohio Valley began to feel their influence. The valuable manufactured products of the East moved in growing volume directly westward across New York and Pennsylvania. The merchants of Marietta, Cincinnati, Louisville, and even of Frankfort and Nashville secured an increasing portion of their merchandise over both northern Ohio routes and via the Pennsylvania canal system. By 1846 more than half of its manufactured imports reached the Ohio basin by this latter route. The value of goods shipped to the West by way of the Erie Canal was nearly $10,000,000 in 1836; by 1853 it was more than $94,000,000. Chicago became an important receiving and distributing point for New York merchandise and, with the opening of the Illinois and Michigan Canal in 1848, St. Louis, which had been an important distributing center for goods imported via New Orleans, began to get increasing shipments by way of the Illinois and Michigan Canal.

For the first time the bulky products of the West began to flow directly eastward. By connecting with the Great Lakes, the canal system of New York had tapped the finest inland waterway in the world.... In the Ohio Basin, produce, which from the first settlement of the West had gone down the river to market, now began to reverse its flow. Produce was carried to Lake Erie by either the Miami or the Ohio Canal and thence via the Erie Canal to the New York markets. Grain and flour from Pennsylvania, Kentucky, and southern Ohio and even some Kentucky tobacco moved to eastern markets by way of the Ohio Canal.... The alternative direct route eastward – up the Ohio and over the Pennsylvania Main Line Canal – also provided an outlet for a number of western products. About 20,000 hogsheads of tobacco annually passed eastward over the Main Line Canal, and by 1850–1852 total shipments of pork and pork products by this route were almost as large as those sent down the river....

Despite the tremendous volume of commerce developed by the canal routes, the Mississippi trade showed no slackening in its growth.... The whole West was growing so rapidly that for the time being there was more than enough business for all channels of trade. The tremendous tonnages reaching Buffalo from the Lake region consisted largely of new production made possible by the Erie Canal. At the same time that produce was being diverted eastward from the Ohio Valley, states tributary to the upper Mississippi – Illinois, Missouri, Iowa, Wisconsin, and Minnesota – were rapidly increasing their shipments down the river. Moreover, the lower Mississippi Valley was one of the most rapidly developing sections of the country, with the result that receipts of cotton and sugar at New Orleans tremendously increased.

Although the rate of growth of commerce on the Mississippi did not slacken, major changes in its nature were taking place. New Orleans became much less important as a distributing center for the manufactured products of the East. The value of eastern products reaching the interior in 1851 was about twice as great by the Hudson and canal as by coastwise shipment and the Mississippi. At the same time the upriver shipments of such products as West Indian coffee and Louisiana sugar and molasses grew greatly as western population increased and the canals of Illinois, Indiana, and Ohio opened up new markets for southern, Caribbean, and South American products.... Hence by 1860 the canals and railroads had almost completely substituted direct trade across the Appalachians for the old indirect route via New Orleans and the sea.

Before through rail lines were completed from New York City to Lake Erie at the beginning of the [1850s], the Erie Canal had developed a tremendous business in transporting westward the manufactured goods of the East. This trade reached its peak in 1853, but as a result of railroad competition, was more than cut in half by 1860.... River traffic was also adversely affected [by the railroads]. Most of the trade on the upper Connecticut simply disappeared soon after rails paralleled the river. After 1852 the volume of goods shipped down the Ohio River to New Orleans declined because of railroad competition, but, so far as Ohio River traffic was concerned, this loss was more than compensated for by increased upriver shipments to the railheads at Pittsburgh and Wheeling, a growing traffic with St. Louis and the upper Mississippi River area, and greatly increased coal shipments....

In tonnage terms, most of the domestic commerce still moved by water in 1860. The direct trade between the West and the north Atlantic seaboard expanded so rapidly during the [1850s] that the railroads, the lakes, and the Erie Canal were all needed to deliver western products to the east. The tonnage carried by the Erie Canal grew tremendously despite railroad competition and did not actually reach its peak until 1880. The Great Lakes served as a gigantic extension of the Erie Canal, and during the [1850s] railroads, pushing westward from Chicago and Milwaukee, acted as feeders to the Great Lakes trade so that its volume, swollen by the corn of Iowa and the wheat of Illinois, Wisconsin, and Minnesota, grew from year to year in almost geometric ratio. By the end of the decade western flour (and wheat equivalent) transported to tidewater via the Erie Canal exceeded 4,000,000 barrels; of this probably about two-thirds came from ports on Lake Michigan.

The railroads also rapidly increased their eastward shipments. The tonnage of through freight carried eastward by the Pennsylvania, Erie, New York Central, and Baltimore and Ohio railroads was not yet quite equal to that transported by the Erie Canal. But it was much more valuable, for the rails transported practically all of the merchandise and livestock, most of the packing house products, and about two-thirds of the flour. As a result, the heavier and bulkier products, such as grain and lumber, made up an increasingly large percentage of lake and canal traffic....

The rapid settlement of the West, the great increase in population, and the phenomenal improvements in transportation which have been emphasized made possible the territorial specialization upon which rested the striking growth of American domestic commerce [between 1815 and 1860]. The direction and magnitude of this commerce was largely determined by the growth of New York City as the great center for foreign importations, and the development of manufacturing in the Atlantic states lying north of Chesapeake Bay. The fundamental pattern of this trade was very similar to that which existed between Great Britain and this country in the colonial and early national period. The South, which in colonial days had sent its great staples directly to England and received manufactured products in return, after 1815 found a growing market for its raw materials – cotton, tobacco, and sugar – in the manufacturing East. The West, an exporter of grain and meat, carried on a similar direct trade with the manufacturing states, but it also provided the South with food products, receiving in exchange drafts on the East which were used to pay for manufactured imports. In similar manner before the Revolution, fish from New England and grain from the Middle Atlantic states had been exported to the West Indies to help permit payment for British imports. But this earlier trade had involved only the fringe of states along the Atlantic, whereas the domestic commerce rapidly developing during the nineteenth century presently involved a whole continent....

The tremendous growth of American internal trade during the forty-five years ending in 1860 was, of course, the result of many interacting factors. Fundamental was the adoption of the new instruments of transportation: canals, steamboats, and railroads. But the many other influences played a part, especially the rapid settlement of the West, the growth of manufacturing, and the increase of foreign trade. Each was partly cause and partly effect; all were mutually interacting forces which taken together produced the transportation revolution and at least the beginnings in America of that whole series of rapid changes which has come to be termed the industrial revolution....

By 1860 the colonial orientation of the American economy...had disappeared, and a national economy had taken its place. No longer were more than nine-tenths of American agriculture and industry concentrated within a narrow strip extending no farther inland than a hundred miles from the Atlantic coast, nor was dependence upon foreign trade and European markets the almost universal characteristic of the economy. The...transportation revolution had resulted in the creation of a new and really national economic orientation....

The growth of domestic commerce had [also] contributed to the decline of merchant capitalism, possibly already past its zenith in 1815, and by 1860 the organization of both foreign and domestic trade had reached a degree of specialization and a country-wide integration typical of modern national economies. Banking and finance had become a separate calling which was further differentiated with the rise of commercial banks, savings banks, insurance companies, note brokers, clearinghouses, and stock exchanges. With the rise of factories, manufacturing had become separated from marketing, and with the transportation revolution the actual moving of goods in foreign and domestic trade had become largely the responsibility of common carriers. Those who actually traded in goods, whether foreign or domestic, had also become highly specialized operators. Among those were the wholesale merchants who bought and sold goods in large quantities for their own account, and whose business had benefited from the decline of the auctions after the 1820s; commission merchants or factors often specializing in a particular product and buying and selling goods for others; brokers who did not actually receive the goods at all but brought buyer and seller together; and retailers, both those who had specialty shops in the large cities and those much more typical the country over who sold to consumers almost every conceivable product and service.

New York had firmly established itself as the great distributing center of the nation for both domestic and foreign goods. Here, centered in Pearl Street, were the jobbers and wholesalers to whose establishments came by coastwise vessel and railroad train country retailers from the South and West.... Retailers and wholesalers flocking to the metropolis on the Hudson divided their time between visiting the countinghouses to buy supplies for the coming season and enjoying a holiday in the big city. But not all storekeepers could afford an annual trip to New York. So regional jobbing centers grew rapidly, especially in the decade preceding 1860, with places like Augusta, Memphis, and Louisville in the South, and Cincinnati, St. Louis and Chicago in the West, becoming of increasing importance. Certain cities became trading centers for particular commodities and developed highly specialized marketing procedures. Thus, by 1860 cotton was sold by sample in New York and New Orleans, and tremendous quantities of grain changed hands in Chicago and Buffalo merely on the basis of recognized grades. Boston had become the leading wool market of the country. St. Louis led in the marketing of furs, while Chicago and Albany were the leading marts for lumber.

This emerging national economy of 1860 had a new orientation. The great cities of the East no longer faced the sea and gave their chief attention to shipping and foreign trade. Their commerce centered increasingly now at the railroad stations, rather than at the docks, and the commercial news from Mobile, Memphis, Louisville, Cleveland and Chicago was awaited with greater interest than that from Liverpool, Marseilles, or Antwerp. But though the American economy now faced the rapidly developing West, the leadership and the organizing genius remained concentrated in the great eastern cities. There, on Wall Street, State Street, and Broad Street, the leaders of the emerging era of finance capitalism were beginning to appear. By means of well-placed investments, by speculation and manipulation on the stock and produce exchanges, and by membership on the boards of directors of banks, insurance companies, cotton mills, and railroads, these rising entrepreneurs, the successors of the older sedentary merchants, were soon to play the directing role in the emerging national economy of stocks and bonds and debentures.

2–2. DOUGLASS C. NORTH, *THE ECONOMIC GROWTH OF THE UNITED STATES 1790–1860*

On the eve of the Civil War the United States had already achieved rapid and sustained economic expansion. We had filled out our territorial boundaries, and the frontier was already encroaching upon the parched lands in the lee of the Rocky Mountains and moving east of the Sierra Nevadas. Territorial acquisition had preceded the frontiersman, but the rapid pace of his westward movement had been a continuous goad. We were an industrial nation second only to Britain in manufacturing. Our expansion had been matched by an acceleration in economic well-being. The obstacles to American economic growth had been removed before the Civil War took place. That war was a costly and bitter interruption.

We have been accustomed to look at this country from 1865 onward to search out the sources of its economic success, or even to see the Civil War as the force which broke the shackles on our potential expansion. Yet the truth is that the critical period in this country's economic development had already passed by that time. Both the westward expansion, which gave us unrivaled natural resources, and the conditions necessary to sustained industrial growth were accomplished. This study is therefore both an essay in American economic history and a study in economic growth....

The analytical framework of this study is a composite of several propositions, the most important of which was a cornerstone of *The Wealth of Nations*. Taken together they reflect certain underlying features of economic behavior which have characterized the development of market economies over the past several centuries.... The gist of the argument is that the timing and pace of an economy's development has been determined by: (1) the success of its export sector, and (2) the characteristics of the export industry and the disposition of the income received from the export sector.

The expanding international economy of the past two centuries has provided the avenue by which one economy after another has accelerated its rate of growth. There are few exceptions to the essential initiating role of a successful export sector in the early stages of accelerated growth of market economies. The reason is that the domestic market has been small and scattered. These economies have been predominantly rural, with a high degree of individual self-sufficiency. Reflecting this aspect of the market, specialization and division of labor have been limited and rudimentary. An expanding external market has provided the means for an increase in the size of the domestic market, growth in money income, and the spread of specialization and division of labor. Under the favorable conditions outlined below (with respect to the disposition of income from the export sector), it has set in motion a chain of consequences leading to sustained growth....

If the export commodity is a plantation type which is relatively labor intensive, with significant increasing returns to scale, then its development will be in marked contrast to one where the export commodity may be most efficiently produced on a family-size farm with relatively smaller absolute amounts of labor required. In the first case, extremely unequal distribution of income will tend to result, with the bulk of the population devoting most of its income to foodstuffs and simple necessities (much of which may be self-sufficient production). At the other end of the income scale the plantation owners will tend to spend most of their income on imported luxury goods. There will be slight encouragement of residentiary types of economic activity. With more equitable distribution of incomes, there is a demand for a broad range of goods and services, part of which will be residentiary, thus inducing investment in other types of economic activities. Trading centers will tend to develop to provide these goods and services, in contrast to the plantation economy, which will merely develop a few urban areas devoted to export of the staple commodity and distribution of imports....

Equally important is the investment induced by the export commodity or service. If the export requires substantial investment in transport, warehousing, port facilities and other types of social overhead investment, external economies are created which facilitate the development of other exports. If the export industry encourages the growth of complementary and subsidiary industries, and if technology, transport costs and resource endowments permit these to be locally produced, further development will be induced. In both social overhead investment and investment in complementary and subsidiary industry, urbanization and increased specialization are promoted and additional residentiary activity geared to the increasing local demand for consumption goods and services develops....

The disposition of income earned from the export industry plays a decisive role in the growth of the region. Related to this argument is the region's propensity to import. To the extent that a region's income directly flows out in the purchase of goods and services rather than having a regional multiplier-accelerator effect, it is inducing growth elsewhere but reaping few of the benefits of increased income from the export sector itself. The *successful* economy grows because the initial developments from the export industry lead to a widening of the export base and growth in the size of the domestic market. Growing demand in the domestic sector leads to an ever widening variety of residentiary industries.

These industries (and services) producing for the local market vary in character. They range from those which must by necessity be residentiary (retail trade, some services, etc.) to those which—as the size of the market permits firms to achieve efficient scale of operations—become substitutes for some imports. In response to profitable opportunities in the economy, there is an inflow of labor and capital to augment the domestic increase. Changing factor proportions, along with the cost reducing consequences of social overhead investments and the improved skills, training and knowledge that come from diversion of capital into investment in education, lead to a broadening of the export base....

Between the end of the second war with England and the firing on Fort Sumter were nearly fifty years of peace, interrupted only briefly by the Mexican War on this continent and the Crimean War abroad. Neither was a major disturbing force, although the latter had repercussions upon economic stability in the 1850's. It was an era of tremendous expansion for the Atlantic economy as a whole and for the United States in particular.

The contrast between the sources of expansion in periods just before and after the War of 1812 is striking. In the former period the Western World was at war, and the rapid development of the American economy for fourteen years reflected our ability to take advantage of this war. The exigencies of war relaxed the mercantilist restrictions of European powers, and war created the demand for shipping and re-exports and the very favorable terms of trade that produced unequalled American prosperity up to 1808.

The period following 1815 was not only one of peace, but one in which artificial national barriers to the free movement of goods, services, productive factors, and ideas were being relaxed. An international economy was emerging in which the parts were interrelated by the forces of comparative prices of goods, services, and productive factors. An analysis of the United States economic development must necessarily be put into the context of the expansion of the Atlantic economy. Institutions and national policies which both impeded and fostered the international exchange of goods, services, productive factors and ideas must be continually brought into view. It was the "anonymous," impersonal forces of the evolving international economy which were the basic influence on the developing Atlantic economy and its constituent parts. National policies and institutional influences modified, rather than generated the economic growth that ensued. The very forces of the Atlantic economy which were inducing expansion in the United States were thereby making this country increasingly independent of the international economic context, so that during these years there was a fundamental shift away from dependence on our own internal economy as the mainspring of expansion.

In 1815 the international context was still critical. The expanding industrialization of England and Europe in the years after the Napoleonic wars was accompanied not only by the gradual relaxation of restrictions on trade and factor mobility, but the resultant structural changes accelerated the movement of productive factors in response to differential rates of return. While the immigration of people and particularly capital into the United States played an important part in our growth in the thirty years after 1815, it was the growth of the cotton textile industry and the demand for cotton which was decisive. In 1815 the previous sources of expansion, the re-export and carrying trade and manufactures, were declining as a result of peacetime competition. The West was still largely unintegrated into the national economy. The United States was left with only cotton as the major expansive force. The vicissitudes of the cotton trade— the speculative expansion of 1818, the radical decline in prices in the 1820s and the boom in the 1830s—were the most important influence upon the varying rates of growth of the economy during this period. Cotton was strategic because it was the major independent variable in the interdependent structure of internal and international trade. The demands for western foodstuffs and northeastern services and manufactures were basically dependent upon the income received from the cotton trade. This dependence resulted not only from the developing regional specialization, but from the characteristics of the South itself. A marked characteristic of the South was that income received from the export of cotton (and sugar, rice and tobacco) flowed directly out of the regional economy again in the purchase of goods and services. The South provided neither the services to market its own exports nor the consumer goods and services to supply its own needs, and had a very high propensity to import. It was the West which provided food for the South and, since the South was the West's major market until the problems of cross-mountain transport had been solved the growth of the market for western foodstuffs was geared to the expansion of the southern cotton economy.

The Northeast provided not only the services to finance, transport, insure, and market the South's cotton, but also supplied the South with manufactured goods, either from its own industry or imported and reshipped to the South. Major markets for the Northeast were the South and the West. Both depended, directly in the first case and indirectly in the second, on the income from the cotton trade.

It was cotton which was the most important influence in the growth in the market size and the consequent expansion of the economy: the slow development of the 1820's, the accelerated growth in the 1830's. In this period of rapid growth, it was cotton that initiated the concomitant expansion in income, in the size of domestic markets, and creation of the social overhead investment (in the course of its role in the marketing of cotton) in the Northeast which were to facilitate the subsequent rapid growth of manufactures. Cotton also accounted for the accelerated pace of westward migration as well as for the movement of people out of self-sufficiency into the market economy.

Cotton was not the only expansive influence in the economy during this period. Clearly there were others, and they will be considered. Had there been no cotton gin, it is certain that the resources directly and indirectly devoted to the cotton trade would have been at least partially absorbed in other types of economic activity. Given the social structure, attitudes and motivation of American society, and the rich quantity and quality of resources which made even the self-sufficient farmer well off as compared with his European counterpart, the United States economy would not have stagnated. But cotton was the commodity for which foreign demand was significantly increasing, it accounted for over half the value of exports and the income directly or indirectly from cotton was the major independent influence on the evolving pattern of interregional trade. Without cotton the development in the size of the market would have been a much more lengthy process, since there was no alternative way to expand the domestic market rapidly without recourse to external demand. In short, cotton was the most important proximate cause of expansion, and by tracing out the resulting interrelationships light may be shed on the pace and character of the economy's development, particularly in the years up to 1843.

... A great deal of economic activity is a passive rather than an active source of economic expansion. It grows up either dependent upon an "active" industry or in response to the growth of income initially generated by the carriers of economic change. In the examination of economic change it is important to distinguish between an independent variable initiating the change and the expansion of dependent economic activity which is induced by the "carrier" industry. This distinction is undoubtedly more difficult to make today than it was before 1860, when transport barriers and distinct patterns of regional specialization and internal trade all pointed to the strategic role of cotton. Direct income from the cotton trade was probably no more than 6 per cent of any plausible estimate of national income which we might employ, but when income from cotton exports, including shipments to textile mills in our own Northeast, grew from $25 million in 1831 to $70 million in 1836, it set in motion the whole process or accelerated expansion which culminated in 1839....

The cotton trade remained an important influence upon the economy until 1860 but its role declined in relative importance after the boom and depression that followed 1839. It is not that income from cotton did not grow. On the contrary, the 1850's represented another prosperous era, though not as wildly speculative as former ones, in which the value of the cotton trade exceeded any former period. However, a major consequence of the expansive period of the 1830s was the creation of conditions that made possible industrialization in the Northeast. Transport facilities developed to connect the East and est more efficiently; a new market for western staples developed in the rapidly urbanizing East and, sporadically, in Europe. The dependence of both the Northeast and the West on the South waned. The discovery of gold in California in 1848 created a third source of expansion outside the South. The Far West was not only a major market for the goods and services of the Northeast, but its one export, gold, played a vital role in the whole expansion of the 1850s.

It should not be forgotten that the United States expansion was taking place within the larger context of the Atlantic economy. While the demand for cotton in England and to a lesser extent in France played perhaps the most prominent part, the terms of trade, relative price levels here and abroad, the movement of productive factors, and the flow of ideas, particularly technological information, were all a part of the interrelated pattern of development.

Throughout the whole period the secular movement of the terms of trade became increasingly favorable. In the expansive surges of 1815–1818 and 1832–1839 they became very favorable, reflecting a rapid rise in the price of American exports. In these two periods, it was cotton that accounted for the rise and appeared to initiate the subsequent flow of capital in response to the increased profitability of opening up and developing new sources of supply of the export staple and western foodstuffs. The consequent divergence of domestic and foreign price levels, and the increase in imports and specie movements, determined the timing of cyclical movements. Attractive employment opportunities during these surges of expansion were the pull which brought immigrants to American shores in increasing numbers.

Expansion in the 1850's, unlike that of the two previous booms, was not preceded by favorable movements of the terms of trade—instead it was the domestic price level which began to rise before the export price index. Cotton played a part in the boom, but it was industrialization in the Northeast and the opening up of the West and Far West which were primarily responsible for the growth of the 1840's and 1850's. The influence of the international economy was felt less in the flow of capital than in the flow of people, with the first big wave of immigration coming in this period.

The foregoing summary has emphasized surges in growth followed by periods of depression, then gradual expansion preceding still another boom. The explanation of these long swings is that these movements are initiated by the movement of prices in the key "carrier" industries. Shifts in supply and demand result in a shift of resources into these areas in periods of rising prices. There is concomitant expansion in the wide variety of subsidiary, complementary, and residentiary activities whose fortunes are tied to the growth of the "carrier" industries and to the rise in income that is initiated by these surges of expansion. The process is a lengthy and cumulative one, ultimately overlayed with speculative excesses; the tremendous expansion in supply results in a painful period of declining prices and readjustment. In the first two expansive periods analyzed here, 1815 to 1818 and 1832 to 1839, cotton was the key industry in both the boom and the subsequent collapse and readjustment. In the last period the sources of expansion are more diffuse, but grain in the West played the most important role.

Underlying the uneven pattern of development were the shape of the supply curve of cotton (or grain) and the way in which the supply curve shifted. During each period of expansion, millions of acres of new land were purchased from the government for cotton production. Once this land had been cleared and a crop or two of corn planted to prepare the soil, the amount of cotton available could be substantially increased, and the supply curve of cotton shifted very sharply to the right. With the depressed cotton prices that followed such expansion, a good deal of this land was devoted to alternative uses. For the most part, it was put to crop and livestock use to feed slaves and reduce the costs of purchasing foodstuffs. In effect, it represented unused capacity with respect to cotton, and any slight increase in cotton prices could and did lead to shifting some of this land into cotton. In the old South, where slaves as such were an important intermediate good, this was clearly a rational redirection of resources during periods of depressed prices.... [The supply curve] was highly elastic over a range of output which included all the available land that had been cleared and readied for crop production and was suitable for cotton. Even with the rapid growth in demand that characterized the cotton textile industry in the first half of the nineteenth century, it took a decade for demand to shift to the right sufficiently to absorb this potential supply. During this decade very little new land was sold in the cotton states, and the expansion of potential capacity was at a much slower rate than during the previous boom. When the growth of demand for cotton finally brought all this potential capacity into production, a further increase in demand resulted in substantial price increases as the supply curve became increasingly inelastic. With the readily available cotton land already in production, higher prices brought forth little additional production in the short run.

While there had been little incentive to buy and clear new land for cotton during the period of low prices, rising prices triggered a land boom in the new South. Millions of acres of virgin land were sold; planters and their slaves migrated in large numbers to open up and exploit the rich land in the Southwest—Alabama, Louisiana, Mississippi, and Arkansas were the major states. A lengthy period intervened between the initial impetus from rising prices and substantial output increases for putting this land into production. While imperfections in the capital market and land speculation partially explain this delay, the more important reasons were the time it took to obtain slaves from the old South, clear the land, and plant a crop or two of corn to prepare the soil.... There was a lag of approximately four years between the peak in land sales and a large increase in cotton production. The consequence was a vast shift to the right in the supply curve of cotton and the beginning of a new period of depressed prices. Cotton output actually fell as some of this land was diverted into corn with the low cotton prices that prevailed after 1839.

In the West, the same general pattern prevailed with respect to wheat and corn. Land sales in the western states paralleled the prices of those staples, with one important difference. Little transportation or other social overhead investment was necessary to increase the supply of cotton in the South. In the West, transportation was the major limiting factor in increasing supply. The accessible lands close to water transportation were taken up first. Initially, the rise in prices brought into cultivation land further and further from cheap transportation. As a result, the supply curve of wheat and corn land was probably less inelastic than cotton as it began to slope upward. However, it also encouraged a boom in land sales and at the same time a growing agitation for large-scale investment in new transportation facilities. Canal and railroad building was a lengthy process, but a completed canal or railroad opened up large amounts of new land. The canal construction era of the 1830's and the railroad construction period of the 1850's each served to make possible, along with the land sales and influx of settlers that accompanied them, a large shift to the right in wheat and corn supplies, with much the same results as cotton.

Interregional Flows – 1815–1860

It is possible to present fairly complete statistics upon our international economic relationships throughout this period, but no complete quantitative picture is available for internal movements of goods, services, and productive factors. Although the statistics are fragmentary, and no attempt has so far been made even to piece them together, there is a wealth of descriptive material in government reports and contemporary books and magazines to provide a general outline and fill in many of the gaps....

While the data on interregional trade are incomplete, the general pattern of this trade has been carefully examined in a number of government studies of United States internal commerce. Yet G. S. Callender's comment of a half-century ago that the significance of this pattern of trade has been slighted by the economic historian is still appropriate. In describing the trade between western farmers and southern planters he said:

> This commerce between different agricultural communities in America has played a more important role in our economic history than seems to have been appreciated. It began in colonial times and shows itself in the trade between the Northern Colonies and the West Indies which was reckoned by the colonists themselves to be of vital importance to their prosperity. It appears again in the first part of the nineteenth century when a trade grew up on our western rivers between the lower South and the new states of the West of exactly the same character as that which went up and down the Atlantic coast between the West Indies and the Northern Colonies during the eighteenth century. It was in both cases a trade between a community of planters using slave labor to produce a few valuable staples which found a ready sale in the markets of the world on one hand, and a community of small farmers (who in many cases were partly fishermen) producing food and crude supplies on the other. The basis of the trade in both cases was the fact that the planter found it more profitable to devote his slave labor to the production of valuable staples to be sold in the markets of the world than to use it in producing the food and other agricultural supplies which he needed. So long as there were other agricultural communities ready and willing to furnish these supplies it was cheaper to procure them by trade than by direct production.

Certainly the pattern of this trade between the West, the South, and the East has long been familiar. While its beginnings antedate the second war with England, it was of negligible importance until the close of the war. With the innovation of the steamboat on the Mississippi in 1816, the West used that artery to ship foodstuffs to the South. The South, in addition to the foreign export of cotton, sugar, tobacco, and rice, shipped these staples to the Northeast and to a lesser extent upriver to the West. The Northeast provided banking, insurance, brokerage, and transport services to the South, and shipped finished goods, both its own and imports to the South and the West. The trade between the Northeast and South was a coastwise trade, while that with the West was overland when it involved valuable manufactured goods which could stand the high cost of wagon transportation, or by coastwise trade to New Orleans, and thence upriver, if they were bulky items. Beginning in the 1830's, this pattern of trade gradually changed. Before 1835 almost all of the produce going eastward over the Erie Canal came only from western New York, but with the completion of the Ohio canals there was a gradual redirection of western produce to the eastern seaboard. It was not until the last two decades of our period that the pattern of internal trade was significantly altered. When, in addition to the Erie and Pennsylvania Canals, East-West railroads were completed in the early 1850s, the nature of internal trade with the South had been fundamentally changed. It is not that the West's trade with the South declined absolutely; on the contrary, it increased and the 1850s were a golden era in Mississippi trade, but percentagewise the growing volume of western foodstuffs and a few mining products, such as lead from Missouri, were going increasingly to eastern markets. At the same time, the West became an important market for eastern finished goods, although the South continued to be a major market for eastern services and manufactures. [Louis B.] Schmidt's succinct summary of this mutual interdependence is worth quoting.

The rise of internal commerce after 1815 made possible a territorial division of labor between the three great sections of the Union—the West, the South, and the East. The markets which were developed for various products opened the way for the division of labor in regions where it had been practically unknown before. Each section tended to devote itself more exclusively to the production of those commodities for which it was best able to provide. There was fostered a mutual economic dependence between sections and the establishment of predominant types of industry in each which were in turn dependent on foreign commerce. The South was thereby enabled to devote itself in particular to the production of a few plantation staples contributing a large and growing surplus for the foreign markets and depending on the West for a large part of its food supply and on the East for the bulk of its manufactured goods and very largely for the conduct of its commerce and banking. The East was devoted chiefly to manufacturing and commerce, supplying the products of its industries as well as the imports and much of the capital for the West and the South while it became to an increasing extent dependent on the food and the fibers of these two sections. The West became a surplus grain- and livestock-producing kingdom, supplying the growing deficits of the South and the East....

This discussion of the interregional trade of the United States is really a means of getting at the income flows between these specialized, interdependent parts. The trade was paralleled by reverse flows of income or at least by claims which were frequently settled by a more circuitous route. We now have some idea of interregional trade, but not of an interregional balance of payments. Unfortunately, no comprehensive figures are available on this score. Contemporaries were aware of the importance of the invisible items in the settlement of claims between the North and the South, not to mention the flow of capital into the West. From their accounts, we can get at least a qualitative picture of this subject supplemented by some contemporary estimates.

It was evident at the time, and indeed the subject of bitter reproach on the part of southern partisans, that the income of the South flowed out to the North and the West.... [T]he reason it flowed out to the North rested not just on the interregional trade, but upon the other items in the balance of payments. The North provided the South with transportation, insurance, and marketing services, as well as a good deal of the capital for plantation expansion. In addition, it provided the summer residence of the wealthy planter class who migrated northward to escape the hot and pestilent summers in the South, so the South paid the North for these services. Their magnitude must remain conjectural to a degree, but they were clearly important. [Thomas P.] Kettell's estimate for 1859 was little more than a guess, but it does give some indication of the likely magnitudes. He estimates southern produce, raw materials, and so on sent north at $462 million, which is balanced by the following credits accruing to the North:

Domestic goods	$240 million
Imported goods	106 million
Interest, brokerage, etc.	63 million
Southern travelers	53 million

While the amount for southern travelers may be excessive, it is doubtful that $63 million was too much to cover insurance, brokerage, interest and transportation accruing to the North. Just one indication of its magnitude can be gained from the *transfer* cost of cotton, that is, the price the planter received compared to the Liverpool price. The various changes are presented in [the following] table.... Most of these changes accrued to the North.

The flow of capital from the North to the South and West was sizable. In addition to the flow resulting from New York being the center of the money market and linked with the English market, long term capital flowed to the South and West in large quantities.

Although there is no quantitative data available on these flows, the ebb and flow of capital to the West was consistent, as far as timing is concerned, with that of foreign capital coming into or leaving the country. Moreover, the terms of trade between the agricultural West and eastern finished goods also showed a pattern similar to that of the international context....

There is better evidence on the internal flows of people. Perhaps the best indication of internal migration is land sales in the southern and western states.... They show surges of migration to the South in 1816–1818, 1832–1839, and only modest inflow into the Southwest in the 1850's. Internal migration was accelerated to the West in each period of expansion, but was greatest in the 1850's. While speculation certainly played a part in the timing of land sales, the evidence of population movements suggests that they bore a close relationship to the westward movement. The movement in the southern states was primarily an intraregional movement from the old South to the new South. The flows into the West came partly from already settled western areas, but particularly from the East....

The timing, pace, and character of American manufacturing development before the Civil War resulted... [primarily from] the growth in the size of the domestic market. ... [T]wo English commissions which investigated United States manufacturing in the 1850's... placed first emphasis on the size and composition of the market. They noted not only the absolute size and rate of growth of the population, but also the high average wealth of the people.... They were most impressed by the standardized method of production which lent itself to mechanical techniques and low unit costs geared to large-scale output of a standardized product. The growing localization of industry, specialization of function, and increasing size of firm were all basically related to the growth in the market, which stemmed from the regional specialization and growth of interregional trade beginning after 1815, but was *really* accelerated with the surge of expansion in the 1830's. The markets for textiles, clothing, boots and shoes, and other consumer goods were national in scope, reflecting the decline of self-sufficiency and the growth of specialization and division of labor. Derived demand for machinery and products of iron expanded in response to the consumer goods industries. The cotton trade was the immediate impetus for this regional specialization, and the growth of cotton income in the 1830's was the most important proximate influence upon the spurt of manufacturing growth of that decade. The growth of specialized methods of distribution and the decline of the auction system betokened this new dimension of the market.

This growing interregional specialization was greatly aided by declining transportation costs. The fall in ocean freight rates, in western river freight rates, and in rates on the Erie and Pennsylvania Canals were important early influences. Even before the advent of the railroad, interregional trade had effectively widened the market for eastern manufactures. The development of industry in Massachusetts in the 1820's and in the other northeastern states in the early 1830's gives evidence of the rapid development of interregional trade dependent upon declining water transportation rates. The spread of railroads in the Northeast between 1835 and 1850 did play an important role in the further growth and localization of industry. This was true of New England in general and Massachusetts in particular, where the most efficient size firms in textiles and in a variety of other industries tended to develop. The effective connection of East and West by railroad in the 1850's further decreased the transfer cost barrier to localized industry....

The development of manufacturing in the Northeast after the sharp readjustment following the War of 1812 centered around a few industries which had already been demonstrated to possess growing markets. Their location in the Northeast was dictated by prior developments there as well as by the natural resource endowment of abundant water power. The linkages associated with the textile industry were an important influence in the development of the 1820's and early 1830's. It was the growth in the size of the market as a consequence of regional specialization which led to acceleration in manufacturing development, and to the specialization of function of the firm in the 1830s. The cotton trade of the South and the decline in transport costs were the proximate influences in this growing regional specialization and the development of interregional trade.

If the growing size of the market made possible the development of manufacturing, it was the quality of entrepreneurial talent and the labor force that could effectively take advantage of these opportunities. The adaptation of foreign inventions, the variety of native innovations, particularly those which cut labor costs, and the rapid spread of new techniques were indicative of the *quality* of labor and entrepreneurial talent. While the underlying aspirations and motivations of people in American society were important, the investment in human capital was a critical factor both in innovations and in the relative ease with which they could spread. The primary source of this quality of the labor force and entrepreneurial talent was the widespread free education system in the Northeast, although the skills of English, and German immigrants were an important supplement.

The surge of expansion that began in 1843 was an era in which the Northeast had ceased being a marginal manufacturing area and could successfully expand into a vast array of industrial goods. By 1860 the *problems* of industrialization were behind in the development of the United States.

Table 2.1 TRANSFER COSTS OF COTTON: CHARGES ON A BALE OF COTTON AT MOBILE

A statement of the Charges incurred at the Port of Mobile, exclusive of Insurance, calculated on a Bale of 420 Pounds, with Freight at 3/4 d., and Prices at the present Rates.

Wharfage, per bale	$.10	
Weighing	.125	
Draying to press	.125	
Storage, average, day	.20	
Factor's commissions, average this season	.80	
Add for freight to city	1.50	
Chargeable to planter		$ 2.85
Brokerage	. 25	
Storage until compressed	.125	
Drayage to vessel or lighter	.08	
Wharfage	.10	
Commission on purchase, average, say	.80	
Freight and primage, say	6.645	
Chargeable to purchaser		$ 8.00
Compressing	.80	
Lighterage to lower bay	.25	
Stowing, (done by the day) say	.25	
Chargeable to vessel		$ 1.30
Total charges on a bale		$12.15
Add port charges at Liverpool	6.00	
Total, on both sides, per bale		$18.15

Source: *Hunt's Merchants' Magazine, and Commercial Review,* March 1840, pp. 267–78.

SUGGESTIONS FOR FURTHER READING

Charles A. Beard, *An Economic Interpretation of the Constitution* (1913).

Thomas Berry, *Western Prices Before 1861* (1943).

Mark Bils, "Tariff Protection and Production in the Early U.S. Cotton Textile Industry," *Journal of Economic History*, 44(1984) 1033–1045.

Victor S. Clark, *History of Manufactures in the United States 1607–1860* (1929).

Clarence Danhof, *Change in Agriculture: The Northern United States, 1820–1870* (1969).

Albert Fishlow, "Antebellum Interregional Trade Reconsidered," *American Economic Review*, (1964) 352–364.

Paul W. Gates, *The Farmer's Age: Agriculture, 1815–1860* (1960).

Claudia D. Goldin and Frank D. Lewis, "The Role of Exports in American Economic Growth During the Napoleonic Wars, 1793–1807," *Explorations in Economic History*, 17(1980) 6–25.

Carter H. Goodrich, *The Government and the Economy, 1783–1861* (1967).

——, *Canals and American Economic Development* (1949).

Erik F. Haites, James Mak, and Gary M. Walton, *Western River Transportation: The Era of Early Internal Development, 1810–1860* (1975).

C. Knick Harley, "International Competitiveness of the Antebellum American Cotton Textile Industry," *Journal of Economic History*, 52(1992) 559–584.

Alice H. Jones, *Wealth of a Nation To Be* (1980).

Diane Lindstrom, *Economic Development in the Philadelphia Region, 1810–1850* (1978).

——, "Southern Dependence on Interregional Grain Supplies: A Review of the Trade Flows, 1840–1860," *Agricultural History*, 44(1970) 101–113.

John Majewski, Christopher Baer, and Daniel B. Klein, "Responding to Relative Decline: The Plank Road Boom of Antebellum New York," *Journal of Economic History*, 53(1993) 106–122.

James Mak and Gary Walton, "Steamboats and the Great Productivity Surge in River Transportation," *Journal of Economic History* 33(1972) 619–640.

Cathy Matson, "The Revolution, the Constitution, and the New Nation," in Stanley L. Engerman and Robert E. Gallman, eds., *The Cambridge Economic History of the United States*, vol. 1 (1996).

Robert A. McGuire and Robert L. Ohsfeldt, "Economic Interests and the American Constitution: A Quantitative Rehabilitation of Charles A. Beard," *Journal of Economic History*, 44(June 1984) 509–519.

Lloyd Mercer, The Antebellum Interregional Trade Hypothesis: A Reexamination of Theory and Evidence," in Roger L. Ransom, Richard Sutch, and Gary M. Walton, eds., *Explorations in the New Economic History* (1982).

Curtis P. Nettels, *The Emergence of a National Economy, 1775–1815* (1962).

Roger L. Ransom, "Interregional Canals and Economic Specialization in the Antebellum United States," *Explorations in Economic History*, 5, 2nd Series (1967).

Nathan Rosenberg, *Technology and American Economic Growth* (1972).

Peter Temin, "Steam and Water Power in the Early 19th Century," *Journal of Economic History*, 26(1966) 187–205.

Paul Uselding, "A Note on the Inter-regional Trade in Manufactures in 1840," *Journal of Economic History*, 35(1976), 428–437.

Robert B. Zevin, *The Growth of Manufacturing in Early Nineteenth-Century New England* (1975).

CHAPTER 3

Railroads and American Economic Growth

INTRODUCTION

Few inventions had as great an impact on American life as the railroad. Without the inexpensive, reliable, and efficient form of internal transportation railroads provided the pace of 19th Century American territorial expansion may have proceeded more slowly. By linking together the different sections of the country into one large national market, the railroads also contributed to the transformation of the 19th Century American economy. The economic success of railroads and the subsequent consolidation of the industry in the decades around the Civil War also gave Americans their first experience with big business and in so doing, produced some of the earliest demands for government regulation of business. But railroads also had a major impact on the American psyche. By reducing travel time from weeks to days and from days to hours, railroads revolutionized Americans' sense of time and space. And as the "iron horse," the term 19th Century Americans often used to describe them, railroads symbolized the growing sense of human mastery of nature made possible by the technological revolution.

In 1828, only fourteen years after the first steam locomotive was built in Great Britain, construction of the great Baltimore & Ohio Railroad began in the United States, a railroad that eventually brought the rich produce of the Ohio River Valley to the port of Baltimore at the head of the Chesapeake Bay. The commercial success of the B & O and other early lines ignited an explosion of railroad construction so that by the eve of the Civil War there were 30,626 miles of railroad track linking together the different regions of the United States. By 1890 the miles of railroad tracks had grown by more than 400%, rising to 129,774.

Railroads became the leading form of internal transportation, rapidly surpassing canals and steamboats because they could move large quantities of passengers and freight faster and more inexpensively than other forms of internal transport. That railroads were generally available twelve months of the year gave them an added advantage over canals and steamboats which could not be used in winter months when waterways froze. The expansion of the railroad network made all sections of the nation readily accessible to all Americans which in turn promoted important changes in the American economy. The advent of railroads made it possible, for example, for American manufactures to ship their wares to remote corners of the nation, thereby providing them with a powerful incentive to expand their size and output. Similarly, because railroads provided the Midwest and later the Trans-Mississippi West with cheap, reliable access to eastern markets and through them to the international market, American farmers were encouraged to expand their output and concentrate increasingly on commercial production. The increasing commercialization of the American economy required, in turn, new and larger centers of business, banking, and finance and in this sense railroads also contributed to the urbanization of the United States.

Initially, most Americans exulted over the railroad, seeing it as not only the source of many real benefits that would improve their lives but also as a symbol of the great progress the United States made as a nation. But the rapid expansion of railroads soon led to the consolidation of many small, independent lines into larger regional and eventually national corporations controlled by immensely powerful and wealthy individuals. In the 1860s, for example, Cornelius Vanderbilt bought up a series of small railroads in New York State to form the New York Central Railroad. By the 1890s Vanderbilt's corporation controlled more than 13,000 miles of track in the northeastern United States. Similarly, the man who beat out Vanderbilt in the 1860s for control of the Erie Railroad, financier Jay Gould, eventually built a railroad empire of more than 16,000 miles of track in the western United States centered on the Union Pacific Railroad. These railroad empires were the first big businesses Americans confronted and they suggested to many that there was a dark side to the industrial revolution then transforming the nation. For once railroads became large national corporations, they seemed to acquire the power to bend market forces to their will. In this sense, railroads served as the model for much of the anti-monopoly sentiment and demand for government regulation of business that dominated the national discourse in the late 19th Century.

Given the many ways that railroads influenced American life in the 19th Century economic historians have long been interested in determining their economic impact. Many have argued that railroads were the single most important factor responsible for the emergence of the industrial economy that transformed the United States into a world economic power by the end of the 19th Century. What sorts of factors do we need to consider in order to determine the railroads' impact on economic growth? 19th Century Americans believed that railroads were the cheapest form of internal transportation, at least until the consolidation movement transformed the industry. Were these impressions always accurate? In addition to their impact on the cost of transportation, in what other ways might railroads have spurred economic growth and promoted the industrialization of the United States? Students of economic history also need to assess the validity of any assumptions inherent in an interpretation. In this case, then, is it safe to assume that if railroads had never been invented the pattern and pace of 19th Century economic growth would have been any different? Can we assume that in the absence of railroads other forms of internal transportation such as canals and steamboats would have been insufficient to meet the demands of an expanding national economy? Is it possible, then, that railroads facilitated the transformation of the 19th Century American economy but were not essential to it?

DOCUMENTS

The ebullience with which Americans initially viewed the railroads is reflected in Document 3–1, an excerpt from an 1867 article published in the *North American Review*, one of the leading journals of the day. In it the author recounts the many positive contributions railroads had made to American life in the first few decades of their existence. Document 3–2, "Danger Ahead," is excerpted from a chapter of the 1873 book *The History of the Grange Movement, or The Farmers' War Against*

Monopolies. It summarizes the complaints and fears of farmers in the United States who believed that through consolidation, the railroads had become a baneful influence on the nation. The farmers' complaints about the economic impact of the railroad empires reflected the emerging discontent late 19th Century Americans felt about the rise of big business. In their continuing efforts to address their complaints farmers formed the Populist Party in 1892, one of the first organized efforts to promote government regulation of business.

3–1. "THE RAILROAD SYSTEM"

Source: *The North American Review*, (CIV) April 1867, pp. 476–511.

The seventh day of the coming August will be the sixtieth anniversary of Robert Fulton's steamboat voyage from New York to Albany. Every one has read the story of that excursion, and has shared in its excitement, from the moment the little steamer…cast off so inauspiciously from the pier in New York, until the steeples of Albany appeared in the distance. Altogether, it makes a day's story hardly less interesting than the story of that famous night which preceded the discovery of America. Eighteen years later, in 1825, steam was first successfully applied to locomotion on land upon the Darlington and Stockton Railroad in England, and not until 1829 was the experiment regarded as one of assured success. At exactly the same time, in this country, the Cumberland Turnpike and its construction was a fiercely agitated national question. It was part of the great system of internal improvement then contemplated; and in identifying with it his name, Henry Clay doubtless thought that he had imperishably connected his memory with a monument more enduring than bronze, —with the Appian Way of America.

From a period long before the Christian era to 1829 there had been no essential improvement in the system of internal communication. In that year it was that the new power first fairly asserted its force. The Liverpool and Manchester road, on which the success of the new motive force was then demonstrated, was a road thirty-two miles in length, and it constituted the only steam railway line in the world which was, in the year 1830…in course of successful operation. Fulton's experiment was made sixty years ago: the last event was only thirty-seven. At present the Cumberland Turnpike is just about as antiquated as the Appian Way, —no more useful, and far less interesting. As to the railroads, it is already impossible exactly to compute, and very difficult even to approximate, the number of miles of their length now operated upon throughout the whole world, or the millions of capital invested in them. For present purposes… there may, in round numbers, be said to be in both hemispheres at least 75,000 miles of railroad in actual use, constructed at a cost varying from $20,000 a mile on the Western prairies to £870,000 sterling a mile for the Metropolitan Railway in London, and averaging throughout the world, perhaps, $80,000 the mile,—thus representing, in round numbers, some $6,000,000,000 of capital in construction alone. These figures, be it remembered, represent only the first thirty-seven years of the life of a growing system which expands with a continually accelerating degree of development, which is every day exercising new influences upon mankind, and forcing upon, them novel questions for immediate solution….

The application of steam to locomotion is vulgarly looked upon as an improvement, an advance of civilization, a great result of science, a fine investment of capital, a wonderful improver of the value of corner lots, a great time-saver, an indispensable agent for the development of new country; but it may be questioned if it is often viewed in its true magnitude, as, with perhaps two exceptions, the most tremendous and far-reaching engine of social revolution which has ever either blessed or cursed the earth. It cannot be time wasted briefly to consider…how deeply and variously this new agent of civilization has already affected human interests. From that consideration perhaps a more just estimate may be formed of the importance of the question now agitated.…

The most apparent and immediate application of steam locomotion is to geographical development. …[T]he attention is at once struck by the new and portentous law of civilized territorial increase which the era of steam has inaugurated. Until as recently as the year 1847, the old Phoenician method of colonization, somewhat improved in details yet prevailed. As the Greeks sent out colonies to the Aegean isles, to Asia Minor, and to Syracuse,— as the Romans conquered the barbarians, and then held them as colonists, — so the Spanish, the Dutch, the French, and the English sent out their offshoots to every quarter of the globe called uncivilized.… As a rule, the growth of these colonies was as slow, in the modern as it had been in the ancient times.…

Steam was applied to locomotion on water and on land respectively in 1807 and 1829. At length, in 1846, vague rumors of regions rich beyond all precedent in golden ores, and only then discovered on the shores of the Pacific, pervaded the whole civilized globe, and, under the influence of steam, a new phase of colonization at once developed itself. To the new gold fields rushed whole populations, and forthwith steam became their servant, and bound them closely with the older world. Where yesterday had been a wilderness, California and Australia took their places among the communities of the globe. The new era was making itself felt, and, under its fostering impulse, communities sprang into life full grown. Without the assistance of steam, settlements would probably have been established, and lingered in slow growth, along the shores of the sea and on the banks of navigable rivers; but the steamboat and the locomotive lent their aid, and the very Arabs of civilization became substantial communities. So far as the inducement of gold was concerned, the same process now going on upon both slopes of the Rocky Mountains was witnessed in the colonization of Mexico and Cuba. With Cuba it succeeded, as the ocean connected the colonist with the world; with Mexico it failed, because colonization was too rapid to be healthy, and the scattered colonists, cut off from and unsupported by the intercourse of their kind, merged into, and both degraded and were degraded by, the semi-civilization of the aborigines. Such will not be the case with Colorado. If that region be indeed, as is claimed by its ex-Governor, "gridironed over with gold, silver, copper, and lead-bearing lodes," then will it very soon experience the influence of the new law of colonization. No long, wearisome, and dangerous wagon road, scarcely marked out across the plains, will connect a nomadic population of semi-barbarous, undomesticated men with a distant civilization which is to them almost a dream of their childhood; but almost at once the ringing grooves of the railroad will connect them with the denser populations of the East and West. A community, embracing multiform industries, will spring up in the wilderness, and every comfort of life and appliance of civilization will flow to a new and opulent market. So the new era of material development, by a process of its own, is peopling and subduing the wilds of America and Australia. This is the present exemplification of a law which dates back only twenty years.

What other possible exemplifications of it await us? What new discoveries of territorial wealth may be made? What region of earth next awaits development? California and Australia have revealed their secrets; — how long will those of Mexico and South America and Africa remain concealed? …We are always inclined to look upon the world as finished, upon known forces as having produced their final results; but results are never complete. Perhaps in 1481 the thinkers of that day may have considered that the printing press had expended its force as a new power; and in 1522 philosophers may have supposed that the ultimate material effects of geographical discovery could be approximately estimated. The one or the other conclusion would probably have been as correct as any attempt at gauging the ultimate effects of the steam system today.

Neither is the extent of the revolution already worked by the new power directly under our notice often appreciated. Its varied influences enter so intimately into our daily life, are so much a part of our acts and thoughts, that they become familiar, and cease to be marvelous. The changes have been so gradual, that we have failed to notice their completeness. Yet most people who observe at all have vaguely felt that there was some element which made our century different from all others, — a century of greater growth, of more rapid development. The young have found things different on attaining manhood from what they remembered in their youth; the middle-aged wondered if change had flashed along in the eyes of their fathers as it did in their own; and the old can easily remember a period less removed from the Middle Ages than from the passing year. Our times are not as those of our fathers. The seventh day of August, 1807, marks an era in human progress, and the years since that day have seen vastly more changes, and a progress vastly more accelerated, than any that preceded them: they have been years of another world.

No power has been so great as to be able to defy the influence of the new force at work in those sixty years, and no locality so obscure as to escape it. From the most powerful of European monarchies to the most insignificant of New England villages, the revolution has been all pervading. Abroad and at home it has equally nationalized people and cosmopolized nations. Its influence has been more potent in peace than of late years in war. The chief bonds of nationality are unities of race, of language, of interest, and of thought. The tendency of steam has universally been towards the gravitation of the parts to the center, — towards the combination and concentration of forces, whether intellectual or physical. Increased communication, increased activity, and increased facilities of trade destroy local interests, local dialects, and local jealousies. The days of small barrier kingdoms and intricate balances of power are well nigh numbered. Whatever is homogeneous is combining all the world over in obedience to an irresistible law. It is the law of gravitation applied to human affairs. One national center regulates the whole daily thought, trade, and language of great nations, and regulates it instantly. In this way, France and England are already bound as closely into two compact wholes, as were formerly the parishes of London or the *arrondissements* of Paris....

On this continent, our own country is the child of steam. With us it has neither combined homogeneous elements, nor forced into conflict those that were incongruous, but it has rapidly disseminated one element over a vast wilderness. The steamboat and railroad alone have rendered existing America possible.

Such are some of the results of peace. The same force has left a deep mark on the results of modern warfare, — a mark no less noticeable from its absence than from its presence. The history of two recent wars, not ten years apart, perfectly illustrates the possible differences of result arising from the regard or disregard of this new element of power. These two are the war in the Crimea and our late Rebellion. Russia failed of success in the Crimea, because she could not avail herself of the steam engine; the Allies succeeded, because they could avail themselves of the steamship. Marseilles and Plymouth were infinitely nearer to Sebastopol than were Moscow and St. Petersburg. Could Russia have concentrated men and munitions with the ease and rapidity of France and England, the war must have had another close. The new element of force and combination, neglected by Russia in 1854, we availed ourselves of with decisive effect in 1864. That one new element of power — wholly left out of their calculations by European military authorities in exercising the gifts of prophecy on the result of our struggle — was the one element which made possible the results we accomplished. They told us of the vastness of the territory to be subdued, of the impossibility of sustaining our armies, of the power of a people acting on the defensive. They pointed to Napoleon's dismal experience in Russia, and wondered and sneered at those who would not learn from the experience of others, or profit from the disasters of the past. They could not realize, and would take no count of, the improved appliances of the age. The result the world knows. It saw a powerful enemy's very existence depending on a frail thread of railroad iron, with the effectual destruction of which perished all hope of resistance; it saw Sherman's three hundred miles of rear, and the base and supplies of eighty thousand fighting men in security three whole days' journey by rail away from the sound of strife; it saw two whole army corps, numbering eighteen thousand men, moved, with all their munitions and a portion of their artillery, thirteen hundred miles round the circumference of a vast theatre of war, from Virginia to Tennessee, in the moment of danger, and this too in the apparently incredibly brief space of only seven days. From Alexander to Napoleon, the possibilities of combination in warfare were in essentials the same. Within thirty years of the death of Napoleon, that was accomplished which to him would have read as the tale of some Arabian night. The changes of thirty years throw deep into the shade those of thirty centuries.

All those yet referred to are but the interior circles of the influences already perceptible from the disturbing action of this one new force. It does not confine itself to nationalizing each several race, but it cosmopolizes nations…. Within the last twenty years, the old New England country town and its inhabitants have equally disappeared. The revolutions of these few years have swept away the last vestiges of colonial thoughts and persons. Who that has ever lived in a New England country town does not remember its old quiet and dullness, its industry, and the slow, steady growth of its prosperity, the staidness of its inhabitants? In the village church and the village street you seemed to see more gray heads than now, and more reverence was paid them. In the country, you met a class of men now wholly gone, — dull, solid, elderly men, men of some property and few ideas, — the legitimate descendants of the English broad-acred squires. They were the country gentry, — the men who went up to the General Court, and had been members of the Governor's Council; they were men of formal manners and of formal dress, — men who remembered Governor Hancock, and had a certain trace of his manners. Today this class is as extinct as the dodo. Railroads have abolished them and their dress and their manners,—they have abolished the very houses they dwelt in. The race of hereditary gentry has gone forever, and the race of hereditary businessmen has usurped its place. Shrewd, anxious, eager, over-worked, the men of today will accomplish vast results, and immensely accelerate the development of the race. They represent the railroad, as the earlier type did the stagecoach….

The same phenomena are witnessed in the regions of thought. It is bolder than of yore. It exerts its influence with a speed and force equally accelerated. The newspaper press is the great engine of modern education; and that press, obeying the laws of gravitation, is everywhere centralized, — the rays of light once scattered are concentrated into one all-powerful focus. Today's metropolitan newspaper, printed by a steam press, is whirled three hundred miles away by a steam engine before the day's last evening edition is in the hands of the carrier. The local press is day by day fighting a losing cause with diminished courage, while the metropolitan press drives it out of circulation and draws from it its brain. Thought draws to intellectual centers as trade draws to commercial centers, and all are railroad centers. Thoughts are quickly exchanged, and act upon each other…. The same problems perplex at once the whole world, and from every quarter light floods in upon their solution. This very question of the relation between communities and their railroad systems is now presenting itself to all the nations at once, and the best solution will result from common experience. The law of competition is brought to bear on national thought. But increased communication has not alone quickened and intensified thought, — it has revolutionized its process. The great feature of the future, if the present view of the influences of the agents at work is correct, will be the rapid uprising of numerous new communities. Of all such communities questioning is a leading characteristic. They have neither faith in, nor reverence for, that which is old. On the contrary, with them age is *prima facie* evidence of badness, and they love novelty for novelty's sake. This mental inclination will ultimately apply the last test to truth, for error has its full chance and is sure of a trial. The burden of proof seems likely to be shifted from the innovator to the conservator. In the rising passion for change, the question seems likely to be, not, is the proposed innovation an improvement? but, is the existing condition certainly better than that proposed?

It is in the domains of trade, however, that the revolution is the most apparent and bewildering, — that the ramifications of cause and effect are most innumerable and interminable.... Increased communication leads to increased activity. Prices seek a level; produce is exchanged; labor goes where it is needed.... In 1807 New York numbered a population of about 75,000. Chicago existed in 1829 only as an uninviting swamp, inhabited by a dozen families, and San Francisco was hardly a name. In 1830 New York contained over 200,000 inhabitants; and today they exceed 800,000.... Between 1829 and 1867 Chicago has increased to 200,000, and San Francisco since 1847 has become a city of 125,000 inhabitants. As to the increased trade of these centers, suffice it as one illustration for all to say, that, whereas the whole wheat trade of Chicago in 1838 was limited to 78 bushels, it had swollen in 1866 to 29,000,000....

The trade revolutions effected by the action of the new power, and the strange tricks of fortune which it has played, furnish a subject of study always instructive, generally amusing, and sometimes sad. Steam has proved itself to be not only the most obedient of slaves, but likewise the most tyrannical of masters. It pulls down as well as builds up. The very forces of nature do not stand in its way. It overcomes the wind and tide, and abolishes the Mississippi River. It is as whimsical as it is powerful. The individual it carries whithersoever he will, but whole communities it carries whither they would not. It destroyed the Southern Confederacy.... It makes the grass grow in the once busy streets of small commercial centers, like Nantucket, Salem, and Charleston. It robs New Orleans of that monopoly of wealth which the Mississippi River once promised to pour into her lap. It promises to make a solitude of the wharves of Boston, and it fills New Hampshire with deserted farms. Then it carries to New York the wealth of the whole world, and makes of her an overgrown monster. It builds up San Francisco like a very palace of Aladdin. It peoples Colorado, Montano [sic.], and Idaho as if by magic, and transfers the seat of empire to what still appears in the maps which ornament our office walls as a wilderness. This is the incomplete work of one half century; but from these beginnings it is not unsafe to draw a few general conclusions. The result of all commercial combination and concentration is necessarily individual inequality and disparity. The wealth and population of our railroad centers is as yet only in the early stages of development. These centers are not, up to this time, even united by rail. In these centers we must ultimately look to see wealth enormously increased, with a population proportioned to it, with all its corresponding depths of vice, of misery, and of poverty. The fortunes of the Astors and Stewarts are but precursors. The sharp spasms of misery and poverty are not yet felt....

...All of these...are the revolutions worked in a single half century by a force which is yet bound up in the swaddling clothes of private and monopolo-corporate interests. Its iron arms have been stretched out in every direction; nothing has escaped their reach, and the most firmly established institutions of man have proved under their touch as plastic as clay. Everything is changing, and will change with increasing rapidity. No human power can stop it. It is useless to cast back regretful glances at the old quiet days of other years and another order of things, — at the middle ages antecedent to 1807. The progressive may exult, and the conservative may repine, but the result will be all the same. We had best go on cheerfully and hopefully, for we are enlisted for the war. We must follow out the era on which we have entered to its logical and ultimate conclusions, for it is useless for men to stand in the way of steam engines. Change is usually ugly, and the whole world, both physical and moral, is now in a period of transition....

3–2. JAMES DABNEY McCABE, "DANGER AHEAD"

Source: James Dabney McCabe, *The History of the Grange Movement, or The Farmer's War Against Monopolies*, Philadelphia: National Publishing Company, 1873, pp. 236–251.

We have…examined hastily some of the evils of the present system of railroad management, and have pointed out some of the troubles likely to arise therefrom. Our purpose in doing so is not to excite unnecessary or ill-advised hostility to the railroad system of the country, but to arouse the people to a sense of the danger with which the mismanagement of this system threatens them. That there is danger, we presume no one will deny….

The power of a railroad corporation is not an imaginary thing. The corporation employs many hundred men, and disburses large sums of money; and it does these things for the avowed purpose of "earning" as much money from the people who are compelled to use the road, as they will pay. It is carrying out a system of operations opposed to the interests of the people, and it is a compact, solid body, under the direction and control of one vigorous mind, and it possesses every chance of success against the people who are generally divided and indisposed to assert their rights, though sensible that they are being injured. It is almost absolute master of the market of the region it supplies. It can benefit or injure a community by liberal tariffs or extortionate rates, as it pleases, and the managers are free to decide which policy shall be pursued. It is subject to no control. It can do as it pleases. It controls hundreds of votes along its line, not one of which will be cast against it in any contest with the public, and the lobby it maintains at the centers of government takes care that no adverse legislation shall stop its encroachments upon the rights of the people. Relying upon its wealth and power, it insolently defies the community to protect itself, and pursues its course of extortion unchecked.

Now, if this be the power of a single road, what shall we say of the vast combinations of roads which are being organized and are in operation throughout the country? Does any one for an instant imagine that these combinations, whose sole object is to enrich themselves, are careful of the rights of the public? The very essence of their system is to make charges as high as possible, and, by combining, prevent competition. They know their roads are a necessity to the public, and that persons using them must pay whatever rates they see fit to impose. They have combined for the purpose of compelling the public to submit to their extortions, and they have no intention of abandoning their design. They are masters of the situation thus far, and they know it….

Few monarchs enjoy as much substantial power as is vested in the hands of Cornelius Vanderbilt of New York who is often called the "Railroad King." A man of unbounded ambition, and with every quality for the successful organization and management of great monopolies, he has, by his genius and daring, placed himself at the head of the railroad interest of the United States…. Vanderbilt…has sought to make himself a dictator in modern civilization, moving forward to this end step by step with a sort of pitiless energy which has seemed to have in it an element of fate. As trade now dominates the world, and railways dominate trade, his object has been to make himself the virtual master of all by making himself absolute lord of the railways….

Not long since, the Presidency of the Lake Shore & Michigan Southern Railroad became vacant by reason of the death of the president, Horace P. Clark. Mr. Clark was the son-in-law and a valuable ally of Commodore Vanderbilt, and at his death the directors transferred the presidency to Vanderbilt…. The election of Commodore Vanderbilt to the presidency of the Lake Shore & Michigan Southern Railway marks another step in the gradual consolidation of our great railroad and financial enterprises. Starting from Chicago…the Lake Shore Railway, running through a country which has been settled for two generations of men, drains the rich peninsula between the lakes, and connects the populous towns of the south shore of Lake Erie with the railway system of the east. At Buffalo it connects with the extensive system of railroads which Mr. Vanderbilt has consolidated within the past few years under the title of the New York Central & Hudson River Railway, and which drain the best counties of New York from Lake Erie to Westchester. Adding to the Central & Hudson the Harlem, which is now operated under a perpetual lease, Mr. Vanderbilt thus controls 2150 miles of railway, constituting the main line between the west and the seaboard, and the chief outlet of such cities as Chicago, Toledo, Cleveland, Buffalo, Rochester, Syracuse, Utica, Lockport, Schenectady, Troy, Albany, Hudson, Poughkeepsie, and the other river-side towns. The property which he thus administers is represented on the Stock Exchange by securities equal to $215,000,000, and its gross income last year was not less than forty-five millions of dollars—more than the whole income of the United States Government a few years ago.

It is impossible to contemplate this vast aggregation of money power and commercial control in the hands of one man without feeling concern for the result.... Yet, not content with the mastery of 2150 miles of railway, involving in a large degree the control of the internal trade of the states of Illinois, Indiana, Ohio, and New York, it is well understood that, in October next, at the annual election of the Western Union Telegraph Company, the Commodore will enter into possession of that great property likewise, with its sixty or seventy thousand miles of wires, its forty millions of capital, and its eight or nine millions of revenue. When this occurs, not only will the commerce of the four chief states of the North be subject to Mr. Vanderbilt—under such feeble restrictions as our Legislatures may impose—but the whole telegraphic correspondence of the country will obey his law. He may prescribe, not only what shall be the price of a barrel of flour in New York, but also when, how, and at what cost citizens may communicate with each other by telegraph.

Of course he will be subject to legislative control. What that will amount to we all know.... It was said that the late James Fisk, Jr., who controlled a paltry 450 miles of [the] Erie [Railroad], running through a half-settled country, could, on an emergency, bring 25,000 votes into the field. At how many votes, then, must we reckon the master of 2150 miles of railway through a thickly settled country, and 70,000 miles of telegraph?

...If...the concentration of these great enterprises in one grasp were likely to be attended with a reduction of the cost of travel and the burdens of trade, or if it insured improved facilities to keep pace with, the development of the country, these would be redeeming features in the Vanderbilt regime. But great as Mr. Vanderbilt undoubtedly is as a railway manager, his greatness shows itself not in increased facilities for travel and trade, but wholly and altogether in economy of administration. He makes money by saving it. Economy is his watchword, his motto.... Now economy in railway administration is admirable from the stockholders' point of view. It is not so good for the traveler.... If it means...filthy cars, wretched stations, general discomfort, and decreased instead of increased accommodation, the prospect of its indefinite extension is not likely to overwhelm the public with delight. It would, of course, be childish to expect Commodore Vanderbilt or any one else to run railroads from philanthropic motives or as charitable institutions. He runs them to make money, and for no other purpose. This being the case, and such being his policy, it is not surprising, considering how extensively railways control commerce, govern prices, and influence our closest interests, that people should feel nervous at the news of this Great Economist capturing another thousand miles of railway, and stretching out his long hand to grasp all the telegraph wires in the country. It is probably unfair to grudge the Central stockholders their dividends. But people who are not so fortunate as to belong to that happy class cannot be blamed for remembering that the Central & Hudson property, which is now made to pay dividends on $115,000,000, was represented in 1862 by only $50,000,000 of stock and bonds, and really cost about $35,000,000, the difference between this sum and $115,000,000 being mostly what is called, in the jargon of the street, "water;" and that if there had been no water mixed with the good old Central wine, the road could have carried passengers at one cent a mile in clean, well-ventilated cars, and have paid the same dividends that it does now....

Now Commodore Vanderbilt is by no means a bad man personally, but he is the representative of one of the most perfect despotisms in existence, and he is human enough to regard the interests of his roads before those of the public. It is not safe to lodge such power as he holds in the hands of any individual, and it is for the people to decide how long such a state of affairs shall continue. His power is exerted against them. His despotism, in common with that of the other monopolies, threatens them in every relation of their national life. He exacts tribute from them in every act of his official existence, and his great wealth is made up of the aggregation of the sums he has wrung from them as a successful leader of a grinding monopoly.

Nor is he the only "dangerous character" before the public. Each of the great railroad monopolies has its representative, who does on a small scale that which Vanderbilt accomplishes in his regal style, and each is dangerous to the community, as being engaged in a struggle against its best interests and most cherished rights and privileges.

Such vast power as these men possess would be a source of danger in the most disinterested hands. It is doubly so in the hands of men who are engaged in such a warfare against the public as the railroads are now carrying on. The people owe it to themselves to curtail their powers, and to render them harmless by subjecting them to a series of regulations which shall compel them to respect the rights of the community to whom they are indebted for the very existence of their roads.

The people have the right to do this, and it should be done promptly. There is no necessity for placing burdens upon the roads heavier than they can bear. They have a right to a fair return for their investments, but they have no right to plunder the public. A series of wise and liberal regulations will protect the people against railroad tyranny and extortion, and at the same time enable the roads to do a profitable business.

ESSAYS

Economic historians have long debated the impact of railroads on the 19th Century American economy. The school of thought which claims that railroads were indispensable to economic growth is represented by the classic article, "Railroads as an Economic Force in American Development" by the late Leland H. Jenks. Jenks, a Professor of Economics and Sociology at Wellesley College, maintained that the railroad as an idea, as a construction enterprise, and as a provider of transportation was an innovative force responsible for the economic changes that transformed the 19th Century American economy. Jenks' belief in the indispensability of railroads was challenged by Robert W. Fogel, the Charles R. Walgreen Distinguished Service Professor of American Institutions at the University of Chicago Graduate School of Business and a 1993 Nobel Laureate in Economics, in a ground breaking article. Professor Fogel employed a quantitative analysis to determine if railroads were essential to the development of the interregional trade in agricultural products which most economic historians see as the key factor in the transformation of the 19th Century economy. He concluded that railroads accounted for a social saving in the interregional trade of approximately 1 percent of national income, suggesting that earlier economic historians had overestimated the indispensability of railroads to the growth of the 19th Century economy.

3–1. LELAND H. JENKS, "RAILROADS AS AN ECONOMIC FORCE IN AMERICAN DEVELOPMENT"

Any attempt to discuss the way in which railroads have promoted the rise of the American economy must assume some theory of economic evolution. The following analysis is based upon [Joseph] Schumpeter's theory of innovations. Briefly this theory holds that economic evolution in capitalistic society is started by innovation in some production function, that is, by new combinations of the factors in the economic process. These innovations may center in new commodities or new services, new types of machinery, new forms of organization, new firms, new resources, or new areas. As Schumpeter makes clear, this is not a general theory of economic, much less of social, change. Innovation is an internal factor operating within a given economic system while the system is also affected by external factors (many of them sociological) and by growth (which means, substantially, change in population and in the sum total of savings made by individuals and firms). These sets of factors interact in economic change. "The changes in the economic process brought about by innovation, together with all their effects, and the response to them by the economic system" constitute economic evolution for Schumpeter.

Railroad development has had three phases or moments which have involved innovation in distinctive ways. I shall consider (1) the railroad as an idea, (2) the railroad as a construction enterprise, and (3) the railroad as a producer of transportation services.

By the railroad as an idea is not meant the original design of steam locomotion on rails. It pertains to the inception in particular areas of particular projects, conceived as likely to be appropriate opportunities for business enterprise. In this sense the idea of any major innovation, such as the railroad, is a potent economic force. For once railway projects have been conceived and plans for their execution elaborated, it becomes easier for other innovating ideas to be entertained. On the one hand, the socio-psychological deterrents against entering upon new ways are lowered. On the other, the characteristics of the prospective future are altered; they assume an aspect more favorable to men and firms with new plans than to men and firms whose position is established. Thus early railway projects were attended by a retinue of satellite innovations.

The first railway projects emerged in the United States in the [1830s] in a situation in which the psychological risks had already been appreciably lowered by the general passion for internal improvements displayed in a plethora of projects for canals, turnpikes, plank roads, bridges, banks, and other enterprises. The earliest railways paralleled, supplemented, or improved transport systems that were already in being. The real railway revolution dates from the [1840s], prior to the California gold discoveries, in projects to cross the Appalachians, to link the seaboard with the interior, the Ohio Valley with the Great Lakes, and, breaking away from the contours of water transport, to unite distant points by more direct routes. It was the determination to build railroads in advance of traffic that gave the "railroad idea" prolonged force in American economic life. The conviction that the railroad would run anywhere at a profit put fresh spurs to American ingenuity and opened closed paddocks of potential enterprise.

Innovations are the work of enterprisers. For the railroad as idea, the role of entrepreneurship was pretty much identical with promotion; and the promoter was rarely limited in outlook to the railroad itself. In action, he was omnicompetent and omnipresent. His imagination leaped readily from the concrete problem of securing authority for a right of way to visions of a countryside filled with nodding grain, settlements of industrious families, and other evidences of progress and civilization. Each railway project involved the sanguine judgment of enterprising individuals and groups in particular, local situations that a certain line would be of direct or indirect pecuniary advantage to themselves. It was linked to specific plans for town promotion and real estate speculation, to combinations for contracting services and supplies or for exploitation of resources, in anticipation of the actual movement of traffic by rail. But as projects multiplied they collectively acquired a symbolic function, dramatizing broader purposes. The railway projector became an exemplification of the power of steam, of the advantages of the corporate form of business organization, of the ability of man to master his environment. The early railway promoter was not only a potential economic agent; he embodied the dream of developing communities, regions, the continent.

Thus, as the barriers to new projects were periodically lowered by the inception of new railway systems, the first moment of the railroad as an economic force was manifested in a wavelike profusion of new enterprises of many sorts. Moreover, its effects in the United States were not exhausted in a decade or so, as they were in England. The railroad idea was periodically renewed for region after region and route after route, as national development, at least facilitated by the earlier railroads, widened the horizons of enterprise.

The second moment of the railroad as an economic force came with the actual construction of new lines.... [R]ailway building proceeded in an undulating pattern, paralleling closely the general contours of major business cycles until the First World War. From 1850 to the [1890s], omitting the years of the Civil War, the rise and fall in new construction in fact led by a perceptible interval most other indices of business conditions. ...[T]here was [also] a long-run trend in new railway construction, which was predominantly upward in absolute figures from the late 1840s to about 1890. ...[F]or the whole period, expansion of railway plant averaged about 10 per cent a year. The trend since 1890 has been irregularly downward....

But how did railway construction as such act as an economic force? How could it be a pace setter? The answer is broadly that it operated directly to create a demand for various factors of production. In response to this demand there were rises in prices or increases in supply or both. Increase of supply could come only from some sort of further innovations, such as the drawing of fresh increments of land, labor, or capital into economic uses or the transfer of such factors to more effective combinations. This process meant the periodic dislocation of the economic structure as well as the disruption of the activities of individuals and communities. At the same time it enhanced the opportunities for enterprisers having a high degree of flexibility, pioneering individuals and groups, the agents of innumerable innovating firms and procedures.

The land for railroad construction was largely new land, previously not of economic use. It cost virtually nothing to the railway companies, and not very much to anyone else. Socially the land devoted to railroad purposes more than paid for itself by the increment in productivity of adjacent land. This was so obvious to everyone connected with railway building that periodic land booms came to communities even before the rails were laid. The speculative activity thus diffused in anticipation of railroad construction may have brought many creative innovations in its wake. But, by distracting labor and enterprise from productive to parasitic activities, it frequently delayed the realization of the plausible hopes upon which railroad projects were primarily based.

The demand for labor initiated a chapter in the history of immigration and colonization. It also disciplined migratory and local labor power to co-operative industrial effort. But it had wider repercussions. Laborers were paid wages and the wages were spent for goods. They went to market to buy the produce of American farms and mills. Thus the demand for labor stimulated the spread of market economy and the more extensive production of goods and services for distant markets, and thereby contributed to the spread of economic specialization.

The demand for capital functioned in parallel to the demand for labor. I am speaking of real capital, of goods, of the picks and shovels, sleepers and steel rails, engines and rolling stock and bridgework and culverts and ordinary building material, which make up the physical plant of a railroad. The construction moment of railway history brought an initial demand for these durable goods. Hence there was a chance for the innovator in the lumbering industry, in quarries, in iron mills and carriage works. Indeed these industries were hard put to keep pace with railway construction. Until the later [1880s], every boom period found American factories unable to meet the demand for rails, and there were heavy importations from England and Wales. As late as the [1890s], over one fifth of the total output of pig iron in the United States was being rolled into railroad bars.

Much of this demand for durable goods turned eventually into a demand for labor in mine and quarry and mill, into wage payments to labor. And these wages too were spent for consumers' goods and meant widening markets, increased specialization, and, presumably, greater productivity.

Thus the initial impetus of investment in railway construction led in widening arcs to increments of economic activity over the entire American domain, far exceeding in their total volume the original inputs of investment capital. To this feature of modern capitalism, John Maynard Keynes and others have applied the term "multiplier." It is believed that for present-day England the efficiency of the multiplier may suffice to double the impact of a new investment in construction. For nineteenth-century United States, its efficiency seems to have been considerably greater than that.

I have spoken of inputs and investment. In our economy the demand for land and labor and capital has meant another demand, a demand not for an independent factor of production, but for something equally essential, a demand for money capital. In fact, without a supply of money capital there could have been no effective demand for any of the real factors, no railways, and no stimulus from them for economic development. Hence it is convenient to think of the building of railroads as an investment of money capital. To this investment there corresponded in the long run the accumulation of savings. That saving came first and investment in the railroads afterwards is a proposition for which there is little historical evidence, at least in the United States. It is true that the practice of thrift as an individual and family responsibility was built into our social system by the Puritans. But the savings thus made in the middle of the nineteenth century went largely into land, into improvements on the farm, into the mill, the private business, and, in relatively small amounts, into public securities. Few railroads were originally financed by direct subscription of the shareholders at par in ready cash.

In final analysis, the funds for railway construction came from the extension of credit by American banks and from foreign exchange supplied by European investors. This was accomplished by many devices which called into play the charitable cupidity of contractors and iron manufacturers on both sides of the Atlantic, and the lively anticipations of property owners in the area which the railroad was to develop. Some of the shares were sold at a heavy discount to local residents, but more were given outright for land, for legal and legislative services, for banking accommodation, or as a bonus to promote the sale of bonds. Frequently there was a construction company…which took all the securities in payment for the road and operated it pending the completion of construction. Since the books of these organizations have been conveniently mislaid, it will always be impossible to ascertain what our railroads really cost originally in money capital. The construction companies turned over whole blocks of securities to manufacturers and contractors in payment for goods and services. These enterprisers usually seem to have pledged the securities with banks for working capital in the process of supplying the goods. In New York and elsewhere, speculators and specialists in railway finance, operating also on bank loans, facilitated this inflationary process by their dealings in stocks and bonds and daily risked the credit of the railway companies in their furious contests of bulls and bears.

The American banking mechanism did not have to bear this periodic strain alone. Every burst of new railway construction, in the [1830s], in the [1850s], at the close of the Civil

War, through the [1880s], and again from 1904 to 1907, meant new investments from abroad by British, Dutch, and German capitalists. Schumpeter states that the boom from 1866 to 1873, which doubled our railway mileage, was entirely financed by an estimated two billion dollars of capital imported during those years. It is incorrect to suppose... that any such amount of foreign money was at that time invested directly in the railways. British, Dutch, and German investors were then buying nearly half of the Civil War debt... to the amount of more than a billion dollars par. The railroads obtained directly only about half a billion. The purchase of government bonds by foreigners, however, released savings and bank resources for railway, industrial, and commercial promotion in the United States. In no subsequent period was the impact of foreign capital as momentous; but it is easy to exaggerate its importance. Although something like one fifth of the nominal value of American railroads was foreign-owned in 1873, the whole volume of foreign claims amounted to only 6 or 7 per cent of national wealth. While in the course of subsequent fluctuations foreign ownership of railroad securities may have reached the proportions of one third in 1890 and nearly as much just before 1914, yet at these later dates it constituted a smaller proportion of the total national wealth than it had in 1873. According to the estimates, foreign investments did not keep pace with the growth of the national wealth....

Whatever the source or timing of the application of money capital, the financing of railroad construction encouraged innovations in financial enterprise: the development of stock exchanges and their techniques; the specialization of firms, old and new, in investment banking and in security brokerage; the specialization of banking institutions (especially trust companies) as trustees and registration agents for securities, and as agents for distributing capital and interest payments; the rise of legal firms specializing in corporation law and in adjusting construction activities to the intricacies of the American political system....

With financial innovation came a transformation of the role of the enterpriser in connection with particular railway systems. In the initial moments of construction, the typical enterpriser was still pretty much the omnicompetent pioneer, the individual of imagination, daring, and energy. Like General W. J. Palmer of the Denver and Rio Grande, he considered himself an agent of civilization, an embodiment of collective purpose. No aspect of the task of railway building was too technical for his consideration and none too petty. In looking for the enterpriser of particular lines, official titles should not deceive. There was usually one man or a small informal group of unspecialized associates who could get things done, who could deal effectively at the same time with laborers, suppliers, politicians, and the local citizenry, and could command the confidence of sources of credit. At the construction moment, administration of a large formal organization was not necessarily involved. The mechanism of subcontracting provided a pattern for the cooperation of innumerable lesser enterprisers of a similar type.

Such enterprisers were rarely able, however, to cope with recurrent financial involvements. The elaboration of the superstructure of railroad securities sooner or later compelled a more formal division of tasks and responsibilities in the continuance of construction. In some cases this involved a shift of the center of decision from the engineer-promoter to financial and legal experts either within or outside the railroad organization. The financier-enterpriser assumed many guises, now entering upon new construction to win stock exchange battles, now basing a program of calculated expansion upon a re-ordering of company accounts, now entering belatedly, as did William Rockefeller in Northwestern, the race for competitive bigness. There was inescapably a narrowing of horizon; the financier-enterpriser could decide freely only problems stated in financial terms, and he focused his attention chiefly on relations with potential intermediaries and rivals for the supply of capital.

Thus the second moment of the railroad as an economic force came with a demand for the factors of production in new construction, accompanied by the rise of new techniques and institutions of finance, by the aggregation of capital in mobile forms, and by the gradual displacement of the omnicompetent type of enterpriser.

The third moment to be surveyed is that of the railroad as a going concern, a complex of tracks and engines and cars and managers and employees engaged in the business of carrying passengers and freight. By rendering this transportation service, the railroad in operation has doubtless added directly to the real income of the United States, and indirectly to economic expansion. There appears to be no satisfactory technique for giving a precise measure to the extent of this contribution. It seems that the railways carried irregularly increasing ton-miles of freight until 1929, while the aggregate of passenger-miles expanded until 1920. The quanta involved, said to be from 13 billions of freight in 1870 to 450 billions in 1929, are certainly enormous....

It is commonly assumed that the great contribution of railroad transportation came from the reduction of shipping costs. As compared with pre-motorized forms of highway transportation, the advantage of the railroad has always been obvious. There is no convincing evidence, however, that railways have ever carried freight at lower costs either to shippers or to society than canals or waterways. The advantages that early railways showed over canals, such as speed, flexibility of service, and special adaptability to short hauls, are analogous to those of modern highway transport over the railroad. It was far more important that the railroad brought transportation to areas that without it could have had scarcely any commercial existence at all.... [T]he very existence of most American communities and regions, of particular farms and industrial firms and aggregates, was made possible by the railroad....

That the railroad tends to attract factors of production to its right of way needs no comment; this perception lay at the heart of the American railroad innovation. ...[T]his supply of potential traffic does not distribute itself at random. It is polarized first about line terminals, and secondarily about traffic intersections. There is a further tendency. Irrespective of rate differentials, the service of the railroad is of greatest advantage to large shippers requiring a fairly regular flow of traffic. Thus railroad transportation provides a considerable addition to the external economies that firms can realize from large-scale operations. Such phenomena as the ecological structure of wholesale trade, the localization and concentration of primary processing establishments, and the vertical integration of production units in spite of their geographical separation are thus functionally related to railroad transportation service. In more concrete terms, attention may be directed to the initial localization of the textile industry in New England, the development of the factory system in some other industries at points remote from water power and dependent upon rail supply of coal, the establishment of stockyards in Chicago and other terminals, the rise of assembly plants, and generally the concentration, at terminals convenient to the source of supply, of industries processing and reducing the bulk of raw materials. In all these respects, railway transportation has worked in the same direction as, but in different areas from, water transport. It has functioned differently from the realized and probable tendencies of highway traffic....

It must be clear that to yield real income and participate in expansion are not the same as to be, a force for economic development. On the economic structure, the impact of the railway as a going concern was most decisive in the early years of the expansion of each system and in many respects came from the network as a whole rather than from any particular part. In time many other forces reinforced the polarizing tendency of the railroad. Urban centers tended to generate conditions that made for their own growth into metropolises. The returns to railways from increasing density tended to increase at slackening rates. Change in the railways gradually became more a matter of adjustment to external innovations than a primary source of disturbance to the economic structure.

As early as the [1880s], railway systems that had been daring ventures only a decade before found themselves embarking on extensions and improvements, not as acts of innovating faith, but to enable them to handle traffic that had been offered them or to keep somebody else from getting the business. In region after region development initiated by the railroad outran the plans of the projectors. The business of the railroad came increasingly to consist not in starting something but in keeping pace with what others were doing. That the railway would carry freight at known rates and with gradual change in the quality of service came to be part of the normal expectations of every business firm, a stable part of an environment which, of course, might still be disturbed by other innovations. While the real income accruing to society from railway transportation probably continued to grow until 1920, the railroad functioned decreasingly as a pace setter or as an inciting force in the expansion of which it was a part....

3–2. ROBERT WILLIAM FOGEL, "A QUANTITATIVE APPROACH TO THE STUDY OF RAILROADS IN AMERICAN ECONOMIC GROWTH"

Leland Jenks's article describing the pervasive impact of the railroad on the American economy first as an idea, then as a construction enterprise, and finally as a purveyor of cheap transportation, has become a classic of economic history. The particular contribution of the Jenks article was not the novelty of its viewpoint, but the neat way in which it summarized the conclusions both of those who lived during the "railroad revolution" and those who later analyzed it through the lens of elapsed time. Out of this summary the railroad emerges as the most important innovation of the last two-thirds of the nineteenth century. It appears as the *sine qua non* of American economic growth, the prime force behind the westward movement of agriculture, the rise of the corporation, the rapid growth of modern manufacturing industry, the regional location of industry, the pattern of urbanization, and the structure of interregional trade....

The idea of a crucial nexus between the railroad and the forward surge of the American economy following 1840 appears to be supported by an avalanche of factual evidence. There is, first of all, the impact of the railroad on the growth of cities. Atlanta was transformed from a spot in the wilderness to a thriving metropolis as a result of the construction of the Western and Atlantic. Chicago eclipsed St. Louis as the commercial emporium of the West by virtue of its superior railroad connections. And Louisville throttled the growth of Cincinnati by its ability to deny the "Porkopolis" rail connection with the South. Further, the decisive victory of the railroads over canals and rivers in the contest for the nation's freight is beyond dispute. One waterway after another was abandoned as a result of its inability to compete with the locomotive. The Pennsylvania Main Line Canal was driven out by the Pennsylvania Railroad, the Blackstone by the Providence and Worcester Railroad, and the Middlesex by the Boston and Lowell line. The Mississippi, which in the early decades of the nineteenth century was the main traffic highway of the center of the continent, had fallen into relative disuse by the end of the century. In 1851–1852 boats carried six times as much freight as railroads; in 1889 the railroads carried five times as much freight as boats.

Finally, there is the high correlation between new railroad construction and both population growth and commercial activity. Illinois, Michigan, and Ohio, for example, experienced a marked increase in population, construction, and manufacturing following the completion of rail lines within and across their borders. For the country as a whole, the undulations in indexes of total output seem to follow closely the cycles in railroad construction. Of particular note is the apparent upsurge in manufacturing output which paralleled the boom in railroad construction. Between 1839 and 1859 railroad mileage in the United States increased by 26,000 miles. The construction of such an immense transportation network required a large volume of manufactured goods, especially iron, lumber, and transportation equipment. Between 1841 and 1850, for example, when railroad mileage increased by 160 per cent, lumber production rose by 150 per cent and pig iron by 100 per cent.

The evidence is impressive. But it demonstrates only an association between the growth of the rail network and the growth of the economy. It fails to establish a causal relationship between the railroad and the regional reorganization of trade, the change in the structure of output, the rise in per capita income, or the various other strategic changes that characterized the American economy of the last century. It does not establish even *prima facie* that the railroad was a necessary condition for these developments. Such a conclusion depends not merely on the traditional evidence, but also on implicit assumptions in its interpretation.

One cannot, for example, leap from data that demonstrate the victory of railroads over waterways in the competition for freight to the conclusion that the development of the railroad network (particularly the trunk lines) was a prerequisite for the rapid, continuous growth of the internal market. The only inference that one can safely draw is that railroads were producing the same (or a similar) service at a lower cost to the buyer. For if rail transportation was a perfect, or nearly perfect, substitute for the canal, all that was required for a large shift from canal to railroad was a small price differential in favor of the latter. Whether the shift produced a significant increase in the size of the internal market depends not on the volume of goods transferred from one medium to the other, but on the magnitude of the associated reduction in transportation costs. If the reduction in cost achieved by the railroads was small, and if canals and rivers could have supplied all or most of the service that railroads were providing without increasing unit charges, then the presence of the railroads did not substantially widen the market, and their absence would not have kept it substantially narrower. The conclusion that the railroad was a necessary condition for the widening of the internal market flows not from a body of observed data, but from the assumption that the cost per unit of transportation service was significantly less by rail than by water.

Other propositions regarding the role of the railroad involve even stronger assumptions than the one just cited. The view that the quantity of manufactured goods used in the construction and maintenance of the railroad was of decisive importance in the upward surge of manufacturing industry during the two decades preceding the Civil War involves a minimum of three assumptions. It not only assumes that the volume of the goods purchased by the railroad was large relative to the total output of the supply industries, but also that railroad purchases were directed toward domestic rather than foreign markets. It assumes further that if there had been no railroad, the demand for manufactured goods by the other forms of transportation would have been significantly less or its impact strategically different from the demand associated with railroads.

The preceding argument is aimed not at refuting the view that the railroad played a decisive role in American development during the nineteenth century, but rather at demonstrating that the empirical base on which this view rests is not nearly so substantial as is usually presumed. The fact that the traditional interpretation involves a number of basic assumptions is not in itself a cause for rejecting it. In the absence of data, the economic historian has no alternative but to make the best possible guess. Without such guesses or assumptions, no analysis is possible. The only question is, "How good are the guesses?" Is there any way of testing them?

It is always easier to point out the need to test a given set of assumptions than to propose a feasible method for testing them. The remainder of this paper deals with the problems involved in evaluating one of the most common presumptions regarding the influence of the railroad on American economic development. The question to be considered is: did the interregional distribution of agricultural products—a striking feature of the American economy of the nineteenth century—depend on the existence of the long-haul railroad? To answer the question, I define a concept of "social saving" in interregional transportation attributable to the existence of the railroad, and propose a method of measuring it. The discussion that follows turns largely on the consistency between the size of this "social saving" and the hypothesis that railroads were a necessary condition for interregional agricultural trade.... The basic issue posed by this paper is the feasibility of applying the analytical techniques of contemporary economics to the re-evaluation of one of the major questions in American history—the influence of railroads on economic growth.

The massive change in the geographical pattern of agricultural output during the nineteenth century has been a leading theme of American historiography. The meager data at the start of the century strongly suggest that the main sections of the nation were agriculturally self-sufficient. By 1890 the North Atlantic, South Atlantic, and South Central divisions, containing twenty-five states and 60 per cent of the nation's population, had become a deficit area in various agricultural commodities, particularly foodstuffs. The greatest deficits appear in the North Atlantic region, that is, New England, New York, New Jersey, and Pennsylvania. In 1890 this division produced only 36 per cent of its estimated wheat consumption, 45 per cent of the corn requirement, 33 per cent of the beef requirement, and 27 per cent of the pork requirement. The South produced a bigger share of its local needs, but it too had to look outside its borders for a significant part of its food supply. The local supply of foodstuffs in the deficit regions appears even more inadequate when the product needed for the export market is added to domestic consumption. In the North Atlantic division, for example, local production of wheat supplied only 24 per cent of the combined local and export requirement.

In contrast to the decline in regional self-sufficiency in foodstuffs in the East and South, the North Central division of the country had become a great agricultural surplus area. Virgin territory at the start of the century, these twelve states were producing 71 per cent of the country's cereal grains by 1890 and were also the national center of cattle and swine production. The magnitude of their surpluses is well illustrated by wheat. In the crop year 1890–1891, the twelve states produced 440,000,000 bushels. At five bushels per capita this was enough to feed 88,000,000 people—four times the region's population. Approximately two thirds of the grain surplus of the North Central states was consumed in the East and South, and one third was exported to Europe and South America.

The process by which the agricultural surpluses of the Midwest were distributed can be divided into three stages. In the case of grain, the first stage was the concentration of the surplus in the great primary markets of the Midwest: Chicago, Minneapolis, Duluth, Milwaukee, Peoria, Kansas City, St. Louis, Cincinnati, Toledo, and Detroit. Over 80 per cent of the grain that entered into interregional trade was shipped from the farms to these cities. The second stage involved the shipment of the grain from the primary markets to some ninety secondary markets in the East and South. Among the most important secondary markets were New York City, Baltimore, Boston, Philadelphia, New Orleans, Albany (NY), Portland (ME), Pittsburgh, Birmingham, and Savannah. The third stage was the distribution of the grain within the territory immediately surrounding the secondary markets, and exportation abroad. The distributional pattern of meat products roughly paralleled that of grain. Perhaps the most important difference was that the first stage of the distribution process—concentration of livestock in the primary markets—was dominated by only four cities: Chicago, St. Louis, Kansas City, and Omaha.

With this background it is possible to give more definite meaning to the term "interregional distribution." For the purposes of this paper, "interregional distribution" is defined as the shipments of commodities from the primary markets of the Midwest to the secondary markets of the East and South. For all other shipments—from farms to primary markets and from secondary markets to the points immediately surrounding them—the term "intraregional distribution" is used. Similarly, the term "interregional railroad" is reserved for lines between primary and secondary markets, and the term '"intraregional railroad" is used for all other lines. These terms are useful in distinguishing between the railroad in its role as a long-distance mover of agricultural products and its other functions. It also helps to clarify the hypothesis to be examined in this paper, which can now be stated as follows:

Rail connections between the primary and secondary markets of the nation were a necessary condition for the system of agricultural production and distribution that characterized the American economy of the last half of the nineteenth century. Moreover, the absence of such rail connections would have forced a regional pattern of agricultural production that would have significantly restricted the development of the American economy.

In the year 1890, a certain bundle of agricultural commodities was shipped from the primary markets to the secondary markets. The shipment occurred in a certain pattern, that is, with certain tonnages moving from each primary market city to each secondary market city. This pattern of shipments was carried out by some combination of rail, wagon, and water haulage at some definite cost. With enough data, one could determine both this cost and the alternative cost of shipping exactly the same bundle of goods from the primary to the secondary markets in exactly the same pattern without the railroad. The difference between these two amounts I call the social saving attributable to the railroad in the interregional distribution of agricultural products—or simply "the social saving." This difference is in fact larger than what the true social saving would have been. Forcing the pattern of shipments in the nonrail situation to conform to the pattern that actually existed is equivalent to the imposition of a restraint on society's freedom to adjust to a new technological situation. If society had had to ship interregionally by water and wagon without the railroad, it could have shifted agricultural production from the Midwest to the East and South, and shifted some productive factors out of agriculture altogether. Further, the cities entering our set of secondary markets and the tonnages handled by each were surely influenced by conditions peculiar to rail transportation; in the absence of the railroad some different cities would have entered this set, and the relative importance of those remaining would have changed. Adjustments of this sort would have reduced the loss in national income occasioned by the absence of the railroad, but estimates of their effects lie beyond the limits of tools and data. I propose, therefore, to use the social saving, as defined, as the objective standard for testing the hypothesis stated above....

The social saving is calculated in my estimates for only one year, 1890. Yet the hypothesis to be tested refers to a period covering almost half a century. How sound an inference about the significance of the railroad's role with respect to agricultural development over such a period can be made on the basis of only one year's data? The answer depends on the relative efficiency of the railroad in 1890 as compared to earlier periods. If the railroad was relatively more efficient in 1890 than in any previous year, the social saving per unit of transportation in 1890 would have exceeded the saving per unit in all previous years. The available evidence suggests that this was indeed the case. The four decades between 1850 and 1890 were ones of continuous advance in efficiency. The size, speed, and pulling capacity of the locomotive were steadily increased, as was the weight of the load a freight car could carry. At the same time, the scattered rail lines were integrated into a network, thus eliminating or reducing transshipment costs. Terminal facilities were expanded, and such important loading devices as the grain elevator were brought into general operation. Perhaps the most significant indication of the increase in the railroad's relative efficiency is the very considerable shift of heavy, low-value items away from water carriers. In 1852 boats and barges dominated the interregional transportation of these items, while in 1890 they were carried mainly by the railroad. Since the volume of agricultural commodities transported between regions had also increased over the period in question, it seems apparent that the social saving in 1890 exceeded in absolute amount the saving of previous years. While it is true that national income rose over the period, the amount of agricultural goods shipped interregionally appears to have risen just as rapidly. In the case of wheat, population and production figures suggest that local requirements in the deficit states were at least 1.1 million tons less in 1870 than they were in 1890. Export requirements were 1.8 million tons less. These figures indicate that the quantity shipped interregionally increased by 145 per cent over two decades—showing approximately the same rate of growth as real national income. Thus, if it is shown that the social saving of 1890 was quite small relative to national income, the relationship would hold with equal force for the half-century preceding 1890.

The problem posed here would be trivial if the wagon were the only alternative to the railroad in interregional transportation. By 1890 the average cost of railroad transportation was less than a cent per ton-mile. On the other hand, the cost of wagon transportation was in the neighborhood of twenty-five cents per ton-mile. According to estimates made here, approximately 7.7 million tons of corn and 5.0 million tons of wheat entered into interregional transportation. Taking the differential between rail and wagon transportation at twenty-five cents per ton-mile, the social saving involved in moving these 12.7 million tons one mile would have been $3,180,000. Assuming that on the average the corn and wheat shipped interregionally traveled nine hundred miles, the total social saving would have been $2,860,000,000. Even this figure is low, since wagon rates did not reflect the cost involved in road construction and maintenance. If account were taken of these and other omitted charges, and if a similar calculation were performed for livestock, the figure for the social saving would probably increase by 50 per cent, to four billion dollars, or more than one third of gross national product in 1890.... Such a loss would have pushed the economy back two decades and probably cut the rate of investment by a third. The calculation is very crude, of course, but there seems little doubt that the order of magnitude is correct.

The problem is not trivial, because water transportation was a practical alternative to the railroad in interregional transportation. A glance at a map will show that all of the primary market cities were on navigable waterways. Duluth, Milwaukee, Chicago, Toledo, and Detroit were on the Great Lakes; Omaha and Kansas City were on the Missouri; Minneapolis and St. Louis were on the Mississippi; Cincinnati was on the Ohio; and Peoria was on the Illinois River, midway between the Mississippi and Lake Michigan. The lakes, inland rivers, canals, and coastal waters directly linked the primary market cities to most of the secondary market cities. Of the forty-three most important secondary markets, thirty-two were located on navigable waters still in use in 1890. Seven were on waterways that had been forced into inactivity as a result of railroad competition, but which could have been used in the absence of the railroad. Only four cities were without direct water connection to the Midwest, and each of these was within a relatively short wagonhaul of a major water artery.

The importance of a water-route alternative lies in the fact that on a per ton-mile basis, water rates were not only less than wagon rates but also less than railroad rates. The all-rail rate on wheat from Chicago to New York, for example, was about 0.52 cents per ton-mile, or nearly four times as much as the ton-mile rate by water. This fact does not, of course, imply that the social cost or even the private cost on a given tonnage was less when shipped by water. Water routes were much more circuitous than rail routes, and the time in transit was considerably greater. Loss of cargo was more frequent. Terminal charges were higher. These and other problems raised the cost of water transportation to a point where shipments between most primary and most secondary markets were cheaper by rail than by boat....

Until now, the discussion has been carried on as if all the agricultural commodities that entered into interregional trade were to be included in the estimate. In fact, the estimate will be based on only four commodities: wheat, corn, beef, and pork. These four accounted for 42 per cent of income originating in agriculture in 1889. Neglect of the other products is not so serious as it first seems. What is important is not the share of wheat, corn, beef, and pork in total output, but their share in that part of output which entered interregional trade. Obviously, if none of the neglected 58 per cent of output moved interregionally, the restriction is of no real consequence. The most important of the omitted items is cotton, which represented 11 per cent of output. But relatively little cotton entered interregional transportation as here defined, and a large part of the crop shipped interregionally was carried by water. This is illustrated by the distribution of the 1898–1899 crop. Of the output of that season, 79 per cent was shipped from southern farms to southern seaport cities, and carried from there by boat to Europe or to northern ports in the United States. Another 13 per cent was consumed in the South. Hence, at most only 8 per cent or 225,000 tons of cotton (that is, 900,000 bales) could have entered into interregional rail transportation. But 235,000 tons is only 1.8 per cent of the combined wheat-corn tonnage. The case of dairy products, which accounted for 12 per cent of total product, is similar. There are three main dairy products: milk, butter, and cheese. Of these, milk was entirely an intraregional product. Census data on butter and cheese production in the Midwest indicate that the amount entering interregional trade was about 166,000 tons or 1.3 per cent of the wheat-corn tonnage. Again, while virtually all wool was transported from west to east, it was less than 1 per cent (closer to one half of 1 per cent) of the wheat-corn tonnage. In short, neglected items probably do not account for more than 10 per cent of the goods entering into interregional trade, and would not justify the effort required to include them.

The most direct method of determining the social saving is to find the 1890 pattern of the shipments of the four commodities, and then estimate both the actual cost of the pattern and the cost that would have obtained if the pattern had been executed with only boats and wagons. This method requires the following data: the amount of each commodity shipped from each primary market, the amounts received by each secondary market, the routes over which they were shipped, and the transportation costs by each medium. But not all of these data are available. The total volume of shipments from each of the primary markets can be determined, but not their destination and routes. Receipts of the secondary markets can be estimated, but not the markets from which these goods came. The impasse is, of course, only apparent. The gap in the statistics can be bridged by linear programming techniques which yield the solution at a cheaper cost in terms of data requirements....

The actual method of analysis is simple. It involves a pair of linear programming models for each commodity. The procedure can be illustrated by considering the case of wheat. In 1890, a certain amount of wheat was shipped from the Midwest to the secondary markets. The first linear programming model will find the least cost of carrying the wheat from the primary to the secondary markets without imposing any restraint on the means of transportation that can be used—that is, allowing the shipments to be made in the cheapest manner, regardless of the transportation medium. The second model imposes the restriction that railroads cannot be used, and then finds the least cost of shipping the same quantity of wheat from the primary to the secondary markets. Presumably these two least-cost figures will differ; but this difference will reflect only the absence of the railroad, since the quantities shipped from each of the primary markets and the requirements of each of the secondary markets will be the same in both models. The difference between the two least-cost figures is the estimate of social saving due to the use of the railroad in the interregional transportation of wheat....

The water rates to be used in the second model must (with some exceptions) be those that actually prevailed in 1890. Even if water rates in 1890 equaled marginal costs, their use in the second model would introduce a bias, since these rates applied to a tonnage which is less than the amount specified in the model. To use them is equivalent to assuming that the marginal cost of water transportation was constant over the relevant range. This assumption probably accentuates the upward bias of the estimate. If all costs except the construction of canals and channels are considered variable, then it seems quite reasonable to assume that marginal costs were constant or declining. The basic operating unit in water transportation was the boat, and boat building may have been subject to economics of scale. In any case, most water routes were greatly under-utilized in 1890 and would have been under-utilized even if they had carried some considerable share of the additional interregional tonnage. Maintenance and other operating costs (for example, dredging, repairing locks, supplying water) would have increased only slightly with additional tonnage. To the extent that these tendencies were operative, the 1890 water rates impart an upward bias to the estimate of social saving. Finally, it is important to note that the published 1890 rates did not reflect all of the costs involved in water transportation. In order to avoid introducing a downward bias into the calculations, it will be necessary to take account of such factors as spoilage, transit time and the unavailability of water routes for five months out of the year....

Figures on the shipments of each of the various commodities were taken from the reports of the produce exchanges, the boards of trade or chambers of commerce of each of the primary market cities. These documents contain much highly reliable information, but except in the cases of Chicago, St. Louis, and New York, they have been badly neglected. Table 3.1 gives the preliminary figures on the shipments of corn and wheat from the primary markets....

The estimation of requirements of the secondary markets is much more difficult than the shipments from the primary markets. The problem here is not merely the absence of a convenient series on the requirements of the various secondary markets; with the exception of such obvious places as New York, Baltimore, and New Orleans, there was no way of knowing which of the various cities of the East and South comprised the relevant set of secondary markets.

The first task, then, was to find some basis for dividing the deficit regions into marketing areas and for determining the cities which served as distributing centers of the area. The basic reference for making this division was a study of wholesale grocery territories carried out by the Department of Commerce in the 1920's. This study divided the country into 183 trading areas. Each of the areas was composed of a group of counties served by a single city. The Boston trading area, for example, was determined by a survey of the wholesale firms situated in Boston, and comprised the six counties immediately surrounding the city.

Since grain and provisions were wholesale grocery products, the Department of Commerce survey provided an appropriate framework for the estimates. That the territories it defined pertained to the economy of the 1920's is not a crucial consideration. The basic rail network, especially in the East, was well established by 1890 and remained stable over the ensuing three decades. In the 1920's, trucks had not yet altered existing geographical patterns of trade. They appear to have affected the size of the inventories carried by outlying retailers rather than the boundaries of the marketing areas. The impression that motor vehicles conformed to, rather than altered, pre-existing patterns is buttressed by a study of wholesale territories made in the late 1930's. The trading areas described by this survey were virtually identical with the earlier set.

This demarcation of trading territories made it possible to devise a procedure for estimating the requirements of each territory by commodity. The area requirement for a given commodity was the difference between the area's total demand for the commodity (including exports) and the amount of the commodity supplied from within the area. Thus, to determine the requirements, estimates of both total demand and local supply were needed. The procedure for arriving at these estimates can be illustrated by the case of wheat.

The total demand for wheat in a given area consisted of two parts: the local demand and the export demand. The export demand was determined directly from export statistics provided by the Treasury Department; the local demand had to be estimated indirectly. The local demand for wheat was almost entirely for human consumption. For the country as a whole, about 10 per cent of the annual wheat crop was set aside for seed and about 2 per cent for animal feed. However, the share of wheat demanded for seed in the deficit regions was considerably less than the national share, since wheat production was quite small. This was especially true in New England, where wheat used as seed was only one half of 1 per cent of the quantity consumed by humans. Similarly, the practice of feeding wheat to animals appears to have been practiced primarily in the areas of surplus production. Hence, the estimate of local demand was largely a matter of determining human consumption.

Total human consumption in a trading area was equal to per capita consumption multiplied by the population of the area. Statistics on area population were obtained from the 1890 census. The tentative estimate of average consumption by regions was calculated from a 1909 survey of urban workers conducted by the British Board of Trade. Based on these data, the estimated per capita consumption of wheat is 4.80 bushels per year in the North and 4.70 bushels per year in the South....

The local supply of wheat in a trading area was the sum of the annual local production of wheat and the supply (positive or negative) out of local inventories. The Department of Agriculture has published estimates of the production of wheat in 1890 by states but not by counties. However, county data were needed to determine local production in a trading area. The 1889 census production data by counties were multiplied by the 1890:1889 ratio of output for the state in which the particular county was located. Inventories of wheat were held by two main groups: wholesalers in the central cities of the trading areas, and

Table 3.1 Shipments of Corn and Wheat from Primary Markets, 1890 (thousands of tons)

Primary Market	Wheat	Corn
Chicago	950	2,536
Minneapolis	1,322	53
Duluth-Superior	793	41
Milwaukee	516	7
Peoria	35	211
Kansas City	181	505
St. Louis	522	1,218
Cincinnati	181	70
Toledo	309	463
Detroit	125	32
Total	**4,934**	**5,136**

farmers. It was not possible to obtain data on changes in the inventories of wholesalers. However, reports on the inventories in the hands of farmers on March 1, 1890 and March 1, 1891 were published by the Department of Agriculture. It was therefore possible to estimate the change in farmers' inventories which, as a factor in supply, was probably more significant than the change in wholesalers' inventories.

The estimate of total wheat requirements of all the secondary markets in the deficit regions is given in Table 3.2. It is broken down into a local consumption deficit (obtained by subtracting local production and changes in farm inventories from my estimate of the local demand in each area) and foreign exports. The latter figure is based on the *Commerce and Navigation Reports* of the Treasury Department....

Standard sources such as the *Annual Reports* of the Interstate Commerce Commission, the Treasury Department *Reports on Internal Commerce,* and the report of the Aldrich Committee provide information on less than 10 per cent of the relevant interregional routes. Fortunately, the tariffs filed with the Interstate Commerce Commission under the Interstate Commerce Act of 1887 are available. These files contain the published [shipping] rates on all of the desired routes.

To the extent that rebating took place, published [shipping] rates exceeded actual rates. State and Federal investigations produced voluminous reports and documents on the rebating problem. These contain data that can be used to adjust some of the published rates.... However, some procedure will have to be devised by which one can both check the reliability of the evidence in the public record and estimate rebates for which no direct evidence exists. One possible approach involves the use of published rates for a year like 1910, when rebating was rather generally eliminated. Abstracting from changes in the price level, the fall in average published rates between 1890 and 1910 is attributable to two factors: the elimination of rebating and the decline in actual rates. Therefore, the differences between average published rates in 1890 and in 1910 (adjusted for changes in the price level) are the most that the average rebate could have been. Thus, by multiplying appropriate ratios of average 1910 rates to 1890 rates by the actual 1890 rates, one obtains an estimate of the least that average actual rates could have been in 1890.

Water transportation was dominated by three main routes: the Great Lakes and Erie Canal route, the Mississippi route and the intracoastal route. Every movement from a primary to a secondary market can be divided into a movement along one or more of these lines, plus an additional short movement along some other body of water. Rates on the main water highways are available in board of trade reports, tariffs filed with the Interstate Commerce Commission, and other documents. Thus only a small part of the charge to a shipper will have to be estimated. Moreover, possible deviations between published and actual water rates are less troublesome. To the extent that such deviations existed, the upward bias of the estimated social saving will be further accentuated.

Table 3.2 Estimated Requirements of Secondary Markets (thousands of tons)

	1	2	3
	Local Consumption Deficits	Exports	Total Requirements (Col.1 plus Col.2)
Wheat	3,099	1,916	5,015
Corn	5,415	2,320	7,735
Dressed Pork	729	347	1,076
Dressed Beef	701	304	1,005

There is no reliable way to predict the outcome of the linear programming problems. In computations of this sort, surprises are common. Even if all the required data were compiled, it would be difficult to anticipate such results as the efficient patterns of trade in the rail and nonrail situations or the breakdown of the social saving by products, routes, and regions. However, a crude estimate of the *aggregate* social saving is possible. The calculation that follows involves guesses about average transit distances and average freight rates by both water and rail—averages that cannot reliably be calculated until the linear programming problems are solved. Despite its crudity, the calculation is useful for two reasons. First, it provides a convenient format for demonstrating the ways in which a number of costs—costs that have been considered unquantifiable—can be quantified. Second, it provides a rough idea of the magnitude of the aggregate social saving that one can expect to obtain from the models.

The starting point of the calculation is the difference between the average ton-mile transportation rate by water and by rail. Various experts on transportation have pointed out that water rates were generally less than railroad rates. Thus, over the route from Chicago to New York, the average all-rail rate on wheat in 1890 was 0.523 cents per ton-mile while the average all-water rate was 0.139 cents per ton-mile. Casual examination of the available data suggests that these figures are approximately the same as those applying to all grains on this and other routes. Hence, for the purposes of calculation it will be arbitrarily assumed that the New York to Chicago all-water rate per ton-mile on wheat equaled the average all-water rate (per ton-mile) on all grains over all the relevant routes. The assumption to be made on the all-rail rate is symmetric.

For the crude calculation of the social saving, the average national rate at which grain was actually transported in 1890 is needed. This actual rate must have been less than the all-rail rate. Not all grains shipped interregionally were carried exclusively by rail. Considerable quantities were shipped by a combination of rail and water or completely by water. In contrast to the 0.523 cents all-rail rate per ton-mile on wheat transported from Chicago to New York, the lake-and-rail charge was 0.229 cents, and the lake-and-canal charge was 0.186 cents. The average of these three rates, weighted by the quantities of grain shipped under each one, is 0.434 cents (see Table 3.3). This last figure will be taken as the "actual" national average rate on grains per ton-mile in 1890. In passing, it may be noted that the adjustment produced a figure which is less than a mill below the all-rail rate.

In the case of meat and livestock products, the calculation is based on the St. Louis to New Orleans rates on pork. The all-rail rate was 1.07 cents per ton-mile and the all-water rate was 0.45 cents. Again, these rates are comparable to those that prevailed on other meat products shipped on this and other routes. Furthermore, since the quantity of meat shipped by water was a small part of the total interregional tonnage, no further adjustment need be made; that is, the all-rail rate on pork will be assumed to equal the actual average rate on all meat products.

The quantity of corn, wheat, pork, and beef shipped interregionally in 1890 was approximately equal to the net local deficit of the trading areas plus net exports. Assuming that half of the meat products was shipped as livestock and half as dressed meat, the amount transported interregionally was 15,700,000 tons.

Estimates of average distances are based on a sample of thirty routes (pairs of cities). The sample was randomly drawn from a population of 875 routes. The average rail distance in the sample was 926 miles, and the average water distance was 1,574 miles. Since only small amounts of meat were transported by water, 926 miles will be assumed to be the average distance over which meats were actually shipped in 1890. In the case of grains, an adjustment should be made for the tonnage that was carried partly or wholly by water. The adjusted figure, 1,044 miles, represents the estimate of the average distance over which grains were actually shipped in 1890.

Table 3.3 Estimate of the Average Actual Rate

Type of Transportation	1	2	3
	Rate per ton-mile (cents)	Wheat and Corn (millions of tons)	Col. 1 × Col. 2 (cents)
1. All-water	0.186	1.254	0.2332
2. Water and rail	0.229	2.423	0.5549
3. All-rail	0.523	9.073	4.7451
4. Sum of columns		12.750	5.5333
5. Average actual rate in cents per ton-mile (sum of Col. 3/sum of Col.2)			0.4340

If rates and ton-miles were the only elements entering into the cost of transportation, it would have been cheaper to have shipped inter-regionally by water than by rail. [But] …the social saving calculated on the basis of these elements is negative by about $38,000, 000. This odd result is not difficult to explain. While the estimated actual cost of transportation includes virtually all relevant items, the estimated cost of water transportation does not. In calculating the cost of shipping without the railroad, one must account for six neglected items of cost not reflected in the first approximation: cargo losses in transit, transshipment costs, wagon haulage from water points to secondary markets not on water routes, the cost resulting from the time lost when using a slow medium of transportation, the cost of being unable to use water routes for five months out of the year, and finally, capital costs not reflected in water rates.

When account is taken of the six neglected costs, the loss attributable to the railroad will be transformed into a saving. How big must the neglected costs be to produce a positive saving of 1 per cent of national income? In 1890 gross national product was about 12,000,000, 000 and 1 per cent of this amount is $120,000,000. Without the neglected costs, interregional shipment of the four commodities would have been $38,000,000 cheaper by water than by rail. Consequently, in order to reach a social saving of 1 per cent of gross national product, the neglected costs will have to be approximately $158,000,000.

The literature on the interregional transportation of agricultural products indicates that cargo losses were greater on water shipments than on rail shipments. Insurance rates can be used to estimate the cost of these water transit losses. Since the average value of a loss on a given shipment was approximately equal to the insurance charge on the shipment, the total value of cargo losses in the absence of the railroad would have been approximately equal to the average insurance charge on a water shipment multiplied by the total value of the goods transported interregionally. Moreover, since railroad rates included insurance, this figure would also represent the neglected cost of cargo losses. The calculation is shown in Table 3.4. The cost of insurance (cost of cargo losses) in the absence of the railroad would have been approximately $6,000,000. Subtracting this figure from $158,000,000, there is left $152,000,000 to cover the remaining costs.

Transshipping costs were incurred whenever it became necessary to switch a cargo from one type of vessel to another. Grain shipped from Chicago to New York, for example, was transferred at Buffalo from lake steamers to canal barges. In the absence of the railroad there would probably have been an average of two transshipments on each ton carried from a primary to a secondary market. At a cost of fifty cents per ton per transshipment, transshipping charges on the grain and meat products in question would have been

$16,000,000. Subtracting this amount from $152,000,000, there is left $136,000,000 to cover the remaining costs.

The two indirect costs of water transportation most frequently cited are the cost of time lost in shipping by water and the cost of being unable to use water routes for about five months out of each year. Arguments based on the time factor and the limited season of navigation have been decisive in ruling out the possibility that water transportation could have been a good substitute for the railroad. Once invoked, these arguments are invincible, since the costs involved seem to be limited only by the intuition of the disputants. Without a means of quantifying the cost of time and the cost of the limited season of navigation, the hypothesis posed in this paper cannot be tested.

The key to quantifying the cost of the time that would have been lost in water transportation is the nexus between time and inventories. If entrepreneurs could replace goods the instant they were sold, they would, *ceteris paribus,* carry zero inventories. Inventories are necessary to bridge the gap of time required to deliver a commodity from its supply source to a given point. If, on the average, interregional shipments of agricultural commodities required a month more by water than by rail, it would have been possible to compensate for the time lost through an inventory increase in the secondary markets equal to one twelfth of annual shipments. Hence the cost of the time lost in using water transportation was the 1890 cost of carrying such an additional inventory.

The problems inherent in the limited season of water transportation could also have been met by an increase in inventory. Since water routes were closed for five-twelfths of the year, I will assume that the absence of railroads would have increased the inventories of agricultural commodities held in secondary markets by five-twelfths of the annual interregional shipment....

The cost of time lost in water transportation and the limited season of navigation would thus not have exceeded the cost incurred in carrying an inventory equal to one half of the annual amount of agricultural products that were transported interregionally. As shown in Table 3.4, the Chicago wholesale value of the corn, wheat, beef, and pork shipped interregionally was about $550,000,000. Another $43,000,000 should be added to approximate wholesale value at seaboard. Hence, in the absence of the railroad, the limited season of navigation would have required an increase in the value of inventories of about $297,000,000. The cost of carrying such an additional inventory would have included the forgone opportunity of investing the same amount elsewhere. If it is assumed that on the average capital earned 6 per cent in 1890, the alternative cost of the investment in additional inventory would have been about $18,000,000 per year. To this, one must

Table 3.4 Estimated Cost of Insurance

	1 Tons shipped interregionally	2 Price per ton	3 Value (Col. 1 × Col. 2)	4 Insurance rate as a proportion of value	5 Cost of insurance (Col.3 × Col. 4)
1. Cattle	949,000	$97	$ 92,100,000	.01	$ 921,000
2. Dressed beef	503,000	138	69,400,000	.01	694,000
3. Hogs	1,008,000	79	79,600,000	.01	796,000
4. Dressed pork	538,000	110	59,100,000	.01	592,000
5. Corn	7,735,000	13	1 00,600,000	.01	1,006,000
6. Wheat	5,015,000	30	150,500,000	.01	1,505,000
7. Totals	**15,748,000**		**551,400,000**		**5,514,000**

add about $30,000,000 for storage charges. Subtracting $48,000,000 from $136,000,000 leaves $88,000,000 to account for the two remaining costs.

Cities receiving approximately 10 per cent of the interregional shipments were not on water routes. If these cities were an average of fifty miles from the nearest water point, the cost of wagon haulage (at twenty-five cents per ton-mile) would have been $20,000,000. Subtracting this amount from $88,000,000 leaves $68,000,000 to account for the last item—neglected capital charges.

Water rates failed to reflect capital costs to the extent that rivers and canals were improved or built by the government and financed out of taxes rather than tolls. If a complete statement of these uncompensated expenditures were available, one could easily estimate the neglected capital costs. Data exist on capital expenditures for water transportation, but much work remains to be done to develop a consistent and complete statement of uncompensated investment. Federal expenditures on river improvement over the years between 1802 and 1890 appear to have amounted to $111,000,000. Canals still in operation in 1890 were built at a cost of $155,000,000. In addition, there were abandoned canals which would have been in use in the absence of the interregional railroad. These were built at a cost of $27,000,000. The total of the three items, $293,000,000, may either overstate or understate the uncompensated capital involved in water transportation. Assuming that the various upward and downward biases, the omitted items and the double counting, cancel each other out, at an interest rate of 6 per cent the neglected capital costs would have been about $18,000,000—$50,000,000 short of the amount required to bring the social saving to 1 per cent of gross national product.

Thus casual examination of the available data suggests that the social saving attributable to the railroad in the interregional transportation of agricultural products was about 1 per cent of national income. The calculation is, of course, subject to considerable error; but there are grounds for having confidence in the result. Four of the estimates— those dealing with transshipment, wagon haulage, time lost, and the limited season of navigation— probably overstate the actual cost of water transportation. While the estimates of some of the other items may be too low, it does not seem likely that the errors are large enough to alter substantially the magnitude of the indicated social saving. Suppose, for example, that railroad rates on a ton-mile basis were not above water rates, as has generally been assumed. If the initial water-rail rate differential had actually been zero on all commodities, the elimination of this error would increase the estimated social saving by only $56,000,000. Indeed, if railroad rates are assumed to have been zero, the social saving would rise to only $158,000,000, or about 1.3 per cent of gross national product.

This paper has focused on one aspect of the influence of the railroad on American economic development. A small aggregate social saving in the interregional transportation of agricultural products would not prove that the railroad was unimportant in American development. Conclusions regarding the over-all impact of the railroad require ... a thorough examination of all the avenues through which the most celebrated innovation of the nineteenth century may have exercised a strategic influence on economic growth. In this connection it is important to re-emphasize that the linear programming models referred to earlier will do more than refine the crude estimate of the aggregate social saving. They will provide information on efficient patterns of agricultural distribution both in the rail and nonrail situations, as well as breakdowns of the interregional social saving by regions and commodities. This type of information, supplemented by similar data on intraregional transportation, will facilitate a re-evaluation of such questions as the developmental significance of various commercial rivalries (for example, the triumph of Chicago over St. Louis and Cincinnati), the determinants of the geographic pattern of urbanization, and the extent to which the railroad promoted a more efficient utilization of certain productive resources.

SUGGESTIONS FOR FURTHER READING

Charles E. Ames, *Pioneering the Union Pacific* (1969).

Alfred D. Chandler, *The Railroads: The Nation's First Big Business* (1965).

Paul Cootner, "The Role of Railroads in the United States Economic Growth," *Journal of Economic History*, 23(1963) 477–521.

Paul David, "Transport Innovation and Economic Growth: Professor Fogel On and Off the Rails," *Economic History Review* 2(1969) 506–525.

Albert Fishlow, *American Railroads and the Transformation of the Antebellum Economy* (1965).

Robert W. Fogel, "Notes on the Social Saving Controversy," *Journal of Economic History*, 39(1979) 1–54.

——, *Railroads and American Economic Growth* (1964).

——, *The Union Pacific Railroad* (1960).

Heywood Fleisig, "The Union Pacific Railroad," *Explorations in Economic History*, (Winter 1973).

E.H. Hunt, "Railroad Social Savings in Nineteenth Century America," *American Economic Review*, 57(1967) 909–910.

Albro Martin, *James J. Hill and the Opening of the Northwest* (1976).

Peter D. McClelland, "Railroads, American Growth, and the New Economic History: A Critique," *Journal of Economic History*, 28(1968) 102–123.

W.Z. Ripley, *Railroads: Rates and Regulations* (1912).

W.W. Rostow, *The Stages of Economic Growth: A Non-Communist Manifesto* (1960).

John Stover, *American Railroads* (1961).

CHAPTER 4

The Economics of American Slavery

INTRODUCTION

Early American colonists utilized several forms of unfree labor to address the chronic labor shortage they encountered in the New World. Initially, they employed indentured servants and redemptioners, individuals who agreed to work for a colonist for a fixed term in exchange for their passage to America. But when African slaves were imported to the colonies beginning in 1619 they quickly became the dominant form of unfree labor, especially in the plantation economy that developed in the South. By 1860 there were more than 3.9 million slaves in the United States. Gangs of slave laborers were used initially to produce the main cash crops of the early colonial South, tobacco, rice, and indigo. But following Eli Whitney's invention of the cotton gin in 1793 and the surge in world demand for cotton, slave labor became essential to the cotton culture of the South in the antebellum decades. Slave labor was also employed to a lesser degree in a variety of capacities ranging from household servants to skilled artisans and craftsmen.

The economic advantages of slaves seemed obvious: they served for their entire life rather than for a fixed term; the legal code of the colonies quickly evolved to define them and their children as the property of their master; because they were regarded as property, their master was able to expropriate all of their earnings. But of all the issues American economic historians have addressed perhaps none has inspired more scrutiny or controversy than the economics of American slavery. The debate was initiated in the early 20th Century by the historian Ulrich Bonnell Phillips. Born in Georgia in 1877, the year Reconstruction ended, Phillips was a professor of History at Wisconsin, Tulane, Michigan, and Yale who specialized in the history of slavery in the antebellum South. In his most famous works, *American Negro Slavery* (1918) and *Life and Labor in the Old South* (1929) Phillips maintained that slavery was a profitable labor system only when free labor was scarce and expensive, when demand was high for crops that could be grown on plantation systems, and when slave prices were low. In Phillips' analysis these conditions had prevailed throughout the colonial era, but as world demand fell for tobacco, rice, and indigo in the decades prior to the American Revolution, slavery steadily became an unprofitable labor system. Had it not been for the invention of the cotton gin and the surge in world demand for cotton in the antebellum years, Phillips believed that American slavery might well have disappeared after independence was achieved in 1783. But the revival of slavery was only temporary. The end of the slave trade in 1808, by limiting supply, caused slave prices to rise more rapidly than the price of cotton in the antebellum decades. As a result, Phillips contended that on the eve of the Civil War slavery was unprofitable and was headed for a natural extinction.

Phillips' views on the unprofitability of slavery shaped the scholarly discourse among economic historians for the first half of the 20th Century. But beginning in the 1950s as a new generation of historians came of age and as the modern civil rights revolution unfolded, Phillips' interpretation came under fire. Critics charged, for example, that Phillips' analysis was often influenced by the racist attitudes common to the post-Reconstruction South of his youth. Others faulted Phillips' work for lacking any effort to measure empirically the profitability of slavery. The 1958 publication of a study made by two Harvard economists finally moved the scholarly discourse beyond Phillips' interpretation. In "The Economics of Slavery in the Ante Bellum South," published originally in the *Journal of Political Economy*, Alfred H. Conrad and John R. Meyer measured the rate of return southern planters earned through their investment in slaves. They found that the return on male slaves generally ranged from 5 percent to 8 percent but that on plantations with especially fertile soil the return was as high as 13 percent. They also found that for female slaves, when the children they bore were included in the calculations, planters averaged a 7 percent to 8 percent return. In light of these findings, Conrad and Meyer concluded that slavery was indeed a profitable labor system throughout the antebellum era and thus was not headed towards natural extinction.

Since the publication of Conrad's and Meyer's work economic historians have generally agreed that slavery was a profitable labor system. They continue to debate, however, the extent of its profitability, the comparison of its rate of return to that earned by northern manufacturers, the impact of slavery on the economic growth of the antebellum South, and the relative efficiency of slave labor. How, then, shall we regard the economics of American slavery? Did the return southern planters earned on their investment in slaves compare favorably or unfavorably with the investment of northern manufacturers in factories and machinery? By tying most of that region's capital to an agricultural economy did slavery retard the economic development of the South? How efficient was slave labor? Was it as efficient as free northern farm labor? Was it as efficient as southern non-slave agricultural labor? How did the material conditions of slaves compare to that of northern factory workers?

DOCUMENTS

Fanny Kemble (1809–1893), a British actress from a prominent acting family, was married to the Georgia planter Peirce Butler in the 1830s and 1840s. During her marriage she lived for a time on the Butler family cotton plantation in the sea islands of Georgia and kept a diary of her experiences. Her diary, later published in 1863 as *Journal of a Residence on a Georgian Plantation in 1838–1839*, provides a remarkable first-hand contemporary portrait of life in the slave South. In Document 4–1, an excerpt from her *Journal*, Kemble, a strong critic of slavery, described the variety of ways in which the slaves on her plantation were employed.

Frederick Law Olmsted, the famous 19th-century landscape architect most well known as the designer of New York City's Central Park, was also an accomplished journalist. In the 1850s as the national debate over slavery intensified, the *New York Times* commissioned Olmsted to travel throughout the slave states and report back to northern readers what he observed of life in the South. Olmsted later condensed the journals of his travels into *The Cotton Kingdom*, published in 1861 as the southern states seceded. In Document 4–2, an excerpt from *The Cotton Kingdom*, Olmsted offered a generally critical portrait of life in the South, concluding that slavery had harmed the people and the region more than it had benefited them

Document 4–3, "Management of Negroes Upon Southern States," appeared originally in the June 1851 edition of *DeBow's Review*. Established in 1846 in New Orleans by James D.B. DeBow, the *Review* was one of the leading Southern journals of the antebellum era and one that stoutly defended the slave system. In this article an anonymous Mississippi planter provided a detailed description of the system he used to manage the 150 slaves on his plantation. He stressed that it was in the planter's self interest to treat the slaves fairly, to provide them with decent food, clothing, and shelter.

4–1. FREDERICK LAW OLMSTED, *THE COTTON KINGDOM*

…My…observation of the real condition of the people of our Slave States gave me…an impression that the cotton monopoly in some way did them more harm than good; …I propose here, therefore, to show how the main body of the observations of the book arrange themselves…with reference to this question, and also to inquire how far the conclusion to which I think they tend is substantiated by the Census returns of those States.

Coming directly from my farm in New York to Eastern Virginia, I was satisfied, after a few weeks' observation, that most of the people lived very poorly; that the proportion of men improving their condition was much less than in any Northern community; and that the natural resources of the land were strangely unused, or were used with poor economy. It was "the hiring season," and I had daily opportunities of talking with farmers, manufacturers, miners, and laborers, with whom the value of labor and of wages was then the handiest subject of conversation. I soon perceived that labor was much more readily classified and measured with reference to its quality than at the North. The limit of measure I found to be the ordinary day's work of a "prime field-hand," and a prime field-hand, I found universally understood to mean, not a man who would split two cords of wood, or cradle two acres of grain in a day, but a man for whom a "trader" would give a thousand dollars, or more, to take on South, for sale to a cotton planter…. [I]n estimating the market value of his labor, he was viewed…from the trader's point of view, or, as if the question were—What is he worth for cotton?

I soon ascertained that a much larger number of hands, at much larger aggregate wages, was commonly reckoned to be required to accomplish certain results, than would have been the case at the North…. I have been in the habit of watching men at work, and of judging of their industry, their skill, their spirit; in short, of whatever goes to make up their value to their employers, or to the community, as instruments of production; and from day to day I saw that as a landowner or as a citizen in a community largely composed or dependent upon the productive industry of working people of such habits and disposition as I constantly saw evinced in those of Virginia, I should feel disheartened, and myself lose courage, spirit, and industry…. I compared notes with every Northern man I met who had been living for some time in Virginia, and some I found able to give me quite exact statements of personal experience, with which…it could not be doubted that laborers costing…the same wages, had taken four times as long to accomplish certain tasks of rude work in Virginia as at the North, and that in house service, four servants accomplished less, while they required vastly more looking after, than one at the North….

I…spent another month in Virginia, after visiting the cotton States, and I also spent three months in Kentucky and other parts of the Slave States where the climate is unsuitable for the production of cotton, and with the information which I had in the meantime obtained,

I continued to study both the question of fact, and the question of cause. The following conclusions…were established at length in my convictions.

1. The cash value of a slave's labor in Virginia is, practically, the cash value of the same labor minus the cost of its transportation, acclimatizing, and breaking in to cotton-culture in Mississippi.
2. The cost of production, or the development of natural wealth in Virginia, is regulated by the cost of slave labor: (that is to say) the competition of white labor does not materially reduce it; though it doubtless has some effect, at least in certain districts, and with reference to certain productions or branches of industry.
3. Taking infants, aged, invalid, and vicious and knavish slaves into account, the ordinary and average cost of a certain task of labor is more than double in Virginia what it is in the Free States adjoining.
4. The use of land and nearly all other resources of wealth in Virginia is much less valuable than the use of similar property in the adjoining Free States, these resources having no real value until labor is applied to them. (The Census returns of 1850 show that the sale value of farm lands by the acre in Virginia is less than one-third the value of farm lands in the adjoining Free State of Pennsylvania, and less than one-fifth than that of the farm lands of the neighboring Free State of New Jersey.)
5. Beyond the bare necessities of existence, poor shelter, poor clothing, and the crudest diet, the mass of the citizen class of Virginia earn very little and are very poor—immeasurably poorer than the mass of the people of the adjoining Free States.
6. So far as this poverty is to be attributed to personal constitution, character, and choice, it is not the result of climate.
7. What is true of Virginia is measurably true of all the border Slave States, though in special cases the resistance of slavery to a competition of free labor is more easily overcome. In proportion as this is the case, the cost of production is less, the value of production greater, the comfort of the people is greater; they are advancing in wealth as they are in intelligence, which is the best form or result of wealth.

I went on my way into the so-called cotton States, within which I traveled over, first and last, at least three thousand miles of roads, from which not a cotton plant was to be seen, and the people living by the side of which certainly had not been made rich by cotton or anything else. And for every mile of road-side upon which I saw any evidence of cotton production, I am sure that I saw a hundred of forest or waste land, with only now and then an acre or two of poor corn half smothered in weeds; for every rich man's house, I am sure that I passed a dozen shabby and half-furnished cottages, and at least a hundred cabins—mere hovels, such as none but a poor farmer would house his cattle in at the North. And I [found]… a much larger number of what poor men at the North would themselves describe as poor men: not that they were destitute of certain things which are cheap at the South,—fuel for instance,—but that they were almost wholly destitute of things the possession of which, at the North, would indicate that a man had begun to accumulate capital—more destitute of these, on an average, than our day laborers. In short, except in certain limited districts…I found the same state of things which I had seen in Virginia, but in a more aggravated form.

At least five hundred white men told me something of their own lives and fortunes, across their own tables, and with the means of measuring the weight of their words before my eyes; and I know that while men seldom want an abundance of coarse food in the cotton States, the proportion of the free white men who live as well in any respect as our working classes at the North, on an average, is small, and the citizens of the cotton States, as a whole, are poor. They work little, and that little, badly; they earn little, they sell little; they buy little, and they have little—very little—of the common comforts and consolations of civilized life. Their destitution is not material only; it is intellectual and it is moral. I know not what virtues they have that rude men everywhere have not; but those which are commonly attributed to them, I am sure that they lack: they are not generous or hospitable; and, to be plain, I must say that their talk is not the talk of even courageous men elsewhere. They boast and lack self-restraint, yet, when not excited, are habitually reserved and guarded in expressions of opinion very much like cowardly men elsewhere.

But, much cotton is produced in the cotton States, and by the labor of somebody; much cotton is sold and somebody must be paid for it; there are rich people; there are good markets; there is hospitality, refinement, virtue, courage, and urbanity at the South. All this is proverbially true. Who produces the cotton? who is paid for it? where are, and who are, the rich and gentle people?

I can answer in part at least.

I have been on plantations on the Mississippi, the Red River, and the Brazos bottoms, whereon I was assured that ten bales of cotton to each average prime field-hand had been raised. The soil was a perfect garden mould, well drained and guarded by levees against the floods; it was admirably tilled; I have seen but few Northern farms so well tilled: the laborers were, to a large degree, tall, slender, sinewy, young men, who worked from dawn to dusk, not with spirit, but with steadiness and constancy. They had good tools; their rations of bacon and corn were brought to them in the field, and eaten with efficient dispatch between the cotton plants. They had the best sort of gins and presses, so situated that from them cotton bales could be rolled in five minutes to steamboats, bound direct to the ports on the Gulf [of Mexico]. They were superintended by skilful and vigilant overseers. These plantations were all large, so large as to yet contain much fresh land, ready to be worked as soon as the cultivated fields gave out in fertility. If it was true that ten bales of cotton to the hand had been raised on them, then their net profit for the year had been not less than two hundred and fifty dollars for each hand employed. Even at seven bales to the hand the profits of cotton planting are enormous. Men who have plantations producing at this rate, can well afford to buy fresh hands at fourteen hundred dollars a head. They can even afford to employ such hands for a year or two in clearing land, ditching, leveeing, fencing, and other preparatory work, buying, meantime, all the corn and bacon they need, and getting the best kind of tools and cattle, and paying fifteen per cent per annum interest on all the capital required for this, as many of them do. All this can be well afforded to establish new plantations favorably situated, on fresh soil, if there is a reasonable probability that they can after all be made to produce half a dozen seven-bale crops. And a great many large plantations do produce seven bales to the hand for years in succession. A great many more produce seven bales occasionally. A few produce even ten bales occasionally, though by no means as often as is reported....

The area of land on which cotton may be raised with profit is practically limitless; it is cheap; even the best land is cheap; but to the large planter it is much more valuable when held in large parcels, for obvious reasons, than when in small; consequently the best land can hardly be obtained in small tracts or without the use of a considerable capital. But there are millions of acres of land yet untouched, which if leveed and drained and fenced, and well cultivated, might be made to produce with good luck seven or more bales to the hand. It would cost comparatively little to accomplish it—one lucky crop would repay all the outlay for land and improvements—if it were not for "the hands." The supply of hands is limited. It does not increase in the ratio of the increase of the cotton demand. If cotton should double in price next year, or become worth its weight in gold, the number of negroes in the United States would not increase four per cent unless the African slave-trade were reestablished. Now step into a dealer's "jail" in Memphis, Montgomery, Vicksburg, or New Orleans, and you will hear the mezzano of the cotton lottery crying his tickets in this way: "There's a cotton nigger for you! Genuine! Look at his toes! Look at his fingers! There's a pair of legs for you! If you have got the right sile and the right sort of overseer, buy him, and put your trust in Providence! He's just as good for ten bales as I am for a julep at eleven o'clock." And this is just as true as that any named horse is sure to win the Derby. And so the price of good laborers is constantly gambled up to a point, where, if they produce ten bales to the hand, the purchaser will be as fortunate as he who draws the high prize of the lottery; where, if they produce seven bales to the hand, he will still be in luck; where, if rot, or worm, or floods, or untimely rains or frosts occur, reducing the crop to one or two bales to the hand, as is often the case, the purchaser will have drawn a blank.

That, all things considered, the value of the labor of slaves does not, on an average, by any means justify the price paid for it, is constantly asserted by the planters, and it is true. At least beyond question it is true, and I think that I have shown why, that there is no difficulty in finding purchasers for all the good slaves that can be got by traders, at prices considerably more than they are worth for the production of cotton *under ordinary circumstances*. The supply being limited, those who grow cotton on the most productive soils, and with the greatest advantages in all other respects, not only can afford to pay more than others for all the slaves which can be brought into market, but they are driven to a ruinous competition among themselves, and slaves thus get a fictitious value like stocks "in a corner." The buyers indeed are often "cornered," and it is only the rise which almost annually has occurred in the value of cotton that has hitherto saved them from general bankruptcy. Nearly all the large planters carry a heavy load of debt from year to year, till a lucky crop coincident with a rise in the price of cotton relieves them.

The whole number of slaves engaged in cotton culture at the Census of 1850 was reckoned by De Bow to be 1,800,000, the crops at 2,400,000 bales, which is a bale and a third to each head of slaves. This was the largest crop between 1846 and 1852. Other things being equal, for reasons already indicated, the smaller the estate of slaves, the less is their rate of production per head; and, as a rule, the larger the slave estate the larger is the production per head. The number of slaves in cotton plantations held by owners of fifty and upwards is, as nearly as it can be fixed by the Census returns, 420,000.

If these produce on an average only two and a half bales per head (man, woman, and child), and double this is not extraordinary on the large plantations of the Southwest, it leaves an average for the smaller plantations of seven-eighths of a bale per head. These plantations are mostly in the interior, with long haulage and boatage to market. To the small planter in the interior, his cotton crop does not realize, as an average plantation price, more than seven cents a pound, or thirty dollars the bale. Those who plant cotton in this small way usually raise a crop of corn, and some little else, not enough...to supply themselves and their slaves with food; certainly not more than enough to do so on an average. To this the Southern agricultural periodicals frequently testify. They generally raise nothing *for sale,* but cotton. And of cotton their sale, as has been shown, amounted in 1849—a favorable year—to less than the value of twenty-five dollars for each slave, young and old, which they had kept through the year. Deducting those who hold slaves only as domestic servants from the whole number of slaveholders returned by the Census, more than half of all the slaveholders and fully half of all the cotton sellers own each not more than one family on an average of five slaves of all ages. The ordinary total cash income, then, in time of peace of fully half our cotton planters cannot be reckoned at more than one hundred and twenty-five dollars or in extraordinary years like the last at say, one hundred and fifty dollars. From this they must purchase whatever clothing and other necessaries they require for the yearly supply of an average of more than ten persons (five whites and five slaves), as well as obtain tools, mechanics' work and materials, and whatever is necessary for carrying on the work of a plantation, usually of some hundred acres, and must yet save enough to pay the fees of doctors, clergy, and lawyers, if they have had occasion to employ them, and their county and state taxes (we will say nothing of the education of their children...).... A majority of those who sell the cotton crop of the United States must be miserably poor—poorer than the majority of our day laborers at the North.

A similar calculation will indicate that the planters who own on an average two slave families each, can sell scarcely more than three hundred dollars' worth of cotton a year, on an average; which also entirely agrees with my observations. I have seen many a workman's lodging at the North, and in England too, where there was double the amount of luxury that I ever saw in a regular cotton planter's house on plantations of three cabins.

The next class of which the Census furnishes us means of considering separately are planters whose slaves occupy, on an average, seven cabins, lodging five each on an average, including the house servants, aged, invalids, and children. The average income of planters of this class...[is] hardly more than that of a private of the New York Metropolitan Police Force. It is doubtless true that cotton is cultivated profitably, that is to say, so as to produce a fair rate of interest on the capital of the planter, on many plantations of this class; but this can hardly be the case on an average, all things considered.

...[W]here the quarters of a cotton plantation number half a score of cabins or more... there are usually other advantages for the cultivation, cleaning, pressing, shipping, and disposing of cotton by the aid of which the owner obtains a fair return for the capital invested and may be supposed to live, if he knows how, in a moderately comfortable way. The whole number of slaveholders of this large class in all the Slave States is, according to De Bow's Compendium of the Census, 7,929, among which are all the great sugar, rice, and tobacco-planters. Less than seven thousand, certainly, are cotton planters.

A large majority of these live, when they live on their plantations at all, in districts, almost the only white population of which consists of owners and overseers of the same class of plantations with their own. The nearest other whites will be some sand-hill vagabonds, generally miles away, between whom and these planters, intercourse is neither intimate nor friendly.

It is hardly worth while to build much of a bridge for the occasional use of two families, even if they are rich. It is less worth while to go to much pains in making six miles of good road for the use of these families. A school house will hardly be built for the children of six rich men who will all live on an average six miles away from it, while private tutors or governesses can be paid by the earnings of a single field hand. If zeal and fluency can be obtained in a preacher coming occasionally within reach, the interest on the cost of a tolerable education is not likely to be often paid by all who would live within half a day's journey of a house of worship, which can be built anywhere in the midst of a district of large plantations. It is not necessary to multiply illustrations like these. In short, then, if all the wealth produced in a certain district is concentrated in the hands of a few men living remote from each other, it may possibly bring to the district comfortable houses, good servants, fine wines, food and furniture, tutors and governesses, horses and carriages for these few men, but it will not bring thither good roads and bridges, it will not bring thither such means of education and of civilized comfort as are to be drawn from libraries, churches, museums, gardens, theatres, and assembly rooms; it will not bring thither local newspapers, telegraphs, and so on. It will not bring thither that subtle force and discipline which comes of the myriad relations with and duties to a well-constituted community which every member of it is daily exercising, and which is the natural unseen compensation and complement of its more obvious constraints and inconveniences. There is, in fact, a vast range of advantages which our civilization has made so common to us that they are hardly thought of, of which the people of the South are destitute....

One of the grand errors [made is in]... supposing that whatever nourishes wealth and gives power to an ordinary civilized community must command as much for a slave-holding community. The truth has been overlooked that the accumulation of wealth and the power of a nation are contingent not merely upon the primary value of the surplus of productions of which it has to dispose, but very largely also upon the way in which the income from its surplus is distributed and reinvested. Let a man be absent from almost any part of the North twenty years, and he is struck, on his return, by what we call the "improvements" which have been made. Better buildings, churches, school houses, mills, railroads, etc. In New York City alone, for instance, at least two hundred millions of dollars have been reinvested merely in an improved housing of the people; in labor-saving machinery, waterworks, gasworks, etc., as much more. It is not difficult to see where the profits of our manufacturers and merchants are. Again, go into the country and there is no end of substantial proof of twenty years of agricultural prosperity, not alone in roads, canals, bridges, dwellings, barns and fences, but in books and furniture, and gardens, and pictures, and in the better dress and evidently higher education of the people. But where will the returning travelers see the accumulated cotton profits of twenty years in Mississippi? Ask the cotton-planter for them, and he will point in reply, not to dwellings, libraries, churches, school houses, mills, railroads, or anything of the kind; he will point to his negroes—to almost nothing else. Negroes such as stood for five hundred dollars once, now represent a thousand dollars. We must look then in Virginia and those Northern Slave States which have the monopoly of supplying negroes, for the real wealth which the sale of cotton has brought to the South. But where is the evidence of it? where anything to compare with the evidence of accumulated profits to be seen in any Free State? If certain portions of Virginia have been a little improving, others unquestionably have been deteriorating, growing shabbier, more comfortless, less convenient. The total increase in wealth of the population during the last twenty years shows for almost nothing. One year's improvements of a Free State exceed it all.

It is obvious that to the community at large, even in Virginia, the profits of supplying negroes to meet the wants occasioned by the cotton demand, have not compensated for the bar which the high cost of all sorts of human service which the cotton demand has also occasioned has placed upon all other means of accumulating wealth; and this disadvantage of the cotton monopoly is fully experienced by the negro-breeders themselves, in respect to everything else they have to produce or obtain....

4–2. FRANCES ANNE KEMBLE, *JOURNAL OF A RESIDENCE ON A GEORGIAN PLANTATION IN 1838–1839*

Source: Frances Anne Kemble, *Journal of a Residence on a Georgian Plantation in 1838–1839*, New York: Harper & Brothers, 1863.

...One of [our slaves]—the eldest son of our laundrywoman, and Mary's brother, a boy of the name of Aleck (Alexander)—is uncommonly bright and intelligent; he performs all the offices of a well-instructed waiter with great efficiency, and anywhere out of slaveland would be able to earn fourteen or fifteen dollars a month for himself; he is remarkably good tempered and well disposed. The other poor boy is so stupid that he appears sullen from absolute darkness of intellect; instead of being a little lower than the angels, he is scarcely a little higher than the brutes, and to this condition are reduced the majority of his kind by the institutions under which they live. I should tell you that Aleck's parents and kindred have always been about the house of the overseer, and in daily habits of intercourse with him and his wife; and wherever this is the case the effect of involuntary education is evident in the improved intelligence of the degraded race. In a conversation which Mr. —— had this evening with Mr. O——, the overseer, the latter mentioned that two of our carpenters had in their leisure time made a boat, which they had disposed of to some neighboring planter for sixty dollars.

Now, E——, I have no intention of telling you a one sided story or concealing from you what are cited as the advantages which these poor people possess; you, who know that no indulgence is worth simple justice, either to him who gives or him who receives, will not thence conclude that their situation thus mitigated is, therefore, what it should be. On this matter of the sixty dollars earned by Mr. ——'s two men much stress was laid by him and his overseer. I look at it thus: if these men were industrious enough out of their scanty leisure to earn sixty dollars, how much more of remuneration, of comfort, of improvement might they not have achieved were the price of their daily labor duly paid them, instead of being unjustly withheld to support an idle young man and his idle family, i.e., myself and my children.

And here it may be well to inform you that the slaves on this plantation are divided into field hands and mechanics or artisans. The former, the great majority, are the more stupid and brutish of the tribe; the others, who are regularly taught their trades, are not only exceedingly expert at them, but exhibit a greater general activity of intellect, which must necessarily result from even a partial degree of cultivation. There are here a gang (for that is the honorable term) of coopers, of blacksmiths, of bricklayers, of carpenters, all well acquainted with their peculiar trades. The latter constructed the washhand stands, clothespresses, sofas, tables, etc., with which our house is furnished, and they are very neat pieces of workmanship—neither veneered or polished indeed, nor of very costly materials, but of the white pinewood planed as smooth as marble—a species of furniture not very luxurious perhaps, but all the better adapted therefore to the house itself, which is certainly rather more devoid of the conveniences and adornments of modern existence than anything I ever took up my abode in before....

I mentioned to you just now that two of the carpenters had made a boat in their leisure time. I must explain this to you and this will involve the mention of another of Miss [Harriet] Martineau's mistakes with regard to slave labor, at least in many parts of the Southern states. She mentions that on one estate of which she knew, the proprietor had made the experiment, and very successfully, of appointing to each of his slaves a certain task to be performed in the day, which once accomplished, no matter how early, the rest of the four-and-twenty hours were allowed to the laborer to employ as he pleased. She mentions this as a single experiment, and rejoices over it as a decided amelioration in the condition of the slave and one deserving of general adoption. But in the part of Georgia where this estate is situated the custom of task labor is universal and it prevails, I believe, throughout Georgia, South Carolina, and parts of North Carolina; in other parts of the latter state, however—as I was informed by our overseer, who is a native of that state—the estates are small, rather deserving the name of farms, and the laborers are much upon the same footing as the laboring men at the North, working from sunrise to sunset in the fields with the farmer and his sons, and coming in with them to their meals, which they take immediately after the rest of the family. In Louisiana and the new Southwestern slave states, I believe, task labor does not prevail; but it is in those that the condition of the poor human cattle is most deplorable. As you know it was there that the humane calculation was not only made, but openly and unhesitatingly avowed that the planters found it, upon the whole, their most profitable plan to work off (kill with labor) their whole number of slaves about once in seven years, and renew the whole stock....

Well, this task system is pursued on this estate; and thus it is that the two carpenters were enabled to make the boat they sold for sixty dollars. These tasks, of course, profess to be graduated according to the sex, age, and strength of the laborer; but in many instances this is not the case, as I think you will agree when I tell you that on Mr. ——'s first visit to his estates he found that the men and the women who labored in the fields had the same task to perform. This was a noble admission of female equality, was it not?—and thus it had been on the estate for many years past. Mr ——, of course, altered the distribution of the work, diminishing the quantity done by the women....

...The Negroes as I before told you are divided into troops or gangs, as they are called; at the head of each gang is a driver, who stands over them, whip in hand, while they perform their daily task, who renders an account of each individual slave and his work every evening to the overseer, and receives from him directions for their next day's tasks. Each driver is allowed to inflict a dozen lashes upon any refractory slave in the field, and at the time of the offense; they may not, however, extend the chastisement, and if it is found ineffectual, their remedy lies in reporting the unmanageable individual either to the head driver or the overseer, the former of whom has power to inflict three dozen lashes at his own discretion, and the latter as many as he himself sees fit, within the number of fifty; which limit, however, I must tell you, is an arbitrary one on this plantation, appointed by the founder of the estate, Major ——, Mr.——'s grandfather, many of whose regulations, indeed I believe most of them, are still observed in the government of the plantation. Limits of this sort, however, to the power of either driver, head driver, or overseer, may or may not exist elsewhere; they are, to a certain degree, a check upon the power of these individuals; but in the absence of the master, the overseer may confine himself within the limit or not, as he chooses; and as for the master himself, where is his limit? He may, if he likes, flog a slave to death, for the laws which pretend that he may not are a mere pretense, inasmuch as the testimony of a black is never taken against a white; and upon this plantation of ours, and a thousand more, the overseer is the *only* white man, so whence should come the testimony to any crime of his? With regard to the oft-repeated statement that it is not the owner's interest to destroy his human property, it answers nothing; the instances in which men, to gratify the immediate impulse of passion, sacrifice not only their eternal, but their evident, palpable, positive worldly interest, are infinite. Nothing is commoner than for a man under the transient influence of anger to disregard his worldly advantage; and the black slave, whose preservation is indeed supposed to be his owner's interest, may be, will be, and is occasionally sacrificed to the blind impulse of passion.

To return to our head driver, or, as he is familiarly called, headman, Frank—he is second in authority only to the overseer, and exercises rule alike over the drivers and the gangs in the absence of the sovereign white man from the estate, which happens whenever Mr. O—— visits the other two plantations at Woodville and St. Simons. He is sole master and governor of the island, appoints the work, pronounces punishments, gives permission to the men to leave the island (without it they never may do so), and exercises all functions of undisputed mastery over his fellow slaves, for you will observe that all this occurs while he is just as much a slave as any of the rest. Trustworthy, upright, intelligent, he may be flogged tomorrow if Mr. O—— or Mr.—— so please it, and sold the next day, like a cart horse, at the will of the latter. Besides his various other responsibilities, he has the key of all the stores and gives out the people's rations weekly nor is it only the people's provisions that are put under his charge—meat, which is only given out to them occasionally, and provisions for the use of the family are also entrusted to his care. Thus you see, among these *inferior* creatures, their own masters yet look to find...good sense, honesty, self-denial, and all the qualities, mental and moral, that make one man worthy to be trusted by another. From the imperceptible but inevitable effect of the sympathies and influences of human creatures toward and over each other, Frank's intelligence has become uncommonly developed by ultimate communion in the discharge of his duty with the former overseer, a very intelligent man, who has only just left the estate, after managing it for nineteen years; the effect of this intercourse, and of the trust and responsibility laid upon the man, are that he is clearheaded, well judging, active, intelligent, extremely well-mannered, and, being respected, he respects himself. He is as ignorant as the rest of the slaves; but he is always clean and tidy in his person, with a courteousness of demeanor far removed from servility, and exhibits a strong instance of the intolerable and wicked injustice of the system under which he lives, having advanced thus far toward improvement, in spite of all the bars it puts to progress; and here being arrested, not by want of energy, want of sense, or any want of his own, but by being held as another man's property, who can only thus hold him by forbidding him further improvement. When I see that man who keeps himself a good deal aloof from the rest in his leisure hours looking with a countenance of deep thought… over the broad river, which is to him as a prison wall, to the fields and forest beyond, not one inch or branch of which his utmost industry can conquer as his own, or acquire and leave an independent heritage to his children, I marvel what the thoughts of such a man may be. I was in his house today, and the same superiority in cleanliness, comfort, and propriety exhibited itself in his dwelling as in his own personal appearance and that of his wife—a most active, trustworthy, excellent woman, daughter of the oldest, and probably most highly respected of all Mr. ——'s slaves. To the excellent conduct of this woman, and, indeed, every member of her family, both the present and the last overseer bear unqualified testimony.…

4–3. "MANAGEMENT OF NEGROES UPON SOUTHERN ESTATES"

Source: *DeBow's Review*, X (June, 1851), pp. 621–627.

[We regard this as a practical and valuable paper for the planters, and hope that those of them who have been experimenting in the matter, will give us the results.]-EDITOR.

Some very sensible and practical writer in the March No. of "The Review," under the "Agricultural Department," has given us an article upon the management of negroes, which entitles him to the gratitude of the planting community, not only for the sound and useful information it contains, but because it has opened up this subject, to be thought of, written about, and improved upon, until the comforts of our black population shall be greatly increased and their services become more profitable to their owners. Surely there is no subject which demands of the planter more careful consideration than the proper treatment of his slaves by whose labor he lives and for whose conduct and happiness he is responsible in the eyes of God. We very often find planters comparing notes and making suggestions as to the most profitable modes of tilling the soil, erecting gates, fences, farmhouses, machinery, and, indeed, everything else conducive to their comfort and prosperity; but how seldom do we find men comparing notes as to their mode of feeding, clothing, nursing, working, and taking care of those human beings intrusted [sic.] to our charge, whose best condition is slavery, when they are treated with humanity, and their labor properly directed! I have been a reader of agricultural papers for more than twenty years and…I have seldom met with an article laying down general rules for the management of negroes by which their condition could be ameliorated and the master be profited at the same time. One good article upon this subject would be worth more to the master than a hundred theories about "rotations" and "scientific culture;" and infinitely more to the slave than whole volumes dictated by a spurious philanthropy looking to his emancipation. For it is a fact established beyond all controversy, that when the negro is treated with humanity and subjected to constant employment without the labor of thought and the cares incident to the necessity of providing for his own support, he is by far happier than he would be if emancipated and left to think and act and provide for himself. And from the vast amount of experience in the management of slaves, can we not deduce some general, practicable rules for their government that would add to the happiness of both master and servant? I know of no other mode of arriving at this great desideratum, than for planters to give to the public their rules for feeding, clothing, housing and working their slaves and of taking care of them when sick, together with their plantation discipline. In this way, we shall be continually learning something new upon this vitally interesting question, filled as it is with great responsibilities; and while our slaves will be made happier, our profits from their labor will be greater and our consciences be made easier.

...To begin, then, I send you my plantation rules that are printed in the plantation book, which constitute a part of the contract made in the employment of the overseer, and which are observed, so far as my constant and vigilant superintendence can enforce them. My first care has been to select a proper place for my [slave] "Quarter," well protected by the shade of forest trees, sufficiently thinned out to admit a free circulation of air, so situated as to be free from the impurities of stagnant water and to erect comfortable houses for my negroes. Planters do not always reflect that there is more sickness and consequently greater loss of life from the decaying logs of negro houses, open floors, leaky roofs, and crowded rooms, than all other causes combined; and if humanity will not point out the proper remedy, let self-interest for once act as a virtue and prompt him to save the health and lives of his negroes by at once providing comfortable quarters for them. There being upwards of 150 negroes on the plantation, I provide for them 24 houses made of hewn post oak, covered with cypress, 16 by 18, with close plank floors and good chimneys and elevated two feet from the ground. The ground under and around the houses is swept every month and the houses, both inside and out, white-washed twice a year. The houses are situated in a double row from north to south, about 200 feet apart, the doors facing inwards and the houses being in a line about 50 feet apart. At one end of the street stands the overseer's house, workshops, tool house, and wagon sheds; at the other, the grist and saw mill with good cisterns at each end, providing an ample supply of pure water. My experience has satisfied me that spring, well, and lake water are all unhealthy in this climate and that large under-ground cisterns, keeping the water pure and cool, are greatly to be preferred. They are easily and cheaply constructed, very convenient, and save both doctors' bills and loss of life. The negroes are never permitted to sleep before the fire, either lying down or sitting up, if it can be avoided, as they are always prone to sleep with their heads to the fire, are liable to be burnt and to contract disease: but beds with ample clothing are provided for them and in them they are made to sleep.... I allow for each hand that works out, four pounds of clear meat and one peck of meal per week. Their dinners are cooked for them, and carried to the field, always with vegetables, according to the season. There are two houses set apart at mid-day for resting, eating, and sleeping if they desire it and they retire to one of the weather-sheds or the grove to pass this time, not being permitted to remain in the hot sun while at rest. They cook their own suppers and breakfasts, each family being provided with an oven, skillet, and sifter, and each one having a coffee pot, (and generally some coffee to put in it,) with knives and forks, plates, spoons, cups, &c., of their own providing. The wood is regularly furnished them; for, I hold it to be absolutely mean for a man to require a negro to work until daylight closes in and then force him to get wood, some times half a mile off, before he can get a fire, either to warm himself or cook his supper. Every negro has his hen house where he raises poultry which he is not permitted to sell, and he cooks and eats his chickens and eggs for his evening and morning meals to suit him self; besides, every family has a garden, paled in, where they raise such vegetables and fruits as they take a fancy to. A large house is provided as a nursery for the children where all are taken at daylight and placed under the charge of a careful and experienced woman whose sole occupation is to attend to them and see that they are properly fed and attended to and above all things to keep them as dry and as cleanly as possible under the circumstances. The suckling women come in to nurse their children four times during the day; and it is the duty of the nurse to see that they do not perform this duty until they have become properly cool after walking from the field. In consequence of these regulations, I have never lost a child from being burnt to death, or, indeed, by accidents of any description; and although I have had more than thirty born within the last five years, yet I have not lost a single one from teething or the ordinary summer complaints so prevalent amongst the children in this climate.

I give to my negroes four full suits of clothes with two pair of shoes every year and to my women and girls a calico dress and two handkerchiefs extra. I do not permit them to have "truck patches" other than their gardens or to raise anything whatever for market; but in lieu thereof I give to each head of a family and to every single negro on Christmas day, five dollars, and send them to the county town under the charge of the overseer or driver to spend their money. In this way I save my mules from being killed up in summer and my oxen in winter, by working and hauling off their crops; and more than all, the negroes are prevented from acquiring habits of trading in farm produce which invariably leads to stealing, followed by whipping, trouble to the master, and discontent on the part of the slave. I permit no spirits to be brought on the plantation or used by any negro, if I can prevent it; and a violation of this rule, if found out, is always followed by a whipping and a forfeiture of the five dollars next Christmas.

I have a large and comfortable hospital provided for my negroes when they are sick; to this is attached a nurse's room; and when a negro complains of being too unwell to work, he is at once sent to the hospital and put under the charge of a very experienced and careful negro woman who administers the medicine and attends to his diet and where they remain until they are able to work again. This woman is provided with sugar, coffee, molasses, rice, flour and tea and does not permit a patient to taste of meat or vegetables until he is restored to health. Many negroes relapse after the disease is broken, and die, in consequence of remaining in their houses and stuffing themselves with coarse food after their appetites return, and both humanity and economy dictate that this should be prevented. From the system I have pursued I have not lost a hand since the summer of 1845, (except one that was killed by accident,) nor has my physician's bill averaged fifty dollars a year, notwithstanding I live near the edge of the swamp of Big Black River where it is thought to be very unhealthy....

I must not omit to mention that I have a good fiddler, and keep him well supplied with catgut and I make it his duty to play for the negroes every Saturday night until 12 o'clock. They are exceedingly punctual in their attendance at the ball, while Charley's fiddle is always accompanied with Ihurod on the triangle and Sam to "pat."

I also employ a good preacher who regularly preaches to them on the Sabbath day and it is made the duty of every one to come up clean and decent to the place of worship. As Father Garritt regularly calls on Brother Abram, (the foreman of the prayer meetings,) to close the exercises, he gives out and sings his hymn with much unction, and always cocks his eye at Charley, the fiddler, as much as to say, "Old fellow, you had your time last night; now it is mine." ...

These are some of the leading outlines of my management so far as my negroes are concerned. That they are imperfect and could be greatly improved, I readily admit; and it is only with the hope that I shall be able to improve them by the experience of others that I have given them to the public....

A MISSISSIPPI PLANTER

Rules and Regulations for the Government of a Southern Plantation

1. THERE SHALL BE A PLACE FOR EVERYTHING AND EVERYTHING SHALL BE KEPT IN ITS PLACE.
2. On the first days of January and July there shall be an account taken of the number and condition of all the negroes, stock and farming utensils of every description on the premises and the same shall be entered in the plantation book.
3. It shall be the duty of the overseer to call upon the stock-minder once every day to know if the cattle, sheep and hogs have been seen and counted and to find out if any are dead, missing, or lost.
4. It shall be the duty of the overseer at least once in every week to see and count the stock himself and to inspect the fences, gates, and watergaps on the plantation and see that they are in good order.
5. The wagons, carts, and all other implements are to be kept under the sheds and in the houses where they belong except when in use.
6. Each negro man will be permitted to keep his own axe and shall have it forthcoming when required by the overseer. No other tool shall be taken or used by any negro without the permission of the overseer.
7. Humanity, on the part of the overseer, and unqualified obedience on the part of the negroes, are under all circumstances indispensable.
8. Whipping, when necessary, shall be in moderation and never done in a passion; and the driver shall in no instance inflict punishment, except in the presence of the overseer, and when from sickness, he is unable to do it himself.
9. The overseer shall see that the negroes are properly clothed and well fed. He shall lay off a garden of at least six acres and cultivate it as part of his crop and give the negroes as many vegetables as may be necessary.
10. It shall be the duty of the overseer to select a sufficient number of the women each week to wash for all. The clothes shall be well washed, ironed and mended, and distributed to the negroes on Sunday morning; when every negro is expected to wash himself, comb his head, and put on clean clothes. No washing or other labor will be tolerated on the Sabbath.
11. The negroes shall not be worked in the rain or kept out after night except in weighing or putting away cotton.
12. It shall be the duty of the driver at such hours of the night as the overseer may designate, to blow his horn and go around and see that every negro is at his proper place and to report to the overseer any that may be absent; and it shall be the duty of the overseer at some hour between that time and day break to patrol the quarters himself and see that every negro is where he should be.
13. The negro children are to be taken every morning by their mothers and carried to the houses of the nurses; and every cabin shall be kept locked during the day.
14. Sick negroes are to receive particular attention. When they are first reported sick, they are to be examined by the overseer and prescribed for and put under the care of the nurse and not put to work until the disease is broken and the patient beyond the danger of a relapse.
15. When the overseer shall consider it necessary to send for a physician, he shall enter in the plantation book the number of visits and to what negro they are made.
16. When any negro shall die, an hour shall be set apart by the overseer for his burial; and at that hour all business shall cease and every negro on the plantation who is able to do so shall attend the burial.

17. The overseer shall keep a plantation book in which he shall register the birth and name of each negro that is born; the name of each negro that died and specify the disease that killed him. He shall also keep in it the weights of the daily picking of each hand; the mark, number and weight of each bale of cotton and the time of sending the same to market; and all other such occurrences relating to the crop, the weather, and all other matters pertaining to the plantation that he may deem advisable.

18. The overseer shall pitch the crops and work them according to his own judgment with the distinct understanding that a failure to make a bountiful supply of corn and meat for the use of the plantation will be considered as notice that his services will not be required for the succeeding year

19. The negroes, teams, and tools, are to be considered as under the overseer's exclusive management and are not to be interfered with by the employer, only so far as to see that the foregoing rules are strictly observed.

20. The overseer shall under no circumstances create an account against his employer except in the employment of a physician or in the purchase of medicines; but whenever anything is wanted about the plantation he shall apply to his employer for it.

21. Whenever the overseer or his employer shall become dissatisfied, they shall in a frank and friendly manner express the same and, if either party desires it, he shall have the right to settle and separate.

ESSAYS

The first essay is an excerpt from Robert William Fogel's and Stanley L. Engerman's important and still controversial 1974 study, *Time on the Cross: The Economics of American Negro Slavery*. Fogel, the Charles R. Walgreen Distinguished Service Professor of American Institutions at the University of Chicago Graduate School of Business and a 1993 Nobel Laureate in Economics and Engerman, the John Munro Professor of Economics and Professor of History at the University of Rochester, aided by the advent of computers for historical research, compiled the records of thousands of antebellum plantations to create what they believed to be the most complete portrait of America's peculiar institution. Based on the analysis of their huge database, Professors Fogel and Engerman contended that the scholarly interpretation of American slavery was in most cases incorrect. Their findings suggested, for example, that slavery was an extremely profitable system whose rates of return were at least as great as those of the most profitable northern factories; that slavery was not on the brink of extinction on the eve of the Civil War; that slave labor was 35 percent more efficient than northern agricultural labor; that the typical slave ate a more nutritious diet than the typical northern industrial worker; and that in the decades prior to the Civil War the southern economy grew more rapidly than that of the North and the West. In the excerpt which follows Professor Fogel and Engerman develop their contention about the profitability of slavery as a labor system and its contribution to the growth of the antebellum southern economy.

The second essay is an excerpt from the 1981 book, *A Deplorable Scarcity: The Failure of Industrialization in the Slave Economy* by Fred Bateman, Beadles Professor of Economics at the University of Georgia's Terry College of Business, and Thomas Weiss, Professor of Economics Emeritus at the University of Kansas. In it Professors Bateman and Weiss explored the impact of slavery on the antebellum southern economy from a different perspective. Economic historians disagree about the connection between the profitability of slavery and the failure of the antebellum South to industrialize. Those who held that slavery was an unprofitable labor system generally **have** explained the absence of antebellum southern manufacturing as the result of irrational decisions made by planters who continued to invest in an unprofitable labor system out of a determination to preserve the cotton culture. On the other hand, those who maintain that slavery was profitable, such as Professors Fogel and Engerman, explain the failure of the South to industrialize as the result of the planters' rational decision to invest in that economic activity which offered the highest rate of return, thereby implying that manufacturing south of the Mason Dixon line was generally less profitable than plantation agriculture. In Essay 4–2 Professors Bateman and Weiss argue that although southern manufacturing typically offered a higher rate of return than slave agriculture, Southern planters who controlled the vast bulk of that region's investment capital were generally unwilling or unable to divert much capital away from their agricultural pursuits. In this sense, then, Professors Bateman and Weiss concluded that slavery did impede southern economic development.

4–1. ROBERT WILLIAM FOGEL AND STANLEY L. ENGERMAN, *TIME ON THE CROSS*

The Level of Profits and the Capitalist Character of Slavery

...Strange as it may seem, the *systematic* investigation of the average rate of profit on investments in slaves did not begin until more than half a century after U. B. Phillips launched the issue. There were some casual attacks on the problem in the 1930s and 1940s, but for various reasons they were wanting. In general, the authors of these early efforts failed to appreciate the complexity of the problem of calculating profit rates. They gave little thought to the nature of the equations to be used in the calculation, failed to take account of the multiplicity of revenues and costs that had to be estimated, and did little to probe the representativeness of the scattered and incomplete records on which their estimates were based.

The study by Alfred H. Conrad and John R. Meyer marked a decisive turning point in the effort to deal with the question of profits. "From the standpoint of the entrepreneur making an investment in slaves," they wrote, "the basic problems involved in determining profitability are analytically the same as those met in determining the returns from any other kind of capital investment." In posing the problem in this way, Conrad and Meyer were, of course, merely taking up one of Phillips's suggestions. For it was Phillips who originally stressed the similarity between the slave and stock markets. However, while Phillips did not know how to pass from his conceptualization of the problem to the measurement of the rate of return on an investment in slaves, these two economists did.

Conrad and Meyer produced separate estimates of the rates of return on males and females. The computation of the return on male slaves was the simpler case. They first derived the average capital cost per slave, including not only the price of a slave, but also the average value of the land, animals, and equipment used by a slave. Estimates of gross annual earnings were then built up from data on the price of cotton and the physical productivity of slaves. The net figure was obtained by subtracting the maintenance and supervisory costs for slaves from gross earnings. The average length of the stream of net earnings was determined from mortality tables. With these estimates, Conrad and Meyer computed rates of return on male slaves and found that for the majority of antebellum plantations the return varied between 5 and 8 percent, depending on the physical yield per hand and the prevailing farm price of cotton. On the farms in poor upland pine country or in the exhausted lands of the eastern seaboard, the range of rates was merely 2 to 5 percent. However, in the "best lands of the new Southwest the Mississippi alluvium, and the better South Carolina and Alabama plantations" rates ran as high as 10 to 13 percent.

The computation of the rate of return on female slaves was somewhat more complicated. Conrad and Meyer had to take account not only of the productivity of a female in the field, but of such additional matters as the productivity of her offspring between their birth and the time of their sale; maternity, nursery, and rearing costs; and the average number of offspring. Contending that very few females produced less than five or more than ten children that survived to be sold, Conrad and Meyer computed lower and upper limits on the rate of return. These turned out to be 7.1 and 8.1 percent respectively. Thus, planters in the exhausted lands of the upper South who earned only 4 or 5 percent on male slaves, still were able to achieve a return on their total operation equal to alternative opportunities. They did so by selling the offspring of females to planters in the West, thus earning rates of 7 to 8 percent on the other half of their slave force. Proof of such a trade was found not only in the descriptions of contemporaries, but also in the age structure of the slave population. The selling states had a significantly larger proportion of persons under fifteen and over fifty, while the buying states predominated in slaves of the prime working ages.

Rather than ending the controversy on profitability, the study of Conrad and Meyer intensified it. However, because of their work, the debate became much more sharply focused than before. They had clearly identified the crucial variables pertinent to the calculation, and the type of equations on which the calculation had to be based. Subsequent work by over a score of scholars was aimed at correcting their estimates of the values of the relevant variables and at refining their computational equations.

It is interesting that the first wave of criticisms of Conrad and Meyer turned up errors running almost exclusively in one direction — errors that made their estimate of the rate of profit too high. Thus, it was pointed out that their assumption that all slaves lived the average length of life biased the estimated rate of profit upward. They also greatly overestimated the number of slave children per female who lived to reach age eighteen. And they underestimated the amount of capital equipment required for slaves, as well as such varied costs as medical care, the employment of managerial personnel, food, and clothing.

As the debate developed, it became clear that Conrad and Meyer had also erred on the other side. They greatly underestimated the average productivity of a prime hand (a healthy slave between the ages of eighteen and thirty) as well as the productivity of females relative to males. At the same time they overestimated such items as maternity costs and the amount of land, equipment, and livestock required for young and old field hands. They also made the erroneous assumption that the land and physical capital employed by each slave died when he or she died.

To trace the twists and turns of this highly technical debate is beyond the scope of this book.... At this point we wish merely to stress that the net result of the various corrections has been to raise, not lower the Conrad and Meyer estimate of the rate of return. On average, slave owners earned about 10 percent on the market price of their bondsmen. Rates of return were approximately the same for investments in males and females. They were also approximately the same across geographic regions. There were, of course, fluctuations around the average. But, for reasons considered in detail below, over the period from 1820 through 1860, there was no secular trend in the level of profits away from the average.

The discovery of a high and persistent rate of profit on slaves constitutes a serious, and probably irreparable, blow to the thesis that the price of slaves was largely attributable to conspicuous consumption. If conspicuous consumption had increased the market price of slaves over the level indicated by business considerations alone, the expected rate of return from an investment in slaves would have been below that earned on alternative investments. The corrected computations of Conrad and Meyer revealed no such profit deficit. Quite the contrary — the computations yielded average rates of return equal to, or in excess of, the averages which obtained in a variety of nonagricultural enterprises. For example, the average rate of return earned by nine of the most successful New England textile firms over the period from 1844 through 1853 was 10.1 percent. And a group of twelve southern railroads averaged 8.5 percent for the decade 1850–1860.

The finding that the rate of return on slaves was quite high does not rule out the possibility that some planters were willing to pay a premium to buy slaves, or that some planters held excessive numbers of slaves at prevailing prices. However, it does show that the aggregate demand of this category of slaveowners was too limited to raise the market price of slaves above the level dictated by normal business standards; that is, the demand of those slaveowners who desired to hold slaves for conspicuous consumption was quite small relative to the total demand for slaves.

It should be remembered that the proponents of the thesis that slaves were held widely for reasons of conspicuous consumption never provided conclusive proof of their contention. The thesis did not appear to require a rigorous proof, since the assumption that an investment in slaves was unprofitable made conspicuous consumption a plausible rationalization for the willingness of slaveowners to pay "excessive" prices. In this context it appeared to be sufficient merely to cite evidence which suggested that prestige attached to the ownership of slaves. Yet surely prestige attaches to the ownership of most assets of great value which bring high rates of return to their owners. To show that the ownership of slaves and prestige were positively correlated does not settle the issue of causality. Was the price of slaves high because the ownership of slaves brought prestige, or did the ownership of slaves bring prestige because their price was high? To distinguish between these alternatives one needs to know whether the expected return to slaves was below or above alternative rates. It was precisely on this point that exponents of the thesis of conspicuous consumption erred.

The demonstration that an investment in slaves was highly profitable not only undermines the case for conspicuous consumption; it also throws into doubt the contention that

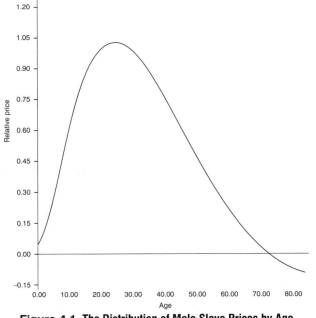

Figure 4.1 The Distribution of Male Slave Prices by Age

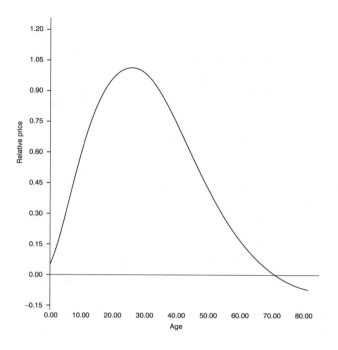

Figure 4.2 Averages of Price Relatives by Age for Males Slaves

southern slaveholders were a "precapitalist," "uncommercial" class which subordinated profit to considerations of power, life-style, and "patriarchal commitments." The point at issue is not whether the slavocracy valued its power, lifestyle, and patriarchal commitments, but whether the pursuit of these objectives generally conflicted with, or significantly undermined, the pursuit of profit.

Paternalism is not intrinsically antagonistic to capitalist enterprise. Nor is it necessarily a barrier to profit maximization. Such well-known and spectacularly profitable firms as the International Business Machines Corporation and Eastman Kodak practice paternalism. Their experience suggests that patriarchal commitments may actually raise profits by inducing labor to be more efficient than it would have been under a less benevolent management. There is no reason to rule out the possibility that paternalism operated in this way for slaveowners. No one has shown that masters who practiced paternalism had lower rates of return on the average than those who were unconcerned or heartless with respect to the welfare of their bondsmen

On the other hand, there is considerable evidence that slaveowners were hard, calculating businessmen who priced slaves, and their other assets, with as much shrewdness as could be expected of any northern capitalist. This point is well illustrated by figure 4.1, which presents over five thousand prices of male slaves. While there was variation in price at each age (as one would expect of slaves who differed in health, attitudes, and capacities), the distribution displays a quite definite pattern. On average, prices rose until the late twenties and then declined. The decline was slow at first but then became more rapid, until advanced ages were reached. The basic pattern in the movement of prices by age is more clearly displayed in figure 4.2. Here each observation represents the average of all the prices for a given age. Figures 4.1 and 4.2 also display the curve, or profile, that best describes the relationship between price and age.

What explains the age pattern of prices? Conspicuous consumption and other nonpecuniary arguments offered to explain the trend in slave prices over time clearly fail here. It seems hardly likely that twenty-six-year-olds were priced twice as high as ten-year-olds because twice as much honor and prestige were attached to the owners of the older than of the younger slaves.

The age-price profile is better explained by the pattern of earnings over the life cycle of slaves. Indeed, the age-price profile implies a corresponding earnings profile.... Net earnings were negative until age eight. Then they became positive and rose to a peak at age thirty-five. It is interesting to note that earnings of sixty-five-year-olds were still positive and, on average, brought an owner as much net income as a slave in the mid-teens. This does not mean that every slave aged sixty-five produced a positive net income for his owner. Some of the elderly were a net loss. However, the income earned by the able-bodied among the elderly was more than enough to compensate for the burden imposed by the incapacitated. The average net income from slaves remained positive until they reached their late seventies. Even after that age the average burden was quite low, since a fair share of the slaves who survived into their eighties still produced positive net incomes.

Thus, the frequent contention that slaveowners preferred to work slaves to death at early ages, in order to avoid the burden of maintenance at late ages, is unfounded. Slaveowners were generally able to employ their bondsmen profitably throughout the life cycle. Planters solved the problem of old age by varying tasks according to the capacities of slaves. There were many occupations on plantations for which the elderly were suited. Women too old to labor in the fields could, for example, be made responsible for the care of slave children or serve as nurses to the sick. They could also be employed as seamstresses, or in spinning cotton and weaving. Elderly men were put in charge of the livestock, or were made responsible for the care of implements. Some became gardeners or household servants. This capacity to utilize the labor of the elderly was probably not so much a feature of slavery *per se* but of the predominantly agrarian nature of slavery. The rise of the problem of what to do with the elderly coincides with the emergence of urbanized, industrial societies. It is a problem that is rarely encountered in the countryside.

...[P]rices of males and females...were virtually identical until age nine, after which female prices rose less rapidly than those of males. At age twenty-seven the female price was about 80 percent of the male price. The ratio fell to 60 percent at age fifty and to less than half at age seventy.

Again, the explanation of this pattern is found in the life cycles of the net earnings of males and females.... For most of the years of their lives, female earnings were below those of males by 20 to 40 percent. Interestingly, prior to age eighteen, female earnings exceeded those of males. This differential is not explained by income produced from children borne by teen-age mothers. As will be shown, earnings from childbearing were quite small during these years. The early advantage in female earnings appears to have been due primarily to a more rapid rate of maturity among women than among men.

In the absence of evidence on the market behavior of slaveowners, it was easy for historians inclined to the romantic to postulate a dichotomy between paternalism and profit-seeking. They took evidence of paternalism to imply that slaveowners must have sacrificed profits to other objectives. Now that the profitability of slavery and the overwhelming dominance of business considerations in the market behavior of slaveowners are firmly established, should we assume that paternalism was an invention of apologists for slavery? That conclusion would be as romantic and naive as the one we have rejected. There is too much evidence of deep personal attachments between owners and their bondsmen to deny that this was a facet of the slave system. "Now my heart is nearly broke," wrote a Louisiana planter on the occasion of the death of the principal slave manager. "I have lost poor *Leven,* one of the most faithful black men [that] ever lived. [H]e was truth and honesty, and without a fault that I ever discovered. He has oversed the plantation nearly three years, and [has] done much better than any white man [had] ever done here, and I lived a quiet life."

Would this expression of affection have been quite so deep if Leven had been inefficient, dishonest, and troublesome? While we do not mean to imply that affection for slaves was purely a function of their earning capacity, we do mean to suggest that it was more usual for affection and productivity to reinforce each other than to conflict with each other. Both cruelty and affection had their place on southern plantations....

The Economic Viability of Slavery After the Revolution and on the Eve of the Civil War

Two episodes during the antebellum era have been singled out as proof that underlying economic forces were working toward the destruction of the slave system. [U.B.] Phillips located one of these episodes in the decade following the close of the American Revolution. [Charles W.] Ramsdell located the other in the decade preceding the Civil War. Phillips based his case on scattered reports by planters who spoke of hard times. "Slave prices everywhere ...," he wrote, "were declining in so disquieting a manner that as late as the end of 1794 George Washington advised a friend to convert his slaves into other forms of property... ." However, Phillips was not able to use the series on slave prices that he so laboriously constructed to test these assertions, since his series only extended back to 1795. He simply accepted the scattered reports of distress as proof that "the peace of 1783 brought depression in all the plantation districts," which lasted for more than a decade and which converted the previously profitable investment in slaves into a heavy burden.

As it turns out, slave prices showed some weakness after the Revolution, but there was not a sustained, severe depression. While slave prices were acutely depressed during the last years of the Revolution, they rebounded to roughly the pre-Revolutionary level by the mid-1780s and remained on a fairly high plateau for the rest of that decade. Between 1784 and 1794 slave prices averaged 89 percent of their pre-Revolutionary level. There was an additional drop of about 5 percent between 1794 and 1795. But this slide was abruptly reversed in 1798.

Furthermore, neither the softening of prices during the early 1790s nor the brief plunge later in the decade necessarily implies that the demand for slaves was declining. It may only show that the supply of slaves was increasing more rapidly than the demand for them. This appears to have been the case. ...[T]he decade of the 1790s was marked by an unprecedented increase in the size of the slave population. Not only was the natural increase large, but slave imports — which exceeded 79,000 — were greater than in any previous decade. Indeed, the decade rate of imports during the 1790s was nearly twice as high as that which prevailed during the previous half century.

Despite the post-Revolutionary softness in prices, the trend in the demand for slaves was strongly upward from 1781 on.... George Washington's apparent gloom was not generally shared by other slaveowners. As a group, slaveowners wanted to increase, not reduce, their holdings of slaves. Even in 1796, when prices were at the lowest point of the post-Revolutionary era, the demand for slaves was over 50 percent higher than it had been in 1772.

The hesitation in the growth of demand for a few years after 1791 may have been due to fear created by the Haitian slave revolt, as well as reactions to the various emancipation laws in northern states. On the other hand, the Haitian revolution could have been responsible for a sudden increase in the supply of slaves in the United States during these years. There are reports which indicate that large numbers of slaveowners from the West Indies sold their slaves to American buyers or fled with them to establish new plantations on the mainland. Southern supply may have been swelled also by the attempt of northern slaveowners to avoid the consequences of emancipation.

In any case, the heavy flow of slaves into the United States clearly contradicts the thesis that slavery was rescued from its deathbed by the rise of the cotton culture. If slavery had become generally unprofitable during the 1780s and 1790s, one would have observed a cessation of slave imports. If the crises had been of substantial proportions, the flow of slaves would have reversed. The United States would have turned from a net importer to a net exporter of slaves, as American planters strove to limit their losses by selling their chattel to areas where slavery was still profitable.

The episode singled out by Ramsdell turns, not on the movement of slave prices, but on the movement of cotton production and cotton prices. He knew very well that slave prices were rising throughout the 1850s. Nevertheless, Ramsdell believed that planters were being irresistibly driven toward the overproduction of cotton and that this undefinable force was tolling the death knell of slavery. He saw clear evidence of the tendency to overproduction in the unprecedented rise in the output of cotton between 1850 and 1860. The increase in production during this decade was greater than the increase over the entire previous century. Moreover, the rate of increase in cotton production accelerated as the decade wore on. Between 1857 and 1860 alone, cotton production increased by 1,500,000 bales. This spectacular rise was more than had been achieved during the four decades stretching from the invention of the cotton gin to the close of the Jacksonian administration.

To Ramsdell, the implication of this compulsion to shift resources into cotton was obvious. The price of cotton was bound to decline — would, indeed, eventually decline to levels so low that slavery would become unprofitable. The signs of the future were already evident, for the leap in output between 1858 and 1860 had initiated the predicted decline in prices. Thus "those who wished it [slavery] destroyed" concluded Ramsdell, "had only to wait a little while — perhaps a generation, probably less."

While one cannot deny that the rise in cotton production during the decade of the 1850s was spectacular, the conclusion that this increase reflected irrational, uncommercial behavior *is* disputable. Neither an extremely rapid growth in output, nor a fall in price are *per se* evidence of overproduction. The output of cotton *cloth,* for example, tripled between 1822 and 1827. At the same time the price of cloth declined by 35 percent. Yet no one has ever accused these northern cloth manufacturers of an irresistible tendency to overproduction. Quite the contrary, their dynamism in responding to the booming market for cloth has been celebrated far and wide. And the capacity of cloth manufacturers to bring down their prices has been taken as a mark of the vitality of the factory system.

There was nothing unusual about the slight decline in cotton prices that occurred between 1857 and 1860. The fact is that the general trend of raw cotton prices was downward from 1802 on.... Although there were fluctuations about this trend, the average annual rate of decrease was 0.7 percent. The basic cause of this long-term decline was the steady increase in productivity. Among the developments which made cotton farming increasingly more efficient were the improvements in the varieties of cottonseeds, the introduction of the cotton gin, the reduction in transportation and other marketing costs, and the relocation of cotton production in the more fertile lands of the New South.

It was, therefore, to be expected that increases in production would generally be associated with declining prices. Since advances in productivity caused costs to fall, profits of planters may have been rising despite declining cotton prices. What is crucial, then, is not the absolute level of prices, but the level of profits. An approximation to the movement of profits may be obtained by examining the deviation of cotton prices from their long-term trend. When cotton prices were above their long-term trend value, profits of planters were likely to have been above normal. When prices were below their trend values, profits on cotton production were likely to have been below normal.

...The 1850s constituted a period of sustained boom in profits for cotton planters. It was an era that outstripped even the fabled prosperity of the 1830s. Nearly every year of the decade was one of above-normal profit. What is more, profits remained high during the last four years of the decade, with prices averaging about 15 percent above their trend values. No wonder cotton production doubled between 1850 and 1860. It was clearly a rational economic response to increase cotton production by over 50 percent between 1857 and 1860. If planters erred, it was not in expanding cotton production by too much. Quite the contrary – they were too conservative. Their expansion had not been adequate to bring prices down to their trend values and profits back to normal (equilibrium) levels.

What was responsible for making the 1850s so prosperous for cotton planters? ... [D]emand for cotton began to increase rapidly beginning in 1846. Over the next fifteen years, the average annual rate of change in demand was about 7 percent per annum.... [T] he supply of cotton generally lagged behind changes in demand. As a consequence, prices and profits tended to be above normal in periods when demand was increasing, and below normal when demand was decreasing or stagnating.

To summarize: The unprecedented increase in cotton production after 1857 was due to a rapid advance in the world demand for U.S. cotton. The lag of cotton supply behind demand caused the price of cotton to rise well above normal levels, creating unusually large profits for planters. While planters responded to this incentive, they did not increase output rapidly enough to return cotton prices and profits to normal levels.

Thus, the tale about the uncommercial planter who was gripped by an irresistible tendency to the overproduction of cotton is sheer fantasy. It is to those who romanticize the antebellum South what the story of the slave-breeding planter was to abolitionist critics — a convenient invention....

The Course of Economic Growth in the South, 1840–1860

The construction of regional income accounts for the nineteenth century, like the estimation of regional efficiency indexes, is an arduous task. Work on these accounts for the census years between 1840 and 1860, which was launched in the early 1950s, is still going on today. Table 4.3 presents the regional income estimates which have now been in use for about half a decade. A recent paper has suggested that the estimate of southern income for 1840 may be too low; the same criticism may also apply to the figure for 1860. If these proposed corrections hold up, it will be necessary to alter some of the details of the analysis

Table 4.3 Per Capita Income by Region for 1840 and 1860 (in 1860 prices)

	1840	1860	Average Annual Rates of Change (percent)
National Average	$ 96	$128	1.4
North:	109	141	1.3
Northeast	129	181	1.7
North Central	65	89	1.6
South:	74	103	1.7
South Atlantic	66	84	1.2
East South Central	69	89	1.3
West South Central	151	184	1.0

that follows, but the main thrust of the argument will not be affected. Rather, the proposed corrections will merely serve to strengthen the argument.

Table 4.3 shows that in both 1840 and 1860 per capita income in the North was higher than in the South. In 1840 the South had an average income which was only 69 percent that of the North's. In 1860 southern per capita income was still only 73 percent as high as in the North.

These figures might appear to sustain [H.R.] Helper's contention that the South was a poverty-ridden, stagnant economy in the process of sinking into "comparative imbecility and obscurity"; that under the burden of slavery the South had been reduced to the status of a colonial nation — "the dependency of a mother country." No such inference is warranted, however, merely because of the existence of a 25 percent gap between the North and the South in the level of per capita income in 1860. Before any conclusion can be drawn, it must first be determined whether the gap means that, by the standards of the time, the South was poor or that the North was extraordinarily rich.

Progress toward the resolution of this issue can be made by disaggregating the North into two subregions: the Northeast, and the north central subregions. This is done in table 4.3, which shows that the northern advantage over the South was due entirely to the extraordinarily high income of the income in the north central states not only less than half as high as in the Northeast; it was 14 percent lower than per capita income in the South. If the South was a poverty-ridden "colonial dependency," how are we to characterize the states that occupy the territory running from the western border of Pennsylvania to the western border of Nebraska — states usually thought of as examples of high prosperity and rapid growth during the antebellum era?

Far from being poverty-stricken, the South was quite rich by the standards of the antebellum era. If we treat the North and South as separate nations and rank them among the countries of the world, the South would stand as the fourth richest nation in the world in 1860. The South was richer than France, richer than Germany, richer than Denmark, richer than any of the countries of Europe except England (see table 4.4). Presentation of southern per capita income in 1860 dollars instead of 1973 dollars tends to cloak the extent of southern economic attainment. The South was not only rich by antebellum standards but also by relatively recent standards. Indeed, a country as advanced as Italy did not achieve the southern level of per capita income until the eve of World War II.

The last point underscores the dubious nature of attempts to classify the South as a "colonial dependency." The South's large purchases of manufactured goods from the North made it no more of a colonial dependency than did the North's heavy purchases of rails from England. The true colonial dependencies, countries such as India and Mexico, had less than one tenth the per capita income of the South in 1860.

The false image of the South as a land of poverty emerged out of the debates on economic policy among southern leaders during the 1850s. As sectional tensions mounted

Table 4.4 The Relative Level of the Per Capita Income of the South in 1860 (Southern per capita income level = 100)

Australia	144	Belgium	92	Italy	49
North	140	France	82	Austria	41
Great Britain	126	Ireland	71	Sweden	41
South	100	Denmark	70	Japan	14
Switzerland	100	Germany	67	Mexico	10
Canada	96	Norway	54	India	9
Netherlands	93				

Southerners became increasingly alarmed by federal policies which they thought were giving economic advantage to the North. They also became increasingly impatient with what they thought was an insufficiently active role by their state and local governments to promote internal improvements and to embrace other policies that would accelerate the southern rate of economic growth. To generate a sense of urgency southern newspapers, journals, economic leaders, and politicians continuously emphasized every new economic attainment of the North and every unrealized objective of the South, every northern advantage and every southern disadvantage. The abolitionist critique on the issue of development was lifted — lock, stock, and barrel — from southern editorials, speeches, and commercial proclamations, sometimes with acknowledgments (as in Olmsted), sometimes without (as in Helper).

The myth of southern backwardness and stagnation thus arose not because of any lack in the southern economic achievement but because the northern achievement was so remarkable, and because the continuous comparisons between the North and South were invariably unfavorable to the South. Compared with any country of Europe except England, however, the South's economic performance was quite strong. That comparison was never invoked by the abolitionists because it made the wrong point. It was rarely invoked by the Southerners because it would encourage complacency when urgency was called for.

Table 4.3 also shows that far from stagnating, per capita income was actually growing 30 percent more rapidly in the South than the North. The South's rate of growth was so rapid (1.7 percent per annum), that it constitutes *prima facie* evidence against the thesis that slavery retarded southern growth. Since few nations have achieved a rate of growth as high as 1.7 percent per annum over sustained periods, those who continue to advance the retardation thesis are implying that in the absence of slavery, the progress of the antebellum South would have exceeded virtually all recorded experience over the past 150 years. France, for example, experienced an average growth rate of 1.55 percent per annum over a 103–year period ending in 1960. Over similar periods the growth rate of the United Kingdom was 1.2 percent and Germany's was 1.43 percent. The long-term annual growth rate for the U.S. as a whole has averaged 1.6 percent. Only Sweden and Japan have been able to sustain long-term growth rates substantially in excess of that achieved by the antebellum South between 1840 and 1860.

When one disaggregates the southern rate of growth by subregions, it turns out that growth within each of the three subregions was less than the growth rate of the South as a whole. This is because part of the South's growth was due to the redistribution of southern population from the older states to the newer ones, particularly to Texas and the other rich states of the west central subregion. It will be noted that this subregion enjoyed an even higher level of per capita income than the Northeast. Approximately 30 percent of the annual growth in per capita income was due to the redistribution of population among subregions and the balance to the growth of per capita income within each of the sub-regions.

One scholar has recently argued that only the growth within subregions is meaningful, that the proportion of the growth rate which is due to the redistribution of the population from east to west is a statistical illusion that ought to be exorcised. The people within each subregion, he states, "could hardly see the realities, advantages, or even any meaning in such economic development."

This viewpoint reflects a fundamental misconception of the process of economic growth. The various industries or subregions of a nation never grow at even rates. Shifting demand for iron, for example, led the U.S. iron industry to grow much more rapidly than cotton textiles between 1842 and 1848, but much more slowly than textiles between 1848 and 1858. Technological progress also proceeds at uneven rates among industries and regions.

The capacity of an economy to grow depends not only on its luck in the marketplace, and its luck or creativity with respect to technological breakthroughs, but on the capacity of the economy to respond to such developments. The ability of an economy to shift labor and other resources from one sector or subregion to another is always a major determinant of its growth. This was true in the North as well as the South. Roughly 16 percent of the northern growth rate between 1840 and 1860 was due to the shift of labor and other resources from agriculture to manufacturing. In other words, if we consider only growth rates within sectors, the rate of growth of northern per capita income between 1840 and 1860 would have been not 1.3 percent but less than 1.1 percent.

To argue that the people within subregions "could hardly see the realities" of growth which could be obtained through shifts between subregions is to misunderstand completely...the dramatic shift of the slave population from a concentration along the Chesapeake Bay in 1790 to a concentration in the cotton belt in 1860. It is precisely because Southerners could perceive the benefits to be achieved from interregional migration, because they could perceive the "meaning in such economic development," that so many of them moved. The large share of the southern growth rate due to interregional migration underscores...the extreme flexibility of the slave economy and the ease with which it "adjusted to the rapidly changing labor requirements of various southern firms and localities."

Equally fallacious are the arguments that the skewed (unequal) income distribution of the South made its markets too small to support a large-scale, modern manufacturing industry, and reduced the rate of investment in physical capital by reducing savings. The assumption that the inequality of the southern income distribution lowered its aggregate savings rate is probably false. This assumption is based on the mistaken belief that large consumption expenditures by the rich necessarily imply low savings. In the fairly typical year of 1925, the per capita consumption of the top one percent of income earners in the United States was about $4,800, while that of the remaining 99 percent was under $550. Certainly this is a pronounced difference, and given normal human reactions this could (and did) lead to discussions of wasteful expenditures by the rich. Yet in 1925 the top one percent had a savings-income ratio of 42.9 percent, and accounted for over 50 percent of estimated personal savings. This suggests the possibility that the effects of large consumption expenditures on southern capital formation may be overstated. Whatever conspicuous consumption did exist was probably carried on mainly by planters who were wealthy by the standards of the times. Their conspicuous consumption probably absorbed only part of their incomes, and their savings rates were probably far in excess of the national average. Given what we now know about the relationship between income and savings, it is quite possible that savings in the South were higher than they would have been with a less skewed income distribution.

In any case, recent work on the southern wealth distribution reveals that previous scholars have generally exaggerated the degree of inequality. Certainly the...contention that 70 percent of nonslaveholding whites lived at the border of starvation is untenable. While the wealth distribution among southern farmers was more unequal than among northern farmers, it was less unequal than the wealth distribution in urban areas. Since the North had a much larger proportion of its population in the cities than in the country-side, the overall inequality of the wealth distribution was roughly the same above and below the Mason-Dixon line for the free populations.

This finding strikes at the heart of the claim that the skewed southern income distribution made the southern market too small to support large-scale manufacturing firms of the type which existed in the Northeast. Even if the income distribution had been more unequal than it was, the fact that planters purchased large quantities of clothing and shoes for slaves from northern firms suggests the existence of a large market for manufacturing goods on plantations. It can, indeed, be argued that the products ordered by planters were more standardized and amenable to mass production techniques than would have been the situation if slaves were themselves the source of demand.

Manufacturing appears to be the only area in which the antebellum South lagged seriously behind the North in physical capital formation. The South did not falter in the financing of railroad construction. The region had 31 percent of the nation's railroad mileage, with per capita mileage only slightly below the national average. This network was financed predominantly by indigenous capital. While the track-to-area ratio was lower in the South than in the rest of the nation, the southern economy was endowed with an unusually favorable system of navigable streams and rivers. Nor were planters lagging behind the rest of the nation in the application of machinery to farming. Expenditures on farming implements and machinery per improved acre were 25 percent higher in the seven leading cotton states than they were for the nation as a whole.

To draw the conclusion that the South was industrially backward, merely because it compared unfavorably with the North, is to repeat the error referred to in the discussion of income levels. Table 4.5 helps to put the South's position as an industrial nation into perspective. In railroad mileage per capita she was virtually tied with the North, and both were far ahead of their nearest competitor. As a manufacturer of cotton textiles, the South ranked sixth in the world, well below Great Britain and the northern United States, but ahead of Germany, Austria-Hungary, and Russia. Of the available indexes of industrial production, the South ranked poorly only in the output of pig iron, falling behind all of the leading nations of Western Europe. The poor showing in iron production, was, of course, due to the South's relatively meager endowments of iron ore and coal. Her resources in these minerals came nowhere near those of the North, Great Britain, France, or Belgium. Thus the South's lag behind the North in industrialization is fully consistent with the proposition that during the antebellum era the South's comparative advantage was in agriculture rather than in manufacturing.

Table 4.5 The Relative Level of Southern Industrialization in 1860 as Revealed by Three Partial Indexes (Southern index levels = 100)

	Index		
	Index of railroad mileage per capita	Index of cotton textile production per capita	Index of pig iron production per capita
South	100	100	100
North	108	401	637
Great Britain	43	1,055	2,728
France	16	136	425
Germany	21	87	231
Russia	1	26	60
Austria-Hungary	9	64	152
Italy	6	23	16
Netherlands	7	41	
Belgium	25	142	1,191
Denmark	5		
Sweden	9	92	779
Switzerland	28	270	
Spain	8	74	
Canada	68		
India	1	2	
Australia	21		

For the most part, it was natural resource endowments which gave the South a comparative advantage in agriculture. But the existence of slavery may also have played a role. To the extent that slavery permitted economies of large scale and raised agricultural productivity, it might have created an economic incentive to shift resources away from industry and into agriculture. But this is not a necessary consequence of the productivity gain. Similarly, while the gain in productivity might have raised southern per capita income, this too is not a necessary consequence of economies of scale. The resolution of these issues depends on the values of certain parameters of the demand and supply equations for cotton and other traded goods. The parameters are quite difficult to estimate. Preliminary work suggests that slavery both retarded industrialization and increased per capita income....

4–2. FRED BATEMAN AND THOMAS WEISS, "PROFITABILITY OF ANTEBELLUM SOUTHERN MANUFACTURING AND THE INVESTMENT RESPONSE"

To many critics, the peculiar conditions in southern product and input markets account for the region's poor industrial performance. Slave labor, with its presumed inefficiencies and its deterrence to the growth of a free work force, is perceived as creating one set of handicaps for producers. Both capital market imperfections and the obstacles to industrialization purportedly erected by planters fearful of change, would have increased production costs for southern manufacturers, making their economic success difficult or impossible. With these forces arrayed against them, and with the presumedly competitive conditions they faced in their product markets, the region's industrial producers would have earned rates of return below their northern and midwestern counterparts, as well as below the yields available in such alternative southern investments as cotton farming. According to this scheme of things, these relatively low rates of return would provide a straightforward explanation for the small size and apparent backwardness of the southern manufacturing sector; additional investment in manufacturing simply was not warranted economically. Southern investors, especially the wealthy planters, would have invested in the more remunerative agricultural operations, while profit-seeking nonsoutherners presumably would have chosen one of the more attractive alternatives within their own regions. Had cotton farming not been the most profitable alternative, or had some planters chosen to diversify their financial interests, there are some writers who think that manufacturing, because of its low rate of return, would still have been shunned....

There is scant evidence to support this. The explanation perforce is quite speculative given the lack of information on the magnitude of alternative returns. Generally, the argument has relied on an implicit assumption that returns in southern manufacturing were below some riskless alternative, and that the returns to cotton farming were equal to that riskless alternative.... The Graniteville Company paid dividends of 10 percent in the mid-fifties and 20 percent in 1860, while the Pendleton Company paid about 7 percent in the early 1850s. While no one can assert that William Gregg's company represented the entire industry, the evidence on his firm leaves some doubt about the purported unprofitability of South Carolina textile mills.

Adherents of a different explanation, one implying that slavery imposed none of these detrimental effects, argue that the overwhelming comparative advantage in cotton growing explains the predominance of agriculture and the limited magnitude of the manufacturing sector.... The question is not simply whether the South possessed a comparative advantage in cotton or some other crop, but whether that advantage was properly exploited given prevailing market conditions. To [Douglass C.] North, [Robert E.] Fogel and [Stanley L.]

Engerman, and others, economically rational southern investors responding appropriately to market signals had allocated resources appropriately.

Like the explanation based on peculiar market conditions, the comparative-advantage argument rests heavily on the estimates of profitability in slavery and slave-based agriculture. Direct evidence on manufacturing investments typically was not considered. Despite this limited perspective, most adherents of this view concluded that the southern economy was working well, implying that risk-adjusted returns were equalized across all investments....

In their study, Fogel and Engerman point out that earlier authors had neglected to consider all the relevant alternatives when evaluating slave investments, noting that the return to some industrial investments was higher than short-term interest rates. The evidence they had—namely, estimates for New England textile firms during the period from 1844 to 1853—suggested that manufacturing returns were equal to their revised estimates of slave profitability. They also considered the issue of comparative advantage and investment allocation from a different viewpoint, regarding the urban-rural distribution of slave labor as a proxy for industrialization, and slave labor investments as a proxy for southern capital in general.... On this basis Fogel and Engerman concluded that southern capital was allocated efficiently among economic sectors. While a conceptual improvement over previous analyses that focused on agriculture alone, this approach relies on a misleading proxy measure of the industrial slaves. In the antebellum economy, urbanization was not synonymous with industrialization anywhere, but especially not in the South. Considerable manufacturing activity occurred in rural environments. Furthermore, a substantial share of the urban slave labor force worked in personal service, not in manufacturing.

The plantation-slave system also has been held responsible for indirectly retarding industrialization by distorting economic signals. Adherents of this position view southern investors as responding rationally to market information that itself was biased by the slave system. In one version, the slave economy's income distribution generated a pattern of demand for manufactured goods that led to a narrowly based industrial system.... Douglass North, in a somewhat different variant, has claimed that the plantation system discouraged investment in social overhead capital, such as transportation, warehouses, and port facilities, which would have enhanced the development of manufacturing....

Not all historians believe that the market worked as well as the comparative advantage argument suggests. Others have proposed that the market functioned poorly and that the failure to industrialize sprang from an "irrationality" on the part of southern investors. They believe that slavery did not drive up the costs of production or hamper the development of domestic markets; instead, the region's investors simply did not respond appropriately to the potentially prosperous conditions in manufacturing. Victor Clark reported "a widespread popular prejudice against manufactures ... and a general disposition to regard the South as unfitted for large industrial undertakings."... The more common position equates this so-called investor irrationality with a desire to preserve slavery and the plantation life.... The primary cause of southern industrial retardation is presumed to be the institution of slavery, but here the argument follows a different path, one which should produce different observable results. The presumption is that manufacturing rates of return were persistently high over the long term because investors reacted insufficiently to reduce or eliminate the excess profits. In the absence of attractive alternatives within their own regions or countries, northerners, midwesterners, or foreigners, could have responded to these high yields. But the traditional argument stresses the failure of southern investors, most notably the cotton planters.

This explanation for the region's industrial backwardness, which is consistent with high rates of return and low levels of investment in manufacturing, has been supported by scattered evidence showing that manufacturing was indeed quite profitable. According to Joseph Robert... and James Hopkins..., the tobacco and hemp industries were apparently thriving. And [Robert] Starobin…has shown that textile manufacturing, iron manufacturing, and rice milling were as profitable as the available alternatives. Some individual producers such as Graniteville, Pendleton, and Tredegar are often cited as examples of what other southern enterprises could have been. Like that of failure, however, this evidence of success is incomplete and of unknown representativeness. The validity of any of these conflicting views hinges on empirical evidence describing the returns to manufacturing and its alternatives. The remainder of this [essay]…provides the first published comprehensive estimates of industrial rates of return, data on which so many historical hypotheses must hinge.

New Evidence on Profitability

An important aspect of this new evidence on the profitability of southern manufacturing is its reflection of the performance of an enormously large number of producers representing all the major antebellum industries. These profitability measures are conceptually identical for these firms and industries, permitting for the first time a comprehensive view of the economic fortunes of varied industries throughout the antebellum South. The census manuscript samples furnish the needed data on capital invested, output value, value of raw material inputs, and wages paid. These figures, which formed the core of our calculations, were supplemented by estimates of depreciation, unreported capital, and miscellaneous costs calculated from evidence obtained from other sources.

The statistics for each firm were combined using the formula below to derive the ratio of net earnings to gross assets. This calculation of the rate of return (r) rests on the assumption that manufacturers made the maintenance and capital replacement expenditures necessary

$$r = \frac{P - (R + W + M + D)}{K_C + K_A}$$

to keep the assets operating perpetually.

The denominator on the right-hand side is the capital investment (K), which consists of two components:

K_C = value of capital invested in business as reported in the census.

K_A = estimate of capital invested in business but unreported in the census (i.e., working capital).

The numerator represents the earnings (E) of the firm, determined by the following variables:

P = value of products (obtained from manuscript census sample).

R = value of raw materials used (obtained from manuscript census sample).

W = wage bill (obtained from manuscript census sample as the reported monthly wage times twelve months).

M = miscellaneous costs (includes maintenance, insurance, rent, contract work, taxes, and sundry expenses not elsewhere specified).

D = depreciation.

…The estimated rates of return are presented in Table 4.6 for the major southern industries, and in Table 4.7 by state and region for all industries combined. The results, which represent the mean of the rates of return earned by the sample firms in each state or industry, are surprising. Manufacturers in almost every industry and state were earning high rates. In all, 130 observations exist (66 in 1850; 64 in 1860) but not all results are reported in the tables. Of the total, however, only a few industries earned a return of 10 percent or less, and most of those were unimportant at that time. Among the major industries, rates ranged upward to around 40 percent. Some less important industries earned even higher returns, as did liquor distilling in 1850 and 1860, and cooperage and meatpacking in 1860. The average for all southern manufacturing was 28 percent in 1860, and 25 percent in

Table 4.6 Mean Rates of Return in Southern Manufacturing, by Industry, 1850 and 1860

Industry	1850	1860
Agricultural implements	n.a.	.20
(9, 40)	(.07)	
Blacksmithing	.21	.32
(213, 119)	(.04)	(.04)
Boots and shoes	.33	.30
(90, 107)	(.06)	(.04)
Brickmaking	.21	.10
(17, 17)	(.07)	(.08)
Clothing	.13	.17
(27, 171)	(.07)	(.10)
Combined milling	.15	.16
(155, 102)	(.03)	(.02)
Cooperage	.26	.57
(18, 12)	(.12)	(.24)
Cotton textiles	−.01	n.a.
(16, 9)	(.05)	
Flour milling	.16	.24
(171, 320)	(.03)	(.02)
Furniture	.24	.16
(74, 36)	(.06)	(.07)
Iron	.24	.38
(27, 23)	(.09)	(.10)
Leather tanning	.27	.22
(196, 133)	(.03)	(.04)
Machinery	.25	.40
(21, 15)	(.08)	(.08)
Meat packing	n.a.	.81
(7, 10)	(.23)	
Printing	n.a.	.35
(3, 17)	(.10)	
Saddlery and harness	.35	.23
(93, 71)	(.07)	(.05)
Sawmilling	.25	.36
(335, 422)	(.03)	(.02)
Tin, copper, and sheet iron	.40	.41
(33, 31)	(.08)	(.10)
Turpentine, tar	.22	.26
(23, 70)	(.10)	(.05)
Wagons, carts, and carriages	.30	.30
(86, 87)	(.04)	(.05)
Woolen textiles	.12	.14
(11, 39)	(.07)	(.09)
All industries	.25	.28
(1951, 1940)	(.01)	(.01)

Figures in parentheses below industry names are the number of firms included in the sample, the first for 1850, the second for 1860. Figures in parentheses below rates are the standard errors.

1850. The typical investor would have recouped his original outlay in 3.5 to 4 years, a feat that even the most conservative could have viewed enthusiastically.

On a state and regional basis (Table 4.7), the returns appear equally lofty. Regionally, they are fairly uniform. In 1850 only in the more prosperous "Other New South" region were producers garnering a substantially higher return than those elsewhere, whereas in 1860 only in the Old South was the average notably below that in the other regions. The range of state returns was wider than for regional returns, from 19 to 38 percent in 1850, and from 20 to 42 percent in 1860. Compared with the other states, South Carolina stands

Table 4.7 Mean Rates of Return in Southern Manufacturing, by State and Region, 1850 and 1860

State and Region	1850	1860
Alluvial	.26	.32
	(.03)	(.03)
Arkansas	.28	.42
	(.05)	(.06)
Mississippi	.25	.28
	(.05)	(.03)
Other New South	.31	.33
	(.02)	(.02)
Alabama	.21	.25
	(.04)	(.03)
Florida	.31	.32
	(.06)	(.05)
Texas	.38	.41
	(.03)	(.04)
Old South	.24	.20
	(.04)	(.02)
South Carolina	.24	.20
	(.04)	(.02)
Upper South .	.22	.25
	(.01)	(.01)
Kentucky	.19	.25
	(.03)	(.03)
North Carolina	.22	.23
	(.03)	(.02)
Tennessee	.31	.41
	(.03)	(.06)
Virginia	.16	.21
	(.02)	(.02)
Weighted Mean for the South	.22	.26

out as the only state where the mean rate of return failed to increase between 1850 and 1860.... South Carolina's inertia is not surprising. That all other states show a different pattern suggests that South Carolina is not regionally representative. When one examines the growth of manufacturing output and investment over the 1850s, South Carolina is the only southern state where per capita manufacturing output declined relative to the country as a whole. Perhaps the pessimism expressed by others regarding the poor opportunities for southern industrialization reflects excessive emphasis on the conditions of this atypical state.

The pervasiveness of such high rates throughout the region is as impressive as the average level. Not merely were such well-known manufactories as the Tredegar Iron Works or the Graniteville Company reaping sizable profits; so were such unheralded establishments as Hugh Moore's sash, door, and blind factory in Alabama, John Odell's mill in South Carolina, and Sylvanus Johnson's flour mill in Virginia. Industrial producers in a few states and industries were realizing fairly low rates of return, but more typically the earnings for most industries within a state were quite high.

Obviously some portion of these measured returns may represent the owner's implicit wage and not part of the return to capital. Unfortunately, because the census did not require owners to report these implicit costs, this item is unreported for some firms but included in the total wage bill for others. For small enterprises operated by the owner with the assistance of a few employees, the owner's salary would constitute a substantial share of total costs. Any underreporting of these costs obviously would overstate measured rates of return. That some owners reported their own wage while others did not, further contributes to the variation in rates of return, particularly for industries heavily populated by small producers.

Nevertheless, adjusting the profits for each firm by imputing an implicit owner's wage would be a questionable procedure. It cannot be argued that all owners were foregoing income. In many cases their main livelihood came from farming; their manufacturing operation represented but a small adjunct to their primary economic interest. In 1860, about one-third of the manufacturers reported their occupation as farmer, and many others owned farms. At least half of the manufacturers were not fully engaged in manufacturing. Thus, a general imputation would be inappropriate, especially for blacksmiths, millers, and coopers, where the calculations would be particularly sensitive to this adjustment. Finally, some of the owners doubtless did report their wage, and many who did not, actually may have had no hand in the operation. Rather than adjust for this factor, we chose a different alternative. To obtain the more relevant and perhaps more precise return to capital figure, only larger firms' returns were calculated. The advantage of this approach is that, if unreported, the owner's income would have represented a smaller fraction of costs and hence not greatly biased the estimated returns. These enterprises also more closely approximate the kind of investments deemed important to regional industrialization. Those who have argued that the South should have had more manufacturing, surely did not mean only more craft operations such as blacksmithing or harness-making. What was desired were the antebellum counterparts to today's "growth industries." Historical studies of northern industrialization stress such industries as textiles, machinery, and iron production, particularly with emphasis on factory production, as favorable to regional development. Thus, the evidence on the returns to large-size units will show more clearly the prospects for this type of production in the antebellum South.

The resultant large-firm estimates presented by industry (Table 4.8) are for firms with a capital investment of $5,000 or more. On average, the returns lie somewhat below those for producers of all sizes. In 1850, the large-size firms earned a return of 19 percent compared with 25 percent for all firms, whereas in 1860 the respective figures were 22

Table 4.8 Rates of Return for Large-Size Southern Firms

Industry	1850	1860
Combined milling	.12	.08
(26, 40)	(.02)	(.03)
Flour milling	.07	.30
(29, 62)	(.07)	(.05)
Iron	.15	.23
(16, 17)	(.10)	(.11)
Leather tanning	.23	.16
(11, 14)	(.08)	(.04)
Machinery	n.a.	.43
(6, 12)	(.08)	
Sawmilling	.43	.27
(53, 98)	(.09)	(.04)
Textiles	.08	.17
(16, 13)	(.03)	(.05)
Tobacco products	n.a.	-.03
(2, 19)	(.04)	
Turpentine & tar	n.a.	.08
(1, 17)	(.07)	
Wagons, carts, & carriages	n.a.	.38
(6, 12)	(.08)	
All industries	.19	.22
(248, 392)	(.03)	(.02)

and 28 percent. These are still high returns, which imply that profitable opportunities of a developmental and capitalistic sort existed in a variety of industries in 1850 and 1860, especially those that traditionally have been viewed as important to industrialization. In 1860, the return in textiles was 17 percent; in machinery production, 43 percent; and in iron manufacturing, 23 percent. Outstanding returns were also earned in such ubiquitous industries as sawmilling and flour milling. The estimates for 1850 similarly document a sizable number of industries in which large establishments realized substantial yields.

Conceivably the aggregate number of these industrial opportunities was too small to create an environment conducive to sustained industrialization. Opportunities simply may not have been highly visible to potential investors. Only one-fifth of all manufacturing enterprises fit this large-size category; although three-fourths of these were earning returns significantly above 10 percent, the total number of such producers approximated 3,000. Scattered throughout the region such opportunities perhaps went largely unnoticed. But it seems more plausible to accept the view espoused by Eugene Genovese and others: that the opportunities existed and were known, but that investors chose to ignore them.

Comparison with Alternative Returns

All informed southern investors surely did not ignore these high rates of return without considering the available alternatives. Some planters obviously raised their level of consumption rather than save and invest in industry, but others obviously considered manufacturing and still chose to invest elsewhere. Indeed, the growing body of literature on slave profitability has suggested that wealthy southerners were quite adept at allocating their capital. Planters bought and sold assets, and if necessary, relocated in order to obtain higher yields. Although there has been debate on these matters, when southern slave investments were viewed in isolation, the region's investment market appears to have worked well.

Our new evidence on manufacturing profitability casts a different light on the behavior of the southern economy. Compared to alternatives available within the region (Table 4.9), the industrial rates of return were not simply high, they were substantially above the returns earned from slavery and slave-based farming....

Relative to slave and agricultural investments, the returns to manufacturing are nearly three times as high as the Fogel-Engerman estimate. These results are startling in light of the accumulating opinion that the market system of 1860 appears to have been working well. If the economy and the manufacturing industries were purely competitive, with unblocked entry, and if the economy were at equilibrium—as realistically it probably was not—these large divergences should not have existed. Clearly there should have been additional manufacturing investment. This new evidence thus raises serious questions about the behavior of planter-investors. There are valid reasons why the market forces

Table 4.9 Rates of Return in Alternative Southern Investments (percentages)

Farm-Slave Return	Best Estimate
Cotton, historical average	5.7
Cotton, current year	10.0
Rice, current year	-3.8
Slave hiring	10.4
Cotton land & capital	10.6

Table 4.10 Manufacturing Rates of Return, by Region, 1850 and 1860

Region	Rate of Return for All Firms		Rate of Return for Large-Size Firms	
	1850	1860	1850	1860
South	.25	.28	.19	.22
	(.01)	(.01)	(.03)	(.02)
East	.18	.22	.13	.20
	(.01)	(.01)	(.01)	(.02)
West	.26	.25	.25	.21
	(.02)	(.01)	(.02)	(.02)
United States	.22	.25	.17	.21
	(.01)	(.01)	(.01)	(.01)

might not have equalized intersectoral returns, but as will be seen below, the southern response nevertheless was woefully inadequate.

The high returns to industry were not unique to this region (see Table 4.10). Rates earned elsewhere show that industrial investors outside the South, who potentially might have responded to the high southern yields, actually had little incentive to choose southern industry over opportunities closer to home. In both 1850 and 1860, the return for all eastern firms was below that in either the West or South, but probably not by enough to compensate for risk attributable to distant investment. Westerners clearly had no incentive to invest in the South; manufacturing enterprises in their region were earning a slightly higher return in 1850 and one only slightly below in 1860. When the evidence is confined to larger producers, the regional differences are virtually eliminated in 1860. Only the 1850 western return stood considerably above that elsewhere, possibly only a statistical quirk due to small sample size. Southern industrial returns were neither low enough to induce southerners to invest elsewhere nor relatively high enough to attract "foreign" capital from other regions.

The Southern Investment Response

The high rates of return common in many southern industries—particularly among the larger firms where unquestionably the return to capital exceeded alternative yields --present a picture at variance with that derived from the agricultural returns alone. Not only do these rates suggest that the southern economy was not performing as well as it should, they also indicate that investors in other regions had no incentive to invest in southern manufacturing, because the returns in their home areas were equally attractive. Conversely, southerners had no apparent reason to invest in industry elsewhere. The intersectoral divergences in yields throughout all regions imply that by market standards, the level of industrialization was too low everywhere, but a more detailed examination of the South indicates that the adjustment process was proceeding more slowly there than elsewhere.

Within the South, the actual response was even more deficient than the profit differentials imply. The inequality of returns was not a one-year phenomenon, but perhaps persisted for a period of at least ten years; and if anything, the variance between the manufacturing and agricultural returns widened during the 1850s. This pattern emerges quite clearly when industrial and agricultural returns are compared on a regional basis. In 1850, the ratio of the manufacturing to the agricultural return was 2.0 in the Alluvial region, 3.4 in the Other New South, 2.4 in the Old South, and 2.2 in the Upper South. By 1860 these ratios were higher in three regions: 2.9 in the Alluvial, 2.5 in the Old South, and 2.5 in the Upper South. Only in the Other New South did the ratio decline....

The persistent and widening differences among returns may be attributable to several forces: lags in the flow of information, market imperfections, or negative expectations regarding the stability of the future profit stream among sectors. Or we may simply be observing two disequilibrium situations. Rapid increases in the demand for manufactured goods, concurrent with technological progress, conceivably worked to raise manufacturing returns more rapidly than additional investment and growing competition were lowering them. But even were this true, it would not be an adequate justification for the performance of the southern economy. The southern response was not only deficient, it was distorted.

If the economy had been functioning properly, but had not adjusted fully, the differences in rates of return would indicate at least the direction in which investment should have gone. Capital investment should have expanded more rapidly in the industries, sectors, or states where higher returns prevailed than in those with lower returns. While differing adjustments in capital accumulation may not have sufficed to equalize returns over a year or even a decade, capital resources should have flowed more rapidly into the higher-yielding alternatives. Southern manufacturing, however, fared poorly even when judged according to this incomplete adjustment standard. We evaluated the southern performance against this standard by testing across states and regions for a correlation between the values of the ratios of manufacturing to agricultural profitability in 1850, against the values of the ratios of the percentage increases in manufacturing and agricultural capital occurring between 1850 and 1860. By using the sectoral ratios rather than only manufacturing returns and investment, the test minimizes the impact of differential growth rates of population and income among the states. These forces would have induced investment in both agriculture and manufacturing. Thus, this approach allows us to focus on the net effect in those areas where the rates of return were higher. As an example, because the 1850 sectoral profitability ratio in Texas exceeded that in Mississippi, it would be expected that the percentage increase in manufacturing capital relative to the increase in agricultural capital would have been higher in the former than in the latter.

The results of the test clearly demonstrated the deficiencies of the southern response. First, the correlation between the ratios of profitability and the ratios of investment was quite low. Furthermore, in each of the four regions and in eight of the ten states, the percentage increase in agricultural capital exceeded that in manufacturing, clearly not in accord with the pattern anticipated on the basis of the relative rates of return among the sectors.

Examining changes in output rather than capital reveals an even more deficient adjustment response. Over the decade 1850–60, only three of the ten slave states saw an increase in manufacturing output that exceeded the rise in the quantity of the chief agricultural staple in each southern state; and one of the three was South Carolina, in which the primary commercial crop, rice, was a declining one. In fact, only in Florida, Texas, and Virginia did the value of industrial output increase faster than the quantity of wheat produced.

The nature of the southern reaction can be appreciated more fully by examining the behavior of investors in other regions, where in general the responses conformed more closely to the pattern that should emerge given the sectoral rates of return. In these areas, where agricultural returns lay below manufacturing returns in 1850, there should have been a larger percentage increase in manufacturing capital than in agricultural over the ensuing decade. Such a response did occur in both the Northeast and West. Of the sixteen nonsouthern states for which data are available, only in four did the agricultural capital stock expand by more than the manufacturing stock. Measured by output, in three of six midwestern states, and for the Midwest as a whole, manufacturing levels increased more rapidly than did the production of wheat, the region's chief export....

The observed adjustment deficiency supports the contention that under slavery the South had not industrialized as fully as possible. The reasons propounded to verify the

South's alleged underdevelopment were not all correct, but given these estimates those reasons have definite credibility. The high rates of return indicate an inefficient economic performance in the South, although equally high returns in other regions suggest that the southern record was not unique....

Using completely different sources, Lance Davis reached remarkably similar conclusions to those inferred by our profit estimates:

> Capital can be said to be immobile if savers are unwilling or unable to make their accumulations available to capital users whose activities yield the highest economic return. Such a failure can occur if there are no effective capital markets, if savers value safety above all else, if they are unwilling to invest their savings in enterprises divorced from their personal experience, or if there are substantial noneconomic rewards to investments whose economic yields are very low. ... Immobile capital seems to be characteristic of most newly developing economies. ... In the United States, such immobilities distorted the pattern of growth throughout the entire nineteenth century....

...[E]vidence that we have compiled supports the position that the inadequate investment response largely reflected the behavior of the planter class. Even though they formed only one-fifth of the free southern population, they exercised a disproportionate influence as they strived to maintain the status of their vested interest, the slave system. Since the preservation of slavery was believed to depend on agricultural success, the planters allegedly retarded industrialization lest it weaken their economic and social position. To some extent the apparently retarding influences were a corollary to the successful exploitation of the region's comparative advantage. The credit and transport systems designed to serve the cotton trade, although not consciously created to prevent the growth of manufacturing, nevertheless may have worked to that end. On the other hand... planters have been viewed as having consciously ignored the signals indicating that the market justified more manufacturing.

Not all planters expressed an exclusivist preference for nonindustrial investments.... Several planters were among the leading industrialists in their states. J. J. Ward, possessing one of the largest slaveholdings in the South, was also one of the twenty largest manufacturers in South Carolina. Approximately one-half of the top twenty firms in most states were owned by planters or large slaveholders. For these men, their industrial investment dominated their agricultural, so although they had substantial farm interests, they were not planters primarily. They, however, were exceptions.

More generally, less than one-fifth of the manufacturers were planters; conversely, only 6 percent of all planters owned manufacturing assets. The data in Table 4.11 reflect the extent to which planters participated directly in manufacturing, as demonstrated by their

Table 4.11 Share of Manufacturers Owning a Plantation, by State, 1860

State	Planters		
	Narrowly Defined	Broadly Defined	Slaveowners (20 or more slaves)
Alabama	.096	.193	.095
Arkansas	.113	.259	.080
Florida	.103	.172	.187
Kentucky	.037	.164	.014
Mississippi	.103	.182	.036
North Carolina	.189	.465	.194
South Carolina	.364	.487	.186
Texas	.080	.168	.046
Virginia	.138	.324	.096
Mean	**.131**	**.266**	**.096**

inclusion in the census of manufacturers as owners of industrial firms. Some other planters may have invested in manufacturing indirectly through the purchase of stock, but such investment was not significant during this period. The figures given here are unlikely to understate the true level of participation.

Measures of the proportion of planters who also owned industrial firms is equally revealing.... Only 6 percent of the wealthy slaveowners, those owning twenty or more slaves, invested any capital in manufacturing. In all but three states, Arkansas, North Carolina, and Virginia, the share of large slaveowners who owned firms fell below 5 percent.

To those planters who did engage in manufacturing, their industrial investment clearly was of secondary importance. In every southern state, the value of the planter's agricultural capital exceeded his manufacturing investment, almost always by a margin in excess of 4 to l. Only in Kentucky, where the average manufacturing investment was approximately $11,000 and the average plantation investment $18,000, were the two even near equality. Elsewhere, the greater relative importance of the agricultural investment ranged from being 4 times larger in Texas to nearly 11 times greater in Mississippi. This stands in contrast to the pattern for other farmers who were engaged in manufacturing. For the large-scale food producers, the comparative importance of the agricultural investment was generally less than 3 to 1, while for those who owned smaller farms the relative levels of the alternative investments were about equal or else favored manufacturing. This is not surprising because the farm investments were small by definition, and to be included in the census, the manufacturing capitalization would have had to exceed the level needed to produce $500 of output.

Not only in this relative sense, however, do the planters' investments appear inconsequential, for a similar picture emerges when the absolute values are considered. The average industrial investment made by planters and other farmers, and the mean size of a manufacturing establishment is indicated in Table 4.12. Only in Arkansas and Kentucky did the typical planter invest substantially more than the mean capital level of a manufacturing enterprise. Elsewhere, the planter investment nearly equaled or fell below that in the average firm. Indeed, the picture described is somewhat favorable to the planters, since it pertains to the group as narrowly defined. If the larger group were considered, the manufacturing interests of this class appear even less noteworthy, because the smaller-sized staple farmers typically invested less in industry than did the highly specialized planter. And, as these data reveal, those who produced food crops on large-sized farms often held a smaller industrial investment than did the planters.

Table 4.12 Capital Invested in Manufacturing by Southern Farmers, 1860

State	Capital Size of Average Firm (thousands of Dollars)	Average Investment (thousands of dollars)		
		Planters	Large-Scale Food Producers	Smaller Farm Owners
Alabama	6.2	1.1	1.3	4.8
Arkansas	2.6	5.6	3.6	3.3
Florida	11.8	2.5	3.8	1.2
Kentucky	5.9	11.0	9.5	1.7
Mississippi	4.5	4.0	3.2	2.6
North Carolina	2.6	2.7	2.1	1.7
South Carolina	5.6	1.5	8.2	4.5
Texas	3.3	3.9	13.7	2.5
Virginia	5.0	4.3	4.0	1.3

Table 4.13 Share of Manufacturing Capital Owned by Farmer-Industrialists, 1860

	All Farmer-Industrialists	Planters (narrowly defined)	Large-Scale Food Producers	Other Farmers
Alabama	.39	.07	.15	.17
Arkansas	.42	.13	.08	.21
Florida	.06	.02	.03	.01
Kentucky	.14	.07	.02	.05
Mississippi	.24	.09	.02	.13
North Carolina	.58	.20	.22	.16
South Carolina	.66	.29	.17	.20
Texas	.54	.09	.24	.21
Virginia	.27	.12	.11	.04
Weighted average	**.33**	**.12**	**.11**	**.10**

Even less involved in manufacturing than either the planters or the large-scale food producers were the small-farm owners. Although the industrial investment of a member of this class was generally as large as its agricultural stake, in absolute terms neither was very significant. Only in Arkansas did the smaller farmers have an industrial investment exceeding the average capital value of a manufacturing establishment. Given their typically meager economic position, the low level of their manufacturing capital is predictable.

This investment pattern illustrates the nature of the capital problem that beset industrialization. The development of southern manufacturing appears to have been retarded by a general inability to transfer capital out of agriculture. Nonplanter southern farmers made only modest contributions, while planters typically held larger industrial investments. However, the planter class posed a peculiar problem. The higher level of the planter's manufacturing investment was a function of greater wealth, not an expression of a stronger preference for manufacturing. Indeed, for the typical planter, the agricultural interest dominated his manufacturing investment. Southern industrialization therefore had to cope with two retardant forces: a general incapacity or unwillingness to transfer resources out of agriculture, and a specific lack of interest on the part of those with substantial amounts of wealth to invest.

The extent to which the agricultural class engaged in manufacturing can be gauged by examining the share of all southern manufacturing assets held by those who also owned farms. The distribution of ownership among various categories of farmers (Table 4.13) shows that in the aggregate only one-third of the manufacturing capital was held by a farmer of any type, while the planter class on average owned only 12 percent. The other wealthy group, the large-scale food producers, claimed a share in industry virtually identical to that of the planters. Combined, these two classes of wealthy farmers owned approximately one-fourth of the region's capital.

The amount of industrial capital held by farmers and planters varied widely across states. In Florida, the planters possessed a mere 2 percent, while in the Carolinas they owned 20 percent or more of the manufacturing sector. There appears to be no pattern to the variation. It does not seem, as one might expect, that planters in the older states of the South owned a larger share of manufacturing because they were more established and had enjoyed a longer time span in which to diversify. The planters of Virginia did not own significantly more than their counterparts in Arkansas, Mississippi, and Texas. Actually, on a broader level, several of the newer cotton states showed greater ownership shares among farmers of all types than did Virginia. In Alabama, Arkansas, and Texas, 40 to 50 percent of the manufacturing capital was in the hands of farmers. Some of this, however, may be merely a statistical phenomenon. In Texas, for example, a handful of men—125 planters—owned one-third of a small industrial sector. More likely, it indicates that agriculture was the dominant source of all capital in these newer states....

There emerges a picture in which the planters and slaveholders, the chief potential source of capital within the South, failed to participate adequately in the development of manufacturing. This failure was crucial to the South, for these wealthy southerners were in a position to shift resources from the agricultural to the industrial sector. The unequal distribution of agricultural income and wealth that many historians associate with the plantation system probably gave the South an unusually great potential for accomplishing the industrial transformation. Unfortunately, only a small link was ever forged, and this despite the high returns available to those willing to invest in manufacturing.

SUGGESTIONS FOR FURTHER READING

John Blassingame, *The Slave Community: Plantation Life in the Antebellum South* (1972).

William Calderhead, "How Extensive was the Border State Slave Trade? A New Look," *Civil War History*, XVIII(1972), 42–55.

Alfred Conrad and John Meyer, "The Economics of Slavery in the Antebellum South," *Journal of Political Economy*, 66(1958), 95-130.

Paul A. David, Herbert Gutman, Richard Sutch, Peter Temin, and Gavin Wright, *Reckoning with Slavery* (1976).

Paul A. David and Peter Temin, "Slavery: The Progressive Institution?" *Journal of Economic History*, 34(1974), 739-783.

Frederick Douglass, *Narrative of the Life of Frederick Douglass* (1993).

Stanley M. Elkins, *Slavery* (1959).

Heywood Fleisig, "Slavery, the Supply of Agricultural Labor, and the Industrialization of the South," *Journal of Economic History*, 36(1976), 572-597.

Robert W. Fogel, "Three Phases of Cliometric Research on Slavery and Its Aftermath," *American Economic Review*, 65(1975), 37-46.

——, *Without Consent or Contract: The Rise and Fall of American Slavery* (1989).

—— and Stanley L. Engerman, "Explaining the Relative Efficiency of Slave Agriculture in the Antebellum South," *American Economic Review*, 67(1977), 275-296.

——, "The Relative Efficiency of Slavery: A Comparison of Northern and Southern Agriculture in 1860," *Explorations in Economic History*, 8(1971), 353-367.

Eugene D. Genovese, *Roll, Jordan, Roll: The World the Slaves Made* (1976).

——, *The Political Economy of Slavery* (1965).

Claudia Goldin, *Urban Slavery in the American South* (1976).

Lewis Gray, *History of Agriculture in the Southern United States to 1860* (1933).

Gerald Gunderson, "Southern Antebellum Income Reconsidered," *Explorations in Economic History*, 10(1973) 151-176.

Herbert G. Gutman, *Slavery and the Numbers Game: A Critique of Time on the Cross* (1975).

James Oakes, *The Ruling Race: A History of American Slaveholders* (1982).

William Parker, ed., *The Structure of the Cotton Economy of the Antebellum South* (1970).

Ulrich B. Phillips, *Life and Labor in the Old South* (1929).

——, The Economic Cost of Slaveholding in the Cotton Belt," *Political Science Quarterly*, 20(1905), 257-275.

Roger L. Ransom, *Conflict and Compromise: The Political Economy of Slavery, Emancipation, and the American Civil War* (1989).

Kenneth M. Stampp, *The Peculiar Institution: Slavery in the Antebellum South* (1956).

Richard Sutch, "The Treatment Received by American Slaves: A Critical Review of the Evidence Presented in *Time on the Cross*," *Explorations in Economic History*, 12(1975), 335-348.

Robert P. Thomas and Richard N. Bean, "The Fishers of Men: The Profits of the Slave Trade," *Journal of Economic History*, 34(1974), 885-914.

Richard K. Vedder, "The Slave Exploitation (Expropriation) Rate," *Explorations in Economic History*, 12(1975), 453-458.

Richard C. Wade, *Slavery in the Cities: The South, 1820-1860* (1964).

Gavin Wright, *The Political Economy of the Cotton South: Households, Markets, and Wealth in the Nineteenth Century* (1978).

CHAPTER 5

Labor in Industrializing America

INTRODUCTION

Work was a central feature of early American life. For many colonial Americans their very survival in the New World was directly linked to labor—carving farmland out of the wilderness, constructing shelter from the materials provided by the forests and fields, eking out a living from the natural environment. But work also held deeper meanings for early Americans. In the market economy of the early Republic the work individuals performed defined their place in their community. Skilled artisans and craftsmen were accorded a higher status than unskilled laborers. Additionally, the Protestant Work Ethic taught that labor was a means to salvation. Through their work individuals learned the discipline which allowed them to lead spiritual and moral lives. But perhaps most importantly, labor was the means by which generations of early Americans realized the new nation's promise of economic opportunity and upward mobility. All of these certitudes were challenged by the rise of industrialism in the early decades of the 19th Century.

The American factory system of production began in 1813 when Francis Cabot Lowell founded the Boston Manufacturing Company and the following year, opened a cotton textile mill in Waltham, Massachusetts. The Boston Manufacturing Company raised capital to build the mill and equip it with power looms through the sale of stock. To staff the large mill the company hired thousands of young, single, mostly female workers from the surrounding farms and villages and housed them in company-owned dormitories. The mill's initial success was so great that seven years after it began operations Boston Manufacturing Company paid investors a 27.5 percent dividend. The success of this first textile mill encouraged the Boston Manufacturing Company to establish Lowell, Massachusetts in 1822 where it built a complex of nine textile factories. The Lowell Factory System, as it came to be known, by utilizing innovative methods to raise capital and to assemble a sizable labor force, and by demonstrating the value of economies of scale in production, helped to spur the industrial revolution that transformed the American economy.

The rise and expansion of the Lowell Factory System posed a series of new and increasingly disturbing challenges to Americans' notions of labor. Because much of industrial work was now done by machines, the skills of many laboring people were substantially devalued. Practically anyone could learn the simple tasks required to operate the factory machinery which, together with the increased number of children and women working in factories, depressed wages. Laborers also lost an enormous amount of the autonomy they had formerly enjoyed over their work lives. With the rise of factories laborers no longer controlled the hours they worked, the wages they earned, or the conditions under which they toiled. The factory system of production also challenged the classical economic belief that there was no such thing as involuntary unemployment for when mills shut down during slow economic times able-bodied willing laborers were left to fend for themselves. And as workers increasingly organized labor unions to address their difficulties in the world of factory work, older notions of the autonomy of individual workers were upset.

The changes in labor brought about by the factory system also raised serious questions to antebellum Americans about the meaning of their nation. As industrialization widened the gap between the rich and the poor, many wondered if the United States could still be regarded as a land of economic opportunity. Did the truth that the Declaration of Independence held to be self-evident, "that all men are created equal," still apply to industrializing America? Was hard work still the path to upward economic mobility? Were the material conditions of northern factory workers better than that of southern slaves? In all of these ways, then, the industrialization of the economy which began with the Boston Manufacturing Company touched off a wide-ranging reassessment of fundamental values and institutions that dominated American life for the remainder of the 19th Century.

In thinking about labor in industrializing America consider the material conditions of working people. What impact did the rise of factories have on wages? Did industrialization contribute to a long-term increase in wages over the course of the 19th Century? Did industrialization promote economic inequality by increasing the premium paid for skilled labor? How was a worker's standard of living affected by industrialization? Does the evidence support the contention of antebellum southern planters that northern factory workers were "wage slaves?" Did industrializing America continue to be a land of economic opportunity for all?

DOCUMENTS

The rise of factories in industrializing America led to a sharp increase in the number of young children employed outside the home, a trend that deeply disturbed many Americans. Not only were these child laborers forced to work long hours for minimal pay, but their employment also deprived them of formal education which often condemned them to a life of hardship. Documents 5–1, 5–2, and 5–3 reveal different aspects of child labor in the early 19th Century. Documents 5–1 and 5–2 are advertisements placed by employers seeking the return of apprentices who had run away. Document 5–3, an 1832 report of an investigation into child labor in New England textile mills, detailed the arduous conditions they faced.

Documents 5–4, 5–5, and 5–6 provide evidence of the working conditions and living standards of factory workers in the 1830s. Document 5–4 was an appeal made to the public by striking journeyman bakers to boycott those employers who had refused their wage demands. In Document 5–5 cotton textile workers in Manayunk, a mill town along the Schuylkill River outside of Philadelphia, described their working conditions. Striking Philadelphia carpenters who sought a wage increase of $0.25 defend their claim in Document 5–6 with a detailed accounting of their cost of living in 1851.

The final two documents describe aspects of labor in the Lowell textile factories. Document 5–7 is a critical appraisal of the factory system made in 1846 by an advocate of labor unions. Document 5–8 provides an account of the sometimes questionable means that Lowell mills used to recruit young women as laborers.

5–1. "FORTY DOLLARS REWARD"

Ran away from the subscriber an indented apprentice to the Cordwainer's business, named John Donnelly, about 18 years of age, thin visage, light complexion, remarkably freckled, uncommonly so on his face, hands and body, and has a large mark on his right or left side, occasioned by the shingles. His hair is sandy colored, and he is about 5 feet, 7 inches high. He took away with him a long blue coat, 1 pair dark mixture trousers, 1 pair white pantaloons, 1 white waistcoat and other clothing. $20 will be paid for him if lodged in any jail where the subcriber may again obtain him, or $40 if brought home to the subscriber. It is expected that he will endeavor to go to sea. Captains of vessels and all other persons are warned not to receive or harbor said runaway at their peril, as they will be dealt with in such cases according to law.

Jeremiah Degrass, No. 355 South Second Street.

5–2. "ONE CENT REWARD"

Ran away on the 9th of October last, an indented apprentice to the Whip and Cane business, named David R. Cole. The above reward will be paid for his apprehension, but no charges. All persons are forbid [sic.] harboring him at their peril.

George W. Burgess

5–3. "REPORT OF COMMITTEE ON EDUCATION"

The Committee appointed to take into consideration the subject of the education of children in manufacturing districts...beg leave to report:

That from statements of facts made to your committee by delegates to this body, the number of youth and children of both sexes under sixteen years of age employed in manufactories constitute about two-fifths of the whole number of persons employed. From the returns from a number of manufactories your committee have made up the following summary which, with some few exceptions and slight variations, they are fully persuaded will serve as a fair specimen of the general state of things. The regular returns made include establishments in Massachusetts, New Hampshire, and Rhode Island which employ altogether something more than four thousand hands. Of these, sixteen hundred are between the ages of seven and sixteen years. In the return from Hope Factory, Rhode Island, it is stated that the practice is to ring the first bell in the morning at ten minutes after the break of day, the second bell at ten minutes after the first, in five minutes after which, or in twenty-five minutes after the break of day, all hands are to be at their labor. The time for shutting the gates at night...is eight o'clock by the factory time, which is from twenty to twenty-five minutes behind the true time. And the only respite from labor during the day is twenty-five minutes at breakfast and the same number at dinner. From the village of Nashua, in the town of Dunstable, N.H., we learn that the time of labor is from the break of day, in the morning, until eight o'clock in the evening; and that the factory time is twenty-five minutes behind the true solar time. From the Arkwright and Harris Mills in Coventry, R.I., it is stated that the last bell in the morning rings and the wheel starts as early as the help can see to work and that a great part of the year, as early as four o'clock. Labor ceases at eight o'clock at night, factory time, and one hour in the day is allowed for meals. From the Rockland Factory in Scituate, R.I., the Richmond Factory, in the same town, the various establishments at Fall River, Mass., and those at Somerworth, N.H., we collect similar details....

From these facts, your committee gather the following conclusions: (1) that on a general average the youth and children that are employed in the cotton mills are compelled to labor at least thirteen and a half, perhaps fourteen hours per day, factory time; and (2) that in addition to this, there are about twenty or twenty-five minutes added, by reason of that time being so much slower than the true solar time, thus making a day of labor to consist of at least fourteen hours, winter and summer, out of which is allowed on an average not to exceed one hour for rest and refreshment. Your committee also learn that in general, no child can be taken from a cotton mill to be placed at school for any length of time, however short, without certain loss of employ; as with very few exceptions, no provision is made by manufacturers to obtain temporary help of this description in order that one class may enjoy the advantages of the school, while the other class is employed in the mill. Nor are parents having a number of children in a mill allowed to withdraw one or more without withdrawing the whole; and for which reason, as such children are generally the offspring of parents whose poverty has made them entirely dependent on the will of their employers...are very seldom taken from the mills to be placed in school.

From all the facts in the case it is with regret that your Committee are absolutely forced to the conclusion that the only opportunities allowed to children...employed in manufactories to obtain an education are on the Sabbath and after half past 8 o'clock of the evening of other days. To these facts, however, your Committee take pleasure in adding two or three others of a more honorable character. It is believed that in the town of Lowell no children are admitted to the labors of the mills under twelve years of age and that the various corporations provide and support a sufficient number of good schools for the education of those that have not attained that age. In the Chicopee Factory Village, Springfield, Mass., and also in the town of New Market, N.H., we also learn that schools are provided and the children actually employed in mills allowed the privilege of attending school during...about one quarter of the year. Your Committee mention these facts as honorable exceptions to the general rule with a desire to do justice to all concerned and the hope that others may be inspired by their example to go much farther still in their efforts to remove the existing evils....

Your committee cannot therefore, without the violation of a solemn trust, withhold their unanimous opinion that the opportunities allowed to children and youth employed in manufactories to obtain an education suitable to the character of American freemen and the wives and mothers of such are altogether inadequate to the purpose; that the evils complained of are unjust and cruel; and are no less than the sacrifice of the dearest interests of thousands of the rising generation of our country to the cupidity and avarice of their employers. And they can see no other result in prospect as likely to eventuate from such practices than generation on generation reared up in profound ignorance and the final prostration of their liberties at the shrine of a powerful aristocracy....

5–4. "STRIKE OF THE JOURNEYMEN BAKERS"

To the Public:

The undersigned Committee, appointed by the General Trades' Union, having now before them a well attested statement of facts which sufficiently prove that the condition of the Journeymen Bakers in this city has been for some time in reality much worse than that of the southern slaves, submit for the inspection of the public a few instances taken from a very long list.

1st. Three men and a boy have had to bake 60 barrels per week, have had to labor 115 hours each week, (doing six men's work) and have received about 50 cents per barrel.

2nd. Four men have had to bake 54 barrels per week, have had to labor 112 hours each week, (doing nearly six men's work) and have received about 60 cents per barrel.

3rd. Five men have had to bake from 65 to 70 barrels per week, have had to labor 115 hours each week, (doing nearly seven men's work) and have received about 40 cents per barrel.

The above facts undoubtedly prove all that we have asserted, and we now call upon the public to know whether those employers who persist in requiring from their men much more than their nature can long bear, *viz*: from 18 to 20 hours labor out of the 24–are to be sustained in their demands, or whether they will not assist the oppressed Journeymen in their present attempt to procure a fair equivalent for their labor.

We have also to state that the General Trades' Union have resolved to support the Journeymen Bakers in their present course and are determined by all just and honorable means to raise them if possible to a fair standing among the other mechanics of the city.

In conclusion we respectfully suggest that the public in general can in no way more effectually support our cause than by bestowing their patronage on those employers who have nobly agreed to give the wages required....

> William Hewitt, Thos. Bonner, David Scott, Robt. Beatty, John H. Bowie
> Committee of the General Trades Union. New York, June 10th, 1834.

5–5. "THE WORKING PEOPLE OF MANAYUNK TO THE PUBLIC"

Fellow Citizens:

Deeply impressed with a sense of our inability to combat single-handed the evils that now threaten us and being fully convinced that the future happiness of ourselves and families depend on our present exertions, we are, with reluctance, obliged to lay our grievances and petition before you, well knowing that we are appealing to an enlightened and generous public. We therefore submit the following with all the candor of feeling with which the human mind is capable of expressing itself and may you judge us according to our merits.

We are obliged by our employers to labor at this season of the year from 5 o'clock in the morning until sunset, being fourteen hours and a half, with an intermission of half an hour for breakfast and an hour for dinner, leaving thirteen hours of hard labor at an unhealthy employment where we never feel a refreshing breeze to cool us, overheated and suffocated as we are, and where we never behold the sun but through a window and an atmosphere thick with the dust and small particles of cotton which we are constantly inhaling to the destruction of our health, our appetite, and strength.

Often do we feel ourselves so weak as to be scarcely able to perform our work on account of the overstrained time we are obliged to labor through the long and sultry days of summer in the impure and unwholesome air of the factories, and the little rest we receive during the night not being sufficient to recruit our exhausted physical energies, we return to our labor in the morning as weary as when we left it; but nevertheless work we must, worn down and debilitated as we are, or our families would soon be in a starving condition, for our wages are barely sufficient to supply us with the necessaries of life. We cannot provide against sickness or difficulties of any kind by laying by a single dollar, for our present wants consume the little we receive and when we are confined to a bed of sickness any length of time we are plunged into the deepest distress which often terminates in total ruin, poverty and pauperism.

Our expenses are perhaps greater than most other working people, because it requires the wages of all the family who are able to work, (save only one small girl to take care of the house and provide meals) to furnish absolute wants, consequently the females have no time either to make their own dresses or those of the children but have of course to apply to trades for every article that is wanted.

"The laborer is worthy of his hire," is a maxim acknowledged to be true in theory by all and yet how different is the practice. Are we not worthy of our hire? Most certainly we are and yet our employers would wish to reduce our present wages twenty per cent! and tell us their reason for so doing is that cotton has risen in value, but is it not a necessary consequence of the rise of cotton that cotton goods will rise also; and what matters it to us what the price of cotton is, our wants are as great when cotton is dear as they are when it is cheap; if our employers make more profit on their goods at any one time than they do at others, they do not give us better wages and is it justice that we should bear all the burthen and submit to a reduction of our wages? No, we could not... submit to it and rivet our chains still closer! We have long suffered the evils of being divided in our sentiments, but the universal oppressions that we now all feel have roused us to a sense of our oppressed condition and we are now determined to be oppressed no longer! We know full well that the attempted reduction in our wages is but the forerunner of greater evils and greater oppressions which would terminate, if not resisted, in slavery....

[Our children]...are obliged at a very early age to enter the factories, to contribute to the support of the family, by which means they are reared in total ignorance of the world, and the consequence of that ignorance is the inculcation of immoral and oftentimes vicious habits which terminates in the disgrace of many of them in public prisons. When on the other hand, if we were relieved of our present oppressions, a reasonable time for labor established, and wages adequate to our labors allowed us, we might then live comfortable, and place our children at some public school, where they might receive instruction sufficient to carry them with propriety through life. But situated as they are, and reared in ignorance, they are trampled upon by every ambitious knave who can boast of a long purse, and made the tools of political as well as avaricious men, who lord it over them as does the southern planter over his slaves!

The female part of the hands employed in the factories are subject to the same burthens that we are without the least allowance made on the part of our employers for their sex or age; they must labor as we do, and suffer as we do; and those of them who are grown to womanhood can barely support themselves by their industry.

We have here drawn but a faint sketch of the oppressions we labor under, but we hope by this to induce the public to examine for themselves. It would be endless to point out in detail all the injustice we suffer from an overbearing aristocracy, but all that we have here stated are facts which cannot be denied.

Adopted at meeting of the Manayunk Working People's Committee, Aug. 23d, 1833.
Wm. Gilmore, Pres. Attest; Wm. F. Small, Secretary.

5–6. "THE COST OF LIVING"

The carpenters of our city are upon strike for an advance of $0.25 a day; this will make $10.50 a week.... Now what will it take to maintain a family [of five]...weekly? A barrel of flour, $5, will last 8 weeks—this will leave flour $0.625 per week; sugar, 4 lbs. at $0.08 per lb., $0.32 per week; butter, 2 lbs. at $0.3125 per lb., $0.625; milk, $0.02 per day, $0.14 per week; butchers meat, 2 lbs. of beef at $0.10 per lb. per day, $1.40 per week; potatoes, half a bushel, $0.50, coffee and tea per week, $0.25, candle light

$0.14 per week; fuel, 3 tons coal, $15 per annum; charcoal, chips, matches, et. cetera, $5 year. This makes $0.40 per week for fuel. Salt, pepper, vinegar, starch, soap, soda, yeast, now and then some cheese, eggs &c., $0.40 a week more for all these sundries; wear and tear and breakage of household articles, such as cups, saucers, plates, dishes, pans, knives, forks &c., $0.25 per week; rent $3.00 per week; bed clothes and bedding $0.20; wearing apparel $2.00 per week; newspapers $0.12.... [The total expenses are $10.37 per week].

I ask, have I made the working man's comforts too high? Where is the money to pay for amusements, for ice creams, his puddings, trips on Sunday up or down the river, in order to get some fresh air; to pay the doctor or apothecary, to pay for pew rent in the church, to purchase books, musical instruments?

5–7. "THE FACTORY SYSTEM"

... We have lately visited the cities of Lowell and Manchester and have had an opportunity of examining the factory system more closely than before. We had distrusted the accounts which we had heard from persons engaged in the Labor Reform now beginning to agitate New England; we could scarcely credit the statements made in relation to the exhausting nature of the labor in the mills and to the manner in which the young women, the operatives, lived in their boarding-houses, six sleeping in a room, poorly ventilated.

We went through many of the mills, talked particularly to a large number of the operatives, and ate at their boarding-houses on purpose to ascertain by personal inspection the facts of the case. We assure our readers that very little information is possessed and no correct judgments formed by the public at large of our factory system which is the first germ of the Industrial or Commercial Feudalism that is to spread over our land....

In Lowell live between seven and eight thousand young women, who are generally daughters of farmers of the different States of New England; some of them are members of families that were rich the generation before....

The operatives work thirteen hours a day in the summer time, and from daylight to dark in the winter. At half past four in the morning the factory bell rings and at five the girls must be in the mills. A clerk, placed as a watch, observes those who are a few minutes behind the time and effectual means are taken to stimulate to punctuality. This is the morning commencement of the industrial discipline (should we not rather say industrial tyranny?) which is established in these Associations of this moral and Christian community. At seven the girls are allowed thirty minutes for breakfast, and at noon thirty minutes more for dinner, except during the first quarter of the year, when the time is extended to forty-five minutes. But within this time they must hurry to their boarding-houses and return to the factory and that through the hot sun or the rain and cold. A meal eaten under such circumstances must be quite unfavorable to digestion and health, as any medical man will inform us. At seven o'clock in the evening the factory bell sounds the close of the day's work.

Thus thirteen hours per day of close attention and monotonous labor are exacted from the young women in these manufactories.... So fatigued, we should say exhausted and worn out...are numbers of the girls, that they go to bed soon after their evening meal and endeavor by a comparatively long sleep to resuscitate their weakened frames for the toils of the coming day. When Capital has got thirteen hours of labor daily out of a being, it can get nothing more. It would be a poor speculation in an industrial point of view to own the operative, for the trouble and expense of providing for times of sickness and old age would more than counterbalance the difference between the price of wages and the expense of board and clothing. The far greater number of fortunes accumulated by the North in comparison with the South shows that hireling labor is more profitable for Capital than slave labor.

Now let us examine the nature of the labor itself and the conditions under which it is performed. Enter with us into the large rooms when the looms are at work. The largest that we saw is in the Amoskeag Mills at Manchester, [N.H.]. It is four hundred feet long and about seventy broad; there are five hundred looms and twenty-one thousand spindles in it. The din and clatter of these five hundred looms under full operation struck us on first entering as something frightful and infernal, for it seemed such an atrocious violation of one of the faculties of the human soul, the sense of hearing. After a while we became somewhat inured to it and by speaking quite close to the ear of an operative and quite loud, we could hold a conversation, and make the inquiries we wished.

The girls attend upon an average three looms; many attend four, but this requires a very active person, and the most unremitting care. However, a great many do it. Attention to two is as much as should be demanded of an operative. This gives us some idea of the application required during the thirteen hours of daily labor. The atmosphere of such a room cannot of course be pure; on the contrary it is charged with cotton filaments and dust, which, we were told, are very injurious to the lungs. On entering the room, although the day was warm, we remarked that the windows were down; we asked the reason and a young woman answered very naively and without seeming to be in the least aware that this privation of fresh air was anything else than perfectly natural, that "when the wind blew, the threads did not work so well." After we had been in the room for fifteen or twenty minutes we found ourselves, as did the persons who accompanied us, in quite a perspiration produced by a certain moisture which we observed in the air, as well as by the heat....

The young women sleep upon an average six in a room; three beds to a room. There is no privacy, no retirement here; it is almost impossible to read or write alone, as the parlor is full and so many sleep in the same chamber. A young woman remarked to us that if she had a letter to write she did it on the head of a band-box sitting on a trunk, as there was not space for a table. So live and toil the young women of our country in the boarding-houses and manufactories which the rich and influential of our land have built for them....

5–8. "OBTAINING OPERATIVES"

... We were not aware until within a few days of the *modus operandi* of the Factory powers in this village of forcing poor girls from their quiet homes to become their tools, and like the southern slaves, to give up her life and liberty to the heartless tyrants and task-masters. Observing a singular looking, "long, low, black" wagon passing along the street, we made inquiries respecting it, and were informed that it was what we term "a slaver." She makes regular trips to the north of the state, cruising around in Vermont and New Hampshire, with a "commander" whose heart must be as black as his craft, who is paid a dollar a head for all he brings to the market and more in proportion to the distance, if they bring them from such a distance that they cannot easily get back. This is done by "hoisting false colors," and representing to the girls that they can tend more machinery than is possible and that the work is so very neat and the wages such that they can dress in silks and spend half their time in reading. Now, is this true? Let those girls who have been thus deceived, answer.

Let us say a word in regard to the manner in which they are stowed in the wagon which may find a similarity only in the manner in which slaves are fastened in the hold of a vessel. It is long and the seats so close that it must be very inconvenient. Is there any humanity in this? Philanthropists may talk of negro slavery but it would be well first to endeavor to emancipate the slaves at home. Let us not stretch our ears to catch the sound of the lash on the flesh of the oppressed black while the oppressed in our very midst are crying out in thunder tones and calling upon us for assistance.

ESSAYS

Because the United States has been regarded as a land of economic opportunity since its inception, economic historians have been interested in the impact early industrialization had on American labor. In the first essay Jeffrey G. Williamson, Laird Bell Professor of Economics at Harvard University, and Peter H. Lindert, Distinguished Professor of Economics at the University of California, Davis, examined the effect 19th-century industrialization had on the premium paid for skilled labor. They argued that during the first wave of industrialization in the antebellum decades wages for skilled workers rose much more rapidly than those for unskilled labor, an advantage they maintained for the remainder of the 19th century. In this sense, they claimed, the early industrialization of the United States promoted a growing inequality in the distribution of wealth. Essay 5–2, however, questions the claims of Professors Williamson and Lindert. Using the pay records of civilians hired by the U.S. Army from 1820 to 1856, Robert A. Margo, Professor of Economics and of African-American Studies at Boston University, and Georgia C. Villaflor, formerly Assistant Professor of Economics at San Diego State University, found no long-term increase in the skill premium. Additionally, the Army pay records suggest that growth in real wages for antebellum labor in the Northeast was slow and erratic.

5–1. JEFFREY G. WILLIAMSON AND PETER H. LINDERT, *AMERICAN INEQUALITY: A MACROECONOMIC HISTORY*

A great deal of information on trends in the inequality of American income and wealth has been gathered since World War II. The seminal contribution was *Shares of Upper Income Groups in Income and Savings* (1953), in which Simon Kuznets first exploited federal income tax returns and national income estimates with systematic and painstaking care. What Kuznets did for income shares, Robert Lampman [*The Share of Top Wealth-Holders in National Wealth, 1922–1956*] (1962) soon did for wealth shares. These two studies by the National Bureau of Economic Research were based on federal taxes on income, which have been levied since 1913, and on wealth at death, which have been levied since 1916....

Kuznets and Lampman found that the gap between rich and poor appeared to decline sharply between the 1920s and mid-century. Numerous studies of trends since World War II failed to find further significant leveling, although some have argued that a modest leveling took place across the postwar years. These twentieth-century distribution trends have quite naturally raised a number of important questions: Why was there a reduction in inequality before mid-century and hardly any since? Are the aggregate trends real, or are they just an artifact of demographic shifts in the age distribution or the rise of more fragmented households? If American income and wealth were much more unequal in the twenties than today, how did they get that way? Compared to the present, was distribution always more unequal before 1929, or was there an earlier period that conforms to the more popular image of an egalitarian America?

It is not easy to illuminate early inequality experience. Data derived from tax returns on income and wealth for the years before World War I are sparse. Prior to 1913 America experimented with federal income taxes only briefly in 1866–1871 and 1894, and even then the tax affected only the very rich. Wealth was taxed only in some localities, such as the precocious states of Massachusetts and Wisconsin. Thus, to establish evidence for the years before 1913, scholars interested in American inequality have had to exploit less conventional data sources.

Several economic historians have risen to the task, finding usable data where none seemed at first to exist. Lee Soltow ["Evidence on Income Inequality in the United States, 1866–1965"] drew on mid-nineteenth-century census materials, most notably the man-uscript censuses of 1850, 1860, and 1870, which recorded household real estate and personal estate holdings. Led by Jackson Turner Main [*The Social Structure of Revolutionary America*] and Alice Hanson Jones [*American Colonial Wealth: Documents and Methods*], colonial historians, have used probate inventories and local tax assessments to explore wealth inequality before the Revolution....

[Our analysis indicates] that there have indeed been important movements in inequality in America over the past three centuries, even when one has made all the possible technical adjustments to the raw data. The ratio of the income or wealth of the richest 10% to that of the poorest 10% does not display an eternal constant. Rather, certain epochs of American history stand out as ones of rising or falling inequality in income and wealth. Furthermore, it appears that these inequality epochs have about the same dates whether they are documented by the behavior of earnings, income, or wealth.

Our survey...offers the tentative conjecture that inequality among *free* Americans before the Revolution was not too different from that which we experience today. Yet, inequality was hardly stable for the long period in between. It now appears that the main epoch of increasing inequality was the last four decades before the Civil War....

Shortly before World War I, the premium on skilled labor was extraordinarily high in America. Skills were very expensive even by West European standards. E.H. Phelps-Brown [*A Century of Pay*] notes that the ratio of skilled to unskilled wages in American building trades, for example, was 2.17 in 1909, while just two years earlier the ratio was as low as 1.54 in the United Kingdom. In contrast, English visitors a century earlier characterized America as a nation endowed with cheap skills and expensive "raw" labor. H.J. Habakkuk [*American and British Technology in the Nineteenth Century*] supplied extensive contemporary comment on the abundance of skilled labor in America during the 1820s. Estimates for the 1820s by Zachariah Allen suggest that American skilled workers had slightly less pay advantage over common labor than in Britain. In short, compared to England (and the Continent), skilled labor may have been relatively cheap in America at the start of modern industrialization. A century later conditions had reversed, and skilled labor was relatively expensive in America.

While these pay ratios and wage relatives have considerable intrinsic interest, one may doubt that their trends are likely to capture long-term overall distribution changes. After all, there are many skill categories and age-experience groups within each occupation. Furthermore, no one occupation can be trusted to reflect the same percentile position on the income spectrum year after year, even though some are always more highly paid than others. The nature of any one job also drifts with time— neither doctors nor the "unskilled" do the same things they did a century ago. In spite of all these reservations, pay ratios do indeed trace out trends that coincide with "true" inequality measures.... We have seen that an extraordinary rise in wealth concentration may have been compressed within the last four antebellum decades. The same impression of an inequality surge between about 1820 and the Civil War reappears when we look at trends in occupational pay structure.

...Pay ratios in Massachusetts building trades reveal a downward drift between 1771 and 1820.... This trend appears to reinforce the view that colonial distributional "quiescence" continues after 1774 up to about 1820. The Massachusetts pay ratios surge thereafter, peaking in the 1850s. Pay ratios in northern cities, skilled to common labor, also rise steeply over the antebellum period, from a low in 1816 to a high in 1856. The ratio of public school teachers' salaries to pay for unskilled common labor, urban or rural, also rises prior to the Civil War, as does the ratio of engineers' to common labor wages. All... document a brief but sharp decline in the skill premium during the Civil War itself.... The [wages of] urban skilled-workers... remain relatively stable up to the early 1890s, and the same is true for the Massachusetts building trades.... Generally, it appears that skill premia, pay ratios, and earnings differentials trace out...[an] "uneven plateau" that is [also] apparent in the late-nineteenth-century wealth distribution....

What is most remarkable [in pay ratios]... is the striking surge in the relative price of skills and an abrupt widening in the pay structure from 1816 to 1856. The movements after 1856 pale by comparison. In four short decades, the American Northeast was transformed from the "Jeffersonian ideal" to a society more typical of developing economies with very wide pay differentials and, presumably, marked inequality in the distribution of wage income. True, the sharp rise following 1816 may be somewhat exaggerated by our choice of 1816 as a base year. It was in the midst of hard times in the urban Northeast following readjustments in the wake of the War of 1812. But the post-Revolutionary wage structure (1781–1790) was quickly regained by the early 1820s, when social overhead construction and capital formation resumed and skilled labor was put back to work. In short, even if we select the 1820s as a base, a surge in antebellum pay differentials is still apparent in our series.

The linked urban skilled-workers [wage] series... is based primarily on manufacturing data from the *Aldrich Report* following 1840. Prior to that date, the series is even more limited, based as it is on payroll data from iron-producing firms in eastern Pennsylvania. Since the series suggests an inequality surge of such dramatic proportions even prior to the Irish immigrations in the late 1840s, it might be wise to pause and consider whether evidence other than the Massachusetts building trades is consistent with our characterization of sharp widening in the early antebellum pay structure. We have only the sketchiest data for the 1830s, [but] we may have understated the rise. For example, when R.G. Layer [*Earnings of Cotton Mill Operatives, 1825–1914*] computed daily earnings of cotton mill employees by department, he found that the dressing department was consistently the highest paid in the antebellum period, while spinners were the lowest. The pay differential rose by 13% from the period 1830–1834 to 1840–1844, whereas our "linked" index rose by 9% over the same period. Further confirmation can be found in Erie Canal payrolls and civil engineers' earnings on internal improvement projects. Between 1830 and 1845, the "skilled-labor wage premium" on internal improvement projects rose by 13.9–15%, while our linked series registers a rise of 14.2%.

Though we encounter no difficulty in confirming a surge in pay differentials during the 1830s, how about the 1840s? Do other wage indicators confirm the epic spreading in pay differentials during the 1840s? Apparently so, since other data fragments from the *Aldrich Report* document the following:... Compared with common laborers, the daily rate for New York bricklayers rose by 18% from 1840 to 1850, while that of carpenters and joiners rose by 37% over the same period; compared with common laborers, "best" machinists' wage relatives in New York increased by 37%, boilermakers' by 8%, and iron molders' by 13%; in Massachusetts, railroad conductors' wage relatives rose by 10% when common labor is used as a base, and by 14% when teamsters are used as a base.

We have dealt at length with the 1830s and 1840s, since measures of pay differentials during these decades of early industrialization are important in dating the nineteenth-century inequality surge in America and thus to economic interpretations of the sources of capitalist inequality. It seems appropriate, therefore, to conclude...by examining some wage data drawn from a New England state where it all began, Massachusetts. N. Rosenberg's ["Anglo-American Wage Differences in the 1820s"] use of Zachariah Allen's data confirmed that in 1825 the average British machinist was paid a premium above common labor of some 105% while his American counterpart earned only a 50% premium. Cheap skills and expensive raw labor are consistent with relative earnings equality in America about 1825. However, the premium on skills surged to 85% by 1837, to 90% during the 1840s, and to 120% by the 1850s. That is, the wage structure in urban Massachusetts in the 1850s was almost exactly like that in England in 1825. It never again reached that height in the three decades that followed.

It should be emphasized again that the pay differentials discussed above relate to *urban* workers in the Northeast. There is some evidence to suggest that *all* workers would be described by a pay-structure index not entirely unlike the northeastern urban index itself. The missing data, of course, relate to "wage gaps" between urban and rural employment, as well as to wage differentials between regions. The development literature makes much of these wage gaps..., the prevailing view being that they rise during early industrialization and growth, thus contributing to nominal wage stretching and inequality economy-wide....

To summarize, during the nineteenth-century surge in wealth inequality, wage stretching, and earnings dispersion, there is no evidence of increasing *spatial* occupational pay differentials. Furthermore, when Civil War effects are accounted for, there is little evidence of increased disparities in *average* regional incomes and labor productivities following 1840, although such disparities may have been on the rise prior to 1840.... The sources of the nineteenth-century inequality surge were not simply manifested by rising income differentials across regions and sectors. Indeed, the sources of the nineteenth-century inequality surge are as likely to be found *within* regions as between them....

American inequality trends confirm the Kuznets hypothesis. Income and wealth inequality did rise sharply with the onset of modern economic growth in the early nineteenth century. Long-term trends toward equality only appear with the advent of mature capitalist development in the twentieth century. In the interim, America generated seven decades of extensive inequality not unlike that experienced in Europe or in much of the contemporary Third World. Thus, in spite of abundant land, alleged equality of opportunity, democratic institutions, and a nineteenth-century reputation as an ideal "poor man's country," America did not avoid the economic inequality commonly believed to be associated with capitalist development.

Data on wages and salaries permit a tentative dating of the nineteenth-century rise in inequality. Between 1816 and 1856 the nominal pay advantage of such skilled groups as engineers, teachers, carpenters, and mechanics rose dramatically over common labor. The advantages thus gained were maintained and even reinforced through 1916; a slight decline in late nineteenth-century pay ratios was followed by another abrupt rise between the 1890s and 1914, the latter surge appearing in the dispersion of high income as well as pay ratios among wage and salary earners. The initial wage structure around 1816 was sufficiently narrow to suggest that there could hardly have been any earlier widening, although there are no reliable colonial wage series to confirm that assertion.

The inequality of personal wealth also seems to have widened dramatically sometime before the Civil War.... The same marked upward drift shows up in regional wealth inequality measures for Massachusetts, for Butler County, Ohio, for Brooklyn and New York City, and for southern slave ownership, although these local trends should be weighted and combined with new data from other regions before they can be accepted as additional evidence of national trends during the century between the Revolutionary and Civil wars.

The measured rise in wealth concentration between 1774 and 1860 apparently occurred sometime after about 1820, to judge from these admittedly meager but additional scraps of local and regional data. If further research confirms this timing, then it appears that the era of rising wealth concentration was also one of wage stretching and increased earnings inequality, in sharp contrast to the egalitarian tones traditionally used to paint the intervening Jacksonian era....

5–2. ROBERT A. MARGO AND GEORGIA C. VILLAFLOR, "THE GROWTH OF WAGES IN ANTEBELLUM AMERICA: NEW EVIDENCE"

The price of labor figures prominently in historical discussions of the antebellum economy. Because data on the income distribution are not available for the antebellum period, changes in income inequality have been proxied by changes in the structure of pay. The growth of wages supplements other measures of the pace of long-term economic change and improvements in living standards before the Civil War, such as per capita incomes. Changes in wages over shorter periods of time and in response to changes in other prices or to specific economic events, like immigration, are central to the labor history of the period. Spatial differences in wages, in conjunction with evidence on internal migration and other prices, yield insights into regional growth patterns and the integration of regional labor markets.

In view of its importance, it is surprising how little is actually known about the antebellum wage structure. Standard nineteenth-century sources...provide little evidence on wage rates before 1850, and what data there are pertain mostly to firms in the Northeast. The behavior of wage rates in other regions before the Civil War is poorly understood.

Recent research has...[used] account books, firm records, census manuscripts, and other materials. Valuable as the studies are, the results are generally limited to particular locations. We surmount this problem by exploiting a previously unutilized body of wage data: the payroll records of civilian employees of the United States Army. Unlike other sources, the payrolls cover all parts of the country. We present here annual estimates of nominal daily wage rates for skilled and unskilled labor at the census region level from 1820 to 1856, and use existing information on the cost of living to construct real-wage indices for the Northeast.

Civilians were employed by the Army throughout the nineteenth century. Workers were hired by quartermasters at army posts. Each month the quartermaster prepared a standardized form, a "Report of Persons and Articles Hired," documenting the pay of civilian workers. We sampled an extensive collection of the reports. For each worker we know when and where he was hired (almost all were male); his nominal wage, daily or monthly, whether he received any army rations, and if so, how many; his occupation or a description of what he did; and his legal status (slave or free, South only).

Our sample includes every extant payroll from 1820 to 1844. From 1844 to 1856 the sample includes every payroll where total retrieval was possible (for example, large cities and the Northeast) and a random selection of reports where total retrieval was impossible (for example, the Southwest during the Mexican War)....

We restrict our attention here to civilians who were skilled artisans (carpenters, masons, painters, plasterers, and blacksmiths), common laborers, and teamsters. We also exclude observations from posts in Florida, in Georgia during the Seminole War, and from the Southwest, Northwest, and Pacific regions.

Table 5.1 shows the distribution of the sample analyzed here by occupation, decade, and fort location within census regions. Over 75 percent of the observations are from forts in the South or the Midwest. The Army hired skilled and unskilled workers in roughly a 45:55 mix, although there were variations across regions. The numbers of observations per decade are large, except in the 1820s and in the Northeast and South Atlantic states in the 1850s. Locations in the West North Central and West South Central states are over-represented compared with the distribution of population within the North and South Central regions. The occupational, temporal, and spatial distributions are not surprising. Large numbers of artisans were hired to maintain and build forts. The army forged a path for western settlement, a role that expanded in scope after 1830.

Although wages at the forts may have some inherent interest, the real value of the sample rests on the assumption that the data faithfully reflect wage rates in the rest of the economy. Except in remote frontier areas, the demand for civilian labor by the Army was too small to have an effect on the local economy or the local labor market. In most respects jobs at the forts resembled their counterparts elsewhere. Some tasks were physically demanding or distasteful ("cleaning the privies"); outside the Army such work must have commanded a wage premium. At certain forts workers faced hazards such as a rampant disease environment or occasional Indian attacks. These factors can be accommodated in the analysis as long as they are known from the occupational descriptions or are related to the location of the fort....

A more serious issue is whether the Army overpaid its civilian workers. The forts were not competitive firms and had little incentive to hire the best workers at the lowest cost. Based on comparisons between wages at the forts and independent evidence on wages for the same location and year, however, systematic overpayment was not common. Table 5.2 shows the most extensive comparisons we can make between forts in New York state and the Erie Canal in the late 1830s and early 1840s, Except in one instance, modal wage rates at the Erie Canal fell within the range of wages observed at the forts. We conclude, tenta-tively, that the army data are reliable for inferring the behavior of wages in the rest of the economy.

Although the sample is large, it is not large enough to calculate annual estimates of wage rates for narrowly defined occupations at specific forts (for example, master masons at St. Louis). Few forts were occupied continuously over the period. None hired every type of worker in every year. The composition of the sample—the distribution of observations between forts and the characteristics of workers and jobs at the forts—changes over time. An analysis that ignored the variations in composition would be misleading.

Our analysis is based on hedonic wage regressions. A hedonic regression controls for variations in sample composition across forts and over time. The dependent variable is the log of the nominal daily wage rate. Monthly wages are converted to daily wages by dividing by 26 days per month. The independent variables are dummy variables for the location of the fort (for example, upstate New York); occupation (for example, teamster or mason); characteristics of the worker or the job associated with especially high or low wages (for example, master carpenter, apprentice mason); whether the worker was paid monthly; the number of army rations (a continuous variable); whether the worker was a slave (South only); the season of the year; and the time period. The time period dummies are single years or groups of years (for example, 1851 to 1853) to which the observation refers.

We estimated two regressions—one for skilled artisans and the other combining common laborers and teamsters—for each of the four census regions. The regressions fit the data reasonably well because 44 to 61 percent of the variance can be explained by the model. The results affirm our belief that the forts generally operated within local

Table 5.1 Distribution of Sample of Civilian Wage Rates by Occupation, Decade, and Fort Location

	Skilled		Unskilled	
	Number	**Percent of Total**	**Number**	**Percent of Total**
Northeast				
1820–1829	189	5.3	246	10.4
1830–1839	1,474	41.5	608	25.7
1840–1849	1,643	46.2	1,333	56.4
1850–1856	249	7.0	297	12.5
Southern New England	379	10.7	122	5.2
Northern New England	583	16.4	71	3.0
New York City	270	7.6	821	34.7
Upstate New York	1,412	39.7	413	17.5
Philadelphia	473	13.3	953	40.3
Carlisle, Pennsylvania	438	12.3	254	10.7
Total	3,555	30.0	2,364	16.7
Midwest				
1820–1829	138	3.9	223	4.6
1830–1839	685	19.6	1,068	21.8
1840–1849	1,456	41.7	1,006	20.5
1850–1856	1,215	34.8	2,603	53.1
Ohio, Western Pennsylvania	66	1.9	345	7.0
Michigan	324	9.3	338	6.9
Iowa, Wisconsin, Minnesota	662	18.9	169	3.4
St. Louis	436	12.5	717	14.6
Kansas	2,006	57.4	3,331	67.9
Total	3,494	29.5	4,900	34.5
South Atlantic				
1820–1829	799	41.5	364	17.6
1830–1839	588	30.8	1,215	58.7
1840–1849	416	21.8	391	18.9
1850–1856	103	5.4	101	4.9
Maryland, Washington, D.C.	449	23.5	262	12.7
Virginia	478	25.1	1,067	51.5
North Carolina	120	6.3	49	2.4
South Carolina	237	12.4	397	19.2
Georgia	622	32.6	296	14.3
Total	1,906	16.1	2,071	14.6
South Central				
1820–1829	268	9.2	298	6.3
1830–1839	1,102	38.0	1,009	21.3
1840–1849	1,106	38.2	I;438	30.4
1850–1856	422	14.6	1,983	41.9
Alabama, Mississippi	148	5.1	158	3.3
Kentucky, Tennessee	371	12.8	330	7.0
Arkansas	1,197	41.3	1,996	42.2
Louisiana	1,182	40.8	2,244	47.5
Total	2,898	24.4	4,728	33.3
Aggregate total	11,853		14,183	

Notes: The unit of observation is a person-month. Percentages may not add to 100 due to rounding. Skilled occupations are carpenters, masons, painters (includes plasterers), and blacksmiths (includes machinists), Unskilled occupations are common laborers and teamsters. Source: Margo-Villaftor sample of "Reports of Persons and Articles Hired," National Archives, Record Group 92

Table 5.2 Daily Wage Rates, 1838–1843: New York Forts and the Erie Canal

	N	New York Forts		Erie Canal	
		Mean	Mode	Range	Mode
Common Laborers and Teamsters					
1838	31	$0.85	$0.75	$0.75–1.00	$0.90
1839	44	0.93	1.00	0.75–1.00	1.00
1840	26	0.77	0.75	0.75–0.88	0.88
1841	71	0.86	0,90	0.50–1.25	0.88
1842	71	0.81	0.88	0.75–0.88	0.88
1843	13	0.75	0.75	0.65–0.88	0.75
Carpenters					
1838	299	1.49	1.50	0.75–1.75	1.25
1839	89	1.51	1.50	1.25–1,75	1.50
1840	115	1.47	1.50	1.25–1.75	1.50
1841	116	1.45	1.63	0.75–2.00	1.50
1842	78	1.34	1.38	1.00–1.75	1.50
1843	23	1.45	1.50	1.00–1.50	1.25
Masons					
1840	60	1.72	1.75	1.38–1.75	1.75
1841	109	1.41	1.50	1.20–1.81	1.75
1842	4	1.35	1.35	1.35–1.35	1..50
1843	9	1.40	1.38	1.38–1.50	1..25

Notes: N = number of observations. New York forts are Ft. Niagara (Buffalo); Madison Barracks (Sacktt's Harbor); Pittsburgh Barracks (Plattsburgh); Ft. Ontario (Syracuse); West Point; Ft, Hamilton, Ft. Columbus, Ft. Lafayette (New York City).

Sources: New York forts from Margo-Villaflor sample; Erie Canal data from Walter B. Smith, "Wage Rates on the Erie Canal," *Journal of Economic History*, 23 (Sept. 1963), pp. 303–4.

labor markets. Wages usually were higher at forts in urban areas or remote locations (for example, northern Maine) than at forts in rural areas. Masons, painters, and blacksmiths earned slightly higher wages (2 to 13 percent) than carpenters. Master artisans received a premium of 48 to 65 percent over journeymen's pay. Although seasonal variations were small, there was a tendency for wages to be lower in the winter. Workers hired on a daily basis received higher wages than the imputed daily wage paid to monthly workers, possibly as a premium for incurring unemployment risk or because monthly workers may have received additional nonwage compensation. Slaves were paid 7 to 24 percent less per day than free labor.

We use the regression coefficients to estimate annual series of nominal daily wage rates for each occupational group and fort location. The estimates pertain to free workers, hired on a daily basis without rations, without characteristics associated with especially high or low wages, and are averaged over the year to account for seasonal variations. Regional estimates are formed by weighting each annual series to reflect the distribution of population and occupations within census regions. The population weights are based on decade-to-decade averages of census-year figures. The occupational weights are derived from the 1850 census.

The limitations of the estimates are numerous. The structure of wages within census regions is held constant by the regression specification, even though the structure of wages across regions is allowed to change over time. The number of observations underlying certain estimates, particularly in the 1820s, is small (less than twelve). When the data are aggregated into time periods some estimates must be interpolated. The weighting procedure is crude and no doubt could be refined. The regressions do not fit the data perfectly, so small changes in wages may not be economically significant.

The estimates...are reported in Appendix Tables 5.4 and 5.5. Decadal averages and average annual rates of growth are given in the appendix tables.

Caveats aside, the estimates appear to be reasonable in terms of trends and levels. Wages began increasing in the late 1820s and early 1830s, peaking in the mid-to-late 1830s, the same general pattern followed by other prices. The drastic deflation following the Panic of 1837 is visible in every region. Wages generally rose during the renewed price inflation of the late 1840s and early 1850s. By the late 1840s levels in the various regions are consistent with census data from 1850.

Although trends in wages were similar throughout the country, there were important differences over shorter periods and in overall rates of growth between occupations and regions. Broadly speaking, overall growth was more rapid among the unskilled than the skilled, and in the North than in the South. Within regions, overall growth was greater and decade-to-decade fluctuations generally larger in the Midwest and South Central states than in the Northeast and the South Atlantic states.

Skilled wages in the Northeast and the Midwest were similar in level in the early 1820s but diverged markedly in favor of the Midwest in the late 1820s. The differences narrowed in the late 1830s through the early 1840s, but again diverged in the late 1840s and early 1850s. The overall rate of growth of skilled wages from the 1820s to the 1850s was slightly higher in the Midwest (1.0 percent per year) than in the Northeast (0.8 percent per year).

Unskilled wages in the 1820s were about 25 percent lower in the Midwest than in the Northeast, but the regional difference disappeared in the early 1830s as wages grew faster in the Midwest. Wages in the Midwest fell below levels in the Northeast in the early 1840s and remained below through the 1850s. Overall, however, unskilled wages grew more rapidly in the Midwest (1.7 percent per year) than in the Northeast (1.1 percent per year) from the 1820s to the 1850s.

Skilled wages in the South Atlantic states changed relatively little from the mid-1820s to the late 1840s, and then increased in the early 1850s to a level 14 percent higher than in the 1820s. In the South Central states, skilled wages rose from the early 1820s to a peak in 1841. Wages fell from 1841 to 1844, rose during the rest of the 1840s, and then remained constant before falling again, in 1856. Overall, skilled wages in the South Central states were 24 percent higher in the 1850s than in the 1820s.

The trend in unskilled wages in the South Atlantic states was basically flat from the 1820s to the 1850s, despite a sharp increase beginning in 1854. Unskilled wages in the South Central states rose from the early 1820s to a peak in 1841, falling sharply from 1841 to 1847. Wages increased from 1847 to 1852, and then fell slightly to 1856. On average, unskilled wages in the South Central states were 23 percent higher in the 1850s than in the 1820s, compared with only a 6 percent increase in the South Atlantic states over the same period.

Indices of real wages for the Northeast based on our nominal wage estimates are... reported in Appendix Table 5.6. The deflator is the "Williamson-Lindert unskilled cost-of-living index." Decadal averages of the indices are given in Appendix Table 5.6.

Real wages changed little on average from the 1820s to the 1830s, and then increased sharply in the early 1840s. From the mid-1840s to 1854 real wages fell by nearly a quarter. Overall, real wages rose at an annual rate of 1.0 percent for artisans and 1.4 percent for common laborers and teamsters from the 1820s to the 1850s.

According to Jeffrey Williamson and Peter Lindert income inequality in America rose from 1820 to 1860. A key element of their explanation of rising inequality was a change in the structure of pay. The price of capital goods fell, and because capital and skills were complementary factors, the demand for skilled labor increased relative to the demand for unskilled labor. The end result was a "surge" in the skill differential—the ratio of skilled to unskilled wages—which they interpret as an increase in income inequality.

The surge hypothesis is controversial. After claiming a surge took place in the Northeast, Williamson and Lindert assert "there is no reason to believe that things were different" elsewhere in the country, but they provide no evidence to support the assertion. Some scholars have questioned the assumption of capital-skill complementarity and whether there was a surge in the Northeast....

Table 5.3 contains estimates of the skill differential, based on the decadal averages in Appendix Tables 5.4 and 5.5. The estimates range from 1.47 to 2.53. The differential was lowest in the Northeast, which may reflect a relative abundance of skilled labor in the region. But, with the exception of the South Atlantic states (where the differential rose 7 percent from the 1820s to the 1850s), there is no evidence of a long-term increase in the skill differential. Simply put, our wage estimates do not support the surge hypothesis.

The absence of a long-term upward trend in the skill differential does not mean there were no important changes over shorter periods. Between 1838 and 1840 the differential in the Northeast increased by 35 percent. The downturn in 1840 was one of the worst in American history. Evidently the brunt of the contraction fell most heavily on unskilled wages. The effects of immigration are also apparent. From 1844 to 1856 the annual number of unskilled immigrants entering the country was 950 percent higher than the average from 1831 to 1840. For skilled artisans the figure was 279 percent. According to our estimates, skill differentials in the Northeast and the Midwest, where the vast majority of immigrants settled, rose 22 and 18 percent from 1844 to 1856. The rise in the differential in the North is consistent with the increase in the relative supply of unskilled immigrants....

Income distribution aside, most economic historians believe the antebellum period was one of substantial economic growth and widespread prosperity. Real per capita income grew at 1.7 percent per annum from 1820 to 1860, comparable to rates of growth after the Civil War. Industrialization took hold in the Northeast, transforming it into the highest per capita income region in the nation. The transportation revolution led to enormous increases in internal trade and internal migration. Productivity growth was rapid and living standards rose throughout the country.

This optimistic assessment of antebellum growth is not shared by some labor historians who, while recognizing that certain groups benefited during the period—mid-western farmers, capitalists, and slaveowners—nevertheless point to a worsening in economic well being among a significant fraction of the nonfarm labor force. The antebellum work place was radically transformed by the rise of the factory system, the deskilling of certain artisanal trades, the use of outwork, and a faster and more regulated pace, all of which contributed to a deterioration in working conditions. Rapid urbanization after 1840 fostered a host of attendant ills, and nutritional status, morbidity, and mortality evidently worsened. Wage workers in urban areas were not isolated from the business cycle, unlike their counterparts in the countryside. Unemployment or underemployment could be hidden in rural areas, but not in the city. Nominal wages lagged behind when prices soared in the mid-1830s and early 1850s, contributing to a wave of strikes and labor agitation. In the late 1840s and early 1850s labor markets in the North were glutted by the increased supply of immigrants. Competition between native and foreign-born workers fostered an outburst of

Table 5.3 Regional Estimates of the Skill Differential, 1821–1856

	Northeast	Midwest	South Atlantic	South Central
1821–1830	1.62	2.53	2.09	1.81
1831–1840	1.68	2.32	2.25	1.87
1841–1850	1.49	1.90	2.11	1.93
1851–1856	1.47	2.11	2.24	1.82

nativism which, along with the changes in work organization, profoundly influenced the course of antebellum politics.

Many of the issues raised in the literature might be resolved by making appropriate adjustments to a real-wage index. Given the limitations of the evidence from the period, it is doubtful if such adjustments could ever be made. Nevertheless, conventionally defined real-wage indices are relevant to the debate. Some scholars flatly deny that real wages rose before the Civil War. Others acknowledge an overall increase, but claim that growth was slow, erratic, and negative at times.

Our real-wage indices for the Northeast tend to favor an intermediate view. The indices do show that real wages in the Northeast increased from 1820 to 1856, but at a slower rate than per capita income growth. Perhaps the most surprising finding is the miniscule rate of increase from the 1820s to the 1830s. Although real wages did rise in the first half of the 1830s, they fell in 1835/36, precisely the timing of the increase in strikes and labor agitation....

But the increase of real wages in the early 1840s is not dependent on the use of a particular deflator. The early 1840s were years of deflation and depression. According to the Williamson-Lindert deflator, the cost of living in the Northeast fell 40 percent from 1837 to 1843. Although nominal wages also fell, the decline was not as large or as prolonged as the decline in prices, and real wages rose for workers who were fully employed. For workers who were unemployed or underemployed (a significant percentage) the increase in real wages overstates the true gains in purchasing power. But any gains were short lived because of the subsequent increase in immigration. Between 1846 and 1854 the number of immigrants arriving annually increased by 274 percent. Over the same period real wages fell 23 percent, and the true decline may have been even greater.

Our wage estimates yield new insights into regional growth patterns and labor-market integration. As such, the estimates supplement other evidence on regional growth: indices of wholesale prices, the volume of internal trade, and sales of public land. Broadly speaking, the estimates for the Midwest and the South confirm regional patterns suggested by other evidence. The 1830s and 1850s were decades of rising prices and economic activity in the Midwest and the South Central states and, so it would appear, rising nominal wages.... Our wage estimates...show steep declines in both regions in the early 1840s and little improvement until late in the decade.... Prices in the South Atlantic states declined from the 1820s to the 1840s, as do our wage estimates for the region....

Wage rates are among the most basic statistics in economic history. We have presented new estimates of nominal and real wages for skilled and unskilled labor in the United States from 1820 to 1856, drawing on a large sample of payrolls of civilian employees of the United States Army.

We find no evidence of a widening in the antebellum pay structure in any part of the country, and therefore no evidence that income inequality increased before the Civil War. Our estimates for the Northeast suggest that real-wage growth during the antebellum period may have been slower and more erratic than previously thought, particularly in the 1820s and 1830s and again in the early 1850s. The real wage indices are sensitive, however, to the use of a particular cost-of-living deflator. It remains to be seen whether similar conclusions hold for the other regions, for which cost-of-living indices are not yet available. Regional trends in wages confirm patterns of regional growth indicated by prices and other economic variables, and suggest the beginnings of the integration of regional labor markets in the North.

Appendix

Table 5.4 Nominal Daily Wage Rates for Artisans, 1821–1856

	Northwest	Midwest	South Atlantic	South Central
1820	$1.55	n.a,	n.a.	$ 1.21
1821	1.10	n.a.	n.a.	1.27
1822	1.39	1.42	n.a.	1.33
1823	1.37	1.41	1.48	1.45
1824	1.37	1.41	1.41	1.43
1825	1.32	1.40	1.56	1.50
1826	1.27	1.39	1.70	1.57
1827	1.45	1.50	1.77	1.56
1828	1.34	1.63	1.59	1.58
1829	1.28	1.75	1.68	1.36
1830	1.23	1.79	1.71	1.51
1831	1.29	1..99	1.73	1.49
1831	1.34	1.95	1.72	1.46
1833	1.32	1.84	1.72	1.55
1834	1.49	1.81	1.75	1.63
1835	1.54	1.78	1.71	1.72
1836	1.64	1.75	1.63	1.84
1837	1.56	2.38	1.65	1.73
1838	1.51	1.93	1.66	1.43
1839	1.60	1.75	1.66	1.76
1840	1.50	1.79	1.65	2.01
1841	1.50	1.69	1.66	2.06
1842	1.37	1.56	1.71	1.84
1843	1.46	1.31	1.50	1.46
1844	1.30	1.39	1.50	1.40
1845	1.55	1.48	1.51	1.60
1846	1.49	1.27	1.51	1.46
1847	1.52	1.46	1.49	1.64
1848	1.43	1.54	1.54	1.55
1849	1.44	1.62	1.57	1.70
1850	1.45	1.70	1.59	1.85
1851	1.43	1.93	1.59	1.86
1852	1.48	1.89	1.73	1.86
1853	1.53	1.02	1.86	1.85
1854	1.64	1.04	1.98	1.80
1855	1.73	1.11	2.10	1.84
1856	1.93	2.16	1.79	1.69
1821–1830	1.31	1.52	1.61	1.47
1831–1840	1.48	1.90	1.69	1.66
1841–1850	1.45	1.50	1.56	1.66
1851–1856	1.63	2.03	1.84	1.82
Rate of growth*	0.78	1.03	0.48	0.76

n.a. = not available; * average annual rate of growth, 1821–1830 to 1851–1856.

Sources: See Table 5.1 and the text.

Table 5.5 Nominal Daily Wage Rates for Unskilled Labor, 1821–1856

	Northeast	Midwest	South Atlantic	South Central
1820	n.a.	$0.73	n.a.	$0.71
1821	0.81	0.74	n.a.	0.77
1822	0.78	0.61	n.a.	0.77
1823	0.78	0.58	n.a.	0.78
1824	0.78	0.57	n.a.	0.77
1825	0.86	0.56	0.76	0.75
1826	0.92	0.55	0.78	0.74
1827	0.87	0.55	0.79	0.81
1828	0.78	0.59	0.80	0.88
1829	0.74	0.61	0.76	0.92
1830	0.74	0.67	0.71	0.94
1831	0.73	0.63	0.70	0.87
1832	0.77	0.67	0.68	0.87
1833	0.76	0.76	0.67	0.86
1834	0.91	0.85	0.65	0.89
1835	0.91	0.85	0.68	0.81
1836	1.06	0.71	0.85	0.96
1837	1.07	1.07	0.89	0.99
1838	0.98	0.81	0.75	0.82
1839	0.87	0.98	0.82	0.92
1840	0.72	0.82	0.81	0.88
1841	0.89	0.78	0.79	1.08
1842	0.91	0.73	0.61	0.98
1843	1.00	0.79	0.72	0.94
1844	1.00	0.77	0.74	0.90
1845	1.00	0.74	0.76	0.81
1846	1.02	0.85	0.77	0.71
1847	0.85	0.71	0.78	0.70
1848	0.93	0.87	0.76	0.75
1849	1.02	0.85	0.74	0.83
1850	1.04	0.83	0.74	0.89
1851	0.99	0.88	0.73	0.94
1852	1.09	0.93	0.72	1.05
1853	1.08	0.89	0.72	1.03
1854	1.13	1.02	0.83	0.98
1855	1.17	1.05	0.89	1.02
1856	1.22	1.01	1.00	0.97
1821–1830	0.81	0.60	0.77	0.81
1831–1840	0.88	0.82	0.75	0.89
1841–1850	0.97	0.79	0.74	0.86
1851–1856	1.11	0.96	0.82	1.00
Rate of growth*	1.13	1.67	0.22	0.75

n.a. = not available; *average annual rate of growth, 1821–1830 to 1851–1856.

Sources: See Table 5.1 and the text

Table 5.6 REAL WAGE INDICES FOR THE NORTHEAST, 1820–1856 (1856 = 100)

	Skilled	Unskilled		Skilled	Unskilled
1820	75.9	n.a.	1839	75.4	64.8
1821	56.2	65.5	1840	84.4	64.1
1822	67.5	59.9	1841	93.8	88.0
1823	67.7	61.0	1842	95.3	100.1
1824	73.9	66.5	1843	107.9	116.9
1825	70.1	72.2	1844	99.1	120.5
1826	69.3	79.5	1845	115.7	118.1
1827	78.2	74.2	1846	111.7	121.0
1828	72.4	66.7	1847	93.6	82.8
1829	69.4	63.4	1848	96.0	98.7
1830	70.0	66.6	1849	96.1	107.7
1831	71.4	63.9	1850	99.8	113..2
1832	75.1	68.3	1851	98.4	107.8
1833	73.5	67.0	1852	92.5	107.8
1834	87.8	84.9	1853	93.3	103.3
1835	80.7	75.4	1854	85.0	92.6
1836	74.0	75.6	1855	84.2	90.0
1837	69.4	75.3	1856	100.0	100.0
1838	69.7	71.5			

Decadal Averages	(1821–30 - 100)	
1821–1830	100.0	100.0
1831–1840	109.5	105.2
184 1–18 5O	145.2	157.8
1851–1856	132.7	148.4
Rate of growth*	1.0	1.4

* Average annual rate of growth, 1821–1830 to 1851–1856.
Notes: Deflator is WillLamson-Lindert cost-of-living index; see text.

Source: See text.

SUGGESTIONS FOR FURTHER READING

Donald R. Adams, Jr. "Wage Rates in the Early National Period: Philadelphia: 1785–1830," *Journal of Economic History*, 28(1968) 404–426.

Simon J. Crowther, "Urban Growth in the Mid-Atlantic States, 1785–1850," *Journal of Economic History*, 36(1976) 624–644.

Allan Dawley, *Class and Community: The Industrial Revolution in Lynn* (1976).

Thomas Dublin, *Women at Work: The Transformation of Work and Community in Lowell, Massachusetts* (1979).

Richard A. Easterlin, "Inter-regional Differences in Per Capita Income, Population, and Total Income, 1840–1950," in *Trends in the American Economy in the Nineteenth Century*, vol. 24 (1960).

Claudia Goldin, *Understanding the Gender Gap: An Economic History of Women* (1990).

Herbert Gutman, *Work, Culture, and Society in Industrializing America* (1977).

Simon Kuznets, "Economic Growth and Income Inequality," *American Economic Review*, 45(1955) 1–28.

R.G. Layer, *Earnings of Cotton Mill Operatives*, 1825–1914 (1955).

Stanley Lebergott, *Manpower in Economic Growth: The American Record Since 1800* (1964).

Jackson Turner Main, "Trends in Wealth Concentration Before 1860," *Journal of Economic History*, 31(1971), 445–447.

Larry Neal and Paul Uselding, "Immigration, A Neglected Source of American Economic Growth: 1790 to 1912," *Oxford Economic Papers*, 24(1972).

Pamela J. Nickless, "A New Look at Productivity in the New England Cotton Textile Industry, 1830–1860," *Journal of Economic History*, 39(1979) 889–910.

Edward E. Pessen, *Most Uncommon Jacksonians: The Radical Leaders of the Early Labor Movement* (1967).

Joseph G. Rayback, *A History of American Labor*, revised edition (1966).

Daniel T. Rodgers, *The Work Ethic in Industrial America, 1850–1920* (1978).

Nathan Rosenberg, "Anglo-American Wage Differences in the 1820s," *Journal of Economic History*, 27(1967) 221–229.

Steven J. Ross, *Workers on the Edge: Work, Leisure, and Politics in Industrializing Cincinnati, 1788–1890* (1985).

Walter B. Smith, "Wage Rates on the Erie Canal, 1828–1881," *Journal of Economic History*, 23(1963), 298–311.

Kenneth L. Sokoloff, "Was the Transition from Artisanal Shop to the Nonmechanized Factory Associated with Gains in Efficiency? Evidence from the U.S. Manufactures Censuses of 1820 and 1850," *Explorations in Economic History*, 21(1984) 351–382.

Lee Soltow, "Economic Inequality in the United States in the Period from 1790 to 1860," *Journal of Economic History*, 31(1971) 822–839.

Stephan Thernstrom, *Poverty and Progress: Social Mobility in a Nineteenth Century City* (1964).

Anthony F.C. Wallace, *Rockdale: The Growth of an American Village in the Early Industrial Revolution* (1978).

Thomas Weiss, "Long-Term Changes in US Agricultural Output Per Worker, 1800–1900," *The Economic History Review*, 46(1993) 324–341.

Sean Wilentz, *Chants Democratic:: New York City and the Rise of the American Working Class, 1788–1850* (1984).

Jeffrey F.Zabler, "Further Evidence on American Wage Differentials, 1800–1830," *Explorations in Economic History*, 10(1972), 109–118.

Jeffrey Williamson, "American Prices and Urban Inequality Since 1820," *Journal of Economic History*, 36(1976) 303–333.

The Rise of Big Business

INTRODUCTION

Although railroads became the nation's first big business prior to the Civil War, the pace of consolidation quickened considerably in the postwar decades. By the early 1880s John D. Rockefeller had formed the Standard Oil Trust which exerted enormous control over the oil industry for the next three decades. In the same period Andrew Carnegie's steel company became the dominant force in the iron and steel industry and the American Sugar Refining Company came to control 98 percent of the production of refined sugar. Practically everywhere Americans turned in the late 19th century—beef, leather, shoes, paper, copper, ice, even life insurance—they were confronted by one or two large national corporations. The rapid emergence of these large, vertically- and horizontally-integrated corporations in the late 19th century produced fundamental changes in the patterns of economic life and fostered a searching re-examination of the values, ideas, and institutions that had previously ordered the nation.

Americans responded to big business with a mixture of awe and fear. In one sense the industrial behemoths were a source of national pride, a tangible symbol of the unparalleled economic growth that catapulted the United States into the world's leading industrial power by 1890. But from the perspective of individual workers and consumers big business inspired more fear and anger. In the market economy of the early Republic individuals had enjoyed a good deal of control over their economic lives. An artisan such as a cooper, for example, could increase his earnings by working longer to produce more barrels or he could raise the price he charged for his wares. In similar fashion, consumers who purchased commodities from the local general store developed a personal relationship with the owner, giving them the ability to haggle over prices. But the rise of a corporate capitalistic economy in the late 19th century stripped individuals of much of this power. As artisans joined the industrial labor force they lost control over their work life. Working people argued increasingly that big business exploited its domination of the labor market to pay unfairly low wages for long, tedious, and sometimes dangerous workdays. Similarly, consumers complained increasingly that the lack of competition among producers resulted in unfairly high prices for commodities of often inferior quality. Small business owners contended that the competitive methods employed by the likes of John D. Rockefeller often drove them into bankruptcy or forced them to sell their business at prices far below their actual value. In general, late 19th century Americans came to see big business as a mixed blessing. Although it greatly expanded the nation's wealth and power, most believed that it had also substantially diminished economic opportunity and equality.

Because late 19th century Americans increasingly viewed big businesses as a Faustian bargain, they protested vigorously against them and often vilified the entrepreneurs who created them. Most of the protest was directed at reducing or controlling the vast power these large corporations were able to exert. Industrial workers, for example, organized themselves into large national labor unions such as the Knights of Labor (1869) and the American Federation of Labor (1886) hoping that such combinations would level the balance of power between labor and management. In this era American farmers also organized themselves into the Farmers' Alliance (1877) which later evolved into the Populist Party (1892). Both aimed to give farmers an effective voice in state and national politics to enact legislation that would provide relief from the abuses of big business. Investigative journalists, labeled "muckrakers" by Theodore Roosevelt, added their voices to the national chorus of complaints against big business. Through such works as Ida Tarbell's "The History of the Standard Oil Corporation" muckrakers sought to expose the unethical and sometimes illegal methods entrepreneurs had used to create their industrial empires in the belief that an informed and aroused public would act to restore democracy and equal opportunity to American life.

One major result of these protests and the general concerns Americans had about big business were new understandings about the role of government and the meaning of private property. Most early Americans had subscribed to the Jeffersonian maxim that "that government is best which governs least," accepting that in the market economy of the early Republic autonomous individuals could best chart their own economic course. But as the corporate capitalistic economy steadily distorted those market forces, late 19th century Americans gradually accepted that in some cases government power had to intervene to restore and maintain equal opportunity. Early Americans similarly held sacred and inviolate the individual's right to property. But as privately-held corporations such as railroads gained the ability to affect an individual's livelihood through the rates they charged, late 19th century Americans redefined private property. In the case of *Munn v. Illinois* (1876) the United States Supreme Court upheld the state's power to regulate rates charged by grain elevators, ruling that private property which was devoted to public use had to yield to the larger well being of the community. This ruling helped to provide a rationale for government regulation of business. The Interstate Commerce Act of 1887 was the first piece of national regulatory legislation. It required that railroads charge consumers "just and reasonable rates." Three years later Congress enacted the Sherman Anti-Trust Act which declared illegal "any combination in restraint of trade or commerce." In the early 20th century the power of the national government was extended to include the regulation of food and drugs, the investigation of unfair business practices, and the supervision of the national banking system.

In their effort to come to grips with the rise of big business economic historians were initially influenced by the attitudes of late 19th century Americans and especially the writings of muckraking journalists such as Ida Tarbell, Upton Sinclair, and Charles E. Russell. They generally regarded large corporations as the personification of entrepreneurs such as John D. Rockefeller and Andrew Carnegie who ruthlessly devoured all competitors and selfishly exploited workers and consumers. In this view big business had a baneful influence on the United States because of the heavy costs it exacted on American democracy and equal opportunity. Matthew Josephson's 1934 work, *The Robber Barons: The Great American Capitalists*, was the classic example of this school of thought. Since the end of World War II economic historians have increasingly challenged this interpretation, arguing that it overlooked the substantial innovations late 19th century entrepreneurs brought to the American economy or that it exaggerated the importance of the entrepreneur to the emergence of big business.

What is the best way to understand the rise of big business and its impact on the United States? Are the late 19th century entrepreneurs best regarded as "robber barons" or as innovative industrial statesmen? Did their efforts to create large integrated corporations pose dire challenges to the nation or provide exceptional benefits? Is it best to view the big businesses as the product of individual effort, of impersonal market forces, or some combination of the two?

DOCUMENTS

Document 6–1 is an excerpt for Ida Tarbell's classic "The History of the Standard Oil Corporation." Originally published as a series of articles in *McClure's Magazine*, one of the leading muckraking journals of the early 20th century, Tarbell exposed to public view for the first time the tactics John D. Rockefeller used to create the Standard Oil Trust. Through her bitter indictment, Rockefeller and Standard Oil came to symbolize monopoly capitalism for Americans of her day. It is worth noting, however, that Tarbell's father was one of the small oil refiners driven out of business by Standard Oil.

Americans' concern with industrial consolidations was heightened considerably by J.P. Morgan's acquisition of Andrew Carnegie's steel company in early 1901. Morgan combined Carnegie Steel with several small firms to create the U.S. Steel Corporation, the first corporation capitalized at $1.0 billion. In May 1901 in response to the formation of U.S. Steel, *The North American Review*, a leading journal of opinion during the era of industrialization, asked several prominent industrialists to debate the costs and benefits of consolidation. In Document 6–2 Russell Sage, one of the major financiers of the late 19th century who made a fortune by speculating in railroad stocks argued that the industrial corporations because of their methods of capitalization undermined the nation's economic stability. James J. Hill, one of the great railroad barons of the era, defended big business in Document 6–3, contending that they were fairly valued because consolidation had greatly increased their earning capacity. In Document 6–4 Charles R. Flint, the founder of the U.S. Rubber Corporation, the American Chicle Corporation, and the Computing-Tabulating-Recording Company, the forerunner of IBM, argued that far from harming the United States, industrial consolidations had brought great benefits to the nation. Through the millions of shares of stock they issued, big businesses spread corporate ownership much more widely which, in turn, led to a more equal distribution of wealth. In the final document F.B. Thurber who together with his brother established H.K. Thurber & Company, the world's largest wholesale grocery business prior to the Panic of 1893, contended that contrary to popular perceptions, industrial consolidations had substantially reduced the price of most consumer products.

6–1. IDA TARBELL, *THE HISTORY OF THE STANDARD OIL COMPANY*

Among the many young men of Cleveland who, from the start, had an eye on the oil-refining business and had begun to take an active part in its development as soon as it was demonstrated that there was a reasonable hope of its being permanent, was a young firm of produce commission merchants. Both members of this firm were keen business men, and one of them had remarkable commercial vision—a genius for seeing the possibilities in material things. This man's name was Rockefeller—John D. Rockefeller. He was but twenty-three years old when he first went into the oil business, but he had already got his feet firmly on the business ladder, and had got them there by his own efforts. The habit of driving good bargains and of saving money had started him....

When young Rockefeller was thirteen years old, his father moved from the farm in Central New York, where the boy had been born (July 8, 1839), to a farm near Cleveland, Ohio. He went to school in Cleveland for three years. In 1855 it became necessary for him to earn his own living.... The position, that of a clerk and bookkeeper, was not lucrative. According to a small ledger which has figured frequently in Mr. Rockefeller's religious instructions, he earned from September 26, 1855, to January, 1856, fifty dollars. "Out of that," Mr. Rockefeller told the young men of his Sunday-school class, "I paid my washerwoman and the lady I boarded with, and I saved a little money to put away."

He proved an admirable accountant—one of the early-and-late sort, who saw everything, forgot nothing and never talked. In 1856 his salary was raised to twenty-five dollars a month, and he went on always "saving a little money to put away." In 1858 came a chance to invest his savings. Among his acquaintances was a young Englishman, M. B. Clark. Older by twelve years than Rockefeller he had left a hard life in England when he was twenty to seek fortune in America.... They were two of a kind, Clark and Rockefeller, and in 1858 they pooled their earnings and started a produce commission business on the Cleveland docks. The venture succeeded. Local historians credit Clark and Rockefeller with doing a business of $450,000 the first year. The [Civil] [W]ar came on, and as neither partner went to the front, they had full chance to take advantage of the opportunity for produce business a great army gives. A greater chance than furnishing army supplies, lucrative as most people found that, was in the oil business (so Clark and Rockefeller began to think), and in 1862, when an Englishman of ability and energy, one Samuel Andrews, asked them to back him in starting a refinery, they put in $4,000 and promised to give more if necessary. Now Andrews was a mechanical genius. He devised new processes, made a better and better quality of oil, got larger and larger percentages of refined from his crude. The little refinery grew big, and Clark and Rockefeller soon had $100,000 or more in it. In the meantime Cleveland was growing as a refining center. The business which in 1860 had been a gamble was by 1865 one of the most promising industries of the town. It was but the beginning—so Mr. Rockefeller thought—and in that year he sold out his share of the commission business and put his money into the oil firm of Rockefeller and Andrews.

In the new firm Andrews attended to the manufacturing. The pushing of the business, the buying and the selling, fell to Rockefeller. From the start his effect was tremendous. He had the frugal man's hatred of waste and disorder, of middlemen and unnecessary manipulation, and he began a vigorous elimination of these from his business. The residuum that other refineries let run into the ground, he sold. Old iron found its way to the junk shop. He bought his oil directly from the wells. He made his own barrels. He watched and saved and contrived. The ability with which he made the smallest bargain furnishes topics to Cleveland story-tellers to-day. Low-voiced, soft-footed, humble, knowing every point in every man's business, he never tired until he got his wares at the lowest possible figure. "John always got the best of the bargain," old men tell you in Cleveland to-day, and they wince though they laugh in telling it. "Smooth," "a savvy fellow," is their description of him. To drive a good bargain was the joy of his life. "The only time I ever saw John Rockefeller enthusiastic," a man told the writer once, "was when a report came in from the creek that his buyer had secured a cargo of oil at a figure much below the market price. He bounded from his chair with a shout of joy, danced up and down, hugged me, threw up his hat, acted so like a madman that I have never forgotten it."

...The firm grew as rapidly as the oil business of the town, and started a second refinery—William A. Rockefeller and Company. They took in a partner, H. M. Flagler, and opened a house in New York for selling oil. Of all these concerns John D. Rockefeller was the head. Finally, in June, 1870, five years after he became an active partner in the refining business, Mr. Rockefeller combined all his companies into one—the Standard Oil Company. The capital of the new concern was $1,000,000. The parties interested in it were John D. Rockefeller, Henry M. Flagler, Samuel Andrews, Stephen V. Harkness, and William Rockefeller....

In the fall of 1871...certain Pennsylvania refiners...brought to them a remarkable scheme...to bring together secretly a large enough body of refiners and shippers to persuade all the railroads handling oil to give to the company formed special rebates on its oil, and drawbacks on that of other people. If they could get such rates it was evident that those outside of their combination could not compete with them long and that they would become eventually the only refiners. They could then limit their output to actual demand, and so keep up prices. This done, they could easily persuade the railroads to transport no crude for exportation, so that the foreigners would be forced to buy American refined. They believed that the price of oil thus exported could easily be advanced fifty per cent. The control of the refining interests would also enable them to fix their own price on crude. As they would be the only buyers and sellers, the speculative character of the business would be done away with.... It was evident that a scheme which aimed at concentrating in the hands of one company the business now operated by scores, and which proposed to effect this consolidation through a practice of the railroads which was contrary to the spirit of their charters, although freely indulged in, must be worked with fine discretion if it ever were to be effective.

The first thing was to get a charter—quietly. At a meeting held in Philadelphia late in the fall of 1871 a friend of one of the gentlemen interested mentioned to him that a certain estate then in liquidation had a charter for sale which gave its owners the right to carry on any kind of business in any country and in any way; that it could be bought for what it would cost to get a charter under the general laws of the state, and that it would be a favor to the heirs to buy it. The opportunity was promptly taken. The name of the charter bought was the " Southern (usually written South) Improvement Company." For a beginning it was as good a name as another, since it said nothing.

With this charter in hand Mr. Rockefeller and Mr. Watson and their associates began to seek converts. In order that their great scheme might not be injured by premature public discussion they asked of each person whom they approached a pledge of secrecy. Two forms of the pledges required before anything was revealed were published later. The first of these, which appeared in the New York *Tribune*, read as follows:

> I, A. B., do faithfully promise upon my honor and faith as a gentleman that I will keep secret all transactions which I may have with the corporation known as the South Improvement Company; that, should I fail to complete any bargains with the said company, all the preliminary conversations shall be kept strictly private; and, finally, that I will not disclose the price for which I dispose of my product, or any other facts which may in any way bring to light the internal workings or organization of the company. All this I do freely promise.
> Signed .... Witnessed by...................

A second, published in a history of the "Southern Improvement Company," ran:

> The undersigned pledge their solemn words of honor that they will not communicate to any one without permission of Z (name of director of Southern Improvement Company) any information that he may convey to them, or any of them, in relation to the Southern Improvement Company.
> .... Witness...........................

...It has frequently been stated that the South Improvement Company represented the bulk of the oil-refining interests in the country. The incorporators of the company in approaching the railroads assured them that this was so. As a matter of fact, however, the thirteen gentlemen...who were the only ones ever holding stock in the concern did not control over one-tenth of the refining business of the United States in 1872. That business in the aggregate amounted to a daily capacity of about 45,000 barrels—from 45,000 to 50,000, Mr. Warden put it—and the stockholders of the South Improvement Company owned a combined capacity of not over 4,600 barrels. In assuring the railroads that they controlled the business, they were dealing with their hopes rather than with facts.

The organization complete, there remained contracts to be made with the railroads. Three systems were to be interested: The Central, which, by its connection with the Lake Shore and Michigan Southern, ran directly into the Oil Regions; the Erie, allied with the Atlantic and Great Western, with a short line likewise tapping the heart of the region; and the Pennsylvania, with the connections known as the Allegheny Valley and Oil Creek Railroad. The persons to be won over were: W. H. Vanderbilt, of the Central; H. F. Clark, president of the Lake Shore and Michigan Southern; Jay Gould, of the Erie; General G. B. McClellan, president of the Atlantic and Great Western; and Tom Scott, of the Pennsylvania. There seems to have been little difficulty in persuading any of these persons to go into the scheme after they had been assured by the leaders that all of the refiners were to be taken in. This was a verbal condition, however, not found in the contracts they signed....

The work of persuasion went on swiftly. By the 18th of January the president of the Pennsylvania road, J. Edgar Thompson, had put his signature to the contract, and soon after Mr. Vanderbilt and Mr. Clark signed for the Central system, and Jay Gould and General McClellan for the Erie. The contracts to which these gentlemen put their names fixed gross rates of freight from all common points, as the leading shipping points within the Oil Regions were called, to all the great refining and shipping centers—New York, Philadelphia, Baltimore, Pittsburg and Cleveland. For example, the open rate on crude to New York was put at $2.56. On this price the South Improvement Company was allowed a rebate of $1.06 for its shipments; but it got not only this rebate, it was given in cash a like amount on each barrel of crude shipped by parties outside the combination.

The open rate from Cleveland to New York was two dollars, and fifty cents of this was turned over to the South Improvement Company, which at the same time received a rebate enabling it to ship for $1.50. Again, an independent refiner in Cleveland paid eighty cents a barrel to get his crude from the Oil Regions to his works, and the railroad sent forty cents of this money to the South Improvement Company. At the same time it cost the Cleveland refiner in the combination but forty cents to get his crude oil. Like drawbacks and rebates were given for all points—Pittsburg, Philadelphia, Boston and Baltimore.

An interesting provision in the contracts was that full waybills of all petroleum shipped over the roads should each day be sent to the South Improvement Company. This, of course, gave them knowledge of just who was doing business outside of their company-of how much business he was doing, and with whom he was doing it. Not only were they to have full knowledge of the business of all shippers—they were to have access to all books of the railroads....

The reason given by the railroads in the contract for granting these extraordinary privileges was that the "magnitude and extent of the business and operations" purposed to be carried on by the South Improvement Company would greatly promote the interest of the railroads and make it desirable for them to encourage their undertaking. The evident advantages received by the railroad were a regular amount of freight—the Pennsylvania was to have forty-five per cent. of the Eastbound shipments, the Erie and Central each 27 1/2 per cent., while West-bound freight was to be divided equally between them, fixed rates, and freedom from the system of cutting which they had all found so harassing and disastrous. That is, the South Improvement Company, which was to include the entire refining capacity of the company, was to act as the evener of the oil business.

It was on the second of January, 1872, that the organization of the South Improvement Company was completed. The day before the Standard Oil Company of Cleveland increased its capital from $1,000,000 to $2,500,000, "all the stockholders of the company being present and voting therefor." …Three weeks after this increase of capital Mr. Rockefeller had the charter and contracts of the South Improvement Company in hand, and was ready to see what they would do in helping him carry out his idea of wholesale combination in Cleveland. There were at that time some twenty-six refineries in the town—some of them very large plants. All of them were feeling more or less the discouraging effects of the last three or four years of railroad discriminations in favor of the Standard Oil Company. To the owners of these refineries Mr. Rockefeller now went one by one, and explained the South Improvement Company. "You see," he told them, "this scheme is bound to work. It means an absolute control by us of the oil business. There is no chance for anyone outside. But we are going to give everybody a chance to come in. You are to turn over your refinery to my appraisers, and I will give you Standard Oil Company stock or cash, as you prefer, for the value we put upon it. I advise you to take the stock. It will be for your good." Certain refiners objected. They did not want to sell. They did want to keep and manage their business. Mr. Rockefeller was regretful, but firm. It was useless to resist, he told the hesitating; they would certainly be crushed if they did not accept his offer, and he pointed out in detail, and with gentleness, how beneficent the scheme really was—preventing the creek refiners from destroying Cleveland, ending competition, keeping up the price of refined oil, and eliminating speculation. Really a wonderful contrivance for the good of the oil business.

That such was Mr. Rockefeller's argument is proved by abundant testimony from different individuals who succumbed to the pressure…. W. H. Doane, whose evidence on the first rebates granted to the Cleveland trade we have already quoted, told the Congressional committee which a few months after Mr. Rockefeller's great coup tried to find out what had happened in Cleveland: "The refineries are all bought up by the Standard Oil works; they were forced to sell; the railroads had put up the rates and it scared them. Men came to me and told me they could not continue their business; they became frightened and disposed of their property." Mr. Doane's own business, that of a crude oil shipper, was entirely ruined, all of his customers but one having sold.

To this same committee Mr. Alexander, of Alexander, Scofield and Company, gave his reason for selling:

> There was a pressure brought to bear upon my mind, and upon almost all citizens of Cleveland engaged in the oil business, to the effect that unless we went into the South Improvement Company we were virtually killed as refiners; that if we did not sell out we should be crushed out…. We sold at a sacrifice, and we were obliged to. There was only one buyer in the market, and we had to sell on their terms or be crushed out, as it was represented to us. It was stated that they had a contract with railroads by which they could run us into the ground if they pleased. After learning what the arrangements were I felt as if, rather than fight such a monopoly, I would withdraw from the business, even at a sacrifice. I think we received about forty or forty-five cents on the dollar on the valuation which we placed upon our refinery. We had spent over $50,000 on our works during the past year, which was nearly all that we received. We had paid out $60,000 or $70,000 before that; we considered our works at their cash value worth seventy-five per cent. of their cost. According to our valuation our establishment was worth $150,000, and we sold it for about $65,000, which was about forty or forty-five per cent. of its value. We sold to one of the members, as I suppose, of the South Improvement Company, Mr. Rockefeller; he is a director in that company; it was sold

in name to the Standard Oil Company, of Cleveland, but the arrangements were, as I understand it, that they were to put it into the South Improvement Company....

A few of the refiners contested before surrendering. Among these was Robert Hanna, an uncle of Mark Hanna, of the firm of Hanna, Baslington and Company. Mr. Hanna had been refining since July, 1869. According to his own sworn statement he had made money, fully sixty per cent. on his investment the first year, and after that thirty per cent. Some time in February, 1872 the Standard Oil Company asked an interview with him and his associates. They wanted to buy his works, they said. "But we don't want to sell," objected Mr. Hanna. "You can never make any more money, in my judgment," said Mr. Rockefeller. "You can't compete with the Standard. We have all the large refineries now. If you refuse to sell, it will end in your being crushed." Hanna and Baslington were not satisfied. They went to see Mr. Watson, president of the South Improvement Company and an officer of the Lake Shore [Railroad], and General Devereux, manager of the Lake Shore road. They were told that the Standard had special rates; that it was useless to try to compete with them. General Devereux explained to the gentlemen that the privileges granted the Standard were the legitimate and necessary advantage of the larger shipper over the smaller, and that if Hanna, Baslington and Company could give the road as large a quantity of oil as the Standard did, with the same regularity, they could have the same rate. General Devereux says they "recognized the propriety" of his excuse. They certainly recognized its authority. They say that they were satisfied they could no longer get rates to and from Cleveland which would enable them to live, and "reluctantly" sold out. It must have been reluctantly, for they had paid $70,000 for their works, and had made thirty per cent a year on an average on their investment, and the Standard appraiser allowed them $40,000. "Truly and really less than one-half of what they were absolutely worth, with a fair and honest competition in the lines of transportation," said Mr. Hanna, eight years later, in an affidavit.

Under the combined threat and persuasion of the Standard, armed with the South Improvement Company scheme, almost the entire independent oil interest of Cleveland collapsed in three months' time. Of the twenty-six refineries, at least twenty-one sold out. From a capacity of probably not over 1,500 barrels of crude a day, the Standard Oil Company rose in three months' time to one of 10,000 barrels. By this maneuver it became master of over one-fifth of the refining capacity of the United States....

6–2. RUSSELL SAGE , "A GRAVE DANGER TO THE COMMUNITY"

Source: *North American Review*, DXXXIV (May, 1901), pp. 641–646.

It is, perhaps, ungracious to sound a harsh note in a company so happy and well content as we are to-day in Wall Street....Why, then, give a danger cry, when perhaps no danger exists?

Because, to me, there seems to be something very sleight-of-hand in the way in which industries are doubling in value, as at the touch of the magician's wand. Here we have a factory—a good, conservative, productive investment which may be turning out anything from toys to locomotives. It falls into the hands of the consolidators, and, whereas it was worth $50,000 yesterday, to-day it is worth $150,000—at least on paper. Stocks are issued; bonds are put out; and loans are solicited, with these stocks as security. The man who owned the factory could probably not have borrowed over $10,000 on it. Now, however, when the $50,000 plant is changed into a stock issue of $150,000 bankers and financiers are asked to advance $60,000 or $70,000 on what is practically the same property, and many of them from all accounts, make the advance.

Under these circumstances, a "squeeze" seems to me inevitable. The Clearing House is reporting, from week to week, an expansion of loans far beyond anything that was dreamed of heretofore. This cannot go on forever; yet, from all appearances, the era of consolidation has only set in.

A reaction must come as soon as the banks realize the situation. A property is not worth $50,000 one day and $150,000 the next simply because a company of men, no matter how big and important they are, say so.

It is truly remarkable, the increase which has taken place in requests for loans based on industrials. No one can even estimate the amount of money that has been advanced on securities of this class; but it is a conservative estimate to say that industrial loans are as ten to one compared with conditions a few years ago. This is apparent from the business offered at my office from day to day. The volume of money in the country is entirely inadequate to meet anything like the demands that are made on collateral of this class. In fact, we have gotten away entirely from the old idea of making the money of the country the basis of our trading. Instead, there is thrown into the business world, to be used as a trading medium, millions upon millions of new stocks, the real value of which is yet to be determined. As soon as this is thoroughly realized, we may look for trouble, pending a re-adjustment. This can be predicted with perfect safety....

The great success of the Standard Oil Company is always adduced by the believers in consolidation, whenever the scheme is attacked. It is true that this company has had enormous success, and that it has benefited the community. It has lowered the price of oil, bringing it down gradually from forty-five cents to seven or eight cents a gallon. Through its excellent management it has evolved methods for using all the by-products of crude oil and, first and last, has added many hundreds of millions to the wealth of the country. It has made its owners, the capitalists, very rich, and it has acted well by its employees and by consumers.

But if consolidation has produced all these things, it has also, in the case of this company, produced a feeling of unrest and disquiet, industrial and political, that threatens, sooner or later, to bring serious results. Every Legislature in the land, almost, has attacked it at one time or another. It has become a by-word among all classes, and is pointed to in every community as one of the dangers of the Republic. Over and over again, it has been the issue in political campaigns. Men who were its competitors have accused its officers of all sorts of practices. Congressional committees have sat in inquiry on it, States have risen against it, criminal courts in many parts of the country have had its alleged crimes on their dockets. Of course, the greater part of this agitation has been entirely unjustifiable. The charges of criminal aggression, when traced, have been found to emanate invariably from irresponsible sources. The complaints of practices have been voiced generally by men who were driven to the wall in trade competition, because they could not dispute the market with a concern so magnificently organized.

But the very groundlessness of most of the complaints ought to be viewed by conservative men as a danger signal. Such complaints, persevered in as they have been, show that the community opposes the idea embodied in this great monopoly, and that it is willing to seize on any pretext to make clear this opposition.

Is it desirable to add to institutions that cause such commotion and keep all the newspapers in the land, rightly or wrongly busy with denunciations? I doubt it. The chief owners of the Standard Oil business have grown so enormously wealthy that in their individual as well as in their corporate capacity they dominate wherever they choose to go. They can make or unmake almost any property, no matter how vast. They can almost compel any man to sell them anything at any price....

Surely that is not a desirable state of affairs, and a condition that breeds it ought hardly to be extended. And with all its vast wealth and domination to-day, the Standard Oil Company started out modestly enough. It built up conservatively from small beginnings. It bought the properties it controls to-day at fair prices, and built them up by the application of close business principles, little by little.

But under the new order it is different. The consolidations of today begin at the very outset with capitalizations that cast all past experiences into the shade, and that almost stagger the imagination. The [U.S.] steel combination now forming... is to start off with a capitalization of $1,000,000,000. This is more than one-half of the National Debt. It is one-seventieth of the entire wealth of the United States. The total money in circulation in the United States, according to the Treasurer's statistics, is $2,113,294,983. It will be seen, therefore, that this company's issue of securities will represent practically one-half of the entire volume of money in America. In a year or two, if precedents count for anything, this capitalization will be very largely increased, and that in spite of the fact that stockholders in the Steel Company, which was the basis of the new combination, got three shares of stock in the new company for one in the old—scores of millions being thus added to the interest-earning securities in the United States, by merely the stroke of a pen. When wealth is created in that way, what security is there for the whole scheme? Not another furnace added to the plant; simply a lifting process, and what was one million before is three millions now. The great experience and strength of the men who produced this change will make us accept the new valuation, and that is all there is in it....

The great railroad combinations we have had thrust on us recently I consider only less dangerous than the industrial combinations, because they are based on sounder considerations. Their stocks and bonds have not, in general, been doubled or trebled, nor unduly inflated. But they are bad, nevertheless. They are sure to arouse the people. And the people, once aroused, are more powerful than the railroad combinations.... Farmers will consider themselves injured by rates, States will inaugurate inimical legislation, and there will be deep hostility to combined capital.

Sir Richard Tangye, the great English iron master and economist, gives us an unprejudiced view of what may come of the wholesale attempt to kill off legitimate competition. He says:

> America will one day awake to the stern reality of the evil and when its terrible nature is fully realized some strong legislation must follow.
>
> I believe if legislation does not step in and treat these men as it would treat other deadly enemies of the state, there will be such an uprising in the States as has not been since the accession of Abraham Lincoln to supreme power. ...

That something may come of Sir Richard Tangye's prophecy of retaliative legislation was made manifest during the last session of Congress. One of the leaders of the Republican party — the party that has always been the friend of capital, as it has been of labor — introduced a measure cutting off the protective duty on the products manufactured by the big steel combination. Nothing came of this measure, but its very introduction was a political straw that should exercise a restraining influence on the capitalists who are rushing pell-mell into the new system of "concentrated management" as they call it.

They had better remain content with the old-fashioned system of honest competition, under which we have grown great as a nation and prosperous as a people.

6–3. JAMES J. HILL, "INDUSTRIAL AND RAILROAD CONSOLIDATIONS: THEIR ADVANTAGES TO THE COMMUNITY"

On one point Mr. Sage is undoubtedly right. There is in the community a general feeling of hostility towards the railroad and industrial consolidations that have been effected and towards those that are now under way.

This hostility is strong, but undefined. Much of it has come, undoubtedly, through the teachings of the newspapers and…through the speeches of political orators. It began when the "trust" came into being as the result of an effort to obviate ruinous competition. The "trust" was found a very cumbersome structure, and the law of the land declared it illegal. It was not a consolidation in any sense of the term, and differed entirely from the business scheme under which the consolidations of today are being effected and operated. Under the "trust" system the stocks of various and competing organizations were trusteed in the hands of a few men, to whom was given absolute and unqualified power to do what they saw fit with the properties placed under their control. It was not on its face a healthy arrangement, and it met with violent opposition on all hands.

The new system in force today is neither illegal nor…harmful to the community. But the people at large have not yet learned to distinguish between the new and the old, and the odium attaching to the "trust" is visited on the consolidation. The old scheme left intact all the corporations it found in existence. In the nature of things, no economy in production could be effected. All the old officers of the individual organizations remained.

Certain plants were shut down to restrict the output, but this process affected only the workingmen who were thrown out of employment. The high-salaried men continued to draw their pay, and large bonuses were paid regularly to the stockholders or owners of the plants that had been put out of business. Increased profits, therefore, could generally be obtained only by an increase of price for the product, which was saddled on the consumer. Under the new system, a different usage prevails. Operating expenses are reduced by combining a number of institutions under one management. Useless officers and unproductive middlemen are cut off. The systems of purchasing and distributing are simplified. Economies are effected by the direct purchase of material in large quantities, or, better still, by adding to the combination a department for the acquisition and control of the sources from which raw material is drawn. Thus, the Carnegie Company, which was the highest type of this system, took its iron from its own mines, made its coke in its own ovens, worked up its material in its own furnaces, and shipped the finished product over its own railroad or in its own vessels….

What has just been effected in the great [U.S.] steel combination is simply an enlargement of the Carnegie plan, and, when the value of the great properties combined is taken into consideration the capitalization of one thousand million dollars is not exorbitant The Carnegie Company by itself was a colossal institution, so colossal that it dominated the steel market absolutely. But because it happened to be a single company, its tremendous proportions aroused no particular opposition. It was considered a fine healthy enterprise… and Mr. Carnegie and his partners were not looked upon in any sense as "trust" magnates. While hostilities to many other concerns were raging at their fiercest, the organization of the Carnegie Company was not once impugned by the anti-consolidationists.

From all accounts, the workmen of the Carnegie Company were among the best paid artisans in America. The company could afford to pay high wages, because its men worked under the most perfect and compact conditions. Nothing was wasted, nothing of the earnings went to middlemen, who are mere leeches sucking sustenance from the business body without giving anything in return.

In the nature of things, a plant bought out or added to the Carnegie Company's properties became, by the mere fact of such addition, greatly more valuable than it possibly could have been under independent management and control. There was lopped off at once the item of executive expenses. There was no president's salary to pay, no vice-president's, no office force. The purchasing agents, with their salaries and commissions, became things of the past. The product was worked up in the most scientific and economical manner and put on the market under the best conditions.

The point, therefore, made by Mr. Sage, that a factory worth $50,000 today is necessarily improperly rated at $150,000 tomorrow, because it has been combined with others under one managerial head, has not all the force that might appear from the bald statement of the facts as Mr. Sage puts it. A property is not necessarily worth only what it represents in the way of real estate, building and plant. It is worth rather what it represents in earning capacity; and, if, under a combination, its earning capacity is trebled, because of the economy of production, it is not unreasonable to say that its value has been trebled, even though nothing tangible has been added to its material assets. Hard and fast rules do not apply to the value of anything. A piece of property worth $1,000 today may be worth $2,000 tomorrow, merely because some improvement has been made in the neighborhood which adds to the rental value of the property in question. Lands showing evidences of iron deposits, which, ten years ago, could have been bought for ten dollars per acre, or even less, are now worth $50,000,000. Not cost, but earning power, is the measure of value....

There are a few men...in the community who can advance good reasons for their opposition [to industrial consolidations]. They are the ones who have been caught between the upper and the nether mill stones; they are the middlemen and the small competitor who was unable to meet the larger concern in open market. To them, consolidation has been a distinct injury. This is apparent, and, under our social and business system inevitable. The aim in business, as in politics, is to do the greatest good to the greatest number; and the greatest number...is apparently benefited by the consolidations. Almost every improvement that helps the masses brings injury to individuals here and there. The building of a railroad into new territory puts the owner of the stage coach out of business. Trolley cars that have sprung up all over the country have done grave damage to the local hackmen and livery stable keepers. But the community which is brought into touch with the outer world by a new railroad, and the village or town that gains the advantage of cheap and quick transportation by means of the trolley car, are benefited so much more than the stage owners and hackmen are injured, that the balance is easily in favor of the improvements.

In all such improvements the chief beneficiary is the workingman. The only asset he has to sell is his time. He cannot afford to pay a quarter for a hack ride, but when the trolley comes and he gets a quick ride for five cents, it is a good business investment for him....

The workingmen benefit also in another direction, where the concern for which they work is backed by ample capital and has the benefit of concentrated management. They are assured the use of the most perfect machinery. A big concern can afford to make improvements and put in the latest machinery, because such improvements and machinery necessarily add to the productiveness of the plant at a rate that will soon make good the expenditure. The smaller concern, while it realizes this fact, is unable to avail itself of the latest appliances, because it has not the necessary capital to invest.

Another advantage of prime importance to the workingmen is that they may easily participate in the profits of these enterprises by investing their savings in the shares of the more solid and prosperous concerns. Over $2,400,000,000 are deposited in the savings banks of the United States, largely made up of the savings of the wage-earners, and this represents only a portion of their accumulations. With these vast resources at command, the workingmen of the country might, in a few years, acquire a large interest in the concerns in which they are employed. The opportunities thus afforded for safe and lucrative investment will enable them to share in the profits, and thus unite the rewards of capital and labor.

The consumer is assured of lower prices when a big concern is the producer, because such a concern must have a steady market for its output in order to keep its machinery busy. The loss of a day is a large item. Therefore, in self-defense the big concern must keep its prices within the figure that will secure the greatest number of purchasers.

Moreover, if the result of these industrial consolidations is to steady and relatively reduce the prices of their products, the gravest of the speculative popular objections to them will be obviated and public opinion will speedily recognize the benefits to the people at large of this new and improved machinery of production. The very motive of self-interest, even the law of self-preservation, dictates a policy which is as necessary to the lasting business prosperity of these concerns as to that popular approval without which they cannot permanently endure.

This is the theory of the new business consolidations, and their promoters, judging by the results attained so far, believe that it will work out—that it is a good policy and a wise one for everybody. Should experience prove that it is not a good condition for the people at large, it will very soon be upset. Politically, the scheme has never been passed upon as yet; and, if it proves a good scheme, it may never be a distinct issue in politics. If the prosperity of the country (much of which, I believe, is due to the consolidations and economies effected so far) continues, the people will be content to let well enough alone. If, however, it is shown that we are on the wrong track, and that consolidations are harmful to the people in general, as has been so frequently stated, the question will undoubtedly be settled at the polls....

There is one thing that the people who deal lightly with the new business scheme, and who want to sweep it aside as a menace, forget. We have reached a stage in our national development where business must be done on a different plan from that which served us well half a century ago. In 1865, when the [Civil] War closed, we had thirty-five millions of people; today we have over seventy millions. That is, we have doubled our population in thirty-five years. If we are advancing at the same rate...we will have over one hundred and fifty millions in 1935. In other words, we are adding at the rate of one and a half to two millions a year to our population. Thirty-five years ago, or even ten years ago, horse-cars served admirably the purposes of urban transportation. Today, we could not possibly get along without the trolley. And as it is with physical conditions, so it must be with economical conditions; we must keep pace with the times. We have reached a period where the old-fashioned methods will prove inadequate, if the masses of the people are to continue in the enjoyment of the prosperity to which they are entitled. There are too many people to be fed, housed and clothed to permit of the wasteful system which would maintain a horde of idle middlemen. People in this country live better today than they ever did before in their lives. This is due, I believe, very largely to the improved methods of production. There are fewer drones in the hive, fewer people who share the results of work without doing any work themselves....

6–4. CHARLES R. FLINT, "INDUSTRIAL CONSOLIDATIONS: WHAT THEY HAVE ACCOMPLISHED FOR CAPITAL AND LABOR"

While Mr. Sage's article has little value as an exposition of facts that exist, it has this merit: Coming from a man who is as wealthy and as prominent as he is, who controls one of the great fortunes of America, the paper offers an excellent vehicle on which the general popular ignorance regarding the question of industrial consolidations may be carried to the public marketplace and exhibited in the stocks.... Out of every ten thousand men in the community, there is hardly one who would not state it as a hard and fast proposition that the industrial enterprises of the country that have been brought together under the present system of consolidation are all outrageously over-capitalized, and that their stocks present about the most hazardous investment conceivable....

As a test of what is really behind the industrial stocks that are being dealt in on the Stock Exchange and on the curb, I have gone into the figures of forty-seven among the most prominent companies.... Industrials, almost without exception, are worth a great deal more, judged by their earning capacity, than they are selling for in the open market. Some of these industrials are earning over 25 per cent a year on their market values, and the average for the entire forty-seven is 13.6 per cent.... Even more astonishing than the earnings on the market value are the earnings on the par value. A very popular impression exists that industrials are composed principally of water. The best answer to this is that the forty-seven companies [analyzed for this study showed] an average earning rate of 7.44 per cent on their total capitalization at par.

Choosing between two evils, Mr. Sage says, if we must have consolidations, the danger lurking in the consolidation of railroads is perhaps not as great, "because," as he puts it, "they are based on sounder considerations. Their stocks and bonds have not been doubled or trebled or unduly inflated." In other words, Mr. Sage concludes that railroad stocks rest on a sounder basis than do industrials.

Even if this statement were accurate, though it is not, it would call for this commentary, that scarcely one of the great railroads of this country whose shares are now quoted at favorable prices on our Exchanges, has not undergone the process of reorganization, growing out of the fact that they were injudiciously organized. And while the common stock of many of these great industrial corporations may be said to have been issued not to represent tangible property, nevertheless, it represents a fair equivalent for tangible property, namely good will or earning power long established, which, for obvious reasons is as rightfully a matter of valuation as the manufacturing plant itself.

...[R]ailroad properties even as they stand today in their reorganized form are not nearly so good an investment as are the industrials, and their only hope of improvement lies in the extensive application of the principle of consolidation which has done so much for the industrial stocks.... If the consolidation movements now on foot by Mr. Hill and Mr. Morgan and the other great railroad men are carried out, railroad values will undoubtedly be much improved. As they stand today, they rank, as earners, about half as high as the industrials..... [Analyzing] thirty-seven railways, including the best properties in the market, they show an average rate of earnings on their market value of 4.85 per cent, and on their par of total capitalization of 4.85 per cent. On the face of it, this would show a very substantial situation so far as the railroads are concerned, placing them as a whole almost on a level with government bonds. Unfortunately, however, the average is more a matter of accident than of anything else, as the earnings fluctuate from 2 per cent, on the market value up to 8 per cent, and from one-half of one per cent, on the par value up to 16 per cent.

Surely, on this comparative showing, there is no better investment anywhere than is offered by the industrial stocks of today. The cold figures dispute absolutely the charge of general overcapitalization, so freely made by people who have but a superficial knowledge of the situation....

To pretend that the industrials, or "trusts," as people are fond of calling them, constitute a political or economic menace is absurd. Instead of concentrating the wealth of the country in the hands of a few people, the consolidations have had exactly the reverse effect. Where, under the old conditions, there were a hundred stockholders, there are to-day a thousand or two thousand. Never before was there such a wide distribution of manufacturing interests. The great bulk of the stocks is held, not by the very rich, but by the moderately well-to-do. The control under the new system is not vested, as it was under the old, in the hands of a few abnormally rich men, but it rests with the majority of stockholders, whose numerical strength is growing every day. The danger to the community today lies not in the centralization of manufactures, in industrial consolidations, but in the centralization of wealth in the hands of a few men. This centralization was made possible by the old conditions of individualism. Unfortunately, the new economic ideas which prevail today arrived so late that they have not proven sufficient, up to this time, to check the accumulation of great fortunes by individuals. As the new scheme works itself out naturally, such accumulations will in the future, be rare. As it is, legislation may be necessary to cope with the evil as we find it today. What would Mr. Sage say to a law limiting individual fortunes?

There is no danger, either to the community or to business, in such consolidation as has been effected in the case of the steel trust. Its capitalization is based on solid properties. That it runs into a thousand millions is not a cause for apprehension, but rather the reverse, for it typifies the acme of scientific business. If its securities equal, as Mr. Sage points out, nearly one-half the amount of money in circulation in America, the country has cause, not to fear, but to rejoice. Money, when based on sound considerations, as our currency is today, is but an expressed form of wealth. Stocks and bonds of the new steel combination, represent quite as much an expressed form of wealth as the currency. They supplement the money in circulation, and, always provided that they are not the mere output of a printing press, serve as tokens of valuable property. Such stocks and bonds are quite as important an item in the wealth of a country as its currency. As the business system of a country expands, the need, relatively, of money grows less. Instead of the actual interchange of gold and silver in commercial transactions, there comes a system of credit. The amount of business transacted on credit in the United States today is over two thousand times as great as that transacted in exchange for gold and silver. As soon as the volume of trade mounts into great proportions, it is impossible to transact it on the basis of an actual exchange of currency. Instead, every means of exchange is utilized. Drafts and checks are the chief mediums now known in the commercial world. Actual money is scarcely ever passed from hand to hand. It is idle, therefore, and absolutely valueless, as an object lesson, to set forth the proportion that any bond issue or stock issue bears to the amount of money in circulation. We have passed the point here in the United States where such a statement carries any weight, and we have passed it because we have grown to such enormous proportions as an industrial nation. Not so very long ago, it was different. Then, a dollar in cash was more important, and it went further because it had more to do....

We traded in times gone by in a measure on the basis of the money in circulation. The result was often disastrous. It left the country in a position where the close-fisted money-lenders had the market at their mercy whenever the notion seized them, or whenever they felt that there was a situation, real or imaginary, that warranted a demand for extortionate interest rates. This condition was a severe handicap to our merchants and manufac-turers.... Now, owing...to an economical and conservative administration of their affairs for the past ten years, they are in a stronger financial condition, and comparatively free from the domination of the money-lender. And, as in the case of individuals, so it is in the nation. Instead of depending upon the good-will of the money-lenders of Europe, instead of trembling, as we used to do, for fear that they would call their loans, we have now reversed the situation. We are no longer borrowers from, but lenders to, Europe. Consequently, the money market has few terrors for us. From a debtor nation we have grown to be a creditor nation, and this is due very largely to the fact that we are conducting our business affairs over here on the most scientific and advanced basis, thanks to the industrial consolidations....

Viewing the matter from every standpoint, the business man is benefited when he operates as a member of a combination instead of as an individual. His property is in the shape of stocks and bonds which he can market at a moment's notice, instead of in the shape of a plant, on which it would be impossible to realize anything like its value at a forced sale. In case of his death, or disability, he leaves to his family a property that runs along uninterruptedly. The death of any one individual has little, if any, effect on the general business prosperity of the combination, and the tokens of interest held by the family of a deceased stockholder continue to bring their return just as steadily as though the man himself stood at the helm. In the case of an individual corporation, no matter how well organized or how well established, business failure is almost inevitable when the head of the corporation dies....

Another great advantage is that a combination can generally arrange to run its best factories on full time. The saving in production in this one item alone—that is, where a factory is run on full time instead of half time—is from 4 per cent to 8 per cent. Over-production, which is one of the most prolific sources of panic, can be largely prevented under the present system and that without throwing any great body of workingmen out of employment....

All these advantages redound directly to the benefit of capital, but indirectly they redound to the benefit of the consumer. They lessen the cost of production, and the consumer is bound to receive his share in this saving.

Labor is immeasurably benefited by the new conditions. The tendency under natural laws would be for wages to gradually decline to the level of the wages paid in other countries, but the industrial combinations have sustained the wages of the American wage-earner. Today, the tendency is to a minimum of profits and a maximum of wages. Any concern whose profits become abnormal at once invites competition. Naturally, these profits are reduced, and the consumer, who is the workingman, reaps the benefit. If the profits are not sufficiently abnormal to invite competition, the workingman again comes to the front, for he demands a larger share of the earnings in the form of increased wages. In either case, then, the wage-earners, as the great body of the community, reap the greatest advantages that come out of more economical production....

America is now at the front in the race for industrial supremacy. The main factor that has placed her there is the system of consolidation which Mr. Sage warns us against. It has won us the lead in less than ten years' trial. Surely, such results do not argue for a restriction, but rather for the continuance and enlightened development, of the system.

6–5. F. B. THURBER, "INDUSTRIAL CONSOLIDATIONS: THE INFLUENCE OF 'TRUSTS' UPON PRICES"

Source: *North American Review*, DXXXIV(May, 1901), pp. 677–686.

A further evolution in the organization of industries by the formation of "a Trust of Trusts" in the steel industry, with a capital approximating a billion of dollars, has given fresh occasion for discussion of the so-called "Trust" question, and has increased the already large number of citizens who fear evil from such consolidations. There is a widespread impression that "Trusts" result in unreasonable prices, through which the many are taxed for the benefit of the few, and it may be interesting to inquire how far this impression is confirmed by the facts...as indicated in the following statistics taken from United States Government reports.

I

The first great organization of industry in the United States was the consolidation of railway lines, and its effect upon the prices of transportation is shown in the Table 6.1.

This result has been attained largely through combinations and consolidations, which, contrary to the impression generally entertained, have not resulted in abolishing competition, but rather in economies of operation and improvement in service, accompanied by a steady reduction in rates....

II

The next great "Trust" was the Standard Oil Company, and its influence on prices is evidenced by the statistics in Table 6.2.

This great decline in the price of oil is attributable partly to the increase in production, but more largely to improvements in manufacture and transportation, which were only attainable through the aggregation of capital in this industry.

III

The next great "Trust" in the order of formation was the American Sugar Refining Company, or the "Sugar Trust," a corporation formed under the laws of the State of New Jersey for the purpose of consolidating the sugar refining interests of the country. Until recently, when additional capital flowed into this channel, it did about eighty-five per cent of the sugar refining business in the United States. The tendency of prices under its influence is shown by the Tables 6.3 and 6.4 giving, respectively, the average price of both raw and refined sugar, with the differing margins, during the nine years prior to and the nine years immediately following its consolidation in 1887.

For nine years after the formation of the "Trust," prices were as shown in Table 6.4.

Table 6.1 Average Receipts Per Ton Per Mile of Leading Railroads (cents)

Railway Line	1870	1880	1890	1899
Lines east of Chicago	1.61	0.87	0.63	0.51
West & Northwest lines	2.61	1.44	1.00	0.92
Southwestern lines	2.95	1.65	1.11	0.93
Southern lines	2.39	1.16	0.80	0.62
Transcontinental lines	4.50	2.21	1.50	0.99
Average	1.99	1.17	0.91	0.70

Table 6.2 Prices of Refined Illuminating Oil, Per Gallon, Exported from the United States (cents)

1871	25.7	1881	10.3	1891	7.0
1872	24.9	1882	9.1	1892	5.9
1873	23.5	1883	8.8	1893	4.9
1874	18.3	1884	9.2	1894	4.2
1875	14.1	1885	8.7	1895	4.9
1876	14.0	1886	8.7	1896	6.8
1877	21.1	1887	7.8	1897	6.3
1878	14.4	1888	7.9	1898	5.7
1879	10.8	1889	7.8	1899	5.6
1880	8.6	1890	7.4	1900	7.8

Table 6.3

Year	Centrifugals, Raw, per lb (cents)	Granulated, Refined, per lb (cents)	Difference per lb (cents)
1879	6.93	8.81	1.88
1880	7.88	9.80	1.92
1881	7.62	9.70	2.08
1882	7.29	9.35	2.06
1883	6.79	8.65	1.86
1884	5.29	6.75	1.46
1885	5.19	6.53	1.34
1886	5.52	6.23	0.71
1887	5.38	6.02	0.64
Average, nine years	6.43	7.98	1.55

Table 6.4

Year	Centrifugals, Raw, per lb (cents)	Granulated, Refined, per lb (cents)	Difference per lb (cents)
1888	5.93	7.18	1.25
1889	6.57	7.89	1.32
1890	5.57	6.27	0.70
1891	3.92	4.65	0.73
1892	3.32	4.35	1.03
1893	3.69	4.84	1.15
1894	3.24	4.12	0.88
1895	3.23	4.12	0.89
1896	3.62	4.53	0.91
Average, nine years	4.34	5.33	0.98

Table 6.5

Year	Centrifugals, Raw, per lb (cents)	Granulated, Refined, per lb (cents)	Difference per lb (cents)
1897	3.56	4.50	0.94
1898	4.24	4.97	0.73
1899	4.42	4.92	0.50
1900	4.57	5.32	0.77
March, 1901	4.09	5.04	0.95
Average, five years	4.17	4.95	0.77

The figures for succeeding years are shown in Table 6.5.

This reduction in price to the consumer has been effected, partly by increased production, and largely through buying the raw material more cheaply than when a large number of separate refiners were competing for the product. Large economies were also effected by closing inferior plants and enlarging and extending superior ones. The American Sugar Refining Company has bought its raw material at cheap rates, but it has given the public the benefit of such purchases, merely retaining as its profit about one-third of a cent per pound, which, considering the nature of the business, is a reasonable one. It employs more labor and pays higher wages than were employed and paid before the organization of this industry.

IV

Among the more recent organizations is the "Paper Trust," known as the International Paper Company, organized in 1897. The contract prices of ordinary newspaper paper for

Table 6.6 Contract Prices for Newspaper for Ten Years (cents per lb.)

1890	3.61	1896	2.35
1891	3.12	1897	2.18
1892	3.12	1898	2.02
1893	2.90	1899	2.00
1894	2.75	1900	2.50
1895	2.40		

Table 6.7

Year	Dollars per ton	Year	Dollars per ton
1890	18.85	1896	12.14
1891	15.95	1897	10.13
1892	14.37	1898	10.33
1893	12.87	1899	19.03
1894	11.38	1900	19.49
1895	12.72	March, 1901	16.50

Table 6.8

1899	English	American
January	22.44	18.00
February	23.24	20.50
March	23.04	22.00
April	23.64	25.00
May	24.90	25.00
June	24.90	25.00
July	25.50	26.00
August	30.96	31.33
September	30.36	32.00
October	32.76	33.00
November	32.76	35.00
December	34.02	35.00

ten years covering a period before and after its formation afford interesting material for study (Table 6.6).

Notwithstanding the advance which, owing to the increased demand, has taken place since 1899, prices for paper are far below those of ten years ago, and it is safe to say that neither the tariff nor trusts have had any appreciable effect upon the price of paper....

The latest and, according to many journalistic utterances, the most startling of the trust organizations is "the billion dollar steel trust." This is a consolidation of trusts in that line; and, while we cannot give figures to show its effect upon future prices, the following figures for iron and steel in the past furnish a basis for future comparison which will be interesting. I foretell results similar to those indicated by the foregoing illustrations in other lines.

The fluctuations in iron and steel have been greater than in most staples, as is shown by the statistics in Table 6.7, giving the prices for "Bessemer pig iron" for a period of ten years.

That the tariff had nothing to do with the advance in prices since 1898 is shown by the comparison shown in Table 6.8 of English and American prices for steel rails for each month during 1899, which illustrates the influence of supply and demand.

The steel trust has not abrogated competition; it has simply elevated it to a higher plane. There are several plants outside of the trust, which are capable of being a David to the Goliath, if the Goliath should prove unreasonable....

The organization of industry has taken place so suddenly that the public has been startled, as a good horse will shy at an umbrella when it is opened suddenly in his face; but let the horse smell the umbrella and see that it is not dangerous and his alarm will subside. Thus will it be with the feeling of the public toward trusts. Their evil will be eliminated, their good will be developed, their usefulness to mankind demonstrated, and the bogy which the rivalries of sensational journalism and partisan politics have conjured up will fade into thin air....

ESSAYS

In the decades after World War II economic historians steadily chipped away at the "robber baron" thesis that had long dominated the historiography about the rise of big business. To them World War II and the unfolding Cold War both clearly demonstrated the benefits of American capitalism over other economic systems and so they often viewed big business more positively than previous generations of Americans. The interpretative school that emerged from this re-examination, while generally not denying that the business leaders of the late 19th century sometimes used questionable tactics, emphasized the positive contributions of these "industrial statesmen." Essay 6–1, an excerpt from the 1986 work by the late Jonathan R. T. Hughes, *The Vital Few: The Entrepreneur and American Economic Progress,* is a representative of this school of thought. In it Professor Hughes, a long-time member of Northwestern University's Economics Department, praised the entrepreneurial innovations Andrew Carnegie used to become the dominant force in the American steel industry. However great the differences were between the "robber baron" thesis and the "industrial statesmen" thesis they agreed on one major point. Both schools of thought saw the big businesses of the late 19th century as the products of powerful individuals.

Glenn Porter, Director Emeritus of the Hagley Museum and Library, and Harold C. Livesay, the Clifford A. Taylor Professor in Liberal Arts at Texas A & M University offer a different way to think about the rise of big business. In Essay 6–2, an excerpt from their 1971 work, *Merchants and Manufacturers: Studies in the Changing Structure of Nineteenth-Century Marketing*, Professors Porter and Livesay suggest that integrated corporations were often the product of impersonal market forces rather than of individual acquisitiveness or genius.

6–1. JONATHAN R. T. HUGHES, "CARNEGIE AND THE AMERICAN STEEL INDUSTRY"

Andrew Carnegie's life contained so much that was great mixed with the absurd, such giant achievements amid the commonplace failures, that the historian's hand necessarily falters momentarily at the prospect of it all. The poor, but deserving, Scottish immigrant lad, laboring in the Allegheny cotton mill lived to carry his version of the American "success story" beyond the sublime, almost beyond belief. He rose to be the greatest innovator in the American steel industry, and in his own lifetime gave away over $350 million of the resulting personal fortune for the benefit, as he saw it, of humanity. He left a host of institutions to influence the future of the world, paid for by the interest on the residue of his personal estate....

Carnegie's life was overshadowed by technological change, the most thoroughgoing revolutionary force man has contrived. Carnegie...became one of the virtuoso industrial innovators in history, imposing technological improvements in the wide-open American steel industry with such skill that none could stand against him....

Carnegie's ... innovations included the first steps toward scientific management in the iron business. First was the introduction of accounting in the shops. He quickly discovered that the cost of each individual process in iron-making was unknown and that only at year end did his competitors really know how their net positions had changed. As an old railway man, Carnegie saw a fabulous opening here. Accountants and strict costing in the shops were introduced. The new system took years to perfect, but from the first was a powerful source of strength to Carnegie. He introduced the Siemens gas furnace into his iron works because his accounting methods showed him that it would raise his profits by cutting his unit costs. His competitors took years to understand this. They thought that the furnaces were "too expensive" because of their high initial costs. Carnegie knew how much they cost per ton of product, a very different sort of information. Carnegie's appreciation of the accountant's art gave him immense advantages in competition with his "practical" Pittsburgh colleagues, whom he was fond of referring to derisively as "the Fathers-in-Israel" because of both their Quaker origins and their hide-bound conservatism. As Carnegie put it:

> One of the chief sources of success in manufacturing is the introduction and strict maintenance of a perfect system of accounting so that responsibility for money or materials can be brought home to every man.

The old rule-of-thumb Pittsburgh was destined to be badly shaken by this man who was a perfectly ruthless competitor. His system of information included the details of his competitors' businesses. He could make calculations fine beyond belief in the iron business of the time. Once, when calculating whether to continue to respect his competitors' steel price agreements, his lieutenant, Charles Schwab, was able to advise Carnegie to cut his competitors down; it would be more profitable to run his vast operations full at one-tenth of a cent less per pound than, at the current prices, to use them at three-fourths of capacity—the amount allotted to him by the "pool." Accounting! As Schwab once described the Carnegie accounting system: "We made a careful ... statement of each manufacture, with the cost as compared with each department. ..." One of Carnegie's employees, Julian Kennedy, recalled that he was expected to show a saving in cost in each accounting period. Even when vacationing in Scotland, Carnegie could detect a 5 percent increase in coke consumption in the accounts of his company's operations which were regularly forwarded to him.

Another important innovation made by Carnegie in the Pittsburgh iron industry was the introduction of chemistry into the blast-furnace operations. To his astonishment Carnegie, upon entering into the iron manufacturing business, learned that the Pittsburgh iron masters really knew very little about the production of iron. The content of the furnace was a mystery until it was poured. "Practical men" ruled at the blast furnace. Carnegie describes the manufacture of pig iron at the beginning of the 1870's:

> The blast furnace manager of that day was... supposed to diagnose the condition of the furnace by instinct, to possess some almost supernatural power of divination, like his congener in the country districts who was reputed to be able to locate ... water ... by means of a hazel rod.

Where might a solution lie? Obviously a chemist might have something beyond rule-of-thumb information to contribute. However, as late as 1867 Sir Lowthian Bell, the great English iron mogul (and himself a chemist), had noted that science had little to offer the ironmaster.

> With regard to the application of science the ironmasters in other countries, as here, can only lament how little chemistry has been able to effect in the blast furnace or puddling process.

Carnegie broke ranks. In 1870 a huge new furnace, the Lucy Furnace (named for his sister-in-law), had been erected at his works and he was determined to increase its efficiency by applying science and getting rid of his "rule-of-thumb-and-intuition" furnace manager. A mere youngster, Henry Curry, a shipping clerk, was raised to manager, and a chemist was hired to find out what happens inside a blast furnace. No one has ever told the story better than Carnegie himself.

> We found the man in a learned German, Dr. Fricke, and great secrets did the doctor open to us. Iron stone from mines that had a high reputation was now found to contain ten, fifteen, and even twenty per cent less iron than it had been credited with. Mines that hitherto had a poor reputation we found to be yielding superior ore. The good was bad and the bad was good, and everything was topsy-turvy. Nine tenths of all the uncertainties of pig-iron making were dispelled under the burning sun of chemical knowledge. ... What fools we had been! But ... we were not as great fools as our competitors. ... We were the first to employ a chemist at blast furnaces. ... The Lucy Furnace became the most profitable branch of our business, because we had almost the entire monopoly of scientific management.

It was years before the "Fathers-in-Israel" understood why the hiring of a chemist was not an extravagance. By then Carnegie, with his cost accounting and chemical analyses, was the industry's most efficient producer by far and it was too late to catch him. His chemist told him where to acquire ore lands, and his partners even bought from his competitors waste materials which were converted into rails at the Carnegie mills.

Carnegie also introduced the modern technique of marketing iron and steel—he went out after business. He solicited. His main customers, railways and manufacturers, had offices in New York City. Instead of waiting in Pittsburgh for their orders to come, Carnegie went out after them. He moved his mother to New York in 1867 and opened an office there, commuting to Pittsburgh whenever his presence was required at his works. Carnegie now became a "commercial traveler on an heroic scale." He was selling iron bridges and rails. No journey was too arduous, and his Keystone bridges began spanning the rivers and gorges of America.

His methods baffled his competitors. Sometimes, as when negotiating a contract with his fellow Scotsman, John Garrett, president of the Baltimore & Ohio Railroad, the "wee drap o' Scotch bluid atween us" gave Carnegie a competitive advantage none could overcome. But Carnegie also had less subtle methods. He lent money to his buyers when necessary; he accepted mortgage bonds as payment; he was as good as any at squeezing special rates out of the railways for shipping his products. He personally marketed his customers' bonds abroad to enable them to buy his bridges. Continuous improvements at his mills allowed him to undercut the competition whenever it was necessary. He *sold* his products on a scale hitherto unknown in the iron business.

...[I]n 1872 Sir Henry Bessemer personally demonstrated his converter to Carnegie and acquired a disciple. Carnegie came home from England...a changed man. He had "seen the future." From then on his world was steel. He now followed his own maxim "Put all good eggs in one basket, and then watch that basket." Carnegie the innovator now created an industrial revolution of his own, either destroying his competitors outright or dragging them "kicking and screaming" into the age of steel. Incredible as it was, the Dunfermline lad, already a millionaire, was not yet 40 and had not yet embarked upon the career which made him a legend. All that began in 1873, at the scene of General Braddock's defeat, near Pittsburgh....

Iron and steel were at the base of the great transformation of the United States into an industrial nation, and in the years 1870–1900, Andrew Carnegie led the fierce competitive battles which made the age of steel so much an American achievement, and the American steel industry the wonder of the manufacturing world.

Carnegie was hardly pioneering when he got back to Pittsburgh in 1872, but he was using an innovation perilously close to the frontier, and he had to undertake his new vocation without his old partners, his brother Thomas, Henry Phipps and Andrew Kloman. They... elected to stay in the iron trade. So Carnegie organized a new company to make steel (he brought brother Thomas and Phipps in later, when they saw the light). He rounded up new partners, sold his holdings of Pullman stock and put up $250,000 of his own money. He bought land at Braddock's and, in 1873, began construction of his steel mill, later to be called the Edgar Thomson Works, after his old chief on the Pennsylvania Railroad....

Once he was in the steel business, Carnegie's competitive instincts were given full rein. Even by 1873, when the Edgar Thomson Works were under construction, many of Carnegie's business habits were evident. He operated his various companies, almost until the end as partnerships. Considering that he was operating in one of the greatest periods of corporation development, this was surprising. But surprising or not, the partnership and not the corporation was Carnegie's instrument... and he built the partnership into a fabulous organizational machine.

Carnegie was a staunch believer in internal financing, plowing back profits into new plant and equipment at the expense of dividends. He left the capital market strictly alone, emphasizing his sizzling contempt for "speculators" and "financiers." Finally, he seemed to have an innate sense of timing as regards the business cycle and learned quickly, and applied the lesson again and again, that cash money goes a long way when the economy is idle, and that taking advantage of low construction costs in depressions meant low production costs when demand revived.

One major advantage of the partnership to Carnegie was his own control; in times of stress, partners who had become financially "embarrassed" could not bring in outside capital by selling equity in the Carnegie companies. If a partner had to raise money, he had to sell out to his other partners or to the wealthiest ones. After the 1873 crash, six of Carnegie's new partners in the Edgar Thomson Works were forced to sell to him and Carnegie ended with 59% of the ownership. He was majority owner from then on, and became quickly the wealthiest man of his time. He resented the notion that he had taken advantage of his partners and always maintained that he had done them a favor by buying them out at the pit of the depression. In later years Carnegie didn't like to recall the rapacious competitor he once was. As he described the acquisition of majority control of Edgar Thomson in later years: "So many of my friends needed money that they begged me to repay them." He did.

Carnegie watched silently as men, including his old boss Thomas Scott, were ruined by calls on stock that had been purchased on credit, and learned the fundamental truth that when the banking system contracts, all of the credit cannot be honored. In 1873 Carnegie, relatively free of current debt personally, found himself esteemed as a "rock" in the industry. His credit was as good as gold, and the "old men" of Pittsburgh ceased to refer to him as a parvenu and a plunger. Carnegie never forgot the lesson. He was convinced thereafter that absolute virtue resided with the man who had cash in depressions. It was of course advantageous on other grounds, too; you could buy extraordinary amounts of labor and materials when prices were low.

In the depression following 1873 the steel men first learned to sweat out Carnegie's virtuoso game of purchasing and rebuilding in depressions. It was Carnegie who initiated, and maintained throughout his lifetime, the policy of continuous cost and price-cutting competition in the steel industry. His competitors were considered enemies, not gentlemanly rivals. The Edgar Thomson Works were built with maximum efficiency and at minimum cost for the best. Carnegie's net marginal returns were enormous compared to those of his competitors. Hendricks quotes one of Carnegie's managers in later years: Carnegie knew

> ... that the real time to extend your operations was when no one else was doing it. Whenever there would be a boom in the steel trade most manufacturers would start in and build new steel works. They would have to pay the very highest prices for the materials that entered into these constructions on account of boom times, and about the time they were ready to operate the bloom was off the peach and the works would have to lie idle.

Or, they could sell out to Carnegie. In 1883 when the steel market began its collapse, the price of rails had been $85 a ton. Soon they were well down toward $27 a ton which they reached in 1885. Carnegie found that his erstwhile competitors at the newly constructed mills at Homestead were "willing" to sell to him. Homestead had been built in the boom to roll steel rails and now lay helpless as Carnegie sold rails profitably below Homestead's costs. The men who built Homestead had openly boasted that they were going to undersell Carnegie. Carnegie summed up the situation bluntly, "They were in no condition to compete with us." He offered the Homestead owners either partnerships, dollar for dollar, or cash. All but one of the Homestead owners took cash. They had already seen enough of Carnegie to satisfy their curiosity (the one who stayed in saw his $50,000 share grow to $8,000,000 in fifteen years). Again, in 1890, the new Duquesne steel works was "swallowed up" by Carnegie after its builders were unable to continue....

He bought in depressions, rebuilt in depressions, restaffed in depressions, then undercut his competitors when business was good. His competitors had to stay awake to remain in the game with him. Efficiency was the result. The whole point of the competitive system, after all, is to reward the efficient producer and chastise the inefficient. In many ways Carnegie was the *laissez-faire* economist's delight; he maximized his profits by competitive ruthlessness and the survivors in the steel industry, by meeting his competition, reduced the price of steel until it became a basic metal....

Before the early 1890's Carnegie's tactics included joining in the multitudinous cartels and pools which the industry tried to maintain to produce monopoly profits. The opportunity was there because of the protective tariff. A tariff of $28 a ton on steel rails, for example, kept out foreign competition and American producers could mulct their compatriots if they could only agree among themselves. Part of the game was to act as if they could agree (such agreements were not illegal before the Sherman Act of 1890). But one fundamental characteristic of a cartel is its instability. The opportunity to undercut the agreed price could hardly be resisted and Carnegie, playing the game, double-crossed his competitors with as much regularity and glee as they double-crossed him....

Carnegie...never liked to cooperate with his enemies. When he entered his first rail pool, he was allotted only a small part of the market by the other members. Carnegie leaped up, announced that he wanted an amount equal to the largest quota, moved his finger around the table from magnate to magnate telling each one his own business and costs and threatening to undercut them all. It was a typical Carnegie display, and it worked.

Until the '90's Carnegie entered pools periodically, using the period of the price agreement to prepare for his next competitive offensive, if there was time. Most of the pools were, in fact, too short-lived. Schwab once said of pools: "... many of them lasted a day, some of them lasted until the gentlemen could go to the telephone from the room in which they were made. ..." Carnegie ceased playing the game with much grace after 1893 when he told a Pittsburgh competitor that he wanted no more price agreements. "The market is mine whenever I want to take it. I see no reason why I should present you with all of my profits."

From the time of the building of the Edgar Thomson Works (it started making rails in 1874), Carnegie's spirit poisoned the would-be convivial atmosphere of the Bessemer Steel Association's meetings—the Pittsburgh rail pool. Even in the late 1870's and early 1880's, before Carnegie's aggressiveness reached its height, his methods were having astonishing effects. It wasn't all Andrew Carnegie, of course—he had help at his mills, but the growth of the competitive steel industry before 1900 was due more to Carnegie personally than is commonly realized today. Carnegie was too good a propagandist and the image of the kindly old philanthropist obscures the man who made Pittsburgh the capital of steel. He could use all the vagaries of the violently fluctuating market to his own advantage. That was remarkable enough. But Carnegie was in a class by himself when it came to choosing his management. Indeed the Carnegie management has been considered by many to be one of his most remarkable achievements. It was also his innovation. It was a singular kind of masterpiece, and the steel industry has never really seen the like of it since 1900....

At first Carnegie had taken partners in when he needed them. Some, like his brother Thomas, Henry Phipps and his cousin George Lauder, had been with Carnegie from childhood. Some men were made partners for special reasons; Andrew Kloman, for example, had the original iron firm that Thomas Carnegie had gone into, staked by Andrew, along with Carnegie partners Thomas Miller and Henry Phipps; Carnegie finally absorbed Kloman and eventually parted with him (Kloman was one of those ruined in 1873). Henry Clay Frick was already the Connellsville coke baron when Carnegie merged with him in order to have the Frick coke ovens integrated with the Carnegie blast furnaces.

Other partners, like William Coleman, went in with Carnegie when he needed capital. But as the Carnegie enterprises grew and Carnegie's personal control became established, young men coming up from the inside were made partners on a merit basis. Stock was set aside for them, paid for out of earnings, and then the fortunate youngsters were full-blown Carnegie partners.

The firm had an agreement, the "Iron-Clad," from 1887 until it was broken by Frick in 1900, which obligated any partner to relinquish his stocks back to the company "at the books" (a valuation which included no "good will" and hence was radically short of what a fair market price might be) if he left the firm. In case of death, the stocks were automatically put back into the treasury and the company had a "protracted" period to pay for them. Carnegie said he was impressed by how much harder commercial fishermen who owned their own boats worked than did those who were merely wage earners. Also Carnegie was terribly sentimental, so long as they did good work, about his friends and cronies and liked to reward good young men by making them associates.

Since a Carnegie partnership was in fact open, free, to any young man, the employees were famous for their diligence. Carnegie kept an eagle eye out for talent in his mills. One of his managers said of him in later years, "... he exceeded any man I ever knew in his ability to pick a man from one place and put him in another with maximum effect... ." His furnace managers competed fiercely with each other, always aware that "the little boss" expected repairs to show an ever increasing efficiency. It might have been slave driving, but the slaves seemed willing. Why not? Any ambitious young man had universal opportunity just sitting there waiting to be taken. No barriers. Moreover, Carnegie believed in giving every bright young man his head. "Every year should be marked by the promotion of one or more of our young men.... We can not have too many of the right sort interested in the profits." In the single year 1898 twenty youngsters were made partners. All had come up from the bottom through the Carnegie mills.

In keeping with the policy of utilizing the best talent, Carnegie never allowed "dead wood" to accumulate. He was perfectly ruthless about partners pulling their own weight. Men who failed to come up to the mark were forced out. In Pittsburgh the "European tour" of unsuccessful Carnegie partners became a standing joke. As Carnegie put it, "If he can win the race he is our race-horse; if not he goes to the cart."

It was a system designed to gain efficiency without regard to personalities. Carnegie, it was said, never inquired about the profits, only about the costs, which he wanted constantly reduced. It was the job of his "young geniuses" to do it—or else. Given the market, Carnegie's profits were determined by his costs. He understood, and many times lectured his sales people about the fact that the price in the market was not their affair. They should just meet the price whatever it was. The technical partners would handle their affairs so that *any* market could be met.

Not only were partnerships dangled in front of bright young men, but so were lavish bonuses for good work. Those who took the bait were known to be the highest paid men in American industry. "I can't afford to pay them any other way" was Carnegie's reply to a question about his young men's high wages. In his *Autobiography* Carnegie noted shrewdly that the most expensive labor is the only kind worth hiring because its high productivity, in a free market, is the cause of its high price.

If Carnegie's incentive system seems a bit hair-raising compared to present-day industrial practices, it is worth considering a few of the astonishing results. The system worked. Perhaps the best known and most spectacular product of Carnegie's system was Charles Schwab. He was hired out of a grocery store as a youth at $1 a day to drive stakes by Capt. William Jones, the great Carnegie superintendent. Within six months Schwab was an assistant manager. He was a superintendent in five years and at barely 30 years of age was president of Carnegie Steel. Carnegie said of Schwab, "I have never met his equal...."

In 1891 most of Carnegie's interests were pulled together in the reorganized Carnegie Steel Co. The capital was valued at a mere $25,000,000, following Carnegie's refusal to count the good will. By then Carnegie had supplied the steel for the first American skyscraper, the Home Insurance Building in Chicago in 1883. (In 1894 Carnegie, Phipps & Co., a special organization, issued the first handbook of steel shapes to guide architects in building skyscrapers. Carnegie's pricing methods were followed there too, selling eleven-story buildings for the price of ten-story buildings.) Carnegie supplied steel for the Brooklyn Bridge, the New York elevated railway, the Washington Monument, railways, and armor plate for the newly developing Navy. Carnegie's company was a wonder of organization, producing all the way from the mines to finished products. Carnegie himself was the "super salesman": the bright young men managed at Pittsburgh.

> There are no other works in the world under one management which have reached this remarkable output or are likely soon to attain it.

So ran a contemporary report....

In 1893 there was another crash, followed by a deep and long-lasting depression. While his competition stared at idle plants, Carnegie used his powerful financial position to play his old game once again. The capacity of Carnegie steel was expanded as never before. Moreover, much of the old plant was destroyed or modernized, so that from 1893 to 1898 most of the mills were rebuilt. When prosperity came again, Carnegie was far under his competitors in production costs. In the 1890's he went all out for vertical integration, self-supply of all inputs from the mines to the retail trade. Carnegie...had been building a vertically integrated system since the days of the Keystone Bridge Co., slowly freeing himself from dependence upon independent suppliers. In the 1890's he completed the process....

The result of these operations was upheaval in the industrial world. Who could stop him? Carnegie had led one of the greatest industrial transformations the world had ever known, the rise of the American steel industry. The nation's industrial machine, based upon cheap steel, was without peer. The resulting rise in national output had in turn nourished the continuing revolution in steelmaking. The process had created the most rapid rise in per capita income the nation had ever known (or has known since, for that matter)....

6–2. GLENN PORTER AND HAROLD C. LIVESAY, "MERCHANTS AND MANUFACTURERS"

During the nineteenth century, the American economy witnessed a process of fundamental change in the marketing of manufactured products. That process mirrored many vital elements in the transformation of the nation's economy from its mercantile, agrarian orientation in the period following the Revolution to its present status as the leading industrial economy in the twentieth century. Changes in distribution played at least as important a role in the story of our economic past as did changes in production, though the attention of historians has primarily been directed at developments in the latter area. This book attempts to redress part of the historical imbalance reflected in the many shelves groaning with the weight of volumes dealing with the means by which Americans have produced manufactured goods.

We have not tried to present a comprehensive history of the marketing of all commodities. The distribution of non-manufactured products, especially unprocessed agricultural products, has already been scrutinized by numerous historians, and many admirable studies have been completed. Consequently we have excluded from our study the marketing of farm and mine products, except in some cases where such goods served as raw materials for manufacturers. Furthermore, although our research has involved an examination of the distribution networks employed in a multitude of nineteenth-century manufacturing industries, what appears here is a study of firms and industries that best illustrate prevailing distribution methods and best explain the causes and directions of change in the broad structural patterns of marketing.

By "distribution system" we mean the channels through which the manufacturer marketed his goods. Some consideration is also given to the means by which the manufacturer obtained his raw materials, since this also involved the distribution of goods—some produced by manufacturers;—but the primary focus is on marketing. We have made no attempt to trace the complete flow of the product through the entire marketing system to its ultimate consumer. Our vantage point is that of the manufacturer; once he had disposed of his goods, he was normally no longer concerned with their subsequent fate. As a consequence of this viewpoint, the book deals almost exclusively with wholesaling, for, insofar as the nineteenth-century producer marketed his goods to independent middlemen, he did so almost entirely to wholesalers, not retailers.

The marketing experience of manufacturing firms clearly indicates that the most important determinants of the marketing system employed by a firm were the nature of the product it manufactured and the nature of the market served by the enterprise. At the close of the eighteenth century, manufacturers shared broadly similar markets. In addition, almost all manufactured products of the time were "generic" goods, regarded by middlemen and by the market as susceptible to similar merchandising techniques. As a result, a uniform distribution system prevailed throughout the entire economy. During the nineteenth century, however, shifts in the makeup of markets and of products in many industries led to fundamental changes in the way goods were distributed. This book describes and analyzes the changes and the reasons behind them, and it delineates and explains the survival of the older marketing order in those segments of the manufacturing sector which remained largely immune to change.

The analytical framework of this study holds that the structure of distribution in America at the beginning of the nineteenth century was in a state of equilibrium. All products, manufactured and otherwise, were distributed through a network of sedentary merchants, who were the dominant element in the economy. Moreover, this pattern was essentially the same as it had been for many centuries throughout the Western world. Although wars, conquests, political upheavals, and religious conflicts had repeatedly upset the social equilibrium, the nature of the market, the methods of production, and the means of transportation and communication had remained relatively static. Consequently the institutions of marketing had exhibited inertial tendencies. In the absence of forces necessitating change, little change had occurred.

As the nineteenth century progressed, however, several basic factors upset the equilibrium and brought widespread changes in the marketing patterns for many manufactured goods. Producers moved to replace merchants in the wholesale distribution of manufactured goods whenever one of two conditions evolved within an industry. First, they did so whenever it became possible for them to market their own products at a lower unit cost than could the mercantile network. Second, they did so whenever it became necessary as a result of shortcomings in the ability or willingness of independent wholesalers to merchandise goods effectively. If neither of these two conditions emerged over time, the producers in a particular industry tended to rely on the independent middlemen who had acted as the channels of distribution from the earliest colonial times.

Neither of the two causal conditions for structural change was widely operative in the American economy until the closing decades of the nineteenth century. Therefore the specialized wholesalers who evolved in the early national period constituted the dominant marketing mechanism for manufactured products until late in the century. It was not generally economically feasible for manufacturers to create and maintain a company wholesale force, because of the diffuse, unconcentrated nature of markets. The manufacturer of the early nineteenth century was a man of very limited horizons; he knew little of the markets outside his immediate area. He relied on his wholesaler to keep abreast of the changing needs of the many small consuming units to which his goods were transferred. Furthermore, the uncertain transportation and slow communications of the times inhibited efforts to establish direct contacts between a producer and his distant customers. By simply selling his goods to an urban wholesaler, the manufacturer avoided all the difficulties and expenses of marketing them to a diffuse, diverse mass of anonymous customers, the problems of arranging transportation for many small lots, and the uncertainties of collecting accounts from the scattered customers. The strength of this advantage lay at the heart of the merchants' long commercial reign. Only when the traditional, diffuse markets changed did the ability to handle his own wholesaling become a genuine possibility for the manufacturer.

The second condition which led manufacturers to bypass merchants, the existence of marketing problems which merchants could not or would not resolve, also did not emerge widely until the latter part of the century. Virtually all goods required neither special handling nor direct contact between producer and customer. The generic nature of products made the utilization of middlemen quite logical. The antebellum industries that constituted exceptions to this generalization were the very industries in which manufacturers were led to take the initiative in distribution.

In the three decades after 1870, changes in the nature of markets and of products brought about one or the other of the two necessary conditions for modifications in the structure of marketing. The first condition—the ability of manufacturers to wholesale more cheaply than merchants—arose in two ways. In many producers' goods industries the rise of the large corporation and the coming of oligopoly brought concentrated markets in which manufacturers sold to a relatively small number of customers who were no longer anonymous and whose orders were much larger than those of firms earlier in the century. In some consumers' goods industries the growth of urban markets produced concentrated markets wherein a firm could enjoy a sufficiently high sales volume in a city to warrant the creation of a permanent sales force there. In both cases the older, diffuse market of many small, scattered consuming units was replaced by a much denser market.

The second condition—the merchandising inadequacy of independent wholesalers— emerged in industries producing new goods that either were technologically complex, expensive items requiring close and often extended contact between manufacturer and consumer or required elaborate, innovative marketing apparatus. Technological advances in marketing facilities made expansion into the national market possible for many firms hitherto restricted to small, local sales. When these producers found existing wholesale channels unwilling or unable to avail themselves of new technology, they had to assume their own wholesaling. The appearance in the latter part of the century of many new products of considerable technological complexity also presented problems the old wholesalers could not solve—problems such as the need for demonstrations, extensive repair facilities, and the necessity for close consultation which resulted from the special needs of the customer. Such changes in the nature of products created marketing challenges undreamed of in the older era of generic, less complicated, less costly manufactured products. The established mercantile system often proved unable to make the needed adjustments and so watched the emergence of new industries in which the independent wholesaler was either entirely absent or considerably less important than he was in more traditional industries.

In those portions of the manufacturing sector where it neither became less costly for manufacturers to replace wholesalers nor became necessary for them to do so because of wholesalers' merchandising inadequacies, the old order endured. Throughout the industries where markets remained diffuse and products remained undifferentiated and inexpensive, the old structure of distribution survived. These industries generally were the least concentrated ones in the emerging twentieth-century economy and were populated by firms that were not examples of the large, modern corporation. They continued to rely on the independent middleman because neither the nature of markets nor that of products changed significantly in the nineteenth century....

In the last half of the nineteenth century, the ancient and honorable dominion of the independent merchant over commerce came to a close. With the development of the modern manufacturing corporation in the last decades of the century, the role of independent middlemen in the distribution of manufactured goods greatly diminished. The rise of the factory and of mass production in the 1850s had tremendously increased the potential production rate of a single firm; the problem that remained for the manufacturers was how to solve the difficulties of mass distribution.

As producers in industry after industry learned to their grief in the decades following the Civil War, efficient production was not enough. Increased production seemed to bring only falling prices, as supply outran demand. The wholesale price index for all commodities in 1865 was 185; it declined fairly steadily thereafter to around eighty at the beginning of the 1890s. Producers struggled mightily with the problem of adjusting output to meet the needs of the market, trying pools, gentlemen's agreements, trusts, and holding companies. During this search for economic order, some manufacturers began to create their own distribution networks and thus to eliminate or greatly reduce the role of the independent middlemen.

While not directly related to their role in the distribution process, one important reason for the decline of merchants was the atrophy of the manufacturers' financial dependence on them. During the 1860s, many manufacturers found that they were able to put their businesses on a cash basis as a result of the wartime boom and the infusion of greenbacks into the economy. This reduced their reliance on credit extended by wholesalers acting as their suppliers and distributors. Of even greater importance was the growing ability of producers to finance their operations out of retained earnings and the concomitant growth of financial intermediaries able and willing to lend funds to promising manufacturing enterprises. These developments hastened the decline of wholesalers in the economy, but their fate in the closing decades of the century was sealed by the increasing tendency of manufacturers in many industries to create their own distribution networks.

Changes in distribution came whenever a large firm faced either a concentrated market or serious problems in the marketing of its products. The independent middleman had always served to bring many buyers and sellers together, to connect and coordinate the diffuse markets of the older economy.

Late in the nineteenth century, however, the structure of markets changed in many industries. The makers of producers' goods such as iron and steel and non-ferrous metals, like the makers of railroad supplies in antebellum days, found that the rise of the large firm and the coming of oligopoly had reduced the numbers and increased the size of buyers and sellers. This resulted in a very different and much more concentrated market in which the network of independent merchants was no longer relevant. Manufacturers could now handle their own wholesaling more efficiently than could the middlemen, and they assumed the functions of the merchants by building their own marketing organizations. In many consumers' goods industries, manufacturers also faced a denser market because of the growth of America's cities, with their concentration of population and hence of customers. As more and more industries grew oligopolistic, manufacturers utilized the significantly improved transportation and communications systems to take over the wholesaling of their own goods in the expanding urban areas. In producers' and consumers' goods industries, manufacturers supplanted the mercantile agents primarily because of changed market conditions, not because of any serious inadequacies in the old distribution network's ability to market the goods effectively. Manufacturers in other industries, however, did encounter distribution problems that the middlemen could not solve.

The latter group of firms produced many of the new goods that appeared in the post-Civil War United States, some of which were quite technologically advanced. Processors of perishable items, such as ice, dressed beef, bananas, beer, and others, employed improved refrigeration techniques to forge marketing organizations that would tap the potential urban markets. Because the old mercantile agents were not in a position to distribute the perishables, producers built costly storage, transport, and marketing facilities, which brought economies of scale in distribution. Makers of complex products, such as industrial machinery, early electrical apparatus, harvesters, office machines, and other commodities, found that the necessity for close and continuing contact between manufacturer and consumer made the commission agents and brokers an unsuitable distribution channel. Accordingly they created their own marketing organizations to provide such services as technical consultation, instruction in the operation of products, replacement parts, and facilities for repairs. In the realm of perishable goods and those requiring intimate, extended contact between producer and customer, the inability of the established distribution channels to provide the facilities and services needed for the new products led manufacturers to bypass the independent middleman and to assume the wholesaling function.

Although erosion was common to the traditional distribution network of most American manufacturing, in some areas the middleman continued to act as the primary wholesale agent. In those industries in which the rise of the large firm and the coming of oligopoly were rare, and in which the structure of markets and the nature of products remained much the same as they had been throughout the nineteenth century, the independent middleman endured. Throughout the complex of industries in which a variety of simple, standard items was sold through many thousands of retailers—in the grocery, drug, hardware, jewelry, liquor, furniture, and dry goods businesses—the jobber continued to assemble and disperse goods through these diffuse markets. The highly unconcentrated structure of such markets made the jobber vital even in those industries dominated by a large firm such as the American Tobacco Company. In the areas in which the independent middleman survived as wholesaler, however, his old role as salesman atrophied because of the coming of national advertising and brand names. Advertising reduced the wholesaler's job to the rather mechanical satisfaction of consumer wants created by the manufacturer's direct appeal to the customer.

By the beginning of the twentieth century, the outlines of the new economic order had emerged. The concentration movement, the changing structure of markets, and the appearance of technologically advanced products that presented serious distribution and marketing problems all spelled the end of the merchant's dominance and the beginning of the manufacturer's preeminence. Only in those sectors of the manufacturing economy which retained many of the characteristics of the older, agrarian-based economy did the independent middleman retain his primary role as wholesaler. The long reign of the merchant had finally come to a close. In many industries the manufacturer of goods had also become their distributor. A new economy dominated by the modern, integrated manufacturing enterprise had arisen.

The changes in the distribution patterns of American manufacturing from 1815 to the opening years of this century reflected the broader pattern of the economy's shifting locus of power. The modern corporation emerged as the dominant institution in our economy and perhaps in our society. The twin engines of change in marketing—the concentration of production and population on the one hand, and the imperatives of advancing technology on the other—also proved to be the forces which shaped the broad outlines of change in all of American civilization. They have determined much of the context of economic, political, and social conflict in modern America....

The pattern of change in distribution which resulted from concentrated urban demand was visible in some firms manufacturing consumers' goods as well as among those making producers' goods. The kind of concentrated market faced by the former was, however, quite different from that encountered by the latter. In the late nineteenth century, two types of concentrated markets appeared in the economy. One involved a relatively few consolidated firms. By and large, it was important to companies competing in the producers' goods sector, as the previous chapter suggested. The other was the dense market presented to makers of consumers' goods by the concentration of population (and hence of customers) in the large cities growing across the land. The new market was accessible via the nearly completed rail network, and thus manufacturers could compete more effectively than ever in a truly national market. Although goods were sold to their ultimate consumers through retail outlets, the concentrated demand represented by the cities led some large firms to create their own wholesaling organizations, which in turn supplied urban customers with a variety of goods. Depending on the industry, all or a part of the wholesaling function passed from the independent middleman to the manufacturer as what Adolf Berle and Gardiner C. Means termed the "modern corporation" rose to dominance in the American economy....

In most cases, the individual firm moved to eliminate the middleman only when the sales volume in a particular city grew large enough to indicate clearly that the firm's products could be marketed more efficiently by a full-time company sales force in that city. In industries that had no special marketing problems, this concentrated demand was usually the result of the rise of the modern corporation and the coming of oligopoly. The assumption of the wholesaling function by producers occurred largely, but not exclusively, among the large, modern corporations born during the period under consideration. It also came about largely, but not exclusively, in industries wherein production was concentrated in the hands of a relatively few firms....

The pioneer industry in this story was, of course, petroleum. In the industry's early years (after E. L. Drake's first successful oil well in 1859), refiners faced no special marketing difficulties for their products. Illuminating oil found ready markets through the same channels that had served to distribute other illuminants (principally coal oil). Commission merchants soon specialized in petroleum products, doing most of their business on a commission basis, but sometimes taking title to these generic goods and selling on consignment. These merchants sold to other wholesalers, including large wholesale grocery and drug merchants, who in turn distributed the items to a mass of local retailers. The marketing of American petroleum goods to foreign countries also was handled by a network of independent merchants. In the period before the dominance of the Rockefeller firm, then, the petroleum industry was a perfect example of the mid-nineteenth-century distribution network.

During the 1870s Standard Oil made a few hesitant moves toward building a company distribution system. It acquired partial control of petroleum marketing firms such as Chess, Carly, and Company of Louisville and Waters-Pierce and Company of Saint Louis. Such marketing enterprises began to make innovations in the bulk transport of petroleum products in special tank cars and also built a storage and distribution network which extended throughout several states.

In the latter part of the seventies and throughout the eighties, Standard moved to take more control of the wholesaling of its products as the growth of cities increased its markets. "The rapid rise in population and incomes," noted Harold Williamson and Arnold Daum, "increased the market for artificial illumination in factories, hotels, office buildings, and homes." Standard's policy of acquiring marketing affiliates continued as the urban markets grew. These specialized wholesaling affiliates assumed the function formerly performed by large grocery and drug wholesalers—they distributed petroleum goods to local grocery and drug jobbers in the nation's towns and cities. Thus Standard replaced middlemen as it began to do a portion of its own wholesaling in urban centers across the country....

The industry that best exemplifies the marketing problems faced by producers of perishable goods and the steps they took to overcome those difficulties is the meat-packing business. In the decades before 1870 the industry was a very diffuse and unconcentrated one. Although processors of cured pork built medium-sized firms that produced pork goods and shipped them great distances, they marketed their output through the old network of independent jobbers. Fresh beef was never transported over great distances in any form other than on the hoof because of its highly perishable nature. Live cattle were moved by rail from the great stockyards in the Midwest, then were butchered and sold in the nation's cities and towns. Processing was thus in the hands of small, local firms that supplied only limited market areas. The development of competition among beef firms in a national market awaited advances in the technology of refrigeration. By the mid-1870s, experimental shipments of dressed beef began arriving in eastern cities, but the refrigerated railroad car was still an imperfect and often unreliable device. Pioneers such as George H. Hammond led the way in the exploration of the applicability of the new technology to the dressed-beef business. The full exploitation of further advances in refrigeration, however, came with the innovations of the man who reshaped the entire structure of the American dressed-beef industry—Gustavus Franklin Swift.

As a young man, Swift had worked in a Massachusetts butcher shop, then had begun his own small wholesale meat business in New England. In 1872 he became a partner in a Boston meat concern operated by James A. Hathaway. Swift came increasingly to handle the buying in the midwestern stockyards, and by 1875 he had established an office in Chicago, the great center of the meat-packing industry. While working in

Chicago, Swift, like George Hammond, conceived of a means by which the beef business might be changed. The enormous potential market for fresh western beef in large eastern cities might be connected with the supply of cattle in midwestern stockyards via the refrigerated railroad car. If cattle could be slaughtered and dressed in the Midwest, and the dressed beef then shipped to the East in refrigerated cars, costs could be substantially reduced. Freight charges would be levied only on the dressed meat rather than on the entire animal. In addition, if slaughtering and processing could be concentrated in large, efficient plants in the Midwest, considerable economies of scale could be realized. Swift presented his proposals to his partner Hathaway, but the older man regarded the scheme as unsound. They dissolved the partnership and Swift proceeded on his own. In 1878 he formed a new partnership with his brother Edwin Swift and began the fight to implement his ideas.

The heart of Swift's plan was to build a nationwide network of branch houses which could store and merchandise the chilled beef. This was necessary because of the inability of established jobbers to handle the perishable meat and because local butchers and packers in the East opposed the sale of western chilled beef. Independent jobbers refused to pay what Swift regarded as fair prices for the beef because they feared it would spoil before they could dispose of it and because they were unable or unwilling to invest in large refrigerated warehouses in which to store the beef until they could sell it. Because the existing channels of distribution for meat proved unsuitable to his needs, Swift created in the 1880s his own system of company-owned jobbing houses (often forming partnerships with local jobbers) in order to achieve outlets to the consuming markets in the nation's urban areas.

The branch houses of Swift and Company consisted of a refrigerated warehouse and a merchandising organization. Dressed beef arrived by refrigerated rail car from the Midwest and was immediately transferred to the chilled storage area. There the sides of beef were further butchered by Swift employees. Sales personnel (in some cases salaried, in some cases working on a commission) contacted local retailers, conferred with them regarding their needs, and closed the sales. Retailers would then call at the branch house (often called a "box" or "cooler") and pick up their goods.

Swift's operations met with much success. Demand increased, and the company opened additional slaughtering and packing plants in cities across the center of the country; in Kansas City, East Saint Louis, Omaha, Saint Paul, Saint Joseph, and Fort Worth new Swift plants arose. In order to meet the needs of his packing plants for larger quantities of ice for refrigeration, Swift also established ice houses in the cities mentioned above.

Swift's innovations proved so successful that other packers soon followed his lead. By the 1890s such firms as Armour, Morris, National Packing, Cudahy Packing, and Swartzchild and Sulzberger had built similar chains of distributing houses in most of the leading cities and in many towns of medium size. By the turn of the century, all the large packing firms merchandised in the way pioneered by Gustavus Swift.

The systems of branch houses, originally built to distribute chilled beef, soon served also to handle the marketing of other products as well. Pork, lamb, and mutton were sold through the branches. When the packers turned to the production of various inedible by-products such as soap and glue, the chain of company-owned jobbing outlets served to market these items in addition to a full line of meat products.

The establishment of networks of branch houses by the packers was, as indicated above, a response to the inadequacies in the existing jobber system. Jobbers were unwilling to bear the heavy costs of adjusting their activities to the problems presented by the handling of chilled beef. The great variety of grades of beef and the variability in quality from one batch to another called for an expertise which jobbers did not have; more important, this variation called for close contact between jobber and supplier in order to insure that supply was carefully adjusted to demand for a perishable product. Furthermore, the jobber—that is, the independent wholesale butcher—had no way of responding to the challenge of the packers unless he joined forces with them, for he did not have access to the supplies of chilled beef. Consequently, many butchers chose to form partnerships with Swift and thus to avoid restriction to the butchering and sale of local cattle and those still carried on the hoof by the railroads.

Swift's branch houses presented complex problems because of the distance of these units from the controlling company and the resulting necessity for intimate contact between the producing plant and the field sales organization in order to control intelligently the flow of goods. Records had to be kept of the exact nature of the supply on hand in the branches and of the supply available (and potentially available) in the plants. A constant flow of communications was required in the form of reports, letters, telegrams, and (later) long-distance telephone contacts between the field organization and the packing plants. Some jobbers chose not to handle fresh beef because of the high costs of maintaining this flow, as well as the variety and varying quality of fresh beef and the costs of constructing refrigerated storage facilities. The result was, of course, that they were replaced by full-time personnel in the field sales organizations of the large packing firms.

Although the packers did largely eliminate the wholesaler from the sale of their processed goods, they made much less of an attempt to remove them as a source for their raw materials, cattle and hogs. The independent cattle commission houses performed their functions in much the same way as they had done before the coming of large firms in the meat-packing business. To be sure, the big packers did systematize their buying of animals and did hire some company-employed buyers to work in the great stockyard centers such as Chicago, Kansas City, Omaha, and others. They continued, however, to buy considerable quantities of their animals from independent commission firms such as Clay, Robinson and Company, Rosenbaum Brothers, Wood Brothers, and the Bowles Livestock Commission Company, all of which had offices in the major stockyards. In addition, the large packing companies never integrated backward to the actual raising of animals. Conditions in the area of raw-material supply afforded few reasons for any serious backward integration because the existing system provided the beef at acceptable prices. The old system of purchasing through independent commission houses continued alongside the operations of buyers employed by the large packers. Swift, Armour, and their fellows faced no problems in supply comparable to those they encountered in the distribution of their processed goods, and hence they made few innovations in that area.

The fresh-beef industry had undergone a transformation by the end of the nineteenth century. In 1870 a mass of local wholesalers handled the output of many local suppliers. As the refrigerated rail car became a reality in the late seventies and early eighties, entrepreneurs moved to utilize this technological advance to break the old patterns by connecting the eastern markets with western sources of supply. The wholesalers did not adapt to the needs of these entrepreneurs, and thus forced them to innovate in marketing. By the nineties the major packing firms had all followed Swift's plan of a nationwide chain of company branch houses equipped and staffed to handle the marketing of chilled beef and other meat items and inedible by-products. Backward integration into purchasing by the large firms also diminished the role of middlemen, but to a lesser extent than did backward integration into the marketing of processed goods. At the turn of the century, independent jobbers sold fresh beef in the small cities and towns, but most of the great market areas—the large cities—had passed into the hands of the manufacturing firms....

Firms in other industries making producers' goods also encountered marketing difficulties that led them to build nationwide marketing organizations by the early years of the twentieth century.

A system of commissioned, exclusive local agents marketing finished producers' goods was developed at mid-century by the McCormick Harvesting Machine Company. During the 1850s McCormick created a network of agencies in the United States and Canada to sell and service farm machines. Its agents pushed the sale of the machines, saw to delivery, collected payment, and agreed to "devote themselves actively to putting up, starting and setting to work the said Reapers." After the Civil War, when the firm produced and sold increasingly complex machines such as binders, the salesman's role as instructor and repairman grew even more important. "The company," wrote the leading historian of the McCormick business, "hesitated to put such a complicated mechanism as a binder in a farmer's hands until it had taught its field force how to operate and repair it." By the early eighties the firm had a large field force of about 150 traveling experts who assisted local agents in instructing farmers in the use of the firm's goods. From 1884 to around 1900, major harvesting machinery producers expanded their distribution systems still further by establishing branch houses and eliminating the old sales system. Much of the impetus for that expansion, however, apparently resulted not from genuine distribution problems but from increased competition, which led to intensive efforts to increase sales. Other firms competing in the industry early in the twentieth century followed the lead of McCormick and its largest competitors.

Makers of various types of office machines provide another example. This industry, like the electrical business, was a new one. For centuries office workers had conducted business without the benefit of anything more complicated than pen, ink, and paper; companies selling such devices as adding machines, cash registers, and typewriters had to overcome the inertia of businessmen. Producers had not only to make a good machine but, equally important, to convince businessmen of the usefulness and reliability of the machine. Advertising helped solve the problem of introducing the goods to potential customers, and the producing firms built marketing organizations designed to merchandise their products efficiently. The Burroughs Adding Machine Company, for example, was founded in 1905 and very quickly created a chain of agencies that specialized in the sale and service of the Burroughs machines. The dealers got the exclusive right to market Burroughs products in a certain geographic area, and they were paid a commission on their sales. The dealers agreed to do nothing else but sell the Burroughs machines, to provide an office and a sales force of appropriate size, and to sell the machines only at the company's price. Burroughs required that the workers at the local dealerships teach all customers how to use the machines and how to care for them properly so as to keep them in good working order. If the machines could not be repaired by the local sales outlet, the dealers were responsible for seeing that they were taken to one of Burroughs' regional repair shops ("Service Stations").

The National Cash Register Company, begun in 1899, marketed in much the same manner as the Burroughs company. National Cash Register utilized local agencies that specialized in its goods and worked on commission. The company's dealers also provided the service of installment purchasing if the customer desired it. John H. Patterson, president of NCR, recognized that the real problem in the growth of his concern was mass distribution, not mass production. "The important things to do are to improve our advertising and improve our sales force. If we get the orders we can easily manufacture the product and make the proper records, but first we must get the orders."

Typewriter makers, like the producers of adding machines and cash registers, often built large marketing systems that provided sales and service to businessmen who desired to make use of the new writing machines. The Remington typewriter firm, for example, had offices in sixteen American cities as early as 1892.

The use of franchised agencies in the harvester, adding machine, and cash register industries made it possible for the producing firm to insure that the needed services of instruction and repair would be performed. The products considered above were widely known, often mechanically superior items, and manufacturers could exercise significant control over their sales outlets because dealers were eager to retain their lucrative franchises.

At the same time, however, manufacturers avoided the large investments that would have been required if they, not the dealers, had had to pay the expenses of the office and of sales and repair personnel, as well as take the risks of selling the goods on credit to consumers. The franchised dealership was less costly than company-owned outlets, and it provided many of their advantages.

The distribution problems described above were not restricted to the makers of finished producers' goods; they also occurred in some industries manufacturing consumer durables. A brief examination of the experience of firms making two such durables, sewing machines and automobiles, will illustrate the range of marketing requirements imposed by some finished consumers' goods.

The sewing machine industry began around 1850, and manufacturers immediately encountered serious problems in distributing the new devices. Edward Clark of the I. M. Singer Company then introduced marketing innovations that cleared the way for his firm's growth and prosperity. Initially, the Singer machines were sold through commissioned agents who worked only in the Singer line. As the 1850s progressed, however, Clark built a network of company-owned sales outlets.

To market the sewing machines adequately, the company had to provide demonstrations and service to customers. Because the sewing machine was a new item, the operation of which was hardly self-evident, sales personnel had to instruct the public in the proper methods of using it. Because it was a moderately complicated piece of machinery, few customers could effect repairs when the machine broke down. Thus a trained company sales force was needed to distribute and repair sewing machines, and to do so more efficiently than the commission agents. As the leading historian of the young Singer firm wrote, "The company learned early in its New York sales offices that adequate selling demanded demonstration and servicing by men who were completely conversant with the mechanical features of the sewing-machine and could adjust or repair them on short notice." By 1856 Edward Clark had concluded that "the only way" to sell the machines was through a nationwide network of company outlets.

The Singer stores had spread into fourteen American cities by 1859, and they provided a wide range of services which furthered the marketing of the firm's products. They engaged in promotional, educational, and service activities, including demonstration, repairs, and the storage of parts, and they furnished information on the credit reliability of local customers, which allowed the company to sell more and more machines by installment plans. The merchandising efforts of the company's own outlets proved so successful that by the mid-1860s Singer had stopped using franchised commission agents.

When the early automobile industry began to expand a half-century after the introduction of sewing machines, its marketing needs proved somewhat similar to those of the Singer company. Unlike the sewing machine firm, auto makers did not turn to company-owned outlets manned by salaried personnel, but they did require that their franchised dealers perform many of the same services provided by the Singer stores and harvester agencies. Auto dealers had to engage solely in the sale of the cars of a single firm, and they enjoyed the exclusive right to market those cars in their particular geographic area. The Ford Motor Company required in its contracts with dealers that they supply full demonstrations and instructions for customers unschooled in the operation of the new vehicles. Furthermore, the dealers agreed to instruct consumers in the proper methods of caring for the cars and to keep on hand a supply of parts and a force of mechanics capable of repairing the autos. Other young automobile firms, such as Packard, Studebaker, Chalmers, and the Waverly Company, marketed their vehicles in much the same way as Ford....

The marketing of goods such as those described here was a very involved proposition. The new, technologically advanced products that entered American markets in the last half of the nineteenth century found little of relevance in the old distribution system, wherein producers sold relatively simple, often standard items to anonymous (to the producers) customers through commercial middlemen. Manufacturers had to figure out new ways to introduce the goods, to instruct customers in the proper use of costly machinery, to effect quick and reliable repairs, to supply needed parts, and to arrange installment purchasing. It no longer sufficed for a manufacturer simply to sell an article to a handy middleman and be done with it. These items carried with them a wide range of requirements which ran from the initial sale through repeated repair jobs. Technical expertise was a necessary element in the composition of the sales and service organizations that evolved to do the job that commission merchants and jobbers could not do. The difficulties of efficiently distributing such goods presented strong challenges to manufacturers, and the pressure of the marketing needs of their products soon led to innovations in merchandising. By the early years of the twentieth century, many firms had responded to the marketing challenge by building extensive company distributing organizations....

The changes in distribution described herein did not, however, result in the complete elimination of the middleman from the American manufacturing scene. In several broad areas of manufactured goods, producers' expansion into distribution was very limited in scope. In those areas the jobber proved very durable because of the survival of many of the conditions which had long made him relevant. In the distribution of the complex of items sold in the grocery, drug, and hardware trades, wholesale marketing continued to be the province of the independent middleman, even in the twentieth century. This chapter and the next will explain the reasons for the survival of middlemen in these sectors of the economy and will point out that, although jobbers endured here, their role changed significantly.

The distribution of manufactured goods through such outlets as hardware, grocery, drug, furniture, dry goods, and jewelry stores represented the only major portion of the economy in which manufacturers continued to face the extremely diffuse and scattered markets that could be served most efficiently by a network of jobbers. The many thousands of retailers who sold goods in these areas dealt in hundreds of different items, most of which were made by many different producers. Oligopoly and concentration of production remained relatively infrequent phenomena in these trades. Manufacturers did not enjoy the concentrated market of a few consolidated firms, and even in major cities, they rarely experienced the high sales volume that would justify their assumption of the jobbing function. Because the goods were standard, uncomplicated, low-cost items (what we have called generic goods), manufacturers encountered none of the distribution problems which marked the merchandising of the products discussed [previously].... A multitude of small manufacturing units sold a mass of simple, standard goods to a mass of small retailers, and that equation perpetuated the need for an interconnecting body of independent middlemen. These themes will be developed more thoroughly in the following chapter, but here we will examine the experience of the tobacco industry. That industry sold to the same diffuse and scattered markets as did producers in the grocery, hardware, and drug businesses, but it was an industry in which the large firm and concentration of production did arise.

The purpose of this [analysis]... is to illustrate that the existence of a diffuse market of many thousands of retailers made the jobber an economically useful agent even in industries dominated by a single large firm. American Tobacco, like other large companies, made some attempts to take over the wholesaling of its goods, but, even when the firm handled a part of the wholesaling operation in major market areas, it continued to find jobbers useful in distributing its goods to the thousands of grocers, druggists, and tobacconists who retailed its products. And, like other large firms processing agricultural goods, American Tobacco made some changes in its purchasing methods for raw materials, though it never felt the need to expand into the full-scale growing of its own tobacco. The middleman was, therefore, never eliminated entirely from the tobacco industry, even though, from the late 1890s to 1911, it was one of the few virtually monopolistic American industries....

In the decade before the formation of the American Tobacco Company, manufacturers made tentative attempts to remove the middleman from both the supply of raw materials and the merchandising of cigarettes. In each case, however, the role of jobbers and tobacco brokers remained very important in the industry.

The major producers obtained most of their leaf tobacco (their prime raw material) through tobacco brokerage houses in the bright-leaf belts of the South. These brokers purchased the leaf at warehouse auctions, stored and dried it in their own warehouses, then resold it to the cigarette manufacturers. Especially in years when there was a serious shortage of crops, this arrangement made it possible for speculators and rehandlers to make handsome profits. One such broker purchased cutters (the particular kind of leaf tobacco used in the production of cigarettes) on the Durham market at thirteen cents per pound, then resold it a, few months later to W. S. Kimball and Company at slightly more than twice that price. Such occurrences were common. Because competition in the cigarette industry became less and less a competition in price of product and increasingly a competition of advertising and gimmickry, producers apparently paid relatively little attention to the cost of raw materials. "The whole attention of these manufacturers," recalled a tobacco broker, "seems to have been taken up with the sale of goods, and it left a good opening for ... speculators and dealers to get a profit out of them."

Manufacturers began in the eighties to create their own purchasing departments in a half-hearted attempt to reduce these' raw-material costs. They made some purchases directly at warehouse auctions in order to eliminate middlemen. Probably in an attempt to avoid bidding against each other and thereby increasing the price, the buyers for each company bought almost exclusively in different auction areas. Allen and Ginter bought most of their leaf in the market at Henderson, North Carolina. W. S. Kimball and Company confined its purchasing to Oxford, North Carolina. The Duke firm bought almost entirely in Durham, but occasionally in Danville, Virginia, which was the market used by the Kinney Tobacco Company. Of the five major producers, only Goodwin and Company apparently had no buyers in the bright-leaf belt.

The big cigarette companies, however, continued to buy most of their leaf through brokers and commission merchants. Purchases through company agents in the latter part of the eighties in most cases amounted to no more than one-fourth of the companies' requirements, the rest coming from commercial middlemen. Only the Duke company made real efforts to eliminate the middleman. Duke, as he later testified, appreciated the value of reducing the role of "the speculator who had been ... buying and selling to the manufacturers, with the exception of Duke's Sons & Co. We had been buying a good part of our tobacco in the loose warehouses direct from the farmer." The independent middleman remained clearly evident at the end of the 1880s.

The major producers also established warehouse storage facilities in the bright-leaf belts during the eighties. The Duke Company, of course, had such warehousing almost from the beginning of its business, for the firm arose in the North Carolina bright-leaf belt. Manufacturers farther removed from the markets found the facilities more difficult to obtain, but most did acquire warehousing. The Kinney company did so very early, opening a rehandling and storage plant in Danville, Virginia, in 1877. There the cutters were re-dried, stemmed, and prized for shipment to their factories in New York and Baltimore. Allen and Ginter established stemmeries and re-drying and storage houses in North Carolina in 1887. W. S. Kimball and Company obtained similar facilities a year later. The warehousing system and the use of company leaf buyers marked significant vertical integration in purchasing well in advance of the combination of the leading producers.

In the distribution of finished goods, as in the supply of raw materials, the cigarette makers made some effort to reduce the importance of middlemen. From its earliest years, the industry sold its products by means of traveling salesmen. The drummer was one means through which the producing companies made potential jobbers and retailers aware of the product. Drummers traveled all over the country, attempting to stimulate demand for cigarettes. They took orders from grocery and drug jobbers, who in turn distributed the goods to the many retailers who sold the cigarettes to their ultimate consumers. From the very earliest days of the industry, then, the manufacturers handled a part of their own wholesaling. The vast majority of the goods, however, were marketed by independent wholesalers.

During the eighties some significant organizational changes occurred in the distribution system. Each of the five leading producers continued to sell to jobbers via traveling salesmen. But the manufacturers organized and maintained a system of company-owned distributing centers in the largest market cities. Connected with these wholesale outlets were generally a manager, a city salesman, and one or two traveling agents. These distributing centers sold cigarettes to the jobbers, who in turn distributed them to the retailers.

The effect of the manufacturers' creation of wholesale outlets in the eighties was primarily to eliminate the commission merchants and perhaps some of the largest urban jobbers from the distribution system for cigarettes. From the very first, cigarette producers had tended to go directly to local jobbers by using traveling salesmen; when several company wholesale offices opened in the eighties, the local independent jobbers could be reached more efficiently. Although the company-owned wholesale outlets sold some cigarettes directly to large urban retailers, the vast majority of their sales went to the jobbers. Although the creation of company branches represented a substantial inroad by manufacturers into the distribution process, the network of local independent jobbers continued to carry the burden of marketing the cigarettes to the thousands of small retailers who ultimately disposed of the goods....

During the years when American Tobacco enjoyed a near monopoly of the tobacco industry, it chose to leave the marketing of its products almost completely in the hands of independent middlemen. As the commissioner of corporations reported in 1909, "The Tobacco Combination [that is, American Tobacco] has followed in general the method of other tobacco manufacturers by disposing of its products through the regular wholesale and retail channels." The rise of the modern corporation and of concentrated production did not lead the tobacco manufacturers to supplant the independent wholesalers and retailers in the tobacco industry. Because the market that the industry served did not change in structure, the old system of distribution continued to be the most economical and efficient. Leaf middlemen were seriously affected by American Tobacco's backward integration in purchasing, but with the rise of the giant combine their counterparts who marketed American Tobacco's goods were left largely intact.

No particular marketing problems arose in the tobacco industry, and the market remained scattered and diffuse. Although the industry sold in the urban markets, the number of retailers remained so large and the volume and value of the individual orders from retailers remained so small that American Tobacco found it logical and efficient to use jobbers. As the *New York Times* observed of the tobacco trade in 1893, it was "done through jobbers, as the smallness of the orders put in by retailers makes a direct dealing on the part of the manufacturers impossible, because it leaves no profit." For American Tobacco to have supplied all its retailers, the company would have had to pay a very sizable force of its own wholesalers. The firm recognized that it would be less costly simply to put its goods through the old channels of grocery and drug jobbers. Because the turnover of items handled by the jobbers for the grocery and drug trades was fairly rapid, the jobbers could also handle tobacco products (which went to the same retailers who took the rest of their line of goods) at a very low cost to manufacturers. American Tobacco produced only a single line of goods, and that line was too narrow to justify the company's doing its own jobbing; a company jobbing force would have spent too much time making sales that were too small to justify the time spent by the jobbers. Therefore, the whole line of goods needed by grocers and drug retailers was most efficiently distributed by middlemen whose full line brought enough small sales in a single visit to a retailer to repay the time spent in the visit.

The economic force of that set of relationships among manufacturers, retailers, and wholesalers in the grocery and drug trades was so strong that virtually all manufacturing concerns whose products are retailed by drug and grocery stores have continued to rely on jobbers for the distribution of their goods, even in the twentieth century. Although the modern tobacco industry hag been concentrated and oligopolistic, the distribution methods of manufacturers have remained much the same as they were before the founding of American Tobacco. A 1939 study of the industry revealed that manufacturers still sold to independent jobbers, most of whom sold a wide range of goods, including tobacco products, groceries, drugs, and alcoholic beverages. The nature of the market that tobacco products found determined the distribution channels through which they would flow, and that has meant the continuing relevance of the jobber.

In one important respect, however, the American Tobacco Company did exert a powerful influence for change in distribution. Although the company chose to leave the jobber network largely intact, the heavy advertising in which the firm engaged significantly altered the role of the jobber. Even before American Tobacco, cigarette manufacturers found heavy advertising to be their most potent weapon for increasing sales, and American did not cease to use massive advertising during its first two decades. In the eighties and even in the nineties tobacco jobbers played an important part in introducing new items and encouraging their sale by engaging in considerable advertising themselves. The role of the jobber in that period was, in short, to act not only as distributor but also as salesman for his goods.

The national advertising of American Tobacco after 1890, however, steadily eclipsed this part of the jobber's activities. The manufacturing firm began to go directly to the consumer via advertising, and the jobber increasingly became only a delivery vehicle, not a salesman. "The function of the cigarette retailer," a scholar of the modern cigarette industry has noted, "is primarily to make change, and the function of the wholesaler is to provide the retailer with what the customers want." The jobber endured in tobacco, but his functions were permanently altered by the advertising of manufacturers. As Nannie M. Tilley said of the tobacco industry in this period, "While existing channels of distribution, wholesale and retail, were not destroyed, they were greatly changed by advertising which drew manufacturer and consumer closer." The significance of the middleman in the tobacco industry declined, but he remained the prime agent of distribution....

By the early years of the twentieth century, the new order in American marketing had emerged in many industries. Although it is impossible to say precisely when most manufactured goods in the U.S. economy came to be distributed by the producers themselves, it seems clear that the marketing revolution occurred between the mid-1890s and World War I.

When the Bureau of the Census conducted the first systematic investigation of the distribution of manufactured products in 1929, the results clearly revealed the dimensions of the change that had taken place in marketing since the early nineteenth century. Independent wholesalers, for so much of our economic past the dominant marketers of manufactured goods, handled less than one-third of the flow of such goods from American factories in 1930. Most manufactured products were marketed in various ways by the producing firms themselves. Almost one-third of the goods were sold directly to industrial consumers, and the rest went to the manufacturers' own wholesale and retail branches, to independent retailers directly (without the use of wholesalers), or directly to home consumers.

The shift toward this new marketing system was quite clearly under way by the turn of the century. In industry after industry, firms developed their own marketing divisions. Just a partial listing of the large companies that by 1910 had built their own systems to distribute their goods in the national market includes: food processing enterprises such as Armour, Swift, Morris, Wilson, Cudahy, Nabisco, United Fruit, Corn Products, American Ice, and National Distillers; metals firms such as U.S. Steel, Bethlehem Steel, Crucible Steel, and National Enameling and Stamping; petroleum products companies such as Standard Oil, Pure Oil, Union Oil of California, Sun Oil, General Asphalt, Texaco, and Gulf; makers of crude chemicals such as du Pont and International Salt; automobile firms such as General Motors, Ford, and Packard; as well as producers of a variety of technologically complex goods— firms such as General Electric, Westinghouse, Pittsburgh Plate Glass, International Harvester, Singer, Eastman Kodak, Worthington Pump and Machine, U.S. Rubber, and Allis-Chalmers.

During the first half of this century, the process of integration forward into marketing continued to spread. By mid-century the vast majority of large corporations were handling some of their own marketing. Of a sample of 153 large manufacturing firms operating in 1948, 79 per cent engaged in wholesaling operations, and 87 per cent were involved in wholesaling and/or retailing activities. Sometimes this occurred in the form of a sales department with offices across the nation, sometimes through company wholesaling and/ or retailing branches that kept inventories, sometimes via the creation of a subsidiary marketing corporation, or through some combination of these methods. Whatever the particular form they assumed, the merchandising activities of manufacturing concerns represented the overturning of an economic order whose lineage in the Western world was centuries old.

In the colonial and early national period, the pattern had been an extension of the European configuration. Virtually all manufactured goods that entered markets other than strictly local ones passed through the hands of sedentary merchants. With the exception of a few industries, this pattern continued without visible prospects of change until the 1870s. The mercantile community experienced internal alterations as a result of expanding trade and specialization after 1815, but these changes did not affect the fundamental dominance of the mercantile community as the agent of distribution or as coordinator of national and regional flows. Merchants acted as merchandisers and as financiers of economic growth. Their financial role began to atrophy after 1860, and they were forced to rely on their specialized marketing activities.

These activities had always rested on the twin pillars of the generic nature of manufactured goods and the diffuse markets in which they were sold. Only when those conditions changed could a new marketing order emerge. The fundamental changes came in the wake of improvements in transportation and communications. These developments made possible the expansion of manufacturing firms into large regional, national, and even international markets. In adapting to these changes, merchants sacrificed versatility for specialization. Once the expansion had occurred, independent wholesalers became vulnerable to changes in the nature of products and of markets.

As the last decades of the nineteenth century unfolded, products and markets changed. Advancing technology brought to many industries new merchandising requirements for their goods. The old economy of simple, uncomplicated products was joined by the many new scientifically and technologically oriented industries that were to become the backbone of the modern American economic system. These new industries found that the traditional marketing arrangements did not function very well for them; consequently they built a new network of manufacturer-dominated merchandising channels. Similarly, the increasing concentration of markets in the wake of the rise of the modern corporation, the emergence of oligopoly, and the concentration of population in urban areas altered the traditional nature of the market for many industries. Many manufacturing firms then found it more efficient to deal directly with their customers and to dispense with much of the old web of commercial intermediaries. These two basic developments, coupled in some industries with backward integration and intracompany sales, spelled the decline of the independent wholesaler in the twentieth-century economy.

Although the independent wholesaler obviously did not disappear from the national scene, he became largely restricted to those broad sectors considered [earlier].... Only where goods remained generic and markets diffuse—in those sectors wherein numerous retailers sold a wide variety of relatively simple goods produced by many manufacturers— did the wholesaler retain his primary distributive role.

The independent wholesalers were unable to adjust to the different economic order of the late nineteenth century primarily because their traditional function was no longer relevant in many industries. They were specialized men of business whose time had simply passed; they cannot fairly be faulted for inadequate will or poor entrepreneurship. Their methods, their organization, their whole orientation toward the economy made them ill equipped to function in the emerging environment of advanced technology and giant corporations. They had served long and well, but their expertise, resources, and training were not adaptable to large portions of the corporate world of the twentieth century.

We have explored in this volume the structure of the marketing of manufactured goods in the nineteenth century, tracing the process of change and suggesting reasons for that change. The evolution of marketing techniques is a part of the over-all story of the fundamental alterations in American society brought about by the metamorphosis from the older, agrarian-oriented, merchant-dominated economy to the modern, industrialized, concentrated economy. Observers have long noted that ours is above all a business civilization; towering office buildings dominate our cities and reflect the values of our civilization as surely as the magnificent cathedrals of the twelfth and thirteenth centuries reflected those of medieval Europe. For more than two centuries after the initial English settlements in what was to become the United States, our business civilization lay in the hands of independent merchants. Their power derived from their strategic position at all the cross-roads of commerce, at the nexus between producer and consumer. When they surrendered their place of leadership, first to the men who built the great manufacturing firms and then to their corporate heirs, they did so in large part as a result of having lost that strategic position. The modern manufacturing corporation assumed the marketing role, not because of a failure of will or vision on the part of the merchants, but because of the alterations in the nature of products and of markets. Once these fundamental dimensions of the economy had changed, there followed a lasting revolution in the relationships between merchants and manufacturers.

SUGGESTIONS FOR FURTHER READING

Jeremy Atack, "Industrial Structure and the Emergence of the Modern Industrial Corporation," *Explorations in Economic History*, 22(1985) 29–52.

Alfred D. Chandler, *The Visible Hand: the Managerial Revolution in American Business* (1977).

Ron Chernow, *Titan: The Life of John D. Rockefeller, Sr.* (2004).

Thomas C. Cochran, *Business in American Life: A History* (1972).

William M. Doyle, "Capital Structure and the Financial Development of the U.S. Sugar Industry, 1875–1905," *Journal of Economic History*, 60(2000), 190–215.

Burton W. Folsom Jr., *The Myth of the Robber Baron: A New Look at the Rise of Big Business in America* (1991).

Louis Galambos, *The Public Image of Big Business, 1880–1940* (1975).

——, "Recasting The Organizational Synthesis: Structure and Process in the Twentieth and Twenty-First Centuries," *Business History Review*, 79(2005), 1–38.

——, "Technology, Political Economy, and Professionalization: Central Themes of the Organizational Synthesis," *Business History Review*, 57(1983) 471–493.

Peter George, *The Emergence of Industrial America: Strategic Factors in American Economic Growth Since 1870* (1982).

Julius Grodinsky, *Jay Gould* (1957).

Matthew Josephson, *The Robber Barons: The Great American Capitalists, 1861–1901* (1934).

Edward C. Kirkland, *Industry Comes of Age: Business, Labor, and Public Policy, 1860–1897* (1961).

Maury Klein, *The Life and Legend of Jay Gould* (1986).

Gabriel Kolko, *Railroads and Regulation, 1877–1916* (1965).

Naomi R. Lamoreaux, *The Great Merger Movement in American Business, 1895–1904* (1985).

Harold C. Livesay, *Andrew Carnegie and the Rise of Big Business* (1975).

Henry Demarest Lloyd, *Wealth Against Commonwealth* (1896).

Blaine McCormick and Burton W. Folsom, Jr., "A Survey of Business Historians on America's Greatest Entrepreneurs," *Business History Review* 77(2003), 703–716.

Allan Nevins, *John D. Rockefeller: The Heroic Age of American Enterprise* (1941).

Anthony P. O'Brien, "Factory Size, Economies of Scale, and the Great Merger Wave of 1898–1902," *Journal of Economic History*, 48(1988), 639–649.

Glenn Porter, *The Rise of Big Business, 1860–1920*, 2nd ed. (1992).

Philip Scranton, *Proprietary Capitalism: The Textile Manufacture at Philadelphia, 1800–1885* (1983).

Andrew Sinclair, *Corsair: The Life of J. Pierpont Morgan* (1981).

Peter Temin, *Iron and Steel in Nineteenth Century America: An Economic Inquiry* (1964).

Oliver Zunz, *Making America Corporate, 1870–1920* (1990).

CHAPTER 7

The "New Era" of the 1920s

From Boom to Bust

INTRODUCTION

As the 1920s opened, America had wearied of its civic obligations at home and its international obligations abroad. The end of the First World War meant that the controls and restrictions imposed by the needs of wartime production could be cast off. The rejection of the League of Nations by the United States Senate made clear that America was intent on withdrawing to its own domestic pursuits. The Harding-Coolidge presidential ticket promised the nation a "return to normalcy," reassuring Americans that the time to pursue private gain rather than some larger public purpose had indeed arrived. With the right policies, growth and prosperity could go on unabated. That prosperity would be shared by all, and poverty would be eradicated. America had entered the New Era.

The 1920s in fact got off to a difficult start. For much of 1920 and the entire year of 1921, the economy suffered through a sharp recession associated with the conversion of the economy back to a peacetime footing. Once the postwar downturn was over, a long economic expansion got underway. Aside from two minor dips in economic activity in 1924 and 1927, the economy performed admirably from 1922 to 1929. By almost any measure, economic performance was impressive. Incomes and production grew rapidly, savings were high, capital formation was strong, prices were stable, and unemployment after 1921 was very low. From 1922 to 1929, GNP grew at an extraordinary average annual rate of 4.7 percent, while unemployment averaged only 3.7 percent. These numbers are all the more imposing when compared to more recent experience: in the post World War II era, GNP growth has averaged between 3 percent and 3.5 percent per annum and the unemployment rate has rarely slipped below 4 percent.

Yet all was not perfect with the American economy. Two sectors were perennial poor performers: agriculture and banking. When major grain producing areas in Europe became battlefields in the Great War, American farmers were encouraged to make up the shortfall. This they willingly did, "planting from hedgerow to hedgerow." When peace returned, European grain production recovered. The resumption of this production, in combination with the expanded capacity in the rest of the world, led to chronic worldwide agricultural overproduction. In America, as the surpluses mounted, farm prices and farmers suffered throughout the 1920s. From 1920 to 1921 farm prices were cut roughly in half. At no point in the remainder of the decade did they return to 1920 levels. Farm foreclosures were a commonplace, fueling the great demographic shift from country to city.

The economic policies of the 20s were in stark counterpoint to the progressive and activist approach followed by the administrations of Theodore Roosevelt and Woodrow Wilson. There is no better illustration of the results of this return to American style laissez-faire than the fate of the banking industry in the 20s. Banks could be either federally chartered or state chartered. The federal government and the various states had entered into what came to be known as a "competition in laxity." Intent on convincing bank organizers to charter with them in order to collect chartering and other fees, federal and state regulators proudly trumpeted the ease with which banking could be conducted under their lax standards. The lack of regulatory oversight allowed far too many poorly managed banks to be chartered.

The weaknesses in agriculture and banking would eventually become mutually reinforcing. As farm foreclosures mounted, bank failures increased, especially in regions where non-performing agricultural loans were concentrated. These weaknesses, ostensibly unimportant in the face of steady and strong economic growth, would play an important role in the debacle to come in the years after 1929.

On the international front, the United States, as a result of its lending to its allies during the First World War, went from the world's largest debtor nation to the world's largest creditor nation. Many debtor nations, especially Germany, became dependent on American loans to remain afloat. The United States never fully embraced its new role as international lender of last resort. Not only did it curtail its international lending toward the end of the decade in deference to the borrowing needs of its own domestic stock market speculators, its maintenance of high tariffs also increased the fragility of the international payments system.

America transformed itself in the 1920s. It was not a decade for the faint-hearted, with its flappers, bootleg liquor and margin accounts. Self-reliance, rugged individualism and faith in unlimited progress were all still part of the national mythology, and all three were to be sorely tested in the decade to come. Much of what we take as life in the modern world emerged in the 1920s: the automobile, the motel, the suburbs, mass communication (especially the radio), mass entertainment, the obsession with professional sports, expensive household appliances, and installment credit. To facilitate this transformation, the Harding-Coolidge-Hoover administrations, firm believers all that the "business of America is business," were committed to keeping the role of government in the economic life of the nation to a minimum. While the Roosevelt and Wilson administrations might have boasted of their many accomplishments (anti-trust laws, the Pure Food and Drug Act, the Federal Trade Commission, the Federal Reserve System and the Federal income tax), the Republican administrations of the 1920s were in no mood to extend government's reach in the marketplace. The centerpiece of their economic policy was the tax cut, with the venerable and very wealthy Secretary of the Treasury, Andrew Mellon, presiding over implementation of the cuts. Aimed at business and the well-to-do, whose enjoyment of the tax cuts was seen as an act of civic virtue, the common man and woman were reassured that the benefits would trickle down to them. The rich were not to be burdened with the payment of taxes; business would not have its profits eroded by the need to produce safe and reliable products or to avoid monopolistic practices. Investment bankers, doing their part to sustain American prosperity, were not to be inconvenienced in floating new issues of securities by cumbersome and sometimes embarrassing disclosure requirements; nor should stockbrokers be forced to abide the interfering hand of the Federal Reserve in setting margin requirements.

Putting aside the matter of governmental oversight, it is clear that some powerful economic forces came into alignment in the 1920s: technological progress, organizational innovation, emergence of new and significant industries, successful exploitation of additional economies of scale and scope, and widespread development of continuous process technologies. These forces gave an enormous boost to productivity growth and greatly expanded employment opportunities. The large enterprises that were either being formed or undergoing expansion following the First World War had a voracious appetite for financial capital. These financial needs could not be satisfied by the banking system. American banking laws generally limited the amount banks could lend to any one borrower. As a result, U.S. corporations turned to the capital markets with a vengeance in the 1920s, placing new issues of common stock and bonds into the hands of the investing public to finance their expansion.

In the 1920s corporate earnings were high and growing; dividend payments and stock prices were moving upward along similar trend lines. The underlying economic fundamentals were entirely consistent with a rising market. The electric utility industry was a growth industry, constructing a vast transmission network and bringing electricity to many households. Electronics was another growth industry; RCA, whose radios were changing the daily life of Americans, was the industry glamour stock. General Motors, following modern management techniques, was surpassing Ford Motor as leader of the automobile industry; its common stock was a strong performer. Then in March of 1928 share prices began a sudden rapid ascent. It is at this point that a speculative bubble may have formed.

The Federal Reserve was greatly agitated by the run-up in share prices, and adopted contractionary monetary policies to combat what it viewed as a dangerous speculation. By the late 1920s the economic expansion was beginning to show signs of fatigue. The full employment economy was generating a high volume of savings. To sustain full employment these savings would have to be matched by a high level of investment spending on plant and equipment, residential housing and inventory. Just when the economy needed this kind of boost and the low interest rates that would make it possible, the Fed switched its policy stance to one of monetary stringency. In January 1928 the Fed began to slow the growth in the monetary aggregates and raised the discount rate from 3.5 percent to 5 percent. An unfortunate side effect of the Fed's approach was that it sacrificed the needs of the domestic economy in the hope of reining in the stock market speculation.

The Fed's high interest rate policy had no effect on the stock market, as share prices continued their upward climb. Funds poured into Wall Street to finance margin accounts, mostly from nonbank sources. General Motors was issuing bonds, not to finance the construction of new assembly lines, but to send the proceeds to New York to be lent in the broker loan market at 12 percent. While Fed policy did not interrupt the ascent of stock prices, its effects on the domestic economy were beginning to show by June and July of 1929. By midyear 1929 the long economic expansion had run its course. Automobile sales had fallen off significantly; industrial production fell in July. Other indicators were to follow: factory payrolls, freight-car loadings, and department store sales.

In the summer and early fall of 1929, in the face of a weakening economy, nervous investors, many of them naive and inexperienced, found the underlying market fundamentals increasingly harder to judge. Many popular stocks had never paid a dividend, leaving investors with little information with which to form expectations. Stock prices hit their cyclical peak in September 1929. Thereafter, with the economic news getting less encouraging each day and the course of corporate earnings more uncertain, investors realized that the earnings growth rates implied by extant market price-earnings ratios were untenable. A mild sell-off got underway, and picked up momentum in October. The market endured spectacular price declines on October 24 and October 29, the infamous Black Thursday and Black Tuesday. The downward spiral was in part propelled by repeated waves of margin calls.

The stock market reached its low for the year in the second week of November; the collapse of the overall economy would soon follow. The New Era had lasted less than ten years. The businessman, glorified and lionized in the 20s, would assume a new role as villain and scapegoat. Government, so recently regarded as the scourge of capitalism, would in time be called upon to restore some semblance of prosperity.

The 1920s leave the student of the period with many questions. What caused the stock market to rise so rapidly beginning in early 1928 and collapse so resoundingly in late 1929? Did a speculative bubble form in the late 20s? If so, what psychological predispositions account for its formation? What role did margin buying play in this collapse? What are the linkages between the stock market and the real economy? What role did the stock market crash of October 1929 play in the onset of the Great Depression? How important was the crash as a causative factor of the Great Depression? How important were underlying economic weaknesses, like the uneven distribution of income, in transmitting the effects of the crash to the real economy? Why did the Fed choose to respond to the speculative mania with monetary contraction? How did this contribute to the economic decline that followed the crash? Lastly, why did the biggest stock market crash of all time, that in October 1987, have virtually no effect on economic activity? While this chapter will not answer all of these questions, some answers will begin to take shape in the readings that follow.

DOCUMENTS

To capture the mood of the 20s, Document 7–1 excerpts selections from "His Method," Chapter IV in Bruce Barton's *The Man Nobody Knows*, the best-selling work of non-fiction for both 1925 and 1926. Regarded by many as the most influential advertising executive of the 1920s, Barton was one of the founding members of the legendary Madison Avenue advertising agency, Batten, Barton, Durstein and Osborne (known more familiarly as BBD&O in the industry) that revolutionized the way products were advertised. In his book Barton argues that Jesus Christ and his disciples were the best marketing organization in history. The ease with which Barton so freely invokes the name of Christ in his best seller amply demonstrates the extent to which business values had permeated American culture.

Samuel Crowther's famous interview of John J. Raskob in the *Ladies Home Journal*, Document 7–2, also measures the temper of the times. Raskob was a leading figure in the investment world. The rise of the stock market was a phenomenon of the end of the decade. Once it gathered momentum, it gripped the nation. Raskob's message is simple: everyone and anyone could be an expert on the stock market; everybody ought to be rich. In his interview he draws on a deep reservoir of optimism about what is possible in America, an optimism that surely fueled the speculative mania of the late 1920s. One irony of that optimism is that it was still so deep so late in the game; his interview appeared in August of 1929.

Document 7–3 is excerpts from "Coolidge Prosperity," Chapter VII in *Only Yesterday* by Frederick Lewis Allen, a longtime editor at *Harper's Magazine*. Published in 1931, it is surprisingly insightful on a decade that had ended only two short years prior to its publication. His description of the mass consumer society that had emerged in America is superb. The America he portrays, with its fascination for autos, movies and household appliances, is the modern one that contemporary generations recognize as the America they live in.

7–1. BRUCE BARTON, *THE MAN NOBODY KNOWS*: CHAPTER IV—HIS METHOD

Many leaders have dared to lay out ambitious programs, but this is the most daring of all:

"Go ye into all the world," Jesus said, "and preach the gospel *to the whole creation.*"

Consider the sublime audacity of that command. To carry Roman civilization across the then known world had cost millions of lives and billions in treasure. To create any sort of reception for a new idea or product today involves a vast machinery of propaganda and expense. Jesus had no funds and no machinery. His organization was a tiny group of uneducated men, one of whom had already abandoned the cause as hopeless, deserting to the enemy. He had come proclaiming a Kingdom and was to end upon a cross; yet he dared to talk of conquering all creation. What was the source of his faith in that handful of followers? By what methods had he trained them? What had they learned from him of the secrets of influencing men?

We speak of the law of "supply and demand," but the words have got turned around. With anything which is not a basic necessity the supply always precedes the demand. Elias Howe invented the sewing machine, but it nearly rusted away before American women could be persuaded to use it. With their sewing finished so quickly what would they ever do with their spare time? Howe had vision, and had made his vision come true; but he could not sell! So his biographer paints a tragic picture—the man who had done more than any other in his generation to lighten the labor of women is forced to attend the funeral of the woman he loved in a borrowed suit of clothes. Nor are men less stubborn than women in opposition to the new idea. The typewriter had been a demonstrated success for years before business men could be persuaded to buy it. How could any one have letters enough to justify the investment of one hundred dollars in a writing machine? Only when the Remingtons sold the Caligraph Company the right to manufacture machines under the Remington patent, and two groups of salesmen set forth in competition, was the resistance broken down....Almost every invention has had a similar battle....

That is the kind of human beings we are— wise in our own conceit, impervious to suggestions, perfectly sure that what's never been done never will be done. Nineteen hundred years ago we were even more impenetrable, for modern science has frequently shot through the hard shell of our complacency ... *"To the whole creation."*... Assuredly there was no demand for a new religion; the world was already over-supplied. And Jesus proposed to send forth eleven men and expect them to substitute his thinking for all existing religious thought...!

This then was what Jesus wished to send to all creation, through the instrumentality of his eleven men. What were his methods of training? How did he meet prospective believers? How did he deal with objections? By what sort of strategy did he interest and persuade...?

Some years later a tired pilgrim arrived in the up-to-date and perfectly self-satisfied city of Athens. He arrived on foot because he had no car-fare. His shoes were sadly worn and his clothing unkempt and covered with dust. One would say that these disadvantages were enough to disqualify him for success in a town so smart and critical, but he had other handicaps more fundamental. He was too short and thickset to be impressive; his eyes had a decided squint; altogether he was not at all the kind of man who commands respect before a crowd. That he should come to the most sophisticated center of the ancient world and expect to make an impression was extraordinary. The principal business of the clever gentlemen of that city was standing around the market-place, there to "hear or to tell some new thing." They were the joke-makers and fashion-setters of their era. They originated new ideas; they did not buy them from the provinces. And as for investing in a new religion—they had hundreds of religions, some new, some fairly new, some old, but all entirely unused....

The critical moment had come. Paul must say something, and no matter what he said, it would be wrong. Suppose he had begun in the usual way: "Good morning, gentlemen, I have something new in the way of a religion which I'd like to explain, if you'll give me just a minute of your time." A boisterous laugh would have ended his talk...a new religion... what did they care about that?

But Paul knew the psychology of the crowd.

"Men of Athens, I congratulate you on having so many fine religions." Nothing in that to which any one could take offense. The sophisticated pressed up a little closer; what was the chap driving at, anyhow? "I've traveled about quite a bit and your assortment is larger and better than I have seen anywhere else. For as I passed up your main street I noticed that you not only have altars erected to all the regular gods and goddesses; you even have one dedicated to the UNKNOWN GOD.

"Let me tell you an interesting coincidence, gentlemen. This God whom you worship without knowing his name, is the very God whom I represent."

Can you see the crowd? Cynical but curious; eager to turn the whole thing into a joke, yet unwilling to miss a chance to hear the latest. Paul stopped short for a moment and voices called out demanding that he go on. It appears later in the narrative that after his talk was over "some mocked, and others said, 'We will hear thee again of this matter.'" It was not a complete victory such as his Master had achieved...; but the audience which had confronted Paul was hostile, and his initial success so cleverly won, that this story deserves a place beside the one which we have just related. Together they help us to understand the great mystery—how a religion, originating in a despised province of a petty country, could so quickly carry around the world. It conquered not because there was any *demand* for another religion but because Jesus knew how, and taught his followers how to catch the attention of the indifferent, and translate a great spiritual conception into terms of practical self-concern.

Surely no one will consider us lacking in reverence if we say that every one of the "principles of modern salesmanship" on which business men so much pride themselves, are brilliantly exemplified in Jesus' talk and work. The first of these and perhaps the most important is the necessity for "putting yourself in step with your prospect." A great sales manager used to illustrate it in this way:

"...The minds of busy men are in motion," he would continue. "They are engaged with something very different from the thought you have to present. You can't jump directly at them and expect to make an effective landing. You must put yourself in the other man's place; try to imagine what he is thinking; let your first remark be in line with his thoughts; follow it by another with which you know he will easily agree. Thus, gradually, your two minds reach a point where they can join without conflict. You encourage him to say 'yes' and 'yes' and 'that's right' and 'I've noticed that myself,' until he says the final 'yes' which is your favorable decision."

Jesus taught all this without ever teaching it. Every one of his conversations, every contact between his mind and others, is worthy of the attentive study of any sales manager. Passing along the shores of a lake one day, he saw two of the men whom he wanted as disciples. *Their* minds were in motion; their hands were busy with their nets; their conversation was about conditions in the fishing trade, and the prospects of a good market for the day's catch. To have broken in on such thinking with the offer of employment as preachers of a new religion would have been to confuse them and invite a certain rebuff. What was Jesus' approach?

"Come with me," he said, "and I will make you fishers of men." Fishers ... that was a word they could understand ... fishers of men ... that was a new idea ... what was he driving at ... fishers of men ...it sounded interesting.

It would be easy to multiply examples, taking each of his parables and pointing out the keen knowledge of human motives on which it is based...We shall have something more to say of these parables—the most powerful advertisements of all tune. For our present purpose the examples already given are enough. They show how instantly he won his audiences. With his very first sentence he put himself in step with them; it was invariably a thought in line with their own thinking, easy for even the dullest to understand, and shrewdly calculated to awaken an appetite for more.

Every salesman knows the value of being able to sense an objection and meet it before it is advanced. Jesus knew that far better... Even very supercilious and self-assured gentlemen hesitated to expose themselves to the thrusts of a mind which could anticipate criticisms before they were uttered, and deal with them so crisply...No argument was left for them except the final one which is always a confession of failure. They had the brute force on their side. They could not stand against his thinking but they could, and did, nail him on the cross.

Not in time, however. Not until his work was finished. Not until he had trained and equipped a force which would carry on with double power because of the very fact of his death...Every year in our country there are thousands of conventions—political, charitable, business. Most of them are a waste. They are conducted on the false assumption that over-selling and exaggeration are potent forces—that the energies of men respond most powerfully to promises of easy victory and soft rewards. The great leaders of the world have known better...

That higher type of leadership which calls forth men's greatest energies by the promise of obstacles rather than the picture of rewards— that was the leadership of Jesus. By it he tempered the soft metal of his disciples' nature into keen hard steel....

Watch the faces and the figures. See the shoulders straighten, the muscles of the lips grow hard. There is power in those faces that will not be withstood—power born of the most transforming appeal which ever fell on human ears. The voice of the speaker was stilled at the cross, but the power carried on. It withstood prisons and scourging; shipwreck and weariness; public condemnation and the loss of personal friends; chains, and the roar of lions and the flames...

Just a few brief years and every member of the original organization was gone, but the "blood of the martyrs was the seed of the church." The Master's training had done its work.

The great Idea prevailed.

7–2. SAMUEL CROWTHER, "EVERYBODY OUGHT TO BE RICH: AN INTERVIEW WITH JOHN J. RASKOB"

Being rich is, of course, a comparative status. A man with a million dollars used to be considered rich, but so many people have at least that much these days, or are earning incomes in excess of a normal return from a million dollars, that a millionaire does not cause any comment.

Fixing a bulk line to define riches is a pointless performance. Let us rather say that a man is rich when he has an income from invested capital which is sufficient to support him and his family in a decent and comfortable manner—to give as much support, let us say, as has ever been given by his earnings. That amount of prosperity ought to be attainable by anyone. A greater share will come to those who have greater ability.

It seems to me to be a primary duty for people to make it their business to understand how wealth is produced and not to take their ideas from writers and speakers who have the gift of words but not the gift of ordinary common sense. Wealth is not created in dens of iniquity, and it is much more to the point to understand what it is all about than to listen to the expounding of new systems which at the best can only make worse the faults of our present system.

It is quite true that wealth is not so evenly distributed as it ought to be and as it can be. And part of the reason for the unequal distribution is the lack of systematic investment and also the lack of even moderately sensible investment.

One class of investors saves money and puts it into savings banks or other mediums that pay only a fixed interest. Such funds are valuable, but they do not lead to wealth. A second class tries to get rich all at once, and buys any wildcat security that comes along with a promise of immense returns. A third class holds that the return from interest is not enough to justify savings, but at the same time has too much sense to buy fake stocks—and so saves nothing at all. Yet all the while wealth has been here for the asking.

The common stocks of this country have in the past ten years increased enormously in value because the business of the country has increased. Ten thousand dollars invested ten years ago in the common stock of General Motors would now be worth more than a million and a half dollars. And General Motors is only one of many first-class industrial corporations.

It may be said that this is a phenomenal increase and that conditions are going to be difficult in the next ten years. That prophecy may be true, but it is not founded on experience. In my opinion the wealth of the country is bound to increase at a very rapid rate. The rapidity of the rate will be determined by the increase in consumption, and under wise investment plans the consumption will steadily increase.

Now anyone may regret that he or she did not have ten thousand dollars ten years ago and did not put it into General Motors or some other good company—and sigh over a lost opportunity. Anyone who firmly believes that the opportunities are all passed and that from now on the country will get worse instead of better is welcome to the opinion and to whatever increment it will bring. I think that we have scarcely started, and I have thought so for many years.

In conjunction with others I have been interested in creating and directing at least a dozen trusts for investment in equity securities. This plan of equity investments is no mere theory with me. The first of these trusts was started in 1907 and the others in the years immediately following. Under all of these the plan provided for the saving of fifteen dollars per month for investment in equity securities only. There were no stocks bought on margin, no money borrowed, nor any stocks bought for a quick turn or resale. All stocks with few exceptions have been bought and held as permanent investments. The fifteen dollars was saved every month and the dividends from the stocks purchased were kept in the trust and reinvested. Three of these trusts are now twenty years old. Fifteen dollars per month equals one hundred and eighty dollars a year. In twenty years, therefore, the total savings amounted to thirty-six hundred dollars. Each of these three trusts is now worth well in excess of eighty thousand dollars. Invested at 6 per cent interest, this eighty thousand dollars would give the trust beneficiary an annual income of four hundred dollars per month, which ordinarily would represent more than the earning power of the beneficiary, because had he been able to earn as much as four hundred dollars per month he could have saved more than fifteen dollars.

Suppose a man marries at the age of twenty-three and begins a regular saving of fifteen dollars a month—and almost anyone who is employed can do that if he tries. If he invests in good common stocks and allows the dividends and rights to accumulate, he will at the end of twenty years have at least eighty thousand dollars and an income from investments of around four hundred dollars a month. He will be rich. And because anyone can do that I am firm in my belief that anyone not only can be rich but ought to be rich.

The obstacles to being rich are two: The trouble of saving, and the trouble of finding a medium for investment.

If Tom is known to have two hundred dollars in the savings bank then everyone is out to get it for some absolutely necessary purpose. More than likely his wife's sister will eventually find the emergency to draw it forth... But if he does withstand all attacks, what good will the money do him? The interest he receives is so small that he has no incentive to save, and since the whole is under his jurisdiction he can depend only upon his own will to save. To save in any such fashion requires a stronger will than the normal.

If he thinks of investing in some stock he has nowhere to turn for advice. He is not big enough to get much attention from his banker, and he has not enough money to go to a broker—or at least he thinks he has not.

Suppose he has a thousand dollars; the bank can only advise him to buy a bond, for the officer will not take the risk of advising a stock and probably has not the experience anyway to give such advice. Tom can get really adequate attention only from some man who has a worthless security to sell, for then all of Tom's money will be profit. The plan that I have had in mind for several years grows out of the success of the plans that we have followed for the executives in the General Motors and the DuPont companies. In 1923, in order to give the executives of General Motors a greater interest in their work, we organized the Managers Securities Company, made up of eighty senior and junior executives. This company bought General Motors common stock to the then market value of thirty-three million dollars. The executives paid five million dollars in cash and borrowed twenty-eight million dollars. The stockholders of the Managers Securities Company are not stockholders of General Motors. They own stock in a company which owns stock in General Motors, so that, as far as General Motors is concerned, the stock is voted as a block according to the instructions of the directors of the Managers Securities Company. This supplies an important interest which can exercise a large influence in shaping the policies of General Motors.

The holdings of the members in the securities company are adjusted in cases of men leaving the employ of the company. The plan of the Managers Securities Company contemplates no dissolution of that company, so that its holdings of General Motors stock will always be *en bloc*. The plan has been enormously successful, and much of the success of the General Motors Corporation has been due to the executives having full responsibility and receiving financial rewards commensurate with that responsibility.

The participation in the Managers Securities Company was arranged in accordance with the position and salary of the executive. Minimum participation required a cash payment of twenty-five thousand dollars when the Managers Security Company was organized. That minimum participation is now worth more than one million dollars.

Recently I have been advocating the formation of an equity securities corporation; that is, a corporation that will invest in common stocks only under proper and careful supervision. This company will buy the common stocks of first-class industrial corporations and issue its own stock certificates against them. This stock will be offered from time to time at a price to correspond exactly with the value of the assets of the corporation and all profit will go to the stockholders. The directors will be men of outstanding character, reputation and integrity. At regular intervals—say quarterly—the whole financial record of the corporation will be published together with all of its holdings and the cost thereof. The corporation will be owned by the public and with every transaction public. I am not at all interested in a private investment trust. The company would not be permitted to borrow money or go into any debt.

In addition to this company, there should be organized a discount company on the same lines as the finance companies of the motor concerns to be used to sell stock of the investing corporation on the installment plan. If Tom had two hundred dollars, this discount company would lend him three hundred dollars and thus enable him to buy five hundred dollars of the equity securities investment company stock, and Tom could arrange to pay off his loan just as he pays off his motorcar loan. When finished he would own outright five hundred dollars of the equity securities investment company stock. That would take his savings out of the free-will class and put them into the compulsory-payment class and his savings would no longer be fair game for relatives, for swindlers or for himself.

People pay for their motor car loans. They will also pay their loans contracted to secure their share in the nation's business. And in the kind of company suggested every increase in value and every right would go to the benefit of the stockholders and be reflected in the price and earning power of their stock. They would share absolutely in the nation's prosperity.

The effect of all this would, to my mind, be very far-reaching. If Tom bought five hundred dollars' worth of stock he would be helping some manufacturer to buy a new lathe or a new machine of some kind, which would add to the wealth of the country, and Tom, by participating in the profits of this machine, would be in a position to buy more goods and cause a demand for more machines. Prosperity is in the nature of an endless chain and we can break it only by our own refusal to see what it is.

Everyone ought to be rich, but it is out of the question to make people rich in spite of themselves.

The millennium is not at hand. One cannot have all play and no work. But it has been sufficiently demonstrated that many of the old and supposedly conservative maxims are as untrue as the radical notions. We can appraise things as they are.

Everyone by this time ought to know that nothing can be gained by stopping the progress of the world and dividing up everything—there would not be enough to divide, in the first place, and, in the second place, most of the world's wealth is not in such form it can be divided.

The socialistic theory of division is, however, no more irrational than some of the more hidebound theories of thrift or of getting rich by saving.

No one can become rich merely by saving. Putting aside a sum each week or month in a sock at no interest, or in a savings bank at ordinary interest, will not provide enough for old age unless life in the meantime be rigorously skimped down to the level of mere existence. And if everyone skimped in any such fashion then the country would be so poor that living at all would hardly be worth while.

Unless we have consumption we shall not have production. Production and consumption go together and a rigid national program of saving would, if carried beyond a point, make for general poverty, for there would be no consumption to call new wealth into being.

Therefore, savings must be looked at not as a present deprivation in order to enjoy more in the future, but as a constructive method of increasing not only one's future but also one's present income.

Saving may be a virtue if undertaken as a kind of mental and moral discipline, but such a course of saving is not to be regarded as a financial plan. Constructive saving in order to increase one's income is a financial operation and to be governed by financial rules; disciplinary saving is another matter entirely. The two have been confused.

Most of the old precepts contrasting the immorality of speculation with the morality of sound investment have no basis in fact. They have just been so often repeated as true that they are taken as true. If one buys a debt—that is, takes a secured bond or mortgage at a fixed rate of interest—then that is supposed to be an investment. In the case of the debt, the principal sum as well as the interest is fixed and the investor cannot get more than he contracts for. The law guards against getting more and also it regulates the procedure by which the lender can take the property of the borrower in case of default. But the law cannot say that the property of the debtor will be worth the principal sum of the debt when it falls due; the creditor must take that chance.

The investor in a debt strictly limits his possible gain, but he does not limit his loss. He speculates in only one direction in so far as the actual return in dollars and cents is concerned. But in addition he speculates against the interest rate. If his security pays 4 per cent and money is worth 6 or 7 per cent then he is lending at less than the current rate; if money is worth 3 per cent, then he is lending at more than he could otherwise get.

The buyer of a common share in an enterprise limits neither his gains nor his losses. However, he excludes one element of speculation—the change in the value of money. For whatever earnings he gets will be in current money values. If he buys shares in a wholly new and untried enterprise, then his hazards are great, but if he buys into established enterprises, then he takes no more chance than does the investor who buys a debt.

It is difficult to see why a bond or mortgage should be considered as a more conservative investment than a good stock, for the only difference in practice is that the bond can never be worth more than its face value or return more than the interest, while a stock can be worth more than was paid for it and can return a limitless profit.

One may lose on either a bond or a stock. If a company fails it will usually be reorganized and in that case the bonds will have to give way to new money and possibly they will be scaled down. The common stockholders may lose all, or again they may get another kind of stock which may or may not eventually have a value. In a failure, neither the bondholders nor the stockholders will find any great cause for happiness- but there are very few failures among the larger corporations.

A first mortgage on improved real estate is supposedly a very safe investment, but the value of realty shifts quickly and even the most experienced investors in real-estate mortgages have to foreclose an appreciable percentage of their mortgages and buy in the properties to protect themselves. It may be years before the property can be sold again.

I would rather buy real estate than buy mortgages on it, for then I have the chance of gaining more than I paid. On a mortgage I cannot get back more than I lend, but I may get back less.

The line between investment and speculation is a very hazy one, and a definition is not to be found in the legal form of a security or in limiting the possible return on the money. The difference is rather in the approach.

Placing a bet is very different from placing one's money with a corporation which has thoroughly demonstrated that it can normally earn profits and has a reasonable expectation of earning greater profits. That may be called speculation, but it would be more accurate to think of the operation as going into business with men who have demonstrated that they know how to do business.

The old view of debt was quite as illogical as the old view of investment. It was beyond the conception of anyone that debt could be constructive. Every old saw about debt—and there must be a thousand of them- is bound up with borrowing instead of earning. We now know that borrowing may be a method of earning and beneficial to everyone concerned. Suppose a man needs a certain amount of money in order to buy a set of tools or anything else which will increase his income. He can take one of two courses.

He can save the money and in the course of time buy his tools, or he can, if the proper facilities are provided, borrow the money at a reasonable rate of interest, buy the tools and immediately so increase his income that he can pay off his debt and own the tools within half the time that it would have taken him to save the money and pay cash. That loan enables him at once to create more wealth than before and consequently makes him a more valuable citizen. By increasing his power to produce he also increases his power to consume and therefore he increases the power of others to produce in order to fill his new needs and naturally increases their power to consume, and so on. By borrowing the money instead of saving it he increases his ability to save and steps up prosperity at once.

That is exactly what the automobile has done to the prosperity of the country through the plan of installment payments. The installment plan of paying for automobiles, when it was first launched, ran counter to the old notions of debt. It was opposed by bankers, who saw in it only an incentive for extravagance. It was opposed by manufacturers because they thought people would be led to buy automobiles instead of their products.

The results have been exactly opposite to the prediction. The ability to buy automobiles on credit gave an immediate step-up to their purchase. Manufacturing them, servicing them, building roads for them to run on, and caring for the people who used the roads have brought into existence about ten billion dollars of new wealth each year—which is roughly about the value of the farm crops. The creation of this new wealth gave a large increase to consumption and has brought on our present very solid prosperity.

But without the facility for going into debt or the facility for the consumer's getting credit—call it what you will—this great addition to wealth might never have taken place and certainly not for many years to come. Debt may be a burden, but it is more likely to be an incentive.

The great wealth of this country has been gained by the forces of production and consumption pushing each other for supremacy. The personal fortunes of this country have been made not by saving but by producing.

Mere saving is closely akin to the socialist policy of dividing and likewise runs up against the same objection that there is not enough around to save. The savings that count cannot be static. They must be going into the production of wealth. They may go in as debt and the managers of the wealth-making enterprises take all the profit over and above the interest paid. That has been the course recommended for saving and for the reasons that have been set out—the fallacy of conservative investment which is not conservative at all.

The way to wealth is to get into the profit end of wealth production in this country.

7–3. FREDERICK LEWIS ALLEN, *ONLY YESTERDAY*: CHAPTER VII—COOLIDGE PROSPERITY

Business was booming when Warren Harding died, and in a primitive Vermont farmhouse, by the light of an old-fashioned kerosene lamp, Colonel John Coolidge administered to his son Calvin the oath of office as President of the United States. The hopeless depression of 1921 had given way to the hopeful improvement of 1922 and the rushing revival of 1923.

The prices of common stocks, to be sure, suggested no unreasonable optimism. On August 2, 1923, the day of Harding's death, United States Steel (paying a five-dollar dividend) stood at 87, Atchison (paying six dollars) at 95, New York Central (paying seven) at 97, and American Telephone and Telegraph (paying nine) at 122; and the total turnover for the day on the New York Stock Exchange amounted to only a little over 600,000 shares. The Big Bull Market was still far in the future. Nevertheless the tide of prosperity was in full flood.

Pick up one of those graphs with which statisticians measure the economic ups and downs of the Post-war Decade. You will find that the line of business activity rises to a jagged peak in 1920, drops precipitously into a deep valley in late 1920 and 1921, climbs uncertainly upward through 1922 to another peak at the middle of 1923, dips somewhat in 1924 (but not nearly so far as in 1921), rises again in 1925 and 1926, dips momentarily but slightly toward the end of 1927, and then zigzags up to a perfect Everest of prosperity in 1929—only to plunge down at last into the bottomless abyss of 1930 and 1931.

Hold the graph at arm's-length and glance at it again, and you will see that the clefts of 1924 and 1927 are mere indentations in a lofty and irregular plateau which reaches from early 1923 to late 1929. That plateau represents nearly seven years of unparalleled plenty; nearly seven years during which men and women might he disillusioned about politics and religion and love, but believed that at the end of the rainbow there was at least a pot of negotiable legal tender consisting of the profits of American industry and American salesmanship; nearly seven years during which the businessman was, as Stuart Chase put it, "the dictator of our destinies," ousting "the statesman, the priest, the philosopher, as the creator of standards of ethics and behavior" and becoming "the final authority on the conduct of American society." For nearly seven years the prosperity band-wagon rolled down Main Street.

Not everyone could manage to climb aboard this wagon. Mighty few farmers could get so much as a fingerhold upon it. Some dairymen clung there, to be sure, and fruit-growers and truck-gardeners. For prodigious changes were taking place in the national diet as the result of the public's discovery of the useful vitamin, the propaganda for a more varied menu, and the invention of better methods of shipping perishable foods. Between 1919 and 1926 the national production of milk and milk products increased by one-third and that of ice-cream alone took a 45-per-cent jump. Between 1919 and 1928, as families learned that there were vitamins in celery, spinach, and carrots, and became accustomed to serving fresh vegetables the year round (along with fresh fruits), the acreage of nineteen commercial truck vegetable crops nearly doubled. But the growers of staple crops such as wheat and corn and cotton were in a bad way. Their foreign markets had dwindled under competition from other countries. Women were wearing less and less cotton. Few agricultural raw materials were used in the new economy of automobiles and radios and electricity. And the more efficient the poor farmer became, the more machines he bought to increase his output and thus keep the wolf from the door, the more surely he and his fellows were faced by the specter of overproduction. The index number of all farm prices, which had coasted from 205 in 1920 to 116 in 1921—"perhaps the most terrible toboggan slide in all American agricultural history," to quote Stuart Chase again —regained only a fraction of the ground it had lost: in 1927 it stood at 131. Loudly the poor farmers complained, desperately they and their Norrises and Brookharts and Shipsteads and La Follettes campaigned for federal aid, and by the hundreds of thousands they left the farm for the cities.

There were other industries unrepresented in the triumphal march of progress. Coal-mining suffered, and textile-manufacturing, and shipbuilding, and shoe and leather manufacturing. Whole regions of the country felt the effects of depression in one or more of these industries. The South was held back by cotton, the agricultural Northwest by the dismal condition of the wheat growers, New England by the paralysis of the textile and shoe industries. Nevertheless, the prosperity band-wagon did not lack for occupants, and their good fortune outweighed and outshouted the ill fortune of those who lamented by the roadside.

§ 2

In a position of honor rode the automobile manufacturer. His hour of destiny had struck. By this time paved roads and repair shops and filling stations had become so plentiful that the motorist might sally forth for the day without fear of being stuck in a mudhole or stranded without benefit of gasoline or crippled by a dead spark plug. Automobiles were now made with such precision, for that matter, that the motorist need hardly know a spark plug by sight; thousands of automobile owners had never even lifted the hood to see what the engine looked like. Now that closed cars were in quantity production, furthermore, the motorist had no need of Spartan blood, even in January. And the stylish new models were a delight to the eye. At the beginning of the decade most cars had been somber in color, but with the invention of pyroxylin finishes they broke out (in 1925 and 1926) into a whole rainbow of colors, from Florentine cream to Versailles violet. Bodies were swung lower, expert designers sought new harmonies of line, balloon tires came in, and at last even Henry Ford capitulated to style and beauty.

If any sign had been needed of the central place which the automobile had come to occupy in the mind and heart of the average American, it was furnished when the Model A Ford was brought out in December, 1927. Since the previous spring, when Henry Ford had shut down his gigantic plant, scrapped his Model T and the thousands of machines which brought it into being, and announced that he was going to put a new car on the market, the country had been in a state of suspense. Obviously he would have to make drastic changes. Model T had been losing to Chevrolet its leadership in the enormous low-priced-car market, for the time had come when people were no longer content with ugliness and a maximum speed of forty or forty-five miles an hour; no longer content, either, to roar slowly uphill with a weary left foot jammed against the low-speed pedal while robin's-egg blue Chevrolets swept past in second. Yet equally obviously Henry Ford was the mechanical genius of the age. What miracle would he accomplish?

Rumor after rumor broke into the front pages of the newspapers. So intense was the interest that even the fact that an automobile dealer in Brooklyn had "learned something of the new car through a telegram from his brother Henry" was headline stuff. When the editor of the Brighton, Michigan, Weekly Argus actually snapped a photograph of a new Ford out for a trial spin, newspaper-readers pounced on the picture and avidly discussed its every line. The great day arrived when this newest product of the inventive genius of the age was to be shown to the public. The Ford Motor Company was running in 2,000 daily newspapers a five-day series of full-page advertisements at a total cost of $1,300,000; and everyone who could read was reading them. On December 2, 1927, when Model A was unveiled, one million people—so the Herald-Tribune figured —tried to get into the Ford headquarters in New York to catch a glimpse of it; as Charles Merz later reported in his life of Ford, "one hundred thousand people flocked into the showrooms of the Ford Company in Detroit; mounted police were called out to patrol the crowds in Cleveland; in Kansas City so great a mob stormed Convention Hall that platforms had to be built to lift the new car high enough for everyone to see it." So it went from one end of the United States to the other. Thousands of orders piled up on the Ford books for Niagara Blue roadsters and Arabian Sand phaetons. For weeks and months, every new Ford that appeared on the streets drew a crowd. To the motor-minded American people the first showing of a new kind of automobile was no matter of merely casual or commercial interest. It was one of the great events of the year 1927; not so thrilling as Lindbergh's flight, but rivaling the execution of Sacco and Vanzetti, the Hall-Mills murder trial, the Mississippi flood, and the Dempsey-Tunney fight at Chicago in its capacity to arouse public excitement.

In 1919 there had been 6,771,000 passenger cars in service in the United States; by 1929 there were no less than 23,121,000. There you have possibly the most potent statistic of Coolidge Prosperity. As a footnote to it I suggest the following: even as early as the end of 1923 there were two cars for every three families in "Middletown," a typical American city. The Lynds and their investigators interviewed 123 working-class families of "Middletown" and found that 60 of them had cars. Of these 60, 26 lived in such shabby-looking houses that the investigators thought to ask whether they had bathtubs, and discovered that as many as 21 of the 26 had none. The automobile came even before the tub!

And as it came, it changed the face of America. Villages which had once prospered because they were "on the railroad" languished with economic anaemia; villages on Route 61 bloomed with garages, filling stations, hot-dog stands, chicken-dinner restaurants, tearooms, tourists' rests, camping sites, and affluence. The interurban trolley perished, or survived only as a pathetic anachronism. Railroad after railroad gave up its branch lines, or saw its revenues slowly dwindling under the competition of mammoth interurban buses and trucks snorting along six-lane concrete highways. The whole country was covered with a network of passenger bus-lines. In thousands of towns, at the beginning of the decade a single traffic officer at the junction of Main Street and Central Street had been sufficient for the control of traffic. By the end of the decade, what a difference!—red and green lights, blinkers, one-way streets, boulevard stops, stringent and yet more stringent parking ordinances—and still a shining flow of traffic that backed up for blocks along Main Street every Saturday and Sunday afternoon. Slowly but surely the age of steam was yielding to the gasoline age.

§3

The radio manufacturer occupied a less important seat than the automobile manufacturer on the prosperity bandwagon, but he had the distinction of being the youngest rider. You will remember that there was no such thing as radio broadcasting to the public until the autumn of 1920, but that by the spring of 1922 radio had become a craze— as much talked about as Mah Jong was to be the following year or cross-word puzzles the year after. In 1922 the sales of radio sets, parts, and accessories amounted to $60,000,000. People wondered what would happen when the edge wore off the novelty of hearing a jazz orchestra in Schenectady or in Davenport, Iowa, play "Mr. Gallagher and Mr. Shean." What actually did happen is suggested by the cold figures of total annual radio sales for the next few years:

1922—$ 60,000,000 (as we have just seen)
1923—$136,000,000
1924— $358,000,000
1925—$433,000,000
1926—$506,000,000
1927—$425,600,000
1928—$650,550,000
1929—$842,548,000 (an increase over the 1922 figures of 1,400 per cent!)

Don't hurry past those figures. Study them a moment, remembering that whenever there is a dip in the curve of national prosperity there is likely to be a dip in the sales of almost every popular commodity. There was a dip in national prosperity in 1927, for instance; do you see what it did to radio sales? But there was also a dip in 1924, a worse one in fact. Yet radio sales made in that year the largest proportional increase in the whole period. Why?

Well, for one thing, that was the year in which the embattled Democrats met at Madison Square Garden in New York to pick a standard-bearer, and the deadlock between the hosts of McAdoo and the hosts of Al Smith lasted day after day after day, and millions of Americans heard through loud-speakers the lusty cry of, "Alabama, twenty-four votes for Underwoo—ood!" and discovered that a political convention could be a grand show to listen to and that a seat by the radio was as good as a ticket to the Garden. Better, in fact; for at any moment you could turn a knob and get "Barney Google" or "It Ain't Gonna Rain No More" by way of respite. At the age of three and a half years, radio broadcasting had attained its majority.

Behind those figures of radio sales lies a whole chapter of the life of the Post-war Decade: radio penetrating every third home in the country; giant broadcasting stations with nationwide hook-ups; tenement-house roofs covered with forests of antennae; Roxy and his Gang, the Happiness Boys, the A & P Gypsies, and Rudy Vallee crooning from antique Florentine cabinet sets; Graham McNamee's voice, which had become more familiar to the American public than that of any other citizen of the land, shouting across your living room and mine: "And he did it! Yes, sir, he did it! It's a touchdown! Boy, I want to tell you this is one of the finest games ..."; the Government belatedly asserting itself in 1927 to allocate wave-lengths among competing radio stations; advertisers paying huge sums for the privilege of introducing Beethoven with a few well-chosen words about yeast or toothpaste; and Michael Meehan personally conducting the common stock of the Radio Corporation of America from a 1928 low of 85¼ to a 1929 high of 549.

There were other riders on the prosperity band-wagon. Rayon, cigarettes, refrigerators, telephones, chemical preparations (especially cosmetics), and electrical devices of various sorts all were in growing demand. While the independent storekeeper struggled to hold his own, the amount of retail business done in chain stores and department stores jumped by leaps and bounds. For every $100 worth of business done in 1919, by 1927 the five-and-ten-cent chains were doing $260 worth, the cigar chains $153 worth, the drug chains $224 worth, and the grocery chains $387 worth. Mrs. Smith no longer patronized her "naborhood" store; she climbed into her two-thousand dollar car to drive to the red fronted chain grocery and save twenty-seven cents on her daily purchases. The movies prospered, sending their celluloid reels all over the world and making Charlie Chaplin, Douglas Fairbanks, Gloria Swanson, Rudolph Valentino, and Clara Bow familiar figures to the Eskimo, the Malay, and the heathen Chinee; while at home the attendance at the motion-picture houses of "Middletown" during a single month (December, 1923) amounted to four and a half times the entire population of the city. Men, women, and children, rich and poor, the Middletowners went to the movies at an average rate of better than once a week!

Was this Coolidge Prosperity real? The farmers did not think so. Perhaps the textile manufacturers did not think so. But the figures of corporation profits and wages and incomes left little room for doubt. Consider, for example, two significant facts at opposite ends of the scale of wealth. Between 1922 and 1927, the purchasing power of American wages increased at the rate of more than two per cent annually. And during the three years between 1924 and 1927 alone there was a leap from 75 to 283 in the number of Americans who paid taxes on incomes of more than a million dollars a year.

§4

Why did it happen? What made the United States so prosperous?

Some of the reasons were obvious enough. The war had impoverished Europe and hardly damaged the United States at all; when peace came the Americans found themselves the economic masters of the world. Their young country, with enormous resources in materials and in human energy and with a wide domestic market, was ready to take advantage of this situation. It had developed mass production to a new point of mechanical and managerial efficiency.

The Ford gospel of high wages, low prices, and standardized manufacture on a basis of the most minute division of machine-tending labor was working smoothly not only at Highland Park, but in thousands of other factories. Executives, remembering with a shudder the piled-up inventories of 1921, had learned the lesson of cautious hand-to-mouth buying; and they were surrounded with more expert technical consultants, research men, personnel managers, statisticians, and business forecasters than had ever before invaded that cave of the winds, the conference room. Their confidence was strengthened by their almost superstitious belief that the Republican Administration was their invincible ally. And they were all of them aided by the boom in the automobile industry. The phenomenal activity of this one part of the body economic—which was responsible, directly or indirectly, for the employment of nearly four million men—pumped new life into all the rest.

Prosperity was assisted, too, by two new stimulants to purchasing, each of which mortgaged the future but kept the factories roaring while it was being injected. The first was the increase in installment buying. People were getting to consider it old-fashioned to limit their purchases to the amount of their cash balance; the thing to do was to "exercise their credit." By the latter part of the decade, economists figured that 15 per cent of all retail sales were on an installment basis, and that there were some six billions of "easy payment" paper outstanding. The other stimulant was stock-market speculation. When stocks were skyrocketing in 1928 and 1929 it is probable that hundreds of thousands of people were buying goods with money which represented, essentially, a gamble on the business profits of the nineteen-thirties. It was fun while it lasted.

If these were the principal causes of Coolidge Prosperity, the salesman and the advertising man were at least its agents and evangels. Business had learned as never before the immense importance to it of the ultimate consumer. Unless he could be persuaded to buy and buy lavishly, the whole stream of six-cylinder cars, super-heterodynes, cigarettes, rouge compacts, and electric ice-boxes would be dammed at its outlet. The salesman and the advertising man held the key to this outlet. As competition increased their methods became more strenuous. No longer was it considered enough to recommend one's goods in modest and explicit terms and to place them on the counter in the hope that the ultimate consumer would make up his mind to purchase. The advertiser must plan elaborate national campaigns, consult with psychologists, and employ all the eloquence of poets to cajole, exhort, or intimidate the consumer into buying,—to "break down consumer resistance." Not only was each individual concern struggling to get a larger share of the business in its own field, but whole industries shouted against one another in the public's ear. The embattled candy manufacturers took full-page space in the newspapers to reply to the American Tobacco Company's slogan of "Reach for a Lucky instead of a sweet." Trade journals were quoted by the Reader's Digest as reporting the efforts of the furniture manufacturers to make the people "furniture conscious" and of the clothing manufacturers to make them "tuxedo conscious." The salesman must have the ardor of a zealot, must force his way into people's houses by hook or by crook, must let nothing stand between him and the consummation of his sale. As executives put it, "You can't be an order-taker any longer—you've got to be a salesman." The public, generally speaking, could be relied upon to regard with complacence the most flagrant assaults upon its credulity by the advertiser and the most outrageous invasions of its privacy by the salesman; for the public was in a mood to forgive every sin committed in the holy name of business.

Never before had such pressure been exerted upon salesmen to get results. Many concerns took up the quota system, setting as the objective for each sales representative a figure 20 or 25 per cent beyond that of the previous year, and putting it up to him to reach this figure or lose his employer's favor and perhaps his job. All sorts of sales contests and other ingenious devices were used to stimulate the force. Among the schemes suggested by the Dartnell Company of Chicago, which had more than ten thousand American business organizations subscribing to its service, was that of buying various novelties and sending them to the salesman at weekly intervals: one week a miniature feather duster with a tag urging him to "dust his territory," another week an imitation cannon cracker with the injunction to "make a big noise," and so on. The American Slicing Machine Company offered a turkey at Christmas to every one of its salesmen who beat his quota for the year. "We asked each man," explained the sales manager afterward, "to appoint a child in his family as a mascot, realizing that every one of them would work his head off to make some youngster happy at Christmas. The way these youngsters took hold of the plan was amusing, and at times the intensity of their interest was almost pathetic." The sales manager of another concern reported cheerfully that "one of his stunts" was "to twit one man at the good work of another until he is almost sore enough to be ready to fight." And according to Jesse Rainsford Sprague, still another company invented—and boasted of—a method of goading its salesmen which for sheer inhumanity probably set a record for the whole era of Coolidge Prosperity. It gave a banquet at which the man with the best score was served with oysters, roast turkey, and a most elaborate ice; the man with the second best score had the same dinner but without the oysters; and so on down to the man with the worst score, before whom was laid a small plate of boiled beans and a couple of crackers.

If the salesman was sometimes under pressure such as this, it is not surprising that the consumer felt the pressure, too.

Let two extreme instances (both cited by Jesse Rainsford Sprague) suffice to suggest the trend in business methods. A wholesale drug concern offered to the trade a small table with a railing round its top for the display of "specials"; it was to be set up directly in the path of customers, "whose attention," according to Printer's Ink, "will be attracted to the articles when they fall over it, bump into it, kick their shins upon it, or otherwise come in contact with it." And Selling News awarded one of its cash prizes for "sales ideas" to a vender of electric cleaners who told the following story of commercial prowess. One day he looked up from the street and saw a lady shaking a rug out of a second-story window. "The door leading to her upstairs rooms was open. I went right in and up those stairs without knocking, greeting the lady with the remark: 'Well, I am here right on time. What room do you wish me to start in?' She was very much surprised, assuring me that I had the wrong number. But during my very courteous apologies I had managed to get my cleaner connected and in action. The result was that I walked out minus the cleaner, plus her contract and check for a substantial down payment." The readers of Selling News were apparently not expected to be less than enthusiastic at the prospect of a man invading a woman's apartment and setting up a cleaner in it without permission and under false pretenses. For if you could get away with such exploits, it helped business, and good business helped prosperity, and prosperity was good for the country.

ESSAYS

What caused the stock market boom and collapse of the 1920s? In Essay 7–1 John Kenneth Galbraith, famed Harvard economics professor and ambassador to India in the Kennedy administration, examines the collapse in "Cause and Consequence," Chapter X from his 1954 bestseller *The Great Crash 1929*. In the excerpts from that chapter, Galbraith describes the economy of the 1920s as fundamentally unsound. The uneven distribution of income, the delicate state of the banking system, and the devotion of policymakers to balanced budgets and the gold standard were main culprits. While Galbraith's explanations may not have as many adherents as they once did, they are still an excellent starting point for understanding the causes of the collapse.

Essay 7–2, "A Glimpse of Modernity," Chapter 12 from W. Elliot Brownlee's *Dynamics of Ascent*, casts the 1920s in a very different light from Galbraith. Brownlee, professor of history emeritus at the University of California at Santa Barbara, sees the American economy of the 20s as stable and prosperous, except for two legacies of the First World War: an agricultural sector that had over expanded, and America's unwillingness to accept the leadership role as the world's lender of last resort. In Essay 7–3, "The Stock Market Boom and Crash of 1929 Revisited," Eugene N. White, a Rutgers University economics professor, explores the role of such factors as dividend payments and brokers' loans as explanations for the rapid rise of the stock market in the late 1920s. Finding these explanations inadequate, he leaves open the possibility of a speculative bubble. While readily admitting to the econometric difficulties of establishing the existence of a bubble, White believes the qualitative evidence supports the existence of a bubble in the post 1927 period. The nascent recession of late 1929 burst the bubble, as the Federal Reserve's perverse policy of monetary restriction assured that a serious recession would be transformed into a prolonged contraction.

7–1. JOHN KENNETH GALBRAITH, *THE GREAT CRASH 1929*: CHAPTER IX—CAUSE AND CONSEQUENCE

After the Great Crash came the Great Depression which lasted, with varying severity, for ten years. In 1933, Gross National Product (total production of the economy) was nearly a third less than in 1929. Not until 1937 did the physical volume of production recover to the levels of 1929, and then it promptly slipped back again. Until 1941 the dollar value of production remained below 1929. Between 1930 and 1940 only once, in 1937, did the average number unemployed during the year drop below eight million. In 1933 nearly thirteen million were out of work, or about one in every four in the labor force. In 1938 one person in five was still out of work.

It was during this dreary time that 1929 became a year of myth. People hoped that the country might get back to twenty-nine; in some industries or towns when business was phenomenally good it was almost as good as in twenty-nine; men of outstanding vision, on occasions of exceptional solemnity, were heard to say that 1929 "was no better than Americans deserve."

On the whole, the great stock market crash can be much more readily explained than the depression that followed it. And among the problems involved in assessing the causes of depression none is more intractable than the responsibility to be assigned to the stock market crash. Economics still does not allow final answers on these matters. But, as usual, something can be said.

As already so often emphasized, the collapse in the stock market in the autumn of 1929 was implicit in the speculation that went before. The only question concerning that speculation was how long it would last. Sometime, sooner or later, confidence in the short-run reality of increasing common stock values would weaken. When this happened, some people would sell, and this would destroy the reality of increasing values. Holding for an increase would now become meaningless; the new reality would be falling prices. There would be a rush, pell-mell, to unload. This was the way past speculative orgies had ended. It was the way the end came in 1929. It is the way speculation will end in the future.

We do not know why a great speculative orgy occurred in 1928 and 1929. The long accepted explanation that credit was easy and so people were impelled to borrow money to buy common stocks on margin is obviously nonsense. On numerous occasions before and since credit has been easy, and there has been no speculation whatever. Furthermore, much of the 1928 and 1929 speculation occurred on money borrowed at interest rates which for years before, and in any period since, would have been considered exceptionally astringent. Money, by the ordinary tests, was tight in the late twenties.

Far more important than rate of interest and the supply of credit is the mood. Speculation on a large scale requires a pervasive sense of confidence and optimism and conviction that ordinary people were meant to be rich. People must also have faith in the good intentions and even in the benevolence of others, for it is by the agency of others that they will get rich. In 1929 Professor Dice observed: "The common folks believe in their leaders. We no longer look upon the captains of industry as magnified crooks. Have we not heard their voices over the radio? Are we not familiar with their thoughts, ambitions, and ideals as they have expressed them to us almost as a man talks to his friend?" Such a feeling of trust is essential for a boom. When people are cautious, questioning, misanthropic, suspicious, or mean, they are immune to speculative enthusiasms.

Savings must also be plentiful. Speculation, however it may rely on borrowed funds, must be nourished in part by those who participate. If savings are growing rapidly, people will place a lower marginal value on their accumulation; they will be willing to risk some of it against the prospect of a greatly enhanced return. Speculation, accordingly, is most likely to break out after a substantial period of prosperity, rather than in the early phases of recovery from a depression. Macaulay noted that between the Restoration and the Glorious Revolution Englishmen were at loss to know what to do with their savings and that the "natural effect of this state of things was that a crowd of projectors, ingenious and absurd, honest and knavish, employed themselves in devising new schemes for the employment of redundant capital." Bagehot and others have attributed the South Sea Bubble to roughly the same causes. In 1720 England had enjoyed a long period of prosperity, enhanced in part by war expenditures, and during this time private savings are believed to have grown at an unprecedented rate. Investment outlets were also few and returns low. Accordingly, Englishmen were anxious to place their savings at the disposal of the new enterprises and were quick to believe that the prospects were not fantastic. So it was in 1928 and 1929.

Finally, a speculative outbreak has a greater or less immunizing effect. The ensuing collapse automatically destroys the very mood speculation requires. It follows that an outbreak of speculation provides a reasonable assurance that another outbreak will not immediately occur. With time and the dimming of memory, the immunity wears off. A recurrence becomes possible. Nothing would have induced Americans to launch a speculative adventure in the stock market in 1935. By 1955 the chances are very much better.

As noted, it is easier to account for the boom and crash in the market than to explain their bearing on the depression which followed. The causes of the Great Depression are still far from certain. A lack of certainty, it may also be observed, is not evident in the contemporary writing on the subject. Much of it tells what went wrong and why with marked firmness. However, this paradoxically can itself be an indication of uncertainty. When people are least sure they are often most dogmatic. We do not know what the Russians intend, so we state with great assurance what they will do. We compensate for our inability to foretell the consequences of, say, rearming Germany by asserting positively just what the consequences will be. So it is in economics. Yet, in explaining what happened in 1929 and after, one can distinguish between explanations that might be right and those that are clearly wrong.

A great many people have always felt that a depression was inevitable in the thirties. There had been (at least) seven good years; now by an occult or biblical law of compensation there would have to be seven bad ones. Perhaps, consciously or unconsciously, an argument that was valid for the stock market was brought to bear on the economy in general. Because the market took leave of reality in 1928 and 1929, it had at some time to make a return to reality. The disenchantment was bound to be as painful as the illusions were beguiling. Similarly, the New Era prosperity would some day evaporate; in its wake would come the compensating hardship....

...Nor was the economy of the United States in 1929 subject to such physical pressure or strain as the result of its past level of performance that a depression was bound to come. The notion that the economy requires occasional rest and resuscitation has a measure of plausibility and also a marked viability. During the summer of 1954 a professional economist on President Eisenhower's personal staff explained the then current recession by saying that the economy was enjoying a brief (and presumably well-merited) rest after the exceptional exertions of preceding years. In 1929 the labor force was not tired; it could have continued to produce indefinitely at the best 1929 rate. The capital plant of the country was not depleted. In the preceding years of prosperity, plant had been renewed and improved. In fact, depletion of the capital plant occurred during the ensuing years of idleness when new investment was sharply curtailed. Raw materials in 1929 were ample for the current rate of production. Entrepreneurs were never more eupeptic. Obviously if men, materials, plant, and management were all capable of continued and even enlarged exertions a refreshing pause was not necessary.

Finally, the high production of the twenties did not, as some have suggested, outrun the wants of the people. During these years people were indeed being supplied with an increasing volume of goods. But there is no evidence that their desire for automobiles, clothing, travel, recreation, or even food was sated. On the contrary, all subsequent evidence showed (given the income to spend) a capacity for a large further increase in consumption. A depression was not needed so that people's wants could catch up with their capacity to produce.

What, then, are the plausible causes of the depression? The task of answering can be simplified somewhat by dividing the problem into two parts. First there is the question of why economic activity turned down in 1929. Second there is the vastly more important question of why, having started down, on this unhappy occasion it went down and down and down and remained low for a full decade.

As noted, the Federal Reserve indexes of industrial activity and of factory production, the most comprehensive monthly measures of economic activity then available, reached a peak in June. They then turned down and continued to decline throughout the rest of the year. The turning point in other indicators — factory payrolls, freight-car loadings, and department store sales — came later, and it was October or after before the trend in all of them was clearly down. Still, as economists have generally insisted, and the matter has the high authority of the National Bureau of Economic Research, the economy had weakened in the early summer well before the crash.

This weakening can be variously explained. Production of industrial products, for the moment, had outrun consumer and investment demand for them. The most likely reason is that business concerns, in the characteristic enthusiasm of good times, misjudged the prospective increase in demand and acquired larger inventories than they later found they needed. As a result they curtailed their buying, and this led to a cutback in production. In short, the summer of 1929 marked the beginning of the familiar inventory recession. The proof is not conclusive from the (by present standards) limited figures available. Department store inventories, for which figures are available, seem not to have been out of line early in the year. But a mild slump in department store sales in April could have been a signal for curtailment.

Also there is a chance — one that students of the period have generally favored — that more deep-seated factors were at work and made themselves seriously evident for the first time during that summer. Throughout the twenties production and productivity per worker grew steadily: between 1919 and 1929, output per worker in manufacturing industries increased by about 43 per cent. Wages, salaries, and prices all remained comparatively stable, or in any case underwent no comparable increase. Accordingly, costs fell and with prices the same, profits increased. These profits sustained the spending of the well-to-do, and they also nourished at least some of the expectations behind the stock market boom. Most of all they encouraged a very high level of capital investment. During the twenties, the production of capital goods increased at an average annual rate of 6.4 per cent a year; non-durable consumers' goods, a category which includes such objects of mass consumption as food and clothing, increased at a rate of only 2.8 per cent. (The rate of increase for durable consumers' goods such as cars, dwellings, home furnishings, and the like, much of it representing expenditures of the well-off to well-to-do, was 5.9 per cent.) A large and increasing investment in capital goods was, in other words, a principal device by which the profits were being spent. It follows that anything that interrupted the investment outlays — anything, indeed, which kept them from showing the necessary rate of increase — could cause trouble. When this occurred, compensation through an increase in consumer spending could not automatically be expected. The effect, therefore, of insufficient investment — investment that failed to keep pace with the steady increase in profits — could be falling total demand reflected in turn in falling orders and output. Again there is no final proof of this point, for unfortunately we do not know how rapidly investment had to grow to keep abreast of the current increase in profits. However, the explanation is broadly consistent with the facts.

There are other possible explanations of the downturn. Back of the insufficient advance in investment may have been the high interest rates. Perhaps, although less probably, trouble was transmitted to the economy as a whole from some weak sector like agriculture. Further explanations could be offered. But one thing about this experience is clear. Until well along in the autumn of 1929 the downturn was limited. The recession in business activity was modest and underemployment relatively slight. Up to November it was possible to argue that not much of anything had happened. On other occasions, as noted — in 1924 and 1927 and of late in 1949 — the economy has undergone similar recession. But, unlike these other occasions, in 1929 the recession continued and continued and got violently worse. This is the unique feature of the 1929 experience. This is what we need really to understand.

There seems little question that in 1929, modifying a famous cliche, the economy was fundamentally unsound. This is a circumstance of first-rate importance. Many things were wrong, but five weaknesses seem to have had an especially intimate bearing on the ensuing disaster. They are:

1) The bad distribution of income. In 1929 the rich were indubitably rich. The figures are not entirely satisfactory, but it seems certain that the 5 per cent of the population with the

highest incomes in that year received approximately one third of all personal income. The proportion of personal income received in the form of interest, dividends, and rent — the income, broadly speaking, of the well-to-do — was about twice as great as in the years following the Second World War.

This highly unequal income distribution meant that the economy was dependent on a high level of investment or a high level of luxury consumer spending or both. The rich cannot buy great quantities of bread. If they are to dispose of what they receive it must be on luxuries or by way of investment in new plants and new projects. Both investment and luxury spending are subject, inevitably, to more erratic influences and to wider fluctuations than the bread and rent outlays of the $25-a-week workman. This high-bracket spending and investment was especially susceptible, one may assume, to the crushing news from the stock market in October of 1929.

2) The bad corporate structure. In November 1929, a few weeks after the crash, the Harvard Economic Society gave as a principal reason why a depression need not be feared its reasoned judgment that "business in most lines has been conducted with prudence and conservatism." The fact was that American enterprise in the twenties had opened its hospitable arms to an exceptional number of promoters, grafters, swindlers, impostors, and frauds. This, in the long history of such activities, was a kind of flood tide of corporate larceny.

The most important corporate weakness was inherent in the vast new structure of holding companies and investment trusts. The holding companies controlled large segments of the utility, railroad, and entertainment business. Here, as with the investment trusts, was the constant danger of devastation by reverse leverage. In particular, dividends from the operating companies paid the interest on the bonds of upstream holding companies. The interruption of the dividends meant default *on* the bonds, bankruptcy, and the collapse of the structure. Under these circumstances, the temptation to curtail investment in operating plant in order to continue dividends was obviously strong. This added to deflationary pressures. The latter, in turn, curtailed earnings and helped bring down the corporate pyramids. When this happened, even more retrenchment was inevitable. Income was earmarked for debt repayment. Borrowing for new investment became impossible. It would be hard to imagine a corporate system better designed to continue and accentuate a deflationary spiral.

3) The bad banking structure. Since the early thirties, a generation of Americans has been told, sometimes with amusement, sometimes with indignation, often with outrage, of the banking practices of the late twenties. In fact, many of these practices were made ludicrous only by the depression. Loans which would have been perfectly good were made perfectly foolish by the collapse of the borrower's prices or the markets for his goods or the value of the collateral he had posted. The most responsible bankers — those who saw that their debtors were victims of circumstances far beyond their control and sought to help — were often made to look the worst. The bankers yielded, as did others, to the blithe, optimistic, and immoral mood of times but probably not more so. A depression such as that of 1929–32, were it to begin as this is written, would also be damaging to many currently impeccable banking reputations.

However, although the bankers were not unusually foolish in 1929, the banking structure was inherently weak. The weakness was implicit in the large numbers of independent units. When one bank failed, the assets of others were frozen while depositors elsewhere had a pregnant warning to go and ask for their money. Thus one failure led to other failures, and these spread with a domino effect. Even in the best of times local misfortune or isolated mismanagement could start such a chain reaction. (In the first six months of

1929, 346 banks failed in various parts of the country with aggregate deposits of nearly $115 million.) When income, employment, and values fell as the result of a depression bank failures could quickly become epidemic. This happened after 1929. Again it would be hard to imagine a better arrangement for magnifying the effects of fear. The weak destroyed not only the other weak, but weakened the strong. People everywhere, rich and poor, were made aware of the disaster by the persuasive intelligence that their savings had been destroyed.

Needless to say, such a banking system, once in the convulsions of failure, had a uniquely repressive effect on the spending of its depositors and the investment of its clients.

4) The dubious state of the foreign balance. This is a familiar story. During the First World War, the United States became a creditor on international account. In the decade following, the surplus of exports over imports which once had paid the interest and principal on loans from Europe continued. The high tariffs, which restricted imports and helped to create this surplus of exports remained. However, history and traditional trading habits also accounted for the persistence of the favorable balance, so called.

Before, payments on interest and principal had in effect been deducted from the trade balance. Now that the United States was a creditor, they were added to this balance. The latter, it should be said, was not huge. In only one year (1928) did the excess of exports over imports come to as much as a billion dollars; in 1923 and 1926 it was only about $375,000,000. However, large or small, this difference had to be covered. Other countries which were buying more than they sold, and had debt payments to make in addition, had somehow to find the means for making up the deficit in their transactions with the United States.

During most of the twenties the difference was covered by cash — i.e., gold payments to the United States — and by new private loans by the United States to other countries. Most of the loans were to governments — national, state, or municipal bodies — and a large proportion were to Germany and Central and South America. The underwriters' margins in handling these loans were generous; the public took them up with enthusiasm; competition for the business was keen. If unfortunately corruption and bribery were required as competitive instruments, these were used.

In all respects these operations were as much a part of the New Era as Shenandoah and Blue Ridge. They were also just as fragile, and once the illusions of the New Era were dissipated they came as abruptly to an end. This, in turn, forced a fundamental revision in the foreign economic position of the United States. Countries could not cover their adverse trade balance with the United States with increased payments of gold, at least not for long. This meant that they had either to increase their exports to the United States or reduce their imports or default on their past loans. President Hoover and the Congress moved promptly to eliminate the first possibility — that the accounts would be balanced by larger imports — by sharply increasing the tariff. Accordingly, debts, including war debts, went into default and there was a precipitate fall in American exports. The reduction was not vast in relation to total output of the American economy, but it contributed to the general distress and was especially hard on farmers.

5) The poor state of economic intelligence.... It seems certain that the economists and those who offered economic counsel in the late twenties and early thirties were almost uniquely perverse. In the months and years following the stock market crash, the burden of reputable economic advice was invariably on the side of measures that would make things worse. In November of 1929, Mr. Hoover announced a cut in taxes; in the great no-business conferences that followed he asked business firms to keep up their capital investment and to maintain wages. Both of these measures were on the side of increasing spendable

income, though unfortunately they were largely without effect. The tax reductions were negligible except in the higher income brackets; businessmen who promised to maintain investment and wages, in accordance with a well-understood convention, considered the promise binding only for the period within which it was not financially disadvantageous to do so. As a result investment outlays and wages were not reduced until circumstances would in any case have brought their reduction.

Still, the effort was in the right direction. Thereafter policy was almost entirely on the side of making things worse. Asked how the government could best advance recovery, the sound and responsible adviser urged that the budget be balanced. Both parties agreed on this. For Republicans the balanced budget was, as ever, high doctrine. But the Democratic Party platform of 1932, with an explicitness which politicians rarely advise, also called for a "federal budget annually balanced on the basis of accurate executive estimates within revenues...."

A commitment to a balanced budget is always comprehensive. It then meant there could be no increase in government outlays to expand purchasing power and relieve distress. It meant there could be no further tax reduction. But taken literally it meant much more. From 1930 on the budget was far out of balance, and balance, therefore, meant an increase in taxes, a reduction in spending, or both. The Democratic platform in 1932 called for an "immediate and drastic reduction of governmental expenditures" to accomplish at least a 25 per cent decrease in the cost of government.

The balanced budget was not a subject of thought. Nor was it, as often asserted, precisely a matter of faith. Rather it was a formula. For centuries avoidance of borrowing had protected people from slovenly or reckless public housekeeping. Slovenly or reckless keepers of the public purse had often composed complicated arguments to show why balance of income and outlay was not a mark of virtue. Experience had shown that however convenient this belief might seem in the short run, discomfort or disaster followed in the long run. Those simple precepts of a simple world did not hold amid the growing complexities of the early thirties. Mass unemployment in particular had altered the rules. Events had played a very bad trick on people, but almost no one tried to think out the problem anew.

The balanced budget was not the only strait jacket on policy. There was also the bogey of "going off" the gold standard and, most surprisingly, of risking inflation. Until 1932 the United States added formidably to its gold reserves, and instead of inflation the country was experiencing the most violent deflation in the nation's history. Yet every sober adviser saw dangers here, including the danger of runaway price increases. Americans, though in years now well in the past, had shown a penchant for tinkering with the money supply and enjoying the brief but heady joys of a boom in prices. In 1931 or 1932, the danger or even the feasibility of such a boom was nil. The advisers and counselors were not, however, analyzing the danger or even the possibility. They were serving only as the custodians of bad memories.

The fear of inflation reinforced the demand for the balanced budget. It also limited efforts to make interest rates low, credit plentiful (or at least redundant) and borrowing as easy as possible under the circumstances. Devaluation of the dollar was, of course, flatly ruled out. This directly violated the gold standard rules. At best, in such depression times, monetary policy is a feeble reed on which to lean. The current economic clichés did not allow even the use of that frail weapon. And again, these attitudes were above party. Though himself singularly open-minded, Roosevelt was careful not to offend or disturb his followers. In a speech in Brooklyn toward the close of the 1932 campaign, he said: "The Democratic platform specifically declares, 'We advocate a sound currency to be preserved at all hazards.' That is plain English. In discussing this platform on July 30, I said, 'Sound money is an international necessity, not a domestic consideration for one nation alone.' Far up in the Northwest, at Butte, I repeated the pledge ... In Seattle I reaffirmed my attitude...."

The following February, Mr. Hoover set forth his view, as often before, in a famous letter to the President-elect: It would steady the country greatly if there could be prompt assurance that there will he no tampering or inflation of the currency; that the budget will be unquestionably balanced even if further taxation is necessary; that the Government credit will be maintained by refusal to exhaust it in the issue of securities.

The rejection of both fiscal (tax and expenditure) and monetary policy amounted precisely to a rejection of all affirmative government economic policy. The economic advisers of the day had both the unanimity and the authority to force the leaders of both parties to disavow all the available steps to check deflation and depression. In its own way this was a marked achievement — a triumph of dogma over thought. The consequences were profound.

It is in light of the above weaknesses of the economy that the role of the stock market crash in the great tragedy of the thirties must be seen. The years of self-depreciation by Wall Street to the contrary, the role is one of respectable importance. The collapse in securities values affected in the first instance the wealthy and the well-to-do. But we see that in the world of 1929 this was a vital group. The members disposed of a large proportion of the consumer income; they were the source of a lion's share of personal saving and investment. Anything that struck at the spending or investment by this group would of necessity have broad effects on expenditure and income in the economy at large. Precisely such a blow was struck by the stock market crash. In addition, the crash promptly removed from the economy the support that it had been deriving from the spending of stock market gains.

The stock market crash was also an exceptionally effective way of exploiting the weaknesses of the corporate structure. Operating companies at the end of the holding-company chain were forced by the crash to retrench. The subsequent collapse of these systems and also of the investment trusts effectively destroyed both the ability to borrow and the willingness to lend for investment. What have long looked like purely fiduciary effects were, in fact, quickly translated into declining orders and increasing unemployment.

The crash was also effective in bringing to an end the foreign lending by which the international accounts had been balanced. Now the accounts had, in the main, to be balanced by reduced exports. This put prompt and heavy pressure on export markets for wheat, cotton, and tobacco. Perhaps the foreign loans had only delayed an adjustment in the balance which had one day to come. The stock market crash served nonetheless to precipitate the adjustment with great suddenness at a most unpropitious time. The instinct of farmers who traced their troubles to the stock market was not totally misguided.

Finally, when the misfortune had struck, the attitudes of the time kept anything from being done about it. This, perhaps, was the most disconcerting feature of all. Some people were hungry in 1930 and 1931 and 1932. Others were tortured by the fear that they might go hungry. Yet others suffered the agony of the descent from the honor and respectability that goes with income into poverty. And still others feared that they would be next. Meanwhile everyone suffered from a sense of utter hopelessness. Nothing, it seemed, could be done. And given the ideas which controlled policy, nothing could be done.

Had the economy been fundamentally sound in 1929 the effect of the great stock market crash might have been small. Alternatively, the shock to confidence and the loss of spending by those who were caught in the market might soon have worn off. But business in 1929 was not sound; on the contrary it was exceedingly fragile. It was vulnerable to the kind of blow it received from Wall Street. Those who have emphasized this vulnerability are obviously on strong ground. Yet when a greenhouse succumbs to a hailstorm something more than a purely passive role is normally attributed to the storm. One must accord similar significance to the typhoon which blew out of lower Manhattan in October 1929.

7–2. W. ELLIOT BROWNLEE, *DYNAMICS OF ASCENT*: CHAPTER XII—THE 1920s: A GLIMPSE OF MODERNITY

To understand the economy during the 1920s, we should view it, not as a sick decade, full of foreshadowings of the depression to follow, but as a period that bears a strong resemblance to the best years of the post-World War II era in its rising standard of living, sustained high employment, stable prices, and strong market for articles of mass consumption. Despite our retrospective awareness that a major depression was to follow, the prosperity was unprecedented and was sustained from 1922 through much of 1929, with only modest pauses in 1924 and 1927.

Traditionally, economic historians have emphasized the structural weaknesses of the economy during the 1920s. That such weaknesses existed is indisputable, but historians of the 1920s have usually exaggerated their dimensions and their contribution to the collapse of the economy in 1929. The successes of the period were as important as the failures, and by examining those strong areas we see that the more recent episodes of ability and growth are based on the accomplishments of the 1920s just as well as on the New Deal and the mobilization for World War II. To a large extent the organizational and technological basis of post-Great Depression prosperity developed from the innovations of the 1920s.

The most significant feature of the prosperity of the 1920s for the average American was solid income growth. National income, per capita income, and wages per member of the labor force increased rapidly. Per capita income jumped from an annual average of $517 during the decade between 1909 and 1918 to $612 between 1919 and 1928. Real earnings also grew steadily for employees and at rates substantially greater than even those during the two preceding decades. Between 1900 and 1910 the real earnings of employees increased about 20 percent, and in the following decade, about 12 percent. But during the 1920s these earnings increased about 23 percent. The average employee was also improving his position more rapidly. Between 1900 and 1920 the average real income of employees increased by roughly 25 percent, but during the 1920s alone the increase was about 30 percent. That acceleration of the 1920s was even more dramatic in light of the fact that between 1870 and 1920, a period of very rapid industrialization, the rate of growth of real income per employee was only one-third that between 1920 and 1930.

No direct, reliable evidence exists that accurately describes changes in the distribution of income during the 1920s. However, we do know with a good deal of certainty that during the period of early-nineteenth-century industrialization the distribution of income worsened and that the trend had reversed by at least the 1930s. That reversal may have occurred as early as the 1880s or the decade 1900–1910, and the improvement may have continued during the 1920s. At the same time the position of unskilled workers improved, relative to those with skills; that is, the skilled and unskilled employees converged during the 1920s, suggesting not only that the distribution of income was moving in a more equitable direction during the 1920s, but also that the pace of such movement accelerated during the 1920s, since the wages of the skilled and unskilled had diverged previously.

Prosperity had its blemishes, however. Averages of per capita incomes do not reveal the actual imbalance in the pattern of growth; nor would measures of the distribution of income if they were available. Certain enterprises experienced severe structural problems in the 1920s and these problems constituted the source of regional depression—depression that would only become more severe during the 1930s. The New England textile industry, for example, suffered from the shift of firms to the lower-cost labor markets of the South. Railroads faced stiff competition in freight and passenger service from publicly subsidized highways (including a trunk system initiated by the Federal Aid Road Act of 1916), suffered from uncoordinated and inefficient management, and thus incurred declining passenger revenues, stagnant freight revenues, and subnormal rates of return. Extractive industries, particularly mining, having experienced overexpansion as a result of wartime demands, suffered from depletion and severe new competition. Coal mining was especially unhealthy, barely surviving the competitive inroads made by hydroelectric power, fuel oil, and natural gas: between 1923 and 1929, wages in coal mining fell some 14 percent. The lumber industry faced overexpansion and depleted resources, especially in the northern portion of the Great Lakes states. Finally, agriculture, containing the most severe defects, faced problems of war-induced overexpansion and, in the regions of severest hardship, extreme overpopulation. Significant regional problems resulted from these afflicted industries, and regional income levels diverged during the decade, reversing the trend of the late-nineteenth century. Per capita income in New England rose relative to that in the nation as a whole, despite the sluggishness of textiles, but the West North Central states (containing much of the Great Plains), the South, and the West were not as fortunate as a result of the hard times in lumbering, mining, and agriculture.

Certainly the distribution of income would have been more favorable and the upward movement of per capita income even more impressive with a better-balanced growth. But the really significant phenomenon for reaching an understanding of the 1920s is the high earnings per employee, despite per capita earnings declining in some significant industries and in several regions of the nation.

Accompanying the high levels of income was an unusual degree of price stability and an exceptional record of employment. Consumer prices were extraordinarily stable after the collapse of 1920–1921 and were scarcely any higher in 1929 than they had been in 1922. (The average annual rate of increase in prices was less than 1 percent between 1922 and 1929.) The nation enjoyed the unusually stable price level without incurring a high rate of unemployment; over the same period, strong demand for goods and services caused unemployment to drop to an annual average of only 3.7 percent. That was a significant improvement over the two preceding decades and was a record unmatched during the presumably more enlightened 1950s and 1960s.

The glitter of newness associated with the 1920s was real. Consumers purchased strikingly greater quantities of durable goods, mainly automobiles and electrical appliances, than they had previously and demanded higher levels of services. Although electrical appliances and automobiles had been available during the decade of World War I, large numbers of people demanded them only in the 1920s. Consequently, the production of radios increased over 25 times between 1923 and 1929; that of refrigerators, over 150 times between 1921 and 1929. And passenger car registrations grew from 9.3 million in 1921 to 23.1 million in 1929. Helping to make all this possible was the finance company, newly emergent and extending consumer credit on a large scale, primarily on automobiles but on furniture and appliances as well. By 1929 outstanding installment debts reached over $3 billion, with almost half that representing automobile paper.

The increases in consumer spending on durables were not only absolute gains but gains relative to spending on all consumer goods. These relative increases were possible in part because real and substantial growth in incomes permitted consumers to shift away from purchases of food and clothing, which still accounted for well over half of the flows of goods to consumers. Another aid to the shift in purchasing patterns was the low level of food prices of the 1920s, largely a product of the war and postwar overexpansion of production. In terms of electrifying the household and putting the family in an automobile the 1920s clearly marked a revolution. However, in structural terms this consumer revolution was actually quite modest. In the decade 1909–1918 durable goods accounted for 9.2 percent of consumption purchases; by the next decade their share had increased only slightly, to 10.6 percent. In other words, consumers increased their purchases of other goods and services during the 1920s almost as rapidly as they increased their spending on durables: they purchased not only more radios, automobiles, and kitchen appliances, but also more food, clothing, education, entertainment, and perhaps even gin. Thus, although consumers bought new kinds of durable goods, they did not drastically increase their purchases of durable goods relative to other goods and services. If there was a real revolution in the character of consumption patterns, it was in the early and middle portions of the nineteenth century rather than the 1920s....

As farmers entered the decade of the 1920s they had almost every reason to believe that they would continue to enjoy a prosperity much like that of the golden age of agriculture. Favorable conditions had persisted for almost two decades alter the late 1890s, stretching even into the war and through 1919. Conditioned to expect strong demands, rising farm prices, and buoyant farm incomes, farmers anticipated continued prosperity after the war by making an enormous investment in farm land, much of it marginal, partially in expectation of growing demand for farm production and partially in anticipation of a dramatic, inflation-fed appreciation of the value of farm land. In so doing, farmers were behaving much like manufacturers who built up inventories during the same period.

The dreams and fortunes of the optimistic farmers evaporated when farm prices dropped sharply in May and June of 1920, at the onset of the postwar depression. Farmers who had expanded production and land holdings during the preceding months now found themselves heavily in debt without the ability, in many cases, to cover their fixed expenses. As costly as the economic collapse was in the short run, its long-term impact on agriculture would have been minimal if farm prices had returned to their earlier level and buoyancy. But during the 1920s they remained well below the relative position they had occupied since the late 1890s. The decline reduced purchasing power of farmers in the 1920s to about three-quarters of the wartime level. Net farm income also fell to about 10 percent of the 1919 level and in the 1920s never returned to more than about three-quarters of that level. Consequently, agriculture's share of national income was also in drastic decline. In short, agriculture never fully recovered from the postwar depression before it suffered further blows in the 1930s.

The economic maladies of the farmers lay in the marketplace, in the patterns of supply and demand, just as their successes after 1900 had resulted from the play of market forces. The most damaging element was the slackening of demand for agricultural products, relative to demand for all goods and services. European demand, a strong force for growth during the war, fell off sharply after 1919, as Europeans raised effective tariffs against American produce in order to aid the recovery of their own agriculture. And within the United States the increase in incomes during the 1920s failed to produce a proportionate increase in the demand for agricultural products. Demand for agricultural goods increased rapidly during the 1920s, given the fact that population growth was rapid—more rapid even than during the previous decade—but the declining share of income spent on farm products helps to account for the worsening position of the nation's farmers....

The most difficult aspect of the farm problem of the 1920s was this set of social rigidities, not the price and income problems of commercial farmers. Indeed, the same was true of the depression years of the 1930s. But public policy in both decades took as its primary objective the resolution of the more manageable market problems of the commercial producers. The resistance of the social problem to corrective medicine partly explains the emphasis of public policy, but the more important factor influencing the choice of policy objectives was the decisive political weight of the commercial farmers.

Although certain farmers (such as the California fruit growers) experienced a decade of rising demands and incomes, most had to shoulder the burdens of the overexpansion that World War I had induced. The structural weakness of agriculture was not sufficient to alter the basically prosperous appearance of the economy during the 1920s, but it was responsible for the regional disparities of the decade and would make the impact of the Great Depression even more severe for the nation's farmers.

As has been indicated, by the 1920s the United States was the world's largest creditor, and the fact that it had become the world's largest, most productive economy meant the reinforcement of its creditor position. Advancing the nation even more as a creditor was the growth of American private investment abroad—a growth of more than two and one-half times between 1919 and 1930. Some of this investment served to facilitate international trade and, in this sense, was an extension of the wartime interest in supporting Allied purchases of supplies. As in wartime, the New York banking community played a crucial part in supplying short-term credit. To some extent federal legislation eased the way. The Federal Reserve Act as amended in 1916 allowed national banks to establish foreign branches and to own, in whole or in part, special foreign banking corporations. After the war, Congress passed the Edge Act (December 1919) to expedite the creation of foreign banking corporations involved in the financing of exports. Previously such investment corporations, under law, required state charters, although national banks could invest in them. The concept behind the act was that corporations created under its provisions would sell their own bonds in the United States and then lend the proceeds to foreign importers, taking long-term foreign obligations as collateral. Thus the Edge Act authorized federal incorporation of investment trusts that would act as instruments to support American export trade. Associations formed under the act included Morgan's American and Foreign Banking Corporation and Rockefeller's International Acceptance Bank, which worked out short-term arrangements with Credit Anstalt, the great Austrian bank. By 1931, American investment in such banking organizations totaled about $125 million....

Thus the international economic system, particularly with reference to Europe, depended on the flow of American capital to Germany, reparations payments from Germany to the former Allies, and the repayment of debts to the United States. The system, convoluted as it was, worked reasonably well after the Dawes plan, but it was inherently unstable. If the outflow of capital from the United States ceased, the international house of cards would collapse. This is, in fact, what happened toward the end of the decade. Short-term lending abroad declined in 1928, and long-term lending followed suit a year later. When the loans stopped, the creditors of Germany met again and this time adopted the plan of Owen D. Young, chairman of the General Electric Company. His plan once more sharply reduced the reparations payments. Meanwhile the former Allies were forced to default on their promised debt-repayment schedules, evoking the Hoover moratorium of 1931 which effectively canceled all debt and reparations payments once and for all. At the same time European demand for American exports fell off drastically, reinforcing the domestic depression. The end result was an unusually serious and prolonged hiatus in the international flow of funds and international trade.

The instability of the international economy of the 1920s was rooted in failures of American policy. Although the United States had undergone an enormous transformation in its international role since the nineteenth century, dominant political opinion still assumed that preserving the vitality of the export sector was the key to upholding prosperity at home and that pursuing a short-run policy of squeezing the most out of foreign investments would have no long-term costs. The fact is that if the United States had canceled the debts or had modified them while providing the means to repay the debt through trade, the European economy would have been stronger, Europeans would have had less urgent demands for American capital, American investments in Europe would have been sounder, and the international economy would have rested on a much firmer foundation than was the case in 1929, when it was overly dependent on the health of the United States. The economic and political devastation of World War I clinched the basic, inescapable fact of American superiority in the marketplaces of the world. But the short-sighted American policies of trade promotion, imposing fidelity to wartime contracts, and a firm adherence to the gold standard turned the fact of superiority into a severe problem for maintaining economic stability and growth throughout the world.

In conclusion, although the economy of the 1920s was in numerous significant ways remarkably prosperous and stable, and although the refinement of corporate strategies and structures during the 1920s would prove of inestimable value in the future to an economy seeking higher rates of growth and a larger measure of stability, there were serious exceptions to the generally sturdy pattern—distortions created largely by World War I. The war and public policy had forced an overexpansion of agriculture that resulted in low prices, low incomes, a heavy burden of debt, and an increase in the number of small farmers trapped on marginal, unproductive land. The war also warped the international role of the United States by too rapidly accelerating its transition from debtor to creditor nation. The pace of change was so swift that Americans failed to comprehend the implications of the transition and to recognize the nation's economic self-interest, enacting policies that placed the world economy in an exceedingly precarious position. Both of these structural weaknesses resulting from the war would prolong and intensify the course of the Great Depression.

7–3. EUGENE N. WHITE, "THE STOCK MARKET BOOM AND CRASH OF 1929 REVISITED"

In trying to explain the 1987 stock market crash, many analysts drew obvious but vague comparisons with the events of 1929. Newspapers published a chart showing the bull market of the 1920s superimposed on the 1980s. The degree of similarity between the two periods up to the crash was striking. Yet while analysts noted this close correspondence, they drew few inferences from it. Comparisons proved difficult because the crash of 1929 had received little scholarly attention since Galbraith's *The Great Crash 1929*.

This paper will sort through many of the hypotheses offered to explain the 1929 boom and bust. Most of the factors cited by historians played trivial or insignificant roles. The central issue is whether fundamentals or a bubble drove the bull market upwards. An econometric resolution of this question is unlikely. However, the qualitative evidence assembled in this paper favors the view that a bubble was present in the 1929 market.

Galbraith's classic book still provides the most commonly accepted explanation of the 1929 boom and crash. He argues that a bubble in the stock market was formed during the rapid economic growth of the 1920s. Galbraith emphasizes the irrational element—the mania—that induced the public to invest in the bull market. The rise in the stock market, according to Galbraith's account, depended on "the vested interest in euphoria [that] leads men and women, individuals and institutions to believe that all will be better, that they are meant to be richer and to dismiss as intellectually deficient what is in conflict with that conviction." This eagerness to buy stocks was then fueled by an expansion of credit in the form of brokers' loans that encouraged investors to become dangerously leveraged.

Galbraith and other writers are vague about the causes of the halt in the market, believing that almost any event could have triggered irrational investors to sell. Instead, they focus on the inevitability of the bubble's collapse and suggest several factors that could have exploded public confidence and caused prices to plummet. The vertical price drops on Black Thursday, October 24, and Black Tuesday, October 29, forced margin calls and distress sales of stocks, prompting a further plunge in prices. When the stock ticker ran late, investors panicked and sold their holdings. In the following weeks and months, the market bounced downwards erratically, propelled by and perhaps propelling the depression.

While Galbraith's book makes for compelling reading, there remain many unanswered questions. There is little discussion about how much fundamentals contributed to the bull market and what might have triggered the speculative mania. The argument about easy credit in the form of broker's loans seems strange at a time when the Federal Reserve was pursuing a tight money policy. Furthermore, little has been done to identify the precise role of external events in provoking the collapse. To address these questions, it is necessary to begin with a brief overview of the changes during the 1920s that set the stage for the stock market boom.

After World War I and a postwar recession, the stability and prosperity of the 1920s appeared extraordinary to contemporary observers. From 1922 to 1929, GNP grew at an annual rate of 4.7 percent and unemployment averaged 3.7 percent. Part of this growth may be attributed to the emergence of large-scale commercial and industrial enterprises that took advantage of new continuous process technologies. Coordination by the emerging system of modern management produced more efficient vertically-integrated enterprises that captured economies of scale and scope.

The financial needs of these new enterprises altered the face of American capital markets. Regulations imposed on commercial banks in the nineteenth century severely limited their ability to provide large long-term loans, and firms turned to financing their investments out of retained earnings and bond and stock issues. The market for industrial securities, which first emerged in the 1880s, came of age in the 1920s, as both old and new corporations issued equities to finance new plant and equipment.

Commercial banks did purchase more bonds, but they could not legally trade or acquire equities. To circumvent this restriction, they set up wholly-owned securities affiliates, which permitted them to enter all aspects of investment banking and the brokerage business. The number of affiliates grew rapidly from 10 in 1922 to 114 in 1931. These affiliates attracted many new customers and became big distributors of stocks and bonds, enabling them to become underwriters. By 1930, commercial banks' security affiliates had obtained roughly half the bond originations. By moving into investment banking through their affiliates, commercial banks were thus able to continue servicing the needs of their corporate customers.

While the securities affiliates catered to a broader clientele than most traditional brokerage houses, many small investors might still have shied away from buying securities, lacking sufficient capital to purchase a diversified portfolio of stocks. This obstacle was eliminated by the investment trusts, which served the same function as mutual funds do today. Investment trusts grew from about 40 in 1921 to over 750 in 1929.

Investment trusts were primarily institutions that sold securities to the public and used the proceeds to invest in stocks and bonds. There were two main types: management trusts where managers had discretion over the portfolio and fixed trusts where the portfolio could not be changed.

The growth of the securities market, assisted by the establishment of investment trusts and securities affiliates, allowed firms to substitute stocks and bonds for commercial bank loans. This development began well before the stock market boom, but the pace of change accelerated in the 1920s with the rapid growth of modern industrial enterprise. During this decade, banks found their traditional role as intermediaries sharply reduced. In response, they sought to increase their fee income by offering new financial services, including trusts and insurance. Most importantly, they increased their role as brokers between the saving public and industry. Banks were familiar with their borrowers and conditioned to monitor their activities. However, many of the new investors they served lacked experience in buying stock and monitoring firms, thus creating a favorable condition for a bubble.

Frederick Lewis Allen and Galbraith see the stock market bubble beginning in March 1928. In the months of April and May, [the stock] index increased 15 percent. In his influential account [*Only Yesterday*] of the stock market, Allen dates the boom as beginning on Monday, March 5. In the aggregate indices, there is nothing extraordinary about this date. Allen's reason for selecting this day is the five point rise in General Motors' stock, which by the end of the week had increased 7 percent. Other stocks shared this excellent week, most notably RCA, which rose almost 14 percent.

Allen attributes the initial sharp rise in March to the purchases by big bullish speculators, but this increase can be justified by economic developments. The economy had been in a recession until late 1927. When business picked up, the stock market responded. General Motors was attractive because Ford (still a private company) had shut down to retool for the Model A. With its more advanced management and organization, GM was able to take advantage of this opportunity, increasing production and sales and seizing the leading position in the industry. Its management exuded confidence. At the end of the month, GM's president predicted its price would rise from 180 to 225, and he promised to return to stockholders 60 percent of earnings.

The other stock that dominated the New York Exchange was RCA, the purveyor of a new technology. RCA's sales were growing by 50 percent each year. Its prospects, which looked excellent as the economy recovered, were reaffirmed by the release of the company's 1927 annual report in early March 1928. RCA stock was thus quite attractive, but not because it promised to pay high dividends like General Motors. The company had never paid a dividend, nor would it pay one for many years to come. The only reason to buy RCA in the short-run or even the medium-run was the belief that its business would continue to thrive and the price of its stock would increase in the hope of dividends in the distant future. Expectations of dividends from RCA had to be extremely diffuse.

Many other prominent companies that did not pay dividends caught the public's attention, too. These included Radio-Keith-Orpheum, the Aluminum Company of America, and the United Aircraft and Transport Corporation. Like RCA, these firms used new, developing technologies. The proportion of firms not paying dividends was also high among public utility holdings companies. These included the Commonwealth and Southern Corporation, Electric Bond and Share and the North American Company. The electric utility industry was undergoing a remarkable transformation in the 1920s where consolidation and expansion gave firms great economies of scale in production and transmission. This was another frontier industry with potentially high but uncertain returns.

The attraction of utilities' stocks is revealed...[in the stock]...indices for industrials, railroads, and public utilities. The boom in utilities far outstripped industrials, while the relatively stable, established railroads languished. Although previous writers have not concerned themselves with the prominence of public utilities and high-tech stocks, they were a central feature of the bull market.

Although most historians believe that the 1920s bull market was a bubble and concede only a small role for real factors, some contemporary observers attributed most of the market's rise to fundamentals. At the height of the market in August 1929, when many began to fear that there was excessive speculation, Charles Amos Dice of Ohio State University argued that the higher prices in the stock market were the product of economic fundamentals. Even after the crash in December 1929, Irving Fisher of Yale retained his conviction that the rise in stock prices was justified and wrote, "My own impression has been and still is that the market went up principally because of sound, justified expectations of earnings, and only partly because of unreasoning and unintelligent mania for buying."

Both Dice and Fisher believed that earnings and dividends would continue to grow rapidly because of great economic improvements they saw in the economy. These changes—the systematic application of science to industry, the development of modern management techniques, and mergers that gained economies of scale and scope—are the same ones that economic historians have emphasized to explain growth in the '20s. Thus, although Galbraith ridiculed Dice and Fisher in the aftermath of the crash, their views cannot be dismissed lightly.

The convictions of Fisher and Dice have more recently found support...[in work showing]...that the high stock prices and high price-earnings ratios were a consequence of the expected rapid growth of earnings. Assuming that a price-earnings ratio of 15 would have been normal,...earnings would have had to grow at 9 percent for another 10 years in order for the peak P/E ratio of 20.4 to have been warranted. Since 9 percent was the average growth rate for 1925–1929, [some have] concluded that there was no "speculative orgy."

The argument for a fundamental explanation of the stock market boom holds that the rise in stock prices would have been justified by continued economic growth if policy blunders by the Federal Reserve and the Congress had not plunged the economy into a depression. However, given the normal duration of business cycles, it seems unlikely that the boom could have been sustained that long. Furthermore, it is by no means evident that it was appropriate for the public simply to extrapolate from the growth rate of the past few years.

In analyzing the role of fundamentals, researchers have only had annual data, yet this hides some of the key developments of 1928—1929. Quarterly earnings are not available, but...[a]...quarterly index of dividends for the firms in the Dow-Jones Index from 1922 to 1930...[has been created]...[This] index and the Dow-Jones Industrial Index...[when compared reveal]...the remarkable change that overtook the stock market. From 1922 to 1927 dividends and prices moved together, but while dividends continued to grow rather smoothly in 1928 and 1929, stock prices soared far above them.

The behavior of prices and dividends seems to imply that managers did not share the public's enthusiasm. Investors might have bid up stock prices based on an extrapolation of a few years' earnings growth, but managers did not increase dividends as quickly. The failure of dividends to keep pace with stock prices does not, however, necessarily imply the existence of a bubble, as it is generally believed that managers are hesitant to increase dividends unless they perceive a permanent rise in earnings. Yet, the available evidence suggests that many managers did not believe that their earnings would rise sufficiently fast to justify the prices of their stock. Some executives were alarmed enough to warn the public. In 1928, A. P. Giannini, head of Bancitaly (the future Bank of America) stated that the high price of his bank's stock was unwarranted, prompting a sharp drop. [Other] companies...[have been identified]...where the management publicly stated that the stock was overvalued, notably Canadian Marconi and Brooklyn Edison.

A change in fundamentals may have initiated the boom, but fundamentals probably did not sustain it. The continued disappointment of unrealized dividends and public statements of some managers did not slow the rise in stock prices. This leaves the greater part of the boom to be explained. One favored candidate is easy credit.

Many economic historians believe that the expansion of brokers' loans helped to create the bubble... [Some argue]...that stock market credit was a key element in generating the mania. Galbraith sees the ability to purchase stock on margin as a great speculative lure. A buyer needed only to provide a fraction of the required funds, borrow the rest and enjoy the full capital gain less the interest on the borrowed funds. Even Irving Fisher believed that ability to borrow money encouraged "unwise speculation."

It is easy to understand the presumption that a credit expansion fueled the stock market boom...[An] index of the New York Stock Exchange's brokers' loans and an index of stock prices...are almost indistinguishable, especially for the period of the boom. While this coincidence may seem convincing, it is hard to understand how credit to buy stock could have been easy when credit in general was tight in the second half of the 1920s. The Federal Reserve pursued a contractionary policy beginning in January 1928, with open market sales and a rise in the discount rate from 3½ to 5 percent... [Money] was tight during the whole course of the boom. In 1928 and 1929, high-powered money and the consumer price index fell and M1 grew only slightly in 1929.

The Federal Reserve's tight money policy during these years was a consequence of its fears about the flow of credit to the stock market. The Federal Reserve had always been concerned about excessive credit for speculation. Its founders were influenced by the real bills doctrine and had hoped the new central bank's discounting activities would channel credit away from "speculative" and towards "productive" activities. Although there was general agreement on this issue, the stock market boom created a severe split over policy.

The Federal Reserve Board believed that "direct pressure" could be used to rechannel credit away from speculation. To curb stock market speculation, the Board wanted member banks making loans on securities to be denied access to the discount window. The Federal Reserve Bank of New York contended that the Federal Reserve could not refuse to discount otherwise eligible assets for its individual members and that it was impossible to control credit selectively. It argued that speculation could only be reduced by raising the discount rate. Between February 1929 and August 1929, the directors of the Federal Reserve Bank of New York frequently voted to raise the discount rate, only to be turned down by the Board, which reaffirmed its policy of direct pressure.

Looking at the rapid growth of brokers' loans in 1929, the Federal Reserve Board was understandably frustrated and angry, but it was not because its member banks failed to comply. Loans to brokers by New York member banks on their own account reached a peak at the end of December 1927, and then declined. Loans made by these banks on account for out-of-town banks also grew slowly during the boom. The rapid growth occurred in loans from private investors, corporations and foreign banks in Europe and Japan, which quickly substituted for bank loans.

Historians acknowledge this flexibility of credit, and...[some identify]...the rising supply of brokers' loans from non-bank sources as responsible for fueling the boom. This interpretation, however, ignores the rise in the interest rates on brokers' loans. After moving together with the...[discount rate and commercial paper rate]...for 1926 and 1927, the call and time rates increased sharply. Although the differentials were not constant for the whole boom, they remained very large, suggesting that it was the rising tide of speculation that demanded funds, not any independent creation of credit.

The interest rate differentials also suggest that lenders no longer regarded brokers' loans as very safe and insisted on a substantial premium... [Margin] requirements began to rise sharply in October 1928, soon reaching historic levels. While borrowers may have been quite sanguine about the rise in the market, lenders did not completely share their optimism.

Brokers' loans did not contribute to the stock market boom. Instead, the demand for credit to buy stock pulled funds into the market, forcing a major reallocation of credit in the money and capital markets. As the call rate rose, there was a sharp decline in commercial paper. In September 1927, $600 million in commercial paper was outstanding. By September 1929, it had declined to $265 million.... [Commercial] banks provided more loans and discounts to firms that had previously relied on the commercial paper market. These firms' former lenders moved into the call market from which banks had been discouraged by the Federal Reserve. The growth in the new issues of domestic stock increased dramatically, while issues of domestic bonds and notes declined from $3183 million in 1927 to $2078 million in 1929 and foreign securities fell even more from $1338 million to $673 million. This evidence reaffirms the independent character of the stock market bubble, whose demand for funds and new issues forced major changes in other financial markets.

If loans to buy stock were not cheap and the role of earnings and dividends was restricted, the surge in stock prices requires an alternative explanation. The surviving candidate is that a bubble appeared in the stock market. Although a large literature has explored the existence of bubbles in financial markets, the econometric identification of bubbles is elusive. A large literature has explored existence of bubbles in financial markets. The models consider the possibility that the price of a stock may not reflect simply its market fundamentals—that is, the expected present value of all future dividends—but may also include some bubble element.... [The] problem with bubble tests is that they specify a set of market fundamentals and then ascribe any leftover price movements to a bubble. Thus, one may perceive a bubble only because the model was not correctly specified.

In addition to this problem, these empirical tests have relied on annual data for stock prices and dividends. Annual data may be sufficient to detect long-term bubbles, but they will not pick up the 1928–1929 boom and bust. Furthermore, the data employed is all aggregate.... [Not] all stocks were caught up in a wave of speculation. Railroad stocks were excluded from the boom, while utilities were the favorites of speculators. Fisher's equally weighted stock price index reached its peak in February 1929, indicating that the majority of stocks on the New York Exchange did not fully participate in the boom. Thus, aggregate annual data may not capture a possible bubble in 1928–1929, even if the model is correctly specified.

Although dividend data for this period is almost exclusively annual, price data is more abundant. Using the daily and monthly Dow Jones Industrials index ... runs tests and Box-Pierce tests on the estimated autocorrelations for the period of the boom...[have been performed], ...showing...that prices followed a random walk and that there was no evidence for the market feeding on itself; however ... the power of these tests can be very low.

While it may be currently impossible to determine econometrically whether a bubble was present in the 1928–1929 stock market, considerable qualitative evidence suggests that the necessary conditions were present. [Bubbles] are likely to appear when fundamentals become difficult to assess. Although...bubbles are unlikely in blue chip stocks, the stock market of the 1920s had characteristics favorable to the emergence of bubbles. Fundamentals became difficult to judge because of major changes in industry. In automobiles, there was an abrupt shift from the dominance of the proprietary Ford Motor Co. to the more modern General Motors. While investors had every reason to expect earnings to grow, they lacked the means to evaluate easily the future path of dividends. RCA was also a highly successful firm in a new industry whose technology was rapidly changing. Not only were RCA's prospects uncertain but the absence of any dividend record left investors with little to judge fundamentals. Other high-tech firms and utilities, with no history of dividends and possibly brilliant futures, became favorites in the boom even though their fundamentals were difficult to assess.

The overall sophistication of investors was weakened by the influx of new people into the market. Since the turn of the century, the demands of industrial finance and regulation had reduced the role of commercial banks and increased the need to sell stock to the general public. Even before the boom began, many people who had never bought stock before entered the market. One identifiable group of new investors was women, whom brokers catered to with special programs and even their own rooms to watch the ticker tape. Women's magazines carried articles on how to buy stocks, including John Raskob's famous interview entitled "Everybody Ought to be Rich." While these changes are not easy to quantify, they do provide qualitative evidence on the existence of conditions that enhanced the likelihood of a bubble appearing in the stock market.

The speculative urge that had propelled the market upwards began to falter in the autumn of 1929. The decline and then sudden plunge of the market has been well-chronicled, but the number and variety of explanations for the crash have left its causes unclear.

The students of 1929 have had a tendency to minimize the importance of any single factor precipitating the crash. They treat the demise of the bull market as an endogenous collapse of expectations. Galbraith and...[others]...argue that the stock market was inherently unstable and anything could have shattered the public's confidence. Yet something did convince investors that their expectations of future price increases were no longer justified. Contemporary pundits offered many explanations, including the excessive issues of new stock, decisions by government regulators, the Smoot-Hawley tariff, foreign stock markets, and declining brokers' loans...[Each was] minor or irrelevant...in the crash. Instead, the downturn in the business cycle, made more severe by tight credit, prompted a revision in expectations.

The rising stock market made it attractive for companies to issue new stock. In 1927, $1474 million of new preferred and common shares were issued. By 1929, this reached $5924 million, with over $1 billion of shares issued in September. As in other bubbles, where speculation began with a nearly fixed supply of an asset, rapid price rises called forth significant additions to the supply...[Some suggest]...that the issue of new securities overwhelmed the market. But while these increases were large, they were modest in comparison to the total supply. The value of the stocks listed on the New York exchange alone was $89.7 billion on September 1. In response to this increment in supply, prices might have sagged but not collapsed. New stock issues were, at most, a small contributing factor to the crash.

Utilities were among the high-flying stocks of 1929. Some pundits claimed that Massachusetts' refusal on October 11 to allow Boston Edison to split its stock sent a threatening signal to the market. Regulators denied the request on the grounds that it would encourage further speculation, and they began a rate inquiry. If the crash began in the utilities because of this announcement, there was no sign of anticipation or reaction in the Dow Jones indices. The index for utilities and the index for industrials dropped by the same proportion, under 1 percent on that day. While the regulatory decision was upsetting to the Boston Edison stockholders, it must be considered an irrelevant factor in the crash.

In most explanations of the Great Depression, the passage of the Smoot-Hawley tariff is regarded as a key factor in disrupting the international economy...[Some]...believed that anticipation of the tariff contributed to the crash, while...[others give]...the tariff sole responsibility for the market's collapse. If the tariff was a key factor, it should have especially hurt the export industries through decreased foreign demand by the operation of the foreign trade multipliers and foreign tariff retaliation. Nontradeables and import-competing industries would not have sustained the same injury and might have benefited. After identifying industries as exporters, import-competing or nontradeables,...[it was found] that the stocks of all groups declined approximately the same percentage at the time when the tariffs passage was assured. There is thus no evidence in support of the view that the Smoot-Hawley tariff significantly contributed to the crash.

The failure in Great Britain of the business and financial empire of Clarence Hatry on September 20, 1929, has been cited by Galbraith...[and others]...as an important shock to first the London and then the New York market...London prices [fell] sharply and in advance of New York's. However, this drop does not square with the broad monthly index published by The Bankers' Magazine. By October 18, after Hatry and before the Wall Street plunge, the index had fallen 2.8 percent ... hardly alarming, given larger earlier declines. Furthermore, American Railway stocks accounted for almost half of the 2.8 percent fall. The London market simply reacted to the New York market.

In comparison to the worldwide bull markets of the 1980s, foreign stock markets in the 1920s often moved independently of New York... There was no boom in the Berlin market, which began falling in early 1928. The German decline stemmed partly from the reduction in post-World War I American lending, as investors turned their sights on New York, and partly from the tight monetary policies of the Reichsbank. The weak stock prices in European markets before October 1929 were more a consequence of the stock market boom than a cause of its demise. The Federal Reserve's tight monetary policy forced Great Britain and Germany to raise their discount rates to counter short-term capital's attraction to New York's high interest rates.... For months, the New York Fed had wanted a higher discount rate to tame the stock market. Finally the Board allowed it to raise its discount rate from 5 percent to 6 percent on August 9.... [Falling] prices made real rates much higher in 1929. Responding to a deterioration in their balance of payments, the British increased their bank rate again in September.

This general rise in interest rates did not have any immediately observable effects on brokers' loans. Weekly reports of brokers' loans show that they peaked on October 9 at $3941 million and then fell to $3823 million on October 23. This decline was not a signal of some catastrophe, as there had been larger temporary drops before. As in the months during the boom, brokers' loans responded rather than drove the stock market's decline.

The inadequacy of these explanations leads back to the question whether any abrupt change in dividends or earnings might have set off the crash. The aggregate figures give no hint of new developments. The quarterly dividends of the Dow-Jones industrials show healthy increases in late 1929, rising 12.8 percent in the third quarter and 11.6 percent in the fourth. The first drop of 6.3 percent appears only in the initial quarter of 1930.

However, there was evidence of an oncoming recession. In the absence of any quarterly earnings, the Federal Reserve's index of industrial production may be used as a proxy. This first dropped in July 1929. In August and September, some of the Federal Reserve's other indices began to fall. This mixed news and rising real interest rates, at home and abroad, spelled an incipient recession; and it was all that was necessary to cause stockholders to revise their expectations.

The market drifted downwards in early October. As the volume of trading rose, brokerage firms were swamped, margin calls became more frequent and the ticker began to run behind. When prompt reporting of prices became impossible, investors lost track of their position. Panic selling began on Black Thursday and Black Tuesday. The vertical price drops forced margin calls on impaired accounts and led many others to liquidate their holdings. Although the frenzied selling occasionally abated, the market could not be talked up by bankers or by big investors' purchases of stock.

A more widespread financial crisis threatened as out-of-town banks and other lenders withdrew their loans to brokers. New York city banks stepped into the breach and quickly increased their loans. They were encouraged by the Federal Reserve Bank of New York, which made open market purchases and let its members know that they could borrow freely at the discount window. The direct financial effects of the crash were thus confined to the stock market. The New York Fed's prompt action ensured that there were no panic increases in money market rates and no threat to the banks from defaults on security loans.

This intelligent policy was the doing of the New York Fed; ... the Board disapproved and censured New York. In spite of the recession, the Board maintained its tight money policy. The continued decline in the stock market after October 1929...reflects the economy's policy-aggravated slide into depression. This contrasts the market's recovery in 1988 when no recession was in the making and the Board recognized the importance of monetary ease.

The technological and structural changes in industry in the 1920s promised higher earnings and dividends. While these developments created a stock market boom, they also made fundamentals more difficult to evaluate, thus setting the stage for a bubble. The October panic can be traced to early signs of a recession that made the dissonance between dividends and stock prices clear. When panic selling began, intervention by the Federal Reserve Bank of New York prevented a collapse of the financial system. This response was appropriate, but the same cannot be said for earlier attempts to halt the market. Instead of allowing the stock market bubble to expand and burst of its own accord, the Federal Reserve's policies helped to push the economy further into a recession. Fear of a new speculative fever led the Federal Reserve Board to oppose easier monetary policy after the crash; hence, the tentative revival of the economy in 1930 was not assisted.

Although economists are generally skeptical about policy makers' ability to learn from history, the Federal Reserve did not make the same mistakes in 1987. In the months prior to the crash, the Fed was not preoccupied with speculation. When the collapse came, it followed the example of the New York Fed in 1929 and prevented a spillover to the banking system. Afterwards, it refocused its attention on general economic conditions. Spectacular as the crash of 1987 was, there was no reason for it to precipitate a second Great Depression.

ADDITIONAL READINGS

Allen, Frederick Lewis, Chapter XII: "The Big Bull Market," and Chapter XIII: "Crash!," in *Only Yesterday* (1997).

Barber, Clarence, "On the Origins of the Great Depression," *Southern Economic Journal* 44(1978) 432–56.

Barber, William J., *From New Era to New Deal: Herbert Hoover, the Economists, and American Economic Policy, 1921–1933*(1985).

Cannadine, David, *Mellon: An American Life* (2006).

Chandler, Lester V., *Benjamin Strong, Central Banker* (1958).

Galbraith, John Kenneth, *The Great Crash 1929* (1988).

Hamilton, David E., "From New Era to New Deal: American Farm Policy Between the Wars," in Lawrence Gelfand and Robert Neymeyer, eds., *Agricultural Distress and the Midwest: Past and Present* (1986).

Holt, Charles, "Who Benefitted from the Prosperity of the Twenties?" *Explorations in Economic History* 14 (1977) 277–89.

Kindleberger, Charles P., "The International Causes and Consequences of the Great Crash," *Journal of Portfolio Management*, 6 (Fall 1979) 11–14.

Lebergott, Stanley, *The American Economy: Income, Wealth and Want* (1962), pp. 248–99.

Johnson, H. Thomas, "Postwar Optimism and the Rural Financial Crisis of the 1920s," *Explorations in Economic History* 11 (Winter 1973/1974) 173–92.

Romer, Christina D., "The Great Crash and the Onset of the Great Depression," *Quarterly Journal of Economics* 105 (August 1990) 597–624.

Samuelson, Paul A., "Myths and Realities about the Crash and Depression," *Journal of Portfolio Management*, 6 (Fall 1979) 7–10.

Smiley, Gene, "Did Incomes for Most of the Population Fall from 1923 through 1929?" *Journal of Economic History* 42 (March 1983) 209–16.

Sobel, Robert, *The Great Bull Market: Wall Street in the 1920s* (1968).

Wicker, Elmus R., *Federal Reserve and Monetary Policy 1917–1933* (1966).

Williamson, Jeffrey and Peter Lindert, *American Inequality: A Microeconomic History* (1981), Chapter 12.

CHAPTER 8

The Onset of the Great Depression

INTRODUCTION

The full course of the Great Depression in the United States ran from 1929 to 1941. This period can be divided into three subperiods. The first subperiod, 1929–1933, was the worst, and is called the Great Contraction. The second phase was the painfully slow and partial recovery of the New Deal years, 1933–1936. The third and final phase stretched from the severe recession of 1937–1938 to America's entry into World War II in December 1941.

The Great Contraction dates from July 1929, when the cyclical peak of economic activity was reached, to March 1933, when the banking system collapsed. The economic profile of those four years and eight months is remarkable. It is easily the most precipitous decline in American economic history; no other period remotely approaches the dimensions of the collapse that occurred during the Great Contraction. From 1929 to 1933, real GNP fell by 31 percent; industrial production declined by over 60 percent; the money stock (checking account balances plus currency in circulation) contracted by 30 percent; prices fell by 22 percent; the stock market lost 83 percent of its value measured from the 1929 peak; 5,100 banks, 20 percent of the total, failed; 9,000 banks suspended operations; Treasury bills were yielding less than 0.5 percent; 11 percent of all businesses disappeared through bankruptcy; unemployment peaked at 25 percent in 1933, remaining above double digits until it slipped to 9.9 percent in 1941; in 1940 there were 47 million jobs in the American economy, the same number as in 1929.

By the end of 1929 the American economy was unmistakably in a deep slump. The high interest rates brought on by the Fed's restrictive policies had the predictable effect. Several important interest rate sensitive sectors were hit hard. Construction in general and housing in particular had already been weakening (building permits had peaked in 1928); automobile sales, which had been above 600,000 for the month of March 1929, had fallen below 100,000 for December. Purchases of consumer durables were down substantially in almost all categories by year's end.

The main impact of the market crash of 1929 came in the form of a curtailment of spending on expensive consumer durables. Households viewed their future income streams as less certain in the aftermath of the crash, and cut back on the purchase of houses, automobiles and major appliances. Consistent with this behavior, while department store sales and automobile registrations fell sharply, grocery store and five and dime store sales rose. By April of 1930 the stock market showed some tentative signs of revival (share prices were 20 percent above the post-crash nadir reached in the second week of November 1929), as monetary policy eased slightly as a result of the actions of the Federal Reserve

Bank of New York. This slight and very incomplete recovery of share prices was short-lived. The Federal Reserve Board in Washington, fearing stock speculation might reignite, rebuked the New York District Bank's actions by resuming a system-wide tightening.

The pause in consumer spending was eventually followed by a wave of bank failures in the fall of 1930. Given the precarious state of the economy and the Fed's alternation between perverse policy and inaction, these panics assured that the decline would continue. Between the fall of 1930 and the spring of 1933, the American economy was beset by four distinct waves of bank failures. The first wave in late 1930 emanated out of the agricultural sections of the country, and made painfully clear how the weaknesses in agriculture and banking could combine to pull the economy down. American banking laws had been written to give small and medium size banks a chance to compete successfully with the big city banks. Many of the banks chartered in the 1920s were small town banks that were often undiversified. Rural banks tended to have loan portfolios with a heavy concentration in agricultural loans. When hard times came to farming in the 1920s, many small rural banks shared in the misery. The 1920s had witnessed 5,700 bank failures. The early 1930s were about to see nearly as many failures, but in a much more compressed time frame.

As word spread that a bank with nonperforming loans was unable to meet its depositors' requests for withdrawals, the bank would experience a run. A small bank would be in the unenviable position of having very limited reserves with which to fight a run. Thus, in the days before deposit insurance, many banks failed, taking with them the savings of their depositors and the investment of their stockholders. Often a contagion would be created wherein depositors' suspicions, even though ill-founded, could bring down a well-managed bank. When a depositor closes out a checking account and asks for his balance in currency, these funds can no longer be relent in the banking system. The resulting retrenchment in lending will lead to a contraction in the money stock. In an atmosphere of bank runs and failures, the behavior of banks can also be adversely affected. Hoping to avoid provoking a run on their institution, bank managers may be more selective in granting loans; they may also maintain greater reserves to forestall a serious run. Both the exercise of greater selectivity in lending and the maintenance of a war chest to fight off a run lead to larger excess reserves in the banking system. This will also inhibit the money creation process. What began with the first wave of bank failures in the fall of 1930 would gain momentum with the waves of failures that followed. This ultimately led to a 30 percent contraction of the money supply.

By the end of 1930 industrial production had fallen by 37 percent from its cyclical peak in July 1929. As 1931 unfolded, there was little reason to hope for a turnaround. By this time the depth of the contraction had brought on a collapse in investment spending. Operating at far below capacity, businesses saw no reason to acquire additional plant and equipment. In 1931 some international feedback effects began to operate on the American economy. After World War I the major trading nations of the world, including the United States, were intent on returning to the gold standard. Under this system, nations with trade deficits would settle their accounts by shipping gold to the countries enjoying a trade surplus. Central banks would often raise their domestic interest rates to attract foreign capital and thereby avoid gold outflows. The Fed's actions in 1929 may be partly attributable to this kind of defense of the currency. The situation became greatly exacerbated in September 1931 when Great Britain abandoned the gold standard. Since any country on the gold standard was obligated to convert its currency into gold on the demand of the bearer, the expectation was that foreign holders of dollars would quickly demand gold before the United States, following Britain's lead, also went off the gold standard. The Fed then pursued a policy of high interest rates to counter the potential for a run on the dollar. While this may have provided a temporary respite for the dollar, higher interest rates added to the contractionary forces already at work in the American economy.

In the immediate aftermath of the stock market crash, the Hoover administration, as alarmed and dismayed by the speculative boom as was the Fed, offered repeated assurances to the public that the American economy was "fundamentally sound." President Hoover urged businesses not to cut wages in order to maintain purchasing power. Early on very little was done to counter the gathering storm. Eventually a small and ineffectual reduction in the federal income tax was passed. The Republican Congress proposed higher tariffs to protect American products from foreign competition. The Republican platform in the 1928 presidential campaign had called for higher tariffs on agricultural imports to protect American farmers, regarded then as a dependable constituency of the Republican Party. Departing from the usual practice of ignoring the party platform before its ink is dry, an earnest Herbert Hoover proposed to make good on his party's promise to American farmers. Hearings began in October 1929, and what was eventually passed by Congress and signed by President Hoover was far more extensive than what was called for in the Republican platform. As the tariff bill made its way through Congress, many industries clamored for and won tariff protection. When the infamous Smoot-Hawley tariff bill became law in June 1930, it was the most restrictive ever to be passed. Its passage did provoke retaliation from other countries. While some observers attribute great importance to the Smoot–Hawley tariff as a causative factor in the Great Depression, the American export sector was quite small in 1929. International trade did collapse in the 1930s, but more likely due the collapse in aggregate demand rather than the result of the tariff bill. Perhaps the damage it did came later in inhibiting the recovery of international trade.

At the start of the Great Contraction, President Hoover relied on urging business to refrain from wage cuts and layoffs. He also felt that voluntarism and charitable giving, rather than government programs, should be used to assist the unemployed and indigent. The tax cut enacted was of little help; federal taxes were already so low for most taxpayers that the cut provided a very small stimulus. Two of Hoover's initiatives in 1932 deserve mention. In January 1932 Hoover, against his natural instincts, was convinced by Eugene Meyer, Governor of the Federal Reserve Board, to sign legislation creating the Reconstruction Finance Corporation (RFC). The RFC was given broad authority to extend emergency funding to banks, other financial institutions, and eventually railroads. Currency hoarding and bank failures eased in the months after the establishment of the RFC. By the middle of 1932 more than $1 billion had been lent to over 5,000 financial institutions. The Democratic leadership in Congress felt that the Hoover administration was showing favoritism in the operation of the RFC by lending heavily to the banks of its Republican supporters. They were able to pass legislation that required the RFC to make monthly reports to the president and the Congress disclosing all RFC loans including the names of borrowers and amounts lent. It is believed that this seriously undermined the effectiveness of the RFC, since potential borrowers, fearing the consequences of public disclosure, would be reluctant to borrow. The RFC was a move in the right direction; it did ease stress in the banking system. But it was not undertaken on a scale necessary to reverse the economic decline.

Another plank in the Republican platform of 1928 committed the party to avoid deficit spending and balance the federal budget. By the spring of 1932, with the economic decline generating budget deficits, Hoover believed that it was time to act on this promise. He believed that closing the deficit would lead to less Treasury borrowing and lower interest rates, which would in turn boost bond prices. Increased bond prices would improve the financial position of banks, heavy investors in bonds, especially railroad bonds. Moreover, he felt that closing the deficit would demonstrate the fiscal responsibility of government and promote the restoration of confidence in the business community. In June of 1932 President Hoover signed into law the biggest peacetime tax increase in the history of the United States. No act better demonstrates the state of economic ignorance under which policymakers operated in the early 30s. The federal budget naturally fell into deficit with the onset of the downturn; as economic activity receded, the tax base and tax revenues fell. The Revenue Act of 1932 stands as a woefully misguided policy action.

Passage of the Revenue Act occurred at a seminal moment. In late spring the beneficial effects of the activities of the RFC were beginning to be felt; the Federal Reserve seemed committed to monetary expansion under Congressional threat to rewrite the Federal Reserve Act to compel expansion. But as summer passed and Congress went into recess, the Fed reversed course when increased gold outflows appeared on the horizon. The RFC began the public disclosure of the names of its borrowers. The contractionary effect of the Revenue Act, combined with a new wave of bank failures in the fall of 1932, assured that the economy would resume its downward trajectory. Uncompromising adherence to long-held dogmas made any kind of expansionary policy, monetary or fiscal, impossible; the gold standard hobbled monetary policy, while devotion to balanced budgets kept fiscal policy in check.

The presidential election campaign also added an element of uncertainty in the fall of 1932. Both candidates publicly avowed their belief in fiscal responsibility. At least in the case of Franklin Roosevelt, it was not clear to voters what policy course they would get should he be elected. With Roosevelt's victory at the polls, the long interregnum began, lasting from election day, November 1932, until inauguration day in early March 1933. During this period, there was little communication between the Hoover and Roosevelt camps. Drift and stasis took hold, as Roosevelt remained close-mouthed about his intentions.

As 1933 commenced, currency hoarding and monetary contraction reappeared with unprecedented force. Many states, experiencing serious runs on their banks, declared bank holidays with their businesses and citizens reduced to the use of scrip to conduct transactions. Hoover remained unalterably opposed to deposit insurance and refused to declare a national bank holiday. As several large northern industrial states proclaimed bank holidays, the banking system ground to a halt. Upon assuming office, Roosevelt immediately suspended gold payments and instituted a national bank holiday. All banks were closed; only viable banks were allowed to reopen. By June, legislation instituting deposit insurance under the aegis of the Federal Deposit Insurance Corporation (FDIC) was enacted. The banking system eventually stabilized, and throughout the remainder of the 1930s, only a handful of bank failures occurred. The economy finally bottomed out in 1933 with the unemployment rate reaching 25 percent. The New Deal years were at hand; the long, slow period of recovery was underway.

The Great Contraction raises many issues and questions. What caused the Fed to view the stock market speculation with such disapproval? What accounts for the caution, timidity and inaction shown by the Fed? Was it incompetence and ineptitude? Was it their devotion to the gold standard? Or was it simply that their operating procedures were cumbersome and flawed? What were the linkages between the stock market and the real economy? How are the effects of a crash transmitted to the economy? Must a stock market crash necessarily lead to an economic downturn? Was the Great Depression caused primarily by the monetary contraction, or was it the result of a collapse in spending? Did the Smoot-Hawley tariff play a major or secondary role in the onset of the Great Depression? Is the Great Depression rooted in domestic causes? Or did it emanate from abroad, as Herbert Hoover believed? What international feedback effects worked to make the Great Depression a global phenomenon? How central was the role of bank failures? Could there have been a Great Depression without the waves of bank failures? Would the United States have been better served if it had had a handful of large diversified banks (like most of the industrial world at the time) rather than a system with thousands of banks? Would the RFC have succeeded if it had been tried on a grander scale? Why were policymakers so slavishly devoted to ideas like the gold standard and the balanced budget while unemployment soared and the economy became mired in a deep depression? The documents and essays that follow provide a point of departure for addressing these questions.

DOCUMENTS

The readings in this chapter begin with four contemporary documents. The first two are from prominent economists of the day who offer their explanations for the Great Depression. The next two are major campaign speeches from the election of 1932 in which presidential candidates Herbert Hoover and Franklin Delano Roosevelt debate the economic issues. Document 8–1 is "The World-Wide Depression of 1930," written by Carl Snyder of the Federal Reserve Bank of New York; it appeared in the *American Economic Review* in March of 1931. Snyder compares the business depression of 1930 with past depressions, noting its severity and its unprecedented world-wide sweep. With all economies in depression, he fears that no nation will be in a position to buy commodities at distress prices and spur recovery. With adherence to the gold standard, the high interest rates in the United States were transmitted to other countries, and weakened their economies. This brought on a collapse in commodity prices not seen in previous depressions, affecting the purchasing power of many countries. What he finds most troubling is that these price declines did not appear to be the result of overproduction, which was widely held as the cause of the commodity price deflation. Document 8–2 is excerpts from "The Debt-Deflation Theory of Great Depressions," written in 1933 by Irving Fisher of Yale University, who at the time of its publication was America's most noted and respected economist. According to Fisher, the inventions and technological improvements of the 1920s created new opportunities to invest. Convinced that profits would be substantial, investors were quite willing to borrow to finance their investments. This led to a state of general over-indebtedness. Once this over-extension was recognized, investors would act in unison to liquidate their holdings to pay off their debts. The resultant security and commodity price deflation would bring on bankruptcies, a reduction in economic activity, higher unemployment and a rise in the real rate of interest. Fisher believes the depression could have been avoided if the Fed had pursued a consistent policy of reflation.

Document 8–3 is excerpts from Herbert Hoover's campaign speech, "The Consequences of the Proposed New Deal," delivered on October 21, 1932 in New York's Madison Square Garden. In his speech he claims that the roots of the depression are to be found abroad. He warns America of the social philosophy that informs the New Deal, and claims that it is at odds with America's traditions. Hoover stated that excessive government intrusion would harm economic incentives; voluntary cooperation was lauded along with the actions his administration had taken. After enumerating the Democratic proposals that would destroy the American system, he cited the number of homes electrified, telephones installed, radios owned, and automobiles purchased over the last generation. He made clear his opposition to any public works projects to employ the jobless. To those who saw Hoover as the very model of inaction from 1929 to 1932, this speech provided the underlying rationale for his approach. Document 8–4 is excerpted from Franklin Roosevelt's address to the Commonwealth Club of San Francisco, delivered on September 23, 1932. Rex Tugwell, a member of FDR's Brain Trust, has written that this speech was handed to Roosevelt just minutes before it was to be delivered, affording him no time to suggest revisions. If it appears more like the lecture of a professor of economic history than the speech of a candidate for office, the reason may be that its principal author was another Braintruster, Adolf Berle, an economist and professor of law at Columbia University. Tugwell felt that the tone of the speech did not capture the optimism that Roosevelt still held for the future. In the speech, a very didactic Roosevelt attempts to explain how the American economy had evolved; in its early stages, individualism ruled, as long as the Western frontier was open and land was free. Then, with the arrival of the industrial revolution, the rules of the game changed. While industrialization brought with it an enormous increase in productive capacity, it also gave great power to the financiers and the large corporate enterprises, threatening the economic freedom of the individual. Roosevelt goes so far as to say that "equality of opportunity…no longer exists." He noted how the economic life of the nation had come to be increasingly concentrated in the hands of a small number of large corporations, and that the individual must be protected from this power. While excoriating the Hoover administration for its budget deficits and fiscal irresponsibility, Roosevelt remained vague throughout the campaign on the specifics of what he would do if elected. His Commonwealth Club speech is seen as the most important of his campaign. Without detailing any policy agenda, it does make clear his willingness to expand the role of government in the economic life of the nation. These two campaigns speeches offered two very different visions to the country. Hoover urged the nation to hold fast to its traditional values of self-reliance and individualism, what he called the American system. Roosevelt felt that the system to which Hoover clung so tenaciously no longer existed; the nation needed a New Deal.

8–1. CARL SNYDER, "THE WORLD-WIDE DEPRESSION OF 1930"

A distinguished English visitor, Sir Charles Addis, speaking in New York last month, referred to the prevailing world depression as "the most serious in over one hundred years." This may be termed a highly informed British view; and I do not doubt that if we were to consider the number of countries involved and were, so to speak, to make up a weighted index of them all, it might well be that Sir Charles Addis' description would be justified.

The difficulty involved is precisely a question of measure and of the areas to be included. A hundred years ago, and even less than this the international exchange of goods was relatively small, and so, likewise, was the industrial product, even of the principal industrial nations. In considering so long a period we can only take descriptive data such as have been so carefully done by Dr. Willard Thorp in his work on *Business Annals*. But even here, going back over so long a period, we have material for only two nations, the United States and England. That for France and Germany goes back only to the latter half of the last century.

Quantitative data of any extent, even in this country—the "statistically mad United States," as some of our neighbors think of us—scarcely run back much more than half a century; that is, into the seventies.

But there is, I think, much to suggest that world-wide and synchronous depressions, back of the dark period of the seventies, scarcely existed. If they did, we know relatively little about them. Even for this country our information as to business depressions antedating our Civil War is meager enough. As I have elsewhere pointed out, the evidence is that one of the earliest of our true industrial depressions, that of the forties, did not coincide with the financial disturbances and panic of 1837; nor did the next severe financial crisis of 1857, usher in a drastic industrial setback as has been invariably the case ever since.

It is interesting further to note that the statistical picture even of the seventies is confused, so that, for example, in no year of that depression did railway traffic, as measured in ton miles, fail to increase——so rapid was the growth of our railway systems at that time.

For this country no adequate measures of general production and trade antedate 1875, and there is, of course, nothing like these measures for other countries until a much later period. And even from this date in this country we are confined to a relatively few basic products, like coal and iron and railway traffic, and returns as to bank clearings in the major cities. For the period from 1875, three especial measures of production and trade have been undertaken, that by the American Telephone Company, our own Clearings

Index of Business, and, more recently, a new measure of basic production and manufacture by Professor Warren Persons. These are from monthly data and are the earliest and most detailed quantitative studies of business depressions, covering a long period, with which I am familiar. It is interesting to find that indexes derived from different types of data should still show a fairly close agreement, and to this I may add also the inevitably rather crude measures of the velocity of bank deposits, from 1875, carried out in my department.

Here then are four different types of measures endeavoring to gauge the intensity of business depressions in this country. If we take as our standard, as three of these indexes do, that amazingly steady line of average or normal growth of industry, what we find is that the drop below this line of normal growth is remarkably similar for each of the major depressions covered in this period. This is strikingly true of Professor Persons' most recent calculations.

Taking, then, these types of measures as our guide and applying them to the present time, we find the latest available month, November, registering the lowest point in the present depression, and that point about the same percentage degree of decline from the estimated normal as in previous industrial crises, as in 1921, in 1907, 1893, 1877, and some intermediate periods like 1884 and 1914.

It is unfortunate that, for the most part, our physical data are so largely confined to basic production, which, decade by decade, become less and less representative of the total trade of the nation. But if we take these measures for precisely what they are, and nothing else, we shall not confuse their showing of a 20 to 30 per cent decline below normal as a true measure of the decline in the total trade of the country, which may not be even one-third as much. As they stand, these indexes confirm for this country at least this much of Sir Charles Addis' estimate, that the present depression is one of the most severe of which we have any definite measure.

In other words, as I expressed it last March, before the fact was as evident as it is today, "it is clear that the business cycle in all its force, unaltered and undiminished, is still with us." This definite fact seem to me of deep significance, as expressing the complete absence up to the present time of any kind of adequate procedure for the control, or even the mitigation of the severity of the business cycle in this country.

But if business cycles mean for us precisely what they have meant since their advent, alike in their severity and the havoc which they wreak, unaltered in any measurable degree, this is unfortunately not true for the rest of the world. I do not think there is any careful student of the problem who would not agree that this is the most world-wide depression, if not the most severe, of which we have any record, whether in a hundred years or more. Certainly no other has to the same degree involved in a common cataclysm the most distant portions of the earth. Australia, the Argentine and the Malay States have suffered as much or possibly more than Great Britain, or Japan or the United States.

It is an astonishing and sinister portent. As if in ironic contrast to the fantasies of a "new era" of unending prosperity, so widely prevalent but little more than a year ago, must we from this derive the impression that the business cycle, and industrial depressions, so far from undergoing a progressive amelioration, are steadily extending, if not in intensity at least in area and numbers involved? Viewed from this angle most of our so-called international problems sink to a minor place.

If, for example, the United States were now alone among the chief nations of the world to suffer, the repercussions of this might still be extensive, owing to our highly predominating position as a buyer and consumer of raw materials. But if most of the other countries were fairly prosperous this effect would be mitigated. The other nations would buy our goods at these depressed prices, gold would flow in, bank credit would be automatically expanded, and the usual and apparently invariable mechanism of recovery in trade would be set in motion.

In reality we have had exactly the reverse. None of the major European, countries, save one, shared the general prosperity of the United States in the last six or eight years. On the contrary, some of them, at least, like Great Britain and Germany, have had a struggle with many adverse factors. And the same is true of other great countries, more distant, like Japan and China. The single exception appears to have been France, and the peculiar circumstances of her exemption I shall advert to in a moment.

The collapse of the speculative mania in the United States last year, puncturing conditions of overexpansion in some important lines, reacted then upon a world in none too buoyant a condition and in which many countries were directly dependent upon these United States, either through our immense purchases of raw materials or through loans of billions of dollars, for such well-being as they had enjoyed.

But there was one event of far-reaching effect. This was the high money rates prevailing in the United States, in consequence of our speculative madness, and the inevitable attraction to this country of foreign funds to which this gave rise. The concatenation of circumstances was peculiar.

In the immediate post-war period the United States alone of the great nations was able to enjoy the luxury of redundant hoards of gold. Gold came to us in fabulous quantity. We had gained a billion dollars in the war, owing to our peculiar strategic position, and another billion and a quarter in the six years after the war had ended. While other countries were struggling to escape from the demoralizing influence of huge paper money circulations, this country was able to indulge in a considerable monetary inflation after 1921, on a gold basis; and there seems little reason to question that then, as always, this was one of the dominating factors that made possible a period of such great, though by no means unexampled, prosperity. It was certainly the strongest factor in the tremendous speculative boom, which in many ways was without example in previous history.

Even before the crisis this boom had attracted wide participation from other countries, leading to an inflow of gold, following a huge, and beneficent, exodus. Largely due to heavy importations by France, this country had in 1927–28 sent abroad an enormous sum of gold, near to six hundred millions. But this had no disastrous effect because of the great redundancy of our existing supply. This enormous loss of gold was not, as in most previous periods of the country's history, a menace but, on the contrary, an unquestioned gain, for it enabled Great Britain, France, Germany, and other countries to return to or sustain their gold currencies, and thereby to expand their production and consumption. The exodus was a mark not of weakness but of strength.

But when, in consequence of the lure of rising share prices and our rising interest rates, we began again to draw gold heavily from other countries which could ill afford to lose it, there was the beginning of disturbance. When finally interest rates rose here to extreme figures, this cut off foreign loans in this country and, on the other hand, forced almost all the central banks of the world likewise to raise their discount rates to figures prohibitive to free borrowings by merchants. The result was a severe crimp in credit in almost every nation all around the world; again, save one. And this came precisely at a time when in this country the usual effect of rising interest rates upon business and bank credit had begun to be felt.

At the same time, France was continuing her heavy imports of gold; and this with the concurrent takings of the United States not only absorbed all of the available new monetary gold but brought a severe reduction in the gold stocks of other countries. In the twenty-three months from the beginning of 1929, while the United States absorbed over four hundred millions, France gained nearly eight hundred millions more. There was a considerable gain for Belgium as well. This meant a total absorption of gold of far over a billion of dollars. In the same period sixteen other leading nations lost nearly six hundred millions. Slight wonder that all these other gold standard countries had to resort to high discount rates to protect what gold they had left.

As a result of tin's peculiar and untimely conjuncture the United States and France have not much below three-fifths of the world's visible stock of monetary gold. This amazing gain by these two countries must have been one of the forces to give to the present depression its singular and unexampled universality; and likewise to accentuate the most extraordinary fall in commodity prices, aside from the direct aftermath of war, of which apparently we have any record.

It is this fall in prices, that for some countries has been of almost catastrophic severity, which most distinctly marks off the present depression from its predecessors. Twenty-two years ago, we had, in this country a particularly sharp industrial crisis, the last preceding the World War, amounting, on the indexes of basic production, to something like present proportions. But this depression was short lived and the fall in commodity prices was not heavy. It amounted to something like 5 to 7 per cent on our familiar indexes, while the present fall in prices in this country, measured by these same indexes, has been three times as great. In other nations even heavier.

But there is reason for thinking that, as a mirror of prevailing conditions, even this estimate is inadequate. So far as I can discover we never had in this country, save in 1921 and in 1864–65, so violent a fall in basic commodities as now. I have taken a composite of twenty of the world's leading basic commodities—the largest in point of total value of product—and compared their prices with the average prices of 1928 and the first half of 1929. The average decline in these twenty basic commodities to November, the latest available date, had been 30 per cent.

From the 1928–29 average, rubber had lost 63 per cent; copper, 40 per cent; wheat, 37 per cent; cotton, 4–7 per cent; silk, 52 per cent; tin, 46 per cent; and so on. Save as a post-war price collapse, as in 1921 and 1864, and apparently much the same thing at the end of the Napoleonic wars, it may be doubted if any such drastic fall in the value of the great basic products of the world has ever taken place in more than a century at least. As this fateful shrinkage in the value of these basic products, and manufactures from them, amounts now to tens of billions of dollars, and has correspondingly affected the purchasing power of most of the producing countries around the earth, possibly Sir Charles Addis is justified in describing this as "the most serious depression in over one hundred years."

It may be of interest to make one further observation. It is a popular belief that this almost universal decline was the result of wide-spread "overproduction." Side by side with the decline of prices we have plotted the world production of these same commodities. It is true that in a number of lines there was a quite usual rate of increase in the total product in the years of 1928 and 1929; true, also, that this had led to some notable increases in stocks on hand. Familiar even to the man in the street are the examples of such commodities as rubber, copper, sugar, coffee, and the like. But in few instances was the rate of production in these two years greater than the rate of increase at other times within the last ten or fifteen years—years in which there had not been, save in 1921, any such violent declines in prices.

Further than this it seemed not easy to discover any direct relationship between the rates of increase of the different basic commodities in 1928–29 and their subsequent individual declines in price. Thus, for example, the world's wheat production in 1929 and 1930 was little above the computed line of long-term growth of wheat production, and markedly below the unusually large and, in fact, record crop of 1928. Nor was the average increase of the last five years anything near to the rapid gain from 1919 to 1923. Yet there was not then, nor in 1928–29, any marked decline in the price of wheat. Yet in December the fall in the price of wheat from the average of 1928–29 has amounted to nearly 40 per cent. And one may find similar instances.

In other words, commodities in which there was no unusual rate of increase have fallen in price as much or even more than some commodities in which the expansion seemed exaggerated. And what was true of wheat in 1928 and in the 1919–23 period has been steadily true of a great number of other commodities at varying times within the last decade, and likewise in former times; viz., either that an unusual or exaggerated rate of production has not resulted in any such violent declines in prices as within the last eighteen months, or, if marked declines took place, they did not seem deeply to affect other commodities nor the tenor of prosperity.

When now we come to consider the broad aggregates of world production, this conclusion is more deeply enforced. For several years the League of Nations has compiled a carefully weighted index of world production of sixty-two important commodities. These are of great variety and represent a very broad sampling. In the five years from 1923 to 1928, the average rate of increase was 3.5 per cent per annum, compounded; that is, practically the same as we have found for the United States alone, when crops are included. But the computed gain from 1928 to 1929 was less than 3 per cent!

Was this rate of increase excessive? It happens that a British compilation of twenty great basic commodities carries back to 1920, and this shows the same average rate of increase as the League of Nations' computation, whether we take the increase from 1920 or from 1923. It follows, therefore, that if there was overproduction in 1929, this was likewise true of previous years, when no disastrous price decline occurred.

As this is written we have just completed an index of world production of basic commodities running back forty years, to 1890; and this may later be extended This covers some thirty of the world's chief products. The results are, to my own mind at least, astonishing. The rates of increase shown from 1920, or from 1923, are, of course, substantially identical with the two computations given above. It reveals further that the average rate of increase from 1925 to 1929, inclusive, was under 3 per cent per annum, or less than the average from 1920 to 1925, and still less than from the average of 1919–21 to 1925 (which was about 5 per cent).

If then there was "overproduction" in 1929 or 1928 or 1927, why did not the more rapid growth up to 1925 bring on a world crisis in 1926 or 1927 or 1928? Why at the end of 1929? The world's warehouses and granaries would not store perhaps even five months of the colossal total of the world's basic products. There can never be, anywhere, any huge, or fateful, world-wide accumulation or piling up of goods.

Furthermore, the average rate of growth through the quarter of a century before the War was close to 3 per cent, with relatively little variation save in 1893–94. Where is the wondrous post-war growth of technology and invention, which was "beyond all precedent," if less than a 3 per cent gain in the last five years spells the most severe world-crisis we ever knew?

It is such considerations which cast doubt upon the validity of the popular belief in the effects of overproduction. It would seem that two things are often lost sight of; first, that the evidence of overproduction and of the accumulation of large stocks of commodities and goods almost invariably appears after the economic crisis, and not before. And I am not one who believes that the lack of this evidence is due to the paucity of trustworthy data in this regard.

Secondly, it seems entirely forgotten that constantly, alike in times of prosperity and periods of indifferent financial health, there is always in every line a certain tendency to overproduction. That is to say, producers in every industry are always intent to put forth the utmost quantity that can be sold; and as a result we find, especially for the great basic commodities, wide oscillations in individual prices, at varying times.

What really demands explanation is the phenomenon of the general debacle, when these drastic declines come all together, in a sort of ill-omened unison. It is not what causes the individual catastrophes, but the composite or, as our Continental friends phrase it, the *konjunktur*. And it may be added that here an adequate explanation, if such be forthcoming, will explain precisely this antecedent "overproduction," such as there always is, as well as the subsequent underconsumption.

8–2. IRVING FISHER, "THE DEBT-DEFLATION THEORY OF GREAT DEPRESSIONS"

In *Booms and Depressions*, I have developed, theoretically and statistically, what may be called a debt-deflation theory of great depressions. In the preface, I stated that the results "seem largely new," I spoke thus cautiously because of my unfamiliarity with the vast literature on the subject. Since the book was published its special conclusions have been widely accepted and, so far as I know, no one has yet found them anticipated by previous writers, though several, including myself, have zealously sought to find such anticipations. Two of the best-read authorities in this field assure me that those conclusions are, in the words of one of them, "both new and important."

Partly to specify what some of these special conclusions are which are believed to be new and partly to fit them into the conclusions of other students in this field, I am offering this paper as embodying, in brief, my present "creed" on the whole subject of so-called "cycle theory." My "creed" consists of…"articles" some of which are old and some new. I say "creed" because, for brevity, it is purposely expressed dogmatically and without proof. But it is not a creed in the sense that my faith in it does not rest on evidence and that I am not ready to modify it on presentation of new evidence. On the contrary, it is quite tentative. It may serve as a challenge to others and as raw material to help them work out a better product.

Meanwhile the following [are]…my…tentative conclusions.

While any deviation from equilibrium of any economic variable theoretically may, and doubtless in practice does, set up some sort of oscillations, the important question is: Which of them have been sufficiently great disturbers to afford any substantial explanation of the great booms and depressions of history?…As explanations of the so-called business cycle, or cycles, when these are really serious, I doubt the adequacy of over-production, under-consumption, over-capacity, price-dislocation, maladjustment between agricultural and industrial prices, over-confidence, over-investment, over-saving, over-spending, and the discrepancy between saving and investment.

I venture the opinion, subject to correction on submission of future evidence, that, in the great booms and depressions, each of the above-named factors has played a subordinate role as compared with two dominant factors, namely *over-indebtedness* to start with and *deflation* following soon after; also that where any of the other factors do become conspicuous, they are often merely effects or symptoms of these two. In short, the big bad actors are debt disturbances and price-level disturbances.

While quite ready to change my opinion, I have, at present, a strong conviction that these two economic maladies, the debt disease and the price-level disease (or dollar disease), are, in the great booms and depressions, more important causes than all others put together.

Some of the other and usually minor factors often derive some importance when combined with one or both of the two dominant factors.

Thus over-investment and over-speculation are often important; but they would have far less serious results were they not conducted with borrowed money. That is, over-indebtedness may lend importance to over-investment or to over-speculation.

The same is true as to over-confidence, I fancy that over-confidence seldom does any great harm except when, as, and if, it beguiles its victims into debt.

Another example is the maladjustment between agricultural and industrial prices, which can be shown to be a result of a change in the general price level. Disturbances in these two factors—debt and the purchasing power of the monetary unit—will set up serious disturbances in all, or nearly all, other economic variables. On the other hand, if debt and deflation are absent, other disturbances are powerless to bring on crises comparable in severity to those of 1837, 1873, or 1929–33.

No exhaustive list can be given of the secondary variables affected by the two primary ones, debt and deflation; but they include especially seven, making in all at least nine variables, as follows: debts, circulating media, their velocity of circulation, price levels, net worths, profits, trade, business confidence, interest rates. *The chief interrelations between the nine chief factors may be derived deductively,* assuming, to start with, that general economic equilibrium is disturbed by only the one factor of over-indebtedness, and, in particular, assuming that there is no other influence, whether accidental or designed, tending to affect the price level. Assuming, accordingly, that, at some point of time, a state of over-indebtedness exists, this will tend to lead to liquidation, through the alarm either of debtors or creditors or both. Then we may deduce the following chain of consequences in nine links: (1) *Debt liquidation* leads to *distress selling* and to (2) *Contraction of deposit currency,* as bank loans are paid off, and to a slowing down of velocity of circulation. This contraction of deposits and of their velocity, precipitated by distress selling, causes (3) *A fall in the level of prices,* in other words, a swelling of the dollar. Assuming, as above stated, that this fall of prices is not interfered with by reflation or otherwise, there must be (4) *A still greater fall in the net worths of business,* precipitating bankruptcies and (5) *A like fall in profits,* which in a "capitalistic," that is, a private-profit society, leads the concerns which are running at a loss to make (6) *A reduction in output, in trade and in employment* of labor. These losses, bankruptcies, and unemployment, lead to (7) *Pessimism and loss of confidence,* which in turn lead to (8) *Hoarding and slowing down still more the velocity of circulation.*

The above eight changes cause (9) *Complicated disturbances in the rates of interest,* in particular, a fall in the nominal, or money, rates and a rise in the real, or commodity, rates of interest. Evidently debt and deflation go far toward explaining a great mass of phenomena in a very simple logical way....

But it should be noted that, except for the first and last in the "logical" list, namely debt and interest on debts, *all the fluctuations listed come about through a fall of prices.*

When over-indebtedness stands alone, that is, does *not* lead to a fall of prices, in other words, when its tendency to do so is counter acted by inflationary forces (whether by accident or design), the resulting "cycle" will be far milder and far more regular. Likewise, when a deflation occurs from other than debt causes and without any great volume of debt, the resulting evils are much less. It *is* the combination of both—the debt disease coming first, then precipitating the dollar disease—which works the greatest havoc.

The two diseases act and react on each other. Pathologists are now discovering that a pair of diseases are sometimes worse than either or than the mere sum of both, so to speak. And we all know that a minor disease may lead to a major one. Just as a bad cold leads to pneumonia, so over-indebtedness leads to deflation.

And, vice versa, deflation caused by the debt reacts on the debt. Each dollar of debt still unpaid becomes a bigger dollar, and if the over-indebtedness with which we started was great enough, the liquidation of debts cannot keep up with the fall of prices which it causes.

In that case, the liquidation defeats itself. While it diminishes the number of dollars owed, it may not do so as fast as it increases the value of each dollar owed. Then, *the very effort of individuals to lessen their burden of debts increases it, because of the mass effect of the stampede to liquidate in swelling each dollar owed.* Then we have the great paradox which, I submit, is the chief secret of most, if not all, great depressions: *The more the debtors pay, the more they owe.* The more the economic boat tips, the more it tends to tip. It is not tending to right itself, but is capsizing. But if the over-indebtedness is not sufficiently great to make liquidation thus defeat itself, the situation is different and simpler. It is then more analogous to stable equilibrium; the more the boat rocks the more it will tend to right itself. In that case, we have a truer example of a cycle.

In the "capsizing" type in particular, the worst of it is that real incomes are so rapidly and progressively reduced. Idle men and idle machines spell lessened production and lessened real income, the central factor in all economic science. In this rapid survey, I have not discussed what constitutes over-indebtedness...

It must also take account of the distribution in time of the sums coming due. Debts due at once are more embarrassing than debts due years hence; and those payable at the option of the creditor, than those payable at the convenience of the debtor. Thus debt embarrassment is great for call loans and for early maturities.

For practical purposes, we may roughly measure the total national debt embarrassment by taking the total sum currently due, say within the current year, including rent, taxes, interest, installments, sinking fund requirements, maturities and any other definite or rigid commitments for payment on principal.

The depression out of which we are now (I trust) emerging is an example of a debt-deflation depression of the most serious sort. The debts of 1929 were the greatest known, both nominally and really, up to that time. They were great enough not only to "rock the boat" but to start it capsizing. By March, 1933, liquidation had reduced the debts about 20 per cent, but had increased the dollar about 75 per cent, *so* that the *real* debt, that is the debt as measured in terms of commodities, was increased about 40 per cent [(100%–20%) ×(100%+75%) = 140%].

Unless some counteracting cause comes along to prevent the fall in the price level, such a depression as that of 1929–33 (namely when the more the debtors pay the more they owe) tends to continue, going deeper, in a vicious spiral, for many years. There is then no tendency of the boat to stop tipping until it has capsized. Ultimately, of course, but only after almost universal bankruptcy, the indebtedness must cease to grow greater and begin to grow less. Then comes recovery and a tendency for a new boom-depression sequence. This is the so-called "natural" way out of a depression, via needless and cruel bankruptcy, unemployment, and starvation.

On the other hand, if the foregoing analysis is correct, it is always economically possible to stop or prevent such a depression simply by reflating the price level up to the average level at which outstanding debts were contracted by existing debtors and assumed by existing creditors, and then maintaining that level unchanged. That the price level is controllable is not only claimed by monetary theorists but has recently been evidenced by two great events: (1) Sweden has now for nearly two years maintained a stable price level, practically always within 2 per cent of the chosen par and usually within 1 per cent. (2) The fact that immediate reversal of deflation is easily achieved by the use, or even the prospect of use, of appropriate instrumentalities has just been demonstrated by President Roosevelt.

Those who imagine that Roosevelt's avowed reflation is not the cause of our recovery but that we had "reached the bottom anyway" are very much mistaken. At any rate, they have given no evidence, so far as I have seen, that we had reached the bottom. And if they are right, my analysis must be woefully wrong. According to all the evidence, under that analysis, debt and deflation, which had wrought havoc up to March 4, 1933, were then stronger than ever and, if let alone, would have wreaked greater wreckage than ever, after March 4.

Had no "artificial respiration" been applied, we would soon have seen general bankruptcies of the mortgage guarantee companies, savings banks, life insurance companies, railways, municipalities, and states. By that time the Federal Government would probably have become unable to pay its bills without resort to the printing press, which would itself have been a very belated and unfortunate case of artificial respiration. If even then our rulers should still have insisted on "leaving recovery to nature" and should still have refused to inflate in any way, should vainly have tried to balance the budget and discharge more government employees, to raise taxes, to float, or try to float, more loans, they would soon have ceased to be our rulers. For we would have insolvency of our national government itself, and probably some form of political revolution without waiting for the next legal election. The mid-west farmers had already begun to defy the law.

If all this is true, it would be as silly and immoral to "let nature take her course" as for a physician to neglect a case of pneumonia. It would also be a libel on economic science, which has its therapeutics as truly as medical science.

If reflation can now so easily and quickly reverse the deadly downswing of deflation after nearly four years, when it was gathering increased momentum, it would have been still easier, and at any time, to have stopped it earlier. In fact, under President Hoover, recovery was apparently well started by the Federal Reserve open-market purchases, which revived prices and business from May to September 1932. The efforts were not kept up and recovery was stopped by various circumstances, including the political "campaign of fear."

It would have been still easier to have prevented the depression almost altogether. In fact, in my opinion, this would have been done had Governor Strong of the Federal Reserve Bank of New York lived, or had his policies been embraced by other banks and the Federal Reserve Board and pursued consistently after his death. In that case, there would have been nothing worse than the first crash. We would have had the debt disease, but not the dollar disease—the bad cold but not the pneumonia.

If the debt-deflation theory of great depressions is essentially correct, the question of controlling the price level assumes a new importance; and those in the drivers' seats—the Federal Reserve Board and the Secretary of the Treasury, or, let us hope, a special stabilization commission—will in future be held to a new accountability.

Price level control, or dollar control, would not be a panacea. Even with an ideally stable dollar, we would still be exposed to the debt disease, to the technological-unemployment disease, to over-production, price-dislocation, over-confidence, and many other minor diseases. To find the proper therapy for these diseases will keep economists busy long after we have exterminated the dollar disease.

The over-indebtedness hitherto presupposed must have had its starters. It may be started by many causes, of which the most common appears to be *new opportunities to invest at a big prospective profit,* as compared with ordinary profits and interest, such as through new inventions, new industries, development of new resources, opening of new lands or new markets. Easy money is the great cause of overborrowing. When an investor thinks he can make over 100 per cent per annum by borrowing at 6 per cent, he will be tempted to borrow, and to invest or speculate with borrowed money. This was a prime cause leading to the over-indebtedness of 1929. Inventions and technological improvements created wonderful investment opportunities, and so caused big debts. Other causes were the left-over war debts, domestic and foreign, public and private, the reconstruction loans to foreigners, and the low interest policy adopted to help England get back on the gold standard in 1925.

Each case of over-indebtedness has its own starter or set of starters. The chief starters of the over-indebtedness leading up to the crisis of 1837 were connected with lucrative investment opportunities from developing the West and Southwest in real estate, cotton, canal building (led by the Erie Canal), steamboats, and turnpikes, opening up each side of the Appalachian Mountains to the other. For the over-indebtedness leading up to the crisis of 1873, the chief starters were the exploitation of railways and of western farms following the Homestead Act. The over-indebtedness leading up to the panic of 1893 was chiefly relative to the gold base which had become too small, because of the injection of too much silver. But the panic of 1893 seems to have had less of the debt ingredient than in most cases, though deflation played a leading role.

The starter may, of course, be wholly or in part the pendulum-like back-swing or reaction in recovery from a preceding depression as commonly assumed by cycle theorists. This, of itself, would tend to leave the next depression smaller than the last.

The public psychology of going into debt for gain passes through several more or less distinct phases: (a) the lure of big prospective dividends or gains in *income* in the remote future; (b) the hope of selling at a profit, and realizing a *capital* gain in the immediate future; (c) the vogue of reckless promotions, taking advantage of the habituation of the public to great expectations; (d) the development of downright fraud, imposing on a public which had grown credulous and gullible.

When it is too late the dupes discover scandals like the Hatry, Krueger, and Insull scandals. At least one book has been written to prove that crises are due to frauds of clever promoters. But probably these frauds could never have become so great without the original starters of real opportunities to invest lucratively. There is probably always a very real basis for the "new era" psychology before it runs away with its victims. This was certainly the case before 1929.

In summary, we find that: (1) economic changes include steady trends and unsteady occasional disturbances which act as starters for cyclical oscillations of innumerable kinds; (2) among the many occasional disturbances, are new opportunities to invest, especially because of new inventions; (3) these, with other causes, sometimes conspire to lead to a great volume of over-indebtedness; (4) this, in turn, leads to attempts to liquidate; (5) these, in turn, lead *(unless counteracted by reflation)* to falling prices or a swelling dollar; (6) the dollar may swell faster than the number of dollars owed shrinks; (7) in that case, liquidation does not really liquidate but actually aggravates the debts, and the depression grows worse instead of better, as indicated by all nine factors; (8) the ways out are either *via laissez-faire* (bankruptcy) or scientific medication (reflation), and reflation might just as well have been applied in the first place.

The general correctness of the above "debt-deflation theory of great depressions" is, I believe, evidenced by experience in the present and previous great depressions. Future studies by others will doubtless check up on this opinion. One way is to compare different countries simultaneously. If the "debt-deflation theory" is correct, the infectiousness of depressions internationally is chiefly due to a common gold (or other) monetary standard and there should be found little tendency for a depression to pass from a deflating to an inflating, or stabilizing, country.

As stated at the outset, several features of the above analysis are, as far as I know, new. Some of these are too unimportant or self-evident to stress. The one which I do venture to stress most is the theory that when over-indebtedness is so great as to depress prices faster than liquidation, the mass effort to get out of debt sinks us more deeply into debt. I would also like to emphasize the whole logical articulation of the nine factors, of which debt and deflation are the two chief. I would call attention to *new investment opportunities* as the important "starter" of over-indebtedness. Finally, I would emphasize the important corollary, of the debt-deflation theory; that great depressions are curable and preventable through reflation and stabilization.

8–3. HERBERT HOOVER, "THE CONSEQUENCES OF THE PROPOSED NEW DEAL"

Campaign is more than a contest between two men. It is more than a contest between two parties. It is a contest between two philosophies of government.

We are told by the opposition that we must have a change, that we must have a new deal. It is not the change that comes from normal development of national life to which I object, but the proposal to alter the whole foundations of our national life which have been builded through generations of testing and struggle, and of the principles upon which we have builded the nation. The expressions our opponents use must refer to important changes in our economic and social system and our system of government, otherwise they are nothing but vacuous words. And I realize that in this time of distress many of our people are asking whether our social and economic system is incapable of that great primary function of providing security and comfort of life to all of the firesides of our 25,000,000 homes in America, whether our social system provides for the fundamental development and progress of our people, whether our form of government is capable of originating and sustaining that security and progress.

This question is the basis upon which our opponents are appealing to the people in their fears and distress. They are proposing changes and so-called new deals, which would destroy the very foundations of our American system.

Our people should consider the primary facts before they come to the judgment—not merely through political agitation, the glitter of promise, and the discouragement of temporary hardships—whether they will support changes, which radically affect the whole system, which has been builded up by a hundred and fifty years of the toil of the fathers. They should not approach the question in the despair with which our opponents would clothe it.

Our economic system has received abnormal shocks during the last three years, which temporarily dislocated its normal functioning. These shocks have in large sense come from without our borders, but I say to you that our system of government has enabled us to take such strong action as to prevent the disaster, which would otherwise have come to our Nation. It has enabled us further to develop measures and programs, which are now demonstrating their ability to bring about restoration and progress.

We must go deeper than platitudes and emotional appeals of the public platform in the campaign, if we will penetrate to the full significance of the changes, which our opponents are attempting to float upon the wave of distress and discontent from the difficulties we are passing through. We can find what our opponents would do after searching the record of their appeals to discontent, group and sectional interest. We must search for them in the legislative acts, which they sponsored and passed in the Democratic-controlled House of Representatives in the last session of Congress. We must look into measures for which they voted and which were defeated. We must inquire whether or not the Presidential and Vice-Presidential candidates have disavowed these acts. If they have not, we must conclude that they form a portion and are a substantial indication of the profound changes proposed.

And we must look still further than this as to what revolutionary changes have been proposed by the candidates themselves.

We must look into the type of leaders who are campaigning for the Democratic ticket, whose philosophies have been well known all their lives, whose demands for a change in the American system are frank and forceful. I can respect the sincerity of these men in their desire to change our form of government and our social and economic system, though I shall do my best tonight to prove they are wrong. I refer particularly to Senator Norris, Senator LaFollette, Senator Cutting, Senator Huey Long, Senator Wheeler, William R. Hearst, and other exponents of a social philosophy different from the traditional American one. Unless these men feel assurance of support to their ideas they certainly would not be supporting these candidates and the Democratic Party. The seal of these men indicates that they have sure confidence that they will have voice in the administration of our government.

I may say at once that the changes proposed from all these Democratic principals and allies are of the most profound and penetrating character. If they are brought about this will not be the America which we have known in the past.

Let us pause for a moment and examine the American system of government, of social and economic life, which it is now proposed that we should alter. Our system is the product of our race and of our experience in building a nation to heights unparalleled in the whole history of the world. It is a system peculiar to the American People. It differs essentially from all others in the world. It is an American system.

It is founded on the conception that only through ordered liberty, through freedom to the individual, and equal opportunity to the individual will his initiative and enterprise be summoned to spur the march of progress.

It is by the maintenance of equality of opportunity and therefore of a society absolutely fluid in freedom of the movement of its human particles that our individualism departs from the individualism of Europe. We resent class distinction because there can be no rise for the individual through the frozen strata of classes and no stratification of classes can take place in a mass livened by the free rise of its particles. Thus in our ideals the able and ambitious are able to rise constantly from the bottom to leadership in the community.

This freedom of the individual creates of itself the necessity and the cheerful willingness of men to act co-operatively in a thousand ways and for every purpose as occasion arises; and it permits such voluntary co-operations to be dissolved as soon as they have served their purpose, to be replaced by new voluntary associations for new purposes.

There has thus grown within us, to gigantic importance, a new conception. That is, this voluntary cooperation within the community. Co-operation to perfect the social organizations; co-operation for the care of those in distress; co-operation for the advancement of knowledge, of scientific research, of education; for co-operative action in the advancement of many phases of economic life. This is self-government by the people outside of Government; it is the most powerful development of individual freedom and equal opportunity that has taken place in the century and a half since our fundamental institutions were founded.

It is in the further development of this co-operation and a sense of its responsibility that we should find solution for many of our complex problems, and not by the extension of government into our economic and social life. The greatest function of government is to build up that co-operation, and its most resolute action should be to deny the extension of bureaucracy. We have developed great agencies of co-operation by the assistance of the Government, which promote and protect the interests of individuals and the smaller units of business. The Federal Reserve System, in its strengthening and support of the smaller banks; the Farm Board, in its strengthening and support of the farm co-operatives; the Home Loan banks, in the mobilizing of building and loan associations and savings banks; the Federal land banks, in giving independence and strength to land mortgage associations; the great mobilization of relief to distress, the mobilization of business and industry in measures of recovery, and a score of other activities are not socialism—they are the essence of protection to the development of free men.

The primary conception of this whole American system is not the regimentation of men but the co-operation of free men. It is founded upon the conception of responsibility of the individual to the community, of the responsibility of local government to the State, of the State to the national Government.

...When the political and economic weakness of many nations of Europe, the result of the World War and its aftermath, finally culminated in collapse of their institutions, the delicate adjustments of our economic and social life received a shock unparalleled in our history. No one knows that better than you of New York. No one knows its causes better than you. That the crisis was so great that many of the leading banks sought directly or indirectly to convert their assets into gold or its equivalent with the result that they practically ceased to function as credit institutions; that many of our citizens sought flight for their capital to other countries; that many of them attempted to hoard gold in large amounts. These were but indications of the flight of confidence and of the belief that our Government could not overcome these forces.

...I therefore contend that the problem of today is to continue these measures and policies to restore this American system to its normal functioning, to repair the wounds it has received, to correct the weaknesses and evils, which would defeat that system. To enter upon a series of deep changes to embark upon this inchoate new deal, which has been propounded in this campaign, would be to undermine and destroy our American system.

Before we enter upon such courses, I would like you to consider what the results of this American system have been during the last thirty years—that is, one single generation. For if it can be demonstrated that by means of this, our unequalled political, social, and economic system, we have secured a lift in the standards of living and a diffusion of comfort and hope to men and women, the growth of equal opportunity, the widening of all opportunity, such as had never been seen in the history of the world, then we should not tamper with it or destroy it; but on the contrary we should restore it and, by its gradual improvement and perfection, foster it into new performance for our country and for our children.

Now, if we look back over the last generation we find that the number of our families and, therefore, our homes, has increased from sixteen to twenty-five million, or 62 per cent. In that time we have builded for them 15,000,000 new and better homes. We have equipped 20,000,000 homes with electricity; thereby we have lifted infinite drudgery from women and men. The barriers of time and space have been swept away. Life has been made freer; the intellectual vision of every individual has been expanded by the installation of 20,000,000 telephones, 12,000,000 radios, and the service of 20,000,000 automobiles. Our cities have been made magnificent with beautiful buildings, parks, and playgrounds. Our countryside has been knit together with splendid roads. We have increased by twelve times the use of electrical power and thereby taken sweat from the backs of men. In this broad sweep real wages and purchasing power of men and women have steadily increased. New comforts have steadily come to them. The hours of labor have decreased, the 12-hour day has disappeared, even the 9-hour day has almost gone. We are now advancing the 5-day week. The portals of opportunity to our children have ever widened. While our population grew by but 62 per cent, we have increased the number of children in high schools by 700 per cent, those in institutions of higher learning by 300 per cent. With all our spending, we multiplied by six times the savings in our banks and in our building and loan associations. We multiplied by 1,200 per cent the amount of our life insurance. With the enlargement of our leisure we have come to a fuller life; we gained new visions of hope, we more nearly realize our national aspiration and give increasing scope to the creative power of every individual and expansion of every man's mind.

Three years ago there came a break in this progress. A break of the same type we have met fifteen times a century and yet we have overcome them. But eighteen months later came a further blow by shocks transmitted to us by the earthquakes of the collapse in nations throughout the world as the aftermath of the World War. The workings of our system were dislocated. Millions of men and women are out of jobs. Businessmen and farmers suffer. Their distress is bitter. I do not seek to minimize the depth of it. We may thank God that in view of this storm 30,000,000 still have their jobs; yet this must not distract our thoughts from the suffering of the other 10,000,000.

But I ask you what has happened. These thirty years of incomparable improvement in the scale of living, the advance of comfort and intellectual life, inspiration and ideals did not arise without right principles animating the American system, which produced them. Shall that system be discarded because vote-seeking men appeal to distress and say that the machinery is all wrong and that it must be abandoned or tampered with? Is it not more sensible to realize the simple fact that some extraordinary force has been thrown into the mechanism, temporarily deranging its operation? Is it not wiser to believe that the difficulty is not with the principles upon which our American system is founded and designed through all these generations of inheritance? Should not our purpose be to restore the normal working of that system which has brought to us such immeasurable benefits, and not destroy it?

...I have said before, and I want to repeat on this occasion, that the only method by which we can stop the suffering and unemployment is by returning our people to their normal jobs in their normal homes, carrying on their normal functions of living. This can be done only by sound processes of protecting and stimulating recovery of the existing economic system upon which we have builded our progress thus far—preventing distress and giving such sound employment as we can find in the meantime.

...In order that we may get at the philosophical background of the mind, which pronounces the necessity for profound change in our American system and a new deal, I would call your attention to an address delivered by the Democratic candidate in San Francisco, early in October. He said:

"Our industrial plant is built. The problem just now is whether under existing conditions it is not overbuilt. Our last frontier has long since been reached. There is practically no more free land. There is no safety valve in the Western prairies where we can go for a new start...The mere building of more industrial plants, the organization of more corporations is as likely to be as much a danger as a help...Our task now is not the discovery of natural resources or necessarily the production of more goods, it is the sober, less dramatic business of administering the resources and plants already in hand...establishing markets for surplus production, of meeting the problem of underconsumption, distributing the wealth and products more equitably and adapting the economic organization to the service of the people..."

There are many of these expressions with which no one would quarrel. But I do challenge the whole idea that we have ended the advance of America, that this country has reached the zenith of its power, the height of its development. That is the counsel of despair for the future of America. That is not the spirit by which we shall emerge from this depression. That is not the spirit that made this country. If it is true, every American must abandon the road of countless progress and unlimited opportunity. I deny that the promise of American life has been fulfilled, for that means we have begun the decline and fall. No nation can cease to move forward without degeneration of spirit....

If these measures, these promises, which I have discussed; or these failures to disavow these projects; this attitude of mind, mean anything, they mean the enormous expansion of the Federal Government; they mean the growth of bureaucracy such as we have never seen in our history. No man who has not occupied my position in Washington can fully realize the constant battle which must be carried on against incompetence, corruption, tyranny of government expanded into business activities. If we first examine the effect on our form of government of such a program, we come at once to the effect of the most gigantic increase in expenditure ever known in history. That alone would break down the savings, the wages, the equality of opportunity among our people. These measures would transfer vast responsibilities to the Federal Government from the States, the local governments, and the individuals. But that is not all; they would break down our form of government. Our legislative bodies cannot delegate their authority to any dictator, but without such delegation every member of these bodies is impelled in representation of the interest of his constituents constantly to seek privilege and demand service in the use of such agencies. Every time the Federal Government extends its arm, 531 Senators and Congressmen become actual boards of directors of that business.

...Even if the Government conduct of business could give us the maximum of efficiency instead of least efficiency, it would be purchased at the cost of freedom. It would increase rather than decrease abuse and corruption, stifle initiative and invention, undermine development of leadership, cripple mental and spiritual energies of our people, extinguish equality of opportunity, and dry up the spirit of liberty and progress. Men who are going about this country announcing that they are liberals because of their promises to extend the Government in business are not liberals; they are reactionaries of the United States.

...The very essence of equality of opportunity of our American system is that there shall be no monopoly or domination by any group or section in this country, whether it be business, sectional, or a group interest. On the contrary, our American system demands economic justice as well as political and social justice; it is not a system of *laissez-faire*.

...My countrymen, the proposals of our opponents represent a profound change in American life—less in concrete proposal, bad as that may be, than by implication and by evasion. Dominantly in their spirit they represent a radical departure from the foundations of 150 years, which have made this the greatest nation in the world. This election is not a mere shift from the ins to the outs. It means deciding the direction our Nation will take over a century to come....

8–4. FRANKLIN DELANO ROOSEVELT, "COMMONWEALTH CLUB ADDRESS"

...So began, in American political life, the new day, the day of the individual against the system, the day in which individualism was made the great watchword of American life. The happiest of economic conditions made that day long and splendid. On the Western frontier, land was substantially free. No one, who did not shirk the task of earning a living, was entirely without opportunity to do so. Depressions could, and did, come and go; but they could not alter the fundamental fact that most of the people lived partly by selling their labor and partly by extracting their livelihood from the soil, so that starvation and dislocation were practically impossible. At the very worst there was always the possibility of climbing into a covered wagon and moving west where the unfilled prairies afforded a haven for men to whom the East did not provide a place. So great were our natural resources that we could offer this relief not only to our own people, but to the distressed of all the world; we could invite immigration from Europe, and welcome it with open arms. Traditionally, when a depression came, a new section of land was opened in the West, and even our temporary misfortune served our manifest destiny.

It was the middle of the 19th century that a new force was released and a new dream created. The force was what is called the industrial revolution, the advance of steam and machinery and the rise of the forerunners of the modern industrial plant. The dream was the dream of an economic machine, able to raise the standard of living for everyone; to bring luxury within the reach of the humblest; to annihilate distance by steam power and later by electricity, and to release everyone from the drudgery of the heaviest manual toil. It was to be expected that this would necessarily affect government. Heretofore, government had merely been called upon to produce conditions within which people could live happily, labor peacefully, and rest secure. Now it was called upon to aid in the consummation of this new dream. There was, however, a shadow over the dream. To be made real, it required use of the talents of men of tremendous will, and tremendous ambition, since by no other force could the problems of financing and engineering and new developments be brought to a consummation.

So manifest were the advantages of the machine age, however, that the United States fearlessly, cheerfully, and, I think, rightly, accepted the bitter with the sweet. It was thought that no price was too high to pay for the advantages which we could draw from a finished industrial system. The history of the last half century is accordingly in large measure a history of a group of financial Titans, whose methods were not scrutinized with too much care, and who were honored in proportion as they produced the results, irrespective of the means they used. The financiers who pushed the railroads to the Pacific were always ruthless, we have them today. It has been estimated that the American investor paid for the American railway system more than three times over in the process; but despite that fact the net advantage was to the United States. As long as we had free land; as long as population was growing by leaps and bounds; as long as our industrial plants were insufficient to supply our needs, society chose to give the ambitious man free play and unlimited reward provided only that he produced the economic plant so much desired.

During this period of expansion, there was equal opportunity for all and the business of government was not to interfere but to assist in the development of industry. This was done at the request of businessmen themselves. The tariff was originally imposed for the purpose of "fostering our infant industry", a phrase I think the older among you will remember as a political issue not so long ago. The railroads were subsidized, sometimes by grants of money, oftener by grants of land; some of the most valuable oil lands in the United States were granted to assist the financing of the railroad which pushed through the Southwest. A nascent merchant marine was assisted by grants of money, or by mail subsidies, so that our steam shipping might ply the seven seas. Some of my friends tell me that they do not want the Government in business. With this I agree; but I wonder whether they realize the implications of the past. For while it has been American doctrine that the government must not go into business in competition with private enterprises, still it has been traditional particularly in Republican administrations for business urgently to ask the government to put at private disposal all kinds of government assistance.

The same man who tells you that he does not want to see the government interfere in business-and he means it, and has plenty of good reasons for saying so–is the first to go to Washington and ask the government for a prohibitory tariff on his product. When things get just bad enough-as they did two years ago–he will go with equal speed to the United States government and ask for a loan; and the Reconstruction Finance Corporation is the outcome of it. Each group has sought protection from the government for its own special interest, without realizing that the function of government must be to favor no small group at the expense of its duty to protect the rights of personal freedom and of private property of all its citizens.

In retrospect we can now see that the turn of the tide came with the turn of the century. We were reaching our last frontier; there was no more free land and our industrial combinations had become great uncontrolled and irresponsible units of power within the state. Clearsighted men saw with fear the danger that opportunity would no longer be equal; that the growing corporation, like the feudal baron of old, might threaten the economic freedom of individuals to earn a living. In that hour, our antitrust laws were born. The cry was raised against the great corporations. Theodore Roosevelt, the first great Republican progressive, fought a Presidential campaign on the issue of "trust busting" and talked freely about malefactors of great wealth. If the government had a policy it was rather to turn the clock back, to destroy the large combinations and to return to the time when every man owned his individual small business.

This was impossible; Theodore Roosevelt, abandoning the idea of "trust busting", was forced to work out a difference between "good" trusts and "bad" trusts. The Supreme Court set forth the famous "rule of reason" by which it seems to have meant that a concentration of industrial power was permissible if the method by which it got its power, and the use it made of that power, was reasonable.

Woodrow Wilson, elected in 1912, saw the situation more clearly. Where Jefferson had feared the encroachment of political power on the lives of individuals, Wilson knew that the new power was financial. He says, in the highly centralized economic system, the despot of the twentieth century, on whom great masses of individuals relied for their safety and their livelihood, and whose irresponsibility and greed (if it were not controlled) would reduce them to starvation and penury. The concentration of financial power had not proceeded so far in 1912 as it has today; but it had grown far enough for Mr. Wilson to realize fully its implications. It is interesting, now, to read his speeches.

What is called "radical" today (and I have reason to know whereof I speak) is mild compared to the campaign of Mr. Wilson. "No man can deny," he said, "that the lines of endeavor have more and more narrowed and stiffened; no man who knows anything about the development of industry in this country can have failed to observe that the larger kinds of credit are more and more difficult to obtain unless you obtain them upon terms of uniting your efforts with those who already control the industry of the country, and nobody can fail to observe that every man who tries to set himself up in competition with any process of manufacture which has taken place under the control of large combinations of capital will presently find himself either squeezed out or obliged to sell and allow himself to be absorbed."

Had there been no World War—had Mr. Wilson been able to devote eight years to domestic instead of to international affairs—we might have had a wholly different situation at the present time. However, the then distant roar of European cannon, growing ever louder, forced him to abandon the study of this issue. The problem he saw so clearly is left with us as a legacy; and no one of us on either side of the political controversy can deny that it is a matter of grave concern to the government.

A glance at the situation today only too clearly indicates that equality of opportunity as we have known it no longer exists. Our industrial plant is built; the problem just now is whether under existing conditions it is not overbuilt. Our last frontier has long since been reached, and there is practically no more free land. More than half of our people do not live on the farms or on lands and cannot derive a living by cultivating their own property. There is no safety valve in the form of a Western prairie to which those thrown out of work by the Eastern economic machines can go for a new start. We are not able to invite the immigration from Europe to share our endless plenty. We are now providing a drab living for our own people.

Our system of constantly rising tariffs has at last reacted against us to the point of closing our Canadian frontier on the north, our European markets on the east, many of our Latin American markets to the south, and a goodly proportion of our Pacific markets on the west, through the retaliatory tariffs of those countries. It has forced many of our great industrial institutions who exported their surplus production to such countries, to establish plants in such countries within the tariff walls. This has resulted in the reduction of the operation of their American plants, and opportunity for employment.

Just as freedom to farm has ceased, so also the opportunity in business has narrowed. It still is true that men can start small enterprises, trusting to native shrewdness and ability to keep abreast of competitors; but area after area has been preempted altogether by the great corporations, and even in the fields which still have no great concerns, the small man starts with a handicap. The unfeeling statistics of the past three decades show that the independent business man is running a losing race. Perhaps he is forced to the wall; perhaps he cannot command credit; perhaps he is "squeezed out," in Mr. Wilson's words, by highly organized corporate competitors, as your corner grocery man can tell you.

Recently a careful study was made of the concentration of business in the United States. It showed that our economic life was dominated by some six hundred odd corporations who controlled two-thirds of American industry. Ten million small business men divided the other third. More striking still, it appeared that if the process of concentration goes on at the same rate, at the end of another century we shall have all American industry controlled by a dozen corporations, and run by perhaps a hundred men. Put plainly, we are steering a steady course toward economic oligarchy, if we are not there already.

Clearly, all this calls for a reappraisal of values. A mere builder of more industrial plants, a creator of more railroad systems, and organizer of more corporations, is as likely to be a danger as a help. The day of the great promoter or the financial Titan, to whom we granted anything if only he would build, or develop, is over. Our task now is not discovery or exploitation of natural resources, or necessarily producing more goods. It is the soberer, less dramatic business of administering resources and plants already in hand, of seeking to reestablish foreign markets for our surplus production, of meeting the problem of under consumption, of adjusting production to consumption, of distributing wealth and products more equitably, of adapting existing economic organizations to the service of the people. The day of enlightened administration has come.

Just as in older times the central government was first a haven of refuge, and then a threat, so now in a closer economic system the central and ambitious financial unit is no longer a servant of national desire, but a danger. I would draw the parallel one step farther. We did not think because national government had become a threat in the 18th century that therefore we should abandon the principle of national government. Nor today should we abandon the principle of strong economic units called corporations, merely because their power is susceptible of easy abuse. In other times we dealt with the problem of an unduly ambitious central government by modifying it gradually into a constitutional democratic government. So today we are modifying and controlling our economic units.

As I see it, the task of government in its relation to business is to assist the development of an economic declaration of rights, an economic constitutional order. This is the common task of statesman and business man. It is the minimum requirement of a more permanently safe order of things.

Every man has a right to life; and this means that he has also a right to make a comfortable living. He may by sloth or crime decline to exercise that right; but it may not be denied him. We have no actual famine or death; our industrial and agricultural mechanism can produce enough and to spare. Our government formal and informal, political and economic, owes to every one an avenue to possess himself of a portion of that plenty sufficient for his needs, through his own work.

Every man has a right to his own property; which means a right to be assured, to the fullest extent attainable, in the safety of his savings. By no other means can men carry the burdens of those parts of life which, in the nature of things afford no chance of labor: childhood, sickness, old age. In all thought of property, this right is paramount; all other property rights must yield to it. If, in accord with this principle, we must restrict the operations of the speculator, the manipulator, even the financier, I believe we must accept the restriction as needful, not to hamper individualism but to protect it.

These two requirements must be satisfied, in the main, by the individuals who claim and hold control of the great industrial and financial combinations which dominate so large a part of our industrial life. They have undertaken to be, not business men, but princes-princes of property. I am not prepared to say that the system which produces them is wrong. I am very clear that they must fearlessly and competently assume the responsibility which goes with the power. So many enlightened business men know this that the statement would be little more that a platitude, were it not for an added implication.

This implication is, briefly, that the responsible heads of finance and industry instead of acting each for himself, must work together to achieve the common end. They must, where necessary, sacrifice this or that private advantage; and in reciprocal self-denial must seek a general advantage. It is here that formal government-political government, if you choose, comes in. Whenever in the pursuit of this objective the lone wolf, the unethical competitor, the reckless promoter, the Ishmael or Insull whose hand is against every man's, declines to join in achieving an end recognized as being for the public welfare, and threatens to drag the industry back to a state of anarchy, the government may properly be asked to apply restraint. Likewise, should the group ever use its collective power contrary to public welfare, the government must be swift to enter and protect the public interest.

The government should assume the function of economic regulation only as a last resort, to be tried only when private initiative, inspired by high responsibility, with such assistance and balance as government can give, has finally failed. As yet there has been no final failure, because there has been no attempt, and I decline to assume that this nation is unable to meet the situation...

ESSAYS

Essay 8–1 is co-authored by Milton and Rose Friedman, and was published on the fiftieth anniversary of the 1929 crash. "The Anatomy of Crisis…and the Failure of Policy" later became part of their widely acclaimed book and PBS-TV series, *Free to Choose*. Professor Friedman spent nearly his entire career at the University of Chicago, where he developed a reputation as the staunchest defender of free enterprise and market capitalism. He was the recipient of the Nobel Prize in Economic Science in 1976. For the Friedmans, the cause of the Great Depression is simple: the inaction, the vacillation, and the ineptitude of the Federal Reserve. The Fed stood by and watched as the chaos in the banking system caused the money supply to contract; this brought on the depression. This is the view of the monetarist school; the growth rate of the money stock determines the course of macroeconomic activity. In Essay 8–2, "The Nation in Depression," Christina Romer, an economics professor at Berkeley, offers an alternative to the Friedmans' view, that of the spending school. She believes that the stock market crash led to a significant reduction in spending on consumer durables in the first half of 1930, sending the economy on its downward spiral well in advance of any contraction in the money stock. She asserts that the American experience before 1931 can be easily explained by domestic factors alone; international factors enter the picture starting in 1931. She shows that the depression in the United States was deeper and more prolonged than for any other major industrial country. While she points to domestic spending shocks as initiating the depression, monetary shocks are crucial later on. Furthermore, she attributes the eventual recovery from the depression to the policies of the Roosevelt administration that led to a spectacular increase in the money stock throughout much of the remainder of the decade of the 1930s.

8–1. MILTON AND ROSE D. FRIEDMAN, "THE ANATOMY OF CRISIS"

The Depression that started in the U.S. in mid-1929 was a catastrophe of unprecedented dimension for the U.S.: by 1933, the dollar income of the nation had been halved, total output had been cut by a third, and one of every four potential workers was recorded as unemployed. It was no less a catastrophe for the world. The spread of the Depression to other countries brought lower output, higher unemployment, hunger, and misery everywhere. In Germany, the Depression helped Adolf Hitler rise to power and paved the way for World War II. In Japan, it strengthened the hold of the military clique dedicated to creating a Greater East Asia co-prosperity sphere. In China, the aftermath of the Depression destroyed the monetary system, weakened the ability of the Nationalist government to resist the Japanese and then the Communists, and fostered the final hyperinflation that sealed the doom of the Chiang Kai-shek regime and elevated Mao to power.

In the realm of ideas, the Depression persuaded the public at large that Karl Marx was right in condemning capitalism as a fundamentally unstable system given to ever more serious crises. It converted the public to the view that had earlier gained increasing acceptance among the intellectuals—that government had to play a more active role; that it should intervene actively to offset instability generated by private enterprise; that it should become a balance wheel promoting stability and assuring the security of its citizens. The change in the public's perception of the role of the market, on the one hand, and of the government, on the other, was a major catalyst for the rapid growth of government, and particularly central government, from that day to this.

The Depression produced an equally drastic change in professional economic opinion. It shattered the long-held belief, which had been strengthened during the 1920s, that monetary policy was a potent instrument for promoting economic stability. Opinion shifted almost to the opposite extreme, that "money does not matter." To fill the gap left by the apparent collapse of the reigning theory, the most brilliant economist of the twentieth century, Keynes, offered an alternative theory, launching the Keynesian revolution, which not only captured the economics profession, but provided both an appealing justification and a prescription for extensive government intervention.

Both shifts—in the opinion of the public and of the economics profession—arose from a misunderstanding of what had actually happened. *We now know, as a few knew then, that the Depression reflected a failure of government, not of private enterprise.* And it reflected a failure of government in an area in which the government had long been assigned responsibility—"to coin money, regulate the value thereof, and of foreign coin." The Federal Reserve System, the key monetary authority at the time, imposed a crushing burden on the economy. Its policies produced or facilitated a decline in the quantity of money by one-third from 1929 to 1933. Established in 1913 in response to the panic of 1907, precisely in order to prevent similar episodes, it stood idly by while over one-third of the commercial banks of the nation went out of existence. It presided over a banking panic far more extensive and damaging than any that had ever occurred earlier, ending up succumbing to its own ineptness by closing its own doors for a week during the so-called banking holiday of March 1933.

At the time, and for a considerable period thereafter, the bank failures and subsequent banking panic were interpreted by many knowledgeable observers as having occurred despite the best efforts of the Federal Reserve to ease monetary conditions and to expand the money supply. Only much later did research demonstrate beyond doubt that the facts were quite different. At all times from 1929 to 1933, the Federal Reserve had the power to prevent any decline in the quantity of money, indeed, to expand the money supply to any desired extent. Throughout the Depression, there were persons within the System, as well as outside, calling for the Fed to take the needed action. It was conflict within the System, inertia, drift, and incompetence, not impotence that produced the disastrous failure of monetary policy.

On the scientific side, we now know that the Depression, far from showing that "money does not matter," was a tragic testimonial to the importance of money. Of course, many factors other than monetary policy affected the detailed course of the Depression and help to explain its severity and duration. But it is literally inconceivable that the Depression could have lasted as long as it did or have been as severe as it was if the Fed had acted early to prevent a decline in the quantity of money.

This conclusion would be endorsed today by the vast majority of economists of all shades of professional and political opinion—but was not known to Keynes or most of his contemporaries.

On Monday, October 21, 1907, some five months after the beginning of an economic recession, the Knickerbocker Trust Company, the third largest trust company in New York, began to experience financial difficulties. The next day a "run" on the bank forced it to close (temporarily, as it turned out: it resumed business in March 1908). The closing of the Knickerbocker Trust precipitated runs on other trust companies in New York and then spread to other parts of the country—a banking "panic" was under way of the kind that had occurred every now and then during the nineteenth century.

Within a week, banks throughout the country reacted to the "panic" by "restriction of payments," i.e. the convertibility of deposits into currency—a move that was legally sanctioned in a few states, and tolerated without explicit sanction in the rest.

The restriction of payments did cut short bank failures and end the panicky runs. But it imposed serious inconvenience on business, led to a shortage of coin and currency, and stimulated wooden nickels and all sorts of other temporary substitutes for legal money— for a time it took $104 of deposits to buy $100 of currency. Together, the panic and the restriction, both directly and by forcing a decline in the quantity of money, sharply intensified the recession under way, turning it into one of the most severe that the U.S. had experienced up to that time.

The severe phase was short-lived, however. Banks resumed payments in early 1908, and a few months thereafter economic recovery got under way. The recession lasted in all only 13 months.

This dramatic episode was the key element that accounted for the establishment of the Federal Reserve System in 1913. It made some action in the monetary and banking area politically essential. In the Republican Administration of Theodore Roosevelt, a National Monetary Commission was established, headed by a prominent Republican Senator, Nelson W. Aldrich. In the Democratic Administration of Woodrow Wilson, the Commission's recommendations were rewritten and repackaged by a prominent Democratic Senator, Carter Glass, and enacted as the Federal Reserve Act of 1913.

But what do the terms "run" and "panic" and "restriction of payments'" really mean? Why did they have the effects they did? And how did the Federal Reserve Act propose to prevent similar episodes?

A run on a bank is simply an attempt by many of its depositors simultaneously to "withdraw" their deposits in cash. It arises from a fear that the bank will fail. It represents an attempt by everyone to get "his" money out before it is all gone.

One bank alone can meet a "run" by borrowing from other banks, or by asking its borrowers to repay their loans—which they may be able to do by withdrawing cash from other banks. But if a bank run spreads, all banks together obviously cannot meet the run in this way—there simply is not enough currency in bank vaults to satisfy the demands of all depositors.

Moreover, any attempt to meet a widespread run by drawing down vault cash—unless it succeeds promptly in restoring confidence and ends the run so the cash is re-deposited— will force a much larger reduction in deposits. On the average in 1907, there were $8 of deposits for every $1 of cash in the vaults of banks. For every $1 transferred from the vaults of banks to the mattresses of depositors, deposits had to go down by roughly $8. That is why a run—hoarding of cash by the public—tends to reduce the total money supply.

It is also why we call cash, or its equivalent, "high-powered money." It is also why a run, if not checked, causes such distress. Individual banks, seeking to get cash to meet the demands of their depositors, try to get their borrowers to repay loans, or refuse to renew loans or to extend additional loans—but the borrowers as a whole have nowhere to turn, so banks fail and businesses fail.

How can a "panic" be stopped once it is under way, or better yet, how can it be prevented from starting? One way to stop a panic is the method adopted in 1907: a concerted restriction of payments by the banks. Banks agreed with one another that they would not pay cash on demand to depositors. They stayed open for business by accepting checks on themselves and other banks as "deposits," and settling among themselves only "through the clearing house." That is, they operated through bookkeeping entries—a primitive version of the cashless society of the future that so many expect to develop. Under this system, banks might and did still fail because they were "unsound" banks, but they did not fail simply because they could not promptly convert their perfectly sound assets into cash.

That is a rather drastic way but it worked. As time passed, panic subsided, confidence in banks was restored, the banks resumed payment, and shortly thereafter the recession came to an end and recovery followed.

Another way to stop a panic is to enable sound banks to convert their assets into cash rapidly, not at the expense of other banks but through the creation of additional cash—to provide an emergency printing press, as it were. In principle, if that way worked, it prevented even the temporary disruptions produced by the restriction of payments. That was the way embodied in the Federal Reserve Act. The 12 regional banks established by that Act, operating under the supervision of a Federal Reserve Board in Washington, were given the power in effect to print money in order that they could serve as "lenders of last resort" to the commercial banks. Initially, it was expected that they would operate mostly by direct loans ("rediscounts") to banks. Subsequently, "open-market operations"—the purchase or sale of government bonds—became the main way in which the System added to or subtracted from the amount of cash—the purchases being financed by creating new cash or its equivalent; the sales, by withdrawing cash or its equivalent from the system.

After the Federal Reserve System failed so miserably in the early 1930's to do what it had been set up to do, an effective method of preventing a panic from starting was finally adopted in 1934—the Federal insurance of bank deposits. By giving depositors confidence that they were guaranteed against loss, it prevented the failure or financial difficulties of an unsound bank from spreading the contagion to other banks—the people in the crowded theatre were confident that it was really fireproof. Since 1934, there have been bank failures and some runs on individual banks but no banking panics of the old style.

This method of preventing a panic had frequently been used earlier—though a far more partial and less effective version—by the banks themselves. Time and again, when an individual bank was in financial trouble, or threatened by a run because of rumors of trouble, other banks banded together voluntarily to subscribe to a fund guaranteeing the assets of the bank in trouble. That device prevented many putative panics and cut short others. On still other occasions it failed, either because a satisfactory agreement could not be reached or because confidence was not promptly restored. We shall examine a particularly dramatic and important case of failure below.

In the popular view, the Depression started on Black Thursday, October 25, 1929, when the New York stock market collapsed, the beginning of a slide that left stock prices in 1933 at only about one-sixth their dizzying level in 1929.

The stock market crash was important, but it was a late comer. Business activity reached its peak in August 1929 and had already fallen appreciably before the crash. In fact, the crash simply reflected the emerging economic contraction. But, of course, once it occurred, it helped to deepen the contraction. It spread uncertainty among businessmen and others, who had been bemused by dazzling hopes of a new era. It dampened the willingness of both consumers and business entrepreneurs to spend, and enhanced their desire to strengthen their liquid reserves for emergencies.

These depressing effects of the stock market crash were strongly reinforced by the early fruits of the struggle for power within the Federal Reserve System. At the time of the crash itself, the New York Federal Reserve Bank, almost by conditioned reflex instilled during the era of its previous head, Benjamin Strong, immediately acted on its own to cushion the shock by purchasing government securities. But Strong *was* dead, and the Board regarded this action as smacking of insubordination. It moved rapidly to impose its discipline on New York, and New York yielded.

The result was that thereafter, the System acted very differently than it had under Strong during earlier economic recessions in the 1920's. Instead of actively expanding the money supply by more than the usual amount to offset the contraction, the System allowed the money supply actually to decline slowly throughout 1930. Compared to the collapse from late 1930 to early 1933, the decline in the stock of money up to October 1930 seems mild—a mere 2.6%. But by comparison with past episodes, it was sizable—larger than during the whole of most earlier recessions.

The combined effect was a rather severe recession. Even if the recession had come to an end in late 1930 or early 1931, as it might have done in the absence of the monetary collapse that was to ensue, it would have ranked as one of the most severe recessions on record.

But the worst was yet to come. Until the fall of 1930, the contraction, though severe, had been a garden-variety recession, unmarred by banking difficulties, runs on the banks, or the like. The character of the recession then changed drastically, as a series of bank failures in the Middle West and South undermined confidence in banks and led to widespread attempts to convert deposits into currency.

The contagion finally spread to New York, the financial center of the country. The critical date is December 11, 1930, when the Bank of United States closed its doors—the largest commercial bank ever to have failed up to that time in U.S. history, and a bank moreover, that, although an ordinary commercial bank, had a name that led many at home and abroad to regard it as an official bank. Its failure was therefore a particularly serious blow to confidence.

It is something of an accident that this particular bank played such a key role. It was an accident that the Bank of United States happened to be the particular big bank in a major financial center that failed. Given the structure of the U.S. banking system, plus the policy of drift and indecision that the Federal Reserve System was following, if it had not failed when it did, some other major bank in a major financial center would sooner or later have done so, and its failure would have had similar effects on confidence in banks. But it was also an accident that the Bank of United States itself failed. It was fundamentally a perfectly sound bank. Though liquidated during the worst years of the Depression, it ended up paying off depositors 92.5 cents on the dollar. There is little doubt that if it had been able to continue as an ongoing business, no depositor would have lost a cent.

In the standard pattern of earlier crises, when rumors started to spread about the Bank of United States, efforts were made by the New York State Superintendent of Banking, the Federal Reserve Bank of New York, and the New York Clearing House Association of Banks to devise plans to save the bank through providing a guarantee fund, or merging it with other banks. Until two days before the bank closed, this effort seemed assured of success.

The effort finally failed primarily because of the particular character of the bank plus the prejudices of the banking community. The name itself, with its appeal to immigrants, was resented by other banks. Far more important, the bank was owned and managed by Jews, and served mostly the Jewish community. It was one of a handful of Jewish owned banks, in an industry, that, more than almost any other, has been the preserve of the well-known and well-bred. By no accident, the final rescue plan involved merging the Bank of United States with the only other major bank in New York that was largely owned and run by Jews, plus two much smaller banks that had a similar ethnic character.

The plan failed because the New York Clearing House at the last moment withdrew from the proposed arrangement—purportedly in large part because of the anti-Semitism of some of the leading members of the banking community. At the final meeting of the bankers, Joseph A. Broderick, then the New York State Superintendent of Banking, tried but failed to get them to go along. "I said," he later testified at a court trial, "it [the Bank of United States] had thousands of borrowers, that it financed small merchants, especially Jewish merchants, and that its closing might and probably would result in widespread bankruptcy among those it served. I warned that its closing would result in the closing of at least ten other banks in the city and that it might even affect the savings banks. The influence of the closing might even extend outside the city, I told them.

I reminded them that two or three weeks before they had rescued two of the largest private bankers of the city and had willingly put up the money needed. I recalled that only seven or eight years before that they had come to the aid of one of the biggest trust companies in New York, putting up many times the sum needed to save the Bank of United States but only after some of their heads had been knocked together.

I asked them if their decision to drop the plan was still final. They told me it was. Then I warned them that they were making the most colossal mistake in the banking history of New York."

For the owners and depositors of the Bank of United States, the closing was tragic. The depositors had their funds tied up for years, and never recovered all of them; two of the owners were tried in court, convicted, and served prison sentences for what everybody agreed were technical infractions of the law.

For the country as a whole, the effects were even more far-reaching. Depositors all over the country, frightened about the safety of their deposits, added to the sporadic runs that had started earlier. Banks failed by the droves—352 banks in the month of December 1930 alone.

Had the Federal Reserve System never been established, and had a similar series of runs started, there is little doubt that they would have been met as the 1907 panic was—by a restriction of payments. That would have been a more drastic measure than any actually taken in the final months of 1930 but, by cutting the vicious circle set in train by the search for liquidity, restriction would almost certainly have prevented the subsequent series of bank failures in 1931, 1932, and 1933, just as restriction in 1907 quickly ended bank suspensions then. Indeed, the Bank of United States itself might have been able to reopen, as the Knickerbocker Trust Company did in 1908. The panic over, confidence restored, economic recovery would very likely have begun in early 1931, just as it did in early 1908.

As it was, the existence of the Reserve System prevented this drastic therapeutic measure: directly, by reducing the concern of the stronger banks, who, mistakenly as it turned out, were confident that borrowing from the System offered them a reliable escape mechanism in case of difficulty; indirectly, by lulling the community as a whole, and the banking system in particular, into the belief that such drastic measures were no longer necessary now that the System was there to take care of such matters.

The System could have provided a far better solution by engaging in large-scale open market purchases, thereby providing banks with cash to meet the demands of their depositors. That would have both ended—or at least sharply reduced—the stream of bank failures and would have prevented the public's attempted conversion of deposits into currency from reducing the quantity of money. But unfortunately, the Fed's actions were hesitant and small. In the main it stood idly by, and let the crisis take its course—a pattern of behavior that was to be repeated again and again during the next two years.

It was repeated in the spring of 1931, when a second banking crisis developed. An even more perverse policy was followed in September 1931, when Britain abandoned the gold standard. The Fed reacted—after two years of severe depression—by taking the most deflationary measures in its history, imposing yet another monetary blow on a struggling economy.

In 1932, under strong pressure from Congress, the Fed finally undertook large-scale open market purchases. The favorable effects were just starting to be felt when Congress adjourned—and the Fed promptly terminated its program.

The final episode in this sorry tale was the banking panic of 1933, once again initiated by a series of bank failures, and intensified by the interregnum between Herbert Hoover and Franklin D. Roosevelt, who was elected on November 8, 1932, but not inaugurated until March 4,1933. Herbert Hoover was unwilling to take drastic measures without the cooperation of the President-elect, and FDR was unwilling to assume any responsibility until he was inaugurated.

As panic spread in the New York financial community, the System itself was infected. The head of the New York Federal Reserve Bunk tried to get President Hoover to declare a national banking holiday on his last day in office; failing in that attempt, he joined with the New York Clearing House Banks and the State Superintendent of Banking to persuade Governor Lehman of New York to declare a state banking holiday effective on March 4, 1933, the day of FDR's inauguration—the Federal Reserve Bank closing along with the commercial banks. Similar actions were taken by other governors. A nationwide holiday was finally proclaimed by President Roosevelt on March 6.

The central banking system, set up primarily to render impossible the restriction of payments by commercial banks, itself joined the commercial banks in a more widespread, complete, and economically disturbing restriction of payments than had ever been experienced in the history of the country. One can certainly sympathize with Hoover's comment in his memoirs: "I concluded [the Reserve Board] was indeed a weak reed for a nation to lean on in time of trouble."

At the peak of business in mid-1929, nearly 25,000 commercial banks were in operation in the United States. By early 1933, the number had shrunk to 18,000. When the holiday was ended by President Roosevelt ten days after it began, fewer than 12,000 banks were permitted to open, and only 3,000 additional banks were later permitted to do so. All in all, therefore, roughly 10,000 out of 23,000 banks disappeared during those four years—through failure, merger, or liquidation!

The total stock of money showed an equally drastic decline. For every $3 of deposits and currency in the hands of the public in 1929, only $2 remained in 1933: a monetary collapse without precedent.

These facts are not in question—though it should be stressed that they were not known or available to many contemporary observers including John Maynard Keynes. The real issues are of interpretation. Was the monetary collapse a cause of the economic collapse or a result? Could the System have prevented the monetary collapse? Or did it happen in spite of the best efforts of the Fed—as so many observers at the time concluded? Did the Depression start in the U.S, and spread abroad? Or did forces emanating from abroad convert what might have been a fairly mild recession in the United States into a severe one?

The System itself expressed no doubt about its role. So great is the capacity for self-justification that the Federal Reserve Board could write in its annual report for 1933, "The ability of the Federal Reserve Board to meet enormous demands for currency during the crisis demonstrated the effectiveness of the country's currency system under the Federal

Reserve Act...It is difficult to say what the course of the depression would have been had the Federal Reserve System not pursued a policy of liberal open market purchases." "Oh, what a tangled web we weave, when first we practice to deceive"—ourselves, in this case.

On cause and effect, there is little doubt that the monetary collapse was both. It had partly independent origins in Federal Reserve policy and unquestionably made the economic collapse far worse than it would have been; but also, once the economic collapse started, it intensified the monetary collapse. Bank loans that might have been "good" in a milder recession became "bad," loans in the severe collapse that occurred, weakening the lending banks and encouraging depositors to start a run on them. Failures of business enterprises, growing unemployment, all fostered uncertainty and fear, and a desire to convert assets into the most liquid form. "Feedback" is a pervasive feature of an economic system.

On the System's power to prevent the monetary collapse, the evidence by now is all but conclusive that it clearly had the power to do so. Defenders of the System have offered a series of excuses—but none has proved a defensible explanation of the failure of the System to perform the task its founders had established it to perform.

Moreover, the System not only had the power, it also had the knowledge required to exercise that power. In 1929, 1930, and 1931, the New York Federal Reserve Bank repeatedly urged the System to engage in open market purchases, the key action the System should have taken but did not. New York was overruled not because persuasive evidence was presented that its proposals were not feasible, but on very different grounds, all stemming basically from the struggle for power within the System and confused, indecisive leadership by the Board in Washington. Outside the System, there were also knowledgeable voices calling for the right action. An Illinois congressman, A. J. Sabath, said, on the floor of the House, "I insist it is within the power of the Federal Reserve Board to relieve the financial and commercial distress." Some academic critics expressed similar views—including one who later became the head of one of the Federal Reserve Banks. As already noted, the only important departure from the Fed's passive policy—in 1932—occurred under direct pressure from the Congress.

On the international character of the Depression, the decisive evidence that it spread from the U.S. to the rest of the world comes from the movements of gold. In 1929, the U.S. was on a gold standard in the sense that there was an official price of gold ($20.67 per fine ounce) at which the U.S. government would buy any gold offered or sell anyone gold on demand in return for U.S. currency or its equivalent. Most other major countries were on a so-called gold-exchange standard, under which they might or might not buy and sell literal gold freely, but under which they specified an official price for gold in terms of their own currencies, and undertook to keep the price of their currency in terms of the dollar fixed at the level determined by the two official prices of gold. Under such a system, if the United States spent (or lent or gave) abroad more dollars than the recipients of those dollars wanted to spend (or lend or give) in the U.S., the difference would come back to the United States in the form of a demand for gold. The U.S. would have a net "outflow" of gold; it would "lose" gold—in the technical jargon. Conversely, it would "gain" gold.

Suppose now that the Depression had originated abroad while the U.S. economy continued, for a time, to boom. An early effect would be a decline in foreign purchases of U.S. goods and an increase in U.S. purchases of foreign goods—as the worsening economic conditions abroad reduced the cost, or increased the availability of foreign goods. The effect would be an excess of dollars spent abroad and an outflow of gold from the U.S. Such an outflow of gold would have reduced the Federal Reserve System's "gold reserves" and have induced it to take action to reduce the quantity of money. That is the way in which, in a system of fixed exchange rates, deflationary (or inflationary) pressure is transmitted from one country to another. Had this been the course of events, the Federal Reserve could correctly claim that its actions were a response to pressures coming from abroad.

Conversely, if the Depression originated in the United States, an early effect would have been a decline in U.S. purchases abroad and an increase in U.S. sales abroad, and hence an inflow of gold. This would have brought pressure on foreign countries to reduce the quantity of money and would have been the way the U.S. deflation would have been transmitted to them.

The facts are crystal clear: the U.S. gold stock *rose* from August 1929 to August 1931, the first two years of the contraction—clinching evidence that the United States was in the van of the movement. Had the System followed the rules of the gold standard, it should have reacted to the inflow of gold by expanding the money supply instead of contracting it, as it actually did.

Of course, once the Depression was under way and had been transmitted to other countries, what happened then had a reflex influence on the United States—another example of the feedback that is so ubiquitous in any complex economy. The country in the vanguard of an international movement need not stay there. France, which had accumulated a large stock of gold as a result of returning to the gold standard in 1928 at an exchange rate that undervalued the franc and therefore had much leeway, at some point passed the United States and not only began to add to its gold stock but also, after late 1931, to drain gold from the United States. Its dubious reward for such leadership was that, although the U.S. economy hit bottom when it suspended gold payments in March 1933, the French economy did not hit bottom until April 1935.

One ironic result the inept monetary policy fashioned by the Federal Reserve Board against the advice of the New York Federal Reserve Bank was a complete victory for the Board against both New York *and* the other Federal Reserve Banks in the struggle for power. The myth that private enterprise, including the private banking system, had failed, and that government needed more power to counteract the alleged inherent instability of the free market, meant that the System's failure produced a political environment favorable to giving the Board greater control over the regional banks.

One symbol of the change was the transfer of the Federal Reserve Board from modest offices in the U.S. Treasury Building to a magnificent Greek temple of its own on Constitution Avenue (since supplemented by a massive additional structure).

The final seal on the shift of power was a change in the name of the Board and in the title of the head officers of the regional banks. In central bank circles, the prestigious title is governor, not president. From 1913 to 1935, the head of a regional bank was designated "governor"; the central Washington body was called "The Federal Reserve Board"; only the chairman of the Board was designated "governor"; the remaining members were simply "members of the Federal Reserve Board." The Banking Act of 1935 changed all that. The heads of the regional banks were put in their place by being designated "presidents" instead of "governors"; the cumbrous Governors of the Federal Reserve System replaced the compact "Board", solely in order that each of the members of the Board could be designated a "governor."

Unfortunately, the increase in power, prestige and trappings of office has been accompanied by no corresponding improvement in performance. Since 1935, the system has presided over—a major recession in 1937, a wartime and immediate postwar inflation, and a roller coaster economy since, with alternate rises and falls in inflation, and decreases and increases in unemployment. Each inflationary peak and each temporary inflationary trough has been at a higher and higher level, and with a gradual increase in the average level of unemployment.

The System has not made the same mistake that it made in 1929–1933—of permitting or fostering a monetary collapse—but it has made the opposite mistake, of fostering an unduly rapid growth in the quantity of money and so promoting inflation. In addition, it has continued, by swinging from one extreme to another, to produce booms but also recessions, some mild, some sharp.

In one respect, the System has remained completely consistent throughout: in blaming all problems on external influences beyond its control and taking credit for any and all favorable occurrences. It thereby continues to promote the myth that the private economy is unstable; while its behavior continues to document the reality that government is today the major source of instability.

8–2. CHRISTINA D. ROMER, "THE NATION IN DEPRESSION"

The economic cataclysm of the 1930s was an international phenomenon experienced by countries in all parts of the globe. Countries as diverse as the United States, Germany, Chile, and Japan all experienced significant depressions in the 1930s. Thus, the title of Charles Kindleberger's classic book *The World in Depression* (1973) captures an important feature of the Great Depression. These international aspects, especially the importance of the gold standard in causing the downturn and transmitting depression from one country to another, have been emphasized in recent years...and have successfully changed the focus of much analysis of the Great Depression from the United States to the world economy.

While such a change from American provincialism is surely healthy and warranted, adopting an international perspective on the Great Depression risks losing sight of the many ways in which the U.S. depression differed in timing and severity from depressions elsewhere...[and]...may obscure the many uniquely American causes of America's Great Depression.

This paper examines the ways in which the U.S. experience during the 1930s resembled that of other countries in some regards, and fundamentally differed in other aspects. I also evaluate the evidence on the causes of the Great Depression in the United States and the sources of the eventual recovery. I suggest that the path of American output and unemployment before 1931 can be explained quite well with only domestic factors. Even after 1931, international factors affected American economic conditions mainly through their impact on American policy decisions.

The experiences of various countries during the 1930s are a well-worked topic. This section uses annual data on industrial production for 24 countries to illustrate many salient features of the individual national experiences. I focus on industrial production because this series is often the most accurately measured national indicator of macroeconomic health. Furthermore, many other series that one might think are more representative of a business cycle, such as the unemployment rate or real GNP, are very highly correlated with industrial production.

The Great Depression started in most countries at around the same time. In annual data, the peak in industrial production occurred in 1929 for 13 of the 22 countries for which a peak can be identified. Seven countries peaked in 1930 and two peaked in 1931. The only country to peak in 1928 was Poland, which was a fairly minor industrial country. The countries in which production peaked in 1929 include most of the major industrial producers, such as the United States, Canada, Germany, Japan, and the United Kingdom. France and Sweden were the largest industrial countries to peak in 1930.

Based just on industrial production, there is little in the timing of the onset of the Great Depression to set the United States apart from the 12 other countries tied for first place. If one wanted to argue that the United States was in some sense earlier than the others, the series to analyze would be some indicator of building activity. Construction was the first sector to weaken in the United States and it weakened sooner here than elsewhere. Of the

11 countries for which the League of Nations provides data on building permits or some other indicator of building plans, only the United States and Belgium peaked in 1928. Planned construction did not turn down in countries such as Germany, France, and the United Kingdom until 1929 or later.

While the early downturn in construction is one way in which the onset of the Depression in the United States differed from other countries, more important differences involve the immediate severity of the Great Depression in the United States and the peculiar composition of the decline in American output. For most countries, the first year of the Great Depression was a fairly ordinary bad year. The median decline in output for the 15 countries experiencing a decline was just over 9 percent. Industrial production in the United States, in contrast, declined 21 percent in the first year of the Depression. Thus, the Depression was "great" in the United States sooner than elsewhere.

Another feature of the American experience in 1930 was that the initial fall in industrial production was more concentrated in consumer goods and less concentrated in investment goods than in many other countries. For example, the ratio of the percentage fall in the production of investment goods to the percentage fall in the production of consumption goods was just over two for the United States, but close to three for Canada and over four for Germany. In the United Kingdom, however, the decline in industrial production in 1930 was even more skewed toward consumption goods than in the United States.

As the Great Depression dragged on through 1931 and 1932, nearly all countries experienced a significant depression. However, there was again substantial variation in the peak to trough amplitude across the countries for which the League of Nations collected industrial production data. In this contest the United States was a clear loser, with a peak to trough fall in industrial production of 62 percent. Only Poland also experienced a fall in production of this magnitude...Canada, Czechoslovakia, and Germany experienced peak to trough declines in output approaching that of the United States. On the other hand, several major industrial countries, including the United Kingdom, Japan, and Sweden, experienced remarkably mild downturns. For example, the peak to trough decline in industrial production in the United Kingdom was less than a third as large as that in the United States. France had a reasonably large peak to trough fall in production of just over 40 percent, but between the peak in 1929 and the absolute trough in 1935 there was a significant recovery in 1933.

The timing of the trough in industrial production, on which the preceding amplitudes are based, is remarkably similar across countries. Of the 22 countries for which a trough can be identified, 15 reached their lowest point in 1932...The United States, Germany, and the United Kingdom are among the countries that have a trough in 1932. Japan, along with Chile, Finland, New Zealand, and Norway, hit bottom earlier, in 1931. Czechoslovakian industrial production reached its lowest point in 1933 and French industrial production, as just mentioned, did not reach its absolute minimum until 1935. Production in all of the remaining countries reached its lowest level in 1932.

Based on these turning points, there is no evidence that the United States was particularly unusual in the duration of the declining phase of the Depression; most of the industrial world turned around at roughly the same time. The United States was somewhat unusual, however, in the strength of the initial recovery...Industrial production in 1933 grew faster in the United States than in any other nation, though France, Germany, and Japan were all close behind. U.S. growth slowed noticeably in 1934, but then surged again in 1935 and 1936.

The composition of the growth of industrial production during the early recovery in the United States was also somewhat different from that of many other countries. While the initial downturn had been skewed toward a fall in the production of consumer goods, the initial upturn in the United States was skewed toward an increase in the production of investment goods. According to League of Nations statistics, the output of investment goods in the United States rose 42 percent in 1933, while the output of consumer goods rose 10 percent, a ratio of more than four to one. In Japan and the United Kingdom, in contrast, production of investment goods rose only about twice as fast as production of consumption goods, and in France production of investment goods grew less rapidly than production of consumption goods. Germany had a composition of production growth that was similar to that of the United States.

While various countries began their recoveries at roughly the same time, there was much variation in when each economy was (in some sense) fully recovered. A crude measure of the date of recovery is simply the year in which industrial production reached its pre-Depression peak. This occurred in 1932 for New Zealand; 1933 for Japan, Greece, and Romania; 1934 for Chile, Denmark, Finland, and Sweden; 1935 for Estonia, Hungary, Norway and the United Kingdom; 1936 for Germany; and 1937 for Canada, Austria, and Italy. The United States, Belgium, Czechoslovakia, France, the Netherlands, and Poland did not recover before the end of the sample in 1937. This comparison suggests that the United States was not only among the first countries to slip into depression, but also among the last to recover.

Documenting the timing and severity of the Great Depression in the United States and abroad is more straightforward than explaining what caused the national and international collapse. Not surprisingly, an experience as devastating and complex as the Great Depression has many different causes. Fortunately, the source of the Great Depression is a topic that has generated a vast literature and many fruitful conclusions. This section argues that the path of output and employment in the United States in the 1930s is, contrary to common perception, very well understood. I also suggest that, at least up until the start of the third year of the American Depression, domestic factors were the prime cause of the drastic decline in American output.

At the broadest conceptual level, the Great Depression in the United States can be analyzed quite well with the simple aggregate supply-aggregate demand model familiar to introductory economics students. Between 1929 and 1933, a series of shocks caused aggregate demand to decline repeatedly in the United States. These declines in aggregate demand moved the economy down along an upward-sloping aggregate supply curve. The net result was both progressively worsening unemployment and deflation.

There is substantial disagreement among scholars about why and when the U.S. aggregate supply curve became upward sloping, though nearly all agree that wages and prices were far from perfectly flexible in the 1920s and 1930s. Some studies of price flexibility conclude that wages and prices have been sticky since the turn of the twentieth century, implying that the only thing unique about the Great Depression was the size of the shocks. Other studies, using different data and different specifications, find that wages and prices did not become less flexible until around the time of the Great Depression. For example...[it is argued] nominal wages became particularly rigid in 1929 and 1930 because firms were mistakenly convinced that maintaining wages would be good for business, and suggested that this belief had its origins in the bankruptcies of the early 1920s and President Hoover's oratory. Other factors often cited as explanations for increased rigidity after World War I are the rise of internal labor markets, which replaced day-to-day wage agreements with set pay scales, and the increasing size and market power of American corporations, which broke the lockstep relationship between costs and prices.

There is also substantial disagreement about whether more wage and price flexibility would have prevented aggregate demand movements from having the large real effects that they had in the 1930s. In the conventional textbook model a fall in wages and prices raises real balances, lowers interest rates, and thus stimulates investment. The rise in investment serves to counteract at least some of the fall in demand...[Some] suggest that this traditional model is too simplistic because it ignores the effect of deflation on expectations. Since the expected real interest rate is what matters for investment decisions, deflation, which generates expectations of further deflation, could in fact depress aggregate demand further by raising real rates. Proponents of the debt-deflation hypothesis, first enunciated in the context of the Great Depression by Irving Fisher..., add that unanticipated deflation, by raising the real value of existing debt, raises the risk of default and depresses the economy by limiting credit availability.

Despite this debate on the role of deflation, the fact that prices and wages were not perfectly flexible in the 1920s and 1930s means that movements in aggregate demand had real effects. Thus, the discussion about the causes of the Great Depression in the United States has rightly focused on the source of the collapse in aggregate demand in the late 1920s and early 1930s. The evidence suggests that domestic spending shocks related to the stock market crash were crucial in the first year of the Depression, while monetary shocks were important in later years. The later monetary shocks were partly the result of slavish adherence to the gold standard and partly due to the peculiarities of American financial institutions and policies.

The U.S. economy was clearly cooling off in the summer of 1929... Seasonally-adjusted industrial production peaked in July 1929 and declined slowly between July and October 1929 (falling 3 percent over three months). The source of this slowdown is almost surely the tightening of Federal Reserve policy in 1928...The Federal Reserve began contractionary open market sales of securities in January 1928. This policy did not result in a drastic decline in the money supply because banks greatly increased their borrowing at the discount window...Banks undertook this heavy borrowing because the boom on the stock market led to enough of an increase in the demand for loans that "banks found it profitable to replace unborrowed reserves with borrowed reserves despite the sharply higher cost of doing so."

The interaction of the open market sales and the increased demand for money and brokers' loans caused by the stock market boom...led to a significant increase in both nominal and real interest rates...The nominal commercial paper rate rose from 4.0 percent in the fourth quarter of 1927 to 5.5 percent in the fourth quarter of 1928. The realized real interest rate—calculated by subtracting the change in the producer price index over the following quarter (at an annual rate) from the commercial paper interest rate—rose even more steeply, from 5.6 percent in the fourth quarter of 1927 to 9.5 percent in the fourth quarter of 1928. Regression estimates of the expected real interest rate (that is the nominal rate less expected inflation) also show a substantial rise in real short-term rates.

This rise in interest rates is enough to explain why the economy was slipping into a recession in the middle of 1929. The industries that started to decline first were those that were typically thought to be interest-sensitive. For example, as discussed previously, building permits for new construction in the United States peaked in 1928 and then declined 21 percent between 1928 and 1929. New automobile registrations peaked in November 1928, rebounded slightly in the spring of 1929, and peaked for the last time in July 1929.

The monetary explanation for the onset of recession in the United States is more plausible than alternative explanations that stress the fact that Germany and the United Kingdom experienced a minor recession in 1928 before rebounding somewhat in 1929. Such a recession abroad could have affected the U.S. economy by depressing our exports. However, American exports continued to rise between 1928 and 1929, suggesting that this effect was not present. Furthermore, at their highest, U.S. real exports in the mid-1920s were only a little over 6 percent of real GNP. Therefore, even a large fall in American exports would have been unlikely to depress the U.S. economy greatly.

The likely importance of monetary tightness in mid-1929 suggests that a domestic policy decision was the cause of the onset of the recession that eventually became the Great Depression. However, this policy decision could certainly have had international roots...[It is suggested] that the change in Federal Reserve policy came at least partly in response to an outflow of U.S. gold to France because of an undervaluation of the French franc. Thus, adherence to the gold standard was to some degree responsible for the change in monetary policy...[It is noted]...protection of the gold standard could not have been the only motivation of the Federal Reserve because the monetary stringency continued even after gold inflows began in 1929...[One] view is that "the major factor influencing monetary policy during 1928–1929 was surely the stock market."...By [several] accounts, the Federal Reserve hoped to stem the stock market boom by raising interest rates.

While adherence to the gold standard was probably not the main factor behind the change in U.S. monetary policy in 1928, it was a crucial factor in determining the response of other countries...[It is suggested]...that because the gold stocks of most European countries were already low by the mid-1920s, the increase in the U.S. interest rates, which drew gold to the United States, forced many countries to tighten their monetary policies along with the United States. Thus, the roughly contemporaneous cooling off of most of the world economy can be understood as a feedback effect from U.S. monetary policy aimed at stemming the American stock market boom.

The recession that started in the United States in the summer of 1929 became suddenly worse following the stock market crash in October 1929. Between October and December 1929, industrial production declined nearly 10 percent, and by the end of 1930 the Great Depression had started in earnest in the United States. Indeed, the decline in output during the first 18 months of the Depression was almost as large as in most previous and subsequent recessions in their entirety. For example, the fall in industrial production from the peak in July 1929 to December 1930 was 37 percent, while the peak to trough decline for the recession of 1921 was 40 percent and for that of 1938 was 39 percent. As discussed above, this was not true of most other countries; the rest of the world experienced much milder drops in industrial output in the first year of the Great Depression.

The source of this sharp decline is almost surely not contractionary monetary policy. The monetary contraction in 1928, though significant, was not large by historical standards. For example, while the nominal commercial paper rate rose 1½ percentage points between 1927 and 1928 (fourth quarter to fourth quarter), it rose nearly three percentage points between 1919 and 1920. Realized real rates, which rose just under four percentage points between 1927 and 1928, rose an unbelievable 140 percentage points between 1919 and 1920 because of an enormous drop in producer prices. Furthermore, immediately following the stock market crash, the Federal Reserve Bank of New York bought large amounts of government bonds, thus increasing the stock of high-powered money. Both nominal and real interest rates fell substantially between the fourth quarter of 1929 and the first quarter of 1930; for example, the nominal commercial paper rate fell from 6.25 percent to 4.88 percent over this interval and...estimates of the expected real commercial paper rate fell 9.1 percentage points. Real rates surged up again in the second quarter of 1930, but are not consistently high until after the banking panic in October 1930. Thus, it is hard to see how monetary conditions, working through conventional channels, could have caused the nasty turn that the depression took in late 1929.

The onset of the Great Depression in the United States following the stock market crash was led by a collapse in domestic consumption spending. As discussed above, consumer spending played a larger role in the fall in output in the United States between 1929 and 1930 than in many other countries...[It is pointed] out that consumer spending in the United States declined much more in 1930 than in either 1921 or 1938, the two other significant interwar recessions...It is certainly true that consumption accounted for a much larger fraction of the decline in real GNP in 1930 than in most previous or subsequent recessions. Indeed, the only years of GNP decline outside the Depression when consumption was nearly as important were 1917, when the United States was participating in World War I, and 1908, another year of substantial stock market volatility.

[Net exports were unimportant]...to the onset of the Great Depression in the United States. The fall in net exports in 1930 accounted for just 2 percent of the total decline in real GNP. This is much smaller than the contribution of net exports in the three recessions just before the Great Depression. This suggests that the international downturn had little feedback effect on the U.S. economy through American exports.

The most likely source of the precipitous drop in American consumption following the stock market crash in 1929 is the crash itself. In a previous paper, I showed that the stock market crash in October 1929 and the subsequent gyrations of stock prices through the middle of 1930 generated tremendous uncertainty about future income; the stock price movements did not necessarily make consumers and investors pessimistic about the future, only highly uncertain. This uncertainty is clearly reflected in the forecasts made by contemporary analysts. Not only was there more variation across forecasts of future income immediately following the Great Crash, but the analysts expressed great uncertainty about their forecasts and speculated that consumers and businessmen felt the same way.

The effect of this uncertainty was that consumers and producers immediately cut their spending on irreversible durable goods as they waited for additional information about the future. This effect is seen most clearly in the fact that department store sales and automobile registrations declined precipitously in November and December 1929, while grocery store sales and ten-cent store sales actually rose; this is exactly what one would expect if consumers were shying away from irreversible goods but had not substantially changed their point estimates of future income. The role of the stock market crash in causing the decline in consumer purchases of durable goods is also seen in regressions of the output of consumer durables on total output, lagged output, wealth, and stock market volatility...[that]...suggest that stock market volatility has a significant negative effect on the output of consumer durables and that the tremendous rise in volatility in late 1929 and early 1930 can more than account for all of the fall in the production of consumer durables in 1930. In addition to its effect through uncertainty, the stock market crash may also have depressed consumer spending by decreasing wealth and by shifting households' balance sheets toward illiquidity.

This discussion suggests that both the initial recession in the United States in the summer of 1929 and the acceleration of the decline in late 1929 and 1930 are ultimately attributable to the stock market boom and bust of the late 1920s. The stock market boom is the prime explanation for why the Federal Reserve was pursuing tight monetary policy starting in 1928. The stock market crash is the prime source for the collapse in durable goods purchases starting in November 1929. Pointing to the stock market, of course, only pushes back the mystery one level. However...[it is suggested]...that the boom and bust of stock prices can best be described as a bubble that burst. Since bubbles are, almost by definition, inexplicable events, the stock price swing is legitimately viewed as an exogenous shock. Furthermore, since the stock market boom and crash were, to a first approximation, a uniquely American phenomenon, the onset of the Great Depression in the United States had uniquely American roots.

If the American Great Depression was severe by late 1930, over the next two years it became horrific...After recovering slightly at the start of 1931, industrial production in the United States tumbled steadily from April 1931 until July 1932. Over this 15-month period, industrial production declined nearly 43 percent; by July 1932, the index of industrial production stood at less than half of its peak value in July 1929. Unemployment increased at a rate one would expect given the fall in output; by 1932, the unemployment rate stood at over 24 percent. Prices also behaved as one would expect if the fall in output were caused by a decline in aggregate demand: the producer price index declined by slightly over 40 percent between July 1929 and July 1932.

The source of the continued decline in production in the United States was almost surely a series of banking panics. Beginning with a first minor wave of panics in the fall of 1930...[there followed]...four waves of banking panics in the United States. The second wave occurred in the spring of 1931, the third in the fall of 1931, following Britain's abandonment of the gold standard, and the fourth in the winter of 1933, around the time of Roosevelt's inauguration. Over the four years from 1930 to 1933, more than 9000 banks suspended operations and depositors and stockholders lost roughly $2.5 billion..., the equivalent of 2.4 percent of nominal GNP in 1929.

The impact of these banking failures took many forms. First, the bank failures had a direct impact on the money supply. As depositors became nervous about the safety of banks, the ratio of deposits to currency fell dramatically. This greatly reduced the money multiplier, with the implication that a given stock of high-powered money could then support a much smaller total money supply. Because the Federal Reserve did nothing to increase the stock of high-powered money, the money supply declined sharply. For example, M1 (currency plus demand deposits) declined 28 percent between July 1929 and July 1932. The realized real interest rates were very high in 1931 and 1932. This is what one would expect if the monetary contraction generated substantial deflation and nominal rates were bounded by zero. Regression estimates of the expected real rate also averaged over 10 percent in these two years. Such high real interest rates are no doubt part of the reason that fixed investment plummeted during this phase of the Great Depression.

The banking panics almost surely also affected the economy in ways unrelated to interest rates...[It is believed] that pessimism had replaced uncertainty among consumers and businessmen by the end of 1930. The financial upheaval surely contributed to this pessimism and is likely to have further depressed consumer spending and investment. The financial panics also disrupted the intermediation function of banks...Banks are an important source of funds for small businesses that cannot issue stocks or bonds. When a particular bank fails, all of the long-term relationships and information about local small borrowers accumulated by the bank are lost. It becomes more expensive for another bank to loan to one of the failed bank's customers, because it has to learn all over again which firms are prudent and which are unreliable...This rise in the "cost of credit intermediation" caused by bank failures was important in 1931 and 1932 and explains much of the deepening of the Great Depression in the United States during this time. The disruption of intermediation presumably worked through credit rationing of small borrowers and the related decline in investment.

Having argued that the banking crises of 1931 and later were a crucial cause of the deepening and sustaining of the Great Depression in the United States, the obvious questions are what caused the financial panics and why did the Federal Reserve do so little to contain them. The cause of Federal Reserve inaction is the easier of the two questions to answer...[Some] stress ineptitude and fear as the main culprits. They believe that certainly up through October 1930, the Federal Reserve could have stepped in with expansionary open market operations which would have raised output and put banks on a firmer footing. In particular, they argue that the U.S. gold supply was such that the Federal Reserve could have pursued a unilateral expansionary monetary policy without running into a serious constraint from the gold standard. The Federal Reserve failed to act, ... [some] ... argue, because of a fear that monetary expansion would reignite speculation on the stock market, and because a power vacuum on the Board of Governors led to deadlock and indecision.

After mid-1931, it is harder to make the argument that the Federal Reserve was unconstrained by the gold standard. When Britain abandoned the gold standard in

September 1931, the United States experienced a serious outflow of gold because there was widespread speculation that the U.S. would be forced to devalue soon as well…[It has been argued]…that in this situation the Federal Reserve had no choice but to raise interest rates in hopes of stemming the gold drain. Others disagree, arguing that the Federal Reserve was in a very strong position to withstand the gold outflow because of its still large gold reserves and its legal power to suspend gold reserve requirements if they should become binding. At the very least, the Federal Reserve could have been more willing to discount bills brought to them by member banks at the higher interest rate than they actually were, thereby allowing banks experiencing runs to get much needed cash.

Whatever one's view of the pressure that the gold standard ultimately put on the Federal Reserve's ability to respond to the financial panics in 1931, there is little doubt that the Federal Reserve could have done something to stop the first wave of panics in late 1930. If one believes that the panics built on one another through the effect on income and the effect on expectations, then a different decision by the Federal Reserve in the fall of 1930 might have prevented the later panics that so decimated the U.S. financial system. In this case, one would have to say that American policy mistakes in 1930 played a crucial role in determining the course of output not just in 1930, but in later years as well.

Uniquely American factors are also important for explaining why the United States was so prone to financial panics in the first place…Many countries in the world experienced financial crises in the 1930s. However, the source of the financial fragility in the United States was quite different from that of other countries. For example, the organization of American banking, with its emphasis on small, undiversified banks, made the American financial system particularly susceptible to local shocks and unable to withstand runs. More important, the great expansion of agricultural lending during World War I left the American farm sector unusually heavily in debt. When deflation started in 1930, farmers were the first to default, and this sent undiversified rural banks into failure. The unique conjunction of undiversified banking and a particularly large increase in agricultural indebtedness in the 1920s made the financial panics in the United States both more severe and more persistent than in other countries. Again, the American problems of 1931 and 1932 stem from peculiarly American roots.

In the spring of 1932, the Federal Reserve adopted a noticeably expansionary monetary policy, largely under the threat from Congress that if it did nothing the legislature would intervene. The behavior of expected real interest rates and the path of industrial production suggest that this monetary expansion lowered real interest rates and generated a noticeable recovery in real output in the United States. Industrial production rose 12 percent in the four months between July and November of 1932. However, this monetary expansion ceased when Congress adjourned in July and the Federal Reserve was able to return to its policy of caution. In early 1933, the final wave of banking panics pushed the economy back into depression. Only in April 1933 did the American recovery begin in earnest.

The recovery of the United States from the Great Depression has been alternatively described as very fast and very slow. It was very rapid in the sense that the growth rate of real output was very large in the years between 1933 and 1937 and after 1938. Monthly industrial production increased by 79 percent between the trough in March 1933 and the peak in July 1937…Annual industrial production in 1933 actually increased faster in the United States than in any other country. This expansion was not limited to industrial output. Real GNP grew at an average rate of nearly 10 percent per year in the four years between 1933 and 1937, and again in the three years between the recession of 1938 and the outbreak of World War II in the United States in December 1941.

The recovery was nevertheless slow in the sense that the fall in output in the United States was so severe that, despite these impressive growth rates, real GNP did not return to its pre-Depression level until 1937 and its pre-Depression growth path until around 1942.

This fact leads to the frequently heard statement that the American Depression did not end until the outbreak of World War II.

The war, however, was not the main source of the American recovery, at least not in the way that is typically thought...The U.S. economy began recovering in 1933 primarily because of huge increases in the money supply. Soon after taking office, Roosevelt, using emergency powers granted to him by the Congress, allowed the dollar to depreciate substantially. A new lower price for the dollar was fixed by law in January 1934. This devaluation greatly increased the nominal value of existing American gold stocks. The Treasury could have ignored the increase in the nominal value of its gold reserves and left the money supply unchanged. Instead, the Treasury issued gold certificates equal to the amount of the increase in gold reserves and deposited them at the Federal Reserve. As the government spent the money, these gold certificates were converted into Federal Reserve notes, which are a component of the monetary base. As a result, high-powered money in the United States increased 12 percent between April 1933 and April 1934.

Devaluation also brought with it a large inflow of monetary gold from abroad as foreigners traded gold for the now less expensive dollars. After 1934, gold continued to flow to the United States because of political unrest in Europe. Hitler's increasing belligerence caused Europeans to want to invest in American assets, which required that they buy dollars with gold. The Treasury could have sterilized this gold inflow by borrowing the dollars to trade for the gold. Instead, the Treasury paid for the gold with deposits at the Federal Reserve, and then replenished its account by issuing gold certificates. As a result, high-powered money increased another 40 percent between April 1934 and April 1937.

This increase in high-powered money led to an increase in M1 of almost the same amount: M1 increased 49 percent between April 1933 and April 1937. That M1 did not increase by more than the base is evidence that the money supply was growing during the mid-1930s because of policy decisions and political events in Europe, rather than because of endogenous changes in the money multiplier caused by the recovery itself...Even before the money supply actually increased, devaluation helped to spur recovery by signaling the switch to a more expansionary monetary regime...Devaluation immediately stimulated purchases of farm equipment and other capital goods by generating expectations of future monetary ease, inflation, and real economic growth.

After 1934 the huge increases in the American money supply had exactly the effect on the U.S. economy that a traditional aggregate supply-aggregate demand model would lead one to predict...Real interest rates plummeted in response to the gold inflows. This came about because nominal rates fell slightly and actual and expected inflation rose substantially (the producer price index rose at over 8 percent per year between January 1933 and January 1937). This fall in real interest rates was followed fairly quickly by a recovery of interest-sensitive spending, such as construction spending and consumer purchases of durable goods. This effect can be seen in the fact that the American recovery, more than in other countries, was led by a surge in the output of investment goods. One piece of evidence that suggests a causal link between the fall in interest rates and the surge in particular types of spending in the United States is the fact that American consumer spending on durable goods turned around before consumer spending on services. This indicates that some factor that affected only durables purchases, such as a fall in interest rates, was initiating the recovery.

That increases in the money supply generated the recovery suggests that movements in aggregate demand were as important for ending the Great Depression in the United States as they were for causing it. However, there is an obvious question about whether the increase in the U.S. money supply during the recovery should be considered an accident caused by international developments or the predictable result of conscious American policy. The right interpretation, I believe, is a mixture of both. The political upheaval in

Europe that caused gold to flow to the United States was clearly an international shock. Indeed, there is a very real sense in which the tension leading up to the outbreak of World War II in Europe did help to end the American Depression by causing the U.S. money stock to grow.

On the other hand, the Roosevelt administration consciously chose to devalue and not to sterilize the subsequent gold inflows, precisely because it wanted to increase the money supply and cause inflation. In this way, the international gold flows may simply have provided a convenient way for the executive branch to bypass the overly cautious Federal Reserve. In the absence of such gold flows, Roosevelt and the Congress would quite possibly have used the threat of amending the Federal Reserve's operating procedures to force the Federal Reserve to increase the money supply. However, devaluation was clearly important in any case, because no country could pursue a wildly expansionary monetary policy for a sustained period and still maintain a fixed exchange rate. Thus...the decision to abandon the old gold parity was a crucial precondition for recovery.

The American Depression was unique in many ways. While many countries experienced a depression at roughly the same time as the United States, the onset of decline and the subsequent rebound were much more extreme in the United States than elsewhere. The overall depth of the Great Depression was also larger in the United States than in any country other than Poland. Finally, the American Depression was initiated by a fall in consumption and ended by a rise in investment to a degree that was quite different from the experience of many other industrial countries.

The picture that I have painted of the American Great Depression is one that stresses the importance of national, rather than international, aggregate demand shocks; the experience of the United States during the 1930s differed in important ways from that of other countries because the American experience had many uniquely American roots. The United States slipped into recession in mid-1929 because of tight domestic monetary policy aimed at stemming speculation on the U.S. stock market. The Great Depression started in earnest when the stock market crash in the United States caused consumers and firms to become nervous and therefore to stop buying irreversible durable goods. The American Depression worsened when banking panics swept undiversified and overextended rural banks and the Federal Reserve failed to intervene. Finally, the American Depression ended when the Roosevelt administration chose to increase the money supply tremendously after 1933.

Most of these shocks contain an international element, in one way or another. The tight monetary policy of 1928 was partly aimed at stopping a gold outflow. The Federal Reserve was less able to respond to financial panics in 1931 because expansionary monetary policy would have led to a serious loss of gold. Increasing the money supply after 1933 was very simple because capital flight from Europe brought billions of dollars worth of gold to the United States. Although these international complications were present, they were not decisive. At each stage of the Great Depression, it was ultimately American shocks and American policy decisions that determined the path of American output and employment.

ADDITIONAL READINGS

Bernanke, Ben S., "Nonmonetary Effects of the Financial Crisis in the Propagation of the Great Depression," *American Economic Review* 73 (June 1983) 257–276.

Cargill, Thomas, "Irving Fisher Comments on Benjamin Strong and the Federal Reserve in the 1930s," *Journal of Political Economy* (December 1992) 1273–77.

Chandler, Lester V., *America's Greatest Depression 1929–1941* (1970).

Eichengreen, Barry, *Golden Fetters: The Gold Standard and the Great Depression, 1919–1939* (1992).

Field, Alexander J., "A New Interpretation of the Onset of the Great Depression," *Journal of Economic History* 44 (June 1984) 489–98.

Friedman, Milton and Anna Jacobson Schwartz, *The Great Contraction* (1966).

Garraty, John A., *The Great Depression* (1986).

Hoover, Herbert, *The Memoirs of Herbert Hoover, Volume 3: The Great Depression, 1929–1941* (1952).

Kennedy, Susan Estabrook, *The Banking Crises of 1933* (1973).

Kindleberger, Charles P., *The World in Depression, 1929–1939* (1973).

Kirkwood, John B., "The Great Depression: A Structural Analysis," *Journal of Money, Banking, and Credit* 4 (November 1972) 811–37.

Marshall, James N., "Eugene Meyer (1875–1959)," in Bernard S. Katz, ed., *Biographical Dictionary of the Board of Governors of the Federal Reserve* (1992).

McElvaine, Robert S., *The Great Depression: America, 1929–1941* (1993).

Meltzer, Alan H., "Monetary and Other Explanations of the Start of the Great Depression," *Journal of Monetary Economics* 2 (1976) 455–72.

Parrish, Michael E., *Anxious Decades: America in Prosperity and Depression, 1920–1941* (1992).

Romer, Christina D., "What Ended the Great Depression?" *Journal of Economic History* 52 (December 1992) 757–84.

Rothbard, Murray, *America's Great Depression*, 3rd edn, (1975).

Schwartz, Anna J., "Understanding 1929–1933," in Karl Brunner, ed., *The Great Depression Revisited* (1981).

Stauffer, Richard, "The Bank Failures of 1930–1931," *Journal of Money, Banking and Credit* 13 (1981) 109–113.

Temin, Peter, *Did Monetary Forces Cause the Great Depression?* (1976).

Temin, Peter, *Lessons from the Great Depression* (1989).

Wanniski, Jude, *The Way the World Works* (1977).

CHAPTER 9

Economic Recovery, 1933–1945

The New Deal, World War II, and Keynes

INTRODUCTION

The Roosevelt administration, once it assumed power, acted very speedily to pass a variety of measures aimed variously at recovery, relief and reform. The famed Hundred Days introduced the nation to the specifics of the New Deal. During the period between his election and inauguration, FDR had little to say about what he intended to do. His plan of action, formulated by his Brain Trust and presented to Congress in the spring of 1933, did not represent a coherent attempt to stimulate aggregate demand and thereby restore full employment. The functioning of a large economy was not well understood; such an attempt was not feasible. Surely some of the actions taken did promote recovery, but may at the time been seen as solutions to particular problems. Ending the gold convertibility of the dollar would solve the problem of gold outflows; it would also free monetary policy from the strictures of the gold standard. Declaring a national bank holiday and instituting deposit insurance might restore a functioning banking system; if these measures ended the contagion of runs and bank failures, the monetary contraction would end and recovery could begin. It is in this light that most New Deal initiatives should be viewed.

Progress was painfully slow. The unemployment rate was 22 percent in 1934, falling to 14 percent by 1937. The sharp recession of 1937–1938, called by some a "depression within a depression," was a major setback, with unemployment going back up to 19 percent in 1938. Clearly, the collection of programs broadly included under what is called the New Deal improved conditions over what they had been during the Great Contraction. However, they were never sufficient to bring about a full recovery.

The experiments and improvisations of the New Deal in the spring of 1933, many of them made memorable with their alphabetical names, included: the establishment of deposit insurance through the Federal Deposit Insurance Corporation (FDIC); a program to shore up farm prices by a system of crop restrictions under the Agricultural Adjustment Act (AAA); a program that employed young men to reforest national parks in the Civilian Conservation Corps (CCC); legislation requiring the disclosure of financial information by firms bringing new issues of common stock and bonds to market under the Securities Act of 1933; a new federal agency, the Tennessee Valley Authority (TVA), to develop the resources of one of the major watersheds in the Southeast; and the National Industrial Recovery Act intended to create a system of industry self-government through codes of fair competition supervised by the National Recovery Administration (NRA). New Deal legislation also created the Public Works Administration (PWA), which entered into contracts for major civil works projects. The Banking Act of 1933, also known as the Glass-Steagall Act, required commercial banks to refrain from investment banking, and took the authority to conduct open market operations away from the Federal Reserve District banks and gave it to the Federal Reserve Board. This is but a sample of the programs enacted during the Hundred Days. Yet it suffices to demonstrate the patchwork quilt of recovery, relief and reform that made up what came to be known as the first New Deal.

In assessing the efficacy of the New Deal, one general observation to be made is that it was not attempted on a scale sufficient to have ended the nation's deepest depression. Indeed, it often worked at cross purposes. For example, the National Industrial Recovery Act put the anti-trust laws in abeyance for two years in an attempt to reduce competition and boost business confidence. At the same time, some of its code provisions called for limiting plant use and the expansion of capacity, hardly conducive to increasing employment and output. Perhaps it was a blessing that this act, like the AAA, was, within two years of its passage, found to be unconstitutional by the Supreme Court.

The year 1935, with the next presidential election on the horizon, brought what some call the second New Deal. With the National Industrial Recovery Act declared unconstitutional, a new flurry of legislative activity would help FDR make his case for reelection. Congress passed the Banking Act of 1935, ceding even greater powers over monetary policy to the Federal Reserve Board in Washington; the Social Security Act of 1935 became law; the Works Progress Administration (WPA) was created, offering government employment to the jobless; and labor won the right to bargain collectively with the passage of the National Labor Relations Act. Much of the second New Deal was aimed at reform, redressing some of the perceived inadequacies of the American economic system.

Roosevelt won a resounding reelection victory over Governor Alf Landon of Kansas in November of 1936. The economy continued its slow steady improvement; the unemployment rate was 17 percent in 1936 and 14 percent in 1937. FDR was apparently never genuinely comfortable with deficit spending (early in his first term, he did make good on his campaign promise of greater economy in government by cutting federal salaries and jobs). In 1937, some of his advisers, especially Treasury Secretary Henry Morgenthau, played on his ambivalence about deficit spending by arguing that, with his reelection secured and the economy on the road to recovery, it was now time to balance the budget. Roosevelt, regarded by both his admirers and detractors as the patron saint of government largesse, became the frugal Dutch Calvinist. He agreed to major reductions in government spending in 1937. At roughly the same time, payroll taxes imposed by the new Social Security legislation were just beginning to be deducted from paychecks. Additionally, Marriner Eccles, who had become Governor of the Federal Reserve Board in 1934, had mistakenly come to believe that monetary policy was too expansionary and posed a serious risk of inflation. While interest rates were low and the banking system was flush with excess reserves, this was probably not the result of excessive monetary expansion, but most likely symptomatic of an economy operating well below full capacity. In January 1937, the Fed, at Eccles' insistence, raised member bank reserve requirements by 50 percent; in consequence, the money stock contracted by 5 percent. With spending cut, taxes increased and the money stock contracting, the economy suffered through a severe recession in 1937–1938. One outcome of this downturn was the liberation of FDR from the balanced budget doctrines of his more conservative advisers. Spending on public works projects and other programs was increased; deficit spending was embraced.

For an administration trying to make policy without any reliably accurate model of the economy, experimentation seemed the only option. John Maynard Keynes, the great British economic theorist, met with many Washington officials during his visit to the United States in 1934, including an awkward and unproductive meeting with FDR. But his macroeconomic theory was not published until late 1936. So it is hard to imagine that any part of the New Deal was significantly inspired by Keynesian thought. Nor, for that matter, can Franklin Roosevelt be claimed as a Keynesian.

The economic experience of the United Kingdom in the interwar period was difficult; the unemployment rate fell below double digits in only one year, in the late 30s. There were no roaring twenties in the British Isles. Therefore, it is not surprising that it was a British economist, John Maynard Keynes, who would develop a theory to explain the causes of a deep depression and to recommend policies for its mitigation. Keynes, the son of an economics don at Cambridge University, first came to public notice at the end of the First World War with the publication of *The Economic Consequences of the Peace*, in which he predicted that the harsh terms imposed on Germany at Versailles would lead to another European war. Before Keynes, there was no discipline called macroeconomics. Full employment was considered the steady state norm for a market economy. Infrequent recessions would be brief, mild and most importantly, self-correcting. When such perturbations did occur, orthodox economists would usually put the blame on some ill-advised government action. Although experience was often at odds with this neo-classical view, most economists accepted it as the received wisdom. It was the performance of the British economy in the interwar years, combined with the worldwide depression of the 1930s, which gave Keynes his opening. Defenders of the ruling orthodoxy became increasingly unconvincing as the depression proved to be prolonged and deep with no sign of self-correction. Neo-classical economists were pressed to propose some kind of policy prescription; given the economic conditions then prevailing, they offered what seemed to the non-specialist to be strange and mystifying advice: wage cuts for labor to encourage business to expand production.

Keynes did not share in the belief that a market economy would always right itself. He believed that the weak link in a mature capitalist economy is the level of investment spending. In mature capitalism, a large industrial economy may not have enough investment opportunities to absorb its savings and maintain full employment. He also found that when investment spending falls it has a multiplied effect on the overall level of economic activity, which will fall by some multiple (greater than one) of the decline in investment spending. If market capitalism were to suffer from "fatigue," sensible public policy could save the day. Thoughtful policymakers would simply substitute government spending for the investment spending that business was unable to generate. Again the multiplier effect would translate the spending injected into the expenditure stream by government into a multiplied increase in national income. Before compensatory finance could be effectively practiced, some old dogmas would have to be abandoned. The gold standard would have to go; high interest rates to forestall gold outflows would only further weaken investment spending. The insistence on balanced budgets would have to be forsaken; an economy mired in a prolonged depression needs the stimulative effect of deficit spending.

In December 1936, Keynes published *The General Theory of Employment, Interest and Money*. Though the initial reaction was mixed, in time Keynesian economics became the new ruling orthodoxy. In the United States, Alvin Hansen, a professor of economics at Harvard University, became the leading proponent of Keynesian economics in the United States. While originally skeptical, he drew heavily on Keynesian ideas in the development of his theory of secular stagnation, which contended that the American economy would likely remain in a permanent state of underemployment. Under Hansen's guidance, a new generation of young, bright academic economists, including Paul Samuelson, James Tobin and Robert Solow, was won over to Keynesian economics. Their influence would be keenly felt in the 1960s.

By 1944 real output in the American economy stood 70 percent above that for 1939. By 1943 the unemployment rate was 1.9 percent; in 1944 it was 1.2 percent. In each year 1943 through 1945, government spending soared, the national debt ballooned, and the federal deficit was well in excess of $50 billion. This did not go unnoticed by politicians, policymakers and average citizens. To many it confirmed Keynesian theory. As the war concluded, many economists were fearful that the stagnation of the 1930s would return. Proposals to make the income tax more progressive, increase spending on public works, and expand social security benefits were aimed at boosting aggregate demand. The dire predictions did not come to pass; the savings of American households had piled up during the war years, during which spending on consumer durables had been deferred. At war's end, new household formations surged and Americans went on a spending spree. Distracted by the jubilation that accompanied the Allied victory and reassured by the booming economy, the public showed little interest in the debate over measures to assure continued economic growth and high employment.

When the Full Employment Bill of 1945, with compensatory finance based on the Keynesian framework as one of its guiding principles, was introduced in Congress, it was vigorously opposed by nearly all major business groups. What ultimately gained passage was the Employment Act of 1946, a watered down version of the original bill with the reference to full employment stripped from its name. Instead, its stated purpose was to "promote maximum employment, production, and purchasing power." It also called for the establishment of a Council of Economic Advisers (CEA) within the executive branch to advise the President on economic matters, and required the annual submission of the Economic Report of the President to the Congress. This seemed a very small advance for the cause of activist macroeconomic management. Only with time would the CEA and the Economic Report of the President take on some importance. But the Act did codify into law what was already a recognized fact of political life: the government, specifically the President, was held responsible for the performance of the economy. The age of Keynes was off to a modest beginning.

The 1933–1945 period poses a host of questions. Did the long interregnum between November 1932 and March 1933 serve to intensify uncertainty and deepen the depression? Is there any sense in which the New Deal can be viewed as Keynesian? Was FDR a Keynesian? In terms of promoting recovery, is there any validity to the claim that on balance the New Deal was counterproductive? What got the recovery started? Was it New Deal spending programs? Or was it the shift to greater monetary expansion? Why was the recovery by 1940 still only partial? Did Keynesian-style compensatory fiscal policy simply not work? Or was it never seriously attempted, making its failure more apparent than real? To what extent was the stimulative effect of deficit spending at the federal level offset by the budget surpluses generated by state and local governments? Was it America's entry into World War II that finally restored full employment? Did the performance of the economy during World War II convince politicians and policymakers of the power of Keynesian economics? Has the postwar experience confirmed or contradicted the claims of Keynes and Hansen that mature economies are prone to stagnation? The readings that follow will help in addressing these questions.

DOCUMENTS

The seven documents below are in chronological order, and offer a glimpse of the views of some of the major figures of the period including Tugwell, Roosevelt, Keynes and Hansen. Since the documents span the years 1933 to 1944, they also show the evolution in thought that took place.

The opening document, Document 9–1, is excerpted from an address, "The Economics of the Recovery Program," delivered by Rexford G. Tugwell on November 16, 1933 before the Institute of Arts and Sciences at Columbia University, where he had been a member of the faculty. Tugwell was a key figure in Roosevelt's Brain Trust, one of the principal architects of the first New Deal, and served in several capacities in the Department of Agriculture, most notably as head of the Rural Resettlement Administration. In his address, Tugwell assails the idea that the economic system remains nearly perfectly competitive, and is capable of correcting itself. He claims that the nation had tired of waiting for the recovery to occur on its own, and had demanded a change in policy direction even if this meant violating some long cherished attachments to the principles of laissez-faire. He draws a distinction between the problems besetting agriculture and those in industry. Agriculture has flexible prices and fixed production; industry has rigid prices and flexible production. Farmers needed to restrict their output in the face of declining prices; industry needed more price flexibility to assure that economic downturns would not mean production cuts and unemployment. Presumably the provisions of the Agricultural Adjustment Act and the National Industrial Recovery Act (Tugwell contributed to the design of both acts) attempted to confront these problems. Price rigidity is a familiar theme in New Deal discourse, and was often cited as evidence of a permanent change in the American economy. Tugwell ends his address by warning that with the days of laissez-faire long gone objections to intervention in the economy by government will have a hollow ring. He also takes American universities to task for teaching a political economy that no longer exists.

Document 9–2 is selections from FDR's sixth fireside chat, given on September 30, 1934. In his talk, Roosevelt reviews what he sees as the accomplishments of his still young administration: reform of the banking system, legislation to control the securities industry, and the promotion of recovery through the NRA codes. He promises a review of the NRA codes, largely written by industry, to assure that the public interest is protected. He expresses his regret that labor-management relations have been poor, and hopes to take action to limit work stoppages in the future. Roosevelt believes his program of public works will prevent the emergence of "a permanent army of unemployed." He closes by stating his conviction that his approach offers a middle course between complete state control of business and the laissez-faire that he believes has failed.

Document 9–3 is a magazine article, "Can America Spend Its Way into Recovery?" Written by John Maynard Keynes, it appeared in *Redbook* in December 1934. In the same issue of this popular magazine, Harold Laski, famed political theorist and economist at the London School of Economics, addressed the same question and delivered an answer in the negative. Keynes answered in the affirmative. He argues that if private spending is not sufficient to assure a high level of employment then government must do the necessary spending. He explains the multiplier effect by describing the successive rounds of respending that will occur as a result of the initial injection of government spending. While some kind of socially useful spending may be preferred, spending of any sort would be better than nothing. Keynes notes that deficit spending is not to be feared in a deeply depressed economy, equating public debt to "owing money to one's self." He reminds his readers that with recovery, government support of the unemployed will be reduced while tax receipts increase; those who oppose government spending during a depression postpone the day when the nation's budget will be restored to balance.

Portions of the *Twenty-Seventh Annual Report of the Secretary of Commerce*, published in December 1939, are presented as Document 9–4. It is authored, at least nominally, by Harry Hopkins. He was a fixture in the executive branch throughout the entire Roosevelt presidency and served as Secretary of Commerce from 1938 to 1940. The report provides a detailed recounting of the economic experience of 1929–1939. The collapse of 1929–1933 and the years of recovery 1933–1936 are reviewed. The account of the 1937–1938 recession makes for interesting reading. In this report it is noted that federal expenditures were expanded in 1936. On the strength of these spending increases, economic activity advanced, leading business to expand inventories. This was then followed by a drastic curtailment of federal expenditures; inventory proved to be excessive, new orders fell off, production was cut, and the sharp recession resulted. For Hopkins a major lesson learned in the 1937–1938 downturn is to avoid "abrupt modification" of fiscal policy. He closes on an optimistic note by rejecting secular stagnation as the inevitable fate of the American economy. This may indicate that by 1939 a shift in thinking within the Roosevelt administration had taken place given that early on in FDR's first term many New Dealers had accepted the idea that the American economy had slipped into a chronic state of underemployment.

Excerpts from "Fiscal Policy in the Recovery," Chapter IV in Alvin H. Hansen's *Fiscal Policy and Business Cycles*, published in 1941, are given in Document 9–5. Hansen was a noted professor of economics at Harvard and by 1941 ardently espoused the Keynesian approach.

The recovery program of the Roosevelt administration from 1933 to 1935 is described as a salvaging operation rather than a true expansionist program. The federal government was not consciously trying to stimulate the economy but rather to relieve the distress of parties affected by the depression: the unemployed, farmers, banks, railroads, and state and local governments. While federal expenditures on public works did help make up for cutbacks at the state and local levels, the public works expenditures of the three levels of government taken collectively "made no positive contribution…toward recovery." At just the federal level, and taking all expenditures and tax receipts into account, the federal government did provide a net stimulus to economic activity, though not sufficient to restore full employment. Hansen explains why he believes expenditures on public works are more stimulative than those on relief. He states that vigorous action early in a depression is vital to avoid the deflation and disinvestment witnessed in 1930 and 1931.

Document 9–6 is a speech by Beardsley Ruml who had a varied and full career as a statistician, an educator, and a longtime business executive with R.H. Macy and Company, rising to be its chair in 1945. During the war, the NBC radio network sponsored a program called "For This We Fight," which offered businessmen the opportunity to express their views on problems and issues expected to arise in the postwar period. Ruml appeared on the program on November 15, 1943. At the time of his speech, he was also serving as chair of the New York Federal Reserve Bank. To assure postwar prosperity he says that government should be prepared to step in with a program of compensatory fiscal policy if business activity should falter. He seems remarkably in touch with some of the subtleties of the policy; he mentions that the federal budget need only be balanced over the course of the business cycle and that tax cuts can be made as stimulative as government spending. Ruml sounds very modern in alluding to what would be called today automatic stabilizers and structural deficits. Notable by its absence is any mention of monetary policy, which had fallen out of favor during the Great Depression.

In Document 9–7 are selections from FDR's State of the Union Address delivered on January 11, 1944 as his twenty-eighth fireside chat. Sick with the flu, President Roosevelt was under his physician's orders not to make the trip up to the Capitol. So he spoke to the nation from the White House. Much of this speech is devoted to a discussion of the prosecution of the war. On the home front, Roosevelt urged Congressional passage of bills to tax unreasonable profits, renew price controls, and institute a program of national service for all defense workers for the duration of the war. He unveiled his economic bill of rights and made clear that he would press the Congress to take action on it. His bill of rights declared all men and women entitled to a useful job, adequate provision of the necessities of life, freedom from unfair competition, a decent home, adequate medical care, and a good education. In fairly strong language, Roosevelt warned that if the nation "were to return to the so-called 'normalcy' of the 1920s, then…we shall have yielded to the spirit of fascism here at home." While the war distracted him from his domestic goals, this speech shows that with growing confidence in a successful outcome to the war he had returned to his economic agenda.

9–1. REXFORD G. TUGWELL, *THE BATTLE FOR DEMOCRACY*: CHAPTER XI— THE ECONOMICS OF THE RECOVERY PROGRAM

In the midst of the cross currents of activity in Washington, it is necessary from time to time to stand apart and recall the general outline of the program which is expressing itself in a day-to-day detailed activity. Only as it is considered as a whole will the apparent paradoxes be reconciled and the total effort be comprehended.

The general objective is clear and easily stated—to restore a workable exchangeability among the separate parts of our economic machine and to set it to functioning again; and beyond this to perfect arrangements which may prevent its future disorganization. This means that we must insure adequate income to the farmers, adequate wages to the workers, an adequate return to useful capital, and an adequate remuneration to management. What we want, really, is to provide the opportunity for every individual and every group to work and to be able to consume the product of others' work. This involves a creation of buying power which is coordinate with the creation of goods. We shall not rest nor be diverted to lesser things until that minimum is achieved.

But to outline an objective in such broad terms does not take us far in understanding specific undertakings. What constitutes a workable relationship among income to farmers, wages to workers, and a return to useful capital? Here is a question which we can answer only when we have considered why they are now inadequate. That they are less than our productive capacity entitles us to, there can be no doubt. Consider what our economic machine could have produced if it had been working in the last four years at the same rate as in 1928 and 1929. If all the labor and equipment which have been idle during the depression could have been converted into houses, every second family in the country could have had a brand new $5,000 house; or we could have scrapped the whole American railroad system and rebuilt it three times over. Such is the waste of the last four years; the waste caused by the failure of the economic machine to function properly, a failure to produce and distribute, which makes inadequate the income of nearly every group in the community. So long as the economic machine fails to operate at its potential capacity the income of each group will continue to be insufficient. So long as our economy provides vastly less to each group in the community than our resources in men and materials make possible, the incomes of everyone will be inadequate.

Consider the reaction of the country to the first three years of depression. Down and down went the curves of business activity. Longer and longer grew the lines of idle workers and the rows of idle machines. The whole constituted a challenge to the American people to act *as a body,* to remedy a ridiculous situation which had developed out of their *acting separately.*

Why was this challenge to American intelligence and action not met in the first three years of depression? We have grown up in a tradition which says that if economic forces are let alone all will come out right in the end. In the past we have regarded social interference in the interest of economic continuity as highly improper. This supremely crucial function we abandoned to private initiative, operating through the price system and controlled by competition.

Such a system had worked in the past—haltingly and after a fashion. In the first year of the depression there may have been justification for waiting for recovery in the interest of protecting this principle. In the second year, was there justification? In the third year, with more than a quarter of our working population out of work and agricultural income reduced to a third its former size, had not the time come for positive action by the community as a body instead of by individuals alone?

A year ago the people of this country voted on precisely this question. And with an overwhelming majority they chose a President with a mandate for positive action; and he assumed his delegated duty with a gallantry which the whole nation unmistakably approved. The change involved in this was of major importance in the development of this country. It meant a shift from laissez faire to positive effort. It implied an effort by the community through its government to restore exchangeability by positive action. It placed directly on the shoulders of the new administration the responsibility for bringing about recovery from one of the deepest depressions this country has ever known.

The immediate reasons for this popular demand for positive action are clear. The terrific waste of depression, the hardships suffered by individuals through no fault of their own, the failure of business leadership to cope with the forces of depression, these all led to the insistent demand for change, a demand which would respect no allegiance to theory or preconceptions. How this demand was to be carried out, what action was to be undertaken, was not clear; but a policy of laissez faire was no longer to be countenanced.

What positive measures could be undertaken? Preliminary to their understanding is an assessment of the underlying developments which led to this general demand for governmental activity. This takes us directly into economic analysis. Those people who have so extravagantly praised the beauties of laissez faire have always done so on the assumption of highly flexible prices and a degree of freedom in competition. Actually the breakdown came at a time when our economy was a spotted reality of competition and control—with the control entrusted to irresponsible trustees. In 1929 we did not have a system of free competition and flexible prices. True, in some areas, like farming, we have had highly flexible prices and a considerable number of individuals actively competing in both production and price. If prices throughout our economy had been as flexible as those in the farm area were, it is quite possible that the 1929 depression would have been of minor consequence. The truth was, however, that an important part of our economy had prices which were not responsive—as theoretically they should have been—to changes in supply or demand. At the furthest extreme are railroad and public-utility rates, steel rails and many other goods and services whose prices were fixed over very considerable periods of time. In such occupations and areas, the whole impact of changes in demand are taken in the form of changes in production without any changes in price.

Intermediate between the extremes of flexible price and fixed price, lies most of industry. In this area prices are fixed for shorter periods of time but are periodically revised over longer periods of time. Thus, in varying degrees, changes in demand are met by changes in production, and more slowly and over a longer time only, by changes in price.

This matter of temporary or more permanently fixed prices is vitally important. This fixity is a major disturbing influence in a system which is theoretically competitive. Consider a concrete case—the production of automobiles. The manufacturer of cars will set a wholesale price on his cars at the beginning of the season. Presumably he will set a price which he expects will sell as many cars in the year as will make his total profits at that price as large as possible. Once the price is set, any drop in demand for cars will result, not in a drop in price, but in a drop in production. Men will be discharged and machines will become idle. Because of lessening employment and lessening incomes, there is likely to be a further drop in demand for cars. If this condition were typical of all industry the resulting condition would be one which we describe as depression. It is, of course, true that once or twice a year the prices of cars will be revised. But in the intermediate periods, prices are fixed, and changing demand is reflected only in changing production, with a direct effect on the income of consumers. It is this fact which is of major significance. It is this price inflexibility which causes an initial drop in demand to induce unemployment. In this manner, the rigidity of some prices and the flexibility of others tends to make production in our system unstable, deranging the balance between prices and production in different fields. We have a choice, if the situation is to be remedied, of really restoring competition or of extending the areas of rigidity until they include all prices of real social consequence.

Notice how differently the depression has affected different parts of our economy. In the agricultural area, in which prices are highly flexible, the drop in effective demand during the depression has caused a great drop in prices, while production has declined little. The farmers are working as hard as ever, but they get less for their product. Throughout most of industry, the effect of the depression has been essentially different. Prices have dropped relatively little compared to the drop in agricultural prices. The fall in demand has been met for the most part by reduced production. The income of the workers as a body has dropped as rapidly as that of the farm group, not primarily because wages were lower (though that has been important), but because of being out of employment. Thus, while the cash incomes of farmers as a body and of wage workers as a body have fallen off to an almost equal degree, one has fallen because of a fall in prices and the other because of a fall in production.

This difference in the effect of the depression in agriculture and in industry is of great importance because it suggests that quite different methods for restoring balance must be applied in the different fields. Restoration of balance would require a lowering of production and a lifting of prices in agriculture, but a lifting of production and in some cases even a lowering of prices in industry.

This difference in the effect of the depression on prices and on production is of vital importance. It is the key to many of the apparent conflicts between the agricultural and the industrial programs. Even for different industries the relative effect on prices and on production has been different; some with fatally flexible prices and maintained production, others with rigid prices and flexible production. Perhaps the picture of the depression is best portrayed by thinking of all the different economic activities distributed along a scale according to the amenability of prices to change. As has been suggested, most agricultural activities and certain industries are at one end of the scale and at the other extreme are certain more or less monopolized trades. Between these extremes are ranged the bulk of industry. If we think of the prices and production of different commodities as having been roughly in balance in 1926, the effect of the depression was to reduce prices at the flexible end of the scale and to maintain production there, while at the other end prices were being maintained and production was dropping.

To restore exchangeability in such a situation we can do one of two things: we can lift the flexible prices to the level of the rigid ones, and simultaneously increase production in the fixed-price areas; or we can reduce the rigid prices to the level of the flexible ones, and reduce production in the flexible-price areas.

The advantages of the first path toward the restoration of exchangeability are clear; and it is this path which has been taken by the administration. The major advantage of lifting prices—of lifting most those which have fallen most and lifting not at all those which have not fallen—grows out of the burden of debt created at the old price level. To lower all prices to the level of those which had fallen most would be to overburden the debtors in the country and to endanger the solvency of our many great debtor institutions. Elementary justice thus required a lifting of the flexible prices to parity with the prices which had not dropped, rather than the more difficult course of revising downward those which had remained fixed.

Here, then, is the more immediate objective of recovery: to raise prices in the area of flexibility, to raise production in the area of rigidity, and raise both prices and production in the intermediate areas of industry until all groups attain the ready exchangeability which they once had.

The methods being employed in raising farm prices are foretold. It is well recognized by economists that in the area in which prices are highly flexible, as in agriculture, it is possible to raise prices only by reducing supply or by increasing demand. The total recovery program involves both, though the A.A.A. program, taken alone, involves mostly a reduction in production. ...

When we come to the industrial sector of the recovery program, the immediate objectives are almost exactly the reverse of those in the agricultural sector. The main problem is, in some industries, to raise volume of production and volume of pay rolls without increasing price; in other industries, to raise volume of production and volume of wages with an increase in price but not an increase at all commensurate with the increase in the price of agricultural products.

At first thought you will ask how the wage bill can be increased by an industry without increasing the prices charged. This is the very crux of the recovery program. It was by reducing production and wages in some industries, without a corresponding drop in prices, that we destroyed exchangeability. To restore it the process must be reversed. In many industries the declining volume of production in the last three years has increased overhead costs per unit of product. In order to meet this increasing cost, the industrialists have, on the one hand, maintained prices at nearly their former level, and, on the other hand, have reduced wage rates and employment. In this way they shifted the burden of reduction to the workers, brought on unemployment and destroyed purchasing power. ...

The success or failure of these will not jeopardize the whole. The success or failure of the three great branches of the program—reducing production and raising prices to the farmer, increasing production and raising wages to the industrial worker faster than industrial prices are raised, and the putting into circulation of a new flow of buying power—these are the central core of the recovery drive conceived to be undertaken by the community as a whole. It is, I believe, adequate. It is in many ways unorthodox. It runs counter to the accepted notions of the doctrinaire—convinced believers in laissez faire like it no better than communists. It is tentative, but still carefully hammered out of the iron of reality. We believe it to be the instrument of our present salvation; but we believe in no part of it so fanatically that we are unwilling to change. And this, of course, is the reason for proceeding through permissive powers with a calculated avoidance of any commitment whatever to doctrine.

The sheer hard economics of the situation in which we find ourselves makes certain demands on human nature from which recoil is natural. Sacrifice is demanded. Promise is also offered, of course, but the sacrifice seems much easier to concentrate on than the promise; and those who are squeezed give themselves whole-heartedly to opposition. All the old shibboleths, behind which vested interests have always hidden, are trotted out to do their stuff. The noise is tremendous and all the faint-hearted are quickly intimidated. To pursue a considered program in the midst of this welter of recrimination and special pleading is the task to which we have now to give ourselves.

The center of the present storm is in the economic field. It is natural that economists should be our greatest dependence for guidance as well as for skillful administration. This university and others have not finished their task by thinning the existing ranks and making temporary loans to government. The end of the demand is not in sight; perhaps it never will be. Perhaps it must be assumed as a regular burden from now on. This requires, of course, a return from economics to political economy as the needed discipline. Economics belonged to laissez faire; the world has turned its back on that. The danger is that universities may not find it out, but may continue to turn over and over the sterile dust of free-competitive principles. Men trained in this kind of thinking are handicapped now; it is the greatest single difficulty with economists in government that they can think only of ways to emasculate the government in its dealings with economic phenomena, because they carry in their heads a formula of noninterference. Political economists are what is needed, men not ridden by preconceptions, careful analysts who recognize logical needs and dare to follow them across their concepts to conclusions in simple operating arrangements, even if this requires the government to do novel things. I say this because for a long time I have been saying it and the event has proved the necessity. Some important part of the effort of our universities has gone to stuffing students with preconceptions which are shattered the moment they meet the economic realities of everyday life. The departments of political economy in our universities are not yet conceiving their problem in the terms to which they must ultimately come—or else go the way of the academic classics with which they really belong.

The most grudging consent to our recovery program comes from these departments of economics; they appear to have forgotten how little they liked the logical alternative when they were living with it a year ago. Seemingly they would rather have us fail than to succeed in unorthodox ways. People who find themselves in such a frame of mind belong with the Bourbons, the Malthusians and other historical die-hards after whom deluges have come.

It is quite impossible to predict the shape our newly invented economic institutions may take in the future. That seems to me, in any case, unimportant. What is important is that we have undertaken a venture which is theoretically new in the sense that it calls for control rather than drift. In the years to come much ingenuity will be needed in the effort to isolate and strengthen the nerve centers of industrial civilization. We have yet to discover in determinate fashion what efforts are naturally those of common service, and so require a high degree of socialization, and what ones can safely be left to relatively free individual or group contrivance. We are turning away from the entrusting of crucial decisions, and the operation of institutions whose social consequences are their most characteristic feature, to individuals who are motivated by private interests. It will take a long time to learn how this may be done effectively. But the longest step toward its accomplishment was taken when the new and untrod path was entered on. It is my earnest hope that the university which has been my home during so many active years, and from whose encouragement I and others have drawn strength, may enter on these tasks with courage and determination. The link between this institution and that one which I am at the moment serving in Washington is a natural one. The university is a place for learning and for renewal. It is the source on which government must depend for inspiration, for criticism, for expert service; the source, also, of that political economy out of which the new industrial state must be forged.

9–2. FRANKLIN DELANO ROOSEVELT, SEPTEMBER 30, 1934, "FIRESIDE CHAT"

...Recently the most notable public questions that have concerned us all have had to do with industry and labor and with respect to these, certain developments have taken place which I consider of importance. I am happy to report that after years of uncertainty, culminating in the collapse of the spring of 1933, we are bringing order out of the old chaos with a greater certainty of the employment of labor at a reasonable wage and of more business at a fair profit. These governmental and industrial developments hold promise of new achievements for the nation.

Men may differ as to the particular form of governmental activity with respect to industry and business, but nearly all are agreed that private enterprise in times such as these cannot be left without assistance and without reasonable safeguards lest it destroy not only itself but also our processes of civilization: The underlying necessity for such activity is indeed as strong now as it was years ago when Elihu Root said the following very significant words:

> Instead of the give and take of free individual contract, the tremendous power of organization has combined great aggregations of capital in enormous industrial establishments working through

vast agencies of commerce and employing great masses of men in movements of production and transportation and trade, so great in the mass that each individual concerned in them is quite helpless by himself. The relations between the employer and the employed, between the owners of aggregated capital and the units of organized labor, between the small producer, the small trader, the consumer, and the great transporting and manufacturing and distributing agencies, all present new questions for the solution of which the old reliance upon the free action of individual wills appear quite inadequate. And in many directions, the intervention of that organized control which we call government seems necessary to produce the same result of justice and right conduct which obtained through the attrition of individuals before the new conditions arose.

It was in this spirit thus described by Secretary Root that we approached our task of reviving private enterprise in March, 1933. Our first problem was, of course, the banking situation because, as you know, the banks had collapsed. Some banks could not be saved but the great majority of them, either through their own resources or with government aid, have been restored to complete public confidence. This has given safety to millions of depositors in these banks. Closely following this great constructive effort we have, through various Federal agencies, saved debtors and creditors alike in many other fields of enterprise, such as loans on farm mortgages and home mortgages, loans to the railroads and insurance companies and, finally, help for home owners and industry itself. In all of these efforts the government has come to the assistance of business and with the full expectation that the money used to assist these enterprises will eventually be repaid. I believe it will be.

The second step we have taken in the restoration of normal business enterprise has been to clean up thoroughly unwholesome conditions in the field of investment. In this we have had assistance from many bankers and businessmen, most of whom recognize the past evils in the banking system, in the sale of securities, in the deliberate encouragement of stock gambling, in the sale of unsound mortgages and in many other ways in which the public lost billions of dollars. They saw that without changes in the policies and methods of investment there could be no recovery of public confidence in the security of savings. The country now enjoys the safety of bank savings under the new banking laws, the careful checking of new securities under the Securities Act and the curtailment of bank stock speculation through the Securities Exchange Act. I sincerely hope that as a result people will be discouraged in unhappy efforts to get rich quick by speculating in securities. The average person almost always loses. Only a very small minority of the people of this country believe in gambling as a substitute for the old philosophy of Benjamin Franklin that the way to wealth is through work.

In meeting the problems of industrial recovery the chief agency of the government has been the National Recovery Administration. Under its guidance, trades and industries covering over ninety percent of all industrial employees have adopted codes of fair competition, which have been approved by the President. Under these codes, in the industries covered, child labor has been eliminated. The work day and the work week have been shortened. Minimum wages have been established and other wages adjusted toward a rising standard of living. The emergency purpose of the N.R.A. was to put men to work and since its creation more than four million persons have been re-employed, in great part through the cooperation of American business brought about under the codes.

Benefits of the industrial Recovery Program have come, not only to labor in the form of new jobs, in relief from over-work and in relief from under-pay, but also to the owners and managers of industry because, together with a great increase in the payrolls, there has come a substantial rise in the total of industrial profits—a rise from a deficit figure in the first quarter of 1933 to a level of sustained profits within one year from the inauguration of the N.R.A.

Now it should not be expected that even employed labor and capital would be completely satisfied with present conditions. Employed workers have not by any means all enjoyed a return to the earnings of prosperous times; although millions of hitherto under-privileged workers are today far better paid than ever before. Also, billions of dollars of invested capital have today a greater security of present and future earning power than before. This is because of the establishment of fair, competitive standards and because of relief from unfair competition in wage cutting which depresses markets and destroys purchasing power. But it is an undeniable fact that the restoration of other billions of sound investments to a reasonable earning power could not be brought about in one year. There is no magic formula, no economic panacea, which could simply revive over-night the heavy industries and the trades dependent upon them.

Nevertheless the gains of trade and industry, as a whole, have been substantial. In these gains and in the policies of the Administration there are assurances that hearten all forward-looking men and women with the confidence that we are definitely rebuilding our political and economic system on the lines laid down by the New Deal—lines which as I have so often made clear, are in complete accord with the underlying principles of orderly popular government which Americans have demanded since the white man first came to these shores. We count, in the future as in the past, on the driving power of individual initiative and the incentive of fair private profit, strengthened with the acceptance of those obligations to the public interest which rest upon us all. We have the right to expect that this driving power will be given patriotically and whole-heartedly to our nation.

We have passed through the formative period of code making in the National Recovery Administration and have effected a reorganization of the N.R.A. suited to the needs of the next phase, which is, in turn, a period of preparation for legislation which will determine its permanent form. ...

Let me call your attention to the fact that the National Industrial Recovery Act gave businessmen the opportunity they had sought for years to improve business conditions through what has been called self-government in industry. If the codes which have been written have been too complicated, if they have gone too far in such matters as price fixing and limitation of production, let it be remembered that so far as possible, consistent with the immediate public interest of this past year and the vital necessity of improving labor conditions, the representatives of trade and industry were permitted to write their ideas into the codes. It is now time to review these actions as a whole to determine through deliberative means in the light of experience, from the standpoint of the good of the industries themselves, as well as the general public interest, whether the methods and policies adopted in the emergency have been best calculated to promote industrial recovery and permanent improvement of business and labor conditions. There may be serious question as to the wisdom of many of those devices to control production, or to prevent destructive price cutting which many business organizations have insisted were necessary, or whether their effect may have been to prevent that volume of production which would make possible lower prices and increased employment. Another question arises as to whether in fixing minimum wages on the basis of an hourly or weekly wage we have reached into the heart of the problem which is to provide such annual earnings for the lowest paid worker as will meet his minimum needs. We also question the wisdom of extending code requirements suited to the great industrial centers and to large employers, to the great number of small employers in the smaller communities.

During the last twelve months our industrial recovery has been to some extent retarded by strikes, including a few of major importance. I would not minimize the inevitable losses to employers and employees and to the general public through such conflicts. But I would point out that the extent and severity of labor disputes during this period has been far less than in any previous, comparable period.

When the businessmen of the country were demanding the right to organize themselves adequately to promote their legitimate interests; when the farmers were demanding legislation which would give them opportunities and incentives to organize themselves for a common advance, it was natural that the workers should seek and obtain a statutory declaration of their constitutional right to organize themselves for collective bargaining as embodied in Section 7 (a) of the National Industrial Recovery Act.

Machinery set up by the Federal government has provided some new methods of adjustment. Both employers and employees must share the blame of not using them as fully as they should. The employer who turns away from impartial agencies of peace, who denies freedom of organization to his employees, or fails to make every reasonable effort at a peaceful solution of their differences, is not fully supporting the recovery effort of his government. The workers who turn away from these same impartial agencies and decline to use their good offices to gain their ends are likewise not fully cooperating with their government.

It is time that we made a clean-cut effort to bring about that united action of management and labor, which is one of the high purposes of the Recovery Act. We have passed through more than a year of education. Step by step we have created all the government agencies necessary to insure, as a general rule, industrial peace with justice for all those willing to use these agencies whenever their voluntary bargaining fails to produce a necessary agreement.

There should be at least a full and fair trial given to these means of ending industrial warfare; and in such an effort we should be able to secure for employers and employees and consumers the benefits that all derive from the continuous, peaceful operation of our essential enterprises.

...Closely allied to the N. R. A. is the program of Public Works provided for in the same Act and designed to put more men back to work, both directly on the public works themselves, and indirectly in the industries supplying the materials for these public works.

To those who say that our expenditures for Public Works and other means for recovery are a waste that we cannot afford, I answer that no country, however rich, can afford the waste of its human resources. Demoralization caused by vast unemployment is our greatest extravagance. Morally, it is the greatest menace to our social order. Some people try to tell me that we must make up our minds that for the future we shall permanently have millions of unemployed just as other countries have had them for over a decade. What may be necessary for those countries is not my responsibility to determine. But as for this country, I stand or fall by my refusal to accept as a necessary condition of our future a permanent army of unemployed. On the contrary, we must make it a national principle that we will not tolerate a large army of unemployed and that we will arrange our national economy to end our present unemployment as soon as we can and then to take wise measures against its return. I do not want to think that it is the destiny of any American to remain permanently on relief rolls.

...Nearly all Americans are sensible and calm people. We do not get greatly excited nor is our peace of mind disturbed, whether we be businessmen or workers or farmers, by awesome pronouncements concerning the unconstitutionality of some of our measures of recovery and relief and reform. We are not frightened by reactionary lawyers or political editors. All of these cries have been heard before. More than twenty years ago, when Theodore Roosevelt and Woodrow Wilson were attempting to correct abuses in our national life, the great Chief Justice White said:

There is great danger it seems to me to arise from the constant habit which prevails where anything is opposed or objected to, of referring without rhyme or reason to the Constitution as a means of preventing its accomplishment, thus creating the general impression that the Constitution is but a barrier to progress instead of being the broad highway through which alone true progress may be enjoyed.

In our efforts for recovery we have avoided on the one hand the theory that business should and must be taken over into an all-embracing Government. We have avoided on the other hand the equally untenable theory that it is an interference with liberty to offer reasonable help when private enterprise is in need of help. The course we have followed fits the American practice of Government—a practice of taking action step by step, of regulating only to meet concrete needs—a practice of courageous recognition of change. I believe with Abraham Lincoln, that "The legitimate object of Government is to do for a community of people whatever they need to have done but cannot do at all or cannot do so well for themselves in their separate and individual capacities."

I still believe in ideals. I am not for a return to that definition of Liberty under which for many years a free people were being gradually regimented into the service of the privileged few. I prefer and I am sure you prefer that broader definition of Liberty under which we are moving forward to greater freedom, to greater security for the average man than he has ever known before in the history of America.

9–3. JOHN MAYNARD KEYNES, "CAN AMERICA SPEND ITS WAY INTO RECOVERY?"

Why, obviously! —is my first reflection when I am faced by this question. No one of common sense could doubt it, unless his mind had first been muddled by a 'sound' financier or an 'orthodox' economist. We produce in order to sell. In other words, we produce in response to spending. It is impossible to suppose that we can stimulate production and employment by *refraining* from spending. So, as I have said, the answer is obvious.

But at a second glance, I can see that the question has been so worded as to inspire an insidious doubt. For spending means extravagance. A man who is extravagant soon makes himself poor. How, then, can a nation become rich by doing what must impoverish an individual? By this thought the public is bewildered. Yet a course of behaviour which might make a single individual poor *can* make a nation wealthy.

For when an individual spends, he affects not only himself but others. Spending is a two-sided transaction. If I spend my income on buying something which you can make for me, I have not increased my own income, but I have increased yours. If you respond by buying something which I can make for you, then my income also is increased. Thus, when we are thinking of the nation as a whole, we must take account of the results as a whole. The rest of the community is enriched by an individual's expenditure—for his expenditure is simply an addition to everyone else's income. If everybody spends more freely, everybody is richer and nobody is poorer. Each man benefits from the expenditure of his neighbour, and incomes are increased by just the amount required to provide the wherewithal for the additional expenditure. There is only one limit to the extent to which a nation's income can be increased in this manner, and that is the limit set by the physical capacity to produce. To refrain from spending at a time of depression, not only fails, from the national point of view, to add to wealth—it is profligate: it means waste of available man-power, and waste of available machine power, quite apart from the human misery for which it is responsible. The nation is simply a collection of individuals. If for any reason the individuals who comprise the nation are unwilling, each in his private capacity, to spend sufficient to employ the resources with which the nation is endowed, then it is for the government, the collective representative of all the individuals in the nation, to fill the gap. For the effects of government expenditure are precisely the same as the effects of individual expenditure, and it is the increase in the income of the public which provides the source of the extra government expenditure.

It may sometimes be advantageous for a government to resort for part of its borrowing to the banking system rather than to the public. That makes no difference of principle to the effects of the expenditure. There are many who will raise the horror-struck cry of 'Inflation!' when borrowing from the banks is suggested. I doubt if any of those who speak in this way have a clear idea what they mean by inflation. Expenditure is either beneficial or it is harmful. I say it is beneficial, but whether I am right or wrong, it is hard to see how the effect can be altered if the money spent by the government comes from the banks rather than from the public.

When the government borrows in order to spend, it undoubtedly gets the nation into debt. But the debt of a nation to its own citizens is a very different thing from the debt of a private individual. The nation *is* the citizens who comprise it—no more and no less—and to owe money to them is not very different from owing money to one's self. Insofar as taxes are necessary to shift the interest payments out of one pocket and into the other, this is certainly a disadvantage; but it is a small matter compared with the importance of restoring normal conditions of prosperity. If private individuals refuse to spend, then the government must do it for them. It might be better if they did it for themselves, but that is no argument for not having it done at all.

It is easy, however, to exaggerate the extent to which the government need get into unproductive debt. Let us take, for purposes of illustration, a government hydro-electric power scheme. The government pays out money, which it borrows, to the men employed on the scheme. But the benefit does not stop there. These men who, previously unemployed, are now drawing wages from the government, spend these wages in providing themselves with the necessaries and comforts of existence— shirts, boots and the like. The makers of these shirts and boots, who were hitherto unemployed, spend their wages in their turn, and so set up a fresh wave of additional employment, of additional production, of additional wages, and of additional purchasing power. And so it goes on, until we find that for each man actually employed on the government scheme, three, or perhaps four, additional men are employed in providing for his needs and for the needs of one another. In this way a given rate of government expenditure will give rise to four or five times as much employment as a crude calculation would suggest. Thus there would be some advantage even if the scheme itself were to yield but little revenue hereafter. If, however, it is even a moderately sound scheme capable of yielding (say) three per cent on its cost, the case for it is overwhelmingly established.

That is not all. Unemployment involves a serious financial strain to the municipal, state, and federal governments. The alleviation of unemployment, as a result of government expenditure, means a considerable reduction in outgoings on the support of the unemployed. At the same time the receipts from taxation mount up as the nation's taxable income increases, and as real property values are re-established. These important factors must be allowed for before it is possible to say how far government expenditure involves additional unproductive government debt. The residue cannot be very large. Depression is itself the cause of government deficits, resulting from increased expenditure on the support of the unemployed and the falling-off in the yield of taxation. Public debt is inevitable at a time when private expenditure is inadequate: it is better to incur it actively in providing employment and promoting industrial activity than to suffer it passively as a consequence of poverty and inactivity.

So far I have been advocating government expenditure without much reference to the purpose to which the money is devoted. The predominant issue, as I look at the matter, is to get the money spent. But productive and socially useful expenditure is naturally to be preferred to unproductive expenditure. The arguments for expenditure are very much strengthened if the government, by spending a small sum of money, can induce private individuals and corporations to spend a much larger sum. Thus a government guarantee to facilitate the building of houses is, perhaps, the best measure of all. The government is here operating under the advantage of very considerable leverage; every dollar which there is any risk of the government having to find under its guarantee means a vastly greater number of dollars spent by private persons. There is no better way by which America can spend itself into prosperity than by spending money on building houses. The need is there waiting to be satisfied; the labour and materials are there waiting to be utilised. It will spread employment through every locality. There is no greater social and economic benefit than good houses. There is probably no greater material contribution to civilisation and a sound and healthy life which it lies within our power to make. The man who regards all this as a senseless extravagance which will impoverish the nation, as compared with doing nothing and leaving millions unemployed, should be recognised for a lunatic.

I stress housing, for this seems to me the happiest of the Administration's schemes. But it is difficult to organise quickly any one type of scheme on a sufficient scale. Meanwhile other forms of government expenditure, not so desirable in themselves, are not to be despised. Even pure relief expenditure is much better than nothing. The object must be to raise the total expenditure to a figure which is high enough to push the vast machine of American industry into renewed motion. If demand can be raised sufficiently by emergency measures, business men will find that they cannot meet it without repairs and renewals to their plant, and they will then once again take heart of grace to recover the care-free optimism without which none of us ever has the courage to live our lives as they should be lived.

9–4. TWENTY-SEVENTH ANNUAL REPORT OF THE SECRETARY OF COMMERCE, DECEMBER 1, 1939

...The past fiscal year brought to a close the most significant decade in the economic history of the United States, and it is in terms of the ... developments characterizing that decade that this Department's functions must be considered.

This 10-year period opened at a time of unparalleled prosperity in the United States, at a time when the disruptions of the early postwar years seemed to lie definitely behind us and a vista of ever expanding national well-being ahead. Within a few months, however, the stock market collapsed, and the prospect of ever-rising activity disappeared as deflation set in and the great depression began.

During the early years of the decade, no decisive attempt was made to use the powers of government to stop the deflation or to correct the underlying conditions. It was generally assumed that if "automatic" economic forces were permitted to take their course, the deflation would come to a "natural end" and the way would be cleared for a return to prosperity.

Persistence in this view of the economy and the policies of government which it implied brought us by 1933 to the brink of economic paralysis. Unemployment increased steadily and reached a total far exceeding the proportions of any previous depression. As the financial structure crumbled, banks failed, mortgages on homes and farms were foreclosed, and millions of thrifty folk lost their life savings. Trade dwindled and factories closed. Local governments were caught between mounting tax delinquency and rising requirements for relief. Between 1929 and 1932, the national income declined by more than 50 percent in money terms and more than 40 percent in terms of goods and services.

Similar conditions in some foreign countries resulted in the sweeping away of the existing forms of government. In this country, the overwhelming demand that the Federal Government make full use of its powers to overcome the depression resulted in the reversal of Government policy at the very moment of final and utter collapse of the financial structure.

A vigorous attack upon the depression was at once undertaken. The banks were reopened. Federal grants were made to the States for unemployment relief. Foreclosures on homes and farms were halted. Agricultural adjustment and industrial recovery programs were launched. The financial structure was permanently strengthened by deposit insurance, reform of the banking system, and by long overdue controls of security issuance and trading. Overnight the downward trend was reversed and marked recovery was felt in every part of the Nation.

The Federal program contained many elements that contributed to this recovery, but the fundamental factor was the increase in buying power that it turned back into the markets for industrial and agricultural products. Income payments increased in all sectors of the economy, but the paralyzing deflation had imposed caution and many preferred the greater liquidity of an enlarged cash or a reduced debt position. As a result, the receipts of business, of State and local governments, and of private individuals exceeded their disbursements. Hence it was not these sectors of the economy that gave impetus to the recovery. It was the Federal Government which, by adding more to the stream of income than it withdrew, made expansion of activity possible in spite of the excess of withdrawals in these other areas of the economy. Moreover, this excess of withdrawals constituted an important and continuing drag on the recovery movement, so that the Federal contribution to buying power, which was designed to provide only the initial impetus to expansion, had to be continued for a longer period than would otherwise have been necessary.

Despite these restrictive influences, employment and production rose until in 1937 they approached the levels attained in 1929. The national income increased from 40 billion dollars in 1932 to 72 billion dollars in 1937. Wages, salaries, profits, and property income participated in the increase. Income from farming, from mining and manufacturing, from distribution and finance all increased as activity surged forward. By 1937 the national income was within 15 percent of its 1929 level. In real terms, that is in terms of the flow of goods and services, it was only a shade below that all-time peak.

Purchases of goods by consumers, which had dropped from 51 billion dollars in 1929 to less than 29 billion dollars in 1932, recovered to 44 billion dollars in 1937. In terms of physical volume, however, the decline had been only about 20 percent and the expansion carried us to within 5 percent of the 1929 high. Sales of automobiles were again at prosperity levels, new passenger-car registrations in 1936 and 1937 being exceeded only by those in 1929. Electrical household equipment, such as refrigerators and vacuum cleaners, topped all previous highs. In short, sales of both durable and nondurable consumers' goods expanded broadly and this high level of consumption constituted the basis of the recovery.

Capital outlays of business also recovered in most lines as part of the general upward movement. In 1937 expenditures for new equipment were greater than in any previous year except 1929. Expenditures for both plant and equipment in mining and manufacturing and in agriculture returned to the high levels of the prosperity years.

Investment tended to lag, however, in a few special areas. In the construction field, high prices and costs were an obstacle to expansion. In the railroad equipment industry, activity failed to recover fully, as the slow process of underreplacement had not yet brought plant and equipment facilities to a level consonant with the reduced volume of railroad traffic. The utilities found their capacity ample for the demand that could be obtained under established rate structures. State and local government preferred reduction of debt to extension of services. Investors remembered the losses of the indiscriminate foreign lending of the 20's, and international developments made foreign countries appear even less attractive as an outlet for their investable funds. In total, these fields, which failed to follow the normal pattern of recovery, did much to keep total investment at a reduced level.

Employment followed the general economic pattern of the period. After the large decline, there was recovery that approached previous peak levels. A fairly large volume of unemployment persisted through the recovery, but this represented primarily the increase in the population of working age and to a lesser extent the residual labor force left without jobs by technological improvements that reduced the number of workers required to produce a given output.

In 1937, the recovery gave promise of wiping out the small margins by which the various measures of economic activity fell short of their previous peaks. It also gave promise of bringing the Federal budget again into balance. The cash deficit was reduced from more than 4,000 million dollars in 1936 to less than 400 million dollars in 1937. With the continuation of recovery, even this small excess outlay would have disappeared.

Just at that moment, however, there ensued the sharpest decline on record. In 5 months, from August to January, the rate of industrial production plunged over 30 percent, and business activity was back at the levels of 3 years earlier. What was responsible for this relapse?

This sharp decline in economic activity appears to have been the outgrowth of a number of factors. From early 1934 until the final quarter of 1936, the Government program yielded a recovery that was both broad and balanced, with prices and costs remaining virtually at a constant level. In the last quarter of 1936, however, a number of dislocations began to develop. Following the bulge in Federal income-creating disbursements that resulted from prepayment of the adjusted service certificates, production and sales moved sharply upward. Prices edged toward higher levels. Certain raw material prices advanced rapidly under the influence of world rearmament and the speculative factors engendered by it. Led on by the upturn in consumer demand and attempting to take advantage of or protect themselves against prospective price increases, businessmen began to expand their inventories.

Other factors also contributed to this inventory movement. In some instances, shortages threatened because of the attrition of capacity and skilled labor during the depression. In others, monopolistic conditions created the prospect of higher prices rather than of larger output and capacity. In addition, the transitional difficulties arising from expanding labor organization and the attempts to resist it resulted in actual or threatened interruptions of production. So rapid was the inventory accumulation that even if businessmen had merely discontinued further accumulation, without attempting to liquidate stocks already accumulated, there would have been a substantial recession.

The rise of prices and costs, besides leading to inventory accumulation, restricted several important types of fixed capital expenditure. Residential construction is a notable example. The cost of both building materials and labor moved up substantially from 1936 levels, despite the relatively small decline in these costs during the depression. While, under the stimulus of lower financing costs and rising consumer income, building subsequently revived without a substantial decline in costs, at that time it was sharply curtailed. Contracts awarded for residential construction declined 33 percent during the year.

Early in 1937, the incentives for further accumulation of inventories began to disappear. The effects upon consumers' expenditures of the reduction in the Federal contribution to the income stream began to be felt. Retail prices in the early part of 1937 continued upward, as did the total value of sales, but the volume of goods moving through the market leveled off and began to decline. The labor difficulties were cleared up in some broad areas and the resumption of activity in these areas served for a time to conceal the vulnerable situation created by the rapid accumulation of inventories and the rise of prices and costs. Finally, however, it became clear that new orders were falling off and that inventories were excessive. The result was inevitable—production was curtailed while the excess was being sold off.

With the Federal contribution to buying power drastically curtailed, moreover, production had to fall far to reach the point at which the desired liquidation could take place. The sharp initial drop was then followed by a continuing gradual decline that again threatened a cumulative deflation such as was experienced in 1929–33. This prospect evoked a vigorous application by the Federal Government of the instruments that had proved their effectiveness before. Results were prompt and striking.

The Federal contribution to buying power was steadily increased beginning in March 1938, and June saw national income on the upturn once more. W. P. A. rolls were expanded, public construction was rapidly brought to a new peak, residential construction was promoted, and payments to farmers were increased. Through the operation of these and other parts of the program, recovery was advanced strongly during the fiscal year 1939. At its close, national income payments were flowing at an annual rate of nearly 69 billion dollars, as compared to a rate of 74 billion dollars in August 1937 and of 65 billion dollars in May 1938. If allowance is made for the decline in prices over this 2-year period, total income in terms of goods and services was again near the 1937 peak.

This recovery was in many respects similar to that of 1933–37. Directly and indirectly, Government policies resulted in outlays that reversed the trend in national income. With total income in the hands of consumers again increasing, businessmen again found their markets expanding, and the general level of activity was stepped up. This rising trend also eliminated any tendency on the part of businessmen to dispose of their inventory holdings. Thus inventories, which had been a large negative factor during the preceding year, became a neutral or perhaps even a small positive factor during the fiscal year 1939.

The Federal Reserve index of nondurable production recovered almost to its previous high, remaining closely in line with increasing sales of nondurable goods. Sales of consumers' durable goods also participated fully in the recovery. Sales of 1939 model-year automobiles were about 30 percent greater than 1938 model-year sales. Sales of ranges, refrigerators, and other appliances also showed very substantial increases. The use of installment credit for these and other items, some of which had not previously been sold on credit, meant the entrance into the market of a large volume of purchasing power that could not have been expected on the basis of current incomes alone. It is estimated that consumer credit increased during the year by one-half to 1 billion dollars. This was especially significant because it constituted a sharp reversal of trend; for in the latter part of the preceding fiscal year, consumer credit had declined by more than a billion dollars.

Construction activity also made large gains during this year. Under the stimulus of Federal Housing Administration action to reduce interest rates and ease monthly payments by home owners, residential construction rose to new postdepression highs by the end of 1938. As a result of the increases in residential and public construction, total construction rose sharply in the latter half of 1938. Contracts awarded showed an average increase in the last quarter of more than 70 percent over the corresponding period in 1937 and were maintained throughout the first half of 1939 at the highest level since 1930.

Capital expenditures and employment also followed the general trend, the restrictions on their full recovery being much the same as before. In a number of special areas, the rate of installation of new productive facilities appears to have remained at fairly low levels, and over the economy as a whole, increases in population of working age and improvements in industrial techniques increased the number of workers unable to find employment. At the close of the fiscal year, however, the trend of business activity and employment was upward.

From the experience of the past decade there emerge certain inescapable conclusions which are of the utmost importance for the national economic policy of both government and business. The foremost lesson of the period is that deflation generates cumulative forces which may completely shatter the productive mechanism. Once deflation dominates the economy, it creates a dozen maladjustments for every one it corrects. The cumulative forces it releases undermine sound and unsound parts alike. They affect ever-widening areas of the economy, until the devastation is general and complete. To prevent these disastrous deflations is a fundamental responsibility of government. The experience of certain European countries bears evidence that unchecked deflation is the greatest threat to democracy in the modern world.

The second conclusion is that the tremendous wastes involved in continued deflation are entirely unnecessary. We have, in recent years, developed the techniques necessary to halt a deflationary process and to secure recovery. This was demonstrated in the 1933–37 recovery. The use of the same techniques to reverse the downward trend in 1938 should dispel any doubts on this score. If the instruments created within this 10-year period are used promptly and aggressively, the country need never again be subjected to the intolerable and unnecessary costs of continued deflation.

In this decade it has also been demonstrated that the complexity of our industrial economy requires great care in the use of these techniques. The sharp bulge in Federal income-creating expenditures in 1936 appears to have been a factor in the development of the dangerous inventory accumulation of that year. Again, the sharp reduction of the Federal net contribution, which came at a time when the economy was particularly vulnerable, played a part in the sharp decline of 1937–38. So powerful are these instruments of the Federal Government that their application requires the most careful and consistent adjustment to economic developments and an avoidance of abrupt modification.

Furthermore, particular attention must be given to certain dislocations which may arise in any rapid recovery, whatever its source may be. The accumulation of inventories and the dislocations in the cost-price structure in the boomlet of 1936–37 illustrate the dangers from this direction. The operation of the economy at a low level of activity entails the impairment of equipment, the depletion of stocks, and the loss of labor skills. Subsequently, under the pressure of a recovery movement, bottlenecks, speculative price and cost movements, and inventory bulges tend to develop. These developments may serve to undermine or reverse any substantial recovery movement, unless Government, business, and labor cooperate to maintain balance in the price and income structure.

A final conclusion emerges from the experience of this decade. In spite of broad recovery, we have not succeeded in making full use of our productive resources. There are some who derive from this experience the conclusion that we have reached the limit of our growth, that our economy is saturated and doomed to stagnation. I vigorously reject this view. It is true that the period of our history in which a rapidly increasing population was opening up a new continent has come to an end. We have extended our boundaries to their geographic limits, built great cities, constructed vast transportation networks, opened up our land to cultivation, and equipped our workers with effective capital larger in total amount and higher per worker than in any other nation. But the disappearance of the geographic frontier does not mean the disappearance of the economic frontier. It is true that world markets under existing conditions of international anarchy beyond our control offer more limited opportunities for the export of our goods and our capital than once was the case. Our home market, on the other hand, is limitless. A rising standard of living can provide an indefinitely expanding market for the fruits of our expanding productive capacity. We have only begun to fulfill the unlimited promise of America.

The vast potential expansion that awaits us in this direction may be illustrated by the fact that in 1935–36 there were more than 12 million families whose incomes were below $1,000 a year. If the incomes of all these families had averaged $1,000 a year, or less than $20 a week, their annual expenditures would have been greater by about 4 billion dollars. They would have spent about 1,300 million dollars more on food alone, about 700 million dollars more on housing, about 400 million dollars more on clothing, and an equal amount more for automobiles and other forms of transportation. Expenditures on fuel, light, gas, and household furnishings would have run 600 million dollars a year higher.

To look at the problem from the point of view of prices rather than income, a vast potential market awaits further progress in the application of mass-production techniques. For example, the residential construction of the past few years has been confined primarily to houses costing over $4,000 and hence to families with incomes over $2,000. This group constitutes less than 20 percent of the total population. Nearly 25 million families have incomes of less than $2,000 a year. A reduction of construction costs to make houses available at $2,500 would tap a substantial fraction of this vast potential market. Similarly, in the field of electric power, the Tennessee Valley Authority has found that rate reductions have led within a few years to an increase of 88 percent in the consumption of electricity. If it were feasible to reduce electric rates throughout the Nation to the levels now prevailing in the Tennessee Valley region, the demand for electricity would so expand as to require an investment, in generating and transmission facilities, in wiring and appliances, of billions of dollars. Thus in these two fields alone we have a foreseeable investment frontier of tremendous dimensions awaiting the successful adaptation of modern technology to supply present needs. Additional billions of investment would be required by the industries which serve those directly involved. The release of potential consumption through lowering of costs and prices can open the floodgates of investment.

...The aggressive economic expansion of the past century was nourished by the vigorous optimism of a Nation expanding its frontier and exploiting its natural resources. Today the Federal Government can restore that optimism through a guaranty that the risks of periodic breakdowns will be eliminated, that the consumers' market will expand, and that the process of intensive exploitation can be safely undertaken.

Specifically, while the Federal Government encourages private investment and employment by every means in its power, to the extent that private employment cannot be found the Government must help provide the necessary jobs and support the Nation's buying power through public action. Value given for value received is the only sound principle. The country cannot be poorer when its workers are creating useful works, and future generations will not be poorer for the receipt of this heritage.

The fiscal implications of governmental responsibility for the attainment of full employment of our resources are clear. During periods when the Government is setting a bottom to a deflationary spiral and giving impetus to recovery, an unbalanced budget necessarily develops. As recovery advances and the national income expands, however, government revenues increase, government expenditures decline, and the budget is brought into balance.

In 1936–37, within 1 year, the Federal cash deficit was reduced from more than 4,000 million to less than 400 million dollars. In view of what we now know about the situation which developed in that year, it appears that our progress toward a balanced budget may have been too rapid. This experience, however, provides convincing evidence that the budget will come into balance as we approach full employment of our productive resources.

The maintenance of that balance, once achieved, cannot be dissociated from the maintenance of a balanced economy. To keep the economy in balance at full employment will require the concerted efforts of business, agriculture, labor, and government.

The responsibilities of business and labor in adapting price and wage policies to the requirements of a full-employment economy have been set forth above. A continuing program to bring and keep agriculture in sound relationship with other sectors of the economy is likewise a requisite. The cooperative responsibility of government and agriculture in such a program is vital if a high level of national income is to be sustained.

Other government policies also must be adapted to this requirement. State and local governments, as well as the Federal Government, must shape fiscal and tax policies so as to contribute to the common objective. The tendency in recent years has been toward increasing tax pressure on low-income groups. The trend in the use of sales taxation and other similar measures which restrict consumption should be reversed. At the same time, taxation on business that can be shown to discriminate against equity financing and to impose an undue burden on risk-bearing should be adjusted. The policies of business and labor looking toward the expansion of markets must be reinforced by government policies at every point if the desired common objective is to be reached and held.

It is obvious from the experiences of the past decade that we are confronted with a serious, complex economic problem. This problem demands the calm thinking of the best minds, in and out of government, so that our system can continue nourishing in the finest democratic tradition.

9–5. ALVIN H. HANSEN, *FISCAL POLICY AND BUSINESS CYCLES*: CHAPTER IV—FISCAL POLICY IN THE RECOVERY

Recovery from the deep depression of 1932–33 proceeded by fits and starts, but on the whole at a fairly satisfactory rate, until 1937. The speed of the recovery, up to this point, was clearly one of the most rapid in our history, and probably about as rapid as the economic organism could digest. The recovery was, moreover, one of the longest in American experience.

In 1937, however, the recovery was checked at a point barely exceeding the 1929 total output level, but about 7 per cent below 1929 in terms of per capita output, and far below 1929 in terms of the degree of full employment reached. Thus, before a full recovery was reached, a major depression was allowed to develop until well into 1938. In the second quarter of that year the tide was turned by a positive program of federal expenditures, and by late 1939, stimulated by the war, the 1937 level was recovered, but no new ground conquered. In broad outlines, the recovery made satisfactory progress until August, 1937, and since then has been operating at about 70 to 80 per cent of reasonably full employment.

A combination of circumstances produced the depression of 1937. A part of these could have been avoided, but in part it was a normal reaction from a prolonged upswing. With respect to the mistakes made, careful account should be taken of them for future guidance, and every effort made to avoid them. Some (for example, the labor difficulties) were related to fundamental changes which the American economy was undergoing. But whatever the causes, once the downturn was started, it was a mistake to permit an acceleration of the recession and to countenance contraction at just the point when vigorous expansion should have been undertaken. If a bold program of federal expenditures had been undertaken in September, 1937, when danger signals were sufficiently in evidence, the precipitous stock market crash of October could have been largely averted, and the recovery pushed forward after a moderate and wholesome (in terms of the cost-price situation) setback. Federal expenditures on useful public projects should have been shot up, in fiscal 1938, $2 to $3 billions in excess of the 1937 level—or, in other words, to $10 or $11 billions. We may remind ourselves that $13.5 billions is the figure contemplated for the fiscal year 1941. Had the defense program, or something equivalent, been started in the autumn of 1937, the national income could have been lifted to $85 or $90 billions by 1940.

Despite the fairly good showing made in the recovery up to 1937, the fact is that neither before nor since has the administration pursued a really positive expansionist program. Until 1936, public works outlays fell far short of the level of the twenties, and since then have only slightly exceeded that level. For the most part, the federal government engaged in a salvaging program and not in a program of positive expansion. The salvaging program took the form of refinancing urban and rural debt, rebuilding the weakened capital structure of the banks, and supporting railroads at or near bankruptcy. As we have seen, the Reconstruction Finance Corporation, the Home Owners' Loan Corporation, and the Farm Credit Administration poured $18 billions into these salvaging operations. The federal government stepped into the breach and supported the hard-pressed state and local governments—again a salvaging operation. One has only to consider the items accounting for the increase in recent years in the federal budget to see how true this is. Unable to carry the relief burden and to continue a normal program of public works, the local units turned to the federal government. From 1934–39 inclusive, $13.8 billions of the federal deficit of $18.7 billions is accounted for by the single item of unemployment relief. Other items which greatly relieved the fiscal position of local governments were the Agricultural Adjustment program, involving expenditures of $3.2 billions, and public works (largely as grants-in-aid or as substitutes for diminishing local outlays), amounting to $5.4 billions in the same period.

That a salvaging program of this magnitude was necessary was, of course, due to the unprecedented depth of the depression reached by early 1933. An important lesson that we can learn from this experience is the waste of funds for salvaging purposes which must be incurred if a depression is allowed to cumulate until the national income is cut in two. Under such circumstances the economy dries up like a sponge. Vast governmental expenditures, designed to float the "sponge" to a high level of prosperity, are instead absorbed by the sponge itself. The expenditures seemingly run to waste. This is the salvaging process. Only when the economy has become thoroughly liquid can further funds float it to higher income levels. A deep depression requires vast salvaging expenditures before a vigorous expansionist process can develop.

It is evident that governmental expenditures during the thirties were not of a character well calculated to take the place of private investment as a means to stimulate employment expansion. The deficit was not the result of a long-range program to fill the gap left by the receding tide of private investment. The spending was rather of an emergency type forced upon the government by reason of (1) the distress of unemployed urban workers, (2) the distress of farmers with declining income and overburdened with debt, (3) the weakened capital position of banks, railroads, and other industries, and (4) the weakened fiscal position of state and local governments.

In the early stages of the depression the local governments were forced to bear the brunt of the onrushing deflationary movement. In 1930–31 they made considerable loan expenditures for relief and public works. State and local outlays for construction and maintenance of government plant averaged over $3 billions in 1930–31. By 1932, however, the resources of the local governments were largely exhausted, and a sharp curtailment set in. Federal expenditures on construction and maintenance did not, however, take up this slack until as late as 1936.

…It is evident that the rising federal outlays were quite inadequate until 1936 to hold total government construction to the predepression level. Total outlays were $1.4 billions short of the 1929 level in 1933, and $800 millions in 1934 and 1935. Before one makes a judgment of the efficacy of the federal public works program in the years 1933–35, one must take cognizance of what was happening to state and local outlays on construction. The federal government only helped to hold back the receding tide. Government as a whole made no positive contribution, through public works, toward recovery.

Had it been possible to maintain private fixed capital investment, including producers' plant and equipment, residential and private nonprofit construction, at the $14 billion level of the period 1925–29, it is reasonable to suppose that state and local construction would have remained high and that the total national income could have been sustained. The measure of the decline in private investment in the thirties indicates the magnitude of the task confronting the government.

...During the first three years of the depression, federal expenditures continued, for the most part, along traditional lines at approximately the usual rate to which they had settled down in the twenties. It is true that in the fiscal year 1931 public works had increased to $421 millions, and loans amounted to $263 millions. In the fiscal year 1932, owing especially to the financial difficulties encountered by the banks and the railroads, loans increased to nearly $873 millions. In addition, federal public works were expanded to half a billion dollars, about double the level of the late twenties. In the next fiscal year total expenditures were reduced by $700,000,000 and, except for public works amounting to $472,000,000 and loans of $181,000,000, were close to the predepression level.

Thus, during the first three years of the depression there occurred an average increase in public works and loans of nearly $700 millions per annum. These items account almost wholly for the increase in total expenditures to $4.0 billions, compared with $3.2 billions in 1926–30. From 1933 on, the picture is changed, mainly by: (1) an increase in public works expenditures from an average of $464 millions in 1930–33 to $940 millions per annum in 1934–40; (2) relief expenditures (including direct relief, work relief, W.P.A., C.C.C., etc.) which had grown from zero in 1930–32, and $360 millions in 1933, to $2,243 millions per annum in 1934–40; and (3) the Agricultural Adjustment program, averaging $592 millions per year. Together, these three items account for $3.8 billions, or a half of the $7.8 billions annual expenditures in the period 1934–40. They account for practically all of the excess expenditures of this period over the average of the period 1926–30.

It is evident that the major effort was directed toward salvaging human and capital resources. Altogether, for this purpose, direct federal expenditures amounted to $26 billions during 1934–40, while indirect expenditures through governmental agencies account for some $18 billions.

Tax receipts averaged in the thirties almost exactly the same as in the fiscal years 1926–30, while expenditures averaged $3.5 billions more per annum. Thus, the federal government poured $6.7 billions per year into the income stream and took back $4.0 in the form of taxes, the "net contribution" measured in this crude manner being $2.7 billions per annum. A somewhat more refined, but still not wholly satisfactory, method of measuring the net contribution of the federal government to the money flow has been attempted by Martin Krost. According to this calculation, the net annual contribution of the federal government in 1931–40 was $2.66 billions. While there are important differences from year to year, the average for the entire decade scarcely varies at all from the average excess of all expenditures over all tax receipts.

The so-called "net contribution" of the government may be regarded as similar to private investment expenditures in so far as both are offsets to saving. It is important, however, to take the "net" figure rather than total expenditures, for the reason that a part of government expenditures are financed from funds which are taken from the consumption and not from the savings stream. In contrast, private investment expenditures are in the usual case financed from the savings stream or from new bank funds. ...

There is, moreover, a very important difference between various kinds of governmental expenditures with respect to their potency in generating employment and income. As we have already indicated, the major new expenditure by the federal government was made in the form of relief. Such expenditures, especially in a period of general depression, are likely to be less effective in raising income and employment than expenditures on public works. This thesis, to be sure, is often denied. It has been argued by some that relief expenditures are more potent because the funds are paid out to very needy individuals who will at once spend all, or nearly all, of it in the consumers' market and thereby at once, and to the fullest extent, stimulate employment and output. It is also said that, in the case of public works, the money is paid out to contractors who will use some considerable part of the money to pay off debts at the banks, or liquidate other indebtedness, and, in part, will simply hold the funds idle. Thus, it is said that the commodity market and employment are stimulated less in the case of public works.

Some comments with respect to this controversy are pertinent. In the first place, it should be noted that, while the utilization of the funds paid out in the commodity market is, in the first instance, quicker and more active in the case of relief payments than in the case of public works, this fact is true only for the first round of expenditures. Once the reliefers have bought goods at the stores, the storekeepers will use the money in the second round of expenditures, partly to liquidate debt and, in part, to hold funds idle. In the second and subsequent rounds of expenditures there is no clear presumption that one case is different from the other. Thus, this part of the argument, while valid up to a certain point, can easily be greatly exaggerated. On the other hand, more important, I think, is the difference in the induced consequences of the two kinds of expenditures upon investment and employment. In the case of relief expenditures, the additional purchases by reliefers is relatively small compared to the large volume of consumption expenditures made by the community as a whole, even in periods of deep depression. The additional purchases are spread very thinly over the vast consumption industries, thus giving very little stimulus to increased output, and are, therefore, likely to induce hardly any increase in employment. This is true because there is sufficient slack in the consumption industries to permit the additional output without taking on additional workers, and frequently even without increasing part-time employment. Thus, the induced employment from relief expenditures is likely to be very insignificant.

On the other hand, public works expenditures are likely to have a much greater induced effect on employment, for the following reasons. In a period of serious depression, it is the construction and heavy industries—those relating to fixed capital production—which are seriously depressed. Employment has fallen to a mere fraction of the level reached in the boom, and construction and heavy industries output is at a low capacity level. Many construction companies have gone into bankruptcy and passed out of the picture. Many heavy goods industries are largely shut down, and in these even replacement capital expenditures are likely to be running at a low level. But when orders come in for construction projects, workers are re-employed and the plant is reconditioned. Public works expenditures of $4 billions or $5 billions would have a tremendous effect upon re-employment and upon capital expenditures. It should be noted that an expenditure of the magnitude of $4 billions to $5 billions is fairly large, even in relation to total fixed capital construction in boom times. From 1925 to 1929, private fixed capital investment, including plant, equipment, housing, and nonprofit construction, amounted to $14 billions per annum. Thus, an injection of from $4 billions to $5 billions of public works would represent a really large figure in relation to even prosperity levels of activity in the capital goods industries. On the other hand, as noted above, a similar amount spent on relief is a very small proportion of the total consumption expenditures. A public works program of relatively moderate proportions will, therefore, induce a very large increase in employment in the construction and heavy goods industries. Thus, the leverage effect of a public works program on employment, taking account of both consumption and investment repercussions, is relatively large.

The magnitude of public expenditures, whether for governmental capital projects or for community consumption, required to counteract a depression as intense as that of the early thirties is enormous. If we underestimate the task to be performed, we are prone to disappointment over quite inadequate efforts from which too much was expected. ...

It would not have been necessary for the government to fill the entire gap left by the receding tide of private investment. Yet in the earlier years—1930 and 1931—it is probable that, in order to have prevented any considerable decline, the outlays would have had to be approximately equal to the decline in private investment. It is a great mistake to assume, as some have, that a mere announcement by the government that it will fill the gap if private enterprise failed to do so would alone be sufficient, and that therefore very small expenditures would, in fact, be necessary. This overly optimistic view fails to take cognizance of the high degree of saturation reached by private investment at the end of a major boom. Private investment, on the scale of the late twenties, could not uninterruptedly have been maintained, even on the basis of favorable expectations with respect to vigorous government action and reasonably satisfactory maintenance of the national income. Not until depreciation, obsolescence, growth of population, and new technological developments had again enlarged the outlet for private investment could the government safely assume that private investment would again become reasonably adequate.

But one can also exaggerate the government's load. This is true for the reason that vigorous governmental action (for example, in 1930 and 1931) could have stopped the secondary cumulation of the deflation. While large private outlays on *new* investment could not have been expected in the early thirties, the disinvestment which occurred could have been largely prevented. Had the government stepped into the breach and maintained the national income on a moderately high scale, private capital expenditures would not have fallen anywhere near as low as they actually did. For these reasons, had the government decided to take vigorous action, the gap left by the declining private investment in 1930–35 would have had to be filled only in part by the governmental outlays.

It is in the first years of a depression that especially vigorous governmental policy is necessary. Bold action at that stage can prevent the drastic disinvestment which the cumulative secondary deflation will surely bring if it is allowed to run its course. Moreover, if the secondary deflation can be prevented, it will not be necessary later to engage in large salvaging operations, which, valuable and necessary though they be, must nevertheless yield disappointing results from the standpoint of the goal of a positive recovery.

Not only are the timing, magnitude, and character of expenditures important; equally significant is the manner of financing. New and burdensome consumption taxes were imposed both by the federal government and by state and local units in the thirties. Federal consumption-tax receipts increased from $1.1 billions in 1933 to $2.2 billions in 1935. To this was subsequently added the social security payroll taxes. The local governmental units resorted more and more to consumption taxes, until by 1938 they were collecting $2.5 billions from these sources, not including the unemployment insurance payroll taxes. Consumption taxes are repressive in character and tend to place a drag on recovery.

Thus, to sum up, various factors tended to reduce the effectiveness of the fiscal recovery program as it actually developed. Large expenditures of a purely salvaging character had to be made, especially in 1933–35. The gross inadequacy of public works expenditures forced undue reliance on the less stimulating relief expenditures. And, finally, a drag was placed upon recovery by reason of the increase in consumption taxes.

9–6. BEARDSLEY RUML, SPEECH GIVEN ON NOVEMBER 15, 1943, "FINANCING POST WAR PROSPERITY: CONTROLLING BOOMS AND DEPRESSIONS"

Today most businessmen agree that our Number One task after the war is to provide jobs for people who are able and willing to work. This is the goal of high production and high employment at which all of us are shooting. By far the greater part of the jobs will be provided by private business. But we must also understand that if business is to assume its full responsibility, it must have the active cooperation of government in keeping employment and production at high levels.

Government can give this help in two ways. It can provide jobs through the ordinary and well-recognized government services, such as education, or through other means such as regular or special public works projects. The other means government can use is to manage its own money affairs in such a way as to encourage and support business activity of all kinds.

I should emphasize that the various things that the government does with and about money matters—which includes taxation, borrowing and lending policy, interest rates and many other things—should have a unified sense of direction. This was definitely not true of our policy during the thirties. Some agencies of government felt that by spending money they could reasonably hope to create jobs and in many cases they did. Other agencies were unwittingly following deflationary policies. The policy of one agency was in direct conflict with the policy of other agencies. In the postwar period we shall, of necessity, have more unified control. Government policies and agencies must not cancel each other out. They must move in the same direction.

In what direction do we want them to move? Our first goal is to get as much production and create as many jobs as we can. The best way we know of doing this is to keep private business as active as possible. Government policies should foster and encourage this at all times. But whenever private activity slackens, because of the business outlook, the policies of government should replace the purchasing power which has declined because of the falling off of private business. Thus government supports private activity and compensates for any falling below the high unemployment and production that we want. For this reason, such a policy is sometimes referred to as a "compensatory" fiscal policy.

Assuming, then, the general desirability of government to take up the slack in private employment whenever it occurs, it is worth while to point out certain things about this "compensatory" system that are often misunderstood.

In the first place, such a policy does not mean that we will always need to have a deficit in the national budget and operate in the red all the time. In times of high production and high employment we will be able to balance the budget without difficulty. In boom times we will not only be able to balance our budget, but we will want to start paying off our national debt in substantial amounts. We will want to do this in order to provide a brake on a business system that might be entering a false and dangerous boom.

Such a policy does not mean spending for its own sake. At no time would there be any need for wasteful expenditure. When government lends or spends, it should put its money into projects that are really necessary, efficient, and productive.

I repeat that the disbursements of government are not the only way of supporting high production and high employment. Indeed they may not be the best way. Our tax policy will have a great effect on these matters. If we want to keep employment at high levels, one way to do it is to give the average man greater purchasing power by reducing taxes. Why not leave at home, for the individual to spend, the income that otherwise might have to be pumped out again in order to maintain high employment? Such reduction of taxes should be made where it will do the most good in creating demand and in encouraging private enterprise. And note particularly that under this "compensatory" policy we don't have to wait until our national budget is balanced before we start reducing taxes.

I would like to set forth one basic principle that I think should govern our tax policy in the postwar years to come.

We should set our tax rates at a figure that will enable us to balance our national budget when we have a satisfactory high level of employment and production. If we have plenty of jobs and if we are turning out lots of goods and services and our national income is high, we can handle the budget on tax rates substantially lower than they are today. We should set our goals for high production. The war, very dramatically, has shown us what we can achieve if we want to strongly enough. When our national business activity goes above these adequate levels then the same tax rates would bring us enough revenue so that we can start reducing our national debt. If activity falls below these levels we can prudently leave the tax rates where they are. Doing so will reduce the tax payments from individuals and will stimulate business activity. The idea is on the one hand to use a reduction of the national debt to check an excessive business boom and on the other hand to use government fiscal and tax policy when private business activity falls off to expand and increase activity—and thereby provide the jobs we want.

9–7. FRANKLIN DELANO ROOSEVELT, JANUARY 11, 1944, "FIRESIDE CHAT"

…The one supreme objective for the future, which we discussed for each nation individually, and for all the United Nations, can be summed up in one word: Security.

And that means not only physical security which provides safety from attacks by aggressors. It means also economic security, social security, moral security—in a family of nations.

In the plain down-to-earth talks that I had with the Generalissimo and Marshal Stalin and Prime Minister Churchill, it was abundantly clear that they are all most deeply interested in the resumption of peaceful progress by their own peoples—progress toward a better life….

…an equally basic essential to peace—permanent peace—is a decent standard of living for all individual men and women and children in all nations. Freedom from fear is eternally linked with freedom from want. There are people who burrow—burrow through the (our) nation like unseeing moles, and attempt to spread the suspicion that if other nations are encouraged to raise their standards of living, our own American standard of living must of necessity be depressed.

The fact is the very contrary. It has been shown time and again that if the standard of living of any country goes up, so does its purchasing power—and that such a rise encourages a better standard of living in neighboring countries with whom it trades. That is just plain common sense….

In this war, we have been compelled to learn how interdependent upon each other are all groups and sections of the whole population of America.

Increased food costs, for example, will bring new demands for wage increases from all war workers, which will in turn raise all prices of all things including those things which the farmers themselves have to buy. Increased wages or prices will each in turn produce the same results. They all have a particularly disastrous result on all fixed income groups.

And I hope you will remember that all of us in this Government, including myself, represent the fixed income group just as much as we represent business owners, or workers or (and) farmers. This group of fixed-income people include: teachers, and clergy, and policemen, and firemen, and widows and minors who are on fixed incomes, wives and dependents of our soldiers and sailors, and old age pensioners. They and their families add up to more than a quarter of our one hundred and thirty million people. They have few or no high pressure representatives at the Capitol. And in a period of gross inflation they would be the worst sufferers. Let us give them an occasional thought....

...in order to concentrate all of our energies, all of our resources on winning this war, and to maintain a fair and stable economy at home, I recommend that the Congress adopt: First, (1) A realistic and simplified tax law—which will tax all unreasonable profits, both individual and corporate, and reduce the ultimate cost of the war to our sons and our daughters. The tax bill now under consideration by the Congress does not begin to meet this test. Secondly, (2) A continuation of the law for the renegotiation of war contracts —which will prevent exorbitant profits and assure fair prices to the Government. For two long years I have pleaded with the Congress to take undue profits out of war. Third, (3) A cost of food law—which will enable the Government (a) to place a reasonable floor under the prices the farmer may expect for his production; and (b) to place a ceiling on the prices the (a) consumer will have to pay for the necessary food he buys. This should apply, as I have intimated, to necessities only; and this will require public funds to carry it out. It will cost in appropriations about one percent of the present annual cost of the war. Fourth, (4) An early re-enactment of the stabilization statute of October, 1942. This expires this year, June 30th, 1944, and if it is not extended well in advance, the country might just as well expect price chaos by summertime. We cannot have stabilization by wishful thinking. We must take positive action to maintain the integrity of the American dollar. And fifth, (5) A national service law which, for the duration of the war, will prevent strikes, and, with certain appropriate exceptions, will make available for war production or for any other essential services every able-bodied adult in this whole Nation.

These five measures together form a just and equitable whole. I would not recommend a national service law unless the other laws were passed to keep down the cost of living, to share equitably the burdens of taxation, to hold the stabilization line, and to prevent undue profits.

The Federal Government already has the basic power to draft capital and property of all kinds for war purposes on a basis of just compensation. ...

A prompt enactment of a National Service Law would be merely an expression of the universality of this American responsibility. I believe the country will agree that those statements are the solemn truth. National service is the most democratic way to wage a war. Like selective service for the armed forces, it rests on the obligation of each citizen to serve his nation to his utmost where he is best qualified. ...

It does not mean reduction in wages. It does not mean loss of retirement and seniority rights and benefits. It does not mean that any substantial numbers of war workers will be disturbed in their present jobs. Let this (these) fact(s) be wholly clear. There are millions of American men and women who are not in this war at all. That (It) is not because they do not want to be in it. But they want to know where they can best do their share. National service provides that direction.

I know that all civilian war workers will be glad to be able to say many years hence to their grandchildren: "Yes, I, too, was in service in the great war. I was on duty in an airplane factory, and I helped to make hundreds of fighting planes. The Government told me that in doing that I was performing my most useful work in the service of my country."...

...it is time to begin plans and determine the strategy for winning a lasting peace and the establishment of an American standard of living higher than ever known before.

This Republic had its beginning, and grew to its present strength, under the protection of certain inalienable political rights—among them the right of free speech, free press, free worship, trial by jury, freedom from unreasonable searches and seizures. They were our rights to life and liberty.

We have come to a clear realization of the fact, however, that true individual freedom cannot exist without economic security and independence. "Necessitous men are not free men." People who are hungry, people who are out of a job are the stuff of which dictatorships are made.

In our day these economic truths have become accepted as self-evident. We have accepted, so to speak, a second Bill of Rights under which a new basis of security and prosperity can be established for all—regardless of station, or race or creed.

Among these are:

- The right to a useful and remunerative job in the industries, or shops or farms or mines of the nation;
- The right to earn enough to provide adequate food and clothing and recreation;
- The right of (every) farmers to raise and sell their (his) products at a return which will give them (him) and their (his) families (family) a decent living;
- The right of every business man, large and small, to trade in an atmosphere of freedom from unfair competition and domination by monopolies at home or abroad;
- The right of every family to a decent home;
- The right to adequate medical care and the opportunity to achieve and enjoy good health;
- The right to adequate protection from the economic fears of old age, and sickness, and accident and unemployment;
- And finally, the right to a good education.

All of these rights spell security. And after this war is won we must be prepared to move forward, in the implementation of these rights, to new goals of human happiness and well-being.

America's own rightful place in the world depends in large part upon how fully these and similar rights have been carried into practice for all our citizens. For unless there is security here at home there cannot be lasting peace in the world. One of the great American industrialists of our day—a man who has rendered yeoman service to his country in this crisis—recently emphasized the grave dangers of "rightist reaction" in this Nation. Any clear-thinking business men share that concern. Indeed, if such reaction should develop—if history were to repeat itself and we were to return to the so-called "normalcy" of the 1920's—then it is certain that even though we shall have conquered our enemies on the battlefields abroad, we shall have yielded to the spirit of fascism here at home.

I ask the Congress to explore the means for implementing this economic bill of rights—for it is definitely the responsibility of the Congress so to do, and the country knows it. Many of these problems are already before committees of the Congress in the form of proposed legislation. I shall from time to time communicate with the Congress with respect to these and further proposals. In the event that no adequate program of progress is evolved, I am certain that the Nation will be conscious of the fact.

Our fighting men abroad—and their families at home—expect such a program and have the right to insist on it. It is to their demands that this Government should pay heed, rather than to the whining demands of selfish pressure groups who seek to feather their nests while young Americans are dying. I have often said that there are no two fronts for America in this war. There is only one front. There is one line of unity that extends from the hearts of people at home to the men of our attacking forces in our farthest outposts. When we speak of our total effort, we speak of the factory and the field and the mine as well as the battlefield—we speak of the soldier and the civilian, the citizen and his Government. Each and every one of them has a solemn obligation under God to serve this Nation in its most critical hour—to keep this Nation great—to make this Nation greater in a better world.

ESSAYS

In the first essay, the role of fiscal policy in the recovery of the 1930s is examined. Some claimed fiscal policy to be useless; others gave it a large measure of the credit for the substantial, yet partial, recovery of the 1930s. "Fiscal Policy in the Thirties: A Reappraisal" was written by E. Cary Brown, a member of the economics faculty at MIT, and appeared in the *American Economic Review* in December 1956. Brown finds that the fiscal policy of all three levels of government combined was more expansionary than in 1929 in only two years: 1931 and 1936. He notes that the fiscal stimulus provided got weaker as the decade of the '30s wore on. This leads to his oft-quoted statement that "fiscal policy, then, seems to have been an unsuccessful recovery device in the 'thirties—not because it did not work, but because it was not tried." In many ways, Brown's conclusions are very similar to Hansen's: while the federal government's fiscal policy was on balance stimulative, it was not adequate to offset the neutral or contractionary stance of state and local governments. Much of the fiscal stimulus was lost to tax increases at all levels of government. Many state and local governments were required by law to balance their budgets. Brown points out the perverse effects of the Revenue Act of 1932 and the Social Security tax, and concludes that it took the massive expenditures of World War II to demonstrate the full potential of fiscal policy.

Essay 9–2 is selected excerpts from "The General Theory," Chapter 4 in *The Age of Keynes*, written by Robert Lekachman and published in 1966, at about the time that Keynesianism had reached its high tide. Lekachman, an academic economist at several New York City area institutions, was an unabashed admirer of Keynes. His account of the economics of Keynes is made readily accessible to the general reader without compromising any of the essentials of Keynesian theory. Lekachman describes Keynes' attack on the orthodox view based on Say's Law ("supply creates its own demand") that claimed full employment to be the norm in market economies and, aside from a small frictional component, unemployment to be voluntary. Aggregate demand is composed of consumption spending and investment spending. Since only a portion of income is spent, strong investment spending is needed to lift an economy to full employment. Because it is susceptible to changing expectations, investment spending can be quite volatile. Keynes' solution is to substitute government deficit spending for inadequate investment spending. Keynes was skeptical of the power of monetary policy in a deep depression; thus, his theory became associated with fiscal policy, specifically spending on public works projects. Lekachman explains Keynes' belief that the interest rate is a reward for parting with liquidity rather than a reward for saving, and his view that wage cuts are a needlessly roundabout and provocative way to stimulate an economy.

Essay 9–3 is excerpted from "Lessons of World War II," Chapter 8 in *The Fiscal Revolution in America*, published in 1969. Written by Herbert Stein, this book examines fiscal policy from the Hoover to the Kennedy administration. Stein spent many years with the Committee for Economic Development, an economics research organization, before joining The Brookings Institution. Shortly thereafter, in late 1968, he was tapped by president-elect Nixon to be a member of the Council of Economic Advisers, which he later chaired under both Presidents Nixon and Ford. In "Lessons of World War II," Stein notes that the restoration of full employment brought on by World War II led to its elevation as the single most important economic goal for the postwar period. As the belief crept in that secular stagnation would not be America's postwar fate, fiscal policy was seen as a means to combat economic fluctuations rather than stagnation. During the war years, tax revenues began to get more attention in discussions of fiscal policy along with government expenditures. A greater appreciation for the built-in stabilizers developed, whereby tax revenue fell and government spending rose automatically in the face of recessions (with the reverse holding in the case of an economic boom). This recognition eroded the insistence of orthodox policymakers that the budget be balanced every fiscal year. Devotion to fiscal recitude was replaced by the idea that the budget should be balanced at high employment. As the war wound to an end, two contending views of fiscal policy emerged. One view continued to focus on government spending as the instrument of fiscal policy. The other view placed greater reliance on the built-in stabilizers, and when fiscal action was warranted, it would give more consideration to the possibility of tax cuts.

9–1. E. CAREY BROWN , "FISCAL POLICY IN THE 'THIRTIES"

The question of how effectively fiscal policy promoted recovery in the 'thirties has agitated a good fraction of the profession at one time or another. The advent of the second world war shifted attention away from this question, and the insight and improvements gained from the major developments in national income measurement and analysis have not been properly reapplied to this highly interesting period. Some recent studies have been made of the dynamic aspects of fiscal policy in the 1937 recession. But I would like to re-examine the direct annual static effects of fiscal policy on demand in the 'thirties, ignoring specific timing problems.

Some measure of the contribution of fiscal policy to effective demand will be needed for this purpose. Early work in this field developed the concept of net-income-creating expenditures of government—a major forward step towards a more careful measurement of the direct effects of fiscal policy. But, important as was this early concept, it has a number of weaknesses in measuring the impact of fiscal policy on total demand. A reformulation is made...and the findings from the application of this revised concept are set forth....

Governmental financial activities make many and varied contributions to demand for goods and services. Government expenditures directly increase demand for output; taxes decrease private demand for it. Monetary activities—open market and similar lending-borrowing actions, and changes in reserve requirements—can also affect rates of private demand. These initial shifts in demand in turn lead to induced changes in private spending. The resulting multiplied effects on income depend among other things on the relationship of governmental taxing and spending to national income. Finally, governmental financial activities can give rise to variations in private demand through substitution effects induced by changes in relative prices or in expectations, and these may either contract or expand private demand still further. It is impossible to include all of these effects in a measure of fiscal contribution to total demand. Some narrowing is necessary....

The concept we will use excludes monetary activities entirely, to the extent this is feasible, by omitting all governmental as well as private lending and borrowing activities. Earlier studies included some of these activities and excluded others.

The results of the statistical manipulations discussed are presented...and the general reader's attention is directed to...the main findings of the study.

Subject to all the limitations of analysis and procedure..., certain broad findings seem to stand out:

1. The direct effects on aggregate full-employment demand of the fiscal policy undertaken by all three levels of government was clearly relatively stronger in the 'thirties than in

1929 in only two years—1931 and 1936—with 1931 markedly higher than 1936....
These were years in which large payments were made under the veterans' adjusted
compensation programs—programs passed by Congress over the vigorous opposition
of both the Hoover and Roosevelt administrations.

If they were eliminated, 1931 would remain clearly above 1929, but 1936 would
fall below it. In three other years—1930, 1932, and 1939— the expansionary effect
of fiscal policy was somewhat higher than in 1929, while in 1934 and 1935 it was
virtually the same. In two years— 1933 and 1937—fiscal policy was markedly less
expansionary than in 1929, and in 1938 slightly less so.

The trend of the direct effects of fiscal policy on aggregate full-employment demand
is definitely downward throughout the 'thirties. For recovery to have been achieved
in this period, private demand would have had to be higher out of a given private
disposable income than it was in 1929. Fiscal policy, then, seems to have been an
unsuccessful recovery device in the 'thirties—not because it did not work, but because
it was not tried. While differing in many details, this finding bears out Hansen's
conclusions reached in 1941: "Despite the fairly good showing made in the recovery up
to 1937, the fact is that neither before nor since has the administration pursued a really
positive expansionist program ... For the most part, the federal government engaged
in a salvaging program and not in a program of positive expansionist program". ...
It is in sharp contrast to Smithies' view: "My main conclusion on government policy
from the experience of the 'thirties is that fiscal policy did prove to be an effective and
indeed the only effective means to recovery."

2. The federal government's fiscal action was more expansionary throughout the 'thirties
   than it was in 1929. In 1929, its fiscal action resulted in a substantial net drag on
   total demand. But this changed sharply in 1931 to an expansionary effect (although
   here again the vetoed veterans' adjusted compensation should be borne in mind).
   Expansion continued throughout the period except for the sharp drop in 1937, which
   represented a shift in demand of over 2 ½ per cent of GNP in one year. It was followed
   by expansionary activity on a fairly large scale, but not of sufficient size to approach
   that of 1934–36.

3. State and local governments' fiscal policy was expansionary through 1933, but
   decreasingly so. By 1934, it had fallen clearly below 1929 and remained in an almost
   neutral position throughout the rest of the period. The federal government's policies
   were little more than adequate in most years of the 'thirties to offset these contractive
   effects of state and local governments. Indeed if we take the seven years from 1933
   on, in only two was the federal share significantly more than enough to offset state
   and local shrinkages.

4. The primary failure of fiscal policy to be expansive in this period is attributable to the
   sharp increase in tax structures enacted at all levels of government. Total government
   purchases of goods and services expanded virtually every year, with federal expansion
   especially marked in 1933 and 1934. But full-employment tax yields more than
   kept pace. Our rough estimates show that in 1929, a year of full employment, all
   governments combined had a deficit (federal surplus and state and local deficit), while
   1933 to 1939, except for 1936, were years of surplus or approximate balance at full
   employment.

The changes made in the tax structure in this period were marked, but their quantitative
impact has been masked by the sharp fall in total income and tax yields. The federal
Revenue Act of 1932 virtually doubled full-employment tax yields and essentially set the
tax structure for the entire period up to the second world war. Since the highly deflationary

impact of this tax law has not been fully appreciated, some of its major provisions are briefly noted here.

The Revenue Act of 1932 pushed up rates virtually across the board, but notably on the lower- and middle-income groups. The scope of the act was clearly the equivalent of major wartime enactments. Personal income tax exemptions were slashed, the normal-tax as well as surtax rates were sharply raised, and the earned-income credit equal to 25 per cent of taxes on low incomes was repealed. Less drastic changes were made in the corporate income tax, but its rate was raised slightly and a $3000 exemption eliminated. Estate tax rates were pushed up, exemptions sharply reduced, and a gift tax was provided. Congress toyed with a manufacturers' sales tax, but finally rejected it in favor of a broad new list of excise taxes and substantially higher rates for the old ones. While some of these excises were later repealed, most remained throughout the decade. Somewhat later in the 'thirties, processing taxes made further temporary inroads on demand, and the social security taxes began in 1937 to exert a pronounced effect.

State and local government were also active in new revenue legislation throughout this period. The major changes were to find the state governments moving heavily into general sales and excise taxation, personal and corporate income taxes, and the gasoline tax.

In brief, then, it took the massive expenditures forced on the nation by the second world war to realize the full potentialities of fiscal policy. Until then, the record fails to show its effective use as a recovery measure. Indeed, the general expansionary policy seems stronger in the early part than in the later part of the decade.

9–2. ROBERT LEKACHMAN, *THE AGE OF KEYNES*: CHAPTER 4—THE GENERAL THEORY

The first draft of *The General Theory* was completed in 1934. Written in close communion with a brilliant group of young Cambridge economists, among them R. F. Kahn, Joan Robinson, and J. E. Meade, the proofs were circulated first to D. H. Robertson, then to the distinguished older economist R. G. Hawtrey, and finally to R. F. Harrod, Keynes's loyal Oxford admirer and ultimate biographer. To Keynes's distress his old friend and colleague Robertson proved unsympathetic to the strategy and the terminology alike of *The General Theory*. He was unprepared to depart as widely from the economics of Marshall and Pigou as the impatient Keynes was. Even Harrod, by his own account, endeavored to dissuade Keynes from an all-out assault on "classical" economics. Keynes was not to be dissuaded. When *The General Theory* officially appeared, its contents were therefore no surprise at least to the Cambridge inner circle who had participated in its production and the Cambridge students who had heard Keynes's lectures in 1934 and 1935.

Three decades after its appearance, *The General Theory* remains a difficult, technical treatise even for specialists. It is full of subtleties of exposition, some necessary, some the consequence of obscure thought, and some apparently designed to infuriate members of his own profession. But it was also a book with a powerful central message. This was a blast at the assumption that there were mechanisms of economic adjustment in capitalist societies which automatically produced conditions of full employment of men and resources. No doubt Keynes exaggerated the uniformity of this opinion among economists, but he was broadly accurate in his judgment that most if not all economists still retained, Great Depression or no Great Depression, a sturdy confidence in the ability of competitive markets to expand employment and production if labor accepted lower wages and businessmen accepted lower prices. Flexible prices and flexible wages were still the best answer that the conventional wisdom of the profession could offer the community.

The thrust of economic analysis is toward the explanation of large numbers of events by a very few abstract principles. When the principles and the events diverge, when existing theories of market equilibrium ill accord with the persistence of unemployment and the gloomy outlook for its alleviation, economists, like labor leaders, may grow discontented. But they will cling to their existing principles until superior principles are invented, for economics is a subject in which bad theory is preferable to no theory at all. Economists like Pigou and Robertson were not blissfully happy with doctrines that preached equilibrium at full employment. In the absence of better theories, they patched up the existing doctrines. Keynes's task, then, was twofold: destruction of bad old doctrine and creation of good new doctrine.

The older theory which Keynes attacked was founded on an old generalization, the nineteenth-century French economist Jean-Baptiste Say's Law of Markets. Often summarized in the aphorism already quoted, "Supply creates its own demand," Say's Law affirmed the impossibility of general overproduction of goods, or general "glut," in Say's word. Equally impossible therefore was general unemployment. Say's reasoning was nearly as concise and simple as his conclusion. Was it not obvious that men produced goods only in order to enjoy the consumption of other goods? Capitalists invested in order to consume their profits in the enjoyment of life. Workers labored in order to consume their wages in acquiring the means of subsistence for themselves and their families. The more that businessmen spent on hiring labor and purchasing raw materials, the larger would be the incomes generated and the capacity of their recipients to purchase goods. Every increase in production soon justified itself by a matching increase in demand. Double production and infallibly you doubled sales. Indeed, the only limit was the amount of resources and the number of employable workers available....

Did this bland and happy tale affront the common sense of the ordinary citizen, who was perfectly aware from his own behavior and observation that no one *had* to spend all of his income, that some might be saved, and that savings seemed to reduce the demand for goods and services? Economists had an answer....

The wage earner or businessman who thriftily saved a portion of his income simply either made the funds available for his own reinvestment in his own business enterprise or, using a bank as an intermediary, loaned the funds to someone who would invest them. In either event, his savings purchased goods just as surely as his expenditures on food, clothing, shelter, and frivolity. Hence, in one fashion or another, the incomes which were paid out to workers, landlords, investors, and lenders returned undiminished as demand for the very goods and services which workers and property owners had cooperated to generate....

Orthodox economic theory thus imputed to the laborer the maximizing, rational, calculating tendencies upon which economic theory has habitually based its explanations of human behavior.

There was a most important corollary of this doctrine: the implication that any individual worker had it in his own power to find or to increase his own employment. All he needed to do was revise his psychic computation of pleasure and pain so as to work more hours at existing wage rates, work the same number of hours at lower wages, or, if unemployed, accept a job offer at a wage rate which previously he had deemed unacceptable. The moral for individual workers and the leaders of their unions was inescapable—the partially or completely unemployed could remedy their situation at any time; all they had to do was accept lower wage rates.

From this inference flowed another. All unemployment was either frictional or voluntary. Where unemployment was frictional, workers who were seasonally idle or between jobs could confidently anticipate re-employment as the season changed or as new jobs became available. All other unemployment had to be interpreted as the voluntary preference of the unemployed. Much as an economist might justify on humane or historical grounds the refusal of a worker to accept a reduction in his standard of life, the economist could not grant him an economic justification....

However, a teasing and unpleasant fact, involuntary unemployment *did* exist. Any observer at all in touch with the social reality of the 1930s knew that quite frequently wages and employment had contracted simultaneously....

Now, according to the reasoning characteristic of classical theory, the response of laborers to declines in their real income was a withholding of a portion of their labor. But was it really sensible to assume that this theoretical reaction also occurred in life? Did workers leave their jobs or work fewer hours every time the price of food and clothing went up? Of course not....

...if ordinary workers were willing to accept jobs at wages *lower* than the previous level of remuneration, then they surely would have been willing to work at the higher real wages of the past. Hence they must have been involuntarily unemployed. If their employers had only felt it worth their while to offer additional employment at lower money and real wages, they would have found willing workers. Thus, economists who were so stubbornly confident that individual employers and individual employees between them determined the level of employment were simply completely mistaken. Often enough nothing an unemployed man or woman could do was capable of having the slightest impact on his own job prospects.

...something vital was missing from the corpus of orthodox economics—nothing less than a theory of aggregate demand. The highest distinction of *The General Theory* was not the explanation of involuntary unemployment; it was the construction of this missing piece of economic apparatus.

Once the theory is stated, the error of conventional economic policy is readily grasped. It becomes plain that the wage- and price-cutting which were approved pre-Keynesian specifics illegitimately leaped from the specific to the general. Any businessman can see that a reduction in his own costs—other things being equal—expands his profits and encourages him to increase his output. The heart of the matter is the failure of other things to remain equal when *all* businessmen reduce wages and costs. When wages in general fall, then the demand for all varieties of consumer goods and services inevitably falls in tune with the declining incomes of workers. At best, then, the demand for goods must fall in much the same proportion as wages. In the aggregate the demand for goods depends upon the incomes which, again in the aggregate, their potential purchasers earn. *One* employer can benefit from a reduction of his workers wages. *All* employers cannot benefit by a general reduction of wages. To believe otherwise is to commit the logical fallacy of composition.

Hence the new Keynesian theory of economic activity was on the one hand an explanation of how the total *supply* of goods and services emerged from the decisions of hordes of individual businessmen, and on the other hand an account of how the total *demand* for goods and services evolved from the spending and saving choices of millions of individual consumers. As Keynes told his new story, events commence with the actions of businessmen. He assumed from the outset that it is individual businessmen or entrepreneurs who provide employment and pay incomes—wages to workers, salaries to executives, interest to bankers, rent to landlords. Entrepreneurs expect to sell the goods which result from the combination of the agents of production at prices which equal at a minimum the sums paid out in the process of producing them —including a normal profit. It follows that when the situation is stable (that is, when aggregate equilibrium is attained), the *aggregate* amount of income and employment which *all* entrepreneurs will offer just matches the volume of the sales which they anticipate making.

When will entrepreneurs wish to expand the employment they offer,—the incomes they provide, and the output they produce? The answer was related by Keynes to the notion of an aggregate *demand* function, which is the other half of the picture. Suppose that *in fact* when entrepreneurs offer a certain amount of employment and produce a certain volume of output, the *actual demand* for the goods they offer for sale exceeds their expectations. Accordingly, most businessmen discover that their stocks (or inventories) of goods are running short. At this point, if they are retailers or wholesalers, they increase their orders to manufacturers; if they are manufacturers, they increase their production. The aggregate demand function measures the volume of sales which corresponds to each possible level of income and output....

...Say's Law blithely assumed that every time businessmen expanded supply, demand simply followed in its train. The beneficent process halted only when full employment of men and resources called a halt to expansion. In the Keynesian universe, equilibrium could be reached at *any* level of employment and income between zero and full employment. Moreover, no theoretical reason existed for saying that one level of employment was more likely to occur than any other level of employment. On the possible scale of values, full employment was simply one possibility among many. It followed that at each and every level of employment other than full employment, involuntary unemployment was more than possible; it was unavoidable. What determined the level of employment was *not* the wage bargain negotiated between laborers and their employers...What determined employment was something quite different. It was the level of aggregate demand for the goods and services of the entire economy.

What elements constituted aggregate demand? What determined its size and therefore the size of employment and income? Keynes started with the simple assumption that the government had a neutral impact upon the economy. He assumed initially that the government removed as much from the stream of national income in the shape of taxes as it placed in the income stream in the form of its own expenditures on materials and labor services. If the net effect of government operations was zero, the two remaining sources of the aggregate demand for goods and services were consumers and investors.

...[I]ncome...[was the determinant] of short-run consumption, ...this was the only force...Keynes was convinced that he had isolated a new truth, and he stated his conviction in the form of a new "law":

...of human nature and from the detailed facts of experience, ...that men are disposed, as a rule and on the average, to increase their consumption as their income increases but not by as much as the increase in their income.

At the time Keynes had very little if any statistical support for the conclusion stated in this "law." Like his illustrious predecessors and colleagues in English economics, he relied confidently upon his knowledge of himself and the world in which he lived. The statistics came later as one of the many consequences of *The General Theory*. A favorite sport of economists and statisticians was "consumption function" construction—a statistical generalization of the actual relations between income and consumption. Although later events as well as these researches demonstrated that the influences upon consumption are more numerous and more complex than Keynes assumed, these same investigations have also tended to certify the broad accuracy of Keynes's "law." Consumers do tend to spend most but not all of the additions to their incomes which come their way. In the United States, statisticians usually assume that consumers will spend between 92 and 94 percent of additions to their disposable income.

As a theoretical contribution, Keynes's definition of an aggregate consumption function was important and suggestive. Alvin Hansen was not alone among economists in assessing it as one of Keynes's major inventions. But whatever its other merits, the consumption function could not explain the *size* of national income and employment. Consumption indeed depended upon national income. What was left as an explanation of national income was necessarily the remaining constituent of aggregate demand—investment. Here at last is the key variable in the Keynesian system. Changes in investment initiate changes in the other economic magnitudes. Increases or decreases in investment generate multiplied effects upon national income and employment. Alterations in national income in their turn produce alterations in the volume of consumer spending.

It is essential, then, to be very clear on this topic. What is investment? What explains its size? In *The General Theory,* Keynes followed the general practice of economists by defining investment as a "real" and not a financial phenomenon. Stocks and bonds are *not* investment. New factories, new tools and machines, and enlargements of business inventories *are* investment....

Such a definition isolates three other investment characteristics. First of all, investments are made by businessmen, not consumers, with the general objective of profitable production and sale. Second, all investments are risky. The businessman who uses his own money or borrowed funds to buy a machine places a bet in effect that he will be able to sell the commodities which the machine produces during its lifetime— two, five, ten, or more years—at profitable prices....

...third...investment is postponable. As a general matter, businessmen need not expand their operations, at least not immediately. Usually, a businessman can even postpone replacing obsolescent equipment with improved models....

...what enters into their decisions? Keynes's answer focused upon a comparison between the *profits* which a prospective investor expected over the lifetime of the machine and the interest charges which he incurred when he borrowed the money to buy the machine.

In an uncertain world, the key word in this analysis was expectation...A powerful theory of investment, accordingly, must elucidate the forces which enter into the long-run expectations of prospective investors, and explain more generally the "state of confidence ...to which practical men always pay the closest and most anxious attention."

The difficulties in the path of understanding are grave. If, said Keynes, we are honest with ourselves, we will at once admit just how little we know about the probable profits of a given investment: "If we speak frankly, we have to admit that our basis of knowledge for estimating the yield ten years hence of a railway, a copper mine, a textile factory, the goodwill of a patent medicine, an Atlantic liner, a building in the City of London amounts to little and sometimes to nothing; or even five years hence."...The bulk of investment is extraordinarily chancy. Its risks are all the greater because stock market speculation intensifies the psychological uncertainties of genuine investment.

Keynes judged that even apart from the influence of stock markets, organized more like gambling casinos than like investment markets, there was an element of instability which was "due to the characteristic of human nature that a large proportion of our positive activities depend on spontaneous optimism. ... Most, probably, of our decisions to do something positive, the full consequences of which will be drawn out over many days to come, can only be taken as a result of animal spirits." As a man of wide practical experience in financial markets, as journalist and speculator, Keynes knew how important the tides of irrational optimism and pessimism were in the decisions of businessmen to invest or to hesitate in the hope of better days. One of the corollaries to Keynes's attitude was an awareness that reforming governments have the usual effect of upsetting the animal spirits of the financial community. "If," remarked Keynes, "the fear of a Labour Government or a New Deal depresses enterprise, this need not be the result either of a reasonable calculation or of a plot with political intent;—it is the mere consequence of upsetting the delicate balance of spontaneous optimism."

Keynes's analysis of investment motivation led him to a still more constricting conclusion. Since the swings of opinion were so frequent and so violent, Keynes questioned the efficacy of interest rate policy. After all, if investors swung in mood between a pessimism which saw profit nowhere and a euphoria which envisaged riches in every financial commitment, small changes of the order of 1 or 2 percent in rates of interest were unlikely to cause substantial effects upon the volume of investment. What remained if one adopted Keynes's skepticism about interest rate tinkering? It seemed apparent that we needed to grant the state "an ever greater responsibility for directly organising investment." The state, unlike the individual businessman, was in a position to "calculate the marginal efficiency of capital-goods on long views and on the basis of the general social advantage."

Taken literally, this position made a substantial increase in state activity inescapable. In fact, the complementary portion of Keynes's theory of investment, his theory of the rate of interest, did provide a possible loophole, given somewhat different assumptions about interest rates and marginal efficiencies of capital. This theory of the rate of interest quickly became and remained one of the most controversial portions of *The General Theory*.

...Keynes's explanation of interest rate determination was decidedly heterodox...For Keynes the rate of interest was a purely monetary phenomenon intimately associated with the preferences of the holders of money, *not* for present over future gratifications, but rather for perfectly liquid assets over less liquid assets. As Keynes saw the issue, some people held money for reasons which had more to do with the level of their incomes than with time preferences of any variety. Businessmen maintained deposit accounts to facilitate their current payments to employees and suppliers. Individuals carried loose cash in order to buy lunches, newspapers, and daily transportation from home to job and back. In such circumstances unspent income had nothing to do with interest rates. What was related to interest rates was yet a third set of activities.

These activities all came under the heading of the speculative motive for holding instead of spending income. What is the nature of the speculator? He is a person engaged in the purchase and sale of securities in accordance with his own estimate of the imminent course of security prices. That speculator who believes stock prices will rise in the near future is a speculator impelled to buy more stock and accordingly hold less money. Very probably he will borrow on margin the better to profit from his judgment. Now, a prediction about stock prices, Keynes pointed out, is inevitably a prediction also about interest rates, since a stock yield—the relationship between stock prices and dividends disbursed—is an interest rate. It follows that when stock prices rise, interest rates *must fall,* for a dollar dividend of a certain amount is a smaller percentage of a higher-priced security.

This is far from the end of the matter. If most speculators are convinced that stock prices are fated to rise and interest rates to fall, they will bid actively for the securities controlled by the minority of pessimists who hold the opposite opinion. But the very attempts of the bulls among the speculators to expand their security holdings will produce the results which caused the actions. To some extent this is another instance of the self-fulfilling prophecy. Stock prices truly rise and yields accordingly do drop. In short, interest rates shift because speculators expect them to shift and act in such a fashion as to validate their own predictions.

The situation is symmetrical. If speculators anticipate a decline in the market and rising yields, logic directs them to dispose of their securities and to sell short into the bargain. They attempt to increase their stock of money in order to purchase securities at a later date and lower prices. However, their effort to sell securities *before* they decline in value has the effect immediately of depressing the stock market, lowering average stock prices, and raising average stock yields. Once more today's rate of interest is the consequence of speculators' expectations about tomorrow's rate of interest. In sum, the rate of interest is indeed a premium, but a premium paid for surrendering cash, the perfectly liquid asset, for securities, imperfectly liquid assets.

Upon this proposition Keynes constructed some substantial conclusions. The most provocative concerned public policy. If the speculators behaved as Keynes insisted they did, the monetary authorities, in this country the Board of Governors of the Federal Reserve System and in England the Directors of the Court of the Bank of England, had strong weapons of reaction in their hands. Thus, if the authorities believed it inadvisable for interest rates to rise even though speculators put selling pressure on the stock market in anticipation of falling security prices and rising stock yields, then they could simply purchase on behalf of the central bank the securities which the speculators unloaded—at unchanged prices and yields. This is the most potent of monetary weapons, open market operations.

Open market operations are perfectly capable of actually lowering interest rates. When the Open Market Committee of the Federal Reserve System begins to purchase securities, its action raises stock prices and lowers security yields. Central banks conventionally buy and sell only government securities, but what happens in this segment of the market quickly spreads to corporate securities, bank loans, and mortgage rates. Thus it is that the rate of interest is within the control of public policy. In effect if not in law, any country's financial authorities can supply speculators with all the money or all the securities they wish. Public authority, after all, prints both the money and the government securities.

This theory of interest completes the Keynesian account of the investment process. Keynesian investors compare marginal efficiencies of capital with rates of interest. A given speculator contemplating a specific purchase will ask himself whether the expected profit (the marginal efficiency of capital) exceeds the cost of the funds he needs to buy the machine (the rate of interest). If the marginal efficiency of capital exceeds the rate of interest, the investor makes his commitment. If the rate of interest is higher than the marginal efficiency of capital, he will refrain. When other elements of the problem are constant, investment increases when either interest rates fall or expected profits rise, and of the two, interest rates are firmly within the power of public agencies.

What happens when a favorable conjuncture of marginal efficiencies and rates of interest causes investors to expand their expenditures? The Keynesian theory sketches a multiplier process. The first impact upon national income is equal to the size of the new investment. New investment orders become income to machine builders and their employees. This is the first step in a sequence. Kahn's multiplier measures the complete change in national income by focusing upon the marginal propensity to consume—the proportion of *additional* income that individuals spend. When the marginal propensity to consume is one-half, the multiplier is two. An extra million dollars of investment accordingly increases national income *first* by a full million, *then* by the half-million which consumers spend out of their increased incomes, *then* by the quarter-million which the next group of income recipients devotes to consumer purchases, and so on. The sum of the increments to national income is two million dollars. In exactly the same fashion, any decrease in investment must diminish national income and employment by amounts greater than the size of the initial decline in investment.

It is plain just how heavily the Keynesian theory of income determination depends upon the behavior of investors and the quantity of investment. The skeleton of the theory is simple enough. Investment is determined by the marginal efficiency of capital and the rate of interest. The marginal efficiency of capital in turn is jointly influenced by the profits expectations of investors and the prices of the machines which they contemplate buying. The rate of interest emerges partly from the liquidity preferences of speculators and partly from the open market decisions made by the monetary authorities. It is within the discretion of these authorities to lower interest rates. If the investment community is receptive, lower rates of interest stimulate investment. If the marginal propensity to consume is high, the investment multiplier will also be large. A huge multiplier implies a very sizable change in national income in response to a comparatively small change in investment. Under ideal conditions, interest rate (or monetary) policy can shift the economy from an unsatisfactory equilibrium level marked by high unemployment to a full-employment equilibrium level.

Ever since the appearance of *The General Theory,* conservative Keynesians have been inclined to rely heavily upon the efficacy of monetary policy. Monetary policy's virtues are substantial. Of all tools of economic policy, interest rate manipulation requires the smallest bureaucracy, the least interference by politicians, and the most expertise... It is rapidly implemented, and it is readily reversible when circumstances alter....

For such reasons as these, monetary policy has been enjoying a revival among economists and public officials. Although nothing in the Keynesian system contradicts the virtues of monetary policy, Keynes himself often doubted that it would suffice to resuscitate a depressed economy, particularly when business confidence had really waned.

Nor was it necessary to rely on monetary policy to do the whole job of economic rescue. Keynes's theoretical construction now at last provided a powerful justification for his old favorite among practical antidepression weapons—public works financed by government deficits...Unemployment and depression were the consequences of a deficiency of aggregate demand for goods and services. If investment flagged, one way to stimulate it was variation of interest rates. Granted. But a surer and a quicker policy was increased government expenditure. All the favorable multiplier effects of expanded private investment could be as reasonably anticipated from an increase in the government's deficit. Analytically, in fact, an increase in government spending, unaccompanied by an increase in taxes, was identical in meaning with an autonomous expansion of private investment.

Naturally, Keynes preferred that kind of public spending which supported projects of social utility—housing, schools, hospitals, parks, and the like....

In his discussion of fiscal policy, Keynes emphasized the public works route to economic expansion. However, the same or substantially the same impact upon national income and employment can be produced by an alternative fiscal technique—tax reduction accompanied by an unchanged level of public expenditure. The 1964 American tax reduction measure... was an experiment with this fiscal device.

However, even though the impact upon national income of a $14 billion reduction in federal taxes may approximate the impact of a $14 billion expansion of public programs, in one important respect the two policies imply different social meanings. Reducing taxes enlarges the sphere of private control over spending, but expansion of public spending widens the sphere of the socially determined allocation of the community's resources. The two routes to prosperity have two different emphases, one on the private economy and one on the public sector. Preference for one rather than the other is likely to be based less on the comparative impact upon national income and more on personal valuations of the importance of outstanding social needs and the merits of the consumer's freedom to allocate the maximum proportion of his own income.

Inevitably, Keynes understated the difficulties in the path of public works as a major administrative device. These, a generation of experience has demonstrated, are not conceptual or theoretical. They are administrative, technical, and political. Particularly in the United States, it is hard to persuade democratic legislatures to take prompt and appropriate action. It is not easy to define the types of public works appropriate to various economic contingencies, nor can the flow of expenditure be readily turned off when the need has passed. The larger the scale of the public work, the more it displays the embarrassing tendency to reach maximum impact on national income and employment after the depression has vanished, when a prudent administration might prefer to curtail rather than enlarge its spending.

Keynes himself envisaged three additional complications. Unless the financing of public works was carefully managed, an additional government demand for funds might have the adverse effects of raising interest rates and discouraging private investment. All the more was it necessary, therefore, to coordinate monetary and fiscal policy. Again, because of the "confused psychology" of investors, public works might have an adverse effect upon their confidence, the marginal efficiency of capital, and the level of private investment. Finally, under conditions where foreign trade is important to the economy—England's constant situation—a portion of the employment benefits from public works flows to other countries, which enjoy the chance to enlarge their exports. Less firmly Keynes suggested a fourth point, that the marginal propensity to consume might decline as the income of the community expanded.

It is worth emphasizing that Keynes's original reservations and those which are derived from American and British experimenting with public works do not invalidate the theoretical case for public works...Put to the choice, no modern government would care to restrict its tools against depression to monetary policy. All sophisticated administrators strive for the appropriate, efficacious mixture of monetary and fiscal measures. The last presidential candidate who believed otherwise finished an extraordinarily bad second in 1964.

In this altered Keynesian universe, what would become of the classical remedy for economic depression—a general reduction in wages? The outcome had its points of paradox. In the end Keynes did not deny that a "reduction of money-wages is quite capable in certain circumstances of affording a stimulus to output, as the classical theory supposes." But as Keynes demonstrated, the manner in which the stimulus operated would be quite different in the Keynesian and the classical systems. Keynes was prepared to claim that even where reductions in money wages might fairly be assumed to increase employment, it was possible to produce the same effects much less painfully by manipulating interest rates instead of wages.

The tale as Keynes told it went like this. To begin with, a general wage reduction was incapable of expanding employment simply because producers' costs were thereby reduced. As incomes dropped because of wage reduction, demand inevitably fell. At best the two movements would offset each other, and real wages and real output would be unaffected. But this was only the preliminary to the argument proper. The appropriate way to identify the impact of wage cuts was to examine their influence upon the key variables of the Keynesian system: the marginal efficiency of capital, the rate of interest, and the propensity to consume.

Keynes commenced with the last of the three. If wages fall, so will prices. Some redistribution of real income will also occur, essentially away from wage earners, whose compensation is flexible, to lenders and landlords, whose compensation is fixed for substantial periods by contracts and leases. On balance this redistribution is unfavorable to spending and employment, for it takes income away from the poor, whose marginal propensity to consume is high, and awards it to the prosperous, whose marginal propensity to consume is taken to be lower. In the circumstances total consumption is likely to be reduced.

What will happen to investment? If money wages at home fall and abroad remain stable, then exports in the wage-reducing country should rise and imports fall. A favorable balance of payments should emerge. Since this is defined as a portion of total investment, total investment accordingly appears to be stimulated. There is a second favorable possibility. The business community may expect the wage reduction to be temporary. If they are convinced that wages will soon recover, investors will find it advantageous to invest now and steal a march on competitors who will be compelled later on to pay higher prices for equipment, since it will be produced by better-paid labor. The third favorable effect of wage reduction is psychological. Businessmen may simply feel more cheerful each time wages drop. As a result, their animal spirits will rise, the marginal efficiency of capital will ascend, and investment will soar.

This is to put the issue in its best light. It is at least equally possible for the consequences of wage reduction to be unfavorable to investment. For one thing debt becomes more burdensome to entrepreneurs when prices sag. For another entrepreneurs are quite likely to interpret a general wage reduction as evidence that wages will continue to decline. Such an expectation is as hostile to further investment as its opposite is favorable. What the psychological and economic sum of these possibilities is, no one can say a priori.

Indeed, there is only one variable which is unequivocally moved in the right direction by wage reduction; the rate of interest. The reasons are these. When wages and prices fall, the amount of money needed by businessmen and consumers simply to finance their current transactions also declines. The funds released from the pockets of consumers and the checking accounts of businessmen become available as speculative balances. These expanded balances permit speculators to bid more vigorously for the available supply of securities. Accordingly, the prices of stocks and bonds rise, their yields decline, and other interest rates follow this downward course. Thus, *if* the influence of wage reduction upon the marginal efficiency of capital and the propensity to consume is no worse than neutral, *then* the decrease in interest rates can be counted upon to stimulate investment, set the multiplier in motion, and enlarge income and employment.

So much, in appearance, Keynes conceded to his antagonists. An Indian-giver, he quickly withdrew his temporary concession. For if in this roundabout way the single favorable result of wage reduction was a lower interest rate, was it not possible to achieve the identical effect in a simpler, quicker, and more equitable fashion? Of course it was. All the monetary authorities needed to do was purchase securities on the open market, enlarge the supply of money, bid up the prices of stocks and bonds, and thus achieve an appropriate reduction in interest rates.

Reducing wages was the royal road to trouble with the trade unions. Its effects were inequitable. Inactive lenders and landlords were favored, and active workers and businessmen suffered. Wage reduction caused general uncertainty and gloom. A simple increase in the supply of money by the central banking authorities was accompanied by none of these drawbacks. Its effects were soothing and inspiriting. The active were encouraged. Investment was stimulated. The burden of debt diminished. All the social classes were more justly handled. By the time he had finished, Keynes had reduced wage policy to the status of an inefficient and unjust substitute for monetary policy. Trade union leaders had been right all along in their reluctance to accept the arguments in favor of money-wage reductions. It was their betters, the economists and the financiers, who were in the wrong....

9–3. HERBERT STEIN, *THE FISCAL REVOLUTION IN AMERICA*: CHAPTER 8—LESSONS OF WORLD WAR II

American fiscal policy came out of World War II much different than it went in. In 1939 fiscal policy, and economic policy generally, had been becalmed. After a decade of depression, and despite a rise of 7 million in employment from 1932, there were still about ten million unemployed, a situation generally recognized as intolerable and yet tolerated. There was widespread agreement that, as things stood, private investment would not be sufficiently vigorous to lift the economy to full employment and keep it there. But the country was unable to adopt either of the two remedies that it was offered. It would not commit itself to permanent deficit spending to compensate for the deficiency of private investment, as it was urged to do by the stagnationists. On the other hand it would not take those steps to encourage private investment that were recommended by conservatives. Contracyclical use of the budget to help stabilize the economy was commonly accepted, either as a systematic policy or as behavior that in a pragmatic economic and political sense was inevitable. But as long as the country could not get over the big issue about stagnation and permanent deficits it could not proceed with the development of practical steps to get the maximum benefits of contracyclical policy.

The war changed all of that radically. Full employment became a national goal in a much more imperative and operational sense than it had ever been during the Depression. The debate over secular stagnation was adjourned, and even those who regarded it as the natural state of the American economy agreed that its arrival would be delayed for some years after the war. The opposition to the works of the New Deal became more discriminating, and this in turn permitted those who generally supported the New Deal to accept the possibility that some criticism might be constructive. Once the more acrimonious issues had been laid aside, attention could turn to the less ideological problems of effective stabilization policy, and some possibilities were found which gave promise of reconciling values and points of view that had formerly seemed in conflict.

All of this came about primarily as a result of conditions created coincidentally and accidentally by the war. The war created full employment, deferred the prospect of secular stagnation, provided a respite from the controversies of the New Deal, involved businessmen in the management of government economic policy, and left behind an enormous federal debt, large budgets, and pay-as-you-go taxation. By the end of the war all of the ingredients of the fiscal revolution, insofar as there has been a revolution up to 1968, were present.

Our interest here is not in the financing of the war but in the ideas which the war generated about the conduct of fiscal policy in peacetime. Therefore, the focus of our story shifts from the making of current fiscal policy decisions to the discussion in the government, in professional economic circles, in business organizations, and in the press, of "plans" for the post-war economy. That full employment was the national goal and that we would not be satisfied with a permanent army of unemployed had been said before the war by President Roosevelt and by others. But this was not understood to mean that the administration had to deliver full employment in any particular year, or even produce a program which promised to lead to full employment on any definite schedule, on pain of being thrown out of office. Even the more limited and specific goal of providing work relief for all the able-bodied unemployed was not taken literally but was met very partially and unevenly during the thirties.

In 1943, Paul Samuelson wrote, "in the years prior to 1939 there were noticeable signs of dwindling interest in the problem of unemployment, which took the form of ostrich-like attempts to 'think' away the very fact of unemployment by recourse to bad arithmetic and doubtful statistical techniques. And even among professional economists there was increased emphasis on the recovery of production and income to 1929 levels."

In 1939 there was no strong liberal, labor, or left opposition driving for a more effective solution to the unemployment problem. While the CIO regularly supported enlarged appropriations for relief, it was otherwise mainly occupied with representing the employed—organizing them and getting wage increases—rather than with doing anything about the unemployed. The intellectual left was preoccupied with the international situation, with its own relations to communism and the Communists, and with remote ideas about general reform of the system. There was no spontaneous movement among those persons still suffering from unemployment, and there were no popular leaders—no Huey Longs or Townsends—to compete with Roosevelt for the support of the forgotten man. The President had become not only a symbol of concern for the masses but the exclusive symbol, and what he would not do no one else would propose to do.

Concern with the shape of the postwar world and postwar America began even before the United States entered the war and rose to a high pitch as the war progressed.

From the beginning, and without exception, full employment was a central feature of the society that had to be constructed in the U.S. Of course, to swear devotion to full employment as a postwar goal in 1943 was much easier than to espouse full employment as an immediate goal in 1939. The postwar promise would not have to be made good for some years; no immediate action or decision was required as a demonstration of good intent. Yet there can be no doubt that the real determination to have full employment increased enormously during the war. Political leaders, government officials, and all private parties directly concerned with influencing economic policy came to give much higher priority to full employment in their own scale of national objectives for peacetime. They also came to believe that the "people" gave it such high priority that no political party or person could hope to be successful unless identified with the achievement of this goal. No party in office could remain in office without delivering full employment. No group could expect to have its views on any aspect of economic policy taken seriously unless it was thought to be constructive on this subject.

The great weight assigned to full employment as a postwar goal certainly resulted from the achievement of full employment during the war against the background of ten years of depression. The generation that lived through 1929 to 1945 knew both how valuable full employment was and how grave was the risk of falling far below it. The high level of prosperity achieved during World War I had not made peacetime prosperity a national goal to be achieved when that war would be over, because peacetime prosperity was part of the "normalcy" to which that generation expected to return. Throughout World War II, on the contrary, the public was very pessimistic about the prospect for full employment after the war, as was shown by many polls taken during that period. Fear of what might happen combined with heightened awareness of the benefits of full employment to raise that goal to the top rank of national objectives.

One important lesson of the war was that the benefits of full employment were not confined to those persons who had previously been unemployed. Aside from the direct effects of military service, everyone, or almost everyone, was much better off than he had ever been before. Although current consumption had not increased for many and had decreased for some, incomes after tax were very much higher, even after discount for higher prices, and the prospect of incomes at wartime levels without wartime taxes was dizzying. It was not only incomes that full employment provided; it was also opportunity and mobility and freedom of many kinds. Therefore the idea spread that full employment was the important and essential means to deliver what every group wanted for itself and had been seeking by other more limited means.

Raising full employment in the scale of common goals did much to elevate fiscal policy as the main instrument for achieving the nation's economic objectives. Fiscal policy promised to be fairly efficient in achieving the full employment goal while being, at least in some variants, neutral with respect to more divisive goals. One could be for active use of fiscal policy to promote high employment without being pro-business or anti-business, or pro-planning or anti-planning. Disputes over these other issues could continue, and did, but no one had to, or could afford to, let his insistence on these other positions stand in the way of supporting a more or less neutral policy for full employment. This characteristic of fiscal policy was shared by monetary policy, but during the war the potentialities of monetary policy were still not highly regarded. When later more weight was to be placed on monetary policy, this only served to enhance the possibility of finding an effective policy for full employment, combining monetary and fiscal instruments, without involving more controversial measures or objectives.

An early example of the acceptance by conservatives of both full employment as the most urgent goal and of fiscal policy as a primary means for achieving it was the establishment of the Committee for Economic Development by a group of leading businessmen in 1942. The committee took as its first objective, specified in its charter, the attainment of high employment. While the charter did not itself prescribe how this was to be done, the committee's research program from the beginning, and the policy statements which began to appear before the end of the war, placed great emphasis on fiscal policy. That this was the original intent is clear from the prominent position in the committee of Beardsley Ruml and Ralph Flanders, both long time supporters of an active fiscal policy.

In December, 1942, *Fortune* magazine, a leading voice of the business community, proposed that the government should commit itself to the maintenance of full employment after the war, to be achieved by government spending if necessary.

Perhaps more significant, and certainly more surprising, was the position taken by the Republican candidate, Thomas Dewey, in the 1944 Presidential election campaign. He said in his speech accepting the nomination:

> It would be a tragedy after this war if Americans returned from our armed forces and failed to find the freedom and opportunity for which they fought. This must be a land where every man and woman has a fair chance to work and get ahead. Never again must free Americans face the specter of long-continued mass unemployment. We Republicans are agreed that full employment shall be a first objective of national policy. And by full employment, I mean a real chance for every man and woman to earn a decent living.

Dewey emphasized the role of government as a "necessary intervenor" to see that workers had jobs, and in his most pointed statement said:

> If at any time there are not sufficient jobs in private employment to go around, then government can and must create additional job opportunities because there must be jobs for all in this country of ours.

The acceptance of full employment as *the* goal and of fiscal policy as *the* means, at least as the last resort, by liberals and inheritors of the New Deal is as significant as their acceptance by conservatives...The assurance of full employment was only one of many ways in which the earlier New Dealers proposed to reform the old order, and fiscal policy was only one of many ways by which they hoped to accomplish the reform. Their discovery that what they and the country really wanted most of all was full employment achieved in the most direct way was important in releasing policy from the stalemate in which it had been stuck before the war. Of course, by 1940 they had achieved much reform, and had discovered that the country was not prepared for more. But their conversion was also due to the war's demonstration of the many-sided blessings of full employment itself and of the irrelevance, to say the least, of many of their programs for that goal. The new attitude of the liberals is best demonstrated by their proposal of the Full Employment Bill....

Acceptance of the active use of fiscal policy was made easier by a radical change in the conception of the economic problem which occurred during the war. In 1938 and 1939 it was widely believed that the United States faced for the indefinite future a problem of persistent economic stagnation. This belief was, after all, natural. We had had nine or ten years of stagnation and had not yet emerged from it. True, there had been fluctuations during the decade, but the basic problem was believed to be the low level around which the economy fluctuated rather than the fluctuations themselves.

There were, as we have seen, two common explanations for this persistent stagnation. One was that a number of historic changes, not caused by policy, had occurred in America which depressed the tendency to invest. These changes included the slowing down of the rate of population growth, the closing of the frontier, and the exhaustion of technological opportunities for investing large amounts of capital such as had been provided by the railroads, electric power, and automobiles. The other explanation was that the policies of the New Deal had made unprofitable and excessively risky the "underlying" investment opportunities that did exist.

It was largely on the basis of the first explanation, the secular stagnation thesis, that active use of fiscal policy was being advocated in the days before the war. But there were a great many people who would not accept the fiscal prescription based on this explanation. They did not like the explanation because it denied the possibility of stimulating investment by modifying policies to which they were opposed. They could not accept the view of investment as a passive response to historical factors, which seemed to deny the dynamic role of the businessmen, in which they took pride and which "legitimized" their incomes and position in society. And they could not accept the never-ending growth of the federal debt to which the thesis seemed to point.

As the war progressed, the secular stagnation argument receded into the background. The possibility of, and need for, an active fiscal policy to deal with fluctuations rather than with stagnation came to the fore. This was a position which conservatives could accept, or at least accept more readily. The fading of secular stagnation as *the* rationale of fiscal policy was partly the result of economic argument. It took a little while after the first promulgation of the stagnation thesis by Alvin Hansen in 1938 before rebuttals from "scientific" sources began to be heard. By 1940 and 1941, however, negative analysis was reaching a flood. It came from Schumpeter, Angell, Hardy, Simons, and many others. The whole thesis was under considerable suspicion by the time George Terborgh dealt it a most damaging blow in his 1945 book, *The Bogey of Economic Maturity*.

This intellectual argument was reinforced by the facts which the war itself created. Even if "secular stagnation" had been an accurate description of our historical legacy as it stood in 1939, the war was itself an historical event of great power which was changing that legacy. The decline in the birth rate was being reversed. The Federal government was making large expenditures for research and development, much of which was expected to have peacetime applications that would call forth private investment. Increased American involvement with the outside world might even take the place, economically, of the vanished frontier on this continent.

All of this was hypothetical, although probably not more so than the original argument for secular stagnation. It might not prevent the arrival of that condition forever or even for a very long time. However, two wartime developments carried more general conviction for a postwar period of moderate but uncertain length. One was the backlog of business and consumers' demand resulting from limited production of plant, equipment, housing, and consumers' durable goods during the war. The other was the enormous accumulation of government securities and bank deposits in private hands that resulted from the big wartime deficits. These two factors combined promised a high postwar demand for goods and services and consequently for labor. The demand might fluctuate, being sometimes excessive and inflationary and at other times deficient, so that there would be need for a policy to moderate fluctuations and prevent them from developing into spirals. But there was no reason to think that a fiscal program to deal with these fluctuations would require persistent deficits. On this minimum position even the stagnationists could agree, with their fingers crossed about how long it would last....

Until the war, fiscal policy to stimulate the economy had always been *spending* policy. President Hoover, as we have seen, had increased expenditures somewhat, and the big demand for a more active policy was a demand for greater spending. Roosevelt substantially stepped up expenditures beginning in 1933, and when he had his own recession to deal with in 1938 he turned to even higher expenditures. Again in 1939 his fiscal proposal for spurring the economy was a proposal for more spending. The one administration-supported tax cut of the Depression had been the temporary reduction of one percentage point in income taxes recommended by Hoover at the end of 1929. Aside from that, the Hoover and Roosevelt regimes not only had not incorporated tax reduction in their recovery policies but had repeatedly and substantially raised taxes.

This governmental emphasis on higher spending rather than lower taxes had ample support in the attitudes of economists during the 1930's. Hundreds of economists had signed petitions in favor of big public works programs during the Hoover administration, but few had opposed the 1932 tax increase and there is no record of recommendations for a tax cut instead. When the intellectual rationale of the New Deal's fiscal policy was being developed, using the Keynesian analysis, the key phrase was deficit spending.

There were several reasons for this concentration on spending rather than tax cuts even by those who accepted or welcomed depression deficits. In its early days, Roosevelt's fiscal policy was largely aimed at achieving certain special effects quickly—notably the employment of people on relief. The idea that jobs might be provided for these people as the indirect consequence of general fiscal measures to stimulate the economy—which would include tax cuts—was not at first appealing to Roosevelt, who found it too round-about a process for his taste. Moreover, even those who relied upon the general process of demand-stimulation by fiscal means, and this probably included Roosevelt in the years after 1937, were skeptical of the effectiveness of tax cuts for that purpose. A federal tax cut was regarded as providing benefits mainly for the rich. With the federal tax system as it existed before the war there was a good deal to this, at least more to it than there has been since, although even then there was a significant burden of excise taxes on average and low incomes. According to the prevailing belief of the time, the rich could not be counted upon to increase their consumption expenditures if their taxes were reduced, but would only save more. At the same time, it was thought that tax reductions would not encourage private investment, which was presumed to be quite rigidly limited by the market for consumers' goods. So, little increase in total spending was foreseen from a cut in taxes. In fact, as we have observed, some kinds of tax increase, such as the imposition of the undistributed profits tax, were expected by their proponents to increase spending.

Other reasons than the presumed ineffectiveness of tax cuts were probably at least as important. Many of the people who were most active in formulating positive fiscal policies in the late 1930's did not want only to increase spending and employment. They wanted a system in which there was full employment plus a high rate of government spending plus a large amount of income redistribution via progressive taxation. They put a high value on the spending not only as a way of providing employment but also as a source of public investment—in resource development and urban improvement, for example. And they wanted redistribution of income after tax, both because they thought it would contribute to economic stability and because they preferred more nearly equal income distribution than would result from market forces alone.

The emphasis of economists on increasing government expenditures rather than cutting taxes as a means of achieving high employment was heightened by their preoccupation with the problem of secular stagnation. Hansen, for example, did consider the possible role of variations of tax rates as a stabilizing measure, but did not regard that kind of policy as relevant for the problem that really concerned him, which was secular stagnation. If the problem of demand deficiency was going to go on forever, one could not visualize cutting taxes forever but could visualize increasing government expenditures forever.

Of course there were people who did not share this preference for large government expenditures and income-redistributing taxation. They might have been expected to make the case for tax reduction as the route to recovery and full employment. To some extent they did. We have already referred to the persistent opposition of the business community to the imposition of certain taxes during the Roosevelt era and in favor of the reduction of others, including the elimination of the undistributed profits tax. This position was commonly supported by the argument that high taxes of certain kinds, specifically taxes on the profits of enterprise, interfered with recovery. But this view of tax policy as a recovery instrument was not the counterpart of the deficit spending programs of the period. In the first place it did not contemplate the creation of deficits. Proponents of tax reduction for recovery were by and large also proponents of balanced budgets, usually with the idea that lower taxes would be accompanied by lower expenditures, but sometimes with the further notion that reduction of particular crucial taxes would increase total revenues as a consequence of its effect in raising the national income. In the second place the conservative advocates of tax reduction during the thirties were not thinking of a continuous flexible program of tax rate adjustment to fluctuating economic conditions.

Thus, proposals for tax reduction during this period did not ordinarily fit within the pattern of a modern program for positive fiscal policy. They did not call for making decisions about tax rates in order to achieve a relation between total revenues and expenditures, whether deficit or surplus, that was appropriate to the varying conditions of the economy. However, it would be a mistake to think that because the tax-reduction proposals of the 1930's did not rely upon modern, Keynesian reasoning they were therefore radically different from the tax-reduction proposals made and adopted in the 1960's.

The big change between the 1930's and the 1960's is not the support of businessmen and conservatives for tax reduction, even in the presence of deficits, but the inclusion of tax variation as an equal, or even senior, partner with expenditure variation in the thinking of advocates of modern, positive fiscal policy. Some early glimpses of this we have already noted. There is Viner in 1931 saying that appropriate policy in a depression is to spend much and tax little. There is Keynes in 1933 nodding to tax reduction but passing on to talk of higher expenditures. There is the Hutchins Committee of 1934, with B. Ruml as a member, suggesting that the effectiveness of the administration's fiscal policy was limited by its exclusive concentration on expenditure increase to the neglect of tax reduction. Again there is Ruml in late 1937 with his lost suggestion of tax forgiveness as a way to halt the recession. But still, there was very little of this before the war.

The mere spelling out of the logic of deficit spending was bound to reveal that it was the deficit, not the spending, that did the trick, and therefore to suggest that the trick could be done by lower taxes as well as by higher spending. This became clear to the New York Times in reflecting on a statement by Marriner Eccles that the government's net contribution to national income was the excess of its expenditures over its receipts. In an editorial of December 28, 1938, the Times pointed out that on this theory we could just as well spend only $4 billion a year and declare a complete tax holiday. "Such a course would at least have the advantage that it would keep expenditures at a manageable level for the day when taxation was once more resumed." But the Times was not really recommending such a policy. The Times of 1938 was still writing as if it regarded the balanced budget as the only reliable standard. The point about the tax holiday was apparently made only with the purpose of ridiculing the idea of deficit spending. During the course of the Temporary National Economic Committee hearings in the spring of 1939 Senator O'Mahoney made a similar observation with a similar intent....

Treating expenditures and taxation separately also led to recognition of two other points. On the most common assumptions a reduction of taxes would have less expansive effect than an equal increase of government expenditures for the purchase of goods and services. This was because taxpayers would increase their expenditure by only part of their tax reduction, saving the remainder. As a corollary to this, an equal increase of expenditures and revenues would be expansive, because the expansive effect of the increase in expenditures would be greater than the contractive effect of the equal tax increase.

By the end of the war economists had become familiar with the idea that there were three routes to full employment: increased expenditures, reduced taxes, or increased expenditures matched with increased taxes, which was the balanced budget route.

The chief policy implication of the progress of fiscal theory during the war years was to focus economists' attention more on taxation as a variable instrument of stabilization policy. Probably the clearest and most influential exposition of this point was Professor Abba Lerner's theory of "functional finance," published in 1943, with its insistence that the function of taxation was to restrain private expenditures, and that taxes should therefore never be higher than was necessary to hold total spending to a non-inflationary rate....

The shift from the secular stagnation problem to the problem of fluctuations in thinking about fiscal policy directed attention to the search for measures that could be flexibly applied in either an anti-deflationary direction or an anti-inflationary direction. When this consideration became important, certain technical advantages of operating on the revenue side of the budget came to the fore. Experience during the 1930s had not been encouraging about the possibility of increasing expenditures quickly without great waste. On the tax side, if the Congress was willing, billions of dollars of after-tax income could be put into people's pockets at the stroke of a pen and there was then no reason to think that people would be slow in spending the money. Further, if a spending program meant a public works construction program, as it did in most formulations, the construction industry might prove too narrow a base upon which to raise the necessary expenditures. In the event of a serious depression, the amount of public-works spending required to sustain or restore the economy might be so large as to inflate construction costs and discourage private investment. There was some evidence that this had happened during the Depression. A tax reduction on a large scale would have much more widely distributed impacts and would be less likely to cause price increases. This defect of a spending program would not be significant if the need for supporting the economy was chronic, because in that case the construction industry could be built up to the necessary size. But if the problem were one of serious *instability,* the attempt to achieve stability by spending on public works might involve major destabilization of the construction industry.

These wartime developments all emphasized the possibility of using revenue variation as a major instrument of active fiscal policy, and perhaps the superiority of the revenue side over the expenditure side on technical grounds. But for many of the leading advocates of active fiscal policy, revenue variation remained a barely recognized stepsister of spending. Alvin Hansen is a leading example of those who recognized the possibility in principle of operating on the revenue side of the budget, but whose practical interest was all in raising federal expenditures.

However, a number of people concerned with postwar fiscal policy began to put tax policy rather than expenditure policy in the center of the picture. The most prolific and influential of these was Beardsley Ruml. In a nationwide radio broadcast in 1943 he briefly outlined a position that he was to reiterate many times in many different ways during the war...

Most of these ideas were repeated and elaborated in a pamphlet, which Ruml wrote with H. Christian Sonne for the National Planning Association in 1944 and which received the "general endorsement" of the Business Committee of that organization....

Ruml was the main bridge between the thinking of economists on fiscal policy and the thinking of businessmen. He served this function, not by "selling" the policy views of contemporary economists to the business community, but by combining what was essential and valid in the analysis of economists as he saw it with the values of businessmen to produce a new synthesis. The general system he developed was basic not only to the postwar thinking of businessmen but also to the postwar national consensus on fiscal policy.

This is not to say that by the end of the war national thinking assigned to tax adjustment the major role in fiscal policy which was evident in the 1960's. It was probably still true in 1945 that "compensatory fiscal policy" or fiscal policy for high employment was commonly understood to refer to expenditure policy. Significantly, when a Full Employment Bill was introduced in the Congress in 1945, calling for all-out use of fiscal policy to achieve that objective, its proponents were still relying chiefly, if not exclusively, upon expenditure policy. But by the end of the war the alternative of a tax adjustment policy had been injected into national thinking and would assume increasing importance thereafter.

An aspect of budgetary behavior that came to much enlarged prominence during the war was built-in flexibility. As applied to taxation, this meant the tendency for revenues to rise when employment and national income rose and for revenues to decline when employment and national income fell, if the tax rates and exemptions were not changed. This variation of revenues resulted, of course, from variation in the size of the tax base to which the tax rates applied. In the case of the federal government the tax base was largely corporate incomes, individual incomes, and sales of a variety of goods, such as alcoholic beverages and tobacco. All of these, and particularly the taxable incomes, tended to vary directly with economic conditions and even more than in proportion to the national income. Thus, if the national income fell by 10 percent, corporate profits would almost certainly fall by much more than 10 percent and individual incomes above the exemption level would also fall more than 10 percent. (Suppose a family with a $5,000 income tax exemption suffers a decline of its income by ten percent, from $10,000 to $9,000. Then its taxable income declines by 20%, from $5,000 to $4,000.)....

The problem essentially was to determine how much total spending—by government, business, and consumers—was consistent with reasonable price stability, what total spending would be with the existing taxes, and what increase of taxes, if any, would be required to hold total spending down to the desired rate. This problem did not have to be solved in a Keynesian way. Professor James W. Angell, for example, approached the problem on the premise that total spending would be determined by the amount of money in circulation, and that fiscal policy would affect total spending through its effect on money in circulation. However, the standard approach was Keynesian in the sense that it assumed a large part of total private spending, including consumption expenditures, to be determined by income, and the main effect of taxation on spending to come through its effect on income after tax. Keynes himself had demonstrated the method for Great Britain in a pamphlet, "How to Pay for the War."...

Balancing the budget at high employment would guard against the grossest errors of fiscal policy, especially against the error of trying to balance the budget in a depression. It would permit the full operation of the built-in stabilizers in the budget, since if the budget balanced at high employment it would automatically run a deficit in depression and a surplus in boom. This would make for stability in the economy even if, in any particular year, tax rates high enough to balance the budget at high employment were not the best of all possible policies to follow. At the same time Ruml, and later the CED, believed that setting tax rates to balance the budget at high employment and leaving them there would make for stability of tax rates, or at least eliminate one cause for instability of tax rates, and they valued that highly.

In the minds of some people, including Ruml, there was an advantage to preserving the budget-balancing principle in some form. The idea was thought to have substantial force in the country as a symbol of sound finance. There was no point to attacking that symbol frontally, creating a great debate, and weakening confidence if it was not necessary to do that in order to enlist the power of the budget against major economic disturbances. Redefining budget-balancing to mean balancing the budget at high employment was one effort to preserve the symbol while making room for a desirable flexibility in the budget....

The developments of the war, the opportunity provided to reflect on the experience of the 1930's, and the further digestion of Keynes led to a convergence of thinking on two points. The first was that the government must take responsibility for the maintenance of full employment, however defined—or, more commonly, not defined. The second was that active fiscal policy must be a major instrument, perhaps the major instrument, for discharging that responsibility. But, as we have seen, two different views of proper and feasible fiscal policy after the war emerged among people who shared these beliefs.

One view was that the government could and should determine its fiscal actions by reference to continuous analysis and forecast of the amount of action which would be just sufficient to give full employment. This view commonly but not always implied that the fiscal action would be on the expenditure side of the budget. The other view was that the government should rely mainly on revenues as the chief instrument of an active fiscal policy, should ordinarily depend upon the automatic, built-in flexibility of revenues as a stabilizing force, and should only take further positive action to change tax rates or, in special circumstances, to vary expenditures in case of extreme departure from the employment goal. In this view the idea of a balanced budget could continue as a guide to fiscal policy, but the guide would have to be stated in a way that allowed for flexibility in the actual relation between revenues and expenditures in accordance with economic conditions. In the first view budget-balancing was a mere shibboleth and had no part to play.

The difference between these views cannot be identified with the difference between Keynesian and anti-Keynesian positions. Both were described in the Keynesian language of the flow of incomes and expenditures, and both accepted the idea, which is both Keynesian and pre-Keynesian, of a compensatory fiscal policy. Neither of these views necessarily implied any position on the most distinctively Keynesian doctrine of the possibility and eventual probability of equilibrium short of full employment. As for the distinction between reliance on tax policy and expenditure policy, Keynesian analysis indicated that either could be effective, and Keynes' writings had referred to both as possible instruments although his discussion had tended to run much more in terms of decisions about government spending. The distinction between the two views was partly a question of the degree of flexibility that could practically be obtained with each instrument and partly a question of the accuracy that could reasonably be expected of the forecasts upon which policy might have to rest. There was no clearly Keynesian position on these questions. The distinction between the two views was also in part a matter of political outlook, of attitude towards the probability and consequences of a rapid secular increase of government spending.

The difference between the two views may have also reflected a difference of ambition with respect to the full-employment goal. Proponents of the more continuously and completely managed policy tended to describe their goal as full employment, whereas those who would have more generally relied on built-in flexibility within the limits of a budget balanced at high employment tended to describe their goal as high employment or the avoidance of serious unemployment. However, this choice of language does not itself determine which policy would in fact have been more successful in minimizing unemployment. That would depend upon how well the alternative policies could actually work.

One point of economic doctrine which was later to be an important difference between the two views had not yet come to the fore. That was the question of the possible contribution of monetary policy, as a supplement to fiscal policy, in economic stabilization. Monetary policy was effectively frozen during the war by the commitment of the Federal Reserve to support the prices of government securities, and wartime experience did not provide the same stimulus to the discussion of monetary policy that it provided for fiscal policy. However, the question became important later, and the people who believed that monetary policy could make a significant contribution tended then also to decide that there was little necessity for continuous recourse to fiscal variations other than those that were built-in.

Of course, it should not be inferred that the whole country, or even that part of the country that wrote and talked about fiscal policy, was divided between these two views. The most common doctrine about how to manage our finances after the war was still that we should get back to balancing the budget. Business organizations' plans for the postwar world usually put this at the head of the paternoster, as did innumerable speeches by Congressmen. However, this talk had as little significance as F. D. Roosevelt's 1932 speech in Pittsburgh about balancing the budget, and probably less. The budget-balancing talk was pure ritual and does not at all detract from the national commitment which existed at the end of the war to use fiscal policy to stabilize the economy around high or full employment. The two views we have distinguished here represent the range of thinking that would be influential in determining how that commitment would be executed.

ADDITIONAL READINGS

Bailey, Stephen K., *Congress Makes a Law: The Story Behind the Employment Act of 1946* (1950).

Berle, Adolf A. and Gardiner C. Means, *The Modern Corporation and Private Property* (1932.)

Fusfeld, Daniel R., *The Economic Thought of Franklin Roosevelt and the Origins of the New Deal* (1956).

Hansen, Alvin H. "Economic Progress and Declining Population," *American Economic Review* 29 (March 1939) 1–15.

Hansen, Alvin H., *Full Recovery or Stagnation* (1938).

Keynes, John Maynard, *The General Theory of Employment, Interest and Money* (1936).

Lekachman, Robert, *The Age of Keynes* (1966).

Moley, Raymond, *The First New Deal* (1966).

Schlesinger, Arthur M., *The Coming of the New Deal* (1959).

Sitkoff, Harvard, ed., *Fifty Years Later: The New Deal Evaluated* (1985).

Smithies, Arthur, "The American Economy in the Thirties," *American Economic Review* 36 (May 1946) 11–27.

Stein, Herbert, *Presidential Economics*, 3rd edn (1994).

Tugwell, Rexford G., *The Brains Trust* (1968).

Terkel, Studs, *Hard Times: An Oral History of the Great Depression* (1970).

Weinstein, Michael M., "Some Macroeconomic Impacts of National Industrial Recovery Act, 1933–1935," in Karl Brunner, ed., *The Great Depression Revisited* (1981).

CHAPTER 10

The Keynesian Consensus, 1946–1968

INTRODUCTION

Upon the conclusion of World War II, there was fear that the American economy would slip back into a depression. This view was not universally shared; some economists believed the threat of secular stagnation, if it posed any threat at all, would be in the longer run. By war's end, the population growth rate was picking up, wartime research had provided a new impetus to technological innovation, and some regarded America's next frontier to be trade with other nations. The argument of the secular stagnationists had been blunted. Yet in some quarters there still remained sufficient concern that the United States would quickly return to 1930s-style economy. Thus, a full employment bill was introduced in Congress; what emerged was the far less ambitious Employment Act of 1946, undoubtedly a result of the influence wielded by those skeptical of the stagnation thesis.

Immediate postwar economic performance was anything but sluggish. As members of the armed forces returned home, household formations rose dramatically. Wartime controls had forced the delay of many consumer purchases. This pent-up demand, backed by the enormous savings accumulated during the war, made for a very robust economy. In 1945 a brief recession occurred as hundreds of thousands of jobs in the defense sector were eliminated (for example, thousands of jobs were lost in the aircraft industry on the West Coast in the course of two months). Strong demand resumed as the conversion to a peacetime economy proceeded. President Truman, beset by so many crises on the international front, was distracted from (some would say uninterested in) economic matters. He took several months to name the members of the first Council of Economic Advisers (CEA). The Council did not flourish under his presidency; he preferred to get his economic advice from businessmen, lawyers and fellow politicians. The Council went largely ignored in the Truman years. The three members of his Council did not mesh well. The Chair, Edwin Nourse, was an academic; the Vice Chair was Leon Keyserling, an inveterate planner and reformer from the New Deal era; the third member was John Clark, a businessman and lawyer. Arguments within the Council made it ineffectual. The incompatibility between the Chair and member Keyserling eventually led to Nourse's departure.

The dispute between Nourse and Keyserling stemmed in part from their differences over what policy actions were advisable as the recession of 1948–1949 took shape. Nourse advocated very limited policy changes, while Keyserling favored a far more activist response. Inflation had been feared when the surge in consumer spending became evident by 1947. The response to this threat may have been too restrictive, and brought on the eleven month downturn that lasted from late 1948 to the fall of 1949. Though some minor countercyclical policy actions were taken in 1949, it would be hard to argue that the Truman administration had entered into a major Keynesian policy initiative. What was not lost on many observers was that a mild recession did not become another depression.

The year 1950 brought with it the Korean War. Defense spending rose considerably, necessitating the reinstitution of wage and price controls. The presidential election of 1952 swept General Eisenhower to victory. His selection of Arthur Burns to chair his CEA suggested a less sympathetic and more skeptical view of Keynesian economics in the White House. It also meant a greater appreciation for monetary policy. Deficit spending would not be viewed favorably in an administration headed by a president who had publicly expressed his reservations about the burden increased government debt would place on future generations.

The Eisenhower years are regarded by many as a kind of "golden age." America, though locked in a Cold War, did remain at peace. The suburbanization of the country was in full flower. The veterans of World War II were busily producing the postwar baby boom generation; economic growth was generally strong. Americans were preoccupied with washers and driers, new cars, new homes in suburban developments, and the latest diversion, television. While most households enjoyed a rising standard of living, the prosperity of the 1950s was not without interruption. The Eisenhower presidency did bring with it three recessions in eight years. The recession of 1953–1954 is usually connected with the unwinding of the Korean War, and the reduction in defense spending that followed in its wake. The inventory recession of 1957–1958 demonstrated that inflation could persist even in an economy experiencing a downturn. The third recession, straddling 1960 and 1961, concluded after Eisenhower had left office, and may have provided the razor thin margin of victory to John F. Kennedy in his race with Richard Nixon.

Three recessions, however mild, in eight years presented the Democrats with an irresistible campaign issue in 1960. JFK promised to "get the country moving again," although little of a precise nature was said about how that was to be done. Kennedy was receptive to new ideas on economic policy. His nominations to the CEA were unmistakably Keynesian, although it seems likely that he was personally unfamiliar with the details of Keynesian economics. The CEA had fallen into disuse during the Truman and Eisenhower administrations. Kennedy was intent on bringing the Council back into prominence in economic policy formulation. He accomplished this by appointing Walter Heller, professor of economics at the University of Minnesota, as chair of his CEA. Heller accepted but not without conditions. First, he insisted that as chair he would also act as the president's chief economic adviser. Additionally, Heller demanded that he be permitted to name the other two members of the CEA. Both stipulations were met, and the second one was vital: Heller could select two likeminded Keynesians to join him on the Council. The other members of the original Kennedy CEA were James Tobin and Kermit Gordon. Tobin, professor of economics at Yale, would in time become a fitting successor to Alvin Hansen as the recognized leader of the neo-Keynesian school in the United States, and a recipient of the Nobel Prize in Economic Science.

Heller began to press Kennedy on the need for a tax cut that would cut tax rates for individuals and corporations. JFK's instincts were conservative when it came to tax cuts and budget deficits. His initial skepticism was overcome by Heller's argument: the tax system acted as a drag on the economy; a tax cut would move the economy to full employment where higher tax receipts would lead to a balanced budget; and the gap between actual and potential output would be closed. Heller faced opposition from two quarters within the administration. Some advisers held to the view that if the economy needed a fiscal stimulus it should be in the form of increased government expenditures. John Kenneth Galbraith ably represented this view by asserting that the United States was all too willing to tolerate public squalor amidst private opulence, and needed to lift itself up through a careful program of public works spending. Treasury Secretary Douglas Dillon and Fed Chair William McChesney Martin, both Republicans, opposed a tax cut for predictably conservative reasons; they were alarmed by the inflationary pressures a major tax cut might generate. In any event, Heller prevailed by emphasizing the political palatability of a tax cut with both a skeptical public and Congress. Slowly Kennedy was convinced that a tax cut would work (James Tobin has related how some of the meetings he had with the president in the Oval Office were but thinly disguised tutorials in the principles of economics; he found JFK to be an eager and able student).

A major turning point was the commencement address delivered by President Kennedy at Yale University in June 1962. In that speech he argued that there was no necessary link between budget deficits and inflation, and that the growth of the national debt posed no risks given that it had declined "as a proportion of our Gross National Product." Both assertions were intended to prepare the nation for the short-term side effects of a reduction in taxes. Kennedy finally embraced tax reduction publicly in a speech before the Economic Club of New York in December 1962 in which he declared tax drag to be hampering economic growth. A tax cut was the main feature of his domestic legislative program for 1963. Heller and his Council did not ignore the possibility of inflation. They had instituted a program of wage-price guideposts for labor and business, overseen by Kermit Gordon. The head of U.S. Steel provoked a celebrated confrontation with President Kennedy when he announced a large price increase in defiance of the guideposts. Kennedy's public jawboning did succeed in getting the price increase rescinded, and helped foster the belief that the guideposts could be an effective tool.

While the Tax Reduction Act of 1964 was not in every detail what Kennedy had proposed, its passage was seen as a fitting way to memorialize the slain president. The tax cut would eliminate fiscal drag and stimulate the economy. The expansion of economic activity would generate higher tax receipts and balance the budget, perhaps even produce a surplus, when a sufficiently high level of employment was achieved. Thus, this policy would eventually restore fiscal discipline, allowing a more expansionary monetary policy. As James Tobin would describe it, this was the ideal policy mix: tight fiscal combined with easy monetary policy. Lower interest rates would encourage capital formation, raise productivity growth, and improve living standards. Between 1964 and 1968, the influence of Keynesian economics reached its high point in the United States. The growth-oriented version practiced by American policymakers came to be known as the New Economics. As a final testament to its importance, *Time* magazine reversed its longstanding rule that only living persons appear on its cover. John Maynard Keynes was on the cover of the December 31, 1965 issue.

The year 1965 was indeed a good one and seemed to bear out all the claims made by Keynesian economists. For the year, economic growth was 5 percent, unemployment stood at 4.2 percent, and the inflation rate remained tame at 1.8 percent. Events quickly intruded on the celebration. America's military spending in support of the government of South Viet Nam began to escalate in 1965. In the previous year President Lyndon B. Johnson had declared a war on poverty and unveiled his Great Society programs. Walter Heller had lobbied both Presidents Kennedy and Johnson to address the problem of poverty in America. Kennedy had warmed to the idea; his successor, Johnson, embraced it enthusiastically. Federal spending increased enormously as Lyndon Johnson tried to fight two wars at once. One of the virtues of the Keynesian prescription for tax reductions was its political palatability; taxpayers and legislators would be agreeably inclined to experiment with a tax cut. But in a democratic society, there may be an asymmetry when the need for a tax increase arises. As the 1960s wore on, federal spending continued to mount and inflationary pressures built. Good Keynesian practice called for a tax increase. The

CEA had been warning President Johnson that a tax increase would be needed. Johnson resisted, fearing that such a move might jeopardize his war on poverty.

The overheated economy experienced a credit crunch in 1966. By mid-year the rate of inflation had doubled, industry was near capacity utilization, labor markets were very tight, and firms experienced a heavy backlog of orders. The Fed decided to impose monetary restraint. The industry most severely affected was residential housing. The increase in interest rates diverted funds from the savings and loan industry, as depositors found rates on Treasury bills and commercial paper to be more attractive than those on certificates of deposit. This process of disintermediation left the savings and loan industry with no mortgage money to lend; in some parts of the country, construction activity came to a virtual standstill. With credit conditions extremely tight, Fed Chair William McChesney Martin initially resisted intense White House pressure to ease. He eventually relented under the mistaken belief that an income tax surcharge would soon be passed, a decision that he later came to regret. Johnson's resistance to a tax increase was worn down by his advisers and the increasingly delicate state of the economy. In his State of the Union Address in January 1967, he called for an income tax surcharge. Congressional opposition stalled the proposal for over a year. Finally in June 1968, President Johnson signed a one-year temporary 10 percent tax surcharge into law. Inflation continued unabated. Some economists thought the surcharge to be too little, too late. Although it was renewed in 1969 at a 5 percent rate, other economists thought that consumer spending responded very little due to the temporary nature of the surcharge. Using Keynesian policies to rein in a surging economy had proven far more difficult than stimulating a sluggish one. The New Economics had no easy answers. The Keynesian consensus was about to unravel.

The postwar economic experience of 1946–1968 raises many questions. What does the postwar performance of the American economy tell us about our ability to manage the macroeconomy? Has it put to rest any fears that the stagnation thesis might be right? Have recessions been less frequent? Have they been less severe? What has Keynesian economics contributed to postwar economic growth and stability? What has been the impact of the enormous growth in the size of the government sector? Has its growth been a force for stability? What has been the enduring legacy of the New Deal? How have the various New Deal initiatives (deposit insurance, security laws, unemployment insurance, Social Security to name a few) affected economic performance in the postwar era? Do they distort economic incentives? Or do they enhance the operation of the automatic stabilizers and therefore contribute to economic stability? Are the New Deal reforms still useful? Why did monetary policy receive so little attention in the early years of the Keynesian consensus? Will political considerations always make balanced economic policy impossible? Will tax cuts and spending increases always prove politically easy? Will the less agreeable remedy for an inflationary economy always prove impossible to administer? Has the Council of Economic advisers proven to be a useful and influential policy body? Has the president of the United States become the chief economist of the nation? Do presidents get too much credit, bear too much blame for economic performance? Does the economic experience of the 1960s call into question the ability of policymakers to fine-tune the economy? Is it possible to chart a path that avoids both inflation and stagnation?

DOCUMENTS

The first document "After the War- Full Employment" written in 1943 by Alvin Hansen, Harvard professor and leading American Keynesian, under the auspices of the National Resources Planning Board strikes a worrisome tone, expressing the fear that depression may return after the war is concluded. While offering assurances that prosperity requires a healthy private sector, it is Keynesian policies with increased spending on welfare and public works projects that will prevent postwar stagnation. The Board may have overplayed its hand by recommending so avowedly in public a major role for government. It displeased some conservatives in Congress and further appropriations for the Board were denied in 1943. The Keynesian consensus was not shared by all and built support slowly. Many of the postwar presidents showed some deference to the Keynesian approach.

Documents 10–2 through 10–5 represent a variety of presidential communications. Each is predicated on an acceptance of Keynesian economics. Document 10–2 is selections from President Truman's "Economic Report to the Congress," dated January 7, 1949. Truman notes that the Employment Act of 1946 calls for maximum employment, and that his administration will work to meet that goal and keep depression from returning. While acknowledging his responsibility to maintain employment, his most immediate concern is inflation. Truman seems to be aware of how Keynesian economics can be used against inflation, which he hopes to contain through a tax increase. Document 10–3 is the commencement address John F. Kennedy delivered at the 1962 Yale University commencement. He used the occasion to dispel some of the myths and illusions that had come to characterize the public debate on the economy. Two of his main points are that big government is not so big when measured against the size of the economy, and that budget deficits are not always inflationary. His remarks can be seen as a sign of his own ongoing conversion to Keynesianism and his belief in the need to prepare the public for the deficits that would initially result from a major tax cut. Walter Heller, Kennedy's chief economic adviser, described this speech "as the most literate and sophisticated dissertation on economics ever delivered by a President."

In Document 10–4, the Economic Report of the President, dated January 28, 1965, it is Lyndon Johnson's happy task to report to Congress on the health of the American economy for the year 1964. The 1964 tax cut had been passed and economic performance for 1964 was strong. President Johnson predicts more strong performance to come as the full effect of the tax cut is felt. He credits government for its role, saying "the vital margin of difference has come from government policies…" Richard Nixon's Annual Budget Message to the Congress, Fiscal Year 1972, issued on January 29, 1971, is Document 10–5. His primary concern is the need to continue with anti-inflationary measures. While making no mention of his wage and price controls, he notes that his budget will "promote orderly economic expansion" by adopting "the idea of the full employment budget," a decidedly Keynesian notion.

10–1. ALVIN H. HANSEN, *AFTER THE WAR—FULL EMPLOYMENT*

The immediate aim of the American people is to preserve and safeguard political freedom. But a military victory for the democracies is not enough. If the victorious democracies muddle through another decade of economic frustration and mass unemployment, we may expect social disintegration and, sooner or later, another international conflagration,

A positive program of post-war economic expansion and full employment, boldly conceived and vigorously pursued, is imperative. Democracies, if they are going to lead the world out of chaos and insecurity, must first and foremost offer their people opportunity, employment, and a rising standard of living.

The fact is that many people dread to think of what is coming. Businessmen, wage-earners, white-collar employees, professional people, farmers—all alike expect and fear a post-war collapse. Demobilization of armies, shut-downs in defense industries, unemployment, deflation, bankruptcy, hard times. Some are hoping for a post-war boom. We got that after the first World War. Not improbably we may get it again. If the war lasts several years, we may have at the end of the war sufficient accumulated shortages in residential housing, in durable consumers' goods such as automobiles, and in the plant and equipment required to supply peacetime consumption demands, to give us a vigorous private investment boom. Indeed, we need to be on the alert to prevent a possible post-war inflation. If in fact we do experience a strong post-war boom, there is, however, the gravest danger that it will lull us to sleep. Sooner or later such a boom will end in a depression, unless we are prepared. If appropriate action is taken, there is no necessity for a post-war collapse.

Everywhere one hears it said that, when this war is over, all countries, including our own, will be impoverished. This view is, however, not sustained by past experience. No country need be impoverished if its productive resources (both capital and human) are intact. The productive resources of this country will be on a considerably higher plane when this war is over than ever before. A larger proportion of our population will be trained to perform skilled and semi-skilled jobs. We shall have enormous productive capacities in all the machine industries. And in special consumers' durable industries, where plant and equipment may have become deficient by reason of the war, we shall be able very quickly, with our large basic machine-producing industries, to expand to meet the peacetime requirements. We shall have, when the war is over, the technical investment boom. Indeed, we need to be on the alert to equipment, the trained and efficient labor, and the natural resources required to produce a substantially higher real income for civilian needs than any ever achieved before in our history. Whether or not we shall, in fact, achieve that level of income will depend upon our intelligence and capacity for cooperative action.

We have to make up our minds as a Nation that we will not permit a post-war depression to overwhelm us. We do not have to take economic defeat after the military victory is won. We can, if we will, maintain business prosperity. We can sustain a continuing demand for goods. We can keep industry going at high levels. We can maintain substantially full employment. We can achieve a society in which everyone capable of and willing to work can find an opportunity to earn a living, to make his contribution, to play his part as a citizen of a progressive, democratic country.

An important gain will, we may hope, be won from the war program in the struggle to achieve and to maintain full employment. We have every reason to expect the national income to rise to around $135 billions, in the calendar year 1943. It will be much easier to muster support for a program to resist a decline from a high income level than it has been in recent years to win approval for an adequate program to *raise* income to full employment from a low level. But we must be vigilant lest this gain slip from our grasp. If we let the income slide from 135 to 100, 80, 70 billion dollars, we will have to make the old uphill fight all over again. We must deliberately set out to hold the new income level and to push it higher as rapidly as increasing productivity will permit.

We do not want the Government to run the whole show. We do not want a totalitarian state. We want freedom of enterprise. We want freedom for collective bargaining between employers and employees. We want freedom for cooperative action. We want freedom of choice of occupation.

If purchasing power is maintained at a high level, we need have no fears that private manufacturers, retailers, wholesalers, and farmers will not come forward and supply the market with the goods demanded by the public—a rich variety of goods at reasonable prices. Private business can and will do the job of production. It is the responsibility of Government to do its part to insure a sustained demand. We know from past experience that private enterprise has done this for limited periods only. It has not been able to insure a continuous and sustained demand. The ever-increasing gigantic powers of production of the modern industrial system, far exceeding that of any earlier experience in history, means that an enormous output has to be reached before full employment is approached. Private industry and Government together must act to maintain and increase output and income sufficiently to provide substantially full employment.

When the war is over the Government cannot just disband the army, close down munition factories, and stop building ships. We want an orderly program of demobilization and reconstruction. We must retain such economic controls as are necessary during the reconversion period, until industry is prepared to match supply with demand. Once industry has caught up with the backlog of deferred demand, the controls can and should be removed. To fulfill our responsibility as a Nation it is necessary to achieve the cooperation of business, labor, farmers, and the Government in the reconversion period and then to go on to the great task of developing a vigorous, expanding and prosperous society.

A positive governmental program looking toward full employment would greatly vitalize and invigorate private enterprise. An expansionist program would permit private enterprise to operate at high output levels. There is plenty of work to do. We need improved manufacturing equipment to produce more and better goods at lower prices. We need to carry on extensive research in the laboratories of our great private corporations, in our universities, and in Government bureaus to create new products and develop new processes. We need to rehabilitate and modernize our transportation system—by land, water, and air. We need continued advance in the techniques of production, distribution, and transportation; in short in all those elements that enter into a higher standard of living. We need to rebuild America—urban redevelopment projects, rural rehabilitation, low-cost housing, express highways, terminal facilities, electrification, flood control, reforestation. Many public developmental projects open fresh outlets for private investment. We need a public health program including expansion of hospital facilities. We need a nutrition program. We need more adequate provision for old age. We need higher educational standards in large sections of our country. We need a program to improve and extend our cultural and recreational facilities. We need an enrichment of the material and spiritual resources of our American way of life. We have seen how it is possible to mobilize the productive capacities of the country for war. We can also mobilize them for peace. Under a program of full employment new enterprises would grow up; old enterprises would expand. Youth would find opportunity and employment.

The notion that we cannot finance our own production is quite without foundation. Every cent expended, private and public becomes income for members of our own society. Costs and income are just opposite sides of the same shield. We can afford as high a standard of living as we are able to produce. We cannot afford to waste our resources of men and material. We cannot afford to use them inefficiently. But we cannot afford idleness,...which in the... decade of the thirties was responsible for the loss of $200 billions of income, judged by 1929 standards. We know that this is an under statement. We know now that our national income could have grown from $80 billions in 1929 to $120 billions by 1940. By these standards we lost $400; billions of income in the decade of the thirties. The public expenditures required to rebuild America, to provide needed social services, and to maintain full employment can be provided for out of the enormous income which the full utilization of our rich productive resources (material and human) makes possible. The costs of producing this income are merely payments to ourselves for the work done. There is not—there cannot be—any financing problem which is not manageable under a full employment income. From a $125 billion income we can raise large tax revenues—large enough to service any level of debt likely to be reached and to cover all other Government outlays—and still retain for private expenditures far more than we had left in former years under a $70 billion income with lower taxes. Taxes are merely one way of paying for social services and public-improvement projects which we need. But it is not necessary or desirable *under all circumstances* to finance all public expenditures from taxes. Whether taxes should equal, fall short of, or exceed expenditures must be decided according to economic conditions.

Everywhere it is said, and constantly reiterated, that we must tighten our belts and reduce our Government debt when peace returns. When is it desirable to pay off part of the debt? Certainly not when there is danger of an impending depression. Under certain conditions it would be desirable to do so. Under other conditions it would be quite unsound policy to retire the debt. Financial responsibility requires a fiscal policy (including governmental expenditures, loans, and taxes) designed to promote economic stability. It would be quite irresponsible to cut expenditures, increase taxes, and reduce the public debt in a period when the effect of such a policy would be to cause a drastic fall in the national income. Equally, it would be financially irresponsible to raise expenditures, lower taxes, and increase the public debt when there is a tendency toward an inflationary boom....

The public debt is something very different from the private debt of an individual. An individual will always improve his asset position if he is able to pay off a part of his debt. But a nation may make itself poor by reducing public debt. This is true because such reduction tends to cause deflation, depression, and unemployment. It is a good thing to retire a part of the public debt if you want to check an excessive boom. It would be ruinous to retire the public debt in a post-war period when unemployment was spreading.

A public debt internally held has none of the essential earmarks of the private debt of an individual. A public debt is an instrument of public policy. It is a means to control the magnitude of the national income and, in conjunction with the tax structure, to affect income distribution.

The war has demonstrated the amazing vitality and productive power of American industry. In 1941, the Federal Reserve Index of Production was 156 or nearly 45 percent higher than in 1929, the peak year of the Twenties. In 1942, the Federal Reserve Index averaged 180 or about 65 percent higher than in 1929. And by the end of the year it reached 196.

In this output record there is conclusive evidence that American industry was achieving, despite the hard times of the decade of the thirties, increased productive capacity. Our business units, it is now demonstrated, did avail themselves of cost reducing improvements; new machines, new techniques, and new processes. We know now that our well-established industries at the end of the decade (1931–40) were well equipped with up-to-date machinery and facilities. Were this not so, how would it have been possible for our economy to produce the prodigious volume of goods which in fact it did produce in 1941 and 1942?

...When the war is over, we shall be confronted with a gap that has to be filled when the $90 billions for war (for fiscal 1944, $100 billions) are curtailed. The problem of the post-war period is to fill this gap largely by an increase in private consumption expenditures and in private capital formation.

From the long-run standpoint, a persistently pursued policy to maintain full employment raises interesting questions with respect to the effect of such a policy on (1) the distribution of income, and (2) the proportion of a full employment income which, it may be expected, would be expended on consumption. In brief, it is reasonable to suppose that the ratio of consumption to income in a full employment economy would automatically tend to be higher than the ratio of consumption 'to income at the peak of a boom in a violently fluctuating economy. A full employment economy would tend automatically toward a distribution of income favorable to high consumption. This affords ground for optimism with respect to the feasibility of a positive program designed to maintain full employment. Such a policy, if successfully pursued, tends to develop repercussions upon the distribution of income which reinforce the program to maintain full employment.

That this is true can best be seen if we analyze the problem of corporate profits in a society continually operating at a full employment level. Peak prosperity profits have never in the past been realized for any considerable period of time. In a highly fluctuating society such as we have known, normal profits are some sort of average of good times and bad times. Thus, for example, in the period 1925–1940, the net income of corporations fluctuated very violently in relation to the total national income. In periods of high prosperity, the ratio of net income of corporations to the total national income was high, while in periods of depression, despite a fall in the national income, the ratio of the net corporate income to the total national income was low. Over the entire 16-year period from 1925–40, inclusive, the corporate net income averaged only 4.6 percent of the national income. It should be remembered, moreover, that this 16-year period included many years of serious depression, so that the average national income was relatively low. In other words, corporate profits constituted only a low percent of a small national income—small in comparison with the income potentially realizable.

In a highly fluctuating society, corporate profits are high in good times and extremely low in bad times, but the average must be adequate to motivate a profit economy and insure its workability. If, however, it were possible to maintain continuously a full-employment national income, it is obvious that corporate profits, representing the same percentage of national income as that averaged over the cycle in the past, would yield an absolute profit figure far above the experience of 1925–40. Yet such a percentage continuously maintained would be much lower than the high ratio of profits to national income reached in a fluctuating society in a few peak boom years.

In a society operating at continuously full employment, it is not probable that peak-prosperity profits (in 1925–29 approximately twice the average for the entire period 1925–40) could indefinitely be maintained. In a fluctuating society such high profits are necessary to offset the losses of the depression years, but it is unreasonable to suppose that profits of the magnitude of boom periods would be realized indefinitely.... Either development would tend toward a more equal distribution of income than has prevailed in the past *in boom periods* when full employment was reached. This is true because of the relative decline in the ratio of business profits to the national income *at full employment levels*. Yet, if a full employment income were continuously maintained, the ratio of business profits to national income over the whole cycle might be greater than that experienced in the past, while the *magnitude* of business profits *would* be considerably greater (even though the average ratio of profit to income were no higher) since the average national income for the whole period would be very much higher if we succeed in achieving substantially full employment.

It must be recognized, however, that there are certain limitations on how far profits can be encroached upon, either through wage increases or price decreases, without encountering unfavorable economic repercussions with respect to the cost-price structure. Wage increases and price reduction are likely to cut across all firms in an industry, whether they make profits or not; and wage increases are likely to spread even to industries which are not making abnormally large profits. Thus, the process of encroachment upon boom-time profits through wage increases and price reduction, if carried too far, may disrupt the appropriate balance in the cost-price system.

Redistribution of income through progressive individual and corporate income taxes is less disruptive of these relations for the reason that such taxes apply only where the profits and income actually emerge. They do not affect the high-cost industries which make no profit. As already indicated, there are limitations upon the process of redistribution of income through the methods of wage increases and price reduction. These methods are feasible up to a certain point, but the point is fixed by the requirements of cost-price balance.

...The following policies are indicated:

Adequate program of public-improvement projects including a nation-wide development of national resources, express highways, urban... and a reorganized public housing program....

Expansion of public-welfare expenditures—Federal aid to education, public health, old-age pensions and family allowances. This involves partly an expanded program, and partly a means of reducing State and local property and consumption taxes, thereby stimulating private consumption....

10–2. HARRY S. TRUMAN, JANUARY 7, 1949, SPECIAL MESSAGE TO THE CONGRESS: THE PRESIDENT'S ECONOMIC REPORT

To the Congress of the United States:

...This third annual Economic Report, under the Employment Act of 1946, affords not only the President but also the Congress and the whole country still another occasion to look to our current economic position, to draw courage from our progress, and to benefit by our mistakes. Now is the time to formulate and execute a practical program of immediate and long-range economic measures pointed toward stability and growth.

The year just ended has tested the strength of our economy, and challenged our ability and willingness to act to protect our prosperity. When 1948 opened, the inflation which had attained threatening proportions in the preceding months was continuing unchecked. Prices were rising everywhere. They brought higher but uneasy profits to business firms. They squeezed the family budget of workers, who in turn sought to press wages upward as the cost of living advanced. The rising spiral created more and more maladjustment among prices, wages, and other incomes.

...Our escape from the danger of a general recession in the spring of 1948 does not mean that no further dangers will appear, or that we can wait until they descend upon us in full force before taking wise preventive measures. We have been granted a breathing spell, but we have not been granted lasting prosperity without further effort and vigilance. So long as the rising course of incomes and activity continues, there will be in operation many of the forces which have been responsible for the long-sustained advance of prices. There are a few sectors of our economy where dangerous inflationary forces continue to be predominant. For example, the shortages of steel and electric power, and the steadily mounting costs of public utility services, add further to the higher costs of production which up to now have been rather readily passed on to the consuming public.

While the prosperity of the postwar years has been great, it has rested in considerable part on somewhat temporary factors which were the aftermath of war. In 1949, we are entering a period of harder tests. The momentum of war-created demand and war-created purchasing power has waned, and we must now rely more fully on currently generated purchasing power to absorb a full output of goods and services. We must be more than ever on the alert, to make sure that withdrawal or lessening of temporary demand factors is not accompanied by a reduction of productive activity and the mounting unemployment to which this would lead.

I believe that prosperity can be continued and that, with proper action, the prospective volume of business investment, consumer spending, and governmental transactions should promote ample employment opportunities for the coming year. But many adjustments in price and income relations need to be made, and these must flow mainly from the wise action of the leaders in our enterprise economy. These leaders should draw sustaining confidence from the fact that it is the policy of the Government under the Employment

Act of 1946 to use all its resources to avoid depression and to maintain continuous prosperity.

These favorable prospects will not be realized automatically. The strength of our economy, the strength of our great Nation, depends upon our capacity and willingness to adopt the salutary policies which are required by changing circumstances and to put them into effect.

In this Economic Report, drawing upon the more detailed information and analysis furnished to me by the Annual Economic Review of the Council of Economic Advisers (transmitted to the Congress herewith), I shall first cover the high points in the current and prospective economic situation, and then propose both policy guides and a program to deal with the situation as I evaluate it.

...As we turn from consideration of the facts of our economic situation to a program of action, there are several broad principles which I believe should guide us. These principles should help us to keep clearly in mind where we want to go and how certain roads rather than others are the surest and quickest way of getting there.

...We should remember that the goal we seek is the greatest prosperity for the whole country and not the special gain of any particular group. That is why the Employment Act of 1946 calls upon the President to present an economic program aimed at continuous "maximum employment, production, and purchasing power." I firmly believe that this goal is attainable.

Maximum employment for 1949 means that nearly 1 million additional job opportunities should be provided for the growing labor force. Maximum production means that our increased labor force and modernized plant should strive for a 3 to 4 percent increase in total output. Maximum purchasing power means that the sum total of market demand by government, business, and consumers, domestic and foreign, should be proportionate to our productive capacity. It must not be more or we shall suffer inflation. It must not be less or we shall suffer unemployment and under-utilization of our resources.

...In order to have a yardstick for appraising strength and weakness in our economy and the adequacy of Government programs, we need concrete objectives for economic growth, and particularly standards for a better balance between production and consumption, income and investment, and prices, profits, and wages which will be conducive to sustained economic progress. In the Annual Economic Review of the Council of Economic Advisers, transmitted herewith, there is a detailed treatment of our growth possibilities over the next few years. This shows how our employment, our output, and our standards of living can rise if we encourage and place major reliance upon our free enterprise system, conserve and develop our natural and human resources, retain our faith in responsible Government, and do not relax our efforts.

This study by the Council of Economic Advisers shows that action is now needed on the long range programs which I set forth in the concluding section of this Economic Report.

We are dedicated to the principle that economic stability and economic justice are compatible ends. The fact that our total purchasing power is now at record levels cannot blind us to the equally important fact that the incomes of many people have not risen apace with the cost of living and that they have become the victims of inflation. A prosperity that is too uneven in the distribution of its fruits cannot last.

We must fulfill the requirements of our essential programs—national defense, international reconstruction, and domestic improvements and welfare—even if doing so may require the temporary exercise of selective controls in our economy. We want the greatest amount of economic freedom that is consistent with the security and welfare of the people; but we do not want to sacrifice that security and welfare because of narrow and selfish concepts as to the acceptable limits of government action. If we could have the amount of national defense that we need, make the contribution to international reconstruction to which we are committed, and at the same time maintain and expand our standards of living now and in the future without any kind of selective controls over the economy, that would be most highly desirable. And it is possible that we may not, in fact, be forced to use such controls. But we would rather have these relatively unpleasant restrictions on our freedom of action for a while than imperil our security or allow our human and material resources to deteriorate.

The vigorous commitment by the Government to an anti-inflation policy should not obscure the fact that the Government is equally committed to an anti-depression policy. In fact, curbing inflation is the first step toward preventing depression. And in times like the present, when the economic situation has mixed elements, the Government needs both anti-inflationary weapons and anti-deflationary weapons so that it will be ready for either contingency. It may even be necessary to employ both types of measures concurrently in some combination, for some prices or incomes could rise too rapidly while others could be falling dangerously. The same dictates of prudent policy which call for higher taxes in a period of inflation would call for tax adjustments designed to counteract any serious recessionary movement.

...It is essential to sound fiscal policy to have a budget surplus now. This is our most effective weapon against inflation. It will enable us to reduce our debt now; it would be much more difficult to do so in less prosperous times.

I recommend legislation to increase the Government revenue from taxation by 4 billion dollars a year. The principal source of additional revenue should be additional taxes upon corporate profits, which can be applied without unduly interfering with prospects for continued business expansion and with assurance that profits, after taxes and dividends, will be sufficient for investments and contingencies.

...On previous occasions I have recommended that adequate means be provided in order that monetary authorities may at all times be in a position to carry out their traditional function of exerting effective restraint upon excessive credit expansion in an inflationary period and conversely of easing credit conditions in a time of deflationary pressures. The temporary authority to increase reserve requirements of member banks of the Federal Reserve System, granted by the Congress last August, will expire on June 30, 1949. The expiration of this authority without further action of the Congress would automatically release a substantial volume of bank reserves irrespective of credit needs at the time. The Congress should promptly provide continuing authority to the Board of Governors of the Federal Reserve System to require banks to hold supplemental reserves up to the limits requested last August, 10 percent against demand deposits and 4 percent against time deposits. This authority to the Board of Governors should not be confined to member banks of the Federal Reserve System but should be applicable to all banks insured by the Federal Deposit Insurance Corporation. ...

10–3. JOHN F. KENNEDY, JUNE 11, 1962, COMMENCEMENT ADDRESS AT YALE UNIVERSITY

As every past generation has had to disenthrall itself from an inheritance of truisms and stereotypes, so in our own time we must move on from the reassuring repetition of stale phrases to a new, difficult, but essential confrontation with reality.

For the great enemy of truth is very often not the lie—deliberate, contrived and dishonest—but the myth—persistent, persuasive, and unrealistic. Too often we hold fast to the clichés of our forebears. We subject all facts to a prefabricated set of interpretations. We enjoy the comfort of opinion without the discomfort of thought.

Mythology distracts us everywhere—in government as in business, in politics as in economics, in foreign affairs as in domestic affairs. But today I want to particularly consider the myth and reality in our national economy. In recent months many have come to feel, as I do, that the dialog between the parties— between business and government, between the government and the public—is clogged by illusion and platitude and fails to reflect the true realities of contemporary American society....

There are three great areas of our domestic affairs in which, today, there is a danger that illusion may prevent effective action. They are, first, the question of the size and the shape of the government's responsibilities; second, the question of public fiscal policy; and third, the matter of confidence, business confidence or public confidence, or simply confidence in America. I want to talk about all three, and I want to talk about them carefully and dispassionately—and I emphasize that I am concerned here not with political debate but with finding ways to separate false problems from real ones.

Let us take first the question of the size and shape of government. The myth here is that government is big, and bad—and steadily getting bigger and worse. Obviously this myth has some excuse for existence. It is true that in recent history each new administration has spent much more money than its predecessor. Thus President Roosevelt outspent President Hoover, and with allowances for the special case of the Second World War, President Truman outspent President Roosevelt. Just to prove that this was not a partisan matter, President Eisenhower then outspent President Truman by the handsome figure of $182 billion. It is even possible, some think, that this trend will continue.

But does it follow from this that big government is growing relatively bigger? It does not—for the fact is for the last 15 years, the Federal Government—and also the Federal debt—and also the Federal bureaucracy—have grown less rapidly than the economy as a whole. If we leave defense and space expenditures aside, the Federal Government since the Second World War has expanded less than any other major sector of our national life—less than industry, less than commerce, less than agriculture, less than higher education, and very much less than the noise about big government....

Next, let us turn to the problem of our fiscal policy. Here the myths are legion and the truth hard to find....

Still in the area of fiscal policy, let me say a word about deficits. The myth persists that Federal deficits create inflation and budget surpluses prevent it. Yet sizeable budget surpluses after the war did not prevent inflation, and persistent deficits for the last several years have not upset our basic price stability. Obviously deficits are sometimes dangerous—and so are surpluses. But honest assessment plainly requires a more sophisticated view than the old and automatic cliché that deficits automatically bring inflation.

There are myths also about our public debt. It is widely supposed that this debt is growing at a dangerously rapid rate. In fact, both the debt per person and the debt as a proportion of our national product have declined sharply since the Second World War. In absolute terms the national debt since the end of World War II has increased only 8 percent, while private debt was increasing 305 percent, and the debts of state and local governments—on whom people frequently suggest we should place additional burdens—the debts of state and local governments have increased 378 percent. Moreover, debts public and private, are neither good nor bad, in and of themselves. Borrowing can lead to over-extension and collapse—but it can also lead to expansion and strength.

There is no single, simple slogan in this field that we can trust.

Finally, I come to the matter of confidence. Confidence is a matter of myth and also a matter of truth—and this time let me make the truth of the matter first.

It is true—and of high importance—that the prosperity of this country depends on the assurance that all major elements within it will live up to their responsibilities. If business were to neglect its obligations to the public, if labor were blind to all public responsibility, above all, if government were to abandon its obvious—and statutory—duty of watchful concern for our economical health—if any of these things should happen, then confidence might well be weakened and the danger of stagnation would increase. This is the true issue of confidence.

But there is also the false issue—and its simplest form is the assertion that any and all of the unfavorable turns of the speculative wheel—however temporary and however plainly speculative in character— are the result of, and I quote, "a lack of confidence in the national administration." This I must tell you, while comforting, is not wholly true. Worse, it obscures the reality—which is also simple. The solid ground of mutual confidence is the necessary partnership of government with all of the sectors of our society in the steady quest for economic progress.

Corporate plans are not based on political confidence in party leaders but on an economic confidence in the Nation's ability to invest and produce and consume. Business had full confidence in the administrations in power in 1929, 1954, 1958, and 1960—but this was not enough to prevent recession when business lacked full confidence in the economy. What matters is the capacity of the Nation as a whole to deal with its economic problems and its opportunities....

What is at stake in our economic decisions today is not some grand warfare of rival ideologies which will sweep the country with passion, but the practical management of a modern economy. What we need is not labels and clichés but more basic discussion of the sophisticated and technical questions involved in keeping a great economic machinery moving ahead.

The national interest lies in high employment and steady expansion of output, in stable prices and a strong dollar. The declaration of such an objective is easy; their attainment in an intricate and interdependent economy and world is a little more difficult. To attain them, we require not some automatic response but hard thought. Let me end by suggesting a few of the real questions on our national agenda.

First, how can our budget and tax policies supply adequate revenues and preserve our balance of payments position without slowing up our economic growth?

Two, how are we to set our interest rates and regulate the flow of money, in ways which will stimulate the economy at home, without weakening the dollar abroad? Given the spectrum of our domestic and international responsibilities, what should be the mix between fiscal and monetary policy?

Let me give several examples from my experience of the complexity of these matters and how political labels and ideological approaches are irrelevant to the solution.

Last week, a distinguished graduate of this school, Senator Proxmire, of the class of 1938, who is ordinarily regarded as a liberal Democrat, suggested that we should follow in meeting our economic problems a stiff fiscal policy, with emphasis on budget balance and an easy monetary policy with low interest rates in order to keep our economy going. In the same week, the Bank for International Settlement in Basel, Switzerland, a conservative organization representing the central bankers of Europe suggested that the appropriate economic policy in the United States should be the very opposite; that we should follow a flexible budget policy, as in Europe, with deficits when the economy is down and a high monetary policy on interest rates, as in Europe, in order to control inflation and protect goals. Both may be right or wrong. It will depend on many different factors.

The point is that this is basically an administrative or executive problem in which political labels or clichés do not give us a solution.

A well-known business journal this morning, as I journeyed to New Haven, raised the prospects that a further budget deficit would bring inflation and encourage the flow of gold. We have had several budget deficits beginning with a $12½ billion budget deficit in

1958, and it is true that in the fall of 1960 we had a gold dollar loss running at $5 billion annually. This would seem to prove the case that a deficit produces inflation and that we lose gold, yet there was no inflation following the deficit of 1958 nor has there been inflation since then.

Our wholesale price index since 1958 has remained completely level in spite of several deficits, because the loss of gold has been due to other reasons: price instability, relative interest rates, relative export-import balances, national security expenditures—all the rest.

Let me give you a third and final example. At the World Bank meeting in September, a number of American bankers attending predicted to their European colleagues that because of the fiscal 1962 budget deficit, there would be a strong inflationary pressure on the dollar and a loss of gold. Their predictions on inflation were shared by many in business and helped push the market up. The recent reality of noninflation helped bring it down. We have had no inflation because we have had other factors in our economy that have contributed to price stability.

I do not suggest that the government is right and they are wrong. The fact of the matter is in the Federal Reserve Board and in the administration this fall, a similar view was held by many well-informed and disinterested men that inflation was the major problem that we would face in the winter of 1962. But it was not. What I do suggest is that these problems are endlessly complicated and yet they go to the future of this country and its ability to prove to the world what we believe it must prove.

I am suggesting that the problems of fiscal and monetary policies in the sixties as opposed to the kinds of problems we faced in the thirties demand subtle challenges for which technical answers, not political answers, must be provided. These are matters upon which government and business may and in many cases will disagree.

They are certainly matters which government and business should be discussing in the most sober, dispassionate and careful way if we are to maintain the kind of vigorous economy upon which our country depends.

How can we develop and sustain strong and stable world markets for basic commodities without unfairness to the consumer and without undue stimulus to the producer? How can we generate the buying power which can consume what we produce on our farms and in our factories? How can we take advantage of the miracles of automation with the great demand that it will put upon highly skilled labor and yet offer employment to the half million of unskilled school dropouts each year who enter the labor market, eight million of them in the 1960's?

How do we eradicate the barriers which separate substantial minorities of our citizens from access to education and employment on equal terms with the rest?

How, in sum, can we make our free economy work at full capacity— that is, provide adequate profits for enterprise, adequate wages for labor, adequate utilization of plant, and opportunity for all

These are the problems that we should be talking about—that the political parties and the various groups in our country should be discussing. They cannot be solved by incantations from the forgotten past. But the example of Western Europe shows that they are capable of solution—that governments, and many of them are conservative governments, prepared to face technical problems without ideological preconceptions, can coordinate the elements of a national economy, and bring about growth and prosperity—a decade of it.

Some conversations I have heard in our own country sound like old records, long-playing, left over from the middle thirties. The debate of the thirties had its great significance and produced great results, but it took place in a different world with different needs and different tasks. It is our responsibility today to live in our own world, and to identify the needs and discharge the tasks of the 1960's.

If there is any current trend toward meeting present problems with old clichés, this is the moment to stop it—before it lands us all in a bog of sterile acrimony.

Discussion is essential; and I am hopeful that the debate of recent weeks, though up to now somewhat barren, may represent the start of a serious dialog of the kind which has led in Europe to such fruitful collaboration among all the elements of economic society and to a decade of unrivaled economic progress. But let us not engage in the wrong argument at the wrong time between the wrong people in the wrong country—while the real problems of our own time grow and multiply, fertilized by our neglect....

10–4. LYNDON B. JOHNSON, JANUARY 28, 1965, ANNUAL MESSAGE TO THE CONGRESS: THE ECONOMIC REPORT OF THE PRESIDENT

To the Congress of the United States:

I am pleased to report that the state of our economy is excellent; that the rising tide of our prosperity, drawing new strength from the 1964 tax cut, is about to enter its fifth consecutive year; that, with sound policy measures, we can look forward to uninterrupted and vigorous expansion in the year ahead.

In the year just ended, we have made notable progress toward the Employment Act's central goal of "...useful employment opportunities, including self-employment, for those able, willing, and seeking to work, and ... maximum employment, production, and purchasing power."

Additional jobs for 1½ million persons have been created in the past year, bringing the total of new jobs since January 1961 to 4½ million. Unemployment dropped from 5.7 percent in 1963 to 5.2 percent in 1964 and was down to 5.0 percent at year's end. Gross National Product (GNP) advanced strongly from $584 billion in 1963 to $622 billion in 1964. Industrial production rose 8 percent in the past twelve months. The average weekly wage in manufacturing stands at a record $106.55, a gain of $3.89 from a year ago and of $17.50 from early 1961.

But high levels of employment, production, and purchasing power cannot rest on a sound base if we are plagued by slow growth, inflation, or a lack of confidence in the dollar. Since 1946, therefore, we have come to recognize that the mandate of the Employment Act implies a series of objectives closely related to the goal of full employment: rapid growth and price stability....

True prosperity means more than the full use of the productive powers available at any given time. It also means the rapid expansion of those powers. In the long run, it is only a growth of over-all productive capacity that can swell individual incomes and raise living standards. Thus, rapid economic growth is clearly an added goal of economic policy. Our gain of $132 billion in GNP since the first quarter of 1961 represents an average growth rate (in constant prices) of 5 percent a year. This contrasts with the average growth rate of 2½ percent a year between 1953 and 1960.

Part of our faster gain in the last four years has narrowed the "gap" that had opened up between our actual output and our potential in the preceding years of slow expansion. But the growth of our potential is also speeding up. Estimated at 3½ percent a year during most of the 1950's, it is estimated at 4 percent in the years ahead; and sound policies can and should raise it above that, even while moving our actual performance closer to our potential....

We can be proud of our recent record on prices; wholesale prices are essentially unchanged from four years ago, and from a year ago. Consumer prices have inched upward at an average rate of 1.2 percent a year since early 1961, and 1.2 percent in the past 12 months.

(Much of this increase probably reflects our inability fully to measure improvements in the quality of consumer goods and services.)

...Thus, the record of our past four years has been one of simultaneous advance toward full employment, rapid growth, price stability, and international balance. We have proved that with proper policies these goals are not mutually inconsistent. They can be mutually reinforcing. The unparalleled economic achievements of these past four years have been founded on the imagination, prudence, and skill of our businessmen, workers, investors, farmers, and consumers. In our basically private economy, gains can come in no other way.

But since 1960 a new factor has emerged to invigorate private efforts. The vital margin of difference has come from Government policies which have sustained a steady, but noninflationary, growth of markets. I believe that 1964 will go down in our economic and political history as the "year of the tax cut." It was not the first time that taxes were cut, of course, nor will it be the last time. But it was the first time our Nation cut taxes for the declared purpose of speeding the advance of the private economy toward "maximum employment, production, and purchasing power." And it was done in a period already prosperous by the standard tests of rising production and incomes. In short, the tax cut was an expression of faith in the American economy...The promise of the tax cut for 1964 was fulfilled. Production, employment, and incomes jumped ahead. Unemployment was whittled down steadily.

Since 1960, the balance between budget expenditures and taxes has been boldly adjusted to the needs of economic growth. We have recognized as self-defeating the effort to balance our budget too quickly in an economy operating well below its potential. And we have recognized as fallacious the idea that economic stimulation can come only from a rapid expansion of Federal spending. Monetary policy has supported fiscal measures. The supply of credit has been wisely tailored to the legitimate credit needs of a noninflationary expansion, while care has been taken to avoid the leakage of short-term funds in response to higher interest rates abroad...A GNP of around $660 billion, with expansion throughout the year, will give us our fifth straight year of substantial economic gains—a record without peacetime precedent.

The productive powers of our dynamic economy are now expanding so rapidly that a gain of $38 billion will do little more than keep up with the expansion of our capacity, and will make only modest inroads into the still too heavy unemployment of our human and physical resources. But unemployment in 1965 should average less than the 5.2 percent of 1964...The road to maximum employment, production, and purchasing power will not be easily or quickly traveled. And it has no final destination. The challenge of maintaining full employment once reached will be as urgent and as difficult as reaching it.

A time of prosperity with no recession in sight is the time to plan our defenses against future dips in business activity. I do not believe recessions are inevitable. Up to now, every past expansion has ended in recession or depression—usually within three years from its start. But the vulnerability of an expansion cannot be determined by the calendar. Imbalance—not old age—is the threat to sustained advance. In principle, public measures can head off recessions before they start. Unforeseen events and mistakes of public or private policy will nonetheless occur. Recessions may be upon us before we recognize their warning signs. We can head them off, or greatly moderate their length and force—if we are able to act promptly. The stimulating force of tax cuts is now generally recognized. The Congress could reinforce confidence that jobs and markets will be sustained by insuring that its procedures will permit rapid action on temporary income tax cuts if recession threatens. Recessions usually arise from a reduction in the intensity of private demand for goods and services. At such a time, it may be appropriate to employ idle or potentially idle resources in sound programs of public expenditure. As in 1964, an expansionary monetary policy will be tempered by the urgency of our balance of payments problem. But barring domestic or international emergency, our monetary and debt-management policies can serve—as they have since 1960—to accommodate the credit needs of a noninflationary expansion. Long-term interest rates, in particular, will continue to be held down by the vast flow of savings into private financial institutions. Long-term borrowers now reasonably plan on the essential stability of long-term interest rates in 1965. Monetary policy must be free of arbitrary restriction. It must be prepared to move quickly—if excessive demand should threaten inflation—if an outflow of liquid funds should unexpectedly worsen our balance of payments. We expect neither of these in 1965. Rather, we expect a continuation of sound and healthy economic expansion.

The Federal Reserve system must be free to accommodate that expansion—in 1965 and in the years beyond 1965. Such an expansion needs to be supported by further orderly growth in money and credit. Clearly, we should place beyond any doubt the ability of the Federal Reserve to meet its responsibility for providing an adequate but not excessive volume of bank reserves. The remarkable price stability of 1959–63 persisted throughout 1964. There is good reason to believe that it will continue in 1965....

...In our economic affairs, as in every other aspect of our lives, ceaseless change is the one constant. Revolutionary changes in technology, in forms of economic organization, in commercial relations with our neighbors, in the structure and education of our labor force converge in our markets. Free choices in free markets—as always—accommodate these tides of change. But the adjustments are sometimes slow or imperfect. And our standards for the performance of our economy are continually on the rise. No longer will we tolerate widespread involuntary idleness, unnecessary human hardship and misery, the impoverishment of whole areas, the spoiling of our natural heritage, the human and physical ugliness of our cities, the ravages of the business cycle, or the arbitrary redistribution of purchasing power through inflation. But as our standards for the performance of our economy have risen, so has our ability to cope with our economic problems.

Economic policy has begun to liberate itself from the preconceptions of an earlier day, and from the bitterness of class or partisan division that becloud rational discussion and hamper rational action. Our tools of economic policy are much better tools than existed a generation ago. We are able to proceed with much greater confidence and flexibility in seeking effective answers to the changing problems of our changing economy. The accomplishments of the past four years are a measure of the constructive response that can be expected from workers, consumers, investors, managers, farmers, and merchants to effective public policies that strive to define and achieve the national interest in full employment with stable prices; rapid economic growth; balance in our external relationships; maximum efficiency in our public and private economies....

These perennial challenges to economic policy are not fully mastered; but we are well on our way to their solution. As increasingly we do master them, economic policy can more than ever become the servant of our quest to make American society not only prosperous but progressive, not only affluent but humane, offering not only higher incomes but wider opportunities, its people enjoying not only full employment but fuller lives.

10–5. RICHARD M. NIXON, JANUARY 29, 1971, ANNUAL BUDGET MESSAGE TO THE CONGRESS, FISCAL YEAR 1972

To the Congress of the United States:

In the 1971 budget, America's priorities were quietly but dramatically reordered: For the first time in 20 years, we spent more to meet human needs than we spent on defense.

In 1972, we must increase our spending for defense in order to carry out the Nation's strategy for peace. Even with this increase, defense spending will drop from 36.5% of total spending in 1971 to 34% in 1972. Outlays for human resources programs, continuing to rise as a share of the total, will be 42% of total spending in 1972.

The 1972 budget has a historic identity of its own.

- *It provides a new balance of responsibility and power in America* by proposing the sharing of Federal revenues with States and communities on a grand scale—and in a way that will both alleviate the paralyzing fiscal crisis of State and local governments and enable citizens to have more of a say in the decisions that directly affect their lives.
- *It introduces a new fairness in American life,* with the development of national strategies to improve the health care of our citizens and to assure, with work incentives and requirements, an income floor for every family in this Nation.
- *It adopts the idea of a "full employment budget,"* in which spending does not exceed the revenues the economy could generate under the existing tax system at a time of full employment. In this way, the budget is used as a tool to promote orderly economic expansion, but the impact of the resulting actual deficit is in sharp contrast to the inflationary pressure created by the deficits of the late sixties, which were the result of excessive spending that went far beyond full employment revenues. *The full employment budget idea is in the nature of a self-fulfilling prophecy: By operating as if we were at full employment, we will help to bring about that full employment.* The 1972 budget reaffirms the determination of the Federal Government to take an activist role in bringing about the kind of prosperity that has rarely existed in the American economy—a prosperity without war and without runaway inflation. In the 1972 budget, the Government accepts responsibility for creating the climate that will lead to steady economic growth with improving productivity and job stability.

Of course, our objective of prosperity without inflation cannot be achieved by budget policy alone. It also requires:—the monetary policy adopted by the independent Federal Reserve System to provide fully for the growing needs of the economy; and—increased restraint in wage and price decisions by labor and business—in their own and the Nation's interest and as a matter of common sense. Only by working together can the budget, monetary policy, and common sense in the private sector make orderly expansion the order of the day.

The full employment 1972 budget—expansionary but not inflationary—does its full share to provide a defense strong enough to protect our national security, higher standards of income and care for the poor and the sick, a reorganized and responsive Federal structure, and the basis for a sound prosperity in a full generation of peace.

Economic Setting

When I took office 2 years ago, rampant inflation was the Nation's principal economic problem. This inflation was a direct result of the economic policies of the period 1966 to 1968, when we were mired in war in Vietnam, and when Federal spending rose sharply. Federal outlays were allowed to exceed full-employment revenues by $6 billion in 1966, $10 billion in 1967, and $25 billion in 1968. Expansive monetary policy in the summer of 1968 helped upset the hoped-for stabilizing impact of an income tax surcharge. The effect of these actions was to turn the thermostat up in an economy that was already hot enough.

My administration acted promptly to move us out of that war and cool the superheated economy.

We controlled Federal spending in 1969 and achieved a budget surplus. Spending was restrained again in 1970. Independently, the Federal Reserve System maintained a monetary policy of restraint which increased in severity throughout calendar year 1969 and continued into early 1970.

The forces of inflation have been durable and persistent—and they remain strong. But their momentum was slowed in calendar year 1969 and early 1970. Excessive demand was eliminated as a source of inflationary pressure during this period. The turnaround of this inflationary trend permitted us to enter the second phase of our plan: to follow more expansive economic policies without losing ground in the battle against inflation.

Budget Policy

Last July, I set forth the budget policy of this administration: "At times the economic situation permits—even calls for—a budget deficit. There is one basic guideline for the budget, however, which we should never violate: except in emergency conditions, expenditures must never be allowed to outrun the revenues that the tax system would produce at reasonably full employment. When the Federal Government's spending actions over an extended period push outlays sharply higher, increased tax rates or inflation inevitably follow."

The principle of holding outlays to revenues at full employment serves three necessary purposes:

- It imposes the discipline of an upper limit on spending, a discipline that is essential because the upward pressures on outlays are relentless.
- It permits Federal tax and spending programs to be planned and conducted in an orderly manner consistent with steady growth in the economy's productive capacity.
- It helps achieve economic stability by automatically imposing restraint during periods of boom and providing stimulus during periods of slack.

The budget policy of this administration is to keep firm control over Federal spending. The outlay total of $229.2 billion in 1972 is the sum of spending for programs that were scrutinized carefully to make certain that they would be managed effectively and efficiently and that they are essential to carry out present laws or to achieve desirable changes in our national priorities.

If this careful scrutiny were not maintained—if we weaken in our resolve to control spending—we would risk permitting outlays to build up a momentum that will carry them beyond full employment receipts in the longer run, and we would risk losing the ability to restrain spending in times when a deficit is undesirable.

ESSAYS

Essay 10–1 is excerpts from "National Budgets and National Policy," by Jacob L. Mosak, a wartime official of the Office of Price Administration. It appeared in the *American Economic Review* in 1946, and calls for a concerted effort by the federal government to plan for the postwar period. It provides a gloomy assessment of the economy's ability to carry itself to full employment. Mosak believes fiscal policy alone may not be sufficient, and that additional ways must be found to boost private expenditures. Essay 10–2 is excerpts from "Achieving Sustained Prosperity," Chapter 2 in Arthur Okun's *The Political Economy of Prosperity*, published in 1970. Okun, reviewing the performance of the economy in the 1960s, argues that recessions could be made a relic of the past if policymakers only had the will to adopt the appropriate stabilization policies. This view would come under question as the difficult 1970s unfolded. Essay 10–3 is excerpted from "The Spread of Keynesian Doctrines and Practices in the United States," written by Walter S. Salant, and published in 1989 as Chapter 2 of *The Political Power of Economic Ideas: Keynesianism across Nations*, edited by Peter A. Hall. Salant, who held several economic advisory posts in the Truman and Roosevelt administrations, thinks Keynesianism had little influence on policy during the New Deal. It was gradually absorbed by government officials, especially those in the civil service, in the postwar period, and had maximum influence in the 60s.

Two longtime antagonists in the Keynesian–Monetarist debate lock horns in Essays 10–4 and 10–5, both from *Monetary vs. Fiscal Policy*, co-authored by Milton Friedman, the monetarist, and Walter Heller, the Keynesian, and published in 1969. In "Is Monetary Policy Being Oversold?," Heller defends discretionary fiscal policy which he credits for the expansion of the 1960s, and warns against the brand of monetary policy advocated by the monetarist school, the monetary rule. Friedman believes both discretionary fiscal policy and discretionary monetary policy have been oversold. He disputes the claims of Keynesians on the impact of the 1964 tax cut, and believes that discretionary monetary policy has an inflationary bias. These two selections offer an excellent perspective on the macroeconomic debate that began by the late 1960s.

10–1. JACOB L. MOSAK, "NATIONAL BUDGETS AND NATIONAL POLICY"

A number of economic models relating to the national budget recently developed on the basis of pre-war income and expenditure patterns have demonstrated that severe depression in the years immediately following the transition period is highly probable in the absence of a national policy to assure full employment. From these models the economists have concluded that in the post-war period (1) national policy must be directed toward changing the income and expenditure patterns so as to increase private expenditures for consumption and tangible investment, and (2) the federal government must assume the responsibility of adjusting its own outlays and revenues so as to maintain aggregate expenditures on goods and services by both government and the private economy at the level required for full-employment production.

The logic underlying these models will be indicated in a later section. The conclusions derived from the models may, however, be arrived at in a very simple manner. In 1944 and the first half of 1945, the American economy produced at an annual rate of about 200 billion dollars of finished goods and services for consumption, business investment and government use. Both the labor force and the output per man hour have been subject to conflicting influences during the war, some of which have tended to raise and others of which have tended to lower the gross national product. There is widespread agreement, however, that when these wartime influences are eliminated, the American economy, in the years immediately following the transition period, will be able to produce the same total volume of goods and services as it did at the peak of the war effort. Our capacity to produce in 1950, in other words, will be about 200 billion dollars gross national product in 1944 prices, and it will steadily increase thereafter as a result of population growth and increases in productivity.

While the capacity to produce will continue at peak levels, government, the largest customer for the national product, a customer which in wartime took one-half of the total, will reduce its orders by about three-fourths. Can markets be found for the 75 billion dollars of gross national product which the government will cease to buy? Can the private economy reasonably be expected to increase its outlays by three-fourths from its present all-time high level? Let us consider the probable changes in private investment and consumer expenditures.

Private investment in housing, plant and equipment, inventories and foreign lending was curtailed during the war. In the peak years, 1929 and 1941, private investment was just under 20 billion dollars whereas it amounted to only 4.5 billions per annum in the first half of 1945. Considerations of past rates of investment, as well as of the present productive capacity of our economy, indicate that the average rate of investment over a period of years in the foreseeable future will not very much exceed the peak reached in a single pre-war year.

Expenditure on consumer goods and services, though higher than in pre-war years, was lower than it would have been at the high wartime levels of income because of shortages, price control and other factors. Consumer durable goods expenditure reached a peak of about 10 billion dollars in 1941, but fell to an annual rate of about 7 billions in the first half of 1945. It may be expected to rise from present levels by some 10 billion dollars per annum. Expenditure on food, clothing, gasoline and consumer services was also curtailed by 5 billions or more per annum at wartime levels of income as a result of shortages. The expenditure on goods has risen relative to disposable income in the first few months of the transition period, and the expenditure on services may also be expected to rise as the supply of services increases. This, however, cannot as yet be taken as evidence that in the post-transition years the total demand for consumer goods and services will be significantly higher in relation to disposable income than it was prior to the war.

Taxes at the peak of the war effort were about 25 billion dollars higher than they would need to be after the war if full employment could be maintained with government expenditures of only 25 billions. A 25-billion-dollar reduction in taxes would certainly increase private expenditures substantially, but undoubtedly by less than 25 billions since a portion of the remitted taxes would serve to increase private savings.

When all these factors are taken into account, however, it is evident that they add up to considerably less than 75 billion dollars of additional private consumption and investment per annum over a period of years. Since any initial deficiency will have repercussions on other private expenditures, the gross national product will fall by considerably more than the initial deficiency. Unless, therefore, the federal government adjusts its revenues and outlays so as to raise the annual aggregate volume of expenditures, both government and private, to the level required for full-employment production, it is evident that mass unemployment and depression will follow. The conclusion is that the government must assume the responsibility and prepare a program to eliminate the deflationary threat of the post-war period.

Dr. Albert G. Hart of the Committee on Economic Development has recently attacked the post-war models in the pages of this journal. His criticism relates to both the model-systems and the policy recommendations of the model-makers. Indeed, although most of his comments are directed against the model-systems, I think it is a fair inference that they stem largely from his objections to the policy recommendations.

Before considering the objections to the policy recommendations, it is worth emphasizing that Hart's criticisms of the model-systems relate only to the question of the adequacy of demand for the potential postwar output. He evidently now agrees that 200 billion dollars is a conservative estimate of the capacity gross national product for 1950. For he estimates the capacity in 1947 to be 186–195 billion dollars in 1944 prices. Allowance for normal increases in both labor force and output per man hour would raise the *lower* end of the range to about 200 billion dollars in 1950. Hart's acceptance of this estimate of our productive capacity represents a great forward step in the clarification of the problem connected with the maintenance of post-war full employment.

The primary objection raised against the recommendations is that they take a one-sided view of the post-war prospects. Hart admits that deflation may be a threat during the next 10 years and probably during the next 5 years, but he maintains that it would be irresponsible to overlook the inflationary dangers in sight for the transition.

I do not believe that the model-builders can be fairly charged with irresponsibility on the inflation front. The American model-builders in question have all participated in helping to prepare and execute the Administration's program to keep inflation in check. They have all emphasized the dangers of price inflation during the earlier part of the transition period. They have, in fact, been accused of desiring to keep price and other anti-inflation controls needlessly during the reconversion period. It is one of the curiosities of our day that many of the economists who have been ridiculing the predictions of the post-war deflationary threat are the very ones who have been pressing for the immediate abolition of price controls.

Even the model-builders who emphasized the threat of *deflation of income* resulting from the reduction in munitions employment, the elimination of overtime and the downgrading of workers insisted that there was simultaneously a threat of *price inflation* in the transition period as a result of the accumulated shortages of housing, consumer durables and other goods and services which would remain short even at the lower levels of income. Although the model-builders supported the movement for increasing wage rates to counteract the threat of income deflation, they exerted every effort to confine collective bargaining for wages within the framework of the price-stabilization program. Their thesis was the same as that advanced by President Truman, namely, that it was possible to increase wages substantially without corresponding price increases. This program required the Administration to assume a calculated risk, but the risk was no greater than that proposed by Hart in his recent Study for the C.E.D. in which he wrote:

> While it lasts, price control must be streamlined and liberalized. The OPA must follow a course of "calculated risk" in suspending controls. Price ceilings must be adjusted if they seriously deter or distort production. Pricing standards should permit the average profit expectations of normal prosperity, The present "earnings" standard for price relief—the 1936–39 average return on net worth, before taxes—should be raised by about one-third. Increases should also be permitted whenever the price of a product fails to cover average total costs of production and not, as at present, average direct costs only. All price adjustments under these standards should be based on actual cost experience of the most recent quarter of "normal" operations, without distinction between "approved" and "unapproved" wage increases.

If the model-builders did not refer to the danger of price inflation in the transition, it was simply because they *explicitly* confined their analysis to the years *following* the transition. For the post-transition period they are agreed that the major threat is depression and mass-unemployment rather than inflation.

In the light of the past fluctuations in economic activity, it is apparent that fiscal and indeed all national economic policy must be sufficiently flexible to counteract either booms or depressions. Hart presents his recommendation for a flexible fiscal policy in such a way as to imply that the model-builders are either opposed or at best indifferent to it. This is a mistake. The model-builders are certainly in favor of a flexible fiscal policy to counteract cyclical fluctuations. The issue is only whether there is also need for a national policy designed to prevent continued unemployment. A flexible fiscal policy, it has been aptly said, corresponds to putting in a properly balanced steering wheel, whereas a policy to prevent continued unemployment corresponds to improving the basic structure of the car. The model-builders want both, whereas their critics appear to be content only with the first.

Although the model-builders have emphasized the need for a comprehensive national policy to maintain stable full employment, the belief is widespread that they are interested only in public spending. The origin of this belief is not difficult to trace. The analysis of the model-builders is Keynesian in the broader sense, and Keynesian theory to the non-critical observer is synonymous with public spending.

It is true, of course, that Keynesian analysis provided the theoretical framework for the justification of the public spending program in the depressed 1930's. Nevertheless a moment's consideration should suffice to refute the charge against Keynesian theory. First, even in the 1930's, public spending was only one element, albeit to many the most dramatic element, of a much broader social and economic policy. Second, the relative concentration on public spending in the thirties was primarily due to (1) the fact that in an emergency which called for quick action, public spending could be increased more quickly than private; and (2) that the country was politically and socially unprepared to take many other measures which might have reduced the need for public spending.

The more our people and our government are educated to the nature of our economic problem, and the more they are prepared to take appropriate steps in raising the level of private expenditure, the less need will there be for public spending. This is in fact one of the major purposes of the analysis of the model-builders.

It is surprising that as trained an economic analyst as Hart should have been so misled by the widespread prejudice on this subject as to write: "The school of economists from which these model systems spring seems to feel that the only lesson economists need to convey to the public is that government spending can remedy depressions."

That the comment just quoted is not based on any economic analysis is evident from the fact that in discussing the model-systems from a purely analytical standpoint, Hart saw clearly that the model-builders were not simply "public spenders." Thus he wrote: "These model-systems are set up on the hypothesis that the major components of the national product are determined by the scale and character of the government's fiscal operations— in a setting, of course, of relationships among the components expressing other economic forces. *This way of viewing the problem emphatically does not commit the model-builder to the assumption that government fiscal policy is the only motive power in the economy.* It merely brings a particular set of variables into the foreground for closer study." (Italics mine.) It is regrettable that between his analytical and his policy discussion there should have occurred such a profound change in Hart.

Most trained economists—even anti-Keynesians—are now agreed that federal deficits are desirable during a depression. Hart goes further even than most anti-Keynesian critics, because he accepts the entire Keynesian analysis concerning the effects of deficits on the national product. As will be shown later, he is more Keynesian than the Keynesians, since his major criticism against the model-builders boils down to nothing more than an objection that they estimate too small an income-multiplier for federal deficits. His argument should, therefore, provide little comfort to other anti-Keynesian critics.

The acceptance of the theoretical analysis of the effect of deficits does not mean that the dispute over the use of deficit policy to maintain full employment has been eliminated. The critics have simply shifted the dispute to the question whether the deficit should be achieved through increased government expenditures or through reduced taxation. In thus shifting their ground they have attributed to the model-builders an arbitrary distinction between the two types of deficits. They suggest that the model-builders believe only the former type of deficit stimulates employment, in contrast to themselves who believe that both types of deficits are expansionary, and/or the latter type is preferable. This is simply wrestling with strawmen. I know of no Keynesian, model-builder or otherwise, who believes that only federal deficits arising from abnormal public spending will increase output whereas federal deficits arising from tax reductions will not. Keynesians argued for a reduction in payroll and excise taxes as an anti-depression measure before the war and for a strong tax program as an anti-inflation measure during the war."

The choice between an additional reduction in taxation or an additional increase in government expenditures can obviously be made only in terms of their relative marginal social utilities. If there is any dispute between Keynesians and their critics on this question it is only on the relative degrees of effectiveness of a given increase in government expenditures as compared to an equal reduction in taxation. Hart states that a billion dollar reduction in taxation would lead to an initial increase in private expenditures "of roughly the same dollar amount." Keynesians generally maintain that a significant part of the tax reduction would serve to increase savings rather than consumption and investment. Since the amount of government expenditures required to maintain full employment would be decreased only to the extent to which private expenditures increased, the reduction in required government expenditures would be less than the tax reduction. Consequently, with a lower volume of taxes, a larger deficit would be required to maintain full employment.

Changes in different taxes will naturally have different effects. A reduction in personal income taxes at the very low income levels or in excises on necessities would lead to a very substantial increase in private consumption, whereas a tax reduction at the higher income levels or at the corporate level would have a much smaller effect. The amount of government expenditures required would, therefore, be smaller in the first case than in the second.

...The models relating to the national budget show that the American economy faces a threat of severe depression in the post-transition years unless the federal government assumes responsibility to maintain stable full employment. This does not mean, as the critics seem to believe, that the model-builders want the government to confine its action to compensatory spending. It means instead that: (1) the government should do all it properly can do to change the pre-war income and expenditure patterns so as to increase private consumption and investment expenditures, and (2) it should adjust its own outlays and revenues so as to maintain total expenditures on goods and services at the level required for full employment. Far from suggesting that full employment could be readily achieved through public spending, the models indicate that even a program relying on both public spending and tax revisions might be inadequate. In other words, we shall need not only a sound fiscal policy but also a change in the private income and expenditure patterns if we are to maintain stable full employment.

10-2. ARTHUR OKUN, *THE POLITICAL ECONOMY OF PROSPERITY*: CHAPTER TWO—ACHIEVING SUSTAINED PROSPERITY

One of the most pleasant assignments of the Council of Economic Advisers under President Johnson was the responsibility for keeping straight the arithmetic on the duration of the nation's economic expansion. By January 1969, we were able to report that the economy had advanced for ninety-five months since the last recession ended early in 1961. Nobody asks me for that statistic any longer; but I still enjoy keeping score. As of this writing (November

1969), the nation is in its one-hundred-and-fifth month of unparalleled, unprecedented, and uninterrupted economic expansion.

The persistence of prosperity has been the outstanding fact of American economic history of the 1960s. The absence of recession for nearly nine years marks a discrete and dramatic departure from the traditional performance of the American economy. Our long-term record of economic progress has been a series of two steps forward followed by one step back. Over the past century, periods of economic expansion have averaged about two and one-half years in length, ending in recession or depression. Before 1961, the longest expansion was an eighty-month period largely during the Second World War, and the holder of second place was the fifty-month extended but incomplete recovery from the Great Depression during the 1930s. The three expansions between 1948 and 1960 lasted forty-five, thirty-five, and twenty-five months.

Reflecting in part the built-in stabilizers of our fiscal and financial system, the postwar recessions were brief and mild as compared with the prewar record. But, until 1961, recessions were not significantly less frequent than previously. Western European nations managed to make prosperity last during the fifties, but the United States did not share this success.

According to the historical record, once the American economy pulled out of a recession, there was a safe period of approximately eighteen months during which a rebound in inventory investment virtually assured the expansion of overall activity. Once that safe period passed, it was about an even bet that an expansion would last another ten months and this estimated life expectancy applied regardless of whether the expansion had already lasted eighteen or thirty-eight months.

Thus, on the basis of previous performance, the odds in February 1961 against the new expansion surviving one hundred and five months were about 400 to 1. For one hundred and eight months, the chance would have been 1/512—the compound probability of getting through nine ten-month periods after the initial safe interval, equivalent to the likelihood of a fair coin coming up heads nine times in a row.

When recessions were a regular feature of the economic environment, they were often viewed as inevitable. Indeed, the Doctor Panglosses saw them as contributors to the health of our best of all possible economies, correcting for the excesses of the boom, purging the poisons out of our productive and financial systems, and restoring vigor for new advances. And the latter-day Machiavellis saw potentially great political significance in the timing of turning points. They spun out fantasies, suggesting or suspecting—depending upon whether their party was in or out of office—that the business cycle would be controlled so that the inevitable recession would come between elections and would be replaced by a vigorous economic recovery during the campaign period.

Professional thinking about overall economic performance was also deeply rooted in the business cycle approach. It focused on our position in terms of the stage of the business cycle, attempted to diagnose how long an expansion could continue, and considered what might be done when a recession took place. Policy was often geared to the simple judgment that sustainable expansion was the good and recession was the bad in the economic tides of the nation. Economic forecasts were concentrated on finding the next turning point—the time when the economy would shift from expansion to contraction or the reverse.

The experience of the sixties has made a marked and lasting change in business cycle mentality. Since November 1968, the monthly Bureau of the Census publication of economic data carries a new title, *Business Conditions Digest,* instead of *Business Cycle Developments.* It continues to be known as BCD, but, as a sign of the times, the "Business Cycle" has disappeared. Today few research economists regard the business cycle as a particularly useful organizing framework for the overall analysis of current economic activity, and few teachers see "business cycles" as an appropriate title for a course to be offered to their students. Now virtually no one espouses the fiscal formula that was most popular with thinking conservatives just a decade ago—that of balancing the federal budget over the course of a business cycle.

In 1965 President Johnson was making a controversial statement when he said: "I do not believe recessions are inevitable." That statement is no longer controversial. Recessions are now generally considered to be fundamentally preventable, like airplane crashes and unlike hurricanes. But we have not banished air crashes from the land, and it is not clear that we have the wisdom or the ability to eliminate recessions. The danger has not disappeared. The forces that produced recurrent recessions are still in the wings, merely waiting for their cue.

Recessions did not just happen; they reflected the vulnerability of an industrial economy to cumulative movements upward and downward. While they have diverse specific causes, cyclical fluctuations can usually be viewed as the result of imbalances between the growth of productive capacity and the growth of final demands for its output. During periods of prosperity, a significant part of the nation's output is used to increase productive capacity through investment in plant and equipment and in business inventories. If the growth of final demand by consumers and government keeps pace and hence sales expand, the increase in fixed and working capital normally turns out to be profitable. The expansionary decisions of businessmen are thus validated, and further expansion is encouraged. The advance then generally keeps rolling along, although it might be deterred by tight-credit or unfavorable cost-price developments.

If, on the other hand, final demand fails to grow sufficiently to make use of growing capacity, businessmen have an incentive to slow down the expansion of the stocks of plant, equipment, and inventories. Even if these capital stocks continue to grow, the mere decline in the rate of expansion of capacity can mean an absolute cutback in the demand for capital goods and for output to be added to inventories. Payrolls and other incomes are thus reduced in some areas; in turn, these income declines lead to more widespread reductions in spending and may generate a decline in total demand. Thus a slowdown in economic activity may be converted into an absolute downturn—a recession or depression.

The balance between final buying and stock building can be upset on either side. Overbuilding of inventories apparently played a key role in the first postwar downturn in 1948. A sharp decline in the government's final demand for defense products precipitated the second postwar recession in 1953. In 1956–57, final demand grew very slowly while productive capacity was expanding rapidly in a major boom for capital goods. In 1959–60, when fiscal and monetary policies were very restrictive, final demand grew too slowly to support even the moderate expansion of capacity that was taking place. Various imbalances have also developed at times in the 1960s, but they have never become so large or so widespread as to turn the economy down. The nature of economic fluctuations has not changed; policies to contain them have made the difference.

The record of economic advance in the sixties has been impressive in strength as well as length. As we caught up and kept up with our productive capacity in eight and one-half years of expansion, our real output grew 51 percent, or 5.0 percent a year, in contrast with our long-term annual average of 3 percent. Real disposable income per capita—our best price-corrected measure of the purchasing power of the average consumer—rose one-third, as much of a gain as in the preceding nineteen years. Corporate profits doubled. The number of civilian jobs increased more than 12 million, enough to match the growth of the labor force and to reduce unemployment by more than 2 million persons.

The record presents a striking contrast to the sluggish growth and recurrent recessions of the late fifties. From 1953 to 1960, the growth of industrial production in the United States averaged only 2.5 percent a year, below the pace of every other industrial nation.

Between 1956 and 1961, real gross national product (GNP) rose at an average rate of 2.1 percent, so far below the 6.4 percent estimated rate of the Soviet Union that it made credible Khrushchev's threat to "bury" us economically. In June 1962, Gunnar Myrdal identified as "the world's greatest problem" neither peace nor race relations, but "economic stagnation" in America.

As the economy entered the sixties staggering rather than soaring, observers drew cosmic implications from its unsatisfactory performance. Some saw it as hopelessly stagnant, arguing that automation and technical progress had altered labor requirements so much as to make high employment an impossibility. We heard dire forecasts raising the specter of automation, the threat of the "triple revolution," the prospect of persistent structural deterioration of labor markets. Thus Robert Theobald predicted:

> Unemployment rates must therefore be expected to rise in the sixties. This unemployment will be concentrated among the unskilled, the older worker and the youngster entering the labor force. Minority groups will also be hard hit. No conceivable rate of economic growth will avoid this result.

In fact, of course, unemployment has fallen sharply during the 1960s. Unemployment rates in the spring of 1969 were not only dramatically lower than in the first quarter of 1961 but also well below those of the spring of 1959, one of the most prosperous quarters of the late fifties. Although teenagers remained victims of high unemployment rates, particularly impressive gains were made by adults who had been at the back of the hiring line.

The attitudes of the early sixties seem dim today. This is proof *par excellence* that at least some controversies in economics get resolved. It also reveals the dangers of cosmic generalizations based on a limited period of experience. Predictions of a chronic dollar shortage, chronic stagnation, chronic secular deterioration in labor markets, and the like have all been sounded in the past generation. And all have been refuted by subsequent developments. Yet the lessons seem to go unheeded. We now see the start of a new wave of cosmic generalizations centering on perpetual inflation, perpetual strength of investment demand, and perpetual credit scarcity. This new wave may already have influenced policy by serving as an intellectual justification for the permanent repeal of the investment tax credit. It will be surprising if the new generalizations hold up much better than their predecessors.

More vigorous and more consistent application of the tools of economic policy contributed to the obsolescence of the business cycle pattern and the refutation of the stagnation myths. The reformed strategy of economic policy did not rest on any new theory: Ever since Keynes, economists had recognized that the federal government could stimulate economic activity by increasing the injection of federal expenditures into the income stream or by reducing the withdrawal of federal tax receipts. For generations they had noted the influence of the cost and availability of credit on expenditures financed with borrowed funds.

Nor were the tools of policy new and different. Some stimulative fiscal actions had been taken under the aegis of the New Deal in the 1930s. The Employment Act of 1946 declared the federal government's continuing responsibility to promote "maximum employment, production, and purchasing power," relying mainly on fiscal and monetary devices. During each of the four postwar recessions, some countercyclical fiscal and monetary measures had been adopted; and each period of inflationary boom had been met with some counteracting policies of economic restraint.

Until the 1960s, however, the use of the federal budget for purposes of economic stabilization often followed a fire-fighting strategy. Deliberate stimulus or restraint through budget deficits or substantial surpluses was applied only when the alarm sounded. At other times, the orthodox rule of balancing the budget seemed to dominate. And because the deliberate application of fiscal policy was widely viewed as an emergency measure, there were considerable inhibitions about initiating a policy program. Any time the President proposed budgetary measures designed to serve economic objectives, he was conceding that the economy was in an emergency and needed the fire department for a rescue operation. That inhibition contributed to delays in the adoption of appropriate antirecessionary measures in each of the four postwar slumps. Similarly, there was eagerness to return to business-as-usual once the recession emergency ended.

These attitudes were particularly pronounced in the late 1950s. Thus, with the unemployment rate near 6 percent, President Eisenhower said in his State of the Union Message of January 1959, "If we cannot live within our means during such a time of rising prosperity, the hope for fiscal integrity will fade." In recalling a decision of the Eisenhower administration not to reverse its restrictive fiscal program early in 1960, Richard Nixon reported, "... There was strong sentiment against using the spending and credit powers of the Federal Government to affect the economy, unless and until conditions clearly indicated a major recession in prospect." As Mr. Nixon's summary makes clear, the restrictive fiscal policy of 1959–60 should not be construed as a conscious and deliberate effort to stop growth in order to eliminate inflationary expectations. Surely, the 1960–61 recession was not intentionally planned by the Eisenhower administration. Nor was a 5 percent rate of unemployment regarded as a minimum for the nation. To be sure, risks were consciously taken on the side of excessive restraint, but these corresponded to the preference for orthodox budgetary principles that largely ignored the economic impact of fiscal policy. The basic strategy was to stick with orthodox principles unless the fire alarm of recession tolled loud and clear. This ruled out the use of stimulative—or even supportive—fiscal policies during periods of expansion.

In the late forties and early fifties, the possible need for stimulative policies even during expansionary periods was widely discussed. But events did not put this strategy to the test during the first postwar decade. Spurred by the Korean buildup in 1950, the economy rose swiftly to—and beyond— full employment in its recovery from the first postwar recession. Again in 1954–55, the rebound from recession was strong and prompt, carrying the nation to essentially full utilization by the close of 1955. From that point on, however, expansion and full utilization did not go hand in hand. The growth of output was very sluggish during the last year and a half of the 1954–57 expansion. Even at its peak in the spring of 1960, the recovery from the 1957–58 recession left the economy far short of full employment. These experiences highlighted the distinction between high employment and cyclical expansion.

Against this background, the strategy of economic policy was reformulated in the sixties. The revised strategy emphasized, as the standard for judging economic performance, whether the economy was living up to its potential rather than merely whether it was advancing. Ideally, total demand should be in balance with the nation's supply capabilities. When the balance is achieved, there is neither the waste of idle resources nor the strain of inflationary pressure. The nation is then actually producing its potential output. The concept of potential output was imprecise and so was its quantification. Yet it helped to deliver and dramatize the verdict that idle resources were a major national extravagance in the late fifties and early sixties. And the quantification, which had been heatedly debated in 1961, held up surprisingly well during the sixties.

The shift of emphasis from the achievement of expansion to the realization of potential had a number of important corollaries. First, by establishing a moving target for economic performance, it stressed the growth of the economy. The supply capabilities of the United States economy advance continually, reflecting both our expanding labor force and the improving productivity that results from advancing technology and investment in human and physical resources. In the late fifties, the growth of potential had amounted to about 3 ½ *percent* per year; the shortfall of actual performance below that pace showed up in rising unemployment. The actual growth performance was unsatisfactory because it failed to take full advantage of our growing supply capabilities, even though new record highs in income and employment were achieved.

Second, the focus on the gap between potential and actual output provided a new scale for the evaluation of economic performance, replacing the dichotomized business cycle standard which viewed expansion as satisfactory and recession as unsatisfactory. This new scale of evaluation, in turn, led to greater activism in economic policy: As long as the economy was not realizing its potential, improvement was needed and government had a responsibility to promote it.

Finally, the promotion of expansion along the path of potential was viewed as the best defense against recession. Two recessions emerged in the 1957–60 period because expansions had not had enough vigor to be self-sustaining. The slow advance failed to make full use of existing capital; hence, incentives to invest deteriorated and the economy turned down. In light of the conclusion that anemic recoveries are likely to die young, the emphasis was shifted from curative to preventive measures. The objective was to promote brisk advance in order to make prosperity durable and self-sustaining.

All of this added up to a coherent view of stabilization policy. Something here was new and different. Arthur Burns has summarized it perceptively:

The central doctrine of this school is that the stage of the business cycle has little relevance to sound economic policy; that policy should be growth-oriented instead of cycle-oriented; that the vital matter is whether a gap exists between actual and potential output; that fiscal deficits and monetary tools need to be used to promote expansion when a gap exists; and that the stimuli should be sufficient to close the gap—provided significant inflationary pressures are not whipped up in the process.

The adoption of these principles led to a more active stabilization policy. The activist strategy was the key that unlocked the door to sustained expansion in the 1960s. The record of economic performance shows serious blemishes, particularly the inflation since 1966. To some degree, these reflect errors of analysis and prediction by economists; to a larger degree, however, they reflect errors of omission in failing to implement the activist strategy.

The expansion can be divided into two distinct parts, which are discussed in some detail below. The remainder of this chapter is devoted to the period from early 1961 until mid-1965, when the main task was to invigorate the economy. The major problem could be simply and clearly diagnosed as inadequate total demand, and the equally simple remedy was stimulative fiscal and monetary policy. By mid-1965, that diagnosis had become accepted and much of the remedy had been applied. Thereafter, the assignment was to hold to a course of noninflationary prosperity, a problem for which the economist does not have a simple and satisfactory solution. It is inherently a much more difficult task, and it was made ever so much more difficult by large increases in defense spending.

As Walter Heller has said: "In 1961, with over five million unemployed and a production gap of nearly $50 billion, the problem of the economic adviser was not what to say, but how to get people to listen." The appropriate remedy required— at least for a time—budgetary deficits and increases in the national debt. There was widespread professional agreement on this prescription. In Herbert Stein's judgment, "If [President Kennedy] had chosen six American economists at random the odds were high that he would have obtained five with the ideas on fiscal policy which his advisers actually had, because those ideas were shared by almost all economists in 1960."

Outside the profession, however, antipathy toward such unorthodox federal budgeting was deeply entrenched; it had been strongly nurtured during the fifties, and remained an obstacle to rational action in 1961. John F. Kennedy had not challenged the orthodox principles during the 1960 election campaign; indeed, he had criticized President Eisenhower's $12 billion budgetary deficit of fiscal 1959. President Kennedy bent but did not break the traditional rules in taking steps to invigorate recovery during 1961 and in heeding the advice of his economists that the Berlin defense buildup did not call for higher taxes. Then the President bowed to the orthodox rules in January 1962, proposing a balanced budget at a time when 6 percent of the labor force was unemployed.

It was only when the expansion faltered in the spring of 1962 that Kennedy reached a fork in the fiscal road. In a memorable commencement address at Yale University in June 1962, he spoke out clearly and strongly against budgetary orthodoxy:

The myth persists that Federal deficits create inflation and budget surpluses prevent it. ... Obviously deficits are sometimes dangerous —and so are surpluses. But honest assessment plainly required a more sophisticated view than the old and automatic cliche that deficits automatically bring inflation....

... What we need is not labels and clichés but more basic discussion of the sophisticated and technical questions involved in keeping a great economic machine moving ahead.

Once President Kennedy called this play, Walter Heller carried the ball and brought the "sophisticated and technical questions" before the public. The press served as the textbook for the biggest course in elementary macroeconomics ever presented. In fact, Professor Heller captured his millions of students with new labels in place of old. The "full employment surplus," "constructive deficit," "fiscal dividend and fiscal drag," and "output gap" were drummed home in repeated lessons. The message was effectively conveyed to the business and financial community and to the nation's legislators by the Secretary of the Treasury, C. Douglas Dillon, and then Under Secretary Henry H. Fowler.

The administrative reform of depreciation guidelines and the enactment of the investment tax credit in 1962 were two new policy initiatives which directly stimulated business investment and made their largest direct contribution to business incomes.

It was probably no coincidence that the first installment of the expansionary strategy worked to benefit directly the groups that seemed particularly hostile to a heterodox, deficit-prone fiscal policy. Remarkably, the proposed investment tax credit was initially viewed as a Grecian gift by many businessmen; their support was enlisted through a major educational effort led by Under Secretary Fowler.

The next stage was bigger, bolder, and more progressive in its distributive impact. Facing up to legislative realities, President Kennedy decided not to ask for an immediate general tax reduction in the summer of 1962. But in August he publicly announced that he would propose a substantial tax reduction in January 1963.

The tax-cut proposal was designed by economists and promoted by economists on economic grounds. As Heller has explained, the size of the proposed tax reduction was based on careful and quantitative professional judgment—although hardly a scientific determination—of that amount of fiscal stimulus appropriate to close the remaining gap between the potential and actual output. With the envisioned shift in fiscal policy, the federal budget would come into approximate balance when the nation attained its potential output, but it would no longer dampen demand with large surpluses at full employment. In addition to the rate reductions, the tax package included many proposals for significant reform of the tax structure to improve equity and efficiency. These reform proposals undoubtedly contributed to the long delay in the enactment of the tax reduction; but, more generally, there was no political consensus during 1963 in favor of the new strategy of relaxing fiscal restraint. While tax reduction was rarely opposed in principle, support for it was sometimes linked to sharp cutbacks in federal outlays that would have vitiated the intent to provide significant fiscal stimulus.

When the tax cut was finally enacted under President Johnson's leadership in February 1964, it was unprecedented in many respects. It was the largest stimulative fiscal action ever undertaken by the federal government in peacetime, cutting individual income tax liabilities by almost one-fifth and corporate tax bills by one-tenth. In combination with the two 1962 tax actions, the new measure reduced the effective rate of corporate taxes by one-fifth compared with its 1961 level. The 1964 tax cut was progressive in its distributive effects. In part, this was the result of the only two significant reforms that were enacted —the minimum standard deduction and the repeal of the dividend credit. In part, it resulted from the slash in the lowest tax rate from 20 to 14 percent, associated with the splitting of the bottom bracket into four segments.

The big tax cut was the first major stimulative measure adopted in the postwar era at a time when the economy was neither in, nor threatened imminently by, recession. And, unlike U.S. tax reductions in the 1920s, late 1940s, and 1954, the 1964 action was taken in a budgetary situation marked by the twin facts that the federal budget was in deficit and federal expenditures were rising.

The tax cut added to demand by leaving more purchasing power in the hands of consumers and businesses. Consumers responded by spending most of that extra income for added goods and services. For businessmen investment became both more profitable and easier to finance out of internal funds. The direct stimulus of the tax cut was multiplied over time. The extra spending it generated meant more jobs and hence more incomes for many families; it strengthened markets and thus encouraged greater investment to expand capacity.

The stimulus of tax reduction dominated the economic scene in 1964 and the first half of 1965. The unemployment rate, which had been fluctuating aimlessly in the range between 5½ and 6 percent all during 1962 and 1963, fell to 5 percent during the course of 1964 and declined further to 4.7 percent during the spring of 1965. The time series on consumer spending registered a sharp take-off early in 1964. According to my estimates, the tax cut added $24 billion (annual rate) to our GNP by the second quarter of 1965, and ultimately provided a lift of $36 billion. The Revenue Act of 1964 provided for two stages of tax reduction: The first was effective in 1964 and the second took place at the beginning of 1965. Beyond the second-stage tax cut, the January 1965 budget program shifted into neutral gear. A major phased reduction of excise taxes was slated to begin at mid-year, and a stimulative liberalization of social security benefits was also envisioned. But other federal budgetary expenditures were expected to grow very little, and defense spending was scheduled to continue downward. Indeed, according to the budget plan, fiscal policy was to shift moderately toward restraint in the first half of 1966 when social security taxes were to rise. There was no new net injection of economic stimulus, and no further downward trend in the budgetary surplus as measured at full employment. As stated by the Council in January 1965: "… The rate of economic advance in the next eighteen months will reflect, to an increasing degree, the strength of private demand. The record of this period should test the economy's ability to advance in high gear with a small, but no longer declining, full-employment surplus."

The economy seemed to be passing the initial stage of that test with flying colors in the first half of 1965. Private demand was somewhat more vigorous than had been anticipated, although not so strong as to cause serious concern. Both consumer spending and business investment forged ahead, and unemployment moved down. Revenue gains from higher personal and corporate incomes flowed into the Treasury, and brought the federal budget into surplus (on a national accounts basis) during the first half of the year. Meanwhile, in May 1965, the duration of economic expansion toppled the previous peacetime record of fifty months.

The nation's balance-of-payments deficit remained a nagging problem, and the quality of some types of credit gave cause for uneasiness. There was also concern lest complacency develop about the economy; this was expressed by the Chairman of the Federal Reserve when he reminded us of "disquieting similarities" between the existing economic scene and that of the late 1920s. Nonetheless, any danger of complacency reflected the exceedingly desirable state of economic activity. After tolerating a high cost of wasted resources and lost output during 1962–63, the nation had finally unleashed the private economy.

The price-cost record of the economy was also generally reassuring, although it was flashing some caution signs by mid-1965. The average of wholesale industrial prices was within 1 percent of its level at the beginning of 1961. It had risen 0.5 percent during the course of 1964, mostly because of nonferrous metals prices, which were pushed up by world supply problems. During the first half of 1965, industrial wholesale prices rose 0.6 percent, with increases more widely dispersed. In manufacturing industries with rapidly rising productivity, price declines, which had previously been common, were going out of style. Yet very few large firms with market power were raising prices to widen profit margins; and there had been no further confrontation between business and government like that in April 1962 when President Kennedy had strongly condemned an increase in steel prices.

Labor costs were remarkably stable in both organized and unorganized areas. In the spring of 1965, unit labor costs in both the total nonfinancial corporate sector of the economy and in manufacturing were *below* their levels of a year earlier. Productivity advanced briskly and wage rates rose only modestly; thus unit labor costs behaved very well, even though the amount of work paid for at premium overtime rates had expanded significantly. Consumer prices were rising moderately by about 1½ percent per year—only a trifle more than in 1960–63—and the price deflator for overall gross national product was advancing at a 1% percent rate.

To be sure, the price record of 1964 and the first half of 1965 was distinctly different from that of earlier years. But it had been recognized all along that the achievement of a high-employment economy would necessarily involve some retreat from the exceptional price stability of the early sixties. When the slack in resource utilization was taken up, it was no surprise to find a departure from the virtually absolute stability of industrial wholesale prices that had ruled in earlier years. The deterioration in our price performance seemed relatively small and readily tolerable. This was not inflation by any definition I know.

The 1964–65 price record generally confirmed the judgment that the Council had made way back in 1961 that an unemployment rate of 4 percent was an appropriate interim target for full utilization of manpower, consistent with the maintenance of a reasonable degree of price stability. It was felt that the achievement of a 4 percent unemployment rate along a smooth path of advance might be accompanied by a 2 percent rate of overall price increase. Such a rate would not be dramatically more rapid than the 1960–63 performance; it seemed likely to be acceptable to the nation and would not be so large as to feed on itself and accelerate through time. Thus in the spring of 1965, the President's Troika—the fiscal advisory group consisting of officials of the Treasury, the Budget Bureau, and the Council of Economic Advisers—was looking ahead to fiscal year 1967 and shaping a program to promote a continuing advance in real output that would bring the unemployment rate gradually down to the 4 percent target.

The prospects for achieving noninflationary high employment had to be viewed in many dimensions. Excise tax cuts were a particularly appropriate form of fiscal stimulus since they countered upward cost pressures. The advance in plant and equipment outlays seemed likely to strengthen our productivity performance. Several newly launched manpower programs were expected to help avoid bottlenecks in labor markets. Moreover, as labor markets began to firm, private business management intensified its own efforts to upgrade and train manpower in ways that would effectively increase both the quality and quantity of our labor supply over the long run. The vigor of foreign competition was another encouraging anti-inflationary sign.

Finally, as one element of the total program, public education on the need for price and wage restraint in areas of market power—the administration's guidepost policy—seemed to be having a favorable influence on decisions by big business and big labor.

The guideposts, first formulated by the Council of Economic Advisers in 1962, were meant to help avoid repetition of the experience in 1956–57 when price-cost stability deteriorated badly in areas of market power. They stressed the arithmetic truth that price stability could be maintained only insofar as gains in money income per unit of input remained within the bounds of advances in national productivity. This formula pointed toward increases of a little more than 3 percent a year in wage rates, paralleling the trend growth of productivity, and toward pricing policies that were geared to unit costs. The guideposts were intended to influence the decisions of large corporations and large unions by enlisting the force of public opinion against the discretionary use of market power to promote inflation. It is impossible to tell just how much influence they had in 1962–65, but there is considerable evidence that they deserve some credit.

The heavy reliance on tax cuts, rather than expenditure increases, in providing fiscal stimulus was a particularly interesting feature of the period. For the first time in history, an expansionary fiscal strategy was pursued without enlarging the relative size of federal expenditures in our economy. From the fourth quarter of 1960 to the second quarter of 1965, the federal sector was the slowest growing major area of the economy. While our gross national product rose 34 percent, total federal outlays—purchases, transfer payments, and so forth—increased 26 percent, or $25 billion. Federal purchases of goods and services were up 20 percent. National defense purchases rose only 7 percent.

Changes in tax laws contributed a net total of $12 billion to the annual rate of private purchasing power by the spring of 1965. Even after increases in social security taxes are netted out, tax cuts provided a third of the total gross stimulative actions undertaken during the four-and-one-half-year period. They accounted for two-thirds of the gross stimulus during the initial one and one-half years of the Johnson presidency, as total federal outlays rose only $5 billion from the last quarter of 1963 to the second quarter of 1965.

This heavy reliance on tax reduction reflected neither an economic judgment on the relative efficacy of the two types of fiscal stimuli nor the administration's assessment of national priorities, but rather the political constraints of the day. A deficit budget might be tolerated by the nation if it stressed tax reduction; it would be much less popular if it featured rapid increases in government spending. Moreover, a crusade for enlarged social programs seemed to have no prospect of success. Indeed, it could not have been launched by simply requesting additional appropriations for existing programs; most of the key authorizing legislation underlying current major social efforts in education, housing, manpower, and health was not yet on the statute books in 1963. The makers of fiscal policy believed that additional federal outlays could add equally well to total demand, but they did not regard this as a realistic alternative. The real choice was between tax cuts and no fiscal stimulus at all.

The stimulus to the economy also reflected a unique partnership between fiscal and monetary policy. Basically, monetary policy was accommodative while fiscal policy was the active partner. The Federal Reserve allowed the demands for liquidity and credit generated by a rapidly expanding economy to be met at stable interest rates. The stability was neither perfect nor complete because of the concern that very low short-term interest rates would worsen our balance-of-payments performance. Hence short rates, such as those on Treasury bills, were nudged upward whenever additional capital outflows seemed to be encouraged by a widening gap between domestic and foreign yields in money markets. Remarkably, this proved to be possible without a major upward impact on the longer-term interest rates that seem to be most important to domestic spending. ...[L]ong-term yields were far more stable in the early sixties than in the late fifties. While the Federal Reserve obviously did not "peg" bond yields, it did aim to stabilize longer-term interest rates. The resulting increases in the quantity of money, bank credit, business loans, and total borrowing all reflected shifts in demands for funds with an essentially passive response on the supply side.

This rate-oriented posture was a major departure from tradition. In previous periods of significant economic expansion, the Federal Reserve had not allowed the supply of credit to expand in pace with growing demands, and interest rates had tended to rise. Monetary policy had thus acted to moderate and contain expansions. But the Fed did not "lean against the wind" during 1961–65. A long as the economy continued to operate below its potential and prices remained stable, the Fed was prepared to provide the liquidity to sustain the advance.

Milton Friedman has attributed to monetary policy the chief causal role in stimulating the expansion of that period....

Friedman's critique raises, first of all, a conceptual issue of whether my study of the impact of the tax cut did "assume away the whole problem." In trying to provide a meaningful answer to the common sense question of what impact the tax cut had on economic activity, one has to make some assumptions about what monetary policy would have been if the tax cut had not been enacted. Monetary conditions are merely one of the many assumptions that must be specified in assessing the impact of the tax bill. It is also necessary, for example, to assume what would have happened to federal expenditures if the tax reduction had not taken place. In my paper, I assumed that they would have been exactly what they were in fact. This, of course, is an arbitrary assumption, but it is a reasonable way to focus on the impact of the tax cut.

The assumptions about monetary factors seem equally reasonable. It is factually clear that the Federal Reserve had conducted an accommodative monetary policy before the tax cut, and that it continued to pursue an accommodative monetary policy for a year and a half afterwards. Both preceding and following the enactment of the tax cut, monetary strategy was geared to provide the reserves needed to stabilize interest rates and the availability of credit. In that sense, monetary policy was unchanged by the tax cut, and I assumed it would have been unchanged if there had been no tax cut. Since interest rates remained remarkably stable during the entire period, it seems reasonable to assume that, in the absence of the tax cut, they would also have been kept stable by an accommodative, rate-oriented monetary policy.

Of course, because of the tax cut, the unchanged rate-oriented monetary policy accommodated a more rapid growth of demand for funds and, hence, provided more growth of the money supply, bank credit, and other related financial flows than would have taken place without the tax cut. An interesting and perfectly reasonable statistical exercise could explore what would have happened after the tax cut if the Federal Reserve had shifted strategy and decided not to accommodate the extra demands for funds. But that exercise is not the way to assess the impact of the tax cut of 1964.

Perhaps this analogy will help. During the early sixties, the Federal Reserve took the position of a ticket seller ready to sell tickets at a fixed price to anyone on line. Given this policy, sales of tickets were determined by the number of people who got on line. One cannot explain adequately why more people saw a show by saying that the ticket seller sold more tickets (at a given price). It doesn't make any more sense to say that the economic stimulus in 1964–65 came from a change in monetary policy. The tax cut does explain why more people got in line; given the willingness of the ticket seller to expand his sales, activity increased. I was concerned with estimating the magnitude of that expansion and, hence, had no reason to ask what would have happened if the ticket seller had refused to sell more tickets.

All of this relates entirely to the issue of whether my study of the tax cut asked the right question, not whether it gave the proper answer to the question it asked. In any comparison of two situations, both involving an accommodative, rate-oriented monetary policy but one with a tax cut and one without it, Friedman would not disagree, to the best of my knowledge, that the tax cut situation would be associated with a higher gross national product.

There are a number of other empirical judgments in comparing hypothetical situations on which "new economists" and "monetarists" can agree. For one thing, I believe that the success of the fiscal strategy depended on the monetary response. If, when the tax cut was enacted, our ticket seller had been reluctant to issue more tickets, interest rates would have risen rather than remaining stable, and credit availability would have been restricted; GNP would then have moved along a lower path than the one that actually resulted. Surely the Fed could have imposed a sufficiently restrictive monetary policy to nullify entirely the expansionary effects of the tax cut.

Moreover, I have no reason to doubt that, in principle, there existed a monetary route to high employment as an alternative to the fiscal route that was traveled. As much additional demand as resulted from the tax cut could have been generated, without fiscal support, by a sufficiently aggressive Federal Reserve policy to increase liquidity and reduce interest rates. The monetary route would have involved significantly lower interest rates. As a political judgment, I am confident that the route would not have been traveled, given the constraints of the balance of payments on lowering interest rates as they were viewed— rightly or wrongly—by the administration and the Federal Reserve, but that is a political judgment.

One can get a debate on empirical economic issues between a monetarist and a new economist by asking whether the monetary route to full employment without the tax cut would have involved the *same* growth of the money supply that in fact took place along the fiscal route. While both would agree that the no-tax-cut situation would have involved lower interest rates, the monetarist would deny that it would have required a larger money supply than was actually experienced. According to the monetarist, we got the GNP we did because of the size of the money supply; and *that* level of total spending for output would have come from *that* money supply regardless of interest rates.

I do not regard this as a very exciting question, but I do have great confidence that the monetarist's answer is wrong. It is one of the best-established empirical propositions in economics that, for a given level of spending, the amount of money people are willing to hold is greater the lower the interest rate.

After reviewing the research in that field, David Laidler reports:

> Of the many experiments that have been performed, only one failed to find a relationship between the demand for money and the rate of interest, and that was carried out by Friedman for the period 1869–1957....

> ... There is an overwhelming body of evidence in favor of the proposition that the demand for money is stably and negatively related to the rate of interest. Of all the issues in monetary economics, this is the one that appears to have been settled most decisively.

This checks with both theory and common sense. The interest return on nonmonetary liquid assets—like thrift accounts and marketable securities—is what people and firms sacrifice in holding money, which yields no interest. Thus lower interest rates provide a reduced incentive to economize on cash balances. Since interest rates would have had to be lower to get the same GNP without the tax cut, a larger money supply would have been necessary to do the job. More generally, because of the link between the demand for money and interest, the relationship between money and income cannot be unique. When the tax cut raised take-home pay, people could and would have spent somewhat more even if the Fed had not provided extra cash balances. In that event, interest rates would have had to rise enough to hold the demand for money down to the available supply.

The ticket analogy to money has to be modified in this case. People need cash tickets to buy goods and services, but they hold an inventory of tickets and can make the tickets turn over faster even if the ticket seller refuses to increase his sales. To be sure, the rise in interest rates resulting from the increased scarcity of money would have curtailed—but not eliminated— the economic expansion generated by the tax cut.

In short, the strong economic expansion of 1964–65 would not have taken place in the face of a highly restrictive monetary strategy. Moreover, the job could in principle have been accomplished by a very expansionary monetary strategy without a stimulative fiscal policy. But the rate-oriented monetary policy that was actually pursued would not in itself have quickened the pace of the economy. It supplied a good set of tires for the economy to move on, but fiscal policy was the engine.

The high-water mark of the economist's prestige in Washington was probably reached late in 1965. At that point, for a brief moment, even congressmen were using the appellation "professor" as a term of respect and approval. There could be no greater tribute to the success of the expansionary policy strategy.

Even under the best of circumstances, with no defense buildup, the attainment of full utilization would have ushered in a new environment with new challenges to economic policy making. In the first place, the growth of output and real incomes was bound to slow down. A significant part of the growth in the 1961–65 period represented a reduction in the initial $50 billion gap between actual and potential output. We were catching up as well as keeping up with productive capacity. Once that catch up was completed, the growth rate could no longer persistently exceed that of potential—about 4 percent per year. A slowdown in growth from a 5½ to a 4 percent rate had to involve some strain and disappointment. With the extra margin in the rapid 5½ percent advance, the national pie was growing so fast that there was unusually little displeasure about the distribution of the pie among labor and business and other groups. Squabbling about fair shares was bound to intensify once the growth rate slowed down. To paraphrase the travel slogan, half the fun of a full-employment economy is getting there.

Second, once full utilization was attained, the range of tolerance for policy error would have to shrink. Because there had been little risk of excessive demand in the early sixties, any growth performance between 4 and 6 percent could be viewed as qualitatively successful: It would be fast enough to reduce unemployment and not so rapid as to jeopardize essential price stability. Once the economy is close to target, however, there are necessarily dangers from both inadequate and excessive demand. In the earlier period, economists knew what to prescribe, and the medicine worked once the patient was persuaded to take it. But in a healthy, prosperous economy, there was no sure tonic. Like physicians, we can cure pneumonia and look great, but we can't keep our patient from catching cold.

Third, in a world of full utilization, the problem of keeping the economy close to a chosen course is compounded by the uncertainties in choosing the course. The ideal rate of utilization is necessarily a difficult compromise between the objective of maximum production and employment, on the one hand, and the objective of price stability, on the other. We have had little experience historically in confronting that hard choice because the nation has so rarely remained on a reasonably satisfactory growth path. Except during wartime inflations, we have not been at full employment long enough to test, under these circumstances, the supply capabilities of the economy, its price-cost performance, or public attitudes toward price increases of various rates.

In 1965 the nation was entering essentially uncharted territory. The economists in government were ready to meet the welcome problems of prosperity. But they recognized that they could not provide a good encore to their success in achieving high-level employment. As Gardner Ackley put the problem in a talk delivered during December 1965:

... The plain fact is that economists simply don't know as much as we would like to know about the terms of trade between price increases and employment gains. We would all like the economy to tread the narrow path of a balanced, parallel growth of demand and capacity—at as high a level of capacity utilization as is consistent with reasonable price stability, and without creating imbalances that would make continuing advance unsustainable. But the macroeconomics of a high employment economy is insufficiently known to allow us to map that path with a high degree of reliability. ...

...It is easy to prescribe expansionary policies in a period of slack. Managing high-level prosperity is a vastly more difficult business and requires vastly superior knowledge. The prestige that our profession has built up in the Government and around the country in recent years could suffer if economists give incorrect policy advice based on inadequate knowledge. We need to improve that knowledge.

10–3. WALTER S. SALANT, IN *THE POLITICAL POWER OF ECONOMIC IDEAS: KEYNESIANISM ACROSS NATIONS*: CHAPTER II—THE SPREAD OF KEYNESIAN DOCTRINES AND PRACTICES IN THE UNITED STATES

This chapter attempts to identify the main channels through which Keynes' major book, *The General Theory of Employment, Interest and Money* (hereafter *GT*), influenced economic policy and practice in the United States.

The title of this chapter obviously implies that Keynes' thinking did greatly influence doctrine and policy in the United States. Because the belief that it did so, at least during and after World War II until the late 1960s or early 1970s, is widespread, we should note at the outset that the truth of this belief has been both questioned and denied. This fact deserves serious consideration, both because it has some merit and because such consideration forces us to think hard about what is meant by Keynesian doctrines and policies.

So far as the New Deal is concerned, the passage of time tends to diminish the importance that today's public attaches to recovery from the Great Depression. That was the greatest and most urgent concern at the time, but as generations pass, memories of it fade into the background. Increasingly, the term *New Deal* is associated with reformist and enduring institutional changes—social security, wage and hour legislation, unemployment insurance, legislation governing labor relations, insurance of bank deposits, government insurance of home mortgages and other housing legislation, government regulation of security issues and securities trading, rural electrification, and other changes in the economic structure of the United States. If these institutional changes are what most people think of as the New Deal, it may be agreed that Keynes and Keynesian policies had nothing to do with them. Probably the time will come, if it is not here already, when the institutional reforms also fade into the background; those who know there was once no deposit insurance, no unemployment benefits, no social security, no health insurance, die and are replaced by those who are not aware that once we did not have these things. Thus, what has been said of science may also be said of ignorance: that it progresses funeral by funeral. Before World War II the Depression was predominant in the thinking about current economics of all but a few, and that is what people have in mind if they assume Keynes' thinking influenced U.S. policy then.

Even with regard to the fiscal policy of the New Deal, however, there is ground for denying that Keynes has much to do with the policies which actually followed. Herbert Stein, in the title of a chapter in his book *The Fiscal Revolution in America,* distinguishes between the "fiscal revolution" and the "Keynesian revolution," and says that "it is possible to describe the evolution of fiscal policy in America up to 1940 without reference to him [Keynes]." Keynes' fiscal ideas, as expressed in his pamphlet *The Means to Prosperity* (1933), in his open letter to Franklin D. Roosevelt in the *New York Times* of December 31, 1933, and in his interview with Roosevelt in 1934, do not appear to have had much influence on the president. Referring to the decision to embark on a spending program in the spring of 1938, Stein says that by then "we had reached the stage in which we would not only accept a deficit in depression but would deliberately and substantially increase expenditures ... for the purpose of raising the general level of the economy. This stage had been reached without a significant contribution from what is now called Keynesianism."

Similar doubts about Keynes' influence have also been expressed with regard to the early years after World War II. Leon Keyserling, who was part of a three-man team revising the first drafts of the Full Employment Bill and also first a member and then chairman of the Council of Economic Advisors from 1946 through 1952, has asserted that "it is a fallacy to think that John Maynard Keynes had anything of substance to do with the idea behind the Employment Act of 1946 or with the policies of the Truman administration." In saying this, Keyserling refers to "Keynes's idea, as it is understood by Americans, as mainly compensatory spending." It is a valuable idea, but it was not the idea underlying the Employment Act of 1946 and it certainly was not the idea underlying the administration of President Truman. ... Compensatory spending (as we understand it *à la* Keynes) was never tried during the Truman administration; it was never needed.

If one accepts the common (noneconomist's) interpretation that Keynes' main idea was his advocacy of compensatory spending, it must be agreed that, although it was central to early drafts of the Full Employment Act, it is not, as will be shown later, the idea underlying the Employment Act of 1946 as that legislation was enacted. One reason for the vigorous objection to the Full Employment Bill by some of its opponents was that they did not want to authorize a policy of compensatory spending. The legislation would not have been enacted had the original prescription of such a policy been retained. When it was cleansed of that idea (and with other changes in earlier versions), it was passed by a vote of 320 to 84 in the House of Representatives and without opposition in the Senate.

These points do give some support to the doubts about Keynes' influence on particular acts of U.S. economic policy, especially before World War II. Nevertheless, Keynes' ideas and the ferment they created changed the intellectual climate. It must be recognized that the ideas expressed in Keynes' *The General Theory of Employment, Interest and Money,* the book that is central to what economists think of as his ideas, included much more than compensatory government spending. Indeed, such spending is hardly mentioned; Keynes' emphasis is elsewhere. His attack on Say's Law was important in undermining the view that aggregate demand could not be insufficient, and in explaining that, during depression or when economic activity was threatening decline, government action to increase or sustain demand was desirable, not useless, let alone destructive, as the neoclassical theory expounded by Hayek and others of the "Austrian" school held.

The effect on the intellectual climate manifested itself in many ways. The idea that government could maintain high levels of employment and output and should accept responsibility for doing so, first expressed officially in the *Annual Report of the Secretary of Commerce for the Fiscal Year 1939,* was written into it by Keynesian economists. Keynesians played an important role in the drafting of the Employment Act, as Stephen Bailey's book about that Act makes clear. Bailey says, however, that "the name of Keynes is being used [by Bailey, presumably] as a symbol for an intellectual movement." There is no question that Keynes' ideas did affect economic doctrines and policies in the United States.

One more word by way of introduction. An attempt by any one person to give a detailed account of the channels through which writings influenced events is bound to be affected by the window through which that writer has seen the developments he describes; they would undoubtedly look different to someone who has seen them from a different view.

In the case of Keynesian doctrines and policies, it makes a difference not only who does the writing but what the subject is. There is a difference, as is well known and made explicit in the title of Axel Leijonhufvud's book, between "Keynesian economics" and the "economics of Keynes." This chapter could be about either or both. At the narrowest extreme one could interpret Keynesian doctrines and practices as being confined to the adoption of countercyclical fiscal policies or policies designed to combat other specific lapses from full use of the economy's labor and capital stock. At the other extreme, the term could be broadly interpreted as the rejection of the paradigm according to which private market forces can be relied on to maintain or restore high output and employment automatically if the government does not interfere with them, and the replacement of that paradigm by another. Between these extremes are many other possible interpretations of Keynesian doctrines and policies, raising many questions of theory or fact.

What is at issue could be any of these questions or all of them. To understand why Keynes' ideas were a novel contribution, it is necessary to know the ideas about both theory and policy that were accepted before *The General Theory* was published.

The widely accepted view of professional economists before the Depression of the 1930s was that in a free market economy unemployment would be limited to the frictional and casual kind. Displacement of workers caused by structural changes would be overcome by the operation of market forces, such as the competition of workers for jobs. When expenditure on capital goods was too little to use all the saving that would be done at high levels of income, interest rates would fall enough to stimulate greater capital expenditure. According to this view, there could be overproduction of specific goods or types of goods, but there could be no general overproduction, except as a temporary result of frictions, including lack of knowledge due to imperfections of communication and similar obstacles to adjustment that would be overcome in time.

At the same time, it was recognized that actual economic activity exhibited cyclical fluctuations. During the 1920s and 1930s, there were intense efforts to explain such fluctuations. This body of business cycle literature and the classical view that there could be no persistent failure of free markets to clear were incompatible, as noted by two observers commenting on Keynes' GT twenty years after its publication.

William A. Salant observes:

> It was in the spirit of classical and neoclassical analysis that a smoothly working economic system would tend toward equilibrium at full employment. The automatic mechanism by which full employment was maintained or restored was not very clearly spelled out. ... Students of the saving-investment process, beginning with Wicksell ... dealt with disturbances in the equilibrium of the classical system. Some of them advocated intervention by the monetary authority in order to offset these disturbances rather than reliance on the automatic self-correcting forces inherent in the system. They did not, however, provide an alternative theory of the determination of the level of output. The Keynesian system did provide such a theory.

Tibor Scitovsky notes that "Keynes coordinated already known bits of economic theorizing, supplied some missing links, and created a coherent theory of employment out of it." He then goes on to say:

Let us bear in mind that before the *General Theory* unemployment was regarded as the result of friction, temporary disequilibrium, or the monopoly power of labor unions. This meant that the business cycle had to be explained within a theoretical framework that made no allowance for the possibility of variations in employment and income. It also meant that business cycle policy had to be formulated without the benefit of a conceptually satisfactory measure of prosperity, such as the level of income or output or employment. This may sound absurd to us today; but it was Keynes's *General Theory* that made us realize its absurdity.

The views about what came to be called macroeconomic theory and about policy that most of the established or rising economists held before publication of the *GT* were well indicated in the book by a group of Harvard economists published in 1934 An example of the orthodox theory, advanced there, is the proposition that saving is simply an indirect form of expenditure, so that a cut in consumption automatically causes an increase in investment (i.e., an increase of spending on capital goods or inventory accumulation).

With regard to policy, the prevailing orthodox view was that the government should not interfere with the working of the market, or should do so only in limited ways. Some of the injunctions against propping up markets through creation of what was regarded as "artificially" easy money were based on the view that depressions grew out of the excesses of the preceding prosperities, and that the resulting mistakes had to be liquidated before a recovery could be "sound." This view, associated with Austrian theorists, notably Friedrich von Hayek *(Prices and Production)* and ridiculed by some of its opponents as the "crime and punishment" theory of the business cycle, regarded demand stimulation through either expansionary monetary policy or government budget deficits as positively harmful because it tended to impede "liquidation" of the mistakes of the preceding prosperity, which was a necessary and perhaps sufficient part of the therapy. The *GT* attacked the theoretical propositions underlying those beliefs. The view that Keynes' important contribution was his attack on the validity of classical and neoclassical theory and the offering of an alternative theory has been strongly advanced by Don Patinkin, who has emphasized in several places that the *GT* is a book about theory, with only incidental references to policy. This view was in fact supported by Keynes himself. In the preface to the *GT* he says, "its main purpose is to deal with different questions of theory, and only in the second place with the applications of this theory to practice."

The more widely held and less sophisticated understanding of Keynesian doctrine is much narrower: that it consisted of advocacy of countercyclical fiscal policy; that is, that when business is slack and there is substantial unemployment, the government should increase its expenditure and/or reduce taxes so as to run a budget deficit, financing it by borrowing from the banking system so that would-be private borrowers will not be deprived of financing, and that during periods of prosperity it should do the opposite.

The orthodoxy of opinion leaders and the general public prevailing prior to the Great Depression held, to the contrary, that the government's budget should be balanced every year, but not for the reasons advanced by professional theorists. The reasons more commonly given were that budget deficits are *necessarily* inflationary regardless of the extent of unemployment of labor, plant, and equipment, and/or that increases in the public debt (or the payment of interest on it?) involve a loss of real national income. These reasons were supplemented by the naive application of "commonsense" precepts of "sound" individual finance to the whole economy. Many other opponents of deficits merely accepted the view of established authority figures.

It should be recognized, however, that before publication of the *GT* and even before publication of Keynes' pamphlet *The Means to Prosperity* (1933), some established and outstanding economists, such as J. M. Clark, James Harvey Rogers, and Jacob Viner, realized that recovery required an expansion of aggregate demand and understood clearly the argument for a planned expansion of loan-financed expenditure. Indeed, J. Ronnie Davis in *The New Economics and the Old Economists,* after examining policy discussions and recommendations in the 1930s, concludes that "a large majority of leading U.S. economists affirmed, as did Keynes, the usefulness of fiscal policy and the uselessness of money wage reductions in fighting business depression" and says that "Keynes cannot claim to have converted leading members of the economics profession to his views on policy; for the reason that the profession already held his views (in some cases, before he did)." Davis emphasizes the prevalence in the early 1930s of those views among economists at the University of Chicago, often thought of as the stronghold of opposition to "Keynesian" policies.

Don Patinkin also supports the view that loan-financed increases in government expenditures during depressions were advocated at the University of Chicago independently of the *GT* and adds that "different policy recommendations can emanate from the same conceptual theoretical framework; and different frameworks can lead to the same policy recommendations." He says, "Those of us who studied at Chicago under Henry Simons did not need the conceptual framework of the *General Theory* to advocate government deficits to combat depressions; ... Simons taught this to his students on the basis of the conceptual framework embodied in Fisher's $MV = PT$. ... Simons was far from being a voice in the wilderness at that time in the United States." Patinkin does not specify when "that time" is, but he does refer to Simons' teaching as independent of Keynes "and, indeed, before the *General Theory*. He also cites Pigou as having stated the same policy conclusion in 1933 from a different conceptual background.

Despite the understanding of Clark, Rogers, and Viner of the need for planned expansion of loan-financed expenditure, in 1932 and even later they nevertheless thought such a program unwise. Clark, in responding to a letter from Senator Wagner in the spring of 1932, expressed the opinion that (in Stein's words) "a policy of financing government expenditures by borrowing during a depression was ordinarily sound. Yet he found the problem 'puzzling' at that particular time, the answer depending in part on certain conditions that he was not in a good position to judge. He was concerned about the danger that additional borrowing, with a credit system abnormally contracted and apparently unable to expand, would lower security values and undermine the shaky collateral on which bank credit rests." Similarly, Viner, in February 1933, after pointing out the advantages of a government deficit financed by monetary expansion, said, "I cannot see any justification for confidence that an aggressive inflationary policy of this sort would not immediately result in a flight from the dollar, in panicky anticipation of the effects in business circles of a grossly unbalanced government budget, and therefore in more injury than good, at least as long as we remained on the gold standard." The reason was the judgment of these economists that, in the shaky financial situation that prevailed after the summer of 1931, the fears of, and opposition to, such a program on the part of domestic and foreign bankers, businessmen, and others would lead to an outflow of capital and declines in security prices, including a fall in the value of collateral for bank loans, that would aggravate the banking crisis and prevent or greatly restrain a recovery of investment. This concern is, in one sense, far from anti-Keynesian. In the *GT* Keynes himself mentions the possibility of such confidence-shaking effects.

Even before the economic situation deteriorated from an ordinary cyclical downturn into devastating depression there were advocates of countercyclical spending. Indeed, there was professional and some official support for such spending during the prosperity of the 1920s. Stein documents this fact with respect to the United States in *The Fiscal Revolution in America,* and George Garvy shows that countercyclical fiscal policy was actively supported by some economists in pre-Hitler Germany. But these supporters either did not have answers to the theoretical objections of classical and neoclassical economists or, if they had such answers, were unable to make them persuasive to supporters of financial orthodoxy before the *GT*.

It is clear that Keynesian doctrine—even in the narrowest definition—was not accepted or even generally respectable up to and through the first Roosevelt administration. Roosevelt himself denounced the budget deficit and advocated balancing the budget during his first (1932) presidential campaign and made moves to cut government expenditures during his first year in office.

In fact the New Deal, at least during Roosevelt's entire first term, was not an exercise in Keynesian economics. The centerpiece of the recovery program in the early years was the National Recovery Administration (NRA), established under the National Industrial Recovery Act, which, among other things, put floors under prices and hourly wages. This legislation did not expand demand for goods and services, and it was the deficiency of demand that was the actual problem.

It should be noted, however, that before the publication of the *GT* some members of the administration did recognize the need to expand demand for goods and services and pressed for the early New Deal legislation partly because they thought that raising prices and money wage rates would promote such expansion. Even the National Labor Relations Act (commonly known as the Wagner Act), which was primarily an aid to unionization of labor, was thought by some to be a means of raising demand.

Most of the federal budget deficits during the first years of the New Deal were the result not of deliberate expansionary fiscal policy but of the Depression and the consequent fall in tax revenues and the expansion of relief and other Depression-related expenditures. Although some economists supported monetary and fiscal expansion, only a few who did so were prominent in the Roosevelt administration before 1937. The original New Deal intellectuals were not mainly economists, and of the economists among them only a few were students of economic fluctuations or of money or of what we now call macroeconomics.

What might be called Keynesian doctrines and practices was not accepted as part of government policy and respectable thinking until Roosevelt's second term, beginning in 1937 and lasting until the expansion of defense and World War II expenditures in the early 1940s. There were five major influences on governmental thinking during this time: (1) The Great Depression itself; (2) Keynes' *The General Theory of Employment, Interest and Money*, published in 1936, which influenced young instructors and graduate students in the economics departments of leading U.S. universities, mainly Harvard, many of whom were recruited into governmental agencies that had responsibility for or influence on fiscal and monetary policies; (3) the development of quantitative estimates of important economic variables and periodic reporting of them, including systematic data on national income and expenditure, at that time not yet developed into the present system of integrated national income and product accounts; (4) the effect of the 1937–1938 recession on thinking about what we now call macroeconomics; and (5) economic expansion in World War II.

The influence of the Great Depression itself is in one sense obvious. It shook faith in the idea that the economy was self-adjusting, or at least that market forces alone could be relied on to restore high employment quickly enough to avoid an unacceptable amount of human suffering and loss of production.

The second major influence, publication of Keynes' *GT*, was followed by several years of critical reviews by the most eminent members of the economics profession. These adverse reviews included one by Alvin Hansen, written before he moved from the University of Minnesota to Harvard and before he became Keynes' most eminent senior supporter. Since many policy ideas that were expressed in the *GT* or could be deduced from it had been advanced earlier by others inside and outside the United States, it may well be asked why this book was so influential and is so widely regarded as revolutionary.

The most plausible explanation arises from the view of Thomas Kuhn about how paradigms are replaced. Prevailing paradigms may become subject to question as facts inconsistent with them come to light, and the questioning intensifies as such facts accumulate. However, they are rarely overthrown unless some alternative theory that accounts for those facts is advanced. In 1971, when I was asked to organize a session on "Keynesians in Government" for the 1971 annual meeting of the American Economic Association, Alvin Hansen threw cold water on the idea of such a session. One of his objections was that it was hard to know whom to identify as a Keynesian. He said, "You mention Eccles for whom I have great respect—a brilliant and original mind—but by no stretch of the imagination a Keynesian. He never knew anything about Keynesian economics. He strongly favored public spending in the deep Depression, but that does not make him a Keynesian." And similarly about Ickes, Wesley Mitchell, and others. Hansen then quoted a statement which he attributed to James Conant: it takes a theory to kill a theory. That idea points to an interpretation of why the *GT* was so important: it provided an alternative to the classical and neoclassical theory, which most of the other supporters of countercyclical fiscal policies did not do. Advocates of the heretical policies were thereby given a theory that they could bring to bear against the theoretical objections of the orthodox.

The perceived lack of correspondence between classical and neoclassical theory on the one hand and the disastrously deep Depression on the other had created an appetite for a more satisfactory explanation of what was going on in the world, an appetite that was until then unsatisfied. In other words, the *GT* made respectable what seemed obvious to commonsense observations of the lay observer but was rejected by sophisticated theorists as fallacy indulged in by amateurs.

There were a number of fallacies in which the orthodox thought the heretics were indulging. One was the amateur's idea that because an increase in one person's money income increases his real income, this conclusion can be generalized: that an increase in everyone's money income will raise total real income. The classical economist "knew" that a general increase in money incomes would simply raise the price level.

Again, as noted earlier, the naive view was that acts of saving might cause underconsumption and thereby reduce aggregate demand. The more sophisticated view denied this; it asserted instead that saving merely diverted some demand for consumption to demand for investment (i.e., spending on capital goods or on increasing inventories). The *GT* made clear that the classical conclusions on these points were not true or not wholly true when resources were unemployed. The idea that "there is no such thing as a free lunch," that is, that an increase of one kind of output involves foregoing another, is now often referred to as something recently learned. Actually, it is what economics had been teaching for approximately two centuries. What Keynes argued and what was actually new was that under some conditions there is a "free lunch." In short, by showing that what classical economics found naive and wrong was sometimes correct, Keynes made the disreputable respectable.

Some of the rebels against orthodox economics were already in the government, although few of them had been students of macroeconomics. By far the most notable was Lauchlin B. Currie, an independent-minded and creative economist who in 1934 had become the main economic advisor to Marriner Eccles, chairman of the Board of Governors of the Federal Reserve System. Before the *GT* was published, this activist economist, whose intellectual fertility is still insufficiently recognized, had independently developed ideas that were not greatly different from those of the *GT*, although his first published reaction to the book was negative. Earlier than most, perhaps even Keynes, Currie had become discouraged about the possibility of obtaining economic recovery through expansionary monetary policy alone and had become convinced that an expansionary fiscal policy involving a government deficit was needed. With his assistant, Martin Krost, at the Federal Reserve, he continued and further developed a statistical series begun at the Treasury designed to measure the monthly net contribution of the federal government's fiscal operations to the flow of money income or purchasing power.

In early 1935 Currie not only estimated the size of what he then called "the pump priming or income producing deficit" of the federal government but attempted to estimate the amount needed to revive privately financed construction, which he thought necessary before "it will become safe to decrease public expenditures." He "hazard[ed] the guess" that "the monthly deficit should range between 400 and 500 millions [dollars]. It is highly questionable whether anything less can make a significant headway against the many forces making for continued depression." This figure compared with his estimate of a monthly average for December 1934 to June 1935 of only 254 million.

Currie goes on to say, "No mention has been made here of the secondary effect of public expenditures for the reason that I know of no way of estimating its magnitude. ... All that I think we can safely affirm is that there is a *tendency* for incomes and expenditures in a given period to be increased by more than the amount of initial spending. Whether such an increase *actually* occurs depends on a large number of circumstances." Largely through the recruiting efforts of Currie and others, or independently through the attractions of the New Deal, young pro-Keynesian economists, mostly graduate students and young instructors from Harvard, were brought into strategic places in the government.

The use of the term *pump priming* to describe the deficit that Currie and Krost calculated is significant as an indicator of how the supporters of loan-financed government expenditures then expected such expenditures to affect the economy. The basic idea is that the increase of such expenditures would stimulate a recovery of business activity and that this, in turn, would induce an expansion of private capital expenditure inducing further expansion so that the recovery could go on by itself. This would permit the increase in government expenditure to be reversed without reversing the recovery, exactly as when a water pump is primed. Currie stated the conditions necessary for this to happen in his 1935 memorandum. Keynes himself stated the idea, without using the apt descriptive metaphor, in 1930 in testimony before Britain's Macmillan Committee. As Keynes notes, if a depression so shakes business confidence and reduces profit expectations that even a very large reduction of interest rates will not stimulate private investment, then "government investment will break the vicious circle. If you can do that for a couple of years, it will have the effect, if my diagnosis is right, of restoring business profits more nearly to normal, and if that can be achieved, then private enterprise will be revived. I believe you have first of all to do something to restore profits and then rely on private enterprise to carry the thing along."

Another development that gained impetus in the early 1930s and was related to the development and spread of Keynesian ideas was the intensification of quantitative work on the economy—the development of statistics on economic variables. Expansion of such work covered all aspects of the economy: production, employment, finance, prices, expenditure on consumption and capital goods, and other variables, and, perhaps most notably, first, the estimation by a group under the leadership of Simon Kuznets and, later, the assembly of these estimates into an integrated whole, now called the National Income and Product Accounts (NIPA). These accounts permitted the student to evaluate the relative importance of components of aggregate production, consumption, and other variables and to trace the aggregates and their components over time.

As Patinkin has made explicit, this quantitative work and *The General Theory* interacted; the book defined concepts that could be quantified and invited quantification, and thereby "defined the framework of research in macroeconomics for many decades which followed," while the quantification put flesh on the bones of the book's concepts. For example, even during the second Roosevelt administration there were no reliable figures on unemployment. Those now used for periods before World War II are postwar estimates based on the scattered information available at that time. Another example relates to the important concept of investment (meaning by that capital formation). In the absence of figures on capital expenditure, its amount was taken to be indicated by the volume of new security issues until an article analyzing the uses of such financing by George Eddy showed that to be a very misleading indicator.

This quantitative work is well described in a book by Joseph Duncan and William Shelton entitled *Revolution in United States Government Statistics, 1926–1976*. As they show in a chapter entitled "National Income and Product Accounts and Their Uses," the prospect and then the actuality of World War II gave a great impetus to this work, and the results of the work, in turn, were used in the development of U.S. economic policy for the prewar defense program and for the prosecution of the war, and in wartime planning for the postwar period. In the early years of the war, several economists—most of them in the government—made quantitative estimates of the potential output of the U.S. economy, both to appraise the feasibility of various proposed defense programs and to help in formulating ideas about the intensity of inflationary pressures that they could be expected to generate. On the quantitative work required for the application of the essentially Keynesian concepts, economists in the U.S. government were the pioneers in the first half of the 1940s. In contrast to academic economists, they were pressured to formulate advice on policy, to face up to applying macro-economic concepts, and, in the process of doing so, to clarify those concepts.

Another influence on official and unofficial thinking about macroeconomic policy was the 1937–1938 recession. The Federal Reserve's index of industrial production plunged 29 percent in the five months between September 1937 and February 1938 and 33 percent in the ten months between July 1937 and May 1938, still the fastest fall on record.

Fiscal actions in 1936 and 1937 were major causes of that recession, and monetary policy may also have been involved, although this is disputed. The budget deficit fell more than $3 billion from 1936 to 1937. That may sound insignificant to us now, but to get a perspective on what its equivalent would have been in 1986, one must consider it as a fraction of the GNP. That would require multiplying by 50 (using round numbers), so it would be equivalent to a change in one year of about 3.5 percent of the 1936 GNP, which would amount to a change of roughly $150 billion in 1986.

That decrease did not reflect either adherence to Keynesian policies or repudiation of them. It was accounted for mainly by two things. One was that expenditures in 1936 had been swollen by the payment of the veterans' "bonus," and none was paid in 1937. The other cause was the coming into effect for the first time in 1937 of the payroll taxes under the new Social Security legislation.

The administration had opposed the bonus and Roosevelt had vetoed the bill, but it was passed over his veto. His veto message offers an answer to the question of how "Keynesian" the administration was during FDR's first term. The message denied the efficacy of "mere spending" for the sake of recovery.

The payroll taxes were of course part of the long-run Social Security plan, the enactment of which was entirely unrelated to recovery policy. Those new taxes were not offset in their effects by payment of Social Security benefits, which did not begin in substantial amounts until 1938.

Federal Reserve policy in 1936–1937 may also have borne some responsibility for the 1937–1938 recession. In the spring of 1936 the price level began to rise sharply, although unemployment, despite its great decline since 1933, was still probably between 16 and 18 percent of the labor force. The Fed was greatly concerned that the rise of prices would continue and that the huge expansion of bank reserves (which greatly exceeded legal requirements) and the money supply might later become too hard to control. Because of this concern, in August 1936 the Fed raised reserve requirements for member banks by 50 percent, announcing at the same time that the existing easy money policy was still unchanged. Then it raised them another one-third through equal increases in March and May of 1937. These increases in legal reserve requirements greatly reduced the excess reserves of member banks, but because they remained at substantial levels, the Fed was again led to express confidence that the increase in legal requirements would have little effect on credit conditions. There seems to be no evidence that the Fed recognized that reserves that were "excess" in a legal sense may not be excessive in an economic sense, although the mere fact that banks held them instead of investing in more earning assets should have suggested that they might not be excess in an economic sense, that the demand of banks for liquidity was high. There were three failures: (1) the Fed apparently did not recognize that banks have a demand for liquidity and that it may exceed levels that satisfy legal requirements. Perhaps this failure is evidence that Keynes' analysis of liquidity had not been completely absorbed; (2) it was not sufficiently appreciated that large unused capacity would make a general demand-induced rise of prices temporary or at least limit it; and (3) it was not recognized that a rise in the price level may reflect a widespread autonomous rise in costs of production at given levels of output. The first two failures may be indications that some aspects of Keynesian views were rejected or not absorbed for years after the 1936–1938 episode. The third was taken into account in *The General Theory*, where Keynes referred to it as a movement in the aggregate supply curve, but he seems to have included it more for formal completeness than because he thought it of great practical importance, for he gave it little emphasis.

The 1937–1938 recession undermined the theory that increased government spending need only get recovery of the economy started, that the resulting expansion would revive private investment, that output and employment would then continue to expand without benefit of the expanded government spending, so that the economy could maintain prosperity on its own and government spending could then return to its normal level, the idea underlying what was felicitously called pump priming. The recession of 1937–1938 persuaded many supporters of this theory that it was incorrect.

The 1937–1938 recession happened to have occurred when macroeconomists were debating Keynes' *General Theory*. One of the book's main themes—the distinguished economist D. H. Robertson thought its *main* theme—was that in a market economy involuntary unemployment could persist. Economists who doubted that the classical and neoclassical theory was applicable to the real world and who supported expansionary fiscal policy as a means to prosperity took the reversal of the recovery as support for this anticlassical idea; the economy's decline when the fiscal stimulus was withdrawn could be interpreted as a relapse to its "normal" state of underemployment equilibrium. A symptom of this new view was Alvin Hansen's book, *Full Recovery or Stagnation?* published in 1938. The displacement of the pump priming idea may be regarded as a step in promoting acceptance of this Keynesian thesis, or at least in having reduced resistance to it.

The discouraging and frustrating recession of 1937–1938 led the administration to abandon "some moves in a budget-balancing direction." In the spring of 1938 Roosevelt was persuaded by his advisors to embark on what Stein calls "the first major and single-minded use of the budget to stimulate the economy."

Perhaps the first official expression of the government's responsibility for maintaining full use of the nation's resources, but with an optimistic rather than the pessimistic tone so often associated with the stagnationist hypothesis, is to be found in the *Annual Report of the Secretary of Commerce for the Fiscal Year 1939* (pp. v-xiv), written by the late Richard V. Gilbert, Director of the Division of Industrial Economics in the Office of the Secretary, with the assistance of his colleague Roderick H. Riley.

When war broke out in Europe in 1939, the United States began to increase its exports to the Allies and to build up its own defenses. As U.S. participation in the war became increasingly likely, some research units in the government began studies of the U.S. production potential, which was still far from being realized. The Keynesians in government, led by Richard Gilbert and Robert Nathan, pressed hard for increases in the defense program unaccompanied at this early stage by curtailment of public and private civilian spending. Indeed, they supported incentives to expand plant capacity so as to realize the still large unused potential. The size of this potential became the subject of intense controversy and, as defense expenditures rose, so did the question of when it was desirable to begin limiting the expansion of demand to avoid or minimize inflation.

It is not necessary to go into those controversies here; it is sufficient to note that the most optimistic views, Gilbert's and Nathan's, as to how large output could be if the economy were operating at full blast were actually exceeded by a wide margin at the peak of wartime production, and that the government economists were miles ahead of those in the universities in efforts to quantify the variables that Keynesian models emphasized. Unemployment, which was later estimated to have been 25 percent of the civilian labor forces in 1933 and 17 percent in 1939, was brought down to less than 2 percent in 1943, 1944, and 1945 under the combined pressure of the great increase in the armed forces and the government's largely loan-financed war expenditures. This economic expansion was widely interpreted as showing how effective an expansion of government spending could be in putting unemployed resources to work. At the same time, of course, it showed the danger of inflation from excessive demand if prices were not controlled.

The elimination of unemployment during World War II was one of the greatest influences on postwar views about the role of government in attaining and maintaining high employment and production, and the possibility of avoiding serious depressions in the future. The idea that this was a responsibility of government had, by war's end, become widespread enough to result in passage of the Employment Act of 1946. Although that legislation, as finally enacted, did not specify the policies by which its goals were to be attained, it did represent a consensus that the government not only had the obligation to try to achieve the Act's objectives but had the power to do so.

By the end of World War II Keynesian theoretical ideas had become much more acceptable to the economics profession. The violent controversy among academic economists during the first few years after publication of the GT, to a large extent intergenerational, had died down—not because many anti-Keynesians had died, because many had been won over.

A few business groups also came to support compensatory fiscal policy. Notable among them were the Committee for Economic Development (CED) and, less prominently, the National Planning Association (NPA). In 1943, well before the end of the war, Beardsley Ruml, an energetic businessman who became an important figure in the CED, publicly advocated an active compensatory fiscal policy, and in 1944 he and H. Christian Sonne, a liberal banker who took the lead in organizing and financing the NPA, wrote a pamphlet which stressed that reduction of tax rates is an alternative to increasing government spending as a way of pursuing a compensatory fiscal policy. They stated their arguments in a way that made the fiscal policy they proposed more acceptable to the business community; instead of saying that deficits should be run when employment and output were low, they said that tax rates should be set at figures that enable the country to balance the budget when employment and production are at a "satisfactory high level."

In addition, the generations of rising undergraduates—both those who would be going into business and those going into other occupations—were increasingly being brought up on Keynesian theory. Although the first postwar college textbook in economics written along Keynesian lines, Lori Tarshis's *Elements of Economics,* was not published until 1947, Tarshis and other economists had been teaching their students and drafting their textbooks for several years before they were actually published. Paul A. Samuelson's *Economics: An Introductory Analysis,* also a Keynesian text, was not published until the following year. Samuelson's textbook had gone through twelve editions as of 1985 and has sold several tens of millions of copies in more than twenty-five languages, so it may be regarded as having educated students all around the world for several decades. Those books were supplemented by Alvin Hansen's *Guide to Keynes* (1953).

Thus, college and university students of economics, from whom the rising generations of government officials, businessmen, journalists, and other opinion leaders would come, were being educated along Keynesian lines. This fact was another important part of the tide toward first the adoption and then the increasing entrenchment of Keynesian views about macroeconomic policy.

If the term *Keynesian doctrine* is used in the loose sense of belief that government has both the ability and the obligation to maintain high output and employment, enactment of the Employment Act of 1946 marked a major step in its official acceptance.

Whether that is also true on a narrower interpretation of the term—as reliance on fiscal policy to accomplish its objectives—is more arguable. Most of those who originally conceived the Employment Act were Keynesians in that sense, too. But the early versions of the bill, which called the proposed law a *Full* Employment Act, were strongly and successfully resisted. One reason was that they made *full* employment the target. Another was that the early versions prescribed countercyclical change in government spending as the means of attaining it. The legislation that was finally enacted was, as Sidney Alexander put it, "completely purged of the fighting words: 'investment and expenditure,' as in 'such Federal investment and expenditure as will be sufficient to bring the aggregate volume of investment and expenditure by [all sources] up to the level required to assure a full employment volume of production'; 'full' as in 'full employment,' and other expressions in the original draft."

As enacted, the legislation deleted that definition of the target and that means of hitting it, and merely permitted the president to do what the original bill would have directed him to do. These changes can be regarded as evidence that acceptance of Keynesian ideas was then limited. The legislation that was enacted set targets—maximum employment, production, and purchasing power—but did not and still does not specify the substantive means of attaining or maintaining them; it only prescribed organizational means for giving the president and the Congress economic advice. However, it did require that the federal government should promote the Act's objectives by means that are "practicable" and "consistent with its needs and obligations and other essential considerations of national policy" and be "calculated to foster and promote free competitive enterprise and the general welfare" (Section 2 of the Employment Act of 1946). Thus, if "Keynesian doctrine" is interpreted to mean fiscal policy, and still more if it is interpreted to mean only countercyclical fiscal policy, the Employment Act of 1946 was not a step in the progressive adoption of Keynesian doctrines and policy.

On a broader view, however, it was. For one thing, the government's acceptance of responsibility for seeking to achieve the specified economic goals can be interpreted to imply that many of the members of Congress who favored the legislation thought that the government had the ability, not merely the desire or obligation, to achieve those goals.

A second reason for considering the Employment Act of 1946 as "Keynesian" is that it is not concerned merely with stabilizing the business cycle. Stability might be maintained at or around levels, including rising trends, of production that are less than the "maximum" potential of the economy on anyone's definition, but the Act sought the "maximum." In that respect it is like *The General Theory,* the main concern of which is the level of output and employment, not cyclical fluctuations.

The emphasis on maintaining maximum employment rather than merely stabilization and the explicit emphasis on growth first came with Truman's Council of Economic Advisors. That council, the first one, was organized by Edwin Nourse, but the emphasis on growth reflected the initiative of Leon Keyserling, one of the original members and Nourse's successor as chairman. Members of the Kennedy Council thought that they initiated the emphasis on growth, as opposed to dampening cyclical fluctuations. They did not initiate that emphasis, but they did revive it.

If the shift of emphasis in policy from stabilization of the cycle to continuing maximum employment is regarded as part of the absorption of Keynesian doctrines and policy into governmental thinking, it should be dated as having occurred during the Truman administration, then reversed or displaced by other considerations or ignored during the Eisenhower administration, and then restored during the Kennedy administration. These shifts may then be regarded as evidence that long-term change in doctrine occurs through a succession of steps, first several in one direction, then a lull or a few steps in the opposite direction, then more in the first direction, and so on.

Aside from restoring the focus of policy to continuing high production and employment, the most important contribution during the 1960s to institutionalizing Keynesianism in government policy was probably the tax cut of 1964. This has been heralded as the beginning of a "new fiscal policy." But Stein evidently does not believe that this can be regarded as one of the first applications of Keynesian doctrine, or even any application of it at all; he observes that "nothing was less in need of a sophisticated theory to explain it than the willingness of Congress to reduce taxes." This observation, however, appears to ignore the fact that there was then a large budget deficit. The proposal to reduce taxes in such a situation met considerable opposition because it was so contrary to fiscal orthodoxy.

From the point of view of 1986 it appears that economic policy ideas and practices in the 1960s represented a high point in the acceptance of Keynesian doctrines by government and private concerns in the United States. Since approximately the mid- or late 1960s those doctrines have been under increasing attack, first by academic monetarists, whose views found increasing acceptance, then by rational-expectations theorists, and more recently by "short-term supply-siders." (I add "short-term" to their usual label to distinguish them and what they say that is new and almost unanimously rejected by trained economists from supply-side considerations that are widely accepted by the profession but are hoary with age.) All these groups have been anti-Keynesian. With the Reagan administration, Keynesians have on the whole been displaced from government positions with macroeconomic responsibilities.

The increase in the acceptability of monetarism does not appear to be related to economic developments in the real world so much as to the persuasiveness of its leading proponents, but the intensified criticism of Keynesian theory and the increase in the influence of the other schools of thought were related to actual developments. Some of these developments were indeed different from what Keynesian theory led its proponents to expect. First, there was the increasing rise in the general price level. If, as is widely believed, this was initiated by excessively expansionary policy when output was at or near its potential, it offered no challenge to Keynesian doctrine; it was a failure to apply that doctrine. But the continuation of that inflation when output was below capacity and there was significant unemployment, and indeed even when both were actually becoming worse (i.e., stagflation), was a challenge to Keynesian doctrine and not at all what was expected by Keynesians, who tended to think mainly of deficiencies of aggregate demand, not of aggregate supply, as the chronic source of macroeconomic problems. The role of the sharp increases in oil prices in 1973–1974 and 1979–1980 on the general price level had not then been fully taken into account. By the time it was, Keynesianism had already been discredited in the eyes of many economists and probably most laymen.

After 1981 those doubts were further intensified by the election and entry into office of a new administration that vigorously repudiated Keynesian doctrines. During 1983 and 1984 the rate of inflation declined while the budget deficit was not only increasing but was surpassing all previous peacetime records in relation to the GNP. This raised further questions in people's minds about the validity of Keynesian doctrines.

Reviewing the past half-century of experience in the United States, several things stand out. The "Keynesianizing" of governmental thought and practice and of opinion leaders was a gradual, evolutionary process. It was not a steady one, however; it included not merely differences in the rates of movement in one direction but at least one reversal of direction. In the United States the intellectuals in government, especially those in the civil service, were more important influences on thought about economic policy than politicians, political parties, or nongovernmental interest groups. From approximately the mid-1930s to the end of World War II, economists in the government were ahead of those in the universities in developing the policy aspects of Keynesian macroeconomic theory and especially in its application to empirical data. The development of quantitative economic data—the national income and product accounts, unemployment statistics, and other statistical information—permitted increasing application of theoretical concepts. By now, data have been developed to a degree unknown and unimagined before World War II. Peacetime government before 1933 was so small that it could not have done much to stabilize the economy by use of fiscal policy even if it had intended to do so. In 1929 the federal government's purchases of goods and services were about 1.4 percent of the gross national product and its total expenditures about 2.6 percent. By 1985 these figures had grown to 8.9 percent and 24.6 percent. It is clear that Keynes had no direct influence on policy in the United States and, until perhaps 1938 or 1939, very little indirect influence. His influence later was on the intellectual atmosphere, and there it was immense.

10–4. WALTER W. HELLER, IN *MONETARY VS. FISCAL POLICY*: IS MONETARY POLICY BEING OVERSOLD?

...Suppose for a moment that a conservative president, heeding—as indeed the Republican candidate seemed to in 1964 —the counsel of the monetarists, (a) persuaded the Federal Reserve Board to set monetary policy on a rigid path of 4 or 5 per cent annual increases in monetary supply, and (b) persuaded the Congress to freeze tax policy into a pattern of once-a-year income tax cuts as Senator Goldwater proposed in '64 and as Arthur Burns seemed to be suggesting last week.

With the controls thus locked into place—I started to say, "with the controls thus on automatic pilot," but that's the wrong figure of speech because the automatic pilot adjusts for changes in the wind and other atmospheric conditions—one can imagine what would happen when the economy encountered the turbulence of recession with its downdrafts in jobs, profits, and incomes. How long could Richard Nixon, for example, stand idly by and deny himself and the country the proven tonic of tax cuts, spending speedups, and easier money? Economic common sense and political sagacity—and he has both—would soon win out, I am sure, over the rigid and static rules that so ill befit an ever changing and dynamic economy. So as a practical matter, I don't expect the country to fall into the trap of lockstep economics in the Nixon Administration or any other administration of the foreseeable future. I fully expect the new Administration to practice active discretionary fiscal and monetary policy....

...Let me turn now to the more positive side of my assignment. Two important tasks remain. The first is to remind you of the potency and effectiveness of fiscal policy. The second is to restate the case for continued and expanded use of discretionary, man-made policy in preference to rigid monetary and fiscal rules.

Again, we need to stop, look, and listen lest we let simplistic or captious criticism operate to deny us the benefits of past experience and thwart the promise of future discretionary action on the monetary and fiscal fronts.

Perhaps the best way to begin is to move back from a day-by-day or month-by-month perspective to ask this broad question: What has been the course of the American economy during the postwar period of an increasingly active and self-conscious fiscal-monetary policy for economic stabilization? Or, for that matter, let's broaden it: what has been the course of the world's advanced industrial economies during this period? The correlation is unmistakable: the more active, informed, and self-conscious fiscal and monetary policies have become, by and large, the more fully employed and stable the affected economies have become. Casual empiricism? Perhaps—yet a powerful and persuasive observation.

Witness the conclusion of the two-and-a-half-year study for the OECD by a group of fiscal experts from eight industrial countries:

> The postwar economic performance of most Western countries in respect of employment, production and growth has been vastly superior to that of the pre-war years. This, in our view, has not been accidental. Governments have increasingly accepted responsibility for the promotion and maintenance of high employment and steady economic growth. The more conscious use of economic policies has undoubtedly played a crucial role in the better performance achieved— an achievement which, from the point of view of the ultimate social objectives of policy, is of paramount importance. Perhaps an even more telling testament to the effectiveness of active modern stabilization-policy is the change in private investment thinking and planning not only in the financial sense of sustained confidence in the future of corporate earnings and stock market values, even in the face of temporary slowdowns in the economy—but more important, in the physical sense of sustained high levels of plant and equipment investment which seem to be replacing the sickening swings that used to be the order of the day.

Why? In good part, I take it to be the result of a constantly deepening conviction in the business and financial community that alert and active fiscal-monetary policy will keep the economy operating at a higher proportion of its potential in the future than in the past; that beyond short and temporary slowdowns, or perhaps even a recession—that's not ruled out in this vast and dynamic economy of ours—lies the prospect of sustained growth in that narrow band around full employment.

Going beyond these general observations, we have to look at specific economic experience for cause-and-effect sequences that demonstrate the potency of fiscal policy. Don't expect me to assert that we have proof, absolute proof, of this causal sequence. But quibbles about exact timing aside, the potency of fiscal policy—both good and bad—has been demonstrated time and again in the past couple of decades.

First, the contrast between the fiscal record and economic consequences of the Vietnam and Korean wars is particularly instructive. In 1950–51, three tax bills that, in today's GNP terms, boosted taxes by $35–40 billion paved the way for some four years of price stability (after an initial spurt that ended by mid-1951) without resort to excessively tight money. In 1966–68, Vietnam escalation coupled with initial Presidential hesitation to ask for a tax boost and later Congressional delay in enacting one led to the opposite result: growing deficits and an accelerating inflation (interrupted only by the late-1966 and early-1967 slowdown after the monetary brakes were slammed on and some fiscal restraints were imposed).

Second, in 1959–60, a growing full-employment surplus which reached a level of more than $10 billion, reinforced by rising interest rates, pushed the economy back into recession after only twenty-five months of expansion. Here we have another prime example of the penalty for failure to act, a penalty that was widely predicted by economists, both liberal *and* conservative, outside the Eisenhower Administration.

Third, the great expansion of the 1960's is another case in point. Deliberate tax cuts and both deliberate and non-deliberate expenditure increases played the key role in the thinking of economic policy makers, in official forecasts of changes in the level of economic activity, and in the actual GNP developments that materialized. And when urgently-recommended steps to increase taxes were not taken, the predicted consequences of overheating and inflation and undue burdens on monetary policy were amply and painfully borne out. Both in the breach and in the observance, fiscal policy demonstrated its potency during the 1960's.

The capstone of postwar policy for putting the U. S. economy more or less permanently into the full-employment orbit was, of course, the great tax cut of 1964. Coupled with the 1962 tax measures to stimulate investment, it reduced both individual and corporate income tax liabilities by one fifth. As for its economic impact: (1) as already noted, it virtually cleared away the last great obstacle to full employment, that $12 to $13 billion full-employment surplus under whose crushing weight we were simply unable to struggle to full employment. Put more starkly, to get full employment without the tax cut would have required $12 to $13 billion of additional private investment to offset a like amount of government saving. (2) Monetary policy played an important supporting role in accommodating the expansionary thrust of the tax cut. The Fed did not permit rising interest rates or tightening credit to choke off its stimulative impact. (3) The pace of economic advance accelerated as expected. By mid-1965, just before Vietnam escalation undid us, the old peacetime record for duration of U. S. expansions, fifty-one months, toppled, and rapidly expanding employment had brought the jobless rate to 4½ per cent. (4) In this process, the tax cut cleared away many of the obstacles of economic myth and misunderstanding that had long blocked the path to full use of our monetary and fiscal tools.

As we near a five-year perspective on the tax cut, we begin to see it as an economic watershed, the end of one era and the beginning of another. It ended an era in which the country felt it could afford to tolerate—or, given the available economic tools and understanding, *needed* to tolerate—chronic unemployment and underutilization of its resources (which characterized eight of the ten years between 1955 and 1965). It ushered in a new era in which the avowed and active use of tax, budget, and monetary instruments would keep the economy operating in the vicinity of full employment, with all the pleasures and pains that the management of prosperity involves (a state that most of our partners in the industrial world have enjoyed and suffered for some time).

But great as its contribution was in removing barriers to full employment and public understanding—and in bearing out the analysis and forecasts in which the tax cut was anchored—it has relatively little to offer us in the management of policy in the narrow band (aside from serving as further confirming evidence on such economic relationships as those reflected in the multiplier).

Why?

Primarily, because the requirement today is for much more nimble and faster action than a chronically or repeatedly underemployed economy typically requires. It was a semantic misfortune that this requirement was put in terms of "fine tuning" in 1967. What we were referring to was simply the need to shift from stimulus to restraint at about mid-year. But given the glee with which the term is being attacked—the critics imply that it means constant fiddling with the fiscal-monetary dials—I'm afraid that "fine tuning" is about to join "the Puritan ethic" in the gallery of gaffes in economic-policy semantics.

Yet, lampooning aside, the term "fine tuning" brings an important issue into focus. For policy tolerances become much narrower in the high-employment economic zone. Fiscal and monetary actions must not only pack a punch, but that punch has to be delivered with greater speed and precision—and with greater courage as well, since inflation is so often the foe in a high-employment, high-growth economy.

That throws the issue of man versus rules, discretion versus automaticity, into bold relief. The monetarists tell the policy maker, in effect, "Don't do something, just stand there." They doubt that we have the economic wisdom, the strength of character, and the institutional capability to operate a successful discretionary policy. In their view, rigid rules would outperform mortal man.

Time and space do not permit a full review here of the case for discretionary and flexible policy. Quite apart from the basic flaw in the concept of living by rules alone— namely, that there is no escape from discretion, if only in setting the rules and changing them from time to time—I have already suggested a couple of practical defects, (1) In anything but a world of flexible price, cost, and exchange adjustments, fixed rates of change in the money stock and tax levels are more likely to be destabilizing than stabilizing. (2) It offends common sense to say that policy should (or would) deny itself the increasingly broad, prompt, and reliable current economic information available to us, let alone, the forecasts grounded in this growing fund of information and knowledge of economic relationships.

Yet, doubts about the limits of discretion persist. In terms of the economic policies of the 60's, they center on (a) the halting performance in dealing with Vietnam-induced inflation in the past three years; (b) the slow response of GNP to last June's tax hike and budget cutback; and (c) occasional errors in official economic forecasts. Close inspection of experience in all three cases offers, I submit, solid reasons for pushing ahead along the path of discretionary policy rather than taking refuge in rigid rules.

First, then, we turn to the lessons of 1966–68. The tendency is to say that we did so poorly in coping with inflation that it bodes ill for the future of discretionary and monetary policy. One can join the chorus of critics of 1966–68 policy without accepting the gloomy inference for the future. A more hopeful inference about our ability and will to cope with excess demand in the future can be drawn from the following facts:

The Economic Advisers' diagnosis of the economy's ills was, in general, correct, and their prescription was apt. As President Johnson recently revealed, his advisers unanimously recommended a tax increase early in 1966 as part of their prescription for what ailed the economy. But Drs. Johnson and Mills were slow to fill the prescription and apply it to the patient. One might add that Dr. Ford and a few others on the other side of the aisle were even slower to accept the diagnosis and prescription.

Some of the difficulties that plagued economic policy were *sui generis*. Can you imagine a repeat of the situation in the second half of 1965 when the Council of Economic Advisers and the Treasury—judging by the speeches of their top men—were not aware of the Pentagon's expenditure plans? Or a period when a block of expenditures as large as those for Vietnam were underestimated again and again to the point where one agency in Washington foot noted an "official" estimate of military expenditures as follows: "For internal use only, but dangerous if swallowed!"

Just as we moved from fiscal fiction and fallacy to fiscal fact and understanding in the course of debate and action on the 1964 tax cut, so it seems to me we learned a great deal in the two-and-a-half-year hassle over the tax increase. The newspaper headline last spring, "Market Rallies on Hope of Tax Boost," is a case in point. Failure to act on taxes was, as predicted, so costly in terms of higher prices, higher interest rates, higher imports, and higher deficits, that the lesson for the future was inescapable. Never again, I should judge, would a President hesitate so long or a Congress sit idly by while inflation takes us by the throat as it did in 1966–68.

Congress did, after all, pass the tax surcharge and the budget cutback. After that unconscionable and costly delay, it was still an act of political courage—coming as it did, just five months before a national election. And judging by the high ratio of incumbents who voted for the surtax in June and won reelection in November, it didn't involve nearly the political penalties that had been feared. That, too, is a good portent for the future.

In the future, the fiscal fight against inflation can ordinarily be fought without resort to the grueling and gruesome process of wringing a tax increase out of Congress. For revenues from existing taxes (the surtax aside) will grow by some $15 billion a year, as an automatic by-product of growth in GNP. It should be a lot easier to exercise fiscal restraint by holding back some of this revenue bounty (i.e., by not declaring "fiscal dividends" through program increases or tax cuts) than it has been to ram a tax increase through a reluctant Congress.

Second, after the long executive and legislative lags on the 10 per cent surtax, how does the advocate of discretionary fiscal action deal with the lag in economic response to this measure after its enactment last June?

By confessing that many, if not most, of us who make specific forecasts have a bit of egg on our face. We expected a cooling off of the economy to be well under way by now, but the overall advance in GNP seems to be holding up better than expected.

By reminding you that the surcharge *is* doing some of the work expected of it, not just in the sense of "think of how much worse off we would be if we hadn't acted, but in the performance of retail sales, which peaked at $29 billion in August (after rising more than $2½ billion during 1968) and have not reached that level since; of real GNP, which forged ahead at an annual rate of nearly 6½ per cent in the first couple of quarters, slowed to 4.9 per cent in the third quarter, seems headed down to about 3½ per cent in the current quarter, and perhaps 1 to 2 per cent in the first couple of quarters next year.

By noting that during the long delay in enacting the fiscal package, cost and price pressures became more intense, and inflationary expectations became more embedded in investment thinking, than most observers realized. Coupled with growing confidence in sustained expansion, this has lessened the risks associated with capital spending and debt. Advances in plant and equipment spending, housing, and durable goods purchases have all exceeded expectations.

I should add that if the expected healthy easing of the economy does occur early next year, it won't provide any clear-cut decision after all on the relative impacts of fiscal and monetary policy. The recent slowdown in the growth of the money supply (at least in its M_1 version) deprives us of what might have been a reasonably clear-cut confrontation. What a sad day for those who had so eagerly awaited a test-tube experiment!

Finally, this brings us to the prickly area of economic forecasting. One of Milton Friedman's main charges against discretionary policy is that economic forecasting is a weak reed on which to lean in guiding policy action. The contrary view, which I hold, is that we cannot operate intelligent economic policies—public or private—without forecasts. We have to make the most reasonable forecast of the future and then be as nimble and flexible as possible in adjusting to unforeseen events and forces.

Official forecasters have, as you know, been leading a mighty exposed life ever since the beginning of President Kennedy's Administration, when we reversed previous practice by laying forecasts on the line publicly. I hope and assume that future administrations will not change this practice.

What's the right test to apply in judging whether forecasting can carry the burden that is required for discretionary policy? The right test, I submit, is not whether annual GNP forecasts are accurate to the nearest $5 or $10 billion, but whether they are sufficiently right in predicting the direction and intensity of change, first, to avoid *wrong* policy advice (for if they do no more than that, they have already at least matched automatic, or lockstep, policy); second, to lead to the *right* policy advice, if not every time, at least a very high proportion of the time.

Now by that reasonable standard, I submit that official forecasts since 1960 have fallen from grace for only four brief periods: early 1962, when we thought the economy was going to be a lot more exuberant than it turned out to be, and we didn't switch our forecast until May of that year; late 1965 and early 1966, when the economic force of Vietnam was at best dimly perceived; the fall of 1966, when economic softness crept up on us unawares and was not recognized for about six weeks; the well known 1968 example we are still experiencing.

But the rest of the time, official economic forecasts have correctly led the President's economic advisers to urge expansionary action from early 1961 to the first half of 1965; to urge restrictive fiscal-monetary policy in 1966; to urge a roller-coaster policy in 1967, consisting of (a) fiscal-monetary ease early in the year to avert recession and then (b) a call for the surtax after mid-year to help ward off resurgent inflation; and to urge, with ever greater intensity, prompt enactment of the surtax in 1968.

That inevitably moves us from the alleged weakness of forecasting to the weakness of the flesh. For what shall it profit us if we can correctly forecast overheating and prescribe the right policy medicine, but Wilbur Mills heedeth us not? Or, as some other wit dimly suggested, that the tax Mills grind exceeding fine, or may even grind to a halt?

That is a none-too-subtle way of bringing me to the point that we need to bend every effort to make fiscal policy—and particularly tax policy—more responsive and flexible. Indeed, if tax rates can be adjusted quickly and flexibly to ebbs and flows of aggregate demand, the penalties for errors in forecasting would be correspondingly reduced. We must find a way to make tax rates more adaptable to economic circumstances, either by granting the President standby power to make temporary cuts and increases in the income tax (subject to Congressional veto); or by setting up speedier Congressional procedures to respond to Presidential requests for quick tax changes to head off recession or inflation; or by developing the executive practice (proposed by a Nixon task force) under which the President would, as part of his budget message each January, propose a positive or negative income surtax (for stabilization purposes).

In winding up these comments, let me say that just as the monetarists have a great deal still to clarify, establish, and correct before they can lay claim to an only-money-matters-much economic policy, so the economic activists—I won't say "fiscalists," because economic activism implies a balanced policy of fiscal and monetary discretion—still have a great deal to learn about operating in the narrow band around full employment; a great deal more to do in improving forecasting; and important worlds to conquer in speeding up the executive and legislative processes and developing the skills to manage the fiscal dividend so as not to let it retard normal expansion, and yet, when the economy overheats, to let it become a welcome fiscal drag.

In my comments today, I referred to the brilliance of the Chicago School. I should also comment on their great consistency over the years. The rest of us—responding to new analysis and evidence, observing basic changes in the economy, and conditioned (or perhaps "burned") by experience and on-the-job training—adapt and modify our views from time to time on such key issues as (a) the role and desirability of government tax incentives for investments; (b) the independence of the Fed; (c) the proper mix of tax cuts, government budget increases, and tax sharing; and (d) yes, even the relative roles of fiscal and monetary policy. In short, we have yet to encounter the revealed and immutable truth.

But the Chicago school just goes rolling along. Miraculously, all the evidence—I really mean, all the admissible evidence—strengthens their conviction, held for decades, that to err is human, and to live by rules is divine. In spite of vast improvements in the promptness, breadth, and accuracy of economic statistics, in spite of important advances in forecasting techniques and performance, in spite of vast strides in public understanding and acceptance of positive economic policy, in spite of encouraging signs of greater responsiveness of executive and legislative officials to informed economic policy advice, the Chicago School still adheres to the proposition that we should put our trust in stable formulas, not in unstable men and institutions.

That's a bit of a caricature, but only a bit. The monetarists have taught us much. We are far richer for their analyses and painstaking research. But we would be far poorer, I believe, for following their policy prescription. It is high time that they stop trying to establish a single variable—money supply—as all-powerful, or nearly so, and stop striving to disestablish another variable—fiscal policy—as impotent, or nearly so. The path to progress in economic policy lies, instead, in a mutual undertaking to work out the best possible combination of fiscal, monetary, and wage-price policies—coupled with measures to speed the rise in productivity—for reconciling sustained high employment with reasonable price stability.

10–5. MILTON FRIEDMAN, IN *MONETARY VS. FISCAL POLICY: HAS FISCAL POLICY BEEN OVERSOLD?*

Let me start by saying that Walter has set up something of a straw man when he says that the issue is not whether money matters, but whether only money matters. I have never myself been able to accept that way of putting the issue. I do not think that it is a meaningful statement. Only money matters for what? If you want to have happiness in your home, the kind of money that matters is not the kind we're talking about now. It isn't Federal Reserve policy; it's income that matters.

More generally, there are many, many different things that matter for many, many different purposes. The key source of misunderstanding about the issue of monetary policy, in my opinion, has been the failure to distinguish clearly what it is that money matters for. What I and those who share my views have emphasized is that the quantity of money is extremely important for nominal magnitudes, for nominal income, for the level of income in dollars—important for what happens to prices. It is not important at all, or, if that's perhaps an exaggeration, not very important, for what happens to real output over the long period.

I have been increasingly impressed that much of the disagreement about this issue stems from the fact that an important element in the Keynesian revolution in economics was the notion that prices are an institutional datum determined outside the system. Once you take that view, once you say that prices are somehow determined elsewhere, then the distinction between nominal magnitudes and real magnitudes disappears. The distinction between magnitudes in dollars and magnitudes in terms of goods and services is no longer important.

That is why the qualifications we have always attached to our statements about the importance of money tend to be overlooked. We have always stressed that money matters a great deal for the development of nominal magnitudes, but not over the long run for real magnitudes. That qualification has tended to be dropped and a straw man has been set up to the effect that we say that money is the only thing that matters for the development of the economy. That's an absurd position, of course, and one that I have never held. The real wealth of a society depends much more on the kind of institutional structure it has, on the abilities, initiative, driving force of its people, on investment potentialities, on technology—on all of those things. That's what really matters from the point of view of the level of output. But, how many dollars will that be valued at? When you ask that question, that's where money matters.

Let me turn more directly to the topics assigned for this session. Is fiscal policy being oversold? Is monetary policy being oversold? I want to stress that my answer is yes to both of those questions. I believe monetary policy is being oversold; I believe fiscal policy is being oversold. What I believe is that fine tuning has been oversold. And this is not a new conclusion. I am delighted to attest to the correctness of Walter's statement that many of our views have not changed over time. It so happens that the facts haven't been inconsistent with them, and, therefore, we haven't had to change them over time.

Just this past week I was reading proof on a collection of technical essays of mine written much earlier that is going to appear next year (1969), and I came across a paper I gave to the Joint Economic Committee in 1958. I would like to quote from that paper, written ten years ago, some sentences which expressed my view at that time, and which still express my view today, on the issue of fine tuning, rather than on the separate issues of monetary and fiscal policy.

I said: "A steady rate of growth in the money supply will not mean perfect stability even though it would prevent the kind of wide fluctuations that we have experienced from time to time in the past. It is tempting to try to go farther and to use monetary changes to offset other factors making for expansion and contraction. ... The available evidence ... casts grave doubts on the possibility of producing any fine adjustments in economic activity by fine adjustments in monetary policy—at least in the present state of knowledge. ... There are thus serious limitations to the possibility of a discretionary monetary policy and much danger that such a policy may make matters worse rather than better."

I went on: "To avoid misunderstanding, it should be emphasized that the problems just discussed are in no way peculiar to monetary policy. ...The basic difficulties and limitations of monetary policy apply with equal force to fiscal policy."

And then I went on, "Political pressures to 'do something' in the face of either relatively mild price rises or relatively mild price and employment declines are clearly very strong indeed in the existing state of public attitudes. The main moral to be drawn from the two preceding points is that yielding to these pressures may frequently do more harm than good. There is a saying that the best is often the enemy of the good, which seems highly relevant. The goal of an extremely high degree of economic stability is certainly a splendid one. Our ability to attain it, however, is limited; we can surely avoid extreme fluctuations; we do not know enough to avoid minor fluctuations; the attempt to do more than we can will itself be a disturbance that may increase rather than reduce instability. But like all such injunctions, this one too must be taken in moderation. It is a plea for a sense of perspective and balance, not for irresponsibility in the face of major problems or for failure to correct past mistakes."

Well, that was a view that I expressed ten years ago, and I do not believe that the evidence of the past ten years gives the lie to that view. I think that the evidence of the past ten years rather reinforces it, rather shows the difficulties of trying to engage in a very fine tuning of economic policy. I would emphasize today even more than I did then my qualifications with respect to monetary policy because thanks fundamentally, I think, to the difficulties that have been experienced with fiscal policy and to the experience of other countries, there has been an enormous shift in opinion.

Walter says we all know that money matters; it's only a question of whether it matters very much. His saying that is, in itself, evidence of the shift in opinion. Before coming up here today I reread the reports of the Council of Economic Advisers that were published when he was chairman of the Council. I do not believe that anybody can read those reports and come out with the conclusion that they say that money matters significantly. While there was some attention paid to money in those reports, it was very limited.

There has been a tremendous change in opinion on this subject since then. And I am afraid that change may go too far. I share very much the doubts that Walter expressed about the closeness of the monetary relations. There is a very good relation on the average. But the relation is not close enough, it is not precise enough, so that you can, with enormous confidence, predict from the changes in the money supply in one quarter precisely what's going to happen in the next quarter or two quarters later.

Indeed, that's the major reason why I'm in favor of a rule. If I thought I could predict precisely, well then, to go back to the statement I quoted from, I would be prepared to make fine adjustments to offset other forces making for change. It's precisely because we don't know how to predict precisely that you cannot in fact use monetary policy effectively for this purpose. So I emphasize that my basic view is that what has been oversold is the notion of fine tuning.

Yet, fiscal policy has, in my view, been oversold in a very different and more basic sense than monetary policy—to turn to the main subject assigned to me. I believe that the rate of change of the money supply by itself—and I'm going to come back to those two words "by itself"—has a very important effect on nominal income and prices in the long run. It has a very important effect on fluctuations in nominal and real income in the short run. That's my basic conclusion about changes in the stock of money.

Now let's turn to fiscal policy. I believe that the state of the government budget matters; matters a great deal—for some things. The state of the government budget determines what fraction of the nation's income is spent through the government and what fraction is spent by individuals privately. The state of the government budget determines what the level of our taxes is, how much of our income we turn over to the government. The state of the government budget has a considerable effect on interest rates. If the federal government runs a large deficit, that means the government has to borrow in the market, which raises the demand for loanable funds and so tends to raise interest rates.

If the government budget shifts to a surplus, that adds to the supply of loanable funds, which tends to lower interest rates. It was no surprise to those of us who stress money that enactment of the surtax was followed by a decline in interest rates. That's precisely what we had predicted and what our analysis leads us to predict. But—and I come to the main point—in my opinion, the state of the budget by itself has no significant effect on the course of nominal income, on inflation, on deflation, or on cyclical fluctuations.

The crucial words in these statements are "by itself" because the whole problem of interpretation is precisely that you are always having changes in monetary policy and that you are always having changes in fiscal policy. And if you want to think clearly about the two separately, you must somehow try to separate the influence of fiscal policy from the influence of monetary policy. The question you want to ask yourself is, "Is what happened to the government budget the major factor that produced a particular change, or is it what happened to monetary variables?"

I recognize, of course, that there is no unique way to separate monetary policy from fiscal policy, but I think there would be wide agreement on the part of most people that by fiscal policy we mean changes in the relation of taxes to spending, and that by monetary policy, we mean changes in certain monetary totals. Some people might want to use as the relevant monetary total the monetary base; some people might want to use the money supply in the sense of currency and demand deposits; some people might want to use a broader money supply.

For the moment, those differences do not matter. What matters is that we ask the question, "What happens if you hold monetary policy constant and you change fiscal policy?" Or, "What happens if you hold fiscal policy constant and you change monetary policy?" Analytically—I'm going to discuss the statistical evidence later—we can separate monetary and fiscal policy by considering a situation in which monetary policy proceeds in a certain way, and we hypothetically consider a big tax increase or a big tax cut. What difference would that make?

In talking about fiscal policy, when I discuss the relation of taxes and expenditures, I don't mean current tax receipts and current payments, because all of us would agree that

that's not solely a question of policy, but partly a result of what happens to the economy. Currently, about the best measure of fiscal policy is to be found in something like the high-employment budget, in the notion of what taxes and expenditures would be at high levels of employment.

I was delighted to see the Council of Economic Advisers, under Walter Heller's chairmanship, follow up the suggestion which had been made in 1947 by the Committee for Economic Development, and independently by me, that we look at fiscal policy in terms of the high-employment budget. The Council provided for the first time some very useful and interesting figures on fiscal policy by itself, namely, on the state of the high-employment budget.

Now it's perfectly clear that fiscal policy can change by itself without a change in monetary policy. You can have a tax cut, let us say, and finance the resulting deficit by borrowing from the market. If you do that, that will have an effect on interest rates, but the money supply need not be affected. Alternatively, the change in fiscal policy can be accompanied by a change in monetary policy. You can have a tax cut and finance the deficit by printing money.

The essence of the pure fiscal position is that it doesn't make any difference which of those you do. The essence of the monetary position that I'm presenting is that it makes an enormous difference which of those you do, that those two kinds of tax cut will have very different effects. That's what I mean by separating the effect of fiscal policy by itself, from the effect of monetary policy by itself.

The fascinating thing to me is that the widespread faith in the potency of fiscal policy—this is flying straight in the face of some words that Walter Heller spoke a few moments ago when he talked about the proven effectiveness of fiscal policy—rests on no evidence whatsoever. It's based on pure assumption. It's based on a priori reasoning.

I'll come back to that point of available evidence a little later and document it more fully. But it is worth dealing briefly with the a priori argument, I think—the argument from first principles—because at first it seems so persuasive. And the question is, "What's wrong with it?" It certainly seems obvious that if you raise taxes, as you did with the surtax, that clearly reduces the disposable income of the people who pay the taxes, leaves them with less to spend, and reduces spending. Surely, that is anti-inflationary. What could be clearer and simpler? How could any fool in his right mind deny so obvious a chain of events?

The trouble is that what I've said so far is only half the story. There's another half to it which is typically left out. If the federal government imposes a surtax, as it did, but keeps on spending roughly the same amount of money, as it did, then that reduces the amount it has to borrow. If it raises $10 billion more in taxes, it now has to borrow $10 billion less. The taxpayers have less money, but the people who would have loaned the government the funds with which to finance their spending have more.

So, you have to ask, "What happens to that $10 billion which the government otherwise would have borrowed?" The answer is that that $10 billion is now available for people to use to pay their taxes with or for people to lend to others. That's why the interest rate can be predicted to fall. The tax increase does reduce the demand for loanable funds on the part of the government. That lowers the interest rate. But the reduction in the interest rate induces somebody else to come and borrow those funds that otherwise would have been available for the government.

It provides the possibility of greater private investment, expenditure on housing, whatever it may be that people are borrowing it for. And so, if you take both sides of the picture to a first approximation, there's a standoff. Taxpayers have $10 billion less, and the people who would have loaned that money to the government have $10 billion more. If there is going to be any net effect, it has to be on a more sophisticated level; it has to be the indirect effect of the reduction in interest rates on other variables. In particular, it has to be a willingness on the part of the populace to hold more money, more nominal money, when the interest rate goes down.

I only sketch this—it isn't intended to be a full analysis—to show that on a purely theoretical level, you cannot come out with a clean case. It could be that fiscal policy is still potent. I don't mean to say that, in abstract theory, these indirect effects could not be strong. Keynes thought they were. And you can perfectly well establish an entirely correct theoretical chain of reasoning whereby those indirect effects would be strong. It is possible, but it's not obvious. And so you have to look at facts. When you look at facts, there's a strong tendency to be anecdotal. After all, it's much more appealing to look at particular episodes. They are more dramatic. They are more immediately accessible. And, especially, when we talk rather than write, they fit into the mode of discourse much better.

There's nothing wrong with doing that. Those individual episodes are relevant evidence, and they are useful to look at—I'm going to look at some—but they are a very small part of the evidence. If we are really going to examine the evidence, we want to look at experience over a long period; we want to look at all the experience, we want to look at the average effect. One swallow doesn't make a spring; one case of confirmation or disconfirmation doesn't settle anything.

I think it will be interesting if you have an experiment in 1969 on the effects of fiscal versus monetary policy. But whichever way it goes, it's only going to be a small part of the total body of accumulated evidence that is available. But let me turn to a couple of episodes.

The one that is most dramatic and that Walter Heller emphasized most is, of course, the 1964 tax cut. Now let me point out to you that, so far as I know, there has been no empirical demonstration that that tax cut had any effect on the total flow of income in the U. S. There has been no demonstration that if monetary policies had been maintained unchanged—I'll come back to that in a moment—the tax cut would have been really expansionary on nominal income. It clearly made interest rates higher than they otherwise would have been. But there is no evidence that by itself it was expansionary on income.

Arthur Okun wrote a paper in the summer of 1965 that he presented at the Statistical Association Meeting that fall which gave a statistical analysis of the effect of the tax cut. It's a very interesting paper; it's a fine thing to have done. I think we ought to have more such examinations. But if you examine what he did, you will find that what he has is an illustrative calculation of, not evidence on, the importance of the tax cut.

What Okun did was to assume away the whole problem because he looked only at the effect of fiscal policy without asking what role monetary policy played during that period. What he did was to say that we could put monetary policy aside, because interest rates didn't change during the period and that, therefore, we could suppose that monetary policy was neutral. As I've just made clear, that really begs the fundamental issue. If monetary policy were really neutral, you would have expected interest rates to go up, not stay constant. You had a tax cut. That meant the government had to borrow more, which would have raised interest rates. If, despite that effect, interest rates didn't go up, monetary policy must have been doing something.

What Art Okun did in that paper was to say: Let us assume that the theory underlying fiscal policy is correct. Then what do the figures say about the numerical value of the multiplier in this episode. He did not present evidence on whether that theory is correct.

To do that, you need to see what happened to money separately. If you look at what happened to money, you will find that the temporal pattern of money supply conforms much better to the temporal pattern of nominal income than does the tax cut. There was a decided tapering off in the growth of money supply in early 1962 through about the first three-quarters of '62. This was reflected in the last part of '62 and early '63 by a tapering off in the economy. You then had a switch in monetary policy. It became more expansive—the quantity of money started growing—and lo and behold, about six or nine or ten months later, before the tax cut had taken effect, income started to rise at a more rapid rate.

In order to make the tax cut responsible for that, you have to argue that anticipation of the tax cut produced an increase in income, and that then, after you had the tax cut, despite the fact that it had been anticipated, it had its full effect all over again. So that episode, while it's a nice dramatic episode, does not, as it has so far been analyzed, provide much evidence.

From what I've said so far, I haven't proved that the tax cut didn't have an expansionary effect. I'm not trying to argue that it has been established conclusively that fiscal policy had no effect in that episode alone. I'm only saying that so far, there is no persuasive statistical, empirical evaluation which gives you reason to say that it had an effect.

1966–1967 is a nice episode. It is a nice controlled experiment. Nature happened to turn one out. In early 1966, April 1966, the Federal Reserve stepped very hard on the monetary brake. The quantity of money, however you measure it, slowed down its rate of growth very sharply. The narrow definition actually declined; the broader definition increased from April to December, but at a much slower pace than it had before. During that same period, the high-employment budget moved toward a larger and larger deficit.

If you were to look at the high-employment budget alone, you would say that we should have had a boom in the early part of 1967. If you were to look at monetary policy alone, you would say that we should have had a slowdown in the early part of 1967. Well, as Walter testified in his talk, we did have a slowdown in the early part of 1967, as you would have expected from the monetary influence, in contrast to what you would have expected from the fiscal influence.

Early in 1967, the Fed turned around, and it is true, as Walter pointed out, that 1967—I guess he was saying '68, but '67 too—comes pretty close to being a record year of monetary expansion. And about six to nine months after the Fed turned around, the economy turned around. We started to have an expanded growth in nominal income.

As for the 1969 possible experiment, it's too soon to say because I do not think that you ought to judge fiscal policy, as you ought not to judge monetary policy, on whether it has an overnight influence of major magnitude. There are lags involved in fiscal policy, as there are in monetary policy. Whether you have an experiment or not depends on how the Federal Reserve behaves. The various monetary totals have been behaving in very different ways, for reasons about which maybe I'll have a chance to say something later. At the moment I'll put it to one side. If the Fed should continue with a very easy policy, of the kind that it had prior to the past two months, that is, if the rate of growth of the money supply defined broadly should continue at its present pace, and if the rate of growth of the narrow money supply should step up and come closer to its usual relation with the rate of growth of the broader money supply, then that would suggest that you would not have a slowdown in the early part of '69.

On the other hand, the fiscal effect would suggest that you would. So you might have another experiment. But whether you do or not, depends on what the Fed does. If the Fed should repeat its behavior of early 1966, if it should step on the brake very hard, then both fiscal and monetary policy will be going in the same direction and you will not have an experiment. But, as I said before, none of this is very satisfactory. This is all episodic. What you need is systematic evidence that takes account of other factors at work, that tries to examine what happens not only at certain critical points of time, but throughout a longer period.

The interesting thing is that those people who speak most loudly about the potency of fiscal policy have produced no such evidence. But there is a great deal of evidence which has been produced primarily by those of us who have argued for the potency of monetary policy. You know, it is always being said that we are unrealistic, that we are abstract and so on. But I think that there is no one who can deny that we have, in the course of the past fifteen years, accumulated an enormous amount of empirical evidence on the questions that are at issue. I'd like to call your attention to some items in that list which are relevant to the particular issue of the potency of fiscal and monetary policy.

I'm going to run over them very hastily. Some sixteen years ago, I wrote an article that compared the Civil War to World War I and World War II. The particular question I asked was, "Do you get a better understanding of what happened to prices during those three wars by looking at what was happening to monetary magnitudes, or by looking at what was happening to fiscal magnitudes?" The answer was completely unambiguous. And nobody has since produced any evidence contradicting that analysis. It turns out that you get a very clear, straight-forward interpretation of price behavior in those three wars by looking at monetary magnitudes; you do not get an explanation by looking at fiscal magnitudes.

Second, Walter Heller was kind enough to comment on the studies that Anna Schwartz and I have done under the auspices of the National Bureau of Economic Research. We have studied the relation between monetary magnitudes and economic magnitudes over the course of a hundred years, roughly a century. During that period, fiscal policy changed enormously. At the beginning of that period, the government budget was negligible. In the period since World War II, the government budget has been mammoth. And yet we found roughly the same kind of a relationship between monetary and economic magnitudes over the whole of that one-hundred-year period.

If fiscal policy were playing a dominant influence, it should have introduced more variability, as Walter properly said it should have, into the relation between money and income in the later part than in the earlier; but as far as we can see, it's a homogeneous universe.

Third, some years back David Meiselman and I published a study directed specifically at the question, "Do monetary magnitudes or autonomous expenditure magnitudes give you a better interpretation of the movements in nominal income over short periods of time?" That article produced a great controversy and a large number of replies and counterreplies. It's a matter of biblical exegesis to trace through the thrusts and counterthrusts of that controversy though I am sure it would be good for all your souls to do so.

But one thing that came out of that controversy is that everybody agreed that the monetary magnitudes did have an important and systematic influence. The complaint that was made against us was the one that Walter makes tonight, that we had gone too far in denying that the autonomous magnitudes exerted an influence.

The most recent study is one by the Federal Reserve Bank of St. Louis, which Walter was good enough to refer to as an unofficial arm of the Chicago School—well, we ought to have one out of twelve anyway. It is an extremely thorough and very fascinating study in which they have related quarter-to-quarter changes in GNP to changes in monetary totals over prior quarters and also to changes in governmental expenditures and taxes. They have been very thorough. Anything that anybody suggested to them which might be wrong with what they initially did, they have tried out. As a result, they have tried out many of the possible permutations and combinations. They have tried the high-employment budget and they have tried other budget concepts. But I'll refer to their findings about the high-employment budget.

What they have done is to try to see whether the monetary or the fiscal magnitudes play a more consistent and systematic role in explaining the course of GNP change over the period 1952 to 1968. That is the right period because Walter Heller is right in pointing to the Federal Reserve-Treasury Accord of 1951 as marking a distinct change in the role of monetary policy and its possibility.

Let me quote their summary conclusion. They say, "This section tested the propositions that the response of economic activity to fiscal actions relative to monetary actions is (I) larger, (II) more predictable, and (III) faster."

Let me repeat this more explicitly. The proposition they tested was that the response of economic activity to fiscal action was larger, more predictable, and faster than the response of the economy to monetary action. "The results of the tests," they say, "were not consistent with any of these propositions. Consequently, either the commonly used measures of fiscal influence do not correctly indicate the degree and the direction of such influence, or there was no measurable net fiscal influence on total spending in the test period." To put it in simpler terms, what they found—far from there being a proven efficiency of fiscal policy—was that, as a statistical matter, the regression coefficients of the high-employment budget surplus or deficit, if the monetary variables are held constant, were not statistically significant.

They found that if you separated expenditures from taxes and treated them separately, expenditures did have some effect but taxes had none. An expenditure increase tended to have a positive influence on income in the first two quarters after the increase, but it had a negative influence in the next two quarters.

Apparently, the expenditure increase had had a short-term influence before it started to work its way through the credit market.

Then there was the delayed effect of the half of the picture that, as I mentioned before, is generally not discussed. That's another piece of evidence. Maybe it's my myopia that leads me not to know the empirical studies the other way around. I would like to have some references to careful, systematic, empirical studies which have analyzed the influence of fiscal policy along with the influence of monetary policy, and which provide some evidence that, for a given quantity of money, or a given monetary-supply policy defined in some other way, fiscal policy has a significant influence on nominal national income and prices.

Surely, I think the time has come to utter the usual poker challenge to those who maintain that fiscal effects are important for inflation and the price level. It seems to me that it is time they put up and gave us some evidence to support the repeated assertions to that effect.

ADDITIONAL READINGS

DeLong, J. Bradford, "Keynesianism, Pennsylvania Avenue Style: Some Economic Consequences of the Employment Act of 1946," *Journal of Economic Perspectives* 10 (Summer 1996) 41–53.

Hargrove, Erwin C. and Samuel A. Morley, *The President and the Council of Economic Advisers: Interviews with CEA Chairmen* (1984.)

Schultze, Charles L., "The CEA: An Inside Voice for Mainstream Economics," *Journal of Economic Perspectives* 10 (Summer 1996) 23–39.

Stein, Herbert, "A Successful Accident: Recollections and Speculations about the CEA," *Journal of Economic Perspectives* 10 (Summer 1996) 3–21.

Stein, Herbert, "What Economic Policy Advisers Do," *The American Enterprise* 2 (March-April 1991) 9.

Tobin, James, "Keynes' Policies in Theory and Practice," *Challenge* (November-December 1983) 5–11.

United States Government, Public Law 304 (Employment Act of 1946), 79th Congress, 2nd Session, Feb. 20, 1946 (1946).

United States Government, Committee of Conference Report, A Bill Declaring a National Policy on Employment, Production, and Purchasing Power, and for Other Purposes, 79th Congress, 2nd Session (1946).

United States Government, Congress, House of Representatives Committee on Executive Department Expenditures, Full Employment Act of 1945: Hearings on H.R. 2202, 79th Congress, 1st Session (1945).

"The Keynesian Revolution," *Time*, Vol. 86, No. 27 (December 31, 1965).

CHAPTER 11

The Collapse of the Keynesian Consensus, 1969–1980

INTRODUCTION

Aside from the 1930s, the decade of the 1970s was the most trying for macroeconomists. The turbulent 70s were characterized by unremitting crises centering around inflation, unemployment and the international payments system. In spite of three recessions in a ten year period, high inflation continued to bedevil the American economy throughout the period. In less than ten years the performance of the economy would help foil the reelection hopes of two incumbent presidents. A new term entered the public policy vocabulary: stagflation, simultaneous high unemployment and high inflation. The decade of the 70s also witnessed the collapse of the Bretton Woods system which had governed international payments in the postwar era. A few short years earlier the ascendency of Keynesian economics seemed assured. Richard Nixon had declared: "I am now a Keynesian." Even Milton Friedman, a major Keynesian foe and originator of monetarism, was moved to utter: "We are all Keynesians now."

The Nixon years opened with the Congress renewing the income tax surcharge in 1969 albeit at a reduced 5 percent rate. The new team of economic advisers hoped to make a "soft landing" through a policy of gradualism in which monetary and fiscal restraint kept inflation under control without raising unemployment. These hopes were dashed as the balance of policy then tipped even more in the direction of restraint. The economy slipped into a recession that lasted from December 1969 until November 1970 with unemployment approaching 6 percent. At the same time inflation showed little improvement. A new companion term to stagflation was coined to describe this kind of downturn: the inflationary recession. Arthur Burns, originally brought into the Nixon administration as Counselor to the President responsible for domestic and economic affairs, replaced William McChesney Martin as Fed chair in 1970 and declared his intention to restore price stability.

Inflation worsened. At the urging of Treasury Secretary John Connally, President Nixon inaugurated his New Economic Policy in August 1971 which called for a ninety day wage and price freeze to be followed by a system of wage and price controls. The controls were to be removed gradually yet as promptly as circumstances allowed as inflation abated. In fact, they lasted longer than the Nixon presidency, lingering into 1974. Nixon always felt that the recession of 1960–1961 cost him the 1960 election. Right or wrong, he was intent on making sure that it did not happen again even if the policy adopted was anathema to most of his Republican supporters. The original game plan was to let the wage and price program reduce inflationary expectations and give tighter monetary and fiscal policy time to work. But as the reelection campaign of 1972 neared, policy soon reversed course in the direction of expansion. With inflation artificially suppressed by the imposition of controls, stimulative macroeconomic policy was used to promote employment growth through the election year. A reignition of inflation (which in fact did occur) could be dealt with after Nixon won reelection.

In this same time frame, some important developments were underway on the international economic scene. As part of the New Economic Policy, the United States closed the gold window, ending the practice of paying gold to foreign central banks for the dollar balances they accrued. In December 1971, the Smithsonian Agreement called for the devaluation of the dollar and set in motion a chain of events leading ultimately to a system of floating exchange rates.

In October 1973 the Arab members of the Organization of Petroleum Exporting Countries (OPEC) imposed an oil embargo on the United States for its support of Israel in the Yom Kippur War. This was followed in November by the first oil price shock in which OPEC quadrupled crude oil prices. From the standpoint of the consuming nations, this was the equivalent of a massive tax increase. The American economy went into a long (1973–1975) and steep recession, the worse since the Great Depression years, with unemployment peaking at 9 percent. Inflation showed no signs of improvement. The recession year of 1974 recorded an inflation rate of 11 percent, the first double digit rate since wartime price controls were removed in 1947. With Nixon's resignation, it was Gerald Ford's turn to wrestle with stagflation. President Ford, not realizing the depth of the downturn, still saw inflation as the main problem and held a domestic economic summit conference in the fall of 1974 to Whip Inflation Now, as the WIN buttons he handed out famously declared. However, another policy reversal was soon underway, as the public debate turned to tax cuts.

The nation was in the grip of a full fledge stagflation. The policy dilemma was clear: stimulate the economy and inflation would worsen; follow restraint and unemployment would worsen. In the early 1960s the Phillips Curve, purporting to show an inverse relationship between the rate of inflation and the rate of unemployment, won widespread acceptance. This relationship seemed to have broken down in the 1970s as the American economy suffered the worst of both worlds: high and rising inflation and unemployment. These problems were further compounded by yet another economic malaise, sluggish productivity growth. The post-1973 wage stagnation, which lasted for over twenty years, is generally attributed to the productivity slowdown that began in the 1970s.

The long recession continued through to March 1975, and was a contributory factor in President Ford's defeat in his bid for reelection by challenger Jimmy Carter. In 1977 President Carter appointed G. William Miller to replace Arthur Burns as Fed chair. Again there were claims, as there were when Nixon selected Burns, that the independence of the Fed was being compromised by a presidential nomination made with the expectation of the pursuit of an expansionary monetary policy. The year 1977 was decent, with inflation stable, unemployment falling and real GDP rising. The macroeconomist's nightmare came in 1979. The Iranian revolution shut down that nation's oil fields and deposed the Shah, and triggered another oil price shock, roughly doubling the posted price of OPEC crude. To offset the contractionary impact of the price shock, monetary and fiscal policy tilted in the direction of ease. In the summer of 1979 Paul Volcker took over from G. William Miller as chair of the Federal Reserve Board, intent on the reassertion of the Fed's independence and the resumption of monetary restraint to fight inflation. A watershed moment in Federal Reserve policymaking came in October 1979 when the Federal Open Market Committee voted to put greater emphasis on the control of the monetary aggregates as an instrument of policy while deemphasizing the federal funds rate.

Economic performance in the election year of 1980 doomed the candidacy of another incumbent president as Ronald Reagan defeated Jimmy Carter. In a presidential debate Reagan had asked his audience: "…are you better off today than you were four years ago?" At the polls the electorate responded with an unequivocal "no." Some argued that the "answer" required a selective reading of the statistics (real per capita disposable income was 7.5 percent higher than in 1976 and unemployment was lower). But the country had just endured two consecutive years of double digit inflation rates, 11.3 percent in 1979 and 13.5 percent in 1980. The misery index, the sum of the inflation rate and the unemployment rate and perhaps a better gauge of public discontent, had gone up substantially. Treasury bill yields and mortgage rates of interest were over 10 percent. In January 1980 the prime rate stood at over 20 percent. For sure the monetarist experiment the Fed began in the fall of 1979 contributed to the poor employment numbers and elevated interest rates. A six month recession began in January 1980, with the unemployment rate peaking at 7.8 percent in July.

The chaotic state of economic performance and policymaking was suitably matched by the disarray in the world of macroeconomic theory. A number of competing theories, all antidotes to what many now regarded as the discredited Keynesian view, came into vogue. The most significant school of thought to emerge was supply-side economics. Its academic pedigree was a dubious one. Many of the key supply-side propositions had little if any empirical support. It was the invention of politicians (including Representative Jack Kemp) and journalists (including *Wall Street Journal* editorial writer Jude Wanniski), as well as economists (including Arthur Laffer). Supply-siders believed that postwar Keynesian demand-side management slighted the economy's supply side and therefore, had an inflationary bias. Economic policy needed to resuscitate the incentives to work, save and invest that had been stifled by an excessively burdensome tax system. Reductions in marginal tax rates allowed income earners to keep more of their gross income, thereby calling forth additional work effort and greater savings to make more capital investment possible. This would increase the aggregate quantity of goods supplied in the economy and serve to counteract inflationary pressures. Reaganomics took its inspiration from supply-side economics by combining the massive tax cut of 1981 with some regulatory reform.

The three Keynesian competitors (supply-side economics, monetarism and rational expectations) shared in common the belief that market capitalism is inherently stable and that government intervention is the source of economic instability. Policymakers should not be allowed to exercise their discretion, but rather should be bound by rules. Thus these schools of thought are sympathetically disposed towards proposals for a balanced budget amendment as a means to eliminate discretionary fiscal policy. They also subscribe to some version of the natural rate of unemployment (in the early 80s estimated to be 5–6 percent). This natural rate hypothesis holds that attempts to push the rate of unemployment below the natural rate will be inflationary.

Monetarism, led by Milton Friedman, had been the earliest entrant in the competition between rules and discretion with the Keynesians. Friedman had long advocated a monetary rule: increase the money stock each year by 3–3½ percent regardless of economic conditions. This would remove discretion from the hands of the monetary authorities. Moreover, monetarists viewed fiscal policy as ineffectual since it crowded out private investment spending. Deficit spending necessitates additional borrowing, causing government to compete with private borrowers for funds in the credit markets. This competition would raise interest rates and discourage some investment spending. Monetarists claimed this crowd-out would be complete; every dollar of increased government spending would displace an equal dollar of private investment spending. To interfere with capital formation, the wellspring of improvement in the standard of living, was misguided and would damage economic performance in the longer run. Consistent with their acceptance of the natural rate hypothesis, monetarists reject the tradeoff between inflation and unemployment implied by the neo-Keynesian Phillips Curve. Monetarists believe there is still much that is unknown about how a modern macroeconomy operates. In deriding fine-tuning, they fault neo-Keynesian policymakers for being too ambitious, almost arrogant, in recommending policy prescriptions that imply an understanding of the underlying economy beyond what is warranted. By the late 1970s yet another alternative to the Keynesian orthodoxy appeared, the theory of rational expectations. Robert Lucas of the University of Chicago received the Nobel Prize in economics for his work as one of the originators of rational expectations. This theory holds as one of its main propositions that market agents (householders and firms) can learn from experience to anticipate certain policy actions, and by anticipating them, thoroughly vitiate them. For example, if in a recession the monetary authority increases the money supply, workers and firms will from past experience immediately anticipate the inflationary impact of the policy action. Workers will demand higher wages and firms will raise prices. Firms will have no incentive to hire more workers, and consumers will have no incentive to buy more of the firm's output. Nothing will change; the policy action will prove ineffective.

As the Keynesian consensus seemed on the verge of complete collapse, each of the other three competing theories was thought to be a candidate to succeed Keynesian economics. Yet this did not happen. Supply-side economics may have overpromised. Cuts in marginal tax rates in 1981 were supposed to generate additional economic activity, enlarge the tax base and increase tax receipts sufficient to avert federal budget deficits. This did not happen. Huge budget deficits were the norm for fifteen years after the Reagan tax cuts. Monetarism had its moment. But it also overpromised. Its monetary rule was supposed to afford a quick and painless way to price stability. Central banks in the United States, the United Kingdom and elsewhere followed the monetarist prescription from 1979 to 1982 only to find that it brought on a deep recession with unemployment in excess of 10 percent. As for rational expectations, its predictions were far from compatible with the performance of the American economy in the aftermath of the Fed's return to monetary ease in the fall of 1982. The Fed's policy was publicly announced and avowedly expansionary. A non-inflationary recovery followed; businesses did not raise prices and labor did not make large wage demands. Years later, Robert Lucas commented as he received his Nobel Prize that: "The Keynesian orthodoxy hasn't been replaced by anything yet." It is fair to say that a majority of macroeconomic models still retain a Keynesian core. Macroeconomic analysis continues to draw heavily on the basic Keynesian model, however imperfect it may be.

The experience of the 1970s raises a number of important questions. What caused the economic volatility? Why did the economy veer sometimes between inflation and contraction, and at others show inflation and contraction? How much of the difficulties of the 1970s is attributable to the OPEC oil price shocks? Did the response of policymakers exacerbate these difficulties? Was the policy response one of stop-go? For example, was it common for a policy of expansion to be abruptly ended and followed by restraint, and vice versa? Does policy lose credibility in such circumstances? Were economic advisers increasingly offering advice in the 1970s meant to advance the political interests of an administration rather than the achievement of economic goals? Is there a political cycle to macroeconomic policy? Do incumbents employ stimulative policies in election years followed by restraint in non-election years? Are market economies driven more by natural forces than the actions of policymakers? Do the actions of policymakers play a more peripheral role? Are their actions sometimes counterproductive? Given the way the Fed behaved in the 70s should its independence be curtailed and monetary policy be put in the hands of the executive branch? What would be the advantages and disadvantages of such a change? Why do economists disagree? Why are there so many competing schools of macroeconomic thought? Why is it so difficult to resolve their differences? The documents and essays that follow will bring some of these questions to the forefront.

DOCUMENTS

Document 11–1 is excerpts from President Gerald Ford's Annual Message to the Congress that accompanied the Economic Report of the President dated January 26, 1976. He states that "there is no simple formula or single act" that will solve the problems of inflation and unemployment that resulted from many years of "excessive stimulation." He proposes a gradual slowing of federal spending along with tax cuts, noting that overly rapid growth would renew inflation. Ford proposes deregulation of the transportation industry as a means to restore competition. Document 11–2 is selections from Walter Heller's "Opening Statement Before the Joint Economic Committee, U.S. Congress, February 6, 1976." Heller expresses his dissatisfaction with the Ford budget, believing that it does not provide sufficient stimulus. He mounts a vigorous defense of traditional demand-side management.

Document 11–3 is selected excerpts from the Full Employment and Balanced Growth Act of 1978. This legislation shows the impatience of its sponsors with the inability of economic policy to achieve full employment. Better known as the Humphrey–Hawkins bill, it was first introduced in 1976. After some modification, it eventually gained passage in 1978. Its authors are clearly trying to legislate full employment, not the maximum employment envisioned by the Employment Act of 1946. Numerical goals are set and other objectives like price stability are made subservient to achieving the employment target. Document 11–4 is Milton Friedman's *Newsweek* column published in the August 2, 1976 issue. He comments on the original version of the Humphrey–Hawkins Full Employment and Balanced Growth Act, as proposed in 1976. The bill called for an employment goal of 3 percent unemployment. Friedman sees this proposal as an unwarranted intrusion of government into the private economy. According to his analysis, any government jobs created under this legislation will lead to a reduction in employment in the private sector. Document 11–5 is a portion of the remarks made by President Jimmy Carter at the announcement of his Economic Renewal Program on August 20, 1980. Perhaps reflecting the policy frustrations of the times, the program is an unusual mixture of disparate policy approaches from traditional demand-side management to industrial policy.

11–1. GERALD R. FORD, JANUARY 26, 1976, ANNUAL MESSAGE TO THE CONGRESS: THE ECONOMIC REPORT OF THE PRESIDENT

To the Congress of the United States:

As we enter 1976, the American public still confronts its two greatest personal concerns: inflation and unemployment. As valid as those concerns are, we should not let them overshadow the very genuine progress we have made in the past year. The underlying fact about our economy is that it is steadily growing healthier. My policies for 1976 are intended to keep us on that upward path.

A year ago the economy was in the midst of a severe recession with no immediate end in sight. Exceptionally strong inflationary forces were just beginning to abate, and the prospects for containing unemployment were not bright.

It is now clear that we have made notable progress. The sharpest recession in the post-World War II period hit bottom last spring, and a substantial recovery is now under way. There were 85.4 million Americans at work in December, 1.3 million more than during March of 1975. While the rate of unemployment remains far too high, it is slowly moving in the right direction. There have also been appreciable advances in reducing the rate of inflation. The increase in the consumer price index was 7 percent between December 1974 and December 1975, down from a rate of more than 12 percent during the previous 12 months.

In reviewing 1975 it is also wise to remember the large number of potentially serious economic problems that did *not* materialize. The financial crisis that some predicted did not occur. The recession did not deepen into a cumulative depression. There was no collapse in international trade and investment. The price of bread never rose to a dollar, nor did the price of gasoline. We did not experience corrosive social unrest as a consequence of our economic difficulties. While I do not regard the events of 1975 as fully satisfactory by any measure, we find it reassuring that our economic system withstood severe strains and displayed inherent strengths during the year. I am confident that with responsible and appropriate policies we can achieve sustained economic progress in the future.

Unfortunately there is no simple formula or single act that will quickly produce full economic health. It has taken many years for excessive stimulation, combined with external shocks like the quintupling of international oil prices, to create the economic difficulties of 1974 and 1975, and it will take several years of sound policies to restore sustained, noninflationary growth. I will not make promises which I know, and you know, cannot be kept. We must restore the strength of the American economy as quickly as we can; but in so doing we cannot ignore the dangers of refueling inflationary forces, because unchecked inflation makes steady growth and full employment impossible. The events of the past several years have once again convincingly demonstrated that accelerating inflation causes instability and disruptions, increases unemployment, and ultimately precludes real prosperity.

It is often said that we must choose between inflation and unemployment, and that the only way to reduce unemployment is to accept chronic inflation or rigid controls. I reject this view. Inflation and unemployment are not opposites but are related symptoms of an unhealthy economy. The latter months of 1974 illustrate the relationship between inflation and unemployment. Sharply rising prices created a climate of uncertainty and were to blame for part of the massive reduction in the purchasing power of household assets placed in savings accounts and investment securities. In turn, consumers cut back on expenditures; and consequently inventories, already swollen by speculative buying, backed up in distribution channels. By the early months of 1975 there were sharp cutbacks in production and employment. Thus inflation played a significant part in the surge of unemployment, and if we have a new round of inflation it is likely to bring still more unemployment. Chronically high unemployment is an intolerable waste of human resources and entails an unacceptable loss of material production. Clearly, we must attack inflation and unemployment at the same time; our policies must be balanced.

My economic program for 1976 has three parts: First, a long-term continuation of the effort to revive the American economy; second, implementation of the many programs necessary to provide cushions for the unemployed during the transition to a healthy economy; and third, the elimination of Government policies and institutions that interfere with price flexibility and vigorous competition.

My key economic goal is to create an economic environment in which sustainable, noninflationary growth can be achieved.

When private spending is depressed, Government can properly absorb private savings and provide fiscal stimulus to the economy. But in the longer run, a viable, steady increase in prosperity is only possible if we have a vigorous private sector. My policies are designed to support the long-term growth of the economy by fostering an environment in which the private sector can flourish.

Increased capital formation is essential to meeting our long-term goals of full employment and noninflationary growth. Although there is no shortage of industrial capacity at the present time, many of our current priorities—to become independent in energy, to improve the environment, to create more jobs, and to raise our living standards—require increased investment. This means that business investment in plant and equipment as a share of gross national product must increase. We must also slow the growth of Federal spending in the years immediately ahead, so that mounting claims by the Federal Government on our economic resources will not prevent an adequate flow of savings into capital investments.

Accordingly, I am recommending that budget savings be refunded to the American taxpayer by means of tax cuts. I have proposed an annual tax cut of $28 billion from 1974 levels, effective July 1, 1976. If we continue in the years ahead to pursue the kind of budgetary restraint which I am recommending, another major tax cut will be feasible by 1979. I strongly believe that the individual wage earner has the right to spend his own money on the goods and services he wants, rather than having the Government increase its control over the disposition of his income.

Regrettably, a full recovery of the economy will take time. Overly rapid growth could lead to a renewed increase in inflation that would ultimately be self-defeating. In the interim we must be mindful of those who have lost their jobs or who are in fear of losing the jobs they hold. While the problems of unemployment can be solved only by restoring the basic strength of our economy, the hardships of unemployment and insecure employment require immediate treatment. In December 1974 and in March 1975, I signed into law major expansion in the duration and coverage of unemployment insurance. These changes eased the financial burden of 3.6 million Americans who were unemployed for a part of last year. Programs in my 1977 fiscal budget will also provide 3.6 million Americans with opportunities for training and employment....

Over the years, Government regulation has also had many other undesirable effects. Besides reducing competition in many instances, it has also imposed on firms enormous burdens, which raise business costs and consumer prices.

Increasing competition from world markets and the need to maintain and improve the standard of living of a growing population require constant improvement of the American market system. For this reason I have asked the Congress to legislate fundamental changes in the laws regulating our railroads, airlines, and trucking firms. The new amendments will free these companies to respond more flexibly to market conditions. I have also urged deregulation of the price of natural gas and sought essential pricing flexibility for the oil and electric utilities industries. We will continue to improve all essential protection for public health and safety, trying at the same time not to increase unnecessarily the cost to the public. My object is to achieve a better combination of market competition and responsible Government regulation. The programs I have advanced in recent months have sought such a balance, and I will continue this course in 1976.

Striking a new regulatory balance is likely to entail some economic and social costs during a period of transition, and changes must therefore be phased in carefully. In the long run, however, a revitalized market system will bring significant benefits to the public, including lower prices.

While our policies focus primarily on the economy of the United States, we recognize that the range of our interests does not stop at our shores. The other major countries of the world are also recovering from the most serious recession they have experienced since the 1930s. Their first economic priority, like ours, is to put their economies on a sustainable, noninflationary growth path. Success in this endeavor, more than anything else, will help developed and developing countries alike achieve higher standards of living.

In recent years the economies of most nations suffered from extraordinarily high inflation rates, due in large part to the quintupling of the world price for oil, and then moved into a deep recession. The simultaneity of this experience demonstrated once again the strong interdependence of the world's economies. Individual countries have become progressively more dependent on each other as a freer flow of goods, services, and capital has fostered greater prosperity throughout the world. Because of this growing interdependence, however, domestic policy objectives cannot be achieved efficiently unless we also take account of economic changes and policy goals in other countries.

In recognition of our growing interdependence, I have consulted closely with the heads of other governments, individually and jointly. At the Economic Summit at Rambouillet last November, I met with the heads of government of five other major industrial countries. There we laid the foundation for closer understanding and consultation on economic policies. During 1975 we also began discussions on international cooperation with both the developed and the less developed countries. This dialogue will assure a better mutual understanding of our problems and aspirations. Finally, I have agreed with my foreign colleagues that, in order to create the proper conditions for lasting and stable growth, we must take important, cooperative steps in monetary matters, trade, and energy. We have directed our trade officials to seek an early conclusion to the continuing negotiations on liberalization of trade. This month in Jamaica we reached significant agreements on strengthening the international monetary system and providing increased support for the developing countries. We have begun to cooperate more closely with oil-consuming countries in the effort become less dependent on imported energy. I intend to consolidate and build upon this progress in 1976.

Of central concern both here and abroad is U.S. energy policy. Without a vigorous and growing industry supplying domestic energy, much of our industrial development in the next 10 years will be uncertain. And unless we can reduce our dependency on Middle East oil, we will not have a sound basis for international cooperation in the development of new fossil fuel and other energy sources.

As an initial step toward greater self-sufficiency, I signed the Energy Policy and Conservation Act in December 1975. I concluded that this act, though deficient in some respects, did provide a vehicle for moving us toward our energy goals. With this mechanism the price of petroleum can be allowed to rise to promote domestic supply and to restrain consumption. At the end of 40 months, under the act, I may remove price controls altogether, and I will utilize the provisions of the act to move toward a free market in petroleum as quickly possible and consistent with our larger economic goals. The act offers flexibility, which I have already used to start dismantling price controls and allocation arrangements in fuel markets where no shortages exist. The legislation establishes a national strategic petroleum reserve which will make our supply of energy more secure and give other nations less inducement to impose an oil embargo.

Measures crucial to our energy future still remain to be enacted, however. Natural gas deregulation is now the most pressing of the issues on energy before Congress: shortages grow year by year, while the country waits for more testimony on supply and demand, or waits for extremely expensive new synthetic gas plants to replace the natural gas production choked off by price controls. I urge the Congress to make deregulation of new natural gas one of its objectives in 1976. The legislation I have proposed in order to assure adequate supplies of fuel for nuclear power plants is also critical. If we are to improve our energy situation, these measures are necessary. They will also reinforce our efforts to remove unnecessary and deleterious Government interference in economic activities where the consumer is adequately protected by market forces.

A year ago I said, "The year 1975 must be the one in which we face our economic problems and start the course toward real solutions." I am pleased with the beginning we have made. The course is a long one, but its benefits for all Americans make the journey worthwhile. The year 1976 must be one in which we will continue our progress toward a better life for all Americans.

11–2. WALTER W. HELLER, FEBRUARY 6, 1976, STATEMENT BEFORE THE JOINT ECONOMIC COMMITTEE, U.S. CONGRESS

...Let me highlight a few points...and then go on to consider some desirable policy moves in the 1976 setting before winding up with an expression of concern over what might be called "the misguiding of the American public" on a number of key economic issues and economic facts. As for the 1976 economic scene, one cannot stress too strongly the importance of differentiating between the direction and level of economic activity. Unless that distinction is constantly borne in mind, the signals for economic policy are likely to be read incorrectly.

The upward course of the U.S. economy in 1976 isn't in doubt. Given the lags in the impact of economic policy, I would say that the first 6 months' performance is pretty well foreordained. It is true, however, that the second half could be imperiled if, first of all, the Federal Reserve were to hit the economy in the solar plexus with a sharp shift toward tighter money and rising interest rates; and second, if the White House and the Congress fail to find a mutually acceptable formula for extending the temporary $18 billion tax cut. Also, full acceptance of Ford's budget would hit the economy with a sickening thud later in 1976—mostly after the election.

Now, on the somewhat perilous assumption that these policy mistakes will not be made, George Perry and I project a somewhat more vigorous rise in real GNP—7 percent year over year—than the private consensus forecast, as well as the administration's forecast.

We project a somewhat stronger rise in both consumption and business capital spending than most forecasters...[and note]...the dazzling upswing in corporate profits. Corporate profits hit a postwar low, it's true, in 1974 at only 8 percent of corporate product. But the newly revised Commerce figures show that after-tax profits rose from an annual rate of $60 billion in the first quarter of last, year to an estimated $88 billion in the fourth quarter: and they will go right on up this year to over $100 billion by the fourth quarter. That's after-tax profits at annual rate.

...Profits, taking out inventory changes, are making a very nice recovery from that 1974 low point. And when we couple those profits with the cash flow from depreciation, and so forth, with the incentive of bigger investment tax credits and better access to capital markets now that the stock market is pepping up again, one can foresee repeated upward revisions of capital spending.

Now, even if the economy, under these favorable policy assumptions—and this is where I get to the level, rather than the direction of the economy—even if it achieves this above-trend pace of expansion that we project, can one really settle for this, let alone accept restrictive White House and Federal Reserve policies for 1977 in light of the present and prospective levels of economic activity?

Now, as 1976 began, the unemployed labor pool equaled well over 9 million workers— and by the way, even with the encouraging news about the unemployment figures today, we are going to find the number hovering around 9 million. But where do I get the 9 million? Well, there are now 7.3 million officially unemployed—plus nearly 1 million discouraged workers—about 900,000; and 3½ million part-time workers who are available for full-time work. That is, 3 million part-time workers who would like to work up to 40 hours a week are averaging 22 hours a week. That adds up to an unemployed labor-pool equivalent of about 9 million.

Second, total output is running at least $150 billion a year below the economy's high-employment potential; and I think that's a very modest number, Mr. Chairman. You know me as an old conservative in these matters. I could say $175, but in order to avoid criticism I put it at $150 billion because there are some that don't feel we can achieve as high a level of employment as some others.

And third, even after a 7–percent gain in output this year, we will end the year with recession like levels of unemployment, at 7¼ percent; of capacity utilization rates in manufacturing, at about 80 percent; and of economic slack, with actual output running about $125 billion below potential output, conservatively measured at 5 percent unemployment.

Now, I say "recession like" advisedly because, looking at the four previous recessions since 1950, the unemployment rate at the bottom of those recessions, in the trough quarter, averaged 6.2 percent. We will be a full percentage point above the bottom of the preceding four recessions.

Capacity utilization at the trough averaged about 77 percent. In other words, you asked about 1977, we will be entering that year at unemployment rates and excess capacity levels comparable to those at the bottom of our previous recessions in this generation.

Now, what about the prospects for inflation? High as it is by national standards, inflation will continue to moderate in 1976. Again, to save time, let me skip to...[my]...concluding statement on this particular point.

Coupling the abatement of food and fuel inflation with the modest impact of demand pressures and an 8-percent average pay increase that we foresee this year, one can reasonably project a 5-percent rise in the GNP deflator, or about 6 percent in the cost of living.

Now, turning to policy. If the President's budget and tax proposals were enacted, the recovery would be dealt a severe blow while the economy is still operating far below target levels. The high employment surplus would rise by $10 billion for the fiscal year 1977, with restrictive pressure becoming particularly sharp during calendar 1977 when the proposed payroll tax increases would go into effect.

Now, that $19 billion a year means a much bigger swing during 1976–77. The special analyses in the President's budget show that there would be a $30 billion jump in fiscal restrictions in 15 months, from the spring of 1976 to the summer of 1977. The Federal budget would be tightening its noose by $30 billion on an economy that is still far from anything resembling full employment. A restrictive swing of that magnitude took a huge toll in jobs and output in 1959–60 and again in 1972–74; and I just hope we don't repeat those disastrous experiences.

Rather than accept the 1977 Ford economy model budget, and an economic policy that resolves all doubts in favor of a go-slow expansion and risk a new recession, the more prudent course would be to follow monetary and fiscal policies that will step up the rate of expansion in 1976 and continue in 1977, until that erosive waste of human and material resources has been brought back within tolerable bounds.

Let me suggest several components of such a policy.

Put Mr. Ford's budget on the course of economic, social, and political responsibility. It would be well within that course for Congress to bring budget spending at least up to a maintenance-of-services level of $414 billion. Indeed, Alice Rivlin puts the baseline budget at $425 billion—$31 billion above Ford's fiscal squeeze budget.

From a purely economic point of view, the minimum task of Congress is to prevent the budget from turning restrictive in the face of recession like levels of unemployment and unused capacity. Perhaps Congress will want to put more tax cuts and less spending in the economic mix that I might prefer. But, one way or another, it must overcome the $19 billion swing toward economic restriction. Indeed, the $19 billion year over year, or $30 billion if you take it from the spring of 1976 to summer of 1977.

The Ford administration and the Federal Reserve are still fighting the last war against inflation. I don't see why they can't see what it took to give us that double-digit inflation in 1973–74 that, by the way, fooled us all—we all did a poor job of forecasting that. We took a five-ply shellacking: A fivefold jump in oil prices, a 40-percent jump in food prices in 2½ years, a double devaluation of the dollar, decontrol of wages and prices, and a worldwide commodity price boom. Those things simply aren't in the cards for 1976–77.

The Congress should do what it can to prevent monetary policy from swinging toward restriction at this stage of the game. I find it, by the way, passing strange that the Federal Reserve, whose Chairman has not been bashful in making known his distaste for monetarist formulas, and the congressional banking committees, whose objectives would be far better served by emphasis on moderate levels of interest rates than by lock-step limits on money supply increases....

...As I say, I find it passing strange that the Federal Reserve and the congressional banking committees have coalesced on monetary policy targets stated exclusively in money supply terms. Interest rates should be brought back into their proper place in setting policy targets—as, indeed, the House Banking Committee has been urging the Federal Reserve to do—but with indifferent success so far.

Arthur Burns showed again, early this week, what damage he can do. Just by manipulating the money supply targets, lowering the floor of his range for technical reasons—which immediately suggests a lower target average for a money supply increase. This quickly boosted short-term rates and took its toll in the stock market.

Social security payroll tax increases today—or next January 1—would be the wrong medicine at the wrong place at the wrong time. It seems particularly paradoxical to consider further cuts in the income tax, our best tax, at the same time that we would boost the payroll tax, which bears hard on the poor, raises business costs, and boosts the cost of living. With contingency reserves above $40 billion, the social security system is in no immediate need of added revenues. And when that need materializes, it is high time to supplement the resources of the system with general revenues, rather than cutting income taxes while boosting payroll taxes.

On income taxes, an adjustment of the proposed cuts to maintain the credits and tax breaks for the lowest income groups—who are still at the bottom of a very deep job barrel and have been hit hard by...inflation this time around—would be very much in order.

Finally, just a word on wage-price policy. Although it now seems beyond the political pale in 1976, the Congress should never forget that a balanced program for full employment must contain some kind of restraint on excessive price increases exacted by concentrated industries and excessive wage increases exacted by overly powerful labor unions. Antitrust can't cope with this problem. A more effective system of flagging down excessive wage and price increases in areas of the economy where competition is not effective as a policeman must be part of a balanced program to overcome intolerable unemployment without incurring intolerable inflation.

Now, there are other policy suggestions I would have made but for the lack of time, something on public service jobs, antirecession grants, getting rid of some of our overregulation and so on....

But I did want to take just a few minutes to talk about the "misguiding" of the American public on economic issues. I cannot conclude these opening remarks without expressing my growing concern over the distressing tendency in recent years to miseducate and, wittingly or unwittingly, mislead the American people on vital issues of economic policy and fact. This process, calculated or not, is contributing to misunderstanding of basic economic relationships, unnecessary anxiety on many fronts, and a loss of faith in the American economy and its public institutions. Let me just cite a few examples.

The Federal Government is depicted as expanding like some monstrous protoplasmic blob that threatens to snuff out economic freedom and initiative. Yet, the facts will show that the Federal budget as a proportion of GNP held virtually steady at about 20 percent from 1953 to 1973. It is projected to rise to 21 percent in fiscal year 1977—but adjusted to a full-employment basis, the figure will be right back at 20 percent.

The expansion, in other words, of the Federal sector relative to the rest of the economy in 24 years—zero.

Or, take the supposed "crushing burden of Federal debt." A striking chart included in last year's budget documents—but not this—shows that the Federal debt held by the public dropped from 82 percent of annual GNP in 1950 to 26 percent in 1974. Seen in this perspective, the public debt is a far different and more manageable problem than the general impression abroad in the land.

A third area of widespread misapprehension of the real problem centers on the large deficits in the Federal budget. Here, two misimpressions are being fostered:

The $70 to $75 billion deficit is being identified with profligacy in spending and fiscal irresponsibility when, in fact, it is almost entirely a hostage to recession. Your witnesses yesterday went over that, and I simply note that if we had something like full employment, revenues would be $50 to $55 billion higher than they are; unemployment compensation would be about $15 billion lower; and other cyclically responsive outlays would be about $5 billion lower. So, almost all of the deficit is a product of recession. Ironically, the selfsame monetary and fiscal authorities whose disastrously tight policies in 1974 helped aggravate the recession and hence the deficit are the ones who are loudest in decrying the deficit as an example of the loss of fiscal discipline.

A related charge is that Government deficits are the root of all inflationary evil. How is it, then, that inflation is ebbing in the face of the largest deficits in history?

A fourth area of anguished misapprehension relates to the social security system. The impression has been given that it is about to go broke. I need not tell this committee how far this is from the truth. May I add, Mr. Chairman, as I speak around the country on economic matters, that's usually question No. 1 by the audiences afterward, "What is going to happen to our social security? We understand that the system is going bankrupt."

How that impression has been so widely disseminated is not quite clear to me....

The financing problems of the social security system can clearly be met.

The fifth example is the mistaken belief that Congress is an instrument of irresponsible and loose spending—an impression that totally ignores the responsible new procedures and spending limits that it is observing. I'm appalled to find out how little understanding there is around the country of what one might call the "sobriety in spending act."

Congress rightly prides itself on its more prudent fiscal posture and procedure. But if the new politics of fiscal responsibility, or austerity, leads to budget parsimony and willy-nilly economic restraints, its benefits will be swamped by its costs. Fiscal responsibility is not synonymous with fiscal restraint.

To hit the economy with a fiscal sledgehammer as Mr. Ford proposes, when economic recovery is still in its adolescence, that's fiscal irresponsibility. I believe we should redefine it to recognize that.

And finally, the continuing barrage of statements and studies, for example, the April release by the Treasury entitled, "U.S. Ranking in Investment and in Real Economic Growth Is Among Lowest of Industrialized Countries, Treasury Study Says," is giving the public a false image of the true strength of the American economy. Only the fine print brings out that:

U.S. productivity is still the best in the world, with even the high-growth countries like France and West Germany having achieved only 80 percent of the U.S. level of productivity.

That the U.S. has been growing steadily more competitive—and these are remarkable numbers which come directly from First National City Bank of New York's monthly bulletin; I always cite impeccably conservative sources when they support my position—

but, the United States has been growing steadily more competitive with its unit labor costs rising only about 10 percent from 1970 to 1974, with Canada showing the next best performance at 29 percent, Germany at 90 percent, and Japan at 100 percent. That is one reason that we had such a good performance in nonagricultural exports as well as agricultural exports last year. And, as a result the U.S. dollar is still the most sought-after currency in the world.

One hesitates to fix the blame for this retrograde movement in the economic education of the American public. Much of it stems, as it has from time immemorial, from the self-serving efforts of particular groups to "sell" particular policies, positions, preferences, and prejudices. Note how many of these positions serve a bias toward smaller government, cutbacks in Federal spending, tax reductions for business, preferential tax treatment of capital investment, and restrictive fiscal and monetary policies.

Clearly, this is not a suggestion that we should be Pollyannas or put our heads in the sand about persistent and troublesome economic problems. But the misunderstandings that are being fostered threaten to thwart rather than facilitate solutions.

To be candid about economic shortcomings and government problems is a virtue. But to denigrate the U.S. economy, and exaggerate its problems and misidentify their sources is certainly a vice. The sooner policymakers talk economic sense instead of nonsense to the American people, the better our chances will be of coping with the truly tough problems we face. Thank you.

11–3. THE FULL EMPLOYMENT AND BALANCED GROWTH ACT OF 1978 (THE HUMPHREY–HAWKINS BILL)

(a) Generally

The Congress declares that it is the continuing policy and responsibility of the Federal Government to use all practicable means, consistent with its needs and obligations and other essential national policies, and with the assistance and cooperation of both small and larger businesses, agriculture, labor, and State and local governments, to coordinate and utilize all its plans, functions, and resources for the purpose of creating and maintaining, in a manner calculated to foster and promote free competitive enterprise and the general welfare, conditions which promote useful employment opportunities, including self-employment, for those able, willing, and seeking to work, and promote full employment and production, increased real income, balanced growth, a balanced Federal budget, adequate productivity growth, proper attention to national priorities, achievement of an improved trade balance through increased exports and improvement in the international competitiveness of agriculture, business, and industry, and reasonable price stability as provided....

(b) Full opportunities for employment

The Congress further declares that inflation is a major national problem requiring improved government policies relating to food, energy, improved and coordinated fiscal and monetary management, the reform of outmoded rules and regulations of the Federal Government, the correction of structural defects in the economy that prevent or seriously impede competition in private markets, and other measures to reduce the rate of inflation....

(f) Expansion of private employment

The Congress further declares that it is the purpose of the Full Employment and Balanced Growth Act of 1978 to maximize and place primary emphasis upon the expansion of private employment, and all programs and policies under such Act shall be in accord with such purpose. Toward this end, the effort to expand jobs to the full employment level shall be in this order of priority to the extent consistent with balanced growth—

(1) expansion of conventional private jobs through improved use of general economic and structural policies, including measures to encourage private sector investment and capital formation;

(2) expansion of private employment through Federal assistance in connection with the priority programs in such Act;

(3) expansion of public employment other than through the provisions of …such Act; and

(4) when recommended by the President under…such Act and subject to the limitations in such section, the creation of employment through the methods set forth in such section.

Medium-term economic goals and policies respecting full employment and balanced growth

(a) Incorporation of necessary programs and policies

In each Economic Report after October 27, 1978, the President shall incorporate (as part of the five-year numerical goals in each Economic Report) medium-term annual numerical goals specified in…this title, and in each President's Budget submitted immediately prior thereto, the President shall incorporate the programs and policies the President deems necessary to achieve such medium-term goals and a balanced Federal budget and to achieve reasonable price stability as rapidly as feasible as provided for in…this title.

(b) Interim numerical goals for initial Economic Reports

The medium-term goals in the first three Economic Reports and, subject to the provisions of subsection (d) of this section, in each Economic Report thereafter shall include (as part of the five-year goals in each Economic Report) interim numerical goals for—

(1) reducing the rate of unemployment, as set forth pursuant to…this title, to not more than 3 per centum among individuals aged twenty and over and 4 per centum among individuals aged sixteen and over within a period not extending beyond the fifth calendar year after the first such Economic Report;

(2) reducing the rate of inflation, as set forth pursuant to…this title, to not more than 3 per centum within a period not extending beyond the fifth calendar year after the first such Economic Report: Provided, That policies and programs for reducing the rate of inflation shall be designed so as not to impede achievement of the goals and timetables specified in clause (1) of this subsection for the reduction of unemployment; and

(3) reducing the share of the Nation's gross national product accounted for by Federal outlays to 21 per centum or less by 1981, and to 20 per centum or less by 1983 and thereafter, or the lowest level consistent with national needs and priorities: Provided, That policies and programs for achieving the goal specified in this clause shall be designed so as not to impede achievement of the goals and timetables specified in clause (1) of this subsection for the reduction of unemployment.

For purposes of this subsection, the first Economic Report shall be the Report issued in the first calendar year after October 27, 1978.

(c) Achievement of full employment, balanced budget, zero inflation rate, and 20 per centum level of Federal outlays as a proportion of gross national product for succeeding Economic Reports

(1) Upon achievement of the 3 and 4 per centum goals specified in subsection (b) (1) of this section, each succeeding Economic Report shall have the goal of achieving as soon as practicable and maintaining thereafter full employment and a balanced budget.

(2) Upon achievement of the 3 per centum goal specified in subsection (b) (2) of this section, each succeeding Economic Report shall have the goal of achieving by 1988 a rate of inflation of zero per centum: Provided, That policies and programs for reducing the rate of inflation shall be designed so as not to impede achievement of the goals and timetables specified in clause (1) of this subsection for the reduction of unemployment.

(3) Upon achievement of the 20 per centum goal specified in subsection (b) (3) of this section, each succeeding Economic Report shall have the goal of establishing the share of an expanding gross national product accounted for by Federal outlays at a level of 20 per centum or less, or the lowest level consistent with national needs and priorities: Provided, That policies and programs for achieving the goal specified in this clause shall be designed so as not to impede achievement of the goals and timetables specified in subsection (b) (1) of this section for the reduction of unemployment.

(d) Review by President; report to Congress; modification of timetables
In the second Economic Report after October 27, 1978, the President shall review the numerical goals and timetables for the reduction of unemployment, inflation, and Federal outlays as a proportion of gross national product, and the goal of balancing the Federal budget; report to the Congress on the degree of progress being made, the programs and policies being used, and any obstacles to achieving such goals and timetables; and, if necessary, propose corrective economic measures toward achievement of such goals and timetables: Provided, That beginning with the second Report and in any subsequent Reports, if the President finds it necessary, the President may recommend modification of the timetable or timetables for the achievement of the goals provided for in subsection (b) of this section and the annual numerical goals to make them consistent with the modified timetable or timetables, and the Congress may take such action as it deems appropriate consistent with title III of the Full Employment and Balanced Growth Act of 1978.

(e) Interim numerical goals for succeeding Economic Reports
If, after achievement of the 3 and 4 per centum goals specified in subsection (b) of this section, the unemployment rate for a year as set forth pursuant to...this title is more than 3 per centum among individuals aged twenty and over or more than 4 per centum among individuals aged sixteen and over, the next Economic Report after such rate is set forth and each succeeding Economic Report shall include (as part of the five-year goals in each Economic Report) the interim numerical goal of reducing unemployment to not more than the levels specified in subsection (b) (1) of this section as soon as practicable but not later than the fifth calendar year after the first such Economic Report, counting as the first calendar year the year in which such Economic Report is issued; Provided, That, if the President finds it necessary, the President may, under the authority provided in subsection (d) of this section, recommend modification of the timetable provided for in this subsection for the reduction of unemployment, and for the purposes of...the Full Employment and Balanced Growth Act of 1978, such recommendation by the President shall be treated as a recommendation made under subsection (d) of this section.

11–4. MILTON FRIEDMAN, "HUMPHREY–HAWKINS"

A centerpiece of the Democratic fall campaign is the "Humphrey–Hawkins Full Employment and Balanced Growth Act of 1976." Support of that bill has become the litmus test of the true-blue Democratic faith of every candidate from Jimmy Carter to the aspirant for dogcatcher.

The present expanded version of the Humphrey–Hawkins bill embraces the earlier Humphrey–Javits bill. It proposes to establish a process of long-range economic planning to achieve "a full-employment goal ... consistent with a rate of unemployment not in excess of 3 per centum of the adult Americans in the civilian labor force, to be attained... within not more than four years after the enactment" of the act, as well as a long list of other goodies.

The best critique of this bill that I have come across was published 200 years ago in that great book, *The Wealth of Nations,* by Adam Smith—the original Adam Smith, not the current imposter who has had the effrontery to adopt that pseudonym.

Wrote Smith: "The statesman, who should attempt to direct private people in what manner they ought to employ their capitals, would not only load himself with a most unnecessary attention, but assume an authority which could safely be trusted, not only to no single person, but to no council or senate whatever, and which would nowhere be so dangerous as in the hands of a man who had folly and presumption enough to fancy himself fit to exercise it."

Has any contemporary political writer described Hubert Humphrey more concisely?

Not to put too fine a point on it, the Humphrey–Hawkins bill is as close to a fraud as has ever served as a campaign document. It is full of pious promises but contains no measures capable of fulfilling those promises. It would not reduce unemployment but simply add to government employment and reduce private employment, in the process making us all poorer and very likely igniting a new inflationary binge.

How can such a bill do otherwise? Easy enough to say that the government will be the employer of last resort. But where does the government get the money? Ultimately, from you and me, by hook or by crook. If it spends, we don't. If it employs people, we don't.

Of course, people on welfare could be relabeled "civil servants assigned to home duty," thereby reducing recorded unemployment without additional spending. But to do more—and Humphrey–Hawkins promises to do far more—requires more government spending. The extra spending could be financed by higher explicit taxes. In that case, taxpayers would have less to spend and would hire fewer people. The extra spending could be financed by higher borrowing. In that case, the lenders, or the borrowers outbid by government, would have less to spend. Government employment would replace employment in building homes or factories. Finally, the government could print the money, which would tax us indirectly via inflation. We would have more pieces of paper to spend but could buy less. For a time, that could mean more government spending without less private spending, but surely by now we have learned that that is a fool's paradise that would not last.

Is anyone so naive as to suppose that the government jobs created will be more productive than the private jobs destroyed?

Why do Democrats believe that Humphrey–Hawkins is such potent political soothing syrup? Do they have such a low opinion of the intelligence of the American people? I do not think so. It is for a very different reason—one that is the source of so many harmful government policies: the visible vs. the invisible effects of government measures.

People hired by government know who is their benefactor. People who lose their jobs or fail to get them because of the government program do not know that that is the source of their problem. The good effects are visible. The bad effects are invisible. The good effects generate votes. The bad effects generate discontent, which is as likely to be directed at private business as at the government.

The great political challenge is to overcome this bias, which has been taking us down the slippery slope to ever bigger government and to the destruction of a free society.

11–5. JIMMY CARTER, AUGUST 28, 1980, REMARKS ANNOUNCING THE ECONOMIC RENEWAL PROGRAM

I'm very delighted to have the Speaker here and distinguished Members of the House and Senate, the Governor of New York, Governor of New Jersey, and others who represent State and local government, members of my Cabinet, and distinguished Americans who've come here representing business and labor, the professions, other elements of life of the greatest nation on Earth.

This is a time of economic testing for our Nation. Inflation has fallen sharply. The recession is near bottom, and we'll recover.

This is no time for an excessive stimulus program, nor is it a time for inflationary tax reductions. We must be responsible, and we must make careful investments in American productivity. We can build in a progressive way a future which America will see that will be creative and will grow more vigorously in this next decade than perhaps any other time since our first industrial revolution over a hundred years ago.

According to a well-known proverb, a journey of a thousand miles begins with one step. We began before now, but each step is important, and the steps that I describe this afternoon will continue that journey toward a more productive and more competitive and a more prosperous American economy. The new steps will put people back to work, reduce taxes, increase public and private investment in the future, and constrain inflation all at the same time. But such progress will be possible only if we regard the past not as a refuge within which we can hide, but a treasury of lessons from which we can learn.

I'd like to consider for a moment a few of those lessons: First, we cannot treat the symptoms of inflation and ignore the underlying causes. Second, inflation and recession augment one another. Third, the longer we ignore our decline in productivity, the more likely we Americans are to live with hard times. The fourth lesson, and it may be the most important of all, is that if a solution is politically attractive it's often economically wrong.

Now, in the heat of an election year, is not the time to seek votes with ill-considered tax cuts that would simply steal back in inflation in the future the few dollars that the average American taxpayer might get. America needs to build muscle, not fat, and I will not accept a preelection bill to cut taxes.

All of us know, who've served in government or in other areas of American life, that there are no simple or easy solutions to serious problems that build up over a long period of time. But there are responsible ways to create productive jobs, and there are responsible ways to restore our technological and competitive lead over all other nations on Earth, and there are responsible ways to strengthen our economy enough to guarantee opportunity and security for every American citizen.

The fundamental challenge to our economy in the 1980's is a difficult combination but one which this program addresses successfully: full employment, stable prices, and real growth, with jobs that attack our declining productivity and our energy dependence, the major causes of inflation and of the recession in the first place. The detailed program which will be explained to all of you after my speech sets forth measures which I will ask the Congress to enact next year.

There are four major goals which I'd like to discuss briefly. First, increase private and public investment to revitalize America's economy. Second, create a forward-looking partnership between government and the private sector to deal with national problems which can only be solved through that cooperation. Third, to help people and communities overcome the effects of industrial dislocations. And fourth, to help to offset the rising individual tax burdens in ways which do not rekindle inflation.

These new proposals will add almost a half-million jobs in the coming year and a total of 1 million jobs by the end of 1982. These are in addition to those that will result from normal recovery and also in addition to the jobs that will result from the new programs already in effect or already on the Hill in existing proposals. We expect to add with these new proposals 2 percent growth to the gross national product of our Nation, increase real investment by 10 percent, and help to hold down inflation at the same time.

We must now build on the progress that we've made already in many vital areas. In the last 3½ years we have added more than 8 million new jobs for workers to America's job rolls. This is more than any other similar period in our Nation or the world's history, in peacetime or in war. Exports have grown substantially. Balance-of-trade figures are very encouraging, and with the 1981 budget we will have cut in half the real annual growth in Federal spending.

We are reducing the anticompetitive regulation of the airlines, trucking, rail, banking, and the communications industries. This is the most fundamental restructuring of the interrelationship between government and the private sector that's taken place since the days of Franklin D. Roosevelt's New Deal.

Above all, after vigorous and painful debate and political decisions, we've put in place now a national energy policy that has already helped to reduce oil imports by 20 percent and has encouraged more drilling to discover new oil and new gas than at any time in the last quarter of a century. And the program, as you well know, has only recently been passed by Congress and is not even yet fully implemented. But we must not just be proud of what has been done. We must continue to build. Our task is nothing less than to revitalize America's economy.

Increasing productivity is the foremost economic challenge of the 1980's. From management we need innovation and more long-range planning. From labor we must have more participation in making the basic decisions, dedicated work, and the skills to take advantage of the most modern tools and technology. From government we must have sound judgment and political courage. And from all Americans there must be a commitment, deep commitment, and also the use of common sense.

We will meet the challenge of a more productive America as if our economic life depended on it—because it does—and this is how we're going to do it. How will we increase private and public investment to revitalize America's economy? The first important step we can take to revitalize America's economy is to provide incentives for greater private investment.

We need a major increase in depreciation allowances to promote investment in modern plants and equipment, and we need dramatic simplification of the tax code so that not only large businesses but also small businesses of our country can benefit.

The investment tax credit, which has been hailed as a bonanza by some, is now of no help to new firms or to distressed industries, because they have no earnings and therefore they pay no taxes and investment tax credits do not help them. Therefore, part of the investment tax credit must be refundable. This is a profound change in concept in American tax policy and will help immediately the small businesses and the new industries, an important source of both technological progress and employment, as you well know, and will also be of special help to those industries which are in distress, such as those which now produce steel and automobiles.

We'll also, of course, implement many of the recommendations that were made earlier this year by the White House Conference on Small Business. To complement the benefits derived from tax-changes for the private sector, we must also expand public investment, especially in crucial areas like energy, technology, transportation, and exports. I'd like to comment on each one of those briefly.

Our energy program already approved for the 1980's, what we've already got planned and committed, is the most massive peacetime undertaking in American history. Its impact will be immense, perhaps greater than any of us at the present time can even envision, ranging from hundreds of thousands who will work in synthetic fuel plants to the millions of individuals who are weatherizing their homes, using solar power, or building our new and fuel-efficient automobiles.

Since I took office we've enacted tax credits and have more than doubled direct spending in order to stimulate energy production and conservation. In addition, we'll create a vast new synthetic fuels industry, and we are seeking new authority to convert utilities from oil to coal and other sources of energy. We need to add substantially more funds for work on energy conservation projects that will help us to fight inflation and to achieve energy security.

Energy, of course, is important. The second thing is technology. Technological advance has provided much of the productive growth of the United States in this last century. We can create literally millions of jobs with new technology in the years ahead. In addition to tax incentives for investment in the latest technology, I favor substantial real growth in Federal support of basic research, and particularly in the great research centers of our colleges and universities.

Mark Twain once defined an American as a person who does things because they haven't been done before. The exciting possibilities for Americans in the 1980's range from lasers for surgery to super-alloys that never rust, from exotic energy technologies to microchips that can make computers as common as radios and as compact as wristwatches. These kinds of advances in technology and in science can well exceed anything that we have seen in this century so far.

The next item is transportation, which is vital to our country. The difference between a healthy transportation network and a broken down highway or a dying railroad is the difference between jobs and joblessness for tens of thousands of Americans, and it's between strength and weakness for our entire Nation. My proposals for major improvements in mass transit, air transportation, and railroad assistance programs are already pending before the Congress. These should be enacted and should be funded without delay, and I'll propose a further significant increase for surface transportation programs. There is simply no more essential investment or element in America's future than a viable, modern, efficient transportation system.

The last item I'd like to mention from the public sector is exports. Americans don't live and breathe exports like some of our European allies and others do. When I took office, exports accounted for 6½ percent of our gross national product. Now, that figure has jumped to 9 percent. This increase has been an essential source of American jobs. One out of every seven jobs in our country now is directly related to producing goods for exports. One out of every three acres of land cultivated in the United States produces food and fiber for exports. Thirty percent of all industrial profits are derived from exports. And we have a great potential for even more growth in jobs and exports in our vast reserves of coal.

We must begin immediately to upgrade our transportation and our port facilities for coal exports. I think you all read the article in the paper Sunday that showed that ships now stand off Norfolk and Hampton Roads and wait 20 or 30 days before they can come there and load their valuable cargo of American coal which is so crucial as a replacement for OPEC oil. Through tax modifications and through a new concept of export trading companies we'll even further expand American exports of both goods and services. This investment in America is important.

The second question is: How can we create a forward-looking partnership between government and the private sector to deal with those kinds of national problems which require that cooperation? To help us revitalize American industry, business, labor, and the government must form a new and a vital partnership. We're all in this together, and the sooner we start acting like it, the better off our Nation will be.

In some areas, such as national security, as you all know, government must play the dominant role. But where government is involved in the economic sphere it will function best not as a boss, but to assist or to cooperate with business and labor only as it's necessary. This can be done. We are cooperating properly now in dealing with coal, steel, and the automobile industries, as well as in many aspects, particularly the new ones, involving our energy program.

The time has now come to extend this experience in cooperation. And this again will be a major change in economic policy for our country. I will establish an Economic Revitalization Board composed of some of the best leaders from American labor, industry, and the public. Cochairmen of this Board will be Irving Shapiro, the chief executive officer of du Pont, and Lane Kirkland, the president of AFL-CIO.

This will be a small group of distinguished Americans, and I'll ask that Board to develop specific recommendations for me, for the Congress, and for the public for an industrial development authority to mobilize both public and private resources, including capital from private markets and from pension funds, to help revitalize American industry in areas most affected by economic dislocations or by industrial bottlenecks. This Board will also consider the integration of industrial development activities now carried out in all the various government agencies, and—this is particularly important— they will address the long-range problems of balancing regulatory costs against the benefits of regulation.

Any project receiving financial assistance must meet tough standards of economic viability. Only a commitment that promotes progress and not obsolescence will be truly in the interests of business, labor, and the American people.

The third question to answer is: How can we help people and communities overcome the effects of industrial dislocations? As we work together on the problems and the intricate issues of economic renewal, we must never forget that we're talking about real people in real places.

Change is inevitable if we are to grow. But as we cope with change, it's my responsibility as President to safeguard communities which are a vital part of our national life and the individual lives of the men, women, and children who are America. That's the whole thrust of one of the most important programs of my Presidency with which almost all of you have helped, that is, economic development in distressed areas. A community cannot exist where there is no work.

We can be proud that direct support of our economic development has increased by over 70 percent just in the last 3 years. We've instituted effective urban and rural programs to stimulate private investment in distressed areas. Funding for programs to promote small business has more than doubled. The Congress now has before it my proposals for substantial increases in economic development financing. But we must do more,

I'll propose a large additional annual increase in funding for economic development for 1981 and for 1982 to create permanent jobs, productive jobs in industries and in regions which are hard hit by industrial change. We also need a special targeted investment tax credit to provide strong incentives for American businesses to invest and to create jobs in those areas which are threatened by economic decline.

These kinds of measures stimulate business, but it cannot help a community when it's already in financial distress. When a community cannot maintain police, fire, education, sanitation services, it loses both its old industry, and it cannot hope to get new industry. In order to help communities like this maintain the services necessary to promote development, I'll propose countercyclical revenue-sharing at a level of $1 billion in 1981.

I'd like to point out that my major domestic program which was new this year is a jobs and training program to help young Americans look forward to a future of hope, not to a life of waste. This is the one action we can take now that will make a difference in the lives of a whole generation of Americans.

I'm also asking the Congress to provide 13 additional weeks of unemployment compensation for eligible workers in high unemployment States. That, by the way, is the only specific recommendation that I intend to send to the Congress at the present time. The other proposals will be made to the Congress for action in the coming year.

And the final question I'd like to answer is: How will we offset the rising individual tax burdens in ways that do not rekindle inflation?

Tax burdens are now scheduled to rise in ways that both increase inflation and slow down our economic recovery. Therefore, I'll ask Congress for three measures next year to deal with this problem in addition to those tax measures designed to stimulate industry.

To help offset the social security tax increases scheduled to take effect in 1981, a social security tax credit for employers and for workers. In addition, the earned income tax credit for working families, those who have income but who have a low income, this to be expanded. And a special tax deduction to counter the inequity that presently exists when a husband and wife both work and who typically have to pay more taxes than two single individuals making the same amount.

All of these policies that I've described to you can be carried out within a responsible budget, so that we can simultaneously promote economic recovery and reduce the pressures of inflation.

To make still further progress we'll consult with business, with labor and other groups about how to improve our voluntary wage and price policies. Because inflation is such a stubborn problem we must design future tax reductions, earned by continued control of Federal spending, in ways that contribute to moderating wage and price increases. For any nation's economy the severe problems come in times of great change. For our Nation this is one of those times. If we keep firmly to our path and attack our problems with courage and responsibility, the result will be an exciting future for our economy and for our Nation.

Let us not forget that this country of ours still has the most productive workforce on Earth. Our standard of living is the highest in the world. Our industrial base is the strongest in world history. We have the greatest human and physical resources of any nation that exists, but we cannot continue to draw them down forever. We must renew those human and natural resources, and we will. That's the basis of the proposal that I'm outlining this afternoon.

Let's don't forget the breadth of what we are discussing. We are embarking on a course to build a major synthetic fuels industry, to double our production and to expand our exports of American coal, to retool our automobile industry in order to produce more fuel-efficient cars and to meet any competition from overseas, to modernize our basic industries like steel, to make our houses and our buildings and our factories more energy efficient, to shift our electric power production from dependence on oil to the use of coal and other fuels, to create a whole new industry, to produce solar and other renewable energy systems, to rebuild our cities and our towns, to continue progress toward a cleaner and a healthier and a safer environment, to expand and to modernize our entire public transportation system, to provide our workforce with skills and jobs to meet a rapidly changing, technological world, to ease the burdens of change and the fear of the future, and to continue to build the homes and produce the goods and the services needed by a growing America.

Our difficult struggle toward economic renewal will be waged in many ways, but we are united in our purpose. We'll put Americans to work fighting the major long-term causes of inflation itself, our declining productivity and our excessive dependence on foreign oil. We'll fight for full employment, at the same time stable prices, at the same time healthy growth. We'll overcome the problems of today together by building for a better future, a better life, for everyone who lives in America.

Thank you very much.

ESSAYS

Essay 11–1 is excerpts from Milton Friedman's presidential address, "The Role of Monetary Policy," delivered on December 29, 1967 at the annual meeting of the American Economic Association. It was published in the *American Economic Review* in March 1968. Friedman argues that early Keynesians dismissed monetary policy, whereas contemporary Keynesians advocate discretionary monetary policy. He disapproves, and reiterates his longstanding support for a monetary rule. James Tobin, leader of the neo-Keynesian school, described this speech as "the single most telling intellectual blow" against the ruling Keynesian orthodoxy. Essay 11–2 is excerpts from Mark H. Willes' "Rational Expectations as a Counterrevolution," which appeared as Chapter 5 in *The Crisis in Economic Theory*, edited by Daniel Bell and Irving Kristol and published in 1981. Willes attacks the Keynesian paradigm from a neo-classical perspective. Keynes is accused of ignoring the behavior of individuals and markets in his model. Willes, who held a variety of positions in the Federal Reserve System, feels the predictions of the Keynesian model were a failure, and that activist policies need to be replaced by stable policies.

Essay 11–3 is excerpts from "The Breakdown of the Keynesian Model," written by Paul Craig Roberts and published in *Public Interest* in 1978. This article was also included in "Hearings Before the Joint Economic Committee of the United States, 95th Congress, 2nd Session, Part 1." Roberts, who served as a Congressional staffer in the late 1970s and helped draft the Kemp–Roth tax bill, has been a leading supply-side economist. He feels Keynesian economics has focused on "the economics of spending" and ignored "the economics of supply." Noting that individuals take marginal tax rates into account when making work effort and savings decisions, Roberts firmly believes that cuts in marginal tax rates are vital. He disputes the findings of Keynesian econometric models that show such cuts do little to increase work effort and savings.

11–1. MILTON FRIEDMAN, "THE ROLE OF MONETARY POLICY"

There is wide agreement about the major goals of economic policy: high employment, stable prices, and rapid growth. There is less agreement that these goals are mutually compatible or, among those who regard them as incompatible, about the terms at which they can and should be substituted for one another. There is least agreement about the role that various instruments of policy can and should play in achieving the several goals.

My topic for tonight is the role of one such instrument—monetary policy. What can it contribute? And how should it be conducted to contribute the most? Opinion on these questions has fluctuated widely. In the first flush of enthusiasm about the newly created Federal Reserve System, many observers attributed the relative stability of the 1920s to the System's capacity for fine tuning—to apply an apt modern term. It came to be widely believed that a new era had arrived in which business cycles had been rendered obsolete by advances in monetary technology. This opinion was shared by economist and layman alike, though, of course, there were some dissonant voices. The Great Contraction destroyed this naive attitude. Opinion swung to the other extreme. Monetary policy was a string. You could pull on it to stop inflation but you could not push on it to halt recession. You could lead a horse to water but you could not make him drink. Such theory by aphorism was soon replaced by Keynes' rigorous and sophisticated analysis.

Keynes offered simultaneously an explanation for the presumed impotence of monetary policy to stem the depression, a nonmonetary interpretation of the depression, and an alternative to monetary policy for meeting the depression and his offering was avidly accepted. If liquidity preference is absolute or nearly so—as Keynes believed likely in times of heavy unemployment—interest rates cannot be lowered by monetary measures. If investment and consumption are little affected by interest rates—as Hansen and many of Keynes other American disciples came to believe—lower interest rates, even if they could be achieved, would do little good. Monetary policy is twice damned. The contraction, set in train, on this view, by a collapse of investment or by a shortage of investment opportunities or by stubborn thriftiness, could not it was argued, have been stopped by monetary measures. But there was available an alternative—fiscal policy. Government spending could make up for insufficient private investment. Tax reductions could undermine stubborn thriftiness.

The wide acceptance of these views in the economics profession meant that for some two decades monetary policy was believed by all but a few reactionary souls to have been rendered obsolete by new economic knowledge. Money did not matter. Its only role was the minor one of keeping interest rates low, in order to hold down interest payments in the government budget, contribute to the "euthanasia of the rentier," and maybe, stimulate investment a bit to assist government spending in maintaining a high level of aggregate demand.

These views produced a widespread adoption of cheap money policies after the war. And they received a rude shock when these policies failed in country after country, when central bank after central bank was forced to give up the pretense that it could indefinitely keep "the" rate of interest at a low level. In this country, the public denouement came with the Federal Reserve-Treasury Accord, in 1951, although the policy of pegging government bond prices was not formally abandoned until 1953. Inflation, stimulated by cheap money policies, not the widely heralded postwar depression, turned out to be the order of the day. The result was the beginning of a revival of belief in the potency of monetary policy.

This revival was strongly fostered among economists by the theoretical developments initiated by Haberler but named for Pigou that pointed out a channel—namely, changes in wealth—whereby changes in the real quantity of money can affect aggregate demand even if they do not alter interest rates. These theoretical developments did not undermine Keynes' argument against the potency of orthodox monetary measures when liquidity preference is absolute since under such circumstances the usual monetary operations involve simply substituting money for other assets without changing total wealth. But they did show how changes in the quantity of money produced in other ways could affect total spending even under such circumstances. And, more fundamentally, they did undermine Keynes' key theoretical proposition, namely, that even in a world of flexible prices, a position of equilibrium at full employment might not exist. Henceforth, unemployment had again to be explained by rigidities or imperfections, not as the natural outcome of a fully operative market process.

The revival of belief in the potency of monetary policy was fostered also by a re-evaluation of the role money played from 1929 to 1933. Keynes and most other economists of the time believed that the Great Contraction in the United States occurred despite aggressive expansionary policies by the monetary authorities—that they did their best but their best was not good enough. Recent studies have demonstrated that the facts are precisely the reverse: the U.S. monetary authorities followed highly deflationary policies. The quantity of money in the United States fell by one-third in the course of the contraction. And it fell not because there were no willing borrowers—not because the horse would not drink. It fell because the Federal Reserve System forced or permitted a sharp reduction in the monetary base, because it failed to exercise the responsibilities assigned to it in the Federal Reserve Act to provide liquidity to the banking system. The Great Contraction is tragic testimony to the power of monetary policy—not, as Keynes and so many of his contemporaries believed, evidence of its impotence.

In the United States the revival of belief in the potency of monetary policy was strengthened also by increasing disillusionment with fiscal policy, not so much with its potential to affect aggregate demand as with the practical and political feasibility of so using it. Expenditures turned out to respond sluggishly and with long lags to attempts to adjust them to the course of economic activity, so emphasis shifted to taxes. But here political factors entered with a vengeance to prevent prompt adjustment to presumed need, as has been so graphically illustrated in the months since I wrote the first draft of this talk. "Fine tuning" is a marvelously evocative phrase in this electronic age, but it has little resemblance to what is possible in practice—not, I might add, an unmixed evil.

It is hard to realize how radical has been the change in professional opinion on the role of money. Hardly an economist today accepts views that were the common coin some two decades ago. Let me cite a few examples.

In a talk published in 1945, E. A. Goldenweiser, then Director of the Research Division of the Federal Reserve Board, described the primary objective of monetary policy as being to "maintain the value of Government bonds ... This country" he wrote, "will have to adjust to a 2½ per cent interest rate as the return on safe, long-time money, because the time has come when returns on pioneering capital can no longer be unlimited as they were in the past."

In a book on *Financing American Prosperity*, edited by Paul Homan and Fritz Machlup and published in 1945, Alvin Hansen devotes nine pages of text to the "savings-investment problem" without finding any need to use the words "interest rate" or any close facsimile thereto. In his contribution to this volume, Fritz Machlup wrote, "Questions regarding the rate of interest, in particular regarding its variation or its stability, may not be among the most vital problems of the postwar economy, but they are certainly among the perplexing ones." In his contribution, John H. Williams—not only professor at Harvard but also a long-time adviser to the New York Federal Reserve Bank—wrote, "I can see no prospect of revival of a general monetary control in the postwar period."

Another of the volumes dealing with postwar policy that appeared at this time, *Planning and Paying for Full Employment*, was edited by Abba P. Lerner and Frank D. Graham and had contributors of all shades of professional opinion—from Henry Simons and Frank Graham to Abba Lerner and Hans Neisser. Yet Albert Halasi, in his excellent summary of the papers, was able to say, "Our contributors do not discuss the question of money supply. ... The contributors make no special mention of credit policy to remedy actual depressions. ... Inflation... might be fought more effectively by raising interest rates ... But ... other anti-inflationary measures ... are preferable." *A Survey of Contemporary Economics*, edited by Howard Ellis and published in 1948, was an "official" attempt to codify the state of economic thought of the time. In, his contribution, Arthur Smithies wrote, "In the field of compensatory action, I believe fiscal policy must shoulder most of the load. Its chief rival, monetary policy, seems to be disqualified on institutional grounds. This country appears to be committed to something like the present low level of interest rates on a long-term basis."

These quotations suggest the flavor of professional thought some two decades ago. If you wish to go further in this humbling inquiry, I recommend that you compare the sections on money—when you can find them—in the Principles texts of the early postwar years with the lengthy sections in the current crop even, or especially, when the early and recent Principles are different editions of the same work.

The pendulum has swung far since then, if not all the way to the position of the late 1920s, at least much closer to that position than to the position of 1945. There are of course many differences between then and now, less in the potency attributed to monetary policy than in the roles assigned to it and the criteria by which the profession believes monetary policy should be guided. Then, the chief roles assigned monetary policy were to promote price stability and to preserve the gold standard; the chief criteria of monetary policy were the state of the "money market," the extent of "speculation" and the movement of gold. Today, primacy is assigned to the promotion of full employment, with the prevention of inflation a continuing but definitely secondary objective. And there is major disagreement about criteria of policy, varying from emphasis on money market conditions, interest rates, and the quantity of money to the belief that the state of employment itself should be the proximate criterion of policy.

I stress nonetheless the similarity between the views that prevailed in the late twenties and those that prevail today because I fear that, now as then, the pendulum may well have swung too far, that, now as then, we are in danger of assigning to monetary policy a larger role than it can perform, in danger of asking it to accomplish tasks that it cannot achieve, and, as a result, in danger of preventing it from making the contribution that it is capable of making.

Unaccustomed as I am to denigrating the importance of money, I therefore shall, as my first task, stress what monetary policy cannot do. I shall then try to outline what it can do and how it can best make its contribution, in the present state of our knowledge—or ignorance.

From the infinite world of negation, I have selected two limitations of monetary policy to discuss: (1) It cannot peg interest rates for more than very limited periods; (2) It cannot peg the rate of unemployment for more than very limited periods. I select these because the contrary has been or is widely believed, because they correspond to the two main unattainable tasks that are at all likely to be assigned to monetary policy, and because essentially the same theoretical analysis covers both.

History has already persuaded many of you about the first limitation. As noted earlier, the failure of cheap money policies was a major source of the reaction against simple-minded Keynesianism. In the United States, this reaction involved widespread recognition that the wartime and postwar pegging of bond prices was a mistake, that the abandonment of this policy was a desirable and inevitable step, and that it had none of the disturbing and disastrous consequences that were so freely predicted at the time.

The limitation derives from a much misunderstood feature of the relation between money and interest rates. Let the Fed set out to keep interest rates down. How will it try to do so? By buying securities. This raises their prices and lowers their yields. In the process, it also increases the quantity of reserves available to banks, hence the amount of bank credit, and, ultimately the total quantity of money. That is why central bankers in particular, and the financial community more broadly, generally believe that an increase in the quantity of money tends to lower interest rates. Academic economists accept the same conclusion, but for different reasons. They see, in their mind's eye, a negatively sloping liquidity preference schedule. How can people be induced to hold a larger quantity of money? Only by bidding down interest rates.

Both are right, up to a point. The *initial* impact of increasing the quantity of money at a faster rate than it has been increasing is to make interest rates lower for a time than they would otherwise have been. But this is only the beginning of the process not the end. The more rapid rate of monetary growth will stimulate spending, both through the impact on investment of lower market interest rates and through the impact on other spending and thereby relative prices of higher cash balances than are desired. But one man's spending is another man's income. Rising income will raise the liquidity preference schedule and the demand for loans; it may also raise prices, which would reduce the real quantity of money. These three effects will reverse the initial downward pressure on interest rates fairly promptly, say, in something less than a year. Together they will tend, after a somewhat longer interval, say, a year or two, to return interest rates to the level they would otherwise have had. Indeed, given the tendency for the economy to overreact, they are highly likely to raise interest rates temporarily beyond that level, setting in motion a cyclical adjustment process.

A fourth effect, when and if it becomes operative, will go even farther, and definitely mean that a higher rate of monetary expansion will correspond to a higher, not lower, level of interest rates than would otherwise have prevailed. Let the higher rate of monetary growth produce rising prices, and let the public come to expect that prices will continue to rise. Borrowers will then be willing to pay and lenders will then demand higher interest rates—as Irving Fisher pointed out decades ago. This price expectation effect is slow to develop and also slow to disappear. Fisher estimated that it took several decades for a full adjustment and more recent work is consistent with his estimates.

These subsequent effects explain why every attempt to keep interest rates at a low level has forced the monetary authority to engage in successively larger and larger open market purchases. They explain why, historically, high and rising nominal interest rates have been associated with rapid growth in the quantity of money, as in Brazil or Chile or in the United States in recent years, and why low and falling interest rates have been associated with slow growth in the quantity of money, as in Switzerland now or in the United States from 1929 to 1933, As an empirical matter, low interest rates are a sign that monetary policy *has been* tight—in the sense that the quantity of money has grown slowly; high interest rates are a sign that monetary policy *has been* easy—in the sense that the quantity of money has grown rapidly. The broadest facts of experience run in precisely the opposite direction from that which the financial community and academic economists have all generally taken for granted.

Paradoxically, the monetary authority could assure low nominal rates of interest—but to do so it would have to start out in what seems like the opposite direction, by engaging in a deflationary monetary policy. Similarly, it could assure high nominal interest rates by engaging in an inflationary policy and accepting a temporary movement in interest rates in the opposite direction.

These considerations not only explain why monetary policy cannot peg interest rates; they also explain why interest rates are such a misleading indicator of whether monetary policy is "tight" or "easy." For that, it is far better to look at the rate of change of the quantity of money.

The second limitation I wish to discuss goes more against the grain of current thinking. Monetary growth, it is widely held, will tend to stimulate employment; monetary contraction, to retard employment. Why, then, cannot the monetary authority adopt a target for employment or unemployment—say, 3 per cent unemployment; be tight when unemployment is less than the target; be easy when unemployment is higher than the target; and in this way peg unemployment at, say, 3 per cent? The reason it cannot is precisely the same as for interest rates—the difference between the immediate and the delayed consequences of such a policy.

...At any moment of time, there is some level of unemployment which has the property that it is consistent with equilibrium in the structure of *real* wage rates. At that level of unemployment, real wage rates are tending on the average to rise at a "normal" secular rate, i.e., at a rate that can be indefinitely maintained so long as capital formation, technological improvements, etc., remain on their long-run trends. A lower level of unemployment is an indication that there is an excess demand for labor that will produce upward pressure on real wage rates. A higher level of unemployment is an indication that there is an excess supply of labor that will produce downward pressure on real wage rates....

...Phillips' analysis of the relation between unemployment and wage change is deservedly celebrated as an important and original contribution. But, unfortunately, it contains a basic defect—the failure to distinguish between *nominal* wages and *real* wages...Implicitly, Phillips wrote his article for a world in which everyone anticipated that nominal prices would be stable and in which that anticipation remained unshaken and immutable whatever happened to actual prices and wages. Suppose, by contrast, that everyone anticipates that prices will rise at a rate of more than 75 per cent a year—as, for example, Brazilians did a few years ago. Then wages must rise at that rate simply to keep real wages unchanged. An excess supply of labor will be reflected in a less rapid rise in nominal wages than in anticipated prices, not in an absolute decline in wages. When Brazil embarked on a policy to bring down the rate of price rise, and succeeded in bringing the price rise down to about 45 per cent a year, there was a sharp initial rise in unemployment because under the influence of earlier anticipations, wages kept rising at a pace that was higher than the new rate of price rise, though lower than earlier. This is the result experienced, and to be expected, of all attempts to reduce the rate of inflation below that widely anticipated.

To avoid misunderstanding, let me emphasize that by using the term "natural" rate of unemployment, I do not mean to suggest that it is immutable and unchangeable. On the contrary, many of the market characteristics that determine its level are man-made and policy-made. In the United States, for example, legal minimum wage rates, the Walsh-Healy and Davis-Bacon Acts, and the strength of labor unions all make the natural rate of unemployment higher than it would otherwise be. Improvements in employment exchanges, in availability of information about job vacancies and labor supply, and so on, would tend to lower the natural rate of unemployment. I use the term "natural"…to try to separate the real forces from monetary forces.

Let us assume that the monetary authority tries to peg the "market" rate of unemployment at a level below the "natural" rate. For definiteness, suppose that it takes 3 per cent as the target rate and that the "natural" rate is higher than 3 per cent. Suppose also that we start out at a time when prices have been stable and when unemployment is higher than 3 per cent. Accordingly, the authority increases the rate of monetary growth. This will be expansionary. By making nominal cash balances higher than people desire, it will tend initially to lower interest rates and in this and other ways to stimulate spending. Income and spending will start to rise.

To begin with, much or most of the rise in income will take the form of an increase in output and employment rather than in prices. People have been expecting prices to be stable, and prices and wages have been set for some time in the future on that basis. It takes time for people to adjust to a new state of demand. Producers will tend to react to the initial expansion in aggregate demand by increasing output, employees by working longer hours, and the unemployed, by taking jobs now offered at former nominal wages. This much is pretty standard doctrine.

But it describes only the initial effects. Because selling prices of products typically respond to an unanticipated rise in nominal demand faster than prices of factors of production, real wages received have gone down—though real wages anticipated by employees went up, since employees implicitly evaluated the wages offered at the earlier price level. Indeed, the simultaneous fall *ex post* in real wages to employers and rise *ex ante* in real wages to employees is what enabled employment to increase. But the decline *ex post* in real wages will soon come to affect anticipations. Employees will start to reckon on rising prices of the things they buy and to demand higher nominal wages for the future. "Market" unemployment is below the "natural" level. There is an excess demand for labor so real wages will tend to rise toward their initial level.

Even though the higher rate of monetary growth continues, the rise in real wages will reverse the decline in unemployment, and then lead to a rise, which will tend to return unemployment to its former level. In order to keep unemployment at its target level of 3 per cent, the monetary authority would have to raise monetary growth still more. As in the interest rate case, the "market" rate can be kept below the "natural" rate only by inflation. And, as in the interest rate case, too, only by accelerating inflation. Conversely, let the monetary authority choose a target rate of unemployment that is above the natural rate, and they will be led to produce a deflation, and an accelerating deflation at that.

What if the monetary authority chose the "natural" rate—either of interest or unemployment—as its target? One problem is that it cannot know what the "natural" rate is. Unfortunately, we have as yet devised no method to estimate accurately and readily the natural rate of either interest or unemployment. And the "natural" rate will itself change from time to time. But the basic problem is that even if the monetary authority knew the "natural" rate, and attempted to peg the market rate at that level, it would not be led to a determinate policy. The "market" rate will vary from the natural rate for all sorts of reasons other than monetary policy. If the monetary authority responds to these variations, it will set in train longer term effects that will make any monetary growth path it follows ultimately consistent with the rule of policy. The actual course of monetary growth will be analogous to a random walk, buffeted this way and that by the forces that produce temporary departures of the market rate from the natural rate.

To state this conclusion differently, there is always a temporary trade-off between inflation and unemployment; there is no permanent trade-off. The temporary trade-off comes not from inflation per se, but from unanticipated inflation, which generally means, from a rising rate of inflation. The widespread belief that there is a permanent trade-off is a sophisticated version of the confusion between "high" and "rising" that we all recognize in simpler forms. A rising rate of inflation may reduce unemployment, a high rate will not.

But how long, you will say, is "temporary"? For interest rates, we have some systematic evidence on how long each of the several effects takes to work itself out. For unemployment, we do not. I can at most venture a personal judgment, based on some examination of the historical evidence, that the initial effects of a higher and unanticipated rate of inflation last for something like two to five years; that this initial effect then begins to be reversed; and that a full adjustment to the new rate of inflation takes about as long for employment as for interest rates, say, a couple of decades. For both interest rates and employment, let me add a qualification. These estimates are for changes in the rate of inflation of the order of magnitude that has been experienced in the United States. For much more sizable changes, such as those experienced in South American countries, the whole adjustment process is greatly speeded up.

To state the general conclusion still differently, the monetary authority controls nominal quantities—directly, the quantity of its own liabilities. In principle, it can use this control to peg a nominal quantity—an exchange rate, the price level, the nominal level of national income, the quantity of money by one or another definition—or to peg the rate of change in a nominal quantity—the rate of inflation or deflation, the rate of growth or decline in nominal national income, the rate of growth of the quantity of money. It cannot use its control over nominal quantities to peg a real quantity—the real rate of interest, the rate of unemployment, the level of real national income, the real quantity of money, the rate of growth of real national income, or the rate of growth of the real quantity of money.

Monetary policy cannot peg these real magnitudes at predetermined levels. But monetary policy can and does have important effects on these real magnitudes. The one is in no way inconsistent with the other.

True, money is only a machine, but it is an extraordinarily efficient machine. Without it, we could not have begun to attain the astounding growth in output and level of living we have experienced in the past two centuries—any more than we could have done so without those other marvelous machines that dot our countryside and enable us, for the most part, simply to do more efficiently what could be done without them at much greater cost in labor.

But money has one feature that these other machines do not share. Because it is so pervasive, when it gets out of order, it throws a monkey wrench into the operation of all the other machines. The Great Contraction is the most dramatic example but not the only one. Every other major contraction in this country has been either produced by monetary disorder or greatly exacerbated by monetary disorder. Every major inflation has been produced by monetary expansion—mostly to meet the overriding demands of war which have forced the creation of money to supplement explicit taxation.

The first and most important lesson that history teaches about what monetary policy can do—and it is a lesson of the most profound importance—is that monetary policy can prevent money itself from being a major source of economic disturbance. This sounds like a negative proposition: avoid major mistakes. In part it is. The Great Contraction might not have occurred at all, and if it had, it would have been far less severe, if the monetary authority had avoided mistakes, or if the monetary arrangements had been those of an earlier time when there was no central authority with the power to make the kinds of mistakes that the Federal Reserve System made. The past few years, to come closer to home, would have been steadier and more productive of economic well-being if the Federal Reserve had avoided drastic and erratic changes of direction, first expanding the money supply at an unduly rapid pace, then, in early 1966, stepping on the brake too hard, then, at the end of reversing itself and resuming expansion until at least November, at a more rapid pace than can long be maintained without appreciable inflation.

Even if the proposition that monetary policy can prevent money itself from being a major source of economic disturbance were a wholly negative proposition, it would be none the less important for that. As it happens, however, it is not a wholly negative proposition. The monetary machine has gotten out of order even when there has been no central authority with anything like the power now possessed by the Fed. In the United States, the 1907 episode and earlier banking panics are examples of how the monetary machine can get out of order largely on its own. There is therefore a positive and important task for the monetary authority—to suggest improvements in the machine that will reduce the chances that it will get out of order, and to use its own powers so as to keep the machine in good working order.

A second thing monetary policy can do is provide a stable background for the economy....

Accomplishing the first task will contribute to this objective, but there is more to it than that. Our economic system will work best when producers and consumers, employers and employees, can proceed with full confidence that the average level of prices will behave in a known way in the future—preferably that it will be highly stable. Under any conceivable institutional arrangements, and certainly under those that now prevail in the United States, there is only a limited amount of flexibility in prices and wages. We need to conserve this flexibility to achieve changes in relative prices and wages that are required to adjust to dynamic changes in tastes and technology. We should not dissipate it simply to achieve changes in the absolute level of prices that serve no economic function.

In an earlier era, the gold standard was relied on to provide confidence in future monetary stability. In its heyday it served that function reasonably well. It clearly no longer does, since there is scarce a country in the world that is prepared to let the gold standard reign unchecked...Such a policy would submit each country to the vagaries not of an impersonal and automatic gold standard but of the policies—deliberate or accidental—of other monetary authorities.

In today's world, if monetary policy is to provide a stable background for the economy it must do so by deliberately employing its powers to that end. I shall come later to how it can do so.

Finally, monetary policy can contribute to offsetting major disturbances in the economic system arising from other sources. If there is an independent secular exhilaration—as the postwar expansion was described by the proponents of secular stagnation—monetary policy can in principle help to hold it in check by a slower rate of monetary growth than would otherwise be desirable. If, as now, an explosive federal budget threatens unprecedented deficits, monetary policy can hold any inflationary dangers in check by a slower rate of monetary growth than would otherwise be desirable. This will temporarily mean higher interest rates than would otherwise prevail—to enable the government to borrow the sums needed to finance the deficit—but by preventing the speeding up of inflation, it may well mean both lower prices and lower nominal interest rates for the long pull. If the end of a substantial war offers the country an opportunity to shift resources from wartime to peacetime production, monetary policy can ease the transition by a higher rate of monetary growth than would otherwise be desirable—though experience is not very encouraging that it can do so without going too far.

I have put this point last, and stated it in qualified terms—as referring to major disturbances—because I believe that the potentiality of monetary policy in offsetting other forces making for instability is far more limited than is commonly believed. We simply do not know enough to be able to recognize minor disturbances when they occur or to be able to predict either what their effects will be with any precision or what monetary policy is required to offset their effects. We do not know enough to be able to achieve stated objectives by delicate, or even fairly coarse, changes in the mix of monetary and fiscal policy. In this area particularly the best is likely to be the enemy of the good. Experience suggests that the path of wisdom is to use monetary policy explicitly to offset other disturbances only when they offer a "clear and present danger."

How should monetary policy be conducted to make the contribution to our goals that it is capable of making? This is clearly not the occasion for presenting a detailed "Program for Monetary Stability"—to use the title of a book in which I tried to do so. I shall restrict myself here to two major requirements for monetary policy that follow fairly directly from the preceding discussion.

The first requirement is that the monetary authority should guide itself by magnitudes that it can control, not by ones that it cannot control. If, as the authority has often done, it takes interest rates or the current unemployment percentage as the immediate criterion of policy, it will be like a space vehicle that has taken a fix on the wrong star. No matter how sensitive and sophisticated its guiding apparatus, the space vehicle will go astray. And so will the monetary authority. Of the various alternative magnitudes that it can control, the most appealing guides for policy are exchange rates, the price level as defined by some index, and the quantity of a monetary total—currency plus adjusted demand deposits, or this total plus commercial bank time deposits, or a still broader total.

For the United States in particular, exchange rates are an undesirable guide. It might be worth requiring the bulk of the economy to adjust to the tiny percentage consisting of foreign trade if that would guarantee freedom from monetary irresponsibility—as it might under a real gold standard. But it is hardly worth doing so simply to adapt to the average of whatever policies monetary authorities in the rest of the world adopt. Far better to let the market, through floating exchange rates, adjust to world conditions the 5 per cent or so of our resources devoted to international trade while reserving monetary policy to promote the effective use of the 95 per cent.

Of the three guides listed, the price level is clearly the most important in its own right. Other things the same, it would be much the best of the alternatives—as so many distinguished economists have urged in the past. But other things are not the same. The link between the policy actions of the monetary authority and the price level, while unquestionably present, is more indirect than the link between the policy actions of the authority and any of the several monetary totals. Moreover, monetary action takes a longer time to affect the price level than to affect the monetary totals and both the time lag and the magnitude of effect vary with circumstances. As a result, we cannot predict at all accurately just what effect a particular monetary action will have on the price level and, equally important, just when it will have that effect. Attempting to control directly the price level is therefore likely to make monetary policy itself a source of economic disturbance because of false stops and starts. Perhaps, as our understanding of monetary phenomena advances, the situation will change. But at the present stage of our understanding, the long way around seems the surer way to our objective. Accordingly, I believe that a monetary total is the best currently available immediate guide or criterion for monetary policy—and I believe that it matters much less which particular total is chosen than that one be chosen.

A second requirement for monetary policy is that the monetary authority avoid sharp swings in policy. In the past, monetary authorities have on occasion moved in the wrong direction—as in the episode of the Great Contraction that I have stressed. More frequently, they have moved in the right direction, albeit often too late, but have erred by moving too far. Too late and too much has been the general practice. For example, in early 1966, it was the right policy for the Federal Reserve to move in a less expansionary direction—though it should have done so at least a year earlier. But when it moved, it went too far, producing the sharpest change in the rate of monetary growth of the post-war era. Again, having gone too far, it was the right policy for the Fed to reverse course at the end of 1966. But again it went too far, not only restoring but exceeding the earlier excessive rate of monetary growth. And this episode is no exception. Time and again this has been the course followed—as in 1919 and 1920, in 1937 and 1938, in 1953 and 1954, in 1959 and 1960.

The reason for the propensity to overreact seems clear: the failure of monetary authorities to allow for the delay between their actions and the subsequent effects on the economy. They tend to determine their actions by today's conditions—but their actions will affect the economy only six or nine or twelve or fifteen months later. Hence they feel impelled to step on the brake, or the accelerator, as the case may be, too hard.

My own prescription is still that the monetary authority go all the way in avoiding such swings by adopting publicly the policy of achieving a steady rate of growth in a specified monetary total. The precise rate of growth, like the precise monetary total, is less important than the adoption of some stated and known rate. I myself have argued for a rate that would on the average achieve rough stability in the level of prices of final products, which I have estimated would call for something like a 3 to 5 per cent per year rate of growth in currency plus all commercial bank deposits or a slightly lower rate of growth in currency plus demand deposits only. But it would be better to have a fixed rate that would on the average produce moderate inflation or moderate deflation, provided it was steady, than to suffer the wide and erratic perturbations we have experienced.

Short of the adoption of such a publicly stated policy of a steady rate of monetary growth, it would constitute a major improvement if the monetary authority followed the self-denying ordinance of avoiding wide swings. It is a matter of record that periods of relative stability in the rate of monetary growth have also been periods of relative stability in economic activity, both in the United States and other countries. Periods of wide swings in the rate of monetary growth have also been periods of wide swings in economic activity.

By setting itself a steady course and keeping to it, the monetary authority could make a major contribution to promoting economic stability. By making that course one of steady but moderate growth in the quantity of money, it would make a major contribution to avoidance of either inflation or deflation of prices. Other forces would still affect the economy, require change and adjustment, and disturb the even tenor of our ways. But steady monetary growth would provide a monetary climate favorable to the effective operation of those basic forces of enterprise, ingenuity, invention, hard work, and thrift that are the true springs of economic growth. That is the most that we can ask from monetary policy at our present stage of knowledge. But that much—and it is a great deal—is clearly within our reach.

11–2. MARK H. WILLES, "'RATIONAL EXPECTATIONS' AS A COUNTER-REVOLUTION"

If there is a crisis in economic theory, it is a crisis in Keynesian economic theory. Most economists, even the Keynesians, seem to agree that there are at least some defects in this theory, although they may disagree passionately about what those defects are and how they should be remedied. Until the early 1970's, the economists who opposed the Keynesians had to be content with pulling a few fish off of their opponents' hooks. But when what has become known as the theory of "rational expectations" began to be developed, these economists found that they could simply dynamite all the fish in the lake. While this may be unsportsmanlike, it does demonstrate an admirable grasp of fundamentals. Today, to continue the metaphor, a fleet of stunned Keynesians is quibbling about which of their few remaining fish are still flopping.

I know how they feel, for I once believed in conventional, Keynesian theory and the economic models based on it. Now, however, I am persuaded that this theory is fundamentally wrong, so wrong that it can never yield adequate models for evaluating policy. Although rational expectations theory is still in its infancy, it has already devastated conventional theory and appears to offer a promising alternative to it.

Rational expectations can be understood as an attempt to apply the principles of classical economics to all economic problems and specifically to macroeconomic policy. These principles have never before been seriously applied to macroeconomic policy making. Rational expectations, then, is a new classical economics.

Classical economics, which dominated economic method in the first part of this century, is built upon two premises. The basic one, seldom disputed, is that individuals optimize. In other words, the model's economic agents—both firms and individuals—seek maximum expected profits or maximum expected utility, within the limitations of their incomes and technologies. The second premise of classical economics, somewhat more controversial, is that markets clear. That is, in each market the amount willingly offered equals the amount willingly bought at a particular price unless legal strictures, discrepancies in information, or government policies prevent it. Equilibrium to a classical economist means that these two premises hold. Equilibrium in each product market means that, at existing prices, the quantities firms want to sell exactly match the quantities consumers want to buy. In labor markets, similarly, at existing wage rates, workers offer as many hours of labor as they want to offer, while firms receive as much labor as they want to hire. Though simple, the classical premises proved remarkably rich for building theory.

All of the early classical models, however, had an important failing. They implied that resources would always be fully employed, that there would never be shortages or unemployment. This failing became obvious during the Great Depression, when millions of people who wanted to work couldn't find jobs and the labor market apparently was not clearing. The classical models of the 1930's could give no explanation for this deep and prolonged depression. They couldn't even account for the existence of ordinary business cycles.

Today, economists have two alternative ways of dealing with this early crisis in economics-they can reject classical premises as the Keynesians have done, or they can seek more coherent and sophisticated versions of the classical premises, as the rational expectations school has done.

To meet the crisis in economic theory engendered by the Great Depression, John Maynard Keynes deliberately rejected the classical premises about the behavior of individuals and markets. In their place he put premises about the behavior of aggregates, such as the general price level and total unemployment. With these new premises, he was able to build a model of an economy in which involuntary unemployment appeared—an economy with a persistent disequilibrium in the labor market. Keynes' method of aggregate-level, disequilibrium modeling is the foundation of macroeconomics, the branch of economics that has dictated economic policy since the New Deal. The classical method of individual-level, equilibrium modeling has been relegated exclusively to microeconomics, where it has had small opportunity to influence macroeconomic policy. It is odd that these two branches of economics should be based on incompatible theories and even odder that Keynesians should accept classical theories for microeconomics but not for macroeconomics, but that is the case today.

Although many outstanding economists have continued to work with the classical method, the Keynesian method has prevailed since the 1930's not only for policy making but for economic modeling. Even the monetarist school, which has perceptively criticized macroeconomic policies, uses aggregate-level premises for its models, just like the Keynesian school. Moreover, virtually all of the large-scale macroeconomic models that businesses and governments use for planning, forecasting, and decision making are, at root, Keynesian.

With the help of these models, economists once hoped to improve policy making. In the early 1960's, when rapid advances in computer technology made highly detailed models possible, many economists—I, for one—believed that the government could control business cycles by manipulating fiscal and monetary policies. We didn't question whether government could accomplish this. We only wondered how to do it most effectively. We asked, for instance, if monetary or fiscal policy produced the most economic growth; we asked how long it took for policy actions to have their effects. Despite these questions, though, we had faith that we could do almost magical things once we properly modeled the economy's major relationships.

We believed that a model could be made to simulate the results of whatever policies we were considering. In this way, we could see in advance what our policies would do to the unemployment rate, the price level, or any other variable in the model. Having a perfected model was like having a crystal ball. We could look into it to see the consequences of our policies—or so we thought.

We also believed that we could generate a mathematical rule to tell us how to change policy in response to new information. To do this, we would have to spell out precisely what we were trying to achieve with the variables in the model. We would have to de-cide, for example, how much more inflation we would accept in return for a bit lower unemployment. With such decisions made, though, we believed that we could turn an economic model into an effective policy maker and that many of our economic worries would then vanish like an egg in a magician's hat.

Such prospects, however naive, motivated a great deal of research to develop economic models for policy making. For example, the Federal Reserve Board of Governors during 1966 and 1967 co-sponsored the development of a large model, the FRB-MIT model, that was designed to be useful for monetary policy making. Universities and private concerns developed other large models of at least a hundred equations representing aggregate behavior for a dozen or more sectors. These models were quickly put to work making forecasts and predicting how the economy would respond to alternative policies.

These economic models flatly failed. As recently as the early 1970's, they uniformly predicted that the United States could push its unemployment rate down to 4 percent if it accepted an inflation rate of about 4 percent. If it accepted a slightly higher inflation rate, according to these models, it could reduce unemployment still further, and with a

5 or 6 percent rate of inflation, it could practically consign unemployment to the history books. Clearly, these predictions were far off the mark. Unemployment did not drop when inflation went up—unemployment went up too. For the last few years, in fact, unemployment and inflation rates have averaged close to 7 or 8 percent.

These mistaken predictions were based on the assumption that there is an exploitable trade-off between inflation and unemployment, a trade-off that is often represented graphically as the Phillips curve. An exploitable trade-off implies that unemployment can be lowered at any time simply by creating a little more inflation, and that high unemployment coinciding with high inflation is an extremely unlikely event. As the crisis in classical economic theory was that it could not explain the vast unemployment of the Depression, so the crisis in Keynesian economic theory is that it cannot explain the debilitating concurrence of high unemployment and high inflation in the 1970's. Keynesian theory by itself provides no explanation for why inflation and unemployment have been rising together.

Even before the rational expectations school developed, economists were beginning to question the foundations of the Keynesian theory, especially its presumption that there is a stable trade-off between inflation and unemployment. In a volume edited by Edmund Phelps in 1969, for example, several economists, recognizing that Keynesian method does not adequately represent individual behavior, tried to construct theories of unemployment and inflation based not on aggregate-level assumptions, but on individual-level assumptions. Again, in 1973, just as the rational expectations school was making its early breakthroughs, Sir John Hicks delivered a series of lectures on *The Crisis in Keynesian Economics* that identified many of the failings of conventional theory.

The rational expectations school, then, is not the only one to see the weaknesses in conventional Keynesian theory, but its criticism of the theory is probably the most basic. According to the rational expectations school, Keynesian method and theory are full of irreparable errors.

Error number 1: irrational expectations.

The rational expectations school has demonstrated that all existing macroeconomic models are useless for policy evaluation, because the method used to construct them dooms them to produce forecasts that are incorrect when policy changes. Any macro model is essentially a group of equations that represent how some aggregate measures are related to one another. Some of these equations, in effect, specify which information agents use to make their decisions about production, employment, or consumption. In any reasonable model, the agents consider information about the future, since they presumably make some decisions based on their expectations of the future. Their expectations of future prices, interest rates, and incomes, for instance, influence their current decisions to save or consume.

Although almost everyone agrees that a model must represent expectations about the future, building a model that represents them is tough. Macro-model builders have generally given their agents "adaptive expectations." Agents who have adaptive expectations expect the future to be essentially a continuation of the past. They expect the future value of any variable in the model—prices, incomes, or anything else—to be an average of its past values and to change very slowly. The average is weighted so that the recent past is more important than the more distant past, but it is always based entirely on the past. The model consequently has no way of formulating expectations for a future that is substantially different from the past.

These kinds of expectations make sense only if relationships among the past and future values of aggregate variables are fixed. They make sense, that is, only if agents can reasonably base their expectations exclusively on historical data. But the assumption that these aggregate relationships change very little, and the related assumption that agents expect them to change very little, can produce ludicrous forecasts when policy changes. If Washington doubled the money supply, eliminated the income tax, and named the Ayatollah Khomeini to the Supreme Court, agents in the adaptive expectations scheme would expect very little change in the economy. Even if Washington changed policy in less extreme ways, such as by passing a windfall profits tax, these agents would expect much too little change in the economy. Adaptive expectations thus amount to irrational expectations.

If economic agents optimize, as most economists agree they do, they cannot be this irrational. Irrationality is unnecessarily expensive—it is more expensive than using the available information efficiently. If agents overlook a series of policies that will obviously increase the price level, they are bypassing large opportunities for economic gain. Workers who overlook such policies, for instance, are signing contracts for slowly rising wages, although foreseeable increases in the price level will quickly erode their buying power. Speculators, likewise, are failing to buy low and sell high, simply because they are ignoring pertinent and readily available information. Irrationality, in short, is not optimizing behavior.

Obviously, agents wouldn't throw their money away willingly. So the economists who defend adaptive expectations claim that agents can be tricked into making wrong decisions by a change of policy. Perhaps agents don't foresee that a policy change is coming, or perhaps they don't understand what its effects will be. It is possible that all these people could be tricked like this once or that some of them could be tricked repeatedly. But it is not very likely that everyone in the economy, on average, could be bamboozled again and again by the same old macroeconomic policies, because they would soon learn what these policies do. As Herbert Stein has said, "The lady in the box cannot be fooled by the illusionist who pretends to saw her in half." If people behave this way, they are not optimizing—not seeking the things they want. They should be studied not by economists but by psychiatrists.

The insight of *rational* expectations is that the equation that best represents agents' expectations is not something as irrational as a weighted average, but is rather the entire model. Agents, this implies, don't know exactly what a particular variable—say, the future price level—will be, but they make the best possible predictions with the information at their disposal. Although they may make mistakes, they don't throw out pertinent information.

With the rational expectations scheme replacing the adaptive expectations scheme, agents in the model take policy changes into account. If a change in policy creates opportunities to make extraordinary profits, they do not ignore them as they do under adaptive expectations. In a rational expectations model of the economy, agents change their decisions to take full advantage of whatever opportunities are produced by a new policy.

It is already possible to impose rational expectations on simple conventional macro models. Simply imposing rational expectations on these models shows how much their forecasts depend on their assumptions about expectations, although it doesn't correct all of their problems. Under the assumption of rational expectations, these models give much different predictions for the effect of a policy change. In a Keynesian model with adaptive expectations, an activist policy such as increasing the money supply generally lowers unemployment and raises output, although it also increases inflation somewhat. But in a similar model with rational expectations, activist policy has no effect on unemployment or real output. It merely boosts inflation. Similarly, in the St. Louis model, a seven-equation monetarist model, monetary expansion normally lowers the unemployment rate over several quarters with only a gradual pickup in the rate of inflation. But after rational expectations is imposed, the trade-off predicted by the model nearly vanishes. Monetary expansion now reduces the unemployment rate only slightly, but quickly pushes the inflation rate into the stratosphere.

Such demonstrations show that policy makers cannot be confident about the forecasts of conventional models unless they are confident that these models accurately portray expectations—which they don't. This may seem self-evident, but it is truly a devastating conclusion. It means that hundreds of laws and thousands of dissertations, books, and articles—including some of my own—have been pointless. It means that all the macroeconomic models that businesses and governments rely on for their economic planning are useless except in the narrowest of circumstances. And that's the *good* news for the Keynesians!

There are even deeper problems with conventional macroeconomic modeling. The Keynesian approach to macro modeling is wrong not just because it muffs expectations. It is fundamentally incapable of providing models valid for policy evaluation first, because it is inherently inconsistent and second, because it depends on arbitrary measures of policy success.

Error number 2: inconsistency.

Conventional modeling is inconsistent because its premises about aggregate behavior are based on conflicting assumptions about individual behavior. In conventional models, the main equations, which represent aggregate functions like consumption and labor supply, are based only indirectly on individual behavior. For one aggregate function the models may assume that agents make their decisions based only on the current period—that they don't consider future income, future taxes, or future price increases. For another function, though, they may assume that agents plan ahead almost infinitely—that they are much more farsighted.

It is fairly obvious that conflicting assumptions like these will lead to serious inconsistencies. If agents decide how much to consume based partly on how much they work, as economists generally agree, then the consumption function cannot be separated from the labor supply function. The same personal decisions about how much to work determine both total consumption and the total supply of labor. Conventional models, however, often treat consumption and labor as unrelated variables, which implies that agents are inconsistent or even schizoid.

The more sophisticated models nod politely to this reality by using some of the same assumptions about agents for both of these functions. Unfortunately, these models have no mechanism for making sure that the individual decisions implied by changes in the labor supply are consistent with those implied by changes in consumption. In these models, policy can cause labor supply to change independent of consumption—something which does not happen in the model's original assumptions, which cannot happen in economic theory, and which does not happen in real life. Policy, likewise, can cause other aggregates to move independently, violating the model's assumptions. This guarantees that Keynesian models will be logically inconsistent.

Aggregate behavior in Keynesian models thus does not correspond with individual optimizing behavior in all conditions. It is, at best, consistent with individual behavior only under some specific conditions. Simplification is of the essence of good science, but the things Keynes has thrown away have made macro models impotent for evaluating policies.

The rational expectations school maintains that only by formulating in a coherent way the decision problem facing individuals can one begin to develop models capable of evaluating policy correctly. *Because aggregate outcomes are only a sum of individual decisions, the aggregate relationships should have no independent existence,* but they do under the Keynesian approach.

Error number 3: arbitrary measures of success.

The third fundamental problem of conventional macroeconomic modeling is that it relies on arbitrary measures of policy success, such as the total unemployment rate and the rate of change in the price level. As measures of a policy's success, these indexes are at best ambiguous, and at worst, misleading.

In classical models or rational expectations models, where agents are assumed to be acting in their own best interests, the success of a policy can be adequately determined. Economists can be confident, for instance, that if they eliminate barriers to trade or decrease uncertainty, they have increased individual welfare. They can know this because all the agents make the decisions that are best for themselves, given their constraints, and because the agents now have fewer constraints. To simplify: Opportunity is almost always good in these models. Optimizing agents will take advantage of new opportunities to make themselves better off in their own terms. Providing more opportunity is a means of increasing people's well-being.

In Keynesian models, in contrast, the success of a policy cannot be clearly determined. Because these models replace individual decisions with aggregate actions, they say nothing about individual welfare. Since these models don't consider people's well-being, the economists have to make guesses about what increases it. Generally, they guess that lower unemployment and greater output increases it. People probably do want these things, but not if the costs—in terms of inflation, lost leisure, economic uncertainty, or anything else—outweigh the benefits. Studies with rational expectations models, in fact, have shown that the costs can easily exceed the benefits. Policies designed to reduce employment fluctuations, even if they succeed, can reduce people's economic welfare over the course of the business cycle.

To simplify again, growth is usually good in Keynesian models, regardless of what it does to individual welfare. Agents are permitted to make themselves better off only in the terms dictated by policy makers, not in their own terms. Economists who rely on these models, then, cannot be sure that they have increased people's well-being, even if their policies actually do what they are supposed to do.

Rational expectations, in sum, avoids the errors of Keynesian economics by applying a few well-established classical principles. It corrects the Keynesian assumption of irrational expectations with the established assumption that agents optimize or, in other words, form the best expectations possible with the information available to them. It avoids Keynesian inconsistencies by building all its theoretical structures on the same foundation, on coherent assumptions about optimizing agents. Finally, it avoids arbitrary Keynesian goals that are only proxies for individual welfare, such as economic growth, by seeking to improve individual welfare in more direct ways.

Taken literally, of course, rational expectations is simply a procedure for economic modeling. On that score it's about as exciting as live bait. But its implications are pure dynamite: Almost everything we thought we knew about macroeconomic policy isn't so. The rational expectations school endorses rational expectations *per se* only as one assumption. A more complete picture is that the school builds on the foundation of classical economics, including the premises that individuals optimize and that markets clear. Using classical premises, it has constructed models that exhibit the main features of business cycles, such as the correlated swings in unemployment and inflation, which the old classical theory couldn't handle. This new classical economics has found cogent grounds for rejecting the Keynesian approach to model building, and it is working to replace it with a new and more consistent approach. The roots of the rational expectations school were already forming in the 1960's, before the crisis in Keynesian economic theory. The literal notion of rational expectations was introduced in a landmark 1961 paper by John F. Muth, who apparently borrowed the concept from engineering literature. Muth's goal was to model expectations the same way economists model other microeconomic behavior: by assuming that agents optimize and use information efficiently when forming their expectations. He was thus able to construct a theory of expectations that was consistent with an economic theory that most economists agree on.

Muth's breakthrough, though, did not convince a significant number of economists to give up their conventional macro models. This task was not accomplished until the early 1970's, when several economists began what, in retrospect, was an all-out assault on existing macroeconomic models. The three that I am most familiar with are Robert Lucas, Thomas Sargent, and Neil Wallace. Lucas proved that a model based on classical principles could generate a correlation between inflation and employment, a correlation which previously had appeared only in conventional models. He thus showed that classical models were more broadly applicable than many economists had thought. His work stimulated Sargent and Wallace, who began to trace some of the implications of the rational expectations hypothesis. They demonstrated that existing models could not be used to evaluate or design policy.

It is no secret that reactions against the new classical economics have been strong. That's understandable, since the rational expectations school strongly attacks ideas many economists have spent their careers refining and denies the usefulness of the models promoted by well-established commercial interests. The most frequent criticism of the school is that its fundamental assumptions—in particular, rational expectations and equilibrium modeling—are unrealistic. One version of this charge is that agents in rational expectations models are preternaturally smart. Of course, individuals don't always use available information efficiently, so the rational expectations assumption isn't completely realistic, but neither is the generally accepted assumption that individuals always optimize. The point is that theories cannot be judged by the realism of their assumptions—superficially unrealistic assumptions can produce realistic results. The assumption that agents use information efficiently is a useful simplification precisely because it gives realistic results. The assumption that agents optimize is useful for the same reason. In fact, the assumption that agents use information efficiently is, at heart, just a logical extension of the assumption that they optimize. Charging rational expectations with being unrealistic, therefore, doesn't bolster the case for conventional models. While models with either rational expectations or adaptive expectations have unrealistic assumptions, models with adaptive expectations have unrealistic results. These models are plainly unrealistic in more important ways —ways that deprive them of any ability to evaluate policy.

Another version of the charge against the rational expectations school is that the premise that markets are continuously clearing —or are in equilibrium—is unrealistic. The alternative, of course, is that markets do not clear or are in disequilibrium. It may well be more realistic to say that some markets do not clear, but again that's not relevant. The relevant issue is what assumptions produce realistic results when used to predict the effects of policies. Existing economic models cannot be used to predict policy effects, and this is in no way changed by resorting to nonclearing markets.

The rational expectations school argues that, for evaluating policy, the economy is best represented by a model that includes continuous equilibrium. Equilibrium modeling is the best strategy available because it is consistent with a useful and fruitful body of economic knowledge. It is linked to the main body of price, value, and welfare theory and is thus able to share the highly refined theorems those fields have already developed. It appears to be able to explain unemployment and the business cycle without discarding what we know about microeconomics.

James Tobin has caricatured this desire to be consistent by commenting: "In other words, if you have lost your purse on a street at night, look for it under the lamppost." He intimates that classical theory, like a lamppost, is applicable only to one area and unable to solve our macroeconomic problems. That really underestimates the capabilities of equilibrium modeling. It is not necessary, after the new advances in classical theory, to resort to disequilibrium models in order to account for unemployment, queues, quantity rationing, or other phenomena that accompany the business cycle. There's no reason, in principle, that these phenomena can't be reproduced by equilibrium modeling—indeed, some of them already have been. Besides, disequilibrium modeling poses enormously complex problems. Efforts to solve these problems would be welcome, but the most promising strategy for devising useful models is clearly equilibrium modeling. The advice of the new classical method is that when you go out at night to look for your lost purse, go with flashlight in hand. Why grope in the dark when a light is available?

Another prominent criticism of rational expectations is that its predictions are valid only under constant policies. Only then, critics argue, could agents know the model well enough to foresee the results of policy. That's really turning things on their heads. Keynesian models, in fact, are the ones limited to constant policies because they do not recognize that people react to a new policy—that if people are faced with a new policy, their decision rules will change.

Rational expectations models may not have solved all of the problems inherent in Keynesian models, but they at least acknowledge that people can and do react to a new policy. Advocates of rational expectations concede that their models have not yet been able to capture fully what happens in the economy when policy changes. But the new method, because it is logically consistent and based firmly on accepted economic principles, has a good chance of producing models that can. The conventional method *in 40 years* has not produced one model that captures what happens when policy changes—and *it is absolutely incapable of doing so.* While Keynesian models can produce very good forecasts as long as policies do not change, they cannot describe how individual agents in the economy make related decisions in response to new policies, as they must if they hope to reproduce the effects of a policy change. An economy in motion is best modeled by having agents change their decisions when the available information changes. This is what rational expectations models try to accomplish—and what Keynesian models forget.

Another false charge is that rational expectations implies that monetary and fiscal policies don't have any real effects on overall employment or production. *Business Week,* for instance, reported: "In essence the rationalists maintain that the government is impotent in the economic sphere" (June 26, 1978). The rational expectations school makes no such claim. In fact, its proponents believe that government has a tremendous influence on economic matters—though it does not have the influence that the Keynesians claim.

The rational expectations school has shown that no one knows much about what happens to the economy when economic policy is changed. The methods of evaluating policy that we thought would work don't—and they cannot be patched up. This means that our policies must be much different than they have been in recent years. Specifically, it means that activist macroeconomic policies—those designed to stimulate economic growth by cutting taxes, increasing government spending, increasing the money supply, or increasing the federal deficit—must be curbed.

Activist policies must be curbed, first, because a growing body of evidence, both empirical and theoretical, suggests that existing models cannot succeed in offsetting the normal fluctuations in output, employment, or other aggregates. They may be able to influence economic activity in some circumstances, but they cannot tame the business cycle.

Second, activist policies must be curbed because most of their effects are uncertain. Although we know that they don't work the way they are supposed to, we don't know— even approximately— what they really do. Every economic theory wisely recommends that policy should be more cautious when its effects are less certain, for the obvious reason that a misconceived policy could make matters worse. Policy makers need to move more slowly, with smaller steps. They must not try to stimulate economic growth with such massive measures as they have been using, because no one can be sure what these measures will accomplish.

Third, activist policies must be curbed because even if we knew what their results would be, we wouldn't know whether they were desirable or not. Policy makers who rely on the Keynesian method cannot let individuals in the economy choose which results are good; they are compelled to choose for them. The result is that activist policies may well be making people generally worse off, unless their preferences exactly match those specified by the policy makers.

Some critics of the new classical economics accept, at least for purposes of argument, the premise of rational expectations in macro models, but nevertheless attempt to justify activist policies. Typically, they have modeled situations in which the government knows what is happening in the business cycle better or sooner than agents. The government then exploits this advantage to fool agents into making decisions they would not make if they knew what it knew. But merely to demonstrate the potential to exploit such information does not establish that it is desirable to do so. In particular, it does not even consider whether simply making this privileged information freely available would make agents better off than tricking them. These attempts, in short, do not result in a verdict in favor of activist policies.

Another common way to justify activist policies is to put various rigidities into a model, such as contracts that lock agents into fixed prices or wage rates over long periods regardless of policy changes or higher inflation. Under these conditions activist policy can work, but only by playing favorites. It requires that the agents with inflexible contracts lose while others win. Even if this inherent favoritism could be excused, such policy making would not be feasible for very long. Any repeated attempts to exploit these rigidities would soon become so expensive that agents, if they optimized, would begin to be wary of rigid contracts. They would find some way to avoid being harmed by these contracts when policy was changed—perhaps they would insist on shorter contracts or escalator clauses.

Instead of activist policies, we need stable policies. Which stable policies are the best is still a matter of debate, but a general approach can be surmised. The government should specify the rules for the economic game—that is, the policies and regulations—so that people know what opportunities are available and understand the probable consequences of their decisions. Tax policies, for example, should be set so that people can know if their relative taxes are going up or down from one year to the next. Spending policies should be announced well in advance and explained so that they don't trick people into making harmful decisions. Regulations on financial markets should be systematic and well announced instead of changing from month to month. Even the regulations pertaining to bankruptcy need to be more predictable, so that future Chrysler Corporations will know in advance what to expect.

For the consequences of the rules to be well understood, the rules must not change very often. The government, of course, would want to be able to change some policies, particularly those that are not succeeding, but it has a responsibility to see that people are not intentionally tricked by a new policy. At present, many of our most important economic policies come as surprises for one reason or another. No one will say what happens at a Federal Open Market Committee meeting. No one will say how much the United States spends to prop upFF the dollar. Congress changes tax laws so fast that labor contracts, wills, and investments often fail to do what people intend. Changes in policy must come more slowly. In the future, perhaps, when our economic knowledge is more sophisticated, we will be able to design fair and well-understood rules for changing policies, but for now we must choose policies that accommodate our ignorance.

An important principle behind this new approach to policy making is that government rules and rule changes should not be based on arbitrary indexes such as the unemployment rate. Rather, they should be based on their ability to improve the general welfare. If a policy can increase efficiency or otherwise make people better off, then use it. But if all it can do is shift some aggregate numbers that may not mean much, why bother? I suspect that this approach to policy making would lead to much less government involvement in the economy than we now have, since it is hard to demonstrate that government involvement has improved welfare. Government may still have a large role as a rule maker, but this is necessarily a passive role. The referee, after all, shouldn't intercept a pass.

Perhaps because of these tentative policy implications, the rational expectations school has sometimes been identified as a conservative branch of economics. "Conservative" is not an entirely accurate term for it, however. It does conserve some classical principles, but it isn't really striving to conserve anything out of a sense of nostalgia or duty to the past. With equal accuracy, in fact, the school might be called radical, for it is attempting to recultivate macroeconomics from the roots up. It might also be called liberal because of its emphasis on individual welfare, rights, and opportunities. Political labels, though, don't quite fit such an academic enterprise. The advocates of rational expectations are seeking a kind of truth, not an ideology. If they persevere and find it, as I believe they will, then the question will be not whether they are left or right, but how much their knowledge can benefit us.

11–3. PAUL CRAIG ROBERTS, "THE BREAKDOWN OF THE KEYNESIAN MODEL"

There is much talk these days about "the crisis in Keynesian economics." That some such crisis exists is evident from the bewilderment and impotence our economic policy makers are displaying in their confrontation with economic reality. But what exactly is the nature of this crisis? What went wrong and what can put it right?

The answer, I would suggest, is almost embarrassingly simple. Today in the United States, public economic policy is formulated in bland disregard of the human incentives upon which the economy relies. Instead it is based on the Keynesian assumption that the gross national product (GNP) and employment are determined only by the level of aggregate demand or total spending in the economy. Unemployment and low rates of economic growth are seen as evidence of insufficient spending. The standard remedy is for government to increase total spending by incurring a deficit in its budget. GNP, it is believed, will then rise by some multiple of the increase in spending. Keynesian economics focuses on estimating the "spending gap" and the "multiplier" so that the necessary deficit can be calculated.

This view of economic policy is enshrined in the large-scale econometric forecasting models upon which both Congress and the Executive Branch rely for simulations of economic policy alternatives. It is a view that is extraordinary in its emphasis on spending.

True, it is obvious that if people did not buy, no one would produce for market. It also seems obvious that the more people buy, the more will be produced and, therefore, that the use of government fiscal policy to increase total demand will increase total production or GNP. All this is so obvious to Keynesians that they believe any fiscal policy that produces an increase in government spending, even a spending increase matched by a tax increase, will produce an increase in GNP.

The concept of the "balanced-budget multiplier" illustrates the primacy that Keynesians give to spending as the determinant of production. According to this concept, government can increase total spending and, thereby, GNP by raising taxes and spending the revenues. The reasoning is as follows. People do not pay the higher taxes only by reducing their spending (consumption); they also reduce their savings. Therefore, when taxes are raised, the decrease in private spending is less than the increase in government spending. Conversely, a cut in tax rates, matched by a decrease in government spending, would result in a reduction in total spending (i.e., saving would increase), a fall in GNP, and a rise in unemployment.

For years after the 1964 Presidential election, college students were asked a standard question on economic exams: What would happen if Barry Goldwater's prescription for a tax cut, matched by a spending cut, were implemented? They missed the answer if they did not reply that there would be a reduction in aggregate demand and, therefore, a fall in GNP and employment. Alas, for too many policy makers that is still the answer.

Since the "balanced-budget multiplier" implies that the greater the increase in taxes and in government spending, the greater the increase in GNP, it is a wonder no one ever asked what happens to production as tax rates rise. This question confronts economic policy with the incentive effects it has disregarded. It should be obvious even to Keynesians that when marginal tax rates are high, people will prefer additional leisure to additional current income, and additional current consumption to additional future income. As work effort and investment decline, production will fall, regardless of how great an increase there might be in aggregate demand. Such a recognition of disincentives implies a recognition of incentives, and Keynesians are gradually having to rethink the answer to their standard question about Barry Goldwater. Once one recognizes that people produce and invest for income, and that income depends on *tax* rates, one has reached the realization that *fiscal policy causes changes not just in demand but also in supply.*

The economics of spending has thoroughly neglected the economics of supply. On the supply side there are two important relative prices governing production. One price determines the choice between additional current income and leisure; the other determines the choice between additional future income (investment) and current consumption. Both prices are affected by the marginal tax rates. The higher the tax rates on earnings, the lower the cost of leisure and current consumption, in terms of foregone after-tax income.

As an illustration, consider the decision to produce. There are two uses of time-work and leisure. Each use has a price relative to the other. The price of additional leisure is the amount of income foregone by not working, and it is influenced by the tax rates. The higher the tax rates, the smaller the amount of after-tax income foregone by enjoying additional leisure. In other words, the higher the tax rates, the lower the relative price of leisure. When the marginal tax rate reaches 100 percent, the relative price of additional leisure becomes zero. At that point, additional leisure becomes a free good, because nothing has to be sacrificed in order to acquire it.

We often hear that a person works the first five months of the year for the government, and then starts working for himself. But that is not the way it goes. The first part of the year, he works for himself; he only begins working for the government when his income reaches taxable levels. The more he earns, the more he works for the government, until rising marginal rates discourage him from further work.

Take the case of a physician who encounters the 50-percent rate after six, eight, or 10 months of work. He is faced with working another six, four, or two months for only 50 percent of his earnings. Such a low after-tax return on their efforts encourages doctors to share practices, to reduce their working hours, and to take longer vacations. The high tax rates thus shrink the tax base by discouraging them from earning additional amounts of taxable income. They also drive up the cost of medical care by reducing the supply of medical services. A tax-rate reduction would raise the relative price of leisure and result in more taxable income earned and also in a greater supply of medical services.

The effect of tax rates on the decision to earn additional taxable income is not limited to physicians or to the top tax bracket; it operates across the spectrum of tax brackets. Studies by Martin Feldstein show that the tax rates on the average worker practically eliminate the gap between his after-tax take-home pay and the level of untaxed unemployment compensation he could be receiving if he did not work. In this case, a marginal tax rate of 30 percent (including state and Federal income taxes and Social Security taxes) reduces the relative price of leisure so much that, by making unemployment competitive with work, it has raised the measured rate of unemployment by 1.25 percent and shrunk GNP and the tax base by the lost production of one million workers.

It is useful to give another example to illustrate that it is not just the top marginal rate that causes losses to GNP, employment, and tax revenues by discouraging people from earning additional taxable income. Blue-collar workers do not yet encounter the top marginal tax rate (although if inflation continues to push up money incomes, and the tax-rate structure remains unadjusted for inflation, it will not be many years before they do). Nevertheless, the marginal tax rates that many blue-collar workers already face are high enough to discourage them from earning additional taxable income. Take the case of a carpenter facing only a 25-percent marginal tax rate. For every additional $100 he earns before income tax, he gets to keep $75. Suppose that his house needs painting and that he can hire a painter for $80 a day and hire himself out for $100 a day. However, since his after-tax earnings are only $75, he saves $5 by painting his own house, so it pays him to choose not to earn the additional $100. In this case, the tax base shrinks by $180—of which $100 is the foregone earnings of the carpenter, and $80 is the lost earnings of the painter who is not hired. (Also, the productive efficiency associated with the division of labor vanishes.)

Suppose, instead, that the marginal tax rate on additional earnings by the carpenter were reduced to 15 percent. In this case, his after-tax earnings would be $85, and it would pay him to hire the painter. The reduction in the marginal tax rate would thus expand the tax base upon which revenues are collected by $180.

Studies by Gary Becker have made it clear that capital and labor are employed by households to produce utility through non-market activities (e.g., a carpenter painting his own house). Utility produced in this way is not purchased with income subject to taxation. Therefore, the amount of household-owned capital and labor supplied in the market will be influenced by marginal tax rates. The lower the after-tax income earned by supplying additional labor and capital in the market, the less the utility that the additional income can provide, and the more likely it is that households can increase their utility by allocating their productive resources to non-market activities. A clear implication of the new household economics is that *the amount of labor and capital supplied in the market is influenced by the marginal tax rates.*

Now consider how relative prices affect the choice concerning the use of income. There are two uses of income, consumption and saving (investment), and each has a price in terms of the other. The price of additional current consumption is the amount of future income foregone by enjoying additional current consumption. The higher the tax rates, the smaller the amount of after-tax future income foregone by enjoying additional current consumption. In other words, the higher the tax rates, the lower the relative price of current consumption.

Take the case of an Englishman facing the 98-percent marginal tax rate on investment income. He has the choice of saving $50,000 at a 17-percent rate of return, which would bring him $8,500 per year before taxes, or purchasing a Rolls Royce. Since the after-tax value of that $8,500 additional income is only $170 per year, the price of additional consumption is very low: He can enjoy having a fine motor car by giving up only $170 per year of additional income. This is why so many Rolls Royces are seen in England today. They are mistaken for signs of prosperity, whereas in fact they are signs of high tax rates on investment income.

A tax-rate reduction would raise the price of current consumption relative to future income, and thus result in more savings, making possible a growth in real investment. A rate reduction not only increases disposable income and total spending, *it also changes the composition of total spending toward more investment.* Thus, labor productivity, employment, and real GNP are raised above the levels that would result from the same amount of total spending more heavily weighted toward current consumption.

The econometric models upon which the government relies for simulations of policy alternatives do not take into account these supply-side effects on GNP of these relative price changes. Consider the alternatives faced by the Keynesian policy maker who wants "to get the economy moving again." His goal is to increase aggregate demand or total spending. How can he do this? He has the choice between the balanced-budget multiplier (i.e., increasing both taxes and government spending) or a deficit. He will discard the balanced-budget multiplier, because it is relatively weak and deficits are more politically acceptable than legislating higher tax rates. Having settled on a deficit, he has to choose how to produce it. He can hold tax revenues constant and increase government spending, or he can hold government spending constant and cut tax revenues. In the latter case, he has a choice between rebates and permanent reductions in tax rates. Wanting the most stimulus for his deficit dollar, he will ask for econometric simulations of his three policy alternatives: a tax rebate, a tax rate reduction, or an increase in government spending programs.

The simulations, all based on Keynesian assumptions, will show that a revenue reduction of a given amount, whether in the form of a rebate of personal income taxes or a reduction in personal-income-tax rates, will raise disposable income—and thereby spending and GNP—by the same amount. The policy maker may prefer the rebate for reasons of "flexibility." The spending stimulus may not be required in the following year, and, if it is, he has the option of providing it either by another rebate or by an increase in government spending programs. But on the basis of the econometric simulation, he will be indifferent as to the choice between rebates or rate reductions. As for his third option, an increase in government spending programs, the simulation may report that, dollar for dollar, an increase in government purchases (as contrasted with transfers) will have a more powerful impact on GNP because the government spends all of the money, whereas if it is returned to consumers they will save part of it. Based on the econometric simulation of his alternatives, he will conclude that there is no compelling economic reason in favor of any of the three, and he will make his choice on a political basis.

But the econometric models have misled the policy maker. Unlike a reduction in personal-income-tax rates, a rebate affects no individual choice at the margin. It does not change the relative prices governing the choices between additional current income and leisure or between additional future income and current consumption. It does not raise the relative prices of leisure and current consumption. Therefore, a rebate directly stimulates neither work nor investment. For any given revenue reduction, a rebate cannot cause as great an increase in GNP as a rate reduction, because it does not affect the choices that would cause people to allocate more time and more income to increasing production for the market.

An increase in government spending fares no better by comparison, and may fare even worse. It too fails to raise the after-tax rewards for work and investment. Furthermore, it increases the percentage of total resources used in the government sector. If the government sector uses resources less efficiently than the private sector, as seems to be the case, the result is a decline in the efficiency with which resources are used—which means GNP would be less than it otherwise would be. Yet the econometric simulations of the policy maker's alternatives will pick up none of the incentive and disincentive effects of these relative price changes. Instead, they focus on the effects of these alternatives on disposable income and on spending.

There are a number of adverse consequences of this extraordinary preoccupation with spending. One is that *the models exaggerate the net tax-revenue losses that result from cutting tax rates.* The only "feedback effect" on the tax base and tax revenues that they provide for is the expansion of GNP in response to an increase in demand. They do not provide for the expansion in GNP that results from higher after-tax rewards for work and investment. The supply-side "feedback effects" are ignored. Similarly, revenue gains from tax-rate increases will be overestimated, because the disincentive effects are left out.

A second consequence follows from the popular misidentification of a tax rebate as a tax cut, and from a similar tendency on the part of most policy makers to see rebates and rate cuts as variations of the same policy instrument. If Milton Friedman is correct that personal consumption is a function of *permanent* income, a temporary rebate has little impact even on spending. Thus, on the basis of experience with rebates, tax cuts *per se* might come to be seen as relatively ineffectual, leaving the field open to proponents of government spending programs.

A third consequence is that the true effects of large tax increases (such as the proposed energy taxes, or the $227-billion increase in the Social Security tax over the next decade) will not be accurately calculated. Policy makers see these tax increases as withdrawals from disposable income and spending, and their only concern is "to put money back" into spending so that aggregate demand does not fall. However, these tax increases change the *relative* prices and incentives of leisure and work, consumption and investment They produce resource reallocations that have adverse implications for employment and the rate of economic growth. Yet the econometric models, as now constructed, flash no warning lights.

Consider what Arthur Laffer, in the *Wall Street Journal,* has called the "tax wedge." The Social Security tax increase provides a good example of this phenomenon. It is a tax on employment, and, as economists should know, a tax on employment will reduce employment. The employer's decision to hire is based on the gross cost to him of an employee. The employee's decision to work is based on his after-tax pay. We know that the higher the price, the less the quantity demanded, and the lower the price, the less the quantity supplied. The Social Security tax both raises the price to the demander and lowers it to the supplier. By increasing the Social Security tax, policy makers reduced both job opportunities and the inclination to work. They raised the cost of labor relative to capital for the employer, and they narrowed the gap between unemployment compensation and after-tax take-home pay for a wider range of workers. Since the revenues available for paying Social Security benefits depend on both the tax rates and the number of people paying into the system, the increase in rates will be offset to some degree by a decrease in the number of people paying into the system. It is hard to see how the Social Security system can be saved by decreasing employment, or how increasing the demand for unemployment compensation is likely to free general revenues for Social Security benefits.

There are at least two other important points on which economic policy is misinformed by the neglect of incentives and of choices made at the margin. One is the impact on GNP of reductions in the corporate-income-tax rate, and the other is the controversy over whether government fiscal policy "crowds out" private investment. Simulations run by the Congressional Budget Office and the House Budget Committee on two of the three large-scale commercial econometric models show *declines* in GNP as a result of reductions in corporate-tax rates. In one of the models, corporate investment did not depend on after-tax profits in a very strong way, but was very sensitive to changes in interest rates. Since interest rates rise as the Treasury increases its borrowing to finance the deficit resulting from the tax cut, investment falls, and *the model predicted a decline in GNP at the result of a tax-rate reduction that increased the profitability of investment.*

The other model predicted that a corporate-tax-rate reduction would slightly raise real GNP after a lag of a couple of quarters, but it predicted a lower nominal GNP for two years. Nominal GNP declined because the corporate-tax-rate reduction reduced the user cost of capital, the price mark-up, and thereby the inflation rate, thus lowering the nominal price level.

To the extent that Keynesians think about the "crowding out" of private investment by fiscal policy, it is in terms of upward pressure on interest rates as a result of government borrowing to finance budget deficits. They do not realize that *investment is crowded out by taxation, regardless of whether the budget is in balance.* To understand how, consider the following example. Suppose that a 10-percent rate of return must be earned if an investment is to be undertaken. In the event that government imposes a 50-percent tax rate on investment income, investments earning 10 percent will no longer be undertaken. Only investments earning 20 percent before tax will return 10 percent after tax. Taxation crowds out investment by reducing the number of profitable investments. When tax rates are reduced, after-tax rates of return rise, and the number of profitable investments increases.

So "crowding out" cannot be correctly analyzed merely in terms of events in the financial markets: "Crowding out" occurs in terms of real output. It is the preempting of production capacity by government outlays, regardless of whether these outlays are financed by taxing, borrowing, or money creation.

A concern with the supply-side effects of fiscal policy is incompatible with the concept of economic policy that currently reigns in the Congress and in the Executive Branch. Members of the House Budget Committee asked Alice Rivlin, Director of the Congressional Budget Office, and Bert Lance, then Director of the Office of Management and Budget, about the neglect of the incentive effects of tax-rate changes on supply and also about the econometric predictions that GNP would fall in response to a reduction in corporate tax rates.

Dr. Rivlin said that she and her staff had been "particularly troubled" by model findings that GNP declines if corporate tax rates are reduced. However, she went on to say:

> Studies have generally found that tax-rate changes are less important than changes in the cost of capital and changes in levels of national output in influencing the level of investment. It follows that an investment tax credit or liberalized depreciation will increase investment more than a corporate-tax-rate reduction of equivalent revenue loss. While we do not believe that corporate-tax-rate cuts reduce investment, it would not be surprising to find that tax cuts had only a minor expansionary effect.

The OMB staff reply to this question was ambiguous.

Both CBO and OMB realized that the question about incentive effects most fundamentally challenged their concept of economic policy. The comments of Rivlin, Lance, and the OMB staff all unequivocally acknowledged that the econometric models upon which they rely for guidance in the choice of economic policy alternatives do not include any relative price effects of changes in personal-income-tax rates. However, since they believe that the performance of the economy is a function of spending levels, not of production incentives, they expressed no concern over this neglect. They said that economic theory and empirical studies leave it unclear whether the neglected supply-side effects are important; regardless of how the issue is resolved, they questioned the practical importance of supply incentives for short-run policy analysis.

There are two parts to this argument. One is that it is unclear whether lowering personal-income-tax rates will increase or reduce work effort. The other is that it is unclear whether any incentive effects on work effort and investment would show up as quantitatively important in a short-run policy framework. The first proposition questions the existence of the incentive effects; the second questions whether they would be effective in time to deal with an immediate problem of economic stabilization.

It is easy to dispose of the latter point. The long-run consists of a series of short-runs. If policies that are effective over a longer period are neglected because they do not have an immediate impact, and if policies that are damaging over the longer period are adopted because they initially have beneficial results, then policy makers will inevitably come to experience, sometime in the future, a period when they will have no solution for the crisis they have provoked. In the United States, that future might be now.

As for the first point, Rivlin acknowledged that a personal-income-tax-rate reduction raises the relative price of leisure, and that work effort will increase as people substitute income for leisure. This is known in economics as the "substitution effect," and it works to increase supply. However, Rivlin also said:

> It is also theoretically arguable that when a tax cut provides people with more after-tax income, many of them will *reduce* effort through what is called the income effect. For most people, leisure has some positive value, and it may even be a "luxury" good; these people could respond to a tax reduction by reducing their working hours, benefiting from more leisure time and still maintaining their after-tax income. For other people who like their work, there may be little or no labor supply response to the income or the substitution effect. In much of the United States economy, work weeks are fixed, leaving little possibility for individuals to make marginal adjustments in hours of work.

In other words, CBO believes that the "income effect" works to decrease supply.

Rivlin then went on to say that it was an empirical question whether the "income effect" offset the "substitution effect," referred to a narrow range of studies that left the question unresolved, and concluded: "In the range of policy options that we have been dealing with, I think the assumption that changes in marginal tax rates have no quantitatively significant effect on labor supply is quite plausible."

But the concept of a targeted or desired level of income unaffected by the cost of acquiring such income is foreign to the price-theoretical perspective of economic science. Rivlin's idea that people respond to a cut in income-tax rates by maintaining their existing income levels while enjoying more leisure implies that, if their tax rates went up, they would work harder in order to maintain their desired income level. Lester Thurow has actually employed this reasoning to argue for a wealth tax. According to Thurow, a wealth tax is a costless way to raise revenues because the "income effect" runs counter to and dominates the "substitution effect." He assumes that people have a targeted level of wealth, irrespective of the cost of acquiring it. Therefore, he says, a tax on wealth will cause people to work harder in order to maintain, after tax, their desired wealth level.

Note the perverse ways in which people respond to incentives and disincentives according to the Rivlin-Thurow line of argument: When tax rates go down and the relative price of leisure rises, people demand more leisure; when tax rates go up and the relative price of leisure falls, people demand less leisure. In economics, any time the "income effect" works counter to the "substitution effect," we have the relatively rare case of what is called an "inferior good" (i.e., people purchase less of it as their income rises). Since income is command over all goods, Rivlin's argument implies that *all* goods are inferior goods: A tax cut will cause people to purchase only more leisure, not more income (i.e., goods). What land of people are these? Well, the only kind of people who fit this land of economic analysis are people who respond to a monetary incentive in perverse ways.

Perhaps Rivlin merely meant to say that lower tax rates would allow people to have a *little* more income for a *little* less work. Even so, as long as she maintains that the "income effect" works counter to the "substitution effect," her argument carries the implication that goods in general are inferior.

Whatever the weight one assigns this point, there is a more fundamental defect in her argument. Notice the stunning inconsistency: People respond to a tax-rate reduction "by reducing their working hours...and still maintaining their after-tax income." But it is impossible for people in *the aggregate* to reduce their work effort and maintain the same level of *aggregate* real income! If people respond to tax cuts by working less, real GNP would fall, and it would be impossible to increase real disposable income, spending, and demand in the aggregate. Rivlin's argument is directed against the effectiveness of incentives in raising aggregate output, but if she were correct, it would mean that Keynesian fiscal policy also is ineffective!

The fatal error in the Rivlin-Thurow argument can be put this way: It derives from trying to aggregate a series of partial equilibrium analyses (individual responses to a change in relative prices) and, in the aggregate, ignoring the *general* equilibrium effects.

There are various ways a non-economist can grasp this point. Assume that the government cuts taxes and maintains a balanced budget by reducing spending. In this case, the higher income accorded the taxpayers whose rates are reduced must be matched by a negative impact on the incomes of recipients of government spending. Some or all of these may be the same people. Assume, for example, that both the tax burden and government spending are evenly distributed. In this case the "income effect" (the substitution of leisure for work) "nets out" for each individual. Since the aggregate income effect is zero, it cannot offset the "substitution effect" (the substitution of work for leisure).

If taxes are cut and government spending is unchanged (resulting in a budget deficit), the nominal disposable income of taxpayers as a group will rise relative to the nominal disposable income of the recipients of government spending as a group. The former will be able to bid real resources away from the latter. The real income gains of the former will be matched by the real income losses of the latter. Since the bidding will raise prices, the real income loss might be suffered by individuals who hold money. Regardless of who loses and who gains, the individual income effects "net out," leaving only the "substitution effects," which unambiguously increase work effort.

There can be no aggregate "income effect" unless the impact of incentives is to raise real aggregate income. Economic theory makes it perfectly clear that a tax-rate reduction will increase work effort and total output.

In the final analysis, Rivlin's argument is not that the supply-side incentive effects are unimportant, but the equally false argument that their impact is perverse—that is, only a tax-rate *increase* can produce a rise in real national income! She may not actually believe any such thing, of course—but that is where her reasoning leads her.

An economist might see the flaw in the Rivlin-Thurow argument, but it is not obvious to politicians. Take something simple, like Rivlin's assertion that a fixed work-week precludes adjustment of the labor supply to tax-rate changes. To an economist her assertion is obviously false, but to the politician it sounds reasonable enough. He will not realize that the "adjustments" will be reflected in absenteeism rates, turnover rates, the average duration of unemployment, labor negotiations for shorter work-weeks and more paid vacation rather than higher wages, and in the quality and intensity of work. Nor will he think of the entrepreneur who, because of high tax rates, loses his incentive to innovate-to make the economy itself (all of us) more productive.

Besides, one has to have an idealistic view of government to believe that politicians even want to know. The Keynesian concept of the economy is that of an unstable private sector that must be stabilized by fiscal and monetary policies of the government. This view has served as a ramp for the expansion of the interests of government. It has also served the interests of economists by transforming them from ivory-tower denizens to public-spirited social activists, a transformation which has much increased their power and enlivened their life styles. Unemployment can always be said to be too high. And the rate of economic growth can always be found to be below "potential." This means that there is always a "scientific" economic reason for expanding government spending programs that enlarge the constituencies of the Congress and of the Federal bureaucracy. From the standpoint of the private interests of policy makers, Keynesian economic policy will always be judged a success.

To write about all of the problems of econometrics and economic policy would require a book, not an article, but one other important problem must be mentioned in closing. Professor Robert Lucas has demonstrated that the standard econometric models assume that the structure of the economy remains invariant under wide variations in policy paths. What this means is that the models assume that people do not learn. But people do learn, and their expectations change as they experience various policies: They may not repeat the same behavior in response to the same policy at different times. Therefore, the policy simulation may always misinform the policy makers. This is not an optimistic note on which to end an article about public policy in a country that believes we need a great deal of it. But our faith in public policy has exceeded our knowledge, and we will find out that, in this area, there is no such thing as free faith.

ADDITIONAL READINGS

Canto, Victor A., Douglas H. Joines and Arthur B. Laffer, *Foundations of Supply-Side Economics: Theory and Evidence* (1982).
Gilder, George, *The Spirit of Enterprise* (1984).
——, *Wealth and Poverty* (1981).
Greider, William, *Secrets of the Temple: How the Federal Reserve Runs the Country* (1987).
Kettl, Donald F., *Leadership at the Fed* (1986).
Mayer, Thomas, *Monetary Policy and the Great Inflation in the United States* (1998).
Neikirk, William R., *Volcker: Portrait of the Money Man* (1987).
Romer, Christina D., and David H. Romer, "Choosing the Federal Reserve Chair: Lessons from History," *Journal of Economic Perspectives* 18 (Winter 2004) 129–162.
Volcker, Paul, *Public Service: The Quiet Crisis* (1988).
Wanniski, Jude, *The Way the World Works* (1977).

CHAPTER 12

Reaganomics

INTRODUCTION

When Ronald Reagan was elected president in 1980 the United States was in the midst of the hardest economic times since the Great Depression. Battered by more than a decade of stagnant growth, rising unemployment, double-digit inflation, and the decline of many of the "smoke-stack" industries that had long been the core of the economy, Americans struggled to understand what had caused the economic decline and how to resolve it. Because this economic decline was preceded by twenty-five years of some of the most spectacular growth and abundance in the nation's history, moreover, the economic malaise of the 1970s was especially perplexing.

The collapse of the Keynesian consensus that had guided economic policy since 1945 added considerably to the nation's travail. Following the apparent success of the 1964 Kennedy tax cut in re-igniting non-inflationary growth, policymakers and economists were confident that Keynesian compensatory fiscal policies gave them the ability to "calibrate" steady economic growth and prosperity. But the simultaneous advent of stagnant economic growth and high rates of inflation, or "stagflation," in the late 1960s undermined the prevailing Keynesian consensus and, as a result, the nation had no clear direction for the formation of economic policy throughout the difficult 1970s.

In 1968 Milton Friedman offered the first serious challenge to the Keynesian consensus when he contended that there were distinct limits to the automatic trade-off between unemployment and inflation expressed in the Phillips Curve. In modern industrial economies, he argued, there was a "natural" level of unemployment and thus any governmental spending to reduce unemployment below that level would only add to the inflationary pressures without significantly adding more jobs. To many observers the subsequent performance of the economy validated Freidman's claims. The "Rational Expectations" school fired another salvo at the Keynesian consensus when it charged that compensatory fiscal policies had become too predictable. In recessionary times, they claimed, businesses anticipated government's countercyclical actions by raising their prices in advance, thereby offsetting the expansionary impact of government action. But of all the challenges to the Keynesian consensus, none garnered more attention and popular support than the Supply Side school of economics that emerged in the mid-1970s. Ronald Reagan eventually aligned his economic policies most closely with this group.

Such supply-side advocates as Congressman Jack Kemp, journalists Jude Wanninski and Irving Kristol, together with economists Arthur B. Laffer and Paul Craig Roberts, took dead aim at two central aspects of the Keynesian paradigm: its exclusively macroeconomic analysis of national economies and its seemingly single-minded concern with stimulating aggregate demand. Sometimes called "neo-classical economics," supply-side analysis sought to refocus economic policy on the microeconomic decisions that inclined individuals to work, to save, and to invest. In contrast to the Keynesian concept of the "balanced-budget multiplier" which held that increased government spending invariably has a net stimulative effect because people pay the higher taxes by reducing both their consumption and their saving, supply-siders argued that beyond a certain point, tax rates act as economic disincentives. Faced with ever increasing tax rates that reduce net income and lower the return on savings and investment, individuals decide to work less in favor of greater leisure, and to save or invest less in favor of greater consumption. According to the supply-side analysis this was the precise cause of the U.S. economic decline that began in the late 1960s. To finance the ever expanding welfare state and the global reach of the U.S. military, taxes had reached such high levels by the late 1960s that economic activity had been stifled. Based on this analysis, the solution to the nation's economic woes seemed simple: cut taxes sharply, reduce government's economic role and individuals will work more productively, save more and invest more.

In 1980 Ronald Reagan made this supply-side prescription for economic revival the central issue in his campaign against Jimmy Carter. Throwing his support behind the Kemp-Roth Tax bill that had been introduced several years earlier, Reagan pledged to cut income taxes by 30 percent over three years, dismantle much of the regulatory state which he claimed needlessly added to production costs, reduce the rate of increase in government spending, and balance the federal budget by 1984. These policies, soon labeled "Reaganomics," had enormous appeal for many Americans in the 1980s because they promised to raise individuals' disposable income by 30 percent and offered what appeared to be a simple solution to the nation's economic difficulties.

Following his election, Reagan moved quickly to implement the main provisions of his plan for economic revival. The centerpiece of Reaganomics was the Economic Recovery Tax Act of 1981, sponsored by Rep. Jack Kemp and Sen. William Roth, which reduced the marginal tax rate by 25 percent over a three-year period and indexed tax brackets to inflation. Over the next several years other components of Reaganomics emerged. Through its deregulation of the telecommunications industry, the dismantling of the Civil Aeronautics Board, and the relaxation of standards for clean air and water, the administration indicated that the government would intervene far less in the private sector than had been true in the previous fifty years. Similarly, in evaluating mergers and acquisitions the Reagan Administration generally ignored the size of the market share a business combination produced, the rule of thumb its predecessors had used in taking anti-trust action. Instead, the Reagan Administration was willing to accept any business combination, regardless of its market share, so long as it could demonstrate that it improved the mix of goods and services in the market place. Finally, throughout his presidency Reagan gave strong support to the restrictive monetary policies of the Fed.

When Reagan's presidency ended in 1988 the economy had improved. Inflation had been substantially tamed, corporate profits surged, and the incomes of most Americans showed real gains. After bottoming out in mid-1982, the economy enjoyed what was at the time the longest peacetime expansion in history, from late 1982 until 1990. Perhaps more importantly, Reaganomics also transformed the national mood. The uncertainty that led many Americans in the 1970s to believe that the nation had entered a new era of limits and slow growth had been replaced by an ebullient self confidence that the nation was once again on the right economic path. But other evidence raised serious questions about the accomplishments of Reaganomics. Despite the claims that supply-side policies would unleash so much economic growth that the federal budget could be balanced by 1984, when Reagan left the White House the deficit had ballooned to the highest peacetime level in U.S. history. Equally troubling was evidence that despite the large tax cuts, neither the rate of personal savings nor of private investment had increased as supply side theory had predicted.

Reaganomics has been controversial since its inception. Historians and economists disagree over what Reagan's economic policies accomplished and how much credit, if any, they deserve for the economic revival of the 1980s and 1990s. Critics then and now argue that it failed to deliver on the promises it made and that by expanding the budget deficit to record proportions actually left the U.S. economy in worse shape than before Reagan took office. Whatever growth was achieved in the 1980s critics charge moreover, was not initiated by the administration's supply-side policies but rather was the result of such long-term supply factors as increased labor and capital, and improved technology. Administration defenders, on the other hand, argue that by significantly reducing the rate of increase in government spending, Reaganomics restored private initiative as the driving force behind American capitalism and was thereby largely responsible for the U.S. economic revival. They also contend that the high deficits were not produced by the tax cuts but by the profligate spending and acknowledge that the tax cuts of the 1980s created unexpected deficits.

Did Reaganomics help or hurt the U.S. economy? In roundly condemning it for what it failed to accomplish, have its critics ignored any positive contributions Reaganomics made to U.S. economic life? Did Reaganomics help restore public confidence, and if so, how important an accomplishment was that? Have defenders of Reaganomics, on the other hand, too easily dismissed many of its unkept promises? Can supporters of Reaganomics demonstrate any real connection between policies enacted in the 1980s and the economic revival of the 1980s and 1990s?

DOCUMENTS

Two years before Ronald Reagan campaigned for the presidency the first serious effort to enact legislation embracing the supply-side philosophy was initiated by an unusual Congressional partnership. Jack Kemp, a former star quarterback for the Buffalo Bills and in the 1970s a Republican congressman representing western New York state, joined with William V. Roth, Jr., a long-serving Republican senator from Delaware and Senate Finance Committee chairman responsible for the individual retirement account that bears his name (Roth IRA), to introduce the Roth–Kemp Tax bill. It proposed to cut the marginal tax rate by 33 percent over a three-year period and to index tax brackets to inflation. Introduced after a decade of stagflation and at a time when many Americans seemed to have lost faith in economic policy, the Roth–Kemp bill evoked strong sentiments. The Roth–Kemp Bill was strongly defended by Arthur Laffer, the economist perhaps most identified publicly with supply-side economics because of his controversial "Laffer Curve." The curve represented in graphic form the relationship between tax rates and revenue yield. Supply siders cited the curve to argue that beyond a certain point, increases in the marginal tax rate, because they discouraged individual economic activity, actually reduced the amount of revenue governments could collect. The Laffer Curve was one of the main pieces of evidence used by advocates of Reaganomics to support their contention that a substantial tax cut was capable of balancing the budget. In Document 12–1 Arthur Laffer vigorously defended his curve and supply-side economics in testimony before the 1978 Joint Economic Hearings on the Roth–Kemp Tax bill.

Many Americans were deeply skeptical about supply-side economics. One of the most powerful dissenting voices was that of economist Walter W. Heller, the chairman of Council of Economic Advisers under John F. Kennedy and the driving force behind the 1964 Kennedy-Johnson tax cut. In Document 12–2, Heller's 1978 testimony before the Joint Economic Committee, the famed economist took strong exception to claims that the Roth–Kemp tax bill was the direct philosophical descendent of the 1964 tax cut. If adopted, Heller warned, the Roth–Kemp bill would dangerously strain U.S. economic capacity and produce huge budget deficits and high inflation.

Document 12–3 is an excerpt from Ronald Reagan's famous speech to a Joint Session of Congress on February 18, 1981. In it the newly inaugurated president detailed his program for economic recovery, soon labeled "Reaganomics." Drawing heavily on supply-side economic theory, the speech also reflected Reagan's characteristic optimism and ebullience, qualities that were especially appealing to many Americans, especially in the economic doldrums of 1981.

12–1. ARTHUR B. LAFFER, PREPARED STATEMENT: THE ROTH–KEMP BILL

In the absence of a "tooth fairy" resources spent by the government are the total tax burden on the economy's productive sector. [Whether] government spending constitutes much needed public services, transfer payments, pure waste, or even worse; these resources must come from the economy's workers and producers. As such, they comprise a major part of the wedge driven between payments made for factor services and payments received by the factors themselves. Taken alone, increases in this wedge per se raise wages paid for factor services, lower wages received by factors and thereby lower the demand for and the supply of productive factor inputs. Output falls.

The Roth–Kemp bill does nothing directly to impact this aggregate wedge. To stop here however would miss not only the essence of the Roth–Kemp bill, but much of the lessons from the history of taxation.

Output depends as much on the constellation of individual factor tax rates as it does on the overall tax burden. If one productive factor is faced with exceptionally burdensome tax rates it will withdraw from the market place. Its departure from the market place will lower output by its production potential and, in turn, reduce the production potential of all other factors with which it is complementary. High productivity and high wages for truck drivers require the existence of trucks for the drivers to drive. If trucks are taxed excessively their numbers will decline as will the wages and productivity of truck drivers. Output will be impacted doubly. In the limiting case when all returns to trucks are confiscated none will exist and wages accruing to truck drivers will be zero. Output, too, will be zero though there [are] no taxes on the earnings of truck drivers. Tax receipts will also be zero.

As a pedagogic device, imagine that we reduce all tax rates in the sample by one-half. The earnings of truck drivers remain untaxed but now earnings accruing to trucks are taxed at 50 percent instead [of] the previous 100 percent. Savers who either abstain from consumption or work harder can now obtain an after tax rate of return by accumulating trucks. There will be more trucks, higher wages, more output and tax receipts will rise. The increase in tax receipts results exclusively from the increase in production and the lowering of tax rates.

The Roth–Kemp bill armed with the experience of similar, but far more extreme, measures carried out by President Kennedy in the early sixties, addresses the current counter productive constellation of individual factor tax rates. By partially redressing the counter productive structure of current tax rates it most likely will lead to a substantial increase in output and, in the course of very few years, will probably reduce the size of government deficits from what they otherwise would have been. Net revenues could well expand even though income tax rates at each and every bracket are reduced. Part of the effect on the deficit, of course, will occur because higher output means less unemployment, less poverty and therefore lower total spending on unemployment benefits and poverty programs. In this sense, the Roth–Kemp bill actually reduces government spending and the overall wedge, albeit indirectly.

People don't work and save to pay taxes. They basically work and save in order to acquire after-tax income. It is the after-tax incentive that drives production, savings and employment.... The Roth–Kemp bill, as the earlier Kennedy tax rate cuts, is precisely a negative income tax surcharge. Its effects will be to lower the progressive nature of income taxes. The Roth–Kemp bill will increase those incentives the most-where the incidence of taxation is currently the highest.

Using the Kennedy income tax rate by way of illustration, when Kennedy came in to office Federal personal income tax rates ranged from 20 percent in the lowest, bracket to 91 percent in the highest bracket. A worker in the lowest bracket who earned $1 on the margin paid 20 cents in taxes and his incentive was 80 cents. In the highest bracket one dollar of marginal earnings yielded 91 cents in taxes and an incentive of 9 cents. By cutting tax rates across the board by about 30 percent the lowest bracket after the Kennedy tax cut was 14 percent and the highest bracket 70 percent. The incentive effects, however, were radically different for the two extremes. The incentive in the lowest bracket was raised from 80 cents on the dollar to 86 cents or an increase of 7½% percent. In the highest bracket where the cut was 23 percent as opposed to 30 percent the incentive was raised from 9 cents on the dollar to 30 cents or an increase in incentive of 233 percent.

The Kennedy era is an excellent example of the type of impact a Roth–Kemp bill could have. While occurring at different times the Kennedy tax program included an across-the-board cut in personal income tax rates. The corporate tax rate was reduced from 52 percent to 48 percent, depreciable lives for legal purposes were shortened and the investment tax credit was instituted....

From 1961 through 1966 real GNP grew on average at a 5.4 percent annual rate. Unemployment rates fell from 6.7 percent in 1961 (5.5 percent in 1962) to 3.8 percent in 1966. Capacity utilization as measured by the Federal Reserve Board rose from 77.3 percent in 1961 to 91.1 percent in 1966. Annual inflation averaged 2.1 percent, 1.6 percent and 1.1 percent for the GNP price deflator, consumer price index and wholesale price index respectively. For some, the behavior of stock prices is perhaps the best indicator of the era's growth. The ratio of the S+P 500 to GNP went from .1104 in 1960 to .1154 in 1967. The low was the 1960 ratio but peaked at .1281 in 1965. Over the 1961–66 period stock prices rose at an annual rate of 5.5 percent and from 1960 through 1967 at an annual rate of 7.8 percent.

During the 1961–1966 period Federal spending rose at a rate lower than GNP growth, 6.2 percent versus 7.5 percent. As a consequence the overall federal wedge fell from 18.75 percent in 1961 to 17.62 percent in 1966. The deficit on the Federal level fell consistently from the $3.1 billion level in 1961 to a surplus of $1.4 billion in 1965 and literal balance in 1966. Defense spending increases during this era were less than non-defense increases.

While the prognosis of dire consequences were the rage in the early 1960's they didn't materialize. In many ways the situation is similar today. Unemployment is high, currently sitting a little above 6.0 percent. Federal spending, or the aggregate wedge, stands about 22.6 percent and S & P stock prices relative to GNP are at .045, close to their all-time low. Inflation is far higher today, running at rates well over 6 percent. The federal deficit in the most recent period is about $45 billion.

While the Federal tax code on the surface appears less distortive today than at the beginning of the Kennedy era other changes have occurred that could even result in more distortions. Additional changes have also occurred that make marginal tax rates relative to average rates even higher now than before. The institution and expansion of State and local taxes, the systematic reduction of real exemptions and credits combined with the highly distortive effects of inflation on the incidence of tax rates on real earnings have resulted in widely divergent marginal tax rates on different factors of production. The effects on incentives of the current structure of taxes are quite conceivably greater today than they were prior to the Kennedy cuts....

In analyzing the Roth–Kemp bill it is important to recognize that the bill is a beginning to a meaningful tax reform, not an end. The need for other legislation does not mitigate the need for Roth–Kemp now. The best cannot be allowed to be the enemy of the good.

The Roth–Kemp bill should also have a good effect on inflation. Inflation is primarily a consequence of too much money chasing too few goods. Excessive money growth has long been recognized as a cause of inflation. It is equally as true, however, that too few goods will also cause prices to rise.

To put this relationship into clear focus, one need only to imagine the following: What would happen to prices in the United States if output were reduced to say, the output level of Luxembourg and the amount of money stayed unchanged? Prices would skyrocket, not fall. Higher unemployment means lower output. As such, high unemployment is, by itself, a cause of high prices.

High prices and rapid inflation increase the prospects for high unemployment. With progressive income tax schedules, high price levels raise tax rates for each level of production. Rapid increases in prices result in firms under-depreciating their plant and equipment and also under-valuing their cost-of-goods sold. Pretax profits are overstated. This results in higher tax rates for businesses for each level of output. The increase in tax rates that result from higher prices and inflation reduce output directly and cause unemployment.

Fortunately, this view has two highly attractive characteristics. First and foremost, this view is supported by a large body of experience. Secondly, the policy implications offer some hope to a world badly afflicted with economic malaise. The Roth–Kemp bill would start the process in the correct direction.

12–2. WALTER W. HELLER, PREPARED STATEMENT: TAX CUTS, THE KEMP–ROTH BILL, AND THE LAFFER CURVE

...[The Roth–Kemp]...bill represents a bold Republican alternative to the now-muted Carter tax proposal. Instead or a single $15 to $20 billion tax cut, it proposes a $98 billion slash via a 33 percent cut in individual income taxes plus a $15.5 billion cut in corporate taxes, both to be phased in over the next three years. Citing the 1964 Kennedy-Johnson tax cut... and a variety of other tax reductions as precedents, the Kemp-Roth supporters claim that their program would unleash such productive energies and generate so much GNP and revenue feedback that it would quickly pay for itself....

As a general observation, it is true that the 1964 tax cut...succeeded, almost exactly as projected, in stimulating the economy. It is also true that the expansion associated with the tax cut and other sources of growth eventually raised income tax revenues above the pre-tax cut level. But in citing the 1964–1965 experience as support for their proposal to cut income taxes by a huge total of $113.5 billion, the Kemp-Roth advocates are misreading: the "verdict of history" in two important respects:

Contrary to their assertion that the Kennedy-Johnson tax cut achieved its economic stimulus and consequent revenue flows "by increasing aggregate supply, by increasing the reward to work and investment," the record is crystal clear that the great bulk of the success of the "great tax cut" that was phased in during 1964–1965 came, as expected, from its stimulus to demand, its release of some $10 billion of consumer purchasing power and another $3 billion or so of corporate funds.

Second, the economic setting for the Kennedy tax cut was sharply different from our setting today. The 1964 cut was injected into an economy characterized by (a) plenty of slack in both labor and product markets, coupled with (b) virtual price stability—inflation averaging about 1.2 percent per year—and stable-to-falling unit labor costs.... So the tax cut was able to activate idle physical and human resources without more than minimal impact on the price level.

As to misrepresentation, I regret to say that on two important counts, the retrospective Kemp-Roth view of the Kennedy-Johnson tax cut is simply wrong:

First, it is said that the Kennedy tax program succeeded for the wrong reasons, that is, virtually ignored the incentive and supply side of the tax equation. On the contrary, President Kennedy's 1963 economic program was a careful blend of measures designed to stimulate both markets and incentives. As he put it in his January 1963 Economic Message: "Only when we have removed the heavy drag our fiscal system now exerts on personal and business purchasing power and on the financial incentives for greater risk taking and personal effort can we expect to restore the high levels of employment and growth we took for granted in the first decade after the war...."

Second, it is asserted that the revenue-generating effect of the 1964 tax cut were not foreseen. Exactly the opposite was true, As President Kennedy said: "The impact of my tax proposals on the budget deficit will be cushioned... most powerfully, in time, by the accelerated growth of taxable income and tax receipts as the economy expands in response to the stimulus of the tax program."

Let me return to the first two points. The core of the 1964 tax cut was a $12 billion-plus boost in after-tax income and profits injected into a slack, non-inflationary economy. At the time, we calculated (a) that actual output was running about $30 to $35 billion below potential output, and (b) that the $12 billion-plus cut—as it was spent and respent and as it energized new investment—would boost consumer spending and business investment by a combined amount of $25 to $30 blllion a year without significantly stepping up inflation.

The true verdict of history is that the tax cut, predominantly operating through the release of purchasing power, worked almost precisely as planned:

The unemployment rate fell from 5.6 percent in January 1964 to 4.5 percent in July 1965 (when escalation in Vietnam began).

Inflation, which had been running at 1.4 percent a year just before the tax cut, crept up to only 1.6 percent by the summer of 1965 (mainly because of food price increases). In other words, the purchasing power punch of the tax cut was converted into higher sales of goods and services, higher output, more jobs, more income, and more tax revenues but not into higher prices.

As a careful quantitative appraisal by Arthur M. Okun (in late 1965) showed, the multiplied impact of the tax cut did indeed raise aggregate demand and GNP by about $30 billion (at annual rates) above what they would have been without the tax cut.

But what about the alternative explanation offered by the Kemp-Roth forces that the 1964 tax cut accomplished all this by quickly expanding supply through its benign effect on incentives?

A great leap forward on the supply side would have to show up in a big jump in trend productivity increases and in the growth of GNP potential. The Kennedy tax program—including both the 1964 tax cuts and the 1962 investment tax stimulants in the form of the investment tax credit and liberalized depreciation guidelines—did in fact improve investment and work incentives and contributed to good, sustained growth in productivity. But no sudden bulge in productivity and potential has been found by any close student of the subject.

Yet it would take precisely such a bulge—many times as big a supply response as the 1964 tax cut produced—to get the kind of results that Senator Roth and Congressman Kemp claim on the basis of estimates by Norman B. Ture. There is no basis in either the 1964 tax cut or any other modern tax cut for Ture's prediction that a Kemp-Roth tax cut would in little more than a year, generate 4 million jobs and boost GNP by $157 billion, and soon boost tax revenues above pre-tax cut levels.

Such findings stretch both credulity and facts. As Rudolph Penner of the American Enterprise Institute puts it, "There can't be two or three or four times more bang in a Kemp-Roth tax cut than we've had with any other."

Given no validated evidence that huge tax cuts would generate huge increases in supply—that is, in productive potential—what would the three-year $98 billion Kemp-Roth tax cut do to budget deficits and inflation? My answer won't surprise you: the huge surge in demand would overwhelm our supply capacity and soon generate soaring deficits and roaring inflation.

Increasingly, supporters of Kemp-Roth are drawing aid and comfort from the "Laffer Curve," a diagram, purporting to show how tax changes can suppress or unleash incentives to work and invest and hence affect tax revenues. Some of my views on the subject are implicit in the foregoing comments. But let me add some thoughts that go beyond the 1964 tax experience:

The Andrew Mellon tax cuts of the 1920s are cited as evidence to support the Laffer thesis. As Jude Wanniski flatly put it (in the "Public Interest," Winter 1978) : "As a result [of the Mellon cuts], the period 1921–1929 was one of phenomenal economic expansion ..." At a time when a relative handful of Americans paid income taxes and Federal spending was less than 5 percent of GNP (in 1929, it was 3 percent), we are asked to believe that Federal income tax reduction powered the growth of GNP from $70 billion in 1921 to $103 billion in 1929...! In short, the whole Laffer thesis and Kemp-Roth initiative rely excessively on post hoc, ergo propter hoc reasoning and on a one-dimensional view of the world. There's more to life than economics, and there's more to economics than taxes.

Apart from such shaky evidence, the alleged miracle effect of tax cuts in generating great surges of work, savings, investment, and productive potential has to face such questions as the following:

Why, in the face of Laffer's assertions, has "Denison's Law" held true through thick and thin for the past 100 years or so? Edward F. Denison of Brookings found that U.S. gross private domestic saving has been virtually invariant year-in and year-out in the face of high taxes, low taxes, or virtually no taxes. Adjusted to a high-employment level, it has held stubbornly at roughly 16 percent of GNP for about a century. And investment has necessarily been stuck right there with it. This simply does not square with the assertion that changes in tax rates touch off big changes in the will to work, save, and invest.

And even if there were something to the Laffer thesis, who is to say that we are in a high enough tax zone to produce those dire effects of higher rates and delightful effects of lower rates that Laffer postulates? Not Dr. William Fellner of AEI: "The U.S. is not yet at high enough tax rates to produce anything like the revenue explosion Laffer is predicting... where the U.S. economy is along such a curve is completely undocumented, unexplored, and unknown."

And how is it that the Kemp-Roth tax cuts could, by increasing take-home pay sharply, lead to such an upsurge in the work ethic when a considerably larger average increase in real take-home pay in the decade of the1960 (mostly as a result of sustained economic growth) produced no similar upsurge? People worked less in response to longer real pay per hour—they took longer vacations and more holidays, and worked shorter work weeks, i.e., they took out part of the proceeds of growth in more leisure. Why wouldn't they do the same with the proceeds of big tax cuts, i.e., respond as much or more to the increase in income (by working less hard to gain a given target income) as they would to the increase in incentives (by working harder as lower taxes made leisure more "expensive")? Or to put it in an economic frame, all the explorations of labor supply, of worker reactions to changes in after-tax income that I know of, cannot even tell us for sure whether the net will to work is increased or decreased by a rise in after-tax income.

The economic slowdown that will confront the Congress and the country at the end of 1978 will leave a lot of red faces around here if Congress simply scuttles the Carter tax cut and does nothing. But if instead Congress adopts the Roth–Kemp super-cut, and thereby guarantees dizzying deficits and sizzling inflation, faces will be even redder.

12–3. RONALD REAGAN, FEBRUARY 18, 1981, WHITE HOUSE REPORT ON THE PROGRAM FOR ECONOMIC RECOVERY

I. A Program for Economic Recovery

Today the Administration is proposing a national recovery plan to reverse the debilitating combination of sustained inflation and economic distress which continues to face the American economy. Were we to stay with existing policies, the results would be readily predictable: a rising government presence in the economy, more inflation, stagnating productivity, and higher unemployment. Indeed, there is reason to fear that if we remain on this course, our economy may suffer even more calamitously.

The program we have developed will break that cycle of negative expectations. It will revitalize economic growth, renew optimism and confidence, and rekindle the Nation's entrepreneurial instincts and creativity.

The benefits to the average American will be striking. Inflation—which is now at double digit rates—will be cut in half by 1986. The American economy will produce 13 million new jobs by 1986, nearly 3 million more than if the status quo in government policy were to prevail. The economy itself should break out of its anemic growth patterns to a much more robust growth trend of 4 to 5 percent a year. These positive results will be accomplished simultaneously with reducing tax burdens, increasing private saving, and raising the living standard of the American family.

The plan is based on sound expenditure, tax, regulatory, and monetary policies. It seeks properly functioning markets, free play of wages and prices, reduced government spending and borrowing, a stable and reliable monetary framework, and reduced government barriers to risk-taking and enterprise. This agenda for the future recognizes that sensible policies which are consistently applied can release the strength of the private sector, improve economic growth, and reduce inflation.

We have forgotten some important lessons in America. High taxes are not the remedy for inflation. Excessively rapid monetary growth cannot lower interest rates. Well-intentioned government regulations do not contribute to economic vitality. In fact, government spending has become so extensive that it contributes to the economic problems it was designed to cure. More government intervention in the economy cannot possibly be a solution to our economic problems.

We must remember a simple truth. The creativity and ambition of the American people are the vital forces of economic growth. The motivation and incentive of our people—to supply new goods and services and earn additional income for their families—are the most precious resources of our Nation's economy. The goal of this Administration is to nurture the strength and vitality of the American people by reducing the burdensome, intrusive role of the Federal Government; by lowering tax rates and cutting spending; and by providing incentives for individuals to work, to save, and to invest. It is our basic belief that only by reducing the growth of government can we increase the growth of the economy.

The U.S. economy faces no insurmountable barriers to sustained growth. It confronts no permanently disabling tradeoffs between inflation and unemployment, between high interest rates and high taxes, or between recession and hyperinflation. We can revive the incentives to work and save. We can restore the willingness to invest in the private capital required to achieve a steadily rising standard of living. Most important, we can regain our faith in the future.

The plan consists of four parts: (1) a substantial reduction in the growth of Federal expenditures; (2) a significant reduction in Federal tax rates; (3) prudent relief of Federal regulatory burdens; and (4) a monetary policy on the part of the independent Federal Reserve System which is consistent with those policies. These four complementary policies form an integrated and comprehensive program....

The leading edge of our program is the comprehensive reduction in the rapid growth of Federal spending.... [O]ur budget restraint is more than "cosmetic" changes in the estimates of Federal expenditures. But we have not adopted a simple-minded "meat ax" approach to budget reductions. Rather, a careful set of guidelines has been used to identify lower-priority programs in virtually every department and agency that can be eliminated, reduced, or postponed.

The second element of the program, which is equally important and urgent, is the reduction in Federal personal income tax rates by 10 percent a year for 3 years in a row. Closely related to this is an incentive to greater investment in production and job creation via faster tax write-offs of new factories and production equipment.

The third key element of our economic expansion program is an ambitious reform of regulations that will reduce the government-imposed barriers to investment, production, and employment. We have suspended for 2 months the unprecedented flood of last-minute rulemaking on the part of the previous Administration. We have eliminated the ineffective and counterproductive wage and price standards of the Council on Wage and Price Stability, and we have taken other steps to eliminate government interference in the marketplace.

The fourth aspect of this comprehensive economic program is a monetary policy to provide the financial environment consistent with a steady return to sustained growth and price stability.... [A] predictable and steady growth in the money supply at more modest levels than often experienced in the past will be a vital contribution to the achievement of the economic goals described in this Report. The planned reduction and subsequent elimination of Federal deficit financing will help the Federal Reserve System perform its important role in achieving economic growth and stability.

The ultimate importance of this program for sustained economic growth will arise not only from the positive effects of the individual components, important as they are. Rather, it will be the dramatic improvement in the underlying economic environment and outlook that will set a new and more positive direction to economic decisions throughout the economy. Protection against inflation and high tax burdens will no longer be an overriding motivation. Once again economic choices—involving working, saving, and investment— will be based primarily on the prospect for real rewards for those productive activities which improve the true economic well-being of our citizens.

II. The Twin Problems of High Inflation and Stagnant Growth

The policies this Administration is putting foward for urgent consideration by the Congress are based on the fact that this Nation now faces its most serious set of economic problems since the 1930s. Inflation has grown from 1 to 1 ½ percent a year in the early 1960s to about 13 percent in the past 2 years; not since World War I have we had 2 years of back-to-back double-digit inflation. At the same time, the rate of economic growth has been slowing and the unemployment rate creeping upward. Productivity growth—the most important single measure of our ability to improve our standard of living—has been declining steadily for more than a decade. In the past 3 years our productivity actually fell.

The most important cause of our economic problems has been the government itself. The Federal Government, through tax, spending, regulatory, and monetary policies, has sacrificed long-term growth and price stability for ephemeral short-term goals. In particular, excessive government spending and overly accommodative monetary policies have combined to give us a climate of continuing inflation. That inflation itself has helped to sap our prospects for growth. In addition, the growing weight of haphazard and inefficient regulation has weakened our productivity growth. High marginal tax rates on business and individuals discourage work, innovation, and the investment necessary to improve productivity and long-run growth. Finally, the resulting stagnant growth contributes further to inflation in a vicious cycle that can only be broken with a plan that attacks broadly on all fronts.

The Role of the Government in Causing Inflation

Surges of inflation are not unusual in history; there were price explosions after both World Wars, as well as smaller outbursts in the 1920s and late 1930s. Therefore, in spite of the role played by food and energy prices in recent inflationary outbursts, it is misleading to concentrate on these transitory factors as fundamental causes of the inflationary bias in the American economy. Even when prices in these markets have been stable, inflation has continued with little relief.

What is unusual about our recent history is the persistence of inflation. Outbursts of high inflation in the last 15 years have not been followed by the customary price stability, but rather by long periods of continued high inflation. This persistence of inflation has crucially affected the way our economy works. People now believe inflation is "here to stay;" they plan accordingly, thereby giving further momentum to inflation. Since there are important long-term relationships between suppliers and customers and between workers and management, long-term contracts, sometimes unwritten, are often based on the view that inflation will persist. This robs the economy of flexibility which might otherwise contribute to reducing inflation.

The Federal Government has greatly contributed to the persistence of high inflation. Overly stimulative fiscal and monetary policies, on average, have financed excessive spending and thus pushed prices upward. Since government accommodation is widely expected to continue, inflation has become embedded in the economy.

When inflationary outbursts occur, policymakers all too often have made a quick turn toward restraint. Such turnabouts, however, have been short-lived and their temporary nature has increasingly been anticipated by savers, investors, and workers. Subsequent declines in employment and growth inevitably call forth stimulative policies before inflation can be brought under control. Such "stop-and-go" policies have only resulted in higher unemployment and lower real growth.

Finally, but equally important, government policies have increased inflation by reducing the potential of our economy to grow—directly through the increasing burdens of taxes and regulations, and indirectly through inflation itself. The result is a vicious circle. Its force can be measured by the statistics of our productivity slowdown, but it is seen more dramatically in the anxiety and concern of our people.

Government Contributes to the Productivity Slowdown

Productivity, popularly measured as output per worker-hour, is an indicator of the efficiency of the economy and consequently of our ability to maintain the rate of improvement in our standard of living. Over the past 15 years, the rate of productivity improvement has slowed, and now virtually halted.

Government policies have been a major contributor to the slowdown but they can be an even more important contributor to the cure. The weight of regulation and the discouragement that results from high marginal tax burdens are key factors, but inflation itself also plays an important role. Reduced capital formation is the most important and visible, but not the only, channel by which this occurs.

By increasing uncertainty about the future, inflation discourages investors from undertaking projects that they would have considered profitable but which, with today's inflationary environment, they consider too risky. Inflation also diverts funds from productive investments into hedging and speculation.

Although recent statistics show that the share of our economy's production devoted to investment is high by historic standards, the magnitude is illusory—an illusion fostered by inflation. Accelerating prices, and the high interest rates and shifting economic policy associated with them, have contributed to an unwillingness to make long-lived investments. As a result, our stock of productive plant and equipment depreciates faster, so that more investment is needed simply to stand still.

The regulatory requirements imposed by the government have likewise served to discourage investment by causing uncertainty in business decision making. In addition, investments to meet regulatory requirements have diverted capital from expanding productive capacity. Some estimates have put regulation-related investment at more than 10 percent of the total level of business investment in recent years. The expanding intrusiveness of the government into the private sector also inhibits innovation and limits the ability of entrepreneurs to produce in the most efficient way.

Inflation, Growth, and the Tax System

The role of the tax system in reducing our past growth, and its potential for improving the prospects for future growth, deserve special attention. By reducing the incentives for investment and innovation, both by individuals and by businesses, the tax system has been a key cause of our stagnation. Restoring the proper incentives will make a major contribution to the long-run vitality of our economy.

The progressivity of the personal income tax system levies rising tax rates on additions to income that merely keep pace with inflation. Households therefore find that even if their gross incomes rise with inflation, their after-tax real income declines. Some households respond to these higher marginal tax burdens by reducing their work effort. "Bracket creep" also encourages taxpayers to seek out "tax shelters," sources of income that offer higher after-tax returns but not necessarily higher before-tax returns than more productive sources, again contributing to economic inefficiency. In the last two decades the Congress has reduced personal income taxes seven times. Nevertheless, average effective tax rates are now about 30 percent higher than their mid-1960's low. Marginal tax rates have climbed in tandem with average rates....

Finally, unless the Congress takes frequent actions to offset the revenue-generating effect of inflation on the progressive personal tax system, the Congress has available for spending unlegislated increases in funds. Inflation in tandem with the tax system thereby impairs the fiscal discipline of the budget process and facilitates higher levels of government spending than would result if the Congress were forced to vote on each tax increase. This offers further encouragement to inflation....

III. Slowing the Growth of Government Spending

The uncontrolled growth of government spending has been a primary cause of the sustained high rate of inflation experienced by the American economy. Perhaps of greater importance, the continued and apparently inexorable expansion of government has contributed to the widespread expectation of persisting—and possibly higher—rates of inflation in the future.

Thus, a central goal of the economic program is to reduce the rate at which government spending increases. In view of the seriousness of the inflationary pressures facing us, the proposed reductions in the Federal budget for the coming fiscal year are the largest ever proposed.

Despite the tendency to refer to "cutting" the budget, it is clear that an expanding population, a growing economy, and a difficult international environment all lead to the need for year-to-year rises in the level of government spending. Thus, the badly needed effort to "cut" the budget really refers to reductions in the amount of increase in spending requested from one year to the next....

It is essential to stress the fundamental principles that guided the development of that program.

First, and most importantly, all members of our society except the truly needy will be asked to contribute to the program for spending control.

Second, we will strengthen our national defense.

Finally, these fundamental principles led to nine specific guidelines that were applied in reducing the budget:

- Preserve "the social safety net."
- Revise entitlements to eliminate unintended benefits.
- Reduce subsidies to middle- and upper-income groups.
- Impose fiscal restraint on other national interest programs.
- Recover costs that can be clearly allocated to users.
- Stretch-out and retarget public sector capital investment programs.
- Reduce overhead and personnel costs of the Federal Government.
- Apply sound economic criteria to subsidy programs.
- Consolidate categorical grant programs into block grants....

IV. Reducing Tax Burdens

An integral part of the comprehensive economic program is a set of tax proposals to improve the after-tax, after-inflation rewards to work, saving, and investment....

Any increase in nominal income moves taxpayers into higher tax brackets, whether the increase is real or merely an adjustment for higher costs of living. As a consequence, taxes rise faster than inflation, raising average tax rates and tax burdens. In fact, every 10 percent increase in income—real or nominal—produces about a 15 percent increase in Federal personal income tax receipts. An average family requiring a $1,500 cost-of-living increase to maintain its standard of living must have $1,900 in wage increases to keep even after taxes.

Individual tax liabilities rose from 9.2 percent of personal income in 1965 to 11.6 percent last year. The average tax burden would have risen far more had not much of the inflation-related tax increases been offset by periodic tax cuts. Marginal tax rates, however, have been allowed to rise sharply for most taxpayers. In 1965, 6 percent of all taxpayers faced marginal rates of 25 percent of more. Today nearly one of every three taxpayers is in at least the 25 percent bracket.

As taxpayers move into higher brackets, incentives to work, save, and invest are reduced since each addition to income yields less after taxes than before. In the late 1960s and the early 1970s, Americans saved between 7 to 9 percent of personal disposable income. In 1979 and 1980, the saving rate was between 5 to 6 percent. The combination of inflation and higher marginal tax rates is undoubtedly a major factor in the lower personal saving rate.

To correct these problems and to improve the after-tax return from work and from saving, the President is asking the Congress to reduce the marginal tax rates for individuals across the board by 10 percent per year for the next 3 years starting July 1, 1981. This would reduce rates in stages from a range of 14 to 70 percent to a range of 10 to 50 percent effective January 1, 1984....

Tax Incentives for Investment

Since the late 1960s the rate of net capital formation (excluding spending mandated to meet environmental standards) has fallen substantially. For the 5 years ending in 1979, increases in real net business fixed capital averaged just over 2 percent of the Nation's real net national product, or one-half the rate for the latter part of the 1960s.

One of the major tasks facing the U.S. economy in the 1980s is to reverse these trends and to promote more capital investment. To combat the decline in productivity growth, to hasten the replacement of energy-inefficient machines and equipment, to comply with government mandates that do not enhance production, we must increase the share of our Nation's resources going to investment. Both improvements in productivity and increases in productive jobs will come from expanded investment....

V. Providing Regulatory Relief

The rapid growth in Federal regulation has retarded economic growth and contributed to inflationary pressures. While there is widespread agreement on the legitimate role of government in protecting the environment, promoting health and safety, safeguarding workers and consumers, and guaranteeing equal opportunity, there is also growing realization that excessive regulation is a very significant factor in our current economic difficulties.

The costs of regulation arise in several ways. First, there are the outlays for the Federal bureaucracy which administers and enforces the regulations. Second, there are the costs to business, nonprofit institutions, and State and local governments of complying with regulations. Finally, there are the longer run and indirect effects of regulation on economic growth and productivity....

During this Administration's first month in office, five major steps have been taken to address the problem of excessive and inefficient regulation. Specifically, we have:

- Established a Task Force on Regulatory Relief chaired by Vice President George Bush

- Abolished the Council on Wage and Price Stability's ineffective program to control wage and price increases
- Postponed the effective dates of pending regulations until the end of March
- Issued an Executive order to strengthen Presidential oversight of the regulatory process
- Accelerated the decontrol of domestic oil....

VI. Controlling Money and Credit

Monetary policy is the responsibility of the Federal Reserve System, an independent agency within the structure of the government. The Administration will do nothing to undermine that independence. At the same time, the success in reducing inflation, increasing real income, and reducing unemployment will depend on effective interaction of monetary policy with other aspects of economic policy.

To achieve the goals of the Administration's economic program, consistent monetary policy must be applied. Thus, it is expected that the rate of money and credit growth will be brought down to levels consistent with noninflationary expansion of the economy.

If monetary policy is too expansive, then inflation during the years ahead will continue to accelerate and the Administration's economic program will be undermined. Inflationary psychology will intensify. Wages, prices, and interest rates will reflect the belief that inflation—and the destructive effects of inflation—will continue.

By contrast, if monetary policy is unduly restrictive, a different set of problems arises, unnecessarily aggravating recession and unemployment. At times in the past, abruptly restrictive policies have prompted excessive reactions toward short-term monetary ease. As a result, frequent policy changes can send confusing signals, and the additional uncertainty undermines long-term investment decisions and economic growth.

With money and credit growth undergoing steady, gradual reduction over a period of years, it will be possible to reduce inflation substantially and permanently. In this regard, the Administration supports the announced objective of the Federal Reserve to continue to seek gradual reduction in the growth of money and credit aggregates during the years ahead. Looking back, it seems clear that if a policy of this kind had been successfully followed in the past, inflation today would be substantially lower and would not appear to be so intractable....

VII. A New Beginning for the Economy

This plan for national recovery represents a substantial break with past policy.

The new policy is based on the premise that the people who make up the economy—workers, managers, savers, investors, buyers, and sellers—do not need the government to make reasoned and intelligent decisions about how best to organize and run their own lives. They continually adapt to best fit the current environment. The most appropriate role for government economic policy is to provide a stable and unfettered environment in which private individuals can confidently plan and make appropriate decisions. The new recovery plan is designed to bring to all aspects of government policy a greater sense of purpose and consistency....

As a result of the policies set forth here, our economy's productive capacity is expected to grow significantly faster than could be achieved with a continuation of past policies. Specifically, real economic activity is projected to recover from the 1980–81 period of weakness and move to a 4 or 5 percent annual growth path through 1986....

In contrast to the inflationary demand-led booms of the 1970s, the most significant growth of economic activity will occur in the supply side of the economy. Not only will a steady expansion in business fixed investment allow our economy to grow without fear of capacity-induced inflation pressures, but it will also increase productivity and reduce the growth of production costs by incorporating new and more high-efficient plants, machinery, and technology into our manufacturing base. The result will be revitalized growth in the real incomes and standards of living of our citizens and significantly reduced inflationary pressures. As our economy responds to a new era of economic policy, unemployment will be significantly reduced.

The Administration's plan for national recovery will take a large step toward improving the international economic environment by repairing domestic conditions. Improving expectations and slowing inflation will enhance the dollar as an international store of value and contribute to greater stability in international financial markets. As interest rates come down and faster U.S. growth contributes to rising world trade, economic expansion in other countries will also accelerate. This Administration will work closely with the other major industrial countries to promote consistency in economic objectives and policies so as to speed a return to noninflationary growth in the world economy. Finally, rising U.S. productivity will enhance our ability to compete with other countries in world markets, easing protectionist pressures at home and thus strengthening our ability to press other countries to reduce their trade barriers and export subsidies. The economic assumptions contained in this message may seem optimistic to some observers. Indeed they do represent a dramatic departure from the trends of recent years—but so do the proposed policies. In fact, if each portion of this comprehensive economic program is put in place—quickly and completely—the economic environment could improve even more rapidly than envisioned in these assumptions.

But, if the program is accepted piecemeal—if only those aspects that are politically palatable are adopted—then this economic policy will be no more than a repeat of what has been tried before. And we already know the results of the stop-and-go policies of the past.

Indeed, if we as a Nation do not take the bold new policy initiatives proposed in this program, we will face a continuation and a worsening of the trends that have developed in the last two decades. We have a rare opportunity to reverse these trends: to stimulate growth, productivity, and employment at the same time that we move toward the elimination of inflation.

ESSAYS

In the first essay, Uwe E. Reinhardt, James Madison Professor of Political Economy at Princeton University, presented a general indictment of Reaganomics. In it Reinhardt argues that the 40th president's economic program was a dismal failure on all counts. Instead of the balanced budget which supply-side theory predicted would follow a large tax cut, Reaganomics produced record deficits. Instead of encouraging Americans to save and invest more, Reinhardt claimed that business formations and the national savings rate were actually lower in the 1980s than during Jimmy Carter's presidency. Finally, despite the supply-side promise to reduce the role of government in the economy, Reinhardt charged that the share of GNP devoted to government actually increased in the Reagan years. "…Whatever Reaganomics may have been," Reinhardt concluded, "it was not supply-side economics."

In Essay 12–2 Martin Feldstein, the George F. Baker Professor of Economics at Harvard University and the chairman of Ronald Reagan's Council of Economic Advisers from 1982 to 1984, offered a temperate defense of supply-side economics. Acknowledging that the predictions of a quick economic transformation made by such "new supply-side extremists" as Jack Kemp and Arthur Laffer were wrong, Feldstein argued nonetheless that Reagan's economic policies helped to validate 'traditional" supply side principles. He maintained that Reaganomics did have a positive effect on the incentive to work and on the GNP, and that the revenue loss caused by the tax cuts was less than its critics predicted.

12–1. UWE E. REINHARDT, "REAGANOMICS, R.I.P."

As the [1987] Congressional Budget Office observes in its latest *Economic and Budget Outlook*, published in January, a verdict on Reaganomics boils down to one of justice between generations. Our fiscal policy since 1981 has allowed people living today to enjoy higher consumption at the expense of those who will be living tomorrow.

It is not clear whether President Reagan actually meant to throw this party or whether things simply got out of hand, as seems to happen so often in his reign. He achieved the presidency through eloquent denunciations of "big-spending government," while more sophisticated Reaganites attacked decades of "Keynesian demand management." By "demand management" they meant federal policies that sought to tease added employment and economic growth out of the economy through added government expenditures, or through transfer programs that channeled income from well-to-do individuals who would have saved and invested it to lower-income groups who spent it on consumption. That fiscal policy, it was argued, treated much too cavalierly the supply side of the economy whence economic growth actually springs.

In 1979, when these "supply-side" complaints were reaching a crescendo, about 62.8 percent of America's total national output was absorbed by personal consumption. About 18 percent went for private investment. About 19 percent was spent by all levels of government to run their operations. Finally, a very tiny sliver –0.1 percent of real GNP— represented the excess of investments by Americans abroad over investments by foreigners made here….

The key element of any supply-side strategy, therefore, must be to reduce the share of GNP going to consumption and government, in order to increase the share set aside for capital formation, a set-aside also known as gross domestic saving. A second element is encouragement of the nation's entrepreneurs to avail themselves of these savings and to invest them wisely.

By the nature of the task, any true supply-side strategy will be multifaceted and complex. Unfortunately, in the late 1970s and in the presidential campaign of 1980, that task was depicted as child's play in the alluring teachings of a new cult led by the economist Arthur Laffer, its affable and verbally facile guru. The cult's message was spread by an equally facile troop of proselytes, some of whom had developed both their verbal skills and the requisite hauteur as writers for the *Wall Street Journal's* supercilious editorial page.

To accomplish the desired shift of resources from consumption into capital formation, the Laffer cult offered a simple and politically appealing strategy: an across-the-board cut in federal income tax rates. The cut in income tax rates would lead to such outbursts of added taxable economic activity that tax revenues would actually increase. American entrepreneurs, enticed by the prospect of higher after-tax rewards, would employ new armies of workers, themselves enticed to work (or to work longer hours) by higher after-tax wages. For capital, the reborn entrepreneurs could count on massive infusions of new savings. These savings would come from American consumers, encouraged by higher after-tax interest rates to cancel planned dinners and vacations for the sake of saving for a better future. (Some members of the cult talked of a doubling of savings as a share of disposable income.) The capital pool would be supplemented by higher business savings made possible by higher after-tax profits.

And, finally, there would be positive government savings at long last. Because the cut in tax rates would raise total federal revenues, the cult assured us, the federal budget would be balanced by 1984. Along with the traditional surpluses of state and local governments, a balanced federal budget would make for a positive contribution to the pool of savings by government as a whole.

Five years later, the sad conclusion of the story can be read right off the many tables included in the *Economic Report of the President*, delivered to Congress in January. Did the pent-up economic energy gush forth as President Reagan and his supply-side cultists had predicted? Did Americans save and invest a larger slice of their GNP? Did legions of hitherto slumbering American entrepreneurs crawl out of the woodwork? And were new jobs created in unprecedented numbers?

Let's begin with a look at the federal budget. Reagan's record can fairly be described as replacing the much-derided policy of "tax and tax, spend and spend" with a policy of "spend even more and just borrow." Combined with an inexorable upward drift in federal spending, the 1981–83 tax cut triggered federal budget deficits that now exceed $200 billion a year. This deficit grew even as the economy recovered from the deep recession of 1982–83. To hope that it will gradually melt away without either substantial tax increases or painful reductions in federal expenditures—spending cuts of a size that Reagan himself has never even dared to propose—is a pipe dream.

It has been suggested that the administration deliberately triggered the large deficits to pressure Congress into overall spending cuts. If that was the strategy, it failed. To be sure, some federal outlays were curbed. There have been cuts in federal support for students and for research, for example, and near-poor working mothers lost their food stamps, welfare, and Medicaid. But for every dollar thus saved, several new dollars were spent. Outlays on national defense almost doubled from $157 billion in 1981 to $273.4 billion in 1986. Interest on the federal debt doubled from $68.7 billion in 1981 to $138 billion in 1986.

Instinctively reluctant to take on any politically powerful group, the president capitulated pre-emptively to the aged, promising rich and poor alike that their path to the federal treasury would remain unobstructed. That promise was kept. Between 1981 and 1986, Social Security benefits increased from $138 billion to almost $200 billion, while outlays on Medicare almost doubled from $41 billion to $74 billion and are slated to exceed $100 billion by 1990.... The president capitulated pre-emptively to the farm lobby as well. In the late 1970s the federal farm price support program absorbed about $4 billion. By 1986 that figure had risen to $26 billion and was heading higher.

A theme vigorously marketed by the president and by his political allies, such as the editors of the *Wall Street Journal*, is that Congress bears sole responsibility for the inexorable upward march of federal expenditures. The implication is that if Congress had only passed the president's budgets, the deficit would have disappeared by now rather than doubling and tripling. Reagan's frequent endorsement of a balanced-budget amendment was meant to underscore this point.

In fact, as the *Wall Street Journal* itself reported in January, Reagan asked Congress to approve expenditures of $4.307 trillion for fiscal years 1982–86 and Congress actually approved $4.342 trillion—only some $35 billion more over five years. In other words, those "big spenders on the Hill" spent less than one percent more than Reagan himself wanted to spend. To be sure, Congress and the president differed over the allocation of the total, as might be expected in a democracy. But the overall budget record demolishes the fantasy of a president valiantly seeking to control a big-spending Congress.

What of that proverbial national pie, the GNP? Did Reaganomics realign the slices in the manner envisaged by the Laffer cult? The remaining cultists like to emphasize growth rates over the period 1982–84 or 1982–85, when the economy climbed out of its steepest postwar recession back to today's more normal plateau. For a more realistic picture that covers the full Reagan era and isn't skewed by the business cycle, let's compare the pie of 1979—the depths of Carterite malaise——with the pie of 1986. The slice of GNP going to personal consumption has *increased* by three percentage points, from 62.8 percent in 1979 to 65.8 percent in 1986. The government's slice also has increased, by 1.3 percentage points, from 19.1 percent to 20.4 percent. The only slice that hasn't increased is the "supply-side" slice—gross private domestic investment.

How could two slices increase, the third not change, and the whole thing still add up to one whole pie? It doesn't. In 1986 total domestic spending by Americans on personal consumption, private investment, and government operations added up to 104 percent of GNP. That is, what we spent on goods and services in 1986 exceeded by four percent(or $150 billion in constant 1982 dollars) what we produced. The extra four percent came from the oft-vilified Japanese, and from the other nations with whom we are running a trade deficit. Between 1979 and 1986, America's "net foreign investments" abroad became "net American borrowing" from abroad. To enable us to have a larger consumption slice, a larger government slice, and about the same investment slice, the foreigners exported us machine tools, Walkmans, BMWs, and fine wines, and we exported to them in return American-made IOUs (bonds and notes) or simply legal titles to American assets (real estate or stock certificates). Unhappily for our children, they will have to redeem these pieces of paper with goods and services some time in the future. Should our children refuse, we shall then redeem the IOUs by simply transferring to foreigners legal title to real assets our kids would otherwise have inherited.

There is nothing wrong with importing capital. Foreign capital helped develop this nation in the last century, and it can help us now. If we had avoided huge government deficits and increased our domestic investment beyond the traditional 18 percent, our children would have plenty of extra money to service the foreign debt and to be better off themselves. But we used the foreign capital to increase our consumption and government spending, not our investment. From 1981 to 1986 savings as a share of disposable personal income fell from 7.5 percent to 3.9 percent. In the last half of 1986, it stood at an annual rate of 2.8 percent— barely a third of the rate at the beginning of the "supply-side" revolution. Foreigners have been making up the difference....

Meanwhile, what of America's entrepreneurs? Has our festival inspired them to new achievements? Reliable data on the penchant for entrepreneurship are not easily had. The president's report to Congress does contain a table on business formation and failures, It shows that between 1980 and 1986 there were actually fewer new business incorporations each year than in 1976–1980. Business failures, on the other hand, increased each year during the 1980s. In the late 1970s the annual rate of failure decreased. The Index of Net Business Formation (1967 = 100) ranged in the high 130s during the late 1970s; it stood at only 121 in 1984–85.

In 1980 the civilian unemployment rate stood at 7.1 percent. In 1986 it stood at 7.0 percent. Now, it has been argued that the unemployment rate is too negative a concept, because it obscures the astounding number of new jobs created during the Reagan era. Was the number really astounding? According to the president's report, total civilian employment stood at 100.4 million in 1981 and at 109.6 million in 1986, a gain of 9.2 percent or 9.2 million jobs. During the preceding five-year period total civilian employment grew from 88.8 million to 100.4 million—a gain of 13 percent, or 11.6 million new jobs.

And finally, what about the size of the pie? Did it grow more rapidly in the 1980s than in the late 1970s? According to the president's report, real GNP in constant 1982 dollars was $2.9586 trillion in 1977 and $3.2438 trillion in 1981. That represents average annual compound growth of 2.4 percent. By 1986 real GNP stood at $3.6765 trillion, which represents average annual compound growth of 2.5 percent over the Reagan years. During 1986 real GNP grew by 2.2 percent, and, in the words of the President's Council of Economic Advisers, "strong growth of real consumption spending [rather than capital formation] was the driving force behind demand growth for most of 1986." Once again, could this be supply-side economics?

Not all facets of the president's economic program have been equally dubious. Inflation has been soundly licked, thanks in part to President Carter's wisdom in appointing Paul Volcker as chairman of the Federal Reserve Board, but also thanks to Reagan's steadfast support of brother Volcker. President Reagan continued the program of deregulation already set in motion by his predecessor in energy and transportation, and he extended it to the financial markets. And Reagan has given strong rhetorical support to the principles of free trade, although the actual share of our imports that are affected by some sort of trade restriction has doubled from 1980 to 1986, from 12 percent to 22 percent.

The peculiar free-lunch populism sold to the nation as "supply-side economics" may be summarized in the following flaky propositions: (1) cutting tax rates increases (government) revenue; (2) inflation can be reduced without a transitional period of unemployment; (3) government expenditures can be greatly reduced without sacrifice of anything by anyone except bureaucrats and welfare queens. The Republic won't collapse because our leaders sold the public on these transparently false propositions—and possibly even believed them themselves. We will simply be left a little poorer in the long run than we could have been under less myopic stewardship. For, whatever Reaganomics may have been, it was not supply-side economics. It was politics as usual, practiced to please or at least not to offend powerful political constituencies, and pushed just one step further in the direction of irresponsibility.

12–2. MARTIN FELDSTEIN, "SUPPLY-SIDE ECONOMICS: OLD TRUTHS AND NEW CLAIMS"

Experience has shown that the notion "supply-side economics" is a malleable one, easily misused by its supporters, maligned by its opponents, and misinterpreted by the public at large. Perhaps now, five years after supply-side economics became a slogan for a changing economic policy, it is possible to assess what supply-side policy really means and how the policies adopted under that banner have fared.

The term, supply-side economics originated as a way of describing an alternative to the demand side emphasis of Keynesian economics. The essence of Keynesian analysis is its conclusion that the level of national income and employment depend on the level of aggregate demand, and that easy money and expanded budget deficits, by stimulating demand, can increase output and employment. Although this may have been an appropriate emphasis during the depression years of the 1930's when Keynes developed his theory, by the 1960's and 1970's it was clear to most economists that it was wrong to focus exclusively on demand and to ignore the factors that increase the potential supply of output—capital accumulation, technical progress, improvements in the quality of the labor force, freedom from regulatory interference, and increases in personal incentives. Many of us also concluded that the persistently high level of measured unemployment did not reflect inadequate demand but was due to government policies like unemployment insurance, welfare restrictions, and the minimum wage that reduced the effective supply of labor.

In all of these ways, many of us were supply siders before we ever heard the term supply-side economics. Indeed, much of our supply-side economics was a return to basic ideas about creating capacity and removing government impediments to individual initiative that were central in Adam Smith's *Wealth of Nations* and in the writings of the classical economists of the nineteenth century. The experience of the 1930's had temporarily made it easy to forget the importance of the supply factors, but by the 1970's they were returning to the mainstream of economics....

It is important in any discussion of supply-side economics to distinguish the traditional supply-side emphasis that characterized most economic policy analysis during the past 200 years from the new supply-side rhetoric that came to the fore as the decade began.

I. The Shift in Policy

Economic policy took a few hesitating steps in the traditional supply-side direction in the late 1970's with deregulation in the transportation industry, a significant reduction in the tax on capital gains, and the partial taxation of unemployment compensation. But it was only in 1981 that Congress enacted the major tax bill that has become the centerpiece of supply-side economics.

The emphasis throughout that tax legislation was on changing marginal tax rates to strengthen incentives for work, saving, investment and risk taking. For individual taxpayers, the basic features of the Economic Recovery Tax Act of 1981 were a 25 percent across-the-board reduction in personal tax rates, an extra tax reduction for two-earner families, an increased exemption for long-term capital gains, and the creation of universal Individual Retirement Accounts that effectively permit the majority of American employees to save as much as they want out of pretax income and pay tax on those savings on a consumption tax basis. Personal tax brackets were also indexed to prevent inflation from raising real tax burdens (although this indexing was only scheduled to begin in 1985). For businesses, the 1981 legislation contained accelerated depreciation schedules that significantly reduced the cost of investment in plant and equipment, and an increased tax credit for research and development.

The Reagan Administration also began an unprecedented reversal of the share of *GNP* absorbed by government nondefense spending. Those outlays declined from 15.1 percent of *GNP* in fiscal year 1980 to 14.1 percent of *GNP* in FY 1984. When the Social Security and Medicare outlays are excluded, this spending declined from 9.3 percent of *GNP* in 1980 to 7.4 percent in 1984. These spending reductions were significant not only because they released resources that could be used to finance tax rate reductions, but also because they were often achieved by shrinking programs that in themselves had adverse incentive effects.

President Reagan also provided strong support for the anti-inflationary Federal Reserve policies. The sharp fall in inflation between 1980 and 1982 significantly reduced the effective tax rates on the return to corporate capital, increasing the real after-tax return to savers as well as reducing the uncertainty of saving and investment.

II. Excessive Claims

These policies were a major step in the direction recommended by supply-side economists of both the new and old varieties. What distinguished the new supply siders from the traditional supply siders as the1980's began was not the policies they advocated, but the claims that they made for those policies.

The traditional supply siders (although I dislike labels, I consider myself one of that group) were content to claim that the pursuit of such tax, spending, and monetary policies would, over the long run, lead to increased real incomes and a higher standard of living. We recognized that the key to this process was increased saving and investment and knew that that would take a long time to have a noticeable effect.

The "new" supply siders were much more extravagant in their claims. They projected rapid growth, dramatic increases in tax revenue, a sharp rise in saving, and a relatively painless reduction in inflation. The height of supply-side hyperbole was the "Laffer curve" proposition that the tax cut would actually increase tax revenue because it would unleash an enormously depressed supply of effort. Another remarkable proposition was the claim that even if the tax cuts did lead to an increased budget deficit, that would not reduce the funds available for investment in plant and equipment because tax changes would raise the saving rate by enough to finance the increased deficit. It was also claimed that the rapid rise in real output that would result from the increased incentive to work would slow the rate of inflation without the need for a rise in unemployment because the increased supply of goods and services could absorb the rising nominal demand.

Probably no single individual made all of those claims—at least not at the same time. And anyone who feels the need to defend his name can argue that the administration's 1981 economic program was not enacted exactly as proposed. Nevertheless, I have no doubt that the loose talk of the supply-side extremists gave fundamentally good policies a bad name and led to quantitative mistakes that not only contributed to subsequent budget deficits, but also made it more difficult to modify policy when those deficits became apparent.

III. Growth and Recovery

To assess the claims of the new supply siders, it is useful to compare the actual growth of real GNP between 1981 and 1985 with the growth that the supply siders initially projected. The record shows that real GNP increased 10.9 percent between 1981 and 1985, only slightly more than half of the 19.1 percent predicted in the Reagan Administration's original economic plan.

This 45 percent shortfall in economic growth cannot be blamed, as some of the new supply siders would now do, on a failure of the Federal Reserve to supply as much money and credit as the plan originally envisioned. The 1981 *Program for Economic Recovery* assumed that "the growth rates of money and credit are gradually reduced from the 1980 levels to one-half those levels by 1986"... while the actual money growth rates have hardly declined at all since 1981.

Although the original forecast of nearly 5 percent a year real growth from 1981 to 1985 was improbable on the basis of both historic experience and economic theory, the shortfall was clearly exacerbated by the recession that depressed GNP from the third quarter of 1981 until the final quarter of 1982. The new supply siders were naively optimistic when they claimed that the double digit inflation of 1980 and 1981 could be halved in a few years without any increase in unemployment simply by increasing output enough through improved incentives to absorb the excess demand.

Most of the new supply siders have now conveniently forgotten the substantial discrepancy between their growth forecast and the subsequent experience. But some of the supply-side extremists even claim that the recovery was delayed because individuals preferred to "consume leisure" and were waiting to return to work until the final stage of the tax rate reduction had occurred. Anyone who believes that that explains the 10.7 percent unemployment in December 1982 has not studied the data on the composition and timing of unemployment or on the relation between the spending upturn and subsequent reductions in unemployment. And those who wish to believe that the cut in the tax rate stimulated a major increase in the number of people wanting to work will be disappointed by the data on labor force participation rates.

During the first four quarters of the recovery, real *GNP* increased at about the average pace of the previous recoveries. In the second year of the recovery, the rise in *GNP* exceeded the past norm. But now, eleven quarters after the recovery began, the cumulative rise in *GNP* has settled back to the middle of the range of past recoveries.

How much of the recovery has been due to the stimulus to increased supply that was provided by the new policies? I have already commented on the lack of evidence of an induced increase in the number of people wanting to work. But it would be equally wrong to view the recovery as the result of the fiscal stimulus to demand as some traditional Keynesians have done....

In fact, the rise in nominal *GNP* since 1982 can be more than fully explained by the traditional relationship to the lagged increase in money (M1). The division of the nominal *GNP* increase between *GNP* and inflation was, however, more favorable than would have been expected on the basis of past experience; somewhere around 2 percent of the 15 percent rise in real *GNP*, since the recovery began cannot be explained by the increase of nominal *GNP* and the past pattern of inflation and might therefore be attributed to supply side factors. However, the rise in the exchange rate fully explains the relatively favorable inflation experience and leaves no unexplained rise in real *GNP*. Of course, it might be argued that supply-side factors contributed to the dollar's rise. Only further research will resolve whether supply side influences have contributed to the rise in real *GNP* since 1981.

Let me emphasize that, to a traditional supply sider like me, the positive but apparently modest supply-side effect is neither surprising nor disappointing. Although we would expect some increase in work effort from the reduction in the highest marginal tax rates, past evidence all points to relatively small changes. The favorable effects of improved incentives for saving and investment can only be expected after a much longer period of time.

IV. Tax Revenue

Perhaps the most dramatic claim of some of the new supply siders was that an across-the-board reduction in tax rates would be self-financing within a few years because of the increased output that results from the enhanced after-tax pay. It is, of course, very difficult to disentangle the effects of the tax legislation from other things that influenced tax revenue. But a very careful study by Lawrence Lindsey... indicates that in 1982 the response of taxpayers did offset about one-third of the effect of the tax cut on federal receipts.

Lindsey reports that about 65 percent of the induced offsetting rise in tax revenue reflects higher pretax wages, salaries, and business profits than would have been anticipated without the change in tax rates and tax rules, 25 percent reflects an increase in realized capital gains, and the remaining 10 percent is due to reductions in various itemized deductions. These induced offsetting effects are very small among taxpayers with incomes below $20,000. Only among tax-payers whose initial marginal tax rates exceeded 50 percent was there evidence that the rate reduction did not reduce federal revenue at all.

Only time will tell whether this first-year tax response overstates the long-term effect (because it reflects a shift in the timing of income receipts and deductions rather than a more fundamental change in behavior) or understates the long-term effect (because it takes time for taxpayers to adjust their behavior to new tax rules). But the effect for 1982 is clearly an economically significant one. Although the increase in taxable income fell far short of the claims made by the overoptimistic new supply siders and may have been due in large part to a restructuring of income (for example, from fringe benefits to cash) rather than an increase in work effort, the rise in taxable income is a reminder that the traditional revenue estimation method that ignores the behavioral response to tax changes can be very misleading....

V. Conclusion

The experience since 1981 has not been kind to the claims of the new supply-side extremists that an across-the-board reduction in tax rates would spur unprecedented growth, reduce inflation painlessly, increase tax revenue, and stimulate a spectacular rise in personal saving. Each of those predictions has proven to be wrong.

But it would be unfortunate if this gave a bad reputation to the traditional supply-side verities that the evolution of a nation's real income depends on its accumulation of physical and intellectual capital and on the quality and efforts of its workforce. Moreover, nothing about the experience since 1981 would cause us to doubt the time-honored conclusion of economists that tax rules influence economic behavior and that high marginal tax rates reduce incentives.

Indeed, the evidence suggests that the reduction in tax rates did have a favorable effect on work incentives and on real *GNP,* and that the resulting loss of tax revenue was significantly less than the traditional revenue estimates would imply. Traditional supply-side considerations are undoubtedly important in the design of economic policies in general and of tax policies in, particular. But the miraculous effects anticipated by some of the new supply-side enthusiasts were, alas, without substance.

SUGGESTIONS FOR FURTHER READING

Martin Anderson, *Revolution: The Reagan Legacy* (1991)
——, *The Ten Causes of the Reagan Boom, 1982–1997* (1998)
Bruce R. Bartlett, *Reaganomics: Supply Side Economics in Action* (1981)
Robert L. Bartley, *Seven Fat Years* (1992)
Lou Cannon, *President Reagan: The Role of a Lifetime* (1991)
George Gilder, *Wealth and Poverty* (1981)
Godfrey Hodgson, *The World Turned Right Side Up: A History of the Conservative Ascendancy in America* (1996)
Jack Kemp, *An American Renaissance: A Strategy for the 1980s* (1979)
Arthur B. Laffer, *Supply Side Economics: Financial Decision-Making for the 80s* (1983)
Robert Lekachman, *Greed is Not Enough: Reaganomics* (1982)
Alfred L. Malabre, Jr., *Beyond Our Means: How America's Long Years of Debt, Deficits and Reckless Borrowing Now Threaten to Overwhelm Us* (1987)
William A. Niskanen, *Reaganomics: An Insider's Account of the Policies and the People* (1988)
Ronald Reagan, *An American Life* (1991)
Donald T. Regan, *For the Record: From Wall Street to Washington* (1988)

Stephen Rousseas, *Political Economy of Reaganomics: A Critique* (1982)
Paul Craig Roberts, *The Supply-Side Revolution: An Insider's Account of Policymaking in Washington,* (1984)
Herbert Stein, *Presidential Economics* (1984)
David A. Stockman, *The Triumph of Politics: How the Reagan Revolution Failed* (1986)
Jude Wanniski, *The Way the World Works* (1989)

CHAPTER 13

Clintonomics and Beyond

INTRODUCTION

As President Bill Clinton assumed office, two issues dominated the economic agenda: recovery from the recession of 1990–1991, and federal budget deficits. The economy he inherited from his predecessor, George H. W. Bush, was going through a painfully slow and nearly jobless recovery. The Bush presidency had been a strange interlude in economic terms; large and growing deficits marked its four years. The cyclical component of the deficit grew as the economy weakened. But the structural component of the deficit was significant too. The structural deficit is that part of the deficit that would persist even if the economy were at full employment. The substantial tax cuts of the early Reagan years had brought on several years of large structural deficits. Beyond this the Bush economy exhibited a curious anomaly: in each of its first fifteen quarters, real GDP growth was below the postwar average of 3–3½ percent. Only in the sixteenth and final quarter of the Bush administration, after the outcome of the election had been decided, was growth above average.

The dilemma facing the Clinton transition team was the choice between a policy course of stimulation to shore up the weak recovery and a policy aimed at deficit reduction. By inauguration day, the team of advisers Clinton had assembled convinced him to pursue the latter course. Clinton announced his intentions in his first State of the Union address under the watchful gaze of Fed chair Alan Greenspan. In what is not a customary display for the person heading an institution known to prize its independence, Greenspan was seated next to the First Lady in the gallery of the Capitol. In his address Clinton stated that his administration would present its plan for deficit reduction in its first budget submission.

The rationale for the Clinton approach does have neo-Keynesian roots. James Tobin was one of the main proponents of a policy mix of tight fiscal and easy monetary policy. Tight fiscal policy meant tax laws that would produce a balanced budget (or perhaps a surplus) at high or full employment. Cyclical deficits were to be tolerated as the natural consequence of the automatic stabilizers that served to stimulate the economy during recessions. Structural deficits, those that persist even at full employment, were not to be tolerated because they would put government in competition with private borrowers and drive up interest rates. If government spending were excessive to the point of threatening inflation, monetary policy would have to be dedicated to keeping inflation at bay, putting added upward pressure on interest rates and discouraging spending in interest rate sensitive sectors of the economy. This is the policy mix that Tobin claimed Reaganomics had produced: easy fiscal and tight monetary policy. The Clinton plan was aimed at the policy mix Tobin had long crusaded for, and so fit comfortably within the Keynesian tradition. From the earliest days of the

Clinton administration, Fed chair Greenspan made it clear that monetary policy could be eased if serious deficit reduction were attempted.

Any realistic hope for deficit reduction requires two politically risky actions: spending cuts and tax increases. The Deficit Reduction Act of 1993 included two new, higher tax brackets (supposed to affect only the top 2 percent of taxpayers), an increase in the gasoline tax, an increase in the portion of Social Security benefits subject to taxes, and reduced growth in government expenditures. Since the recovery was still in a delicate state, many of the provisions called for in the Act would only come into force gradually over time. The opposition of Congressional Republicans was immediate and complete. The final denouement came on the evening of August 6, 1993 when the Senate voted on the Clinton plan. The plan had survived an earlier vote in the House of Representatives by a margin of one vote. The Senate vote on the bill resulted in a 50–50 tie. Passage was assured when Vice President Al Gore cast the deciding vote in favor of the bill. Not one Republican in either house voted for the bill. Outside the senate chamber, Republican Senators lined up before the television cameras predicting economic catastrophe as a result of the vote.

During the 1990–1991 recession and in its aftermath, monetary policy was very expansionary. In 1992, in an unusual move, the Fed eliminated the reserve requirement on personal time deposits (certificates of deposits held by individuals). Yet monetary ease and low interest rates did little to spur private spending. Improvement came in 1993. By 1994 the Fed was concerned with the rapid pace of economic growth. The Fed turned to restraint, making 1994 a year of higher interest rates and weak stock market performance. By September of 1994 the unemployment rate had slipped below 6 percent, widely accepted as the non-accelerating inflation rate of unemployment (NAIRU); by December it stood at 5.5 percent. Ordinarily, the Fed would have tightened further. At about this time, Mr. Greenspan claims to have come to the belief that the accepted relationship between inflation and unemployment had been altered by improved productivity gains which allowed firms to absorp cost increases without resorting to price increases. Greenspan's suspicion was that years of investment in high technology by business, especially information technology, had finally begun to pay off. With productivity growth acting as a brake on inflation and lowering the NAIRU, the Fed no longer felt the need to take early action to choke off expansions before they became inflationary. The results were astounding.

During the four years of the presidency of George H. W. Bush, there was no net job creation. In the eight years that followed, 22 million jobs were created. The unemployment rate averaged about 4 percent for the year in 2000, having dipped as low as 3.8 percent in April. Inflation remained largely in check, falling below 2 percent in two consecutive years in the late '90s. Productivity growth, which had slowed down in the early 1970s, increased. Between 1995 and 2000, output per worker hour improved by over 15 percent. By the late '90s there was evidence that the post-1973 wage stagnation had come to an end. The federal budget went from a deficit of nearly $300 billion in 1992 to virtual balance in 1997. By 2000 the Federal budget had a surplus of over $235 billion. The poverty rate by 2000 was 11.3 percent, the lowest in nearly thirty years. By decade's end the welfare caseload was down, as was the crime rate.

The Clinton administration claimed the credit for the boom of the '90s, while its critics looked elsewhere for an explanation. Many thought Alan Greenspan and the Fed to be responsible. Others looked to the policies of previous administrations for setting the stage for the '90s expansion.

One noteworthy policy initiative of the 1990s on the international side was Congressional approval of the North American Free Trade Agreement (NAFTA) in 1993. By the early 1990s the international competitive position of the United States had been challenged by Japan and other countries on the Pacific Rim. The European Union, though still in its formative stages, presented yet another potentially significant challenge. NAFTA called for Canada, Mexico and the United States to become a free trade zone by eliminating many trade restrictions and scheduling many others to be phased out. Many environmental and labor concerns were raised both before and after ratification. While trade among the three countries has more than doubled since NAFTA was passed, the same can be said for trade between the three signatories and many other non-NAFTA countries. The impact of NAFTA has proven difficult to measure. There have been calls to expand the free trade zone to include Central America. A Western Hemisphere free trade zone has also been proposed.

In 2001 the administration of George W. Bush came into office intent on the passage of large tax cuts. The tax cuts enacted may have provided a mild stimulus in combating the recession of 2001, which lasted from March to November. However, job creation was weak through 2004. This time period also witnessed the resumption of massive Federal budget deficits. By fiscal year 2002 large deficits had returned, exceeding $400 billion by 2004. Some portion of the reported deficits is attributable to the cyclical downturn, but the size of the budget shortfalls signaled the return of large structural deficits.

The major questions raised by the economic experience of the 1990s concern the policies pursued by the Clinton administration. Was the deficit reduction program responsible for the long uninterrupted expansion? Was the Federal Reserve's monetary policy of equal importance? Was the best policy mix used? Why did productivity growth unexpectedly change? Is there any validity to the claim that the foundation for the success of the '90s was put in place by the Reagan and Bush administrations that preceded the boom? To what extent was the '90s prosperity serendipitous? What role did investment in information technology play? Why might years of such investment yield a payoff with a lag of several years? With respect to NAFTA, how can its impact be assessed? Have American consumers benefited at the expense of American workers? Does a NAFTA-style agreement work best when all participating nations have roughly similar educational, workplace and environmental standards? How did the administration of George W. Bush decide to use the Federal budget surplus? What else could have been done with it? Why was job creation so weak during the recovery from the recession? What in the design of the tax cut could have been changed to promote more rapid job creation? Does the fact that much of the debt created to cover Federal budget deficits is held by foreigners have any implications for continued improvements in the American standard of living?

DOCUMENTS

Document 13–1 is excerpts from Bill's Clinton's first state of the union address, delivered on February 17, 1993. In it he unveils his deficit reduction program. Document 13–2 is excerpted from the North American Free Trade Agreement and includes its preamble, objectives and some environmental stipulations. Document 13–3 is the transmittal letter written by President Clinton to the Congress that accompanied his 1999 Economic Report of the President. He reviews the extraordinary performance of the economy during the 1990s, describing it as 'the longest peacetime economic expansion" in American history. He states that in 1993 the "new economic strategy was rooted first and foremost in fiscal discipline." Clearly he attributes the expansion to his deficit reduction program. Document 13- 4 is the remarks of President George W. Bush made on the occasion of his signing the Economic Growth and Tax Relief Reconciliation Act of 2001 on June 7, 2001. In those remarks the focus is on tax relief; no mention is made of how the Act might affect future budgetary balance.

13–1. WILLIAM J. CLINTON, FEBRUARY 17, 1993, STATE OF THE UNION ADDRESS

Address by the President to the Joint Session of Congress, The Capitol, Mr. President, Mr. Speaker, members of the House and the Senate, distinguished Americans here as visitors in this Chamber, as am I. It is nice to have a fresh excuse for giving a long speech.

When Presidents speak to Congress and the nation from this podium, typically, they comment on the full range and challenges and opportunities that face the United States. But this is not an ordinary time, and for all the many tasks that require our attention, I believe tonight one calls on us to focus, to unite, and to act. And that is our economy. For more than anything else, our task tonight as Americans is to make our economy thrive again.

Let me begin by saying that it has been too long, at least three decades, since a President has come and challenged Americans to join him on a great national journey, not merely to consume the bounty of today, but to invest for a much greater one tomorrow....

Like individuals, nations must ultimately decide how they wish to conduct themselves, how they wish to be thought of by those with whom they live, and later, how they wish to be judged by history. Like every individual, man and woman, nations must decide whether they are prepared to rise to the occasions history presents them.

We have always been a people of youthful energy and daring spirit. And at this historic moment, as communism has fallen, as freedom is spreading around the world, as a global economy is taking shape before our eyes, Americans have called for change. And now it is up to those of us in this room to deliver for them....

The conditions which brought us as a nation to this point are well-known: Two decades of low productivity growth, and stagnant wages; persistent unemployment and underemployment; years of huge government deficits and declining investment in our future; exploding health care costs and lack of coverage for millions of Americans; legions of poor children; education and job training opportunities inadequate to the demands of this tough, global economy. For too long we have drifted without a strong sense of purpose or responsibility or community.

And our political system so often has seemed paralyzed by special interest groups, by partisan bickering and by the sheer complexity of our problems. I believe we can do better because we remain the greatest nation on Earth, the world's strongest economy, the world's only military superpower. If we have the vision, the will and the heart to make the changes we must, we can still enter the 21st century with possibilities our parents could not even have imagined, and enter it having secured the American Dream for ourselves and for future generations.

I well remember 12 years ago President Reagan stood at this very podium and told you and the American people that if our national debt were stacked in thousand-dollar bills the stack would reach 67 miles into space. Well, today that stack would reach 267 miles. I tell you this not to assign blame for this problem. There is plenty of blame to go around in both branches of the government and both parties. The time has come for the blame to end. I did not seek this office to place blame. I come here tonight to accept responsibility and I want you to accept responsibility with me. And if we do right by this country, I do not care who gets the credit for it.

The plan I offer you has four fundamental components. First, it shifts our emphasis in public and private spending from consumption to investment—initially by jump-starting the economy in the short-term, and investing in our people, their jobs, and their incomes over the long run. Second, it changes the rhetoric of the past into the actions of the present by honoring work and families in every part of our public decision-making. Third, it substantially reduces the federal deficit honestly and credibly by using in the beginning the most conservative estimates of government revenues, not, as the Executive Branch has done so often in the past, using the most optimistic ones.

And finally, it seeks to earn the trust of the American people by paying for these plans first with cuts in government waste and efficiency; second, with cuts, not gimmicks, in government spending; and by fairness for a change in the way additional burdens are borne.

Tonight I want to talk with you about what government can do because I believe government must do more. But let me say first that the real engine of economic growth in this country is the private sector. And second, that each of us must be an engine of growth and change. The truth is that as government creates more opportunity in this new and different time, we must also demand more responsibility in turn.

Our immediate priority must be to create jobs, create jobs now. Some people say, well, we're in a recovery and we don't have to do that. Well, we all hope we're in a recovery, but we're sure not creating new jobs. And there's no recovery worth its salt that doesn't put the American people back to work.

To create jobs and guarantee a strong recovery, I call on Congress to enact an immediate package of jobs investments of over $30 billion to put people to work now, to create a half a million jobs. Jobs to rebuild our highways and airports, to renovate housing, to bring new life to rural communities and spread hope and opportunity among our nation's youth. Especially, I want to emphasize after the events of last year in Los Angeles and the countless stories of despair in our cities and in our poor rural communities, this proposal will create almost 700,000 new summer jobs for displaced, unemployed young people alone this summer.

And tonight, I invite America's business leaders to join us in this effort so that together we can provide over one million summer jobs in cities and poor rural areas for our young people.

Second, our plan looks beyond today's business cycle because our aspirations extend into the next century. The heart of this plan deals with the long-term. It is an investment program designed to increase public and private investment in areas critical to our economic future. And it has a deficit reduction program that will increase the savings available for the private sector to invest, will lower interest rates, will decrease the percentage of the federal budget claimed by interest payments, and decrease the risk of financial market disruptions that could adversely affect our economy.

Over the long run, all this will bring us a higher rate of economic growth, improved productivity, more high-quality jobs, and an improved economic competitive position in the world. In order to accomplish both increased investment and deficit reduction, something no American government has ever been called upon to do at the same time before, spending must be cut and taxes must raised.

The spending cuts I recommend were carefully thought through in a way to minimize any adverse economic impact, to capture the peace dividend for investment purposes, and to switch the balance in the budget from consumption to more investment. The tax increases and the spending cuts were both designed to assure that the cost of this historic program to face and deal with our problems will be borne by those who could readily afford it the most. Our plan is designed, furthermore, and perhaps in some ways most importantly, to improve the health of American business through lower interest rates, more incentives to invest, and better trained workers.

Because small business has created such a high percentage of all the new jobs in our nation over the last 10 or 15 years, our plan includes the boldest targeted incentives for small business in history. We propose a permanent investment tax credit for the smallest firms in this country, with revenues of under $5 million. That's about 90 percent of the firms in America employing about 40 percent of the work force, but creating a big majority of the net new jobs for more than a decade.

And we propose new rewards for entrepreneurs who take new risks. We propose to give small business access to all the new technologies of our time. And we propose to attack this credit crunch which has denied small business the credit they need to flourish and prosper....

Standing as we are on the edge of a new century, we know that economic growth depends as never before on opening up new markets overseas and expanding the volume of world trade. And so, we will insist on fair trade rules in international markets as a part of a national economic strategy to expand trade, including the successful completion of the latest round of world trade talks and the successful completion of a North American Free Trade Agreement, with appropriate safeguards for our workers and for the environment.

At the same time—and I say this to you in both parties and across America tonight, all the people who are listening—it is not enough to pass a budget or even to have a trade agreement. The world is changing so fast that we must have aggressive, targeted attempts to create the high-wage jobs of the future. That's what all our competitors are doing. We must give special attention to those critical industries that are going to explode in the 21st century, but that are in trouble in America today like aerospace. We must provide special assistance to areas and to workers displaced by cuts in the defense budget and by other unavoidable economic dislocations....

Let me further say that I want to work with all of you on this. I realize this is a complicated issue. But we must address it. And I believe if there is any chance that Republicans and Democrats who disagree on taxes and spending or anything else could agree on one thing, surely we can all look at these numbers and go home and tell our people the truth. We cannot continue these spending patterns in public or private dollars for health care for less and less and less every year. We can do better....

Later this year, we will offer a plan to end welfare as we know it. I have worked on this issue for the better part of a decade. And I know from personal conversations with many people that no one—no one wants to change the welfare system as badly as those who are trapped in it.

I want to offer the people on welfare the education, the training, the child care, the health care they need to get back on their feet, but say, after two years, they must get back to work, too, in private business if possible, in public service if necessary. We have to end welfare as a way of life and make it a path to independence and dignity....

Next, to revolutionize government we have to ensure that we live within our means, and that should start at the top and with the White House. In the last few days I have announced a cut in the White House staff of 25 percent, saving approximately $10 million. I have ordered administrative cuts in budgets of agencies and departments. I have cut the federal bureaucracy—or will over the next four years—by approximately 100,000 positions, for a combined savings of $9 billion. It is time for government to demonstrate in the condition we're in that we can be as frugal as any household in America.

And that's why I also want to congratulate the Congress. I notice the announcement of the leadership today that Congress is taking similar steps to cut its costs. I think that is important. I think it will send a very clear signal to the American people.

But if we really want to cut spending we're going to have to do more, and some of it will be difficult. Tonight I call for an across-the-board freeze in federal government salaries for one year. And thereafter, during this four-year period, I recommend that salaries rise at one point lower than the cost of living allowance normally involved in federal pay increases.

Next, I recommend that we make 150 specific budget cuts, as you know, and that all those who say we should cut more be as specific as I have been.

Finally, let me say to my friends on both sides of the aisle, it is not enough simply to cut government, we have to rethink the whole way it works. When I became President I was amazed at just the way the White House worked in ways that added lots of money to what taxpayers had to pay—outmoded ways that didn't take maximum advantage of technology and didn't do things that any business would have done years ago to save taxpayers' money.

So I want to bring a new spirit of innovation into every government department. I want to push education reform, as I said, not just to spend more money, but to really improve learning. Some things work and some things don't. We ought to be subsidizing the things that work and discouraging the things that don't. I'd like to use that superfund to clean up pollution for a change and not just pay lawyers.

In the aftermath of all the difficulties with the savings and loans, we must use federal bank regulators to protect the security and safety of our financial institutions, but they should not be used to continue the credit crunch and to stop people from making sensible loans.

I'd like for us to not only have welfare reform but to reexamine the whole focus of all of our programs that help people to shift them from entitlement programs to empowerment programs. In the end we want people not to need us anymore. I think that's important.

But in the end we have to get back to the deficit. For years there's been talk about it, but very few credible efforts to deal with it. And now I understand why, having dealt with the real numbers for four weeks. But I believe this plan does—it tackles the budget deficit seriously and over the long-term. It puts in place one of the biggest deficit reductions and one of the biggest changes in federal priorities from consumption to investment in the history of this country at the same time over the next four years.

Let me say to all the people watching us tonight, who will ask me these questions beginning tomorrow as I go around the country and who've asked it in the past, we're not cutting the deficit just because experts say it's the thing to do or because it has some intrinsic merit. We have to cut the deficit because the more we spend paying off the debt, the less tax dollars we have to invest in jobs and education and the future of this country. And the more money we take out of the pool of available savings, the harder it is for people in the private sector to borrow money at affordable interest rates for a college loan for their children, for a home mortgage, or to start a new business.

That's why we've got to reduce the debt—because it is crowding out other activities that we ought to be engaged in and that the American people ought to be engaged in. We cut the deficit so that our children will be able to buy a home, so that our companies can invest in the future and in retraining their workers, so that our government can make the kinds of investments we need to be a stronger and smarter and safer nation.

If we don't act now, you and I might not even recognize this government 10 years from now. If we just stay with the same trends of the last four years, by the end of the decade the deficit will be $635 billion a year, almost 80 percent of our gross domestic product. And paying interest on that debt will be the costliest government program of all. We'll still be the world's largest debtor. And when members of Congress come here, they'll be devoting over 20 cents on the dollar to interest payments, more than half of the budget to health care and to other entitlements. And you'll come here and deliberate and argue over six or seven cents on the dollar, no matter what America's problems are.

We will not be able to have the independence we need to chart the future that we must. And we'll be terribly dependent on foreign funds for a large portion of our investment.

This budget plan by contrast will, by 1997, cut $140 billion in that year alone from the deficit. A real spending cut, a real revenue increase, a real deficit reduction, using the independent numbers of the Congressional Budget Office. Well, you can laugh, my fellow Republicans, but I'll point out that the Congressional Budget Office was normally more conservative in what was going to happen and closer to right than previous Presidents have been.

I did this so that we could argue about priorities with the same set of numbers. I did this so that no one could say I was estimating my way out of this difficulty. I did this because if we can agree together on the most prudent revenues we're likely to get, if the recovery stays and we do right things economically, then it will turn out better for the American people than we say than the last 12 years. Because there were differences over the revenue estimates, you and I know that both parties were given greater elbow room for irresponsibility. This is tightening the rein on the Democrats as well as the Republicans. Let's at least argue about the same set of numbers so the American people will think we're keeping straight with them.

As I said earlier, my recommendation makes more than 150 difficult reductions to cut the federal spending by a total of $246 billion. We are eliminating programs that are no longer needed, such as nuclear power research and development. We're slashing subsidies and canceling wasteful projects. But many of these programs were justified in their time, and a lot of them are difficult for me to recommend reductions in. Some really tough ones for me personally.

I recommend that we reduce interest subsidies to the Rural Electric Administration. That's a difficult thing for me to recommend. But I think that I cannot exempt the things that exist in my state, or in my experience, if I ask you to deal with things that are difficult for you to deal with. We're going to have to have no sacred cows except the fundamental abiding interest of the American people.

I have to say that we all know our government has been just great at building programs. The time has come to show the American people that we can limit them, too; that we can not only start things, that we can actually stop things....

I know this economic plan is ambitious, but I honestly believe it is necessary for the continued greatness of the United States. And I think it is paid for fairly, first by cutting government, then by asking the most of those who benefited the most in the past, and by asking more Americans to contribute today so that all of us can prosper tomorrow.

For the wealthiest—those earning more than $180,000 per year—I ask you all who are listening tonight to support a raise in the top rate for federal income taxes from 31 to 36 percent. We recommend a 10 percent surtax on incomes over $250,000 a year—and we recommend closing some loopholes that let some people get away without paying any tax at all.

For businesses with taxable incomes in excess of $10 million we recommend a raise in the corporate tax rate also to 36 percent, as well as a cut in the deduction for business entertainment expenses. Our plan seeks to attack tax subsidies that actually reward companies more for shutting their operations down here and moving them overseas than for staying here and reinvesting in America.

I say that as someone who believes that American companies should be free to invest around the world and, as a former governor who actively sought investment of foreign companies in my state, but the tax code should not express a preference to American companies for moving somewhere else. And it does in particular cases today.

We will seek to ensure that through effective tax enforcement foreign corporations who do make money in America simply pay the same taxes that American companies make on the same income.

To middle class Americans who have paid a great deal for the last 12 years and from whom I ask a contribution tonight, I will say again as I did on Monday night, you're not going alone anymore, you're certainly not going first and you're not going to pay more for less as you have too often in the past.

I want to emphasize the facts about this plan: 98.8 percent of America's families will have no increase in their income tax rates—only 1.2 percent at the top. Let me be clear: There will also be no new cuts in benefits for Medicare. As we move toward the fourth year, with the explosion in health care costs, as I said, projected to account for 50 percent of the growth of the deficit between now and the year 2000, there must be planned cuts in payments to providers—to doctors, to hospitals, to labs—as a way of controlling health care costs. But I see these only as a stop-gap until we can reform the entire health care system. If you'll help me do that, we can be fair to the providers and to the consumers of health care.

Let me repeat this, because I know it matters to a lot of you on both sides of the aisle. This plan does not make a recommendation for new cuts in Medicare benefits for any beneficiary. Secondly, the only change we are making in Social Security is one that has already been publicized. The plan does ask older Americans with higher incomes who do not rely solely on Social Security to get by to contribute more. This plan will not affect the 80 percent of Social Security recipients who do not pay taxes on Social Security now. Those who do not pay tax on Social Security now will not be affected by this plan.

Our plan does include a broad-based tax on energy. And I want to tell you why I selected this and why I think it's a good idea. I recommend that we adopt a BTU tax on the heat content of energy as the best way to provide us with revenue to lower the deficit because it also combats pollution, promotes energy efficiency, promotes the independence economically of this country, as well as helping to reduce the debt, and because it does not discriminate against any area—unlike a carbon tax that's not too hard on the coal states; unlike a gas tax that's not too tough on people who drive a long way to work; unlike an ad valorem tax it doesn't increase just when the price of an energy source goes up. And it is environmentally responsible. It will help us in the future as well as in the present with the deficit.

Taken together these measures will cost an American family with an income of about $40,000 a year less than $17 a month. It will cost American families with incomes under $30,000 nothing, because of other programs we propose—principally those raising the earned income tax credit.

Because of our publicly-stated determination to reduce the deficit, if we do these things, we will see the continuation of what's happened just since the election. Just since the election, since the Secretary of the Treasury, the Director of the Office of Management and Budget and others who have begun to speak out publicly in favor of a tough deficit reduction plan, interest rates have continued to fall long-term. That means that for the middle class, who will pay something more each month, if they had any credit needs or demands their increased energy costs will be more than offset by lower interest costs for mortgages, consumer loans, credit cards. This can be a wise investment for them and their country now.

I would also point out what the American people already know, and that is, because we're a big, vast country where we drive long distances, we have maintained far lower burdens on energy than any other advanced country. We will still have far lower burdens on energy than any other advanced country. And these will be spread fairly, with real attempts to make sure that no cost is imposed on families with incomes under $30,000 and that the costs are very modest until you get into the higher income groups where the income taxes trigger in.

Now, I ask all of you to consider this: Whatever you think of the tax program, whatever you think of the spending cuts, consider the cost of not changing. Remember the numbers that you all know. If we just keep on doing what we're doing, by the end of the decade we'll have a $650-billion-a-year deficit. If we just keep on doing what we're doing, by the end of the decade, 20 percent of our national income will go to health care every year—twice as much as any other country on the face of the globe. If we just keep on doing what we're doing, over 20 cents on the dollar will have to go to service the debt.

Unless we have the courage now to start building our future and stop borrowing from it, we're condemning ourselves to years of stagnation interrupted by occasional recessions, to slow growth in jobs, to no more growth in income, to more debt, to more disappointment. Worse less—unless we change, unless we increase investment and reduce the debt, to raise productivity so that we can generate both jobs and incomes, we will be condemning our children and our children's children to a lesser life than we enjoyed.

Once Americans looked forward to doubling their living standards every 25 years. At present productivity rates, it will take 100 years to double living standards, until our grandchildren's grandchildren are born. I say that is too long to wait.

Tonight the American people know we have to change. But they're also likely to ask me tomorrow and all of you for the weeks and months ahead whether we have the fortitude to make the changes happen in the right way. They know that as soon as I leave this Chamber and you go home, various interest groups will be out in force lobbying against this or that piece of this plan. And that the forces of conventional wisdom will offer a thousand reasons why we well ought to do this but we just can't do it.

Our people will be watching and wondering, not to see whether you disagree with me on a particular issue, but just to see whether this is going to be business as usual or a real new day. Whether we're all going to conduct ourselves as if we know we're working for them. We must scale the walls of the people's skepticisms, not with our words but with our deeds.

After so many years of gridlock and indecision, after so many hopeful beginnings and so few promising results, the American people are going to be harsh in their judgments of all of us if we fail to seize this moment.

This economic plan can't please everybody. If the package is picked apart, there will be something that will anger each of us, won't please anybody. But if it is taken as a whole, it will help all of us.

So I ask you all to begin by resisting the temptation to focus only on a particular spending cut you don't like or some particular investment that wasn't made. And nobody likes the tax increases, but let's just face facts. For 20 years, through administrations of both parties, incomes have stalled and debt has exploded, and productivity has not grown as it should. We cannot deny the reality of our condition. We have got to play the hand we were dealt and play it as best we can.

My fellow Americans, the test of this plan cannot be what is in it for me, it has got to be what is in it for us.

If we work hard and if we work together, if we rededicate ourselves to creating jobs, to rewarding work, to strengthening our families, to reinventing our government, we can lift our country's fortunes again.

Tonight, I ask everyone in this Chamber and every American to look simply into your heart, to spark your own hopes, to fire your own imagination. There is so much good, so much possibility, so much excitement in this country now, that if we act boldly and honestly, as leaders should, our legacy will be one of prosperity and progress.

This must be America's new direction. Let us summon the courage to seize it.

Thank you. God bless America.

13–2. NORTH AMERICAN FREE TRADE AGREEMENT (NAFTA)

PREAMBLE

The Government of Canada, the Government of the United Mexican States and the Government of the United States of America, resolved to:

STRENGTHEN the special bonds of friendship and cooperation among their nations;
CONTRIBUTE to the harmonious development and expansion of world trade and provide a catalyst to broader international cooperation;
CREATE an expanded and secure market for the goods and services produced in their territories;
REDUCE distortions to trade;
ESTABLISH clear and mutually advantageous rules governing their trade;
ENSURE a predictable commercial framework for business planning and investment;
BUILD on their respective rights and obligations under the General Agreement on Tariffs and Trade and other multilateral and bilateral instruments of cooperation;
ENHANCE the competitiveness of their firms in global markets;
FOSTER creativity and innovation, and promote trade in goods and services that are the subject of intellectual property rights;
CREATE new employment opportunities and improve working conditions and living standards in their respective territories;
UNDERTAKE each of the preceding in a manner consistent with environmental protection and conservation;
PRESERVE their flexibility to safeguard the public welfare;
PROMOTE sustainable development;
STRENGTHEN the development and enforcement of environmental laws and regulations; and
PROTECT, enhance and enforce basic workers' rights;

HAVE AGREED as follows

PART ONE
GENERAL PART

Chapter One Objectives

Article 101: Establishment of the Free Trade Area

The Parties to this Agreement, consistent with Article XXIV of the *General Agreement on Tariffs and Trade*, hereby establish a free trade area.

Article 102: Objectives

1. The objectives of this Agreement, as elaborated more specifically through its principles and rules, including national treatment, most-favored-nation treatment and transparency, are to:
   a. eliminate barriers to trade in, and facilitate the cross-border movement of, goods and services between the territories of the Parties;

b. promote conditions of fair competition in the free trade area;

c. increase substantially investment opportunities in the territories of the Parties;

d. provide adequate and effective protection and enforcement of intellectual property rights in each Party's territory;

e. create effective procedures for the implementation and application of this Agreement, for its joint administration and for the resolution of disputes; and

f. establish a framework for further trilateral, regional and multilateral cooperation to expand and enhance the benefits of this Agreement.

2. The Parties shall interpret and apply the provisions of this Agreement in the light of its objectives set out in paragraph 1 and in accordance with applicable rules of international law.

Article 103: Relation to Other Agreements

1. The Parties affirm their existing rights and obligations with respect to each other under the *General Agreement on Tariffs and Trade* and other agreements to which such Parties are party.

2. In the event of any inconsistency between this Agreement and such other agreements, this Agreement shall prevail to the extent of the inconsistency, except as otherwise provided in this Agreement.

Article 104: Relation to Environmental and Conservation Agreements

1. In the event of any inconsistency between this Agreement and the specific trade obligations set out in:

a. the Convention on International Trade in Endangered Species of Wild Fauna and Flora, done at Washington, March 3, 1973, as amended June 22, 1979,

b. the Montreal Protocol on Substances that Deplete the Ozone Layer, done at Montreal, September 16, 1987, as amended June 29, 1990,

c. the Basel Convention on the Control of Transboundary Movements of Hazardous Wastes and Their Disposal, done at Basel, March 22, 1989, on its entry into force for Canada, Mexico and the United States, or

d. the agreements set out in Annex 104.1, such obligations shall prevail to the extent of the inconsistency, provided that where a Party has a choice among equally effective and reasonably available means of complying with such obligations, the Party chooses the alternative that is the least inconsistent with the other provisions of this Agreement.

2. The Parties may agree in writing to modify Annex 104.1 to include any amendment to an agreement referred to in paragraph 1, and any other environmental or conservation agreement.

Article 105: Extent of Obligations

The Parties shall ensure that all necessary measures are taken in order to give effect to the provisions of this Agreement, including their observance, except as otherwise provided in this Agreement, by state and provincial governments.

Annex 104.1

Bilateral and Other Environmental and Conservation Agreements

1. The Agreement Between the Government of Canada and the Government of the United States of America Concerning the Transboundary Movement of Hazardous Waste, signed at Ottawa, October 28, 1986.
2. The Agreement Between the United States of America and the United Mexican States on Cooperation for the Protection and Improvement of the Environment in the Border Area, signed at La Paz, Baja California Sur, August 14, 1983.

13–3. WILLIAM J. CLINTON, FEBRUARY 4, 1999, ECONOMIC REPORT OF THE PRESIDENT

To the Congress of the United States:

I am pleased to report that the American economy today is healthy and strong. Our Nation is enjoying the longest peacetime economic expansion in its history, with almost 18 million new jobs since 1993, wages rising at twice the rate of inflation, the highest home ownership ever, the smallest welfare rolls in 30 years, and unemployment and inflation at their lowest levels in three decades.

This expansion, unlike recent previous ones, is both wide and deep. All income groups, from the richest to the poorest, have seen their incomes rise since 1993. The typical family income is up more than $3,500, adjusted for inflation. African-American and Hispanic households, who were left behind during the last expansion, have also seen substantial increases in income.

Our Nation's budget is balanced, for the first time in a generation, and we are entering the second year of an era of surpluses: our projections show that we will close out the 1999 fiscal year with a surplus of $79 billion, the largest in the history of the United States. We are on course for budget surpluses for many years to come.

These economic successes are not accidental. They are the result of an economic strategy that we have pursued since 1993. It is a strategy that rests on three pillars: fiscal discipline, investments in education and technology, and expanding exports to the growing world market. Continuing with this proven strategy is the best way to maintain our prosperity and meet the challenges of the 21st century.

Our new economic strategy was rooted first and foremost in fiscal discipline. We made hard fiscal choices in 1993, sending signals to the market that we were serious about dealing with the budget deficits we had inherited. The market responded by lowering long-term interest rates. Lower interest rates in turn helped more people buy homes and borrow for college, helped more entrepreneurs to start businesses, and helped more existing businesses to invest in new technology and equipment. America's economic success has been fueled by the biggest boom in private sector investment in decades—more than $1 trillion in capital was freed for private sector investment. In past expansions, government bought more and spent more to drive the economy. During this expansion, government spending as a share of the economy has fallen.

The second part of our strategy has been to invest in our people. A global economy driven by information and fast-paced technological change creates ever greater demand for skilled workers. That is why, even as we balanced the budget, we substantially increased our annual investment in education and training. We have opened the doors of college to all Americans, with tax credits and more affordable student loans, with more work-study grants and more Pell grants, with education IRAs and the new HOPE Scholarship tax credit that more than 5 million Americans will receive this year. Even as we closed the budget gap, we have expanded the earned income tax credit for almost 20 million low-income working families, giving them hope and helping lift them out of poverty. Even as we cut government spending, we have raised investments in a welfare-to-work jobs initiative and invested $24 billion in our children's health initiative.

Third, to build the American economy, we have focused on opening foreign markets and expanding exports to our trading partners around the world. Until recently, fully one-third of the strong economic growth America has enjoyed in the 1990s has come from exports. That trade has been aided by 270 trade agreements we have signed in the past 6 years.

We have created a strong, healthy, and truly global economy—an economy that is a leader for growth in the world. But common sense, experience, and the example of our competitors abroad show us that we cannot afford to be complacent. Now, at this moment of great plenty, is precisely the time to face the challenges of the next century.

We must maintain our fiscal discipline by saving Social Security for the 21st century—thereby laying the foundations for future economic growth.

By 2030, the number of elderly Americans will double. This is a seismic demographic shift with great consequences for our Nation. We must keep Social Security a rock-solid guarantee. That is why I proposed in my State of the Union address that we invest the surplus to save Social Security. I proposed that we commit 62 percent of the budget surplus for the next 15 years to Social Security. I also proposed investing a small portion in the private sector. This will allow the trust fund to earn a higher return and keep Social Security sound until 2055.

But we must aim higher. We should put Social Security on a sound footing for the next 75 years. We should reduce poverty among elderly women, who are nearly twice as likely to be poor as other seniors. And we should eliminate the limits on what seniors on Social Security can earn. These changes will require difficult but fully achievable choices over and above the dedication of the surplus. Once we have saved Social Security, we must fulfill our obligation to save and improve Medicare and invest in long-term health care. That is why I have called for broader, bipartisan reforms that keep Medicare secure until 2020 through additional savings and modernizing the program with market-oriented purchasing tools, while also providing a long-overdue prescription drug benefit.

By saving the money we will need to save Social Security and Medicare, over the next 15 years we will achieve the lowest ratio of publicly held debt to gross domestic product since 1917. This debt reduction will help keep future interest rates low or drive them even lower, fueling economic growth well into the 21st century.

To spur future growth, we must also encourage private retirement saving. In my State of the Union address I proposed that we use about 12 percent of the surplus to establish new Universal Savings Accounts—USA accounts. These will ensure that all Americans have the means to save. Americans could receive a flat tax credit to contribute to their USA accounts and additional tax credits to match a portion of their savings—with more help for lower income Americans. This is the right way to provide tax relief to the American people.

Education is also key to our Nation's future prosperity. That is why I proposed in my State of the Union address a plan to create 21st-century schools through greater investment and more accountability. Under my plan, States and school districts that accept Federal resources will be required to end social promotion, turn around or close failing schools, support high-quality teachers, and promote innovation, competition, and discipline. My plan also proposes increasing Federal investments to help States and school districts take responsibility for failing schools, to recruit and train new teachers, to expand after school and summer school programs, and to build or fix 5,000 schools.

At this time of continued turmoil in the international economy, we must do more to help create stability and open markets around the world. We must press forward with open trade. It would be a terrible mistake, at this time of economic fragility in so many regions, for the United States to build new walls of protectionism that could set off a chain reaction around the world, imperiling the growth upon which we depend. At the same time, we must do more to make sure that working people are lifted up by trade. We must do more to ensure that spirited economic competition among nations never becomes a race to the bottom in the area of environmental protections or labor standards.

Strengthening the foundations of trade means strengthening the architecture of international finance. The United States must continue to lead in stabilizing the world financial system. When nations around the world descend into economic disruption, consigning populations to poverty, it hurts them and it hurts us. These nations are our trading partners; they buy our products and can ship low-cost products to American consumers.

The U.S. proposal for containing financial contagion has been taken up around the world: interest rates are being cut here and abroad, America is meeting its obligations to the International Monetary Fund, and a new facility has been created at the World Bank to strengthen the social safety net in Asia. And agreement has been reached to establish a new precautionary line of credit, so nations with strong economic policies can quickly get the help they need before financial problems mushroom from concerns to crises.

We must do more to renew our cities and distressed rural areas. My Administration has pursued a new strategy, based on empowerment and investment, and we have seen its success. With the critical assistance of Empowerment Zones, unemployment rates in cities across the country have dropped dramatically. But we have more work to do to bring the spark of private enterprise to neighborhoods that have too long been without hope. That is why my budget includes an innovative "New Markets" initiative to spur $15 billion in new private sector capital investment in businesses in underserved areas through a package of tax credits and guarantees.

Now, on the verge of another American Century, our economy is at the pinnacle of power and success, but challenges remain. Technology and trade and the spread of information have transformed our economy, offering great opportunities but also posing great challenges. All Americans must be equipped with the skills to succeed and prosper in the new economy. America must have the courage to move forward and renew its ideas and institutions to meet new challenges. There are no limits to the world we can create, together, in the century to come.

13–4. GEORGE W. BUSH, JUNE 7, 2001, REMARKS ON SIGNING THE ECONOMIC GROWTH AND TAX RELIEF RECONCILIATION ACT OF 2001

...Thank you very much for being here on this historic moment. Mr. Vice President, Secretary O'Neill, Director Daniels, Secretary Evans and Chao are here, as well. Secretary Abraham, Administrator Christine Todd Whitman, Members of the United States Senate, Members of the House of Representatives, fellow Americans, welcome.

Some months ago, in my speech to the joint session of Congress, I had the honor of introducing Steven Ramos to the Nation. Steven is the network administrator for a school district. His wife, Josefina, teaches at a charter school. They have a little girl named Lianna, and they're trying to save for Lianna's college education. High taxes made saving difficult. Last year they paid nearly $8,000 in Federal income taxes. Well, today we're beginning to make life for the Ramos' a lot easier. Today we start to return some of the Ramos' money and not only their money but the money of everybody who paid taxes in the United States of America.

Across the board tax relief does not happen often in Washington, DC. In fact, since World War II, it has happened only twice: President Kennedy's tax cut in the sixties and President Reagan's tax cuts in the 1980s. And now it's happening for the third time, and it's about time.

A year ago tax relief was said to be a political impossibility. Six months ago it was supposed to be a political liability. Today it becomes reality. It becomes reality because of the bipartisan leadership of the Members of the United States Congress, Members like Bill Thomas of California, Ralph Hall of Texas, Charles Grassley of Iowa, Max Baucus of Montana, Zell Miller of Georgia, John Breaux of Louisiana, Trent Lott of Mississippi and the entire leadership team in the Senate, and Denny Hastert of Illinois and the leadership team in the House of Representatives—some Democrats, many Republicans—who worked tirelessly and effectively to produce this important result.

I also want to pay tribute to the members of my administration who worked with Congress to bring about this day: Vice President Cheney, Secretary O'Neill, Director Daniels, and the team inside the White House of Andy Card and Larry Lindsey, Nick Calio, and their staffs.

With us today are 15 of the many families I met as I toured our country making the case for tax relief—hard-working Americans. I was able to talk about their stories and their struggles and their hopes, which made the case for tax relief much stronger than my words could possible convey. And I want to thank you all for coming.

And here at the White House today are representatives of millions of Americans, including labor union members, small-business owners, and family farmers. Your persistence and determination helped bring us to this day. The American people should be proud of your efforts on their behalf, and I personally thank you all for coming.

Tax relief is a great achievement for the American people. Tax relief is the first achievement produced by the new tone in Washington, and it was produced in record time.

Tax relief is an achievement for families struggling to enter the middle class. For hardworking lower income families, we have cut the bottom rate of Federal income tax from 15 percent to 10 percent. We doubled the per-child tax credit to $1,000 and made it refundable. Tax relief is compassionate, and it is now on the way.

Tax relief is an achievement for middle class families squeezed by high energy prices and credit card debt. Most families can look forward to a $600 tax rebate before they have to pay the September back-to-school bills. And in the years ahead, taxpayers can look forward to steadily declining income tax rates.

Tax relief is an achievement for families that want the Government tax policy to be fair and not penalize them for making good choices, good choices such as marriage and raising a family. So we cut the marriage penalty.

Tax relief makes the code more fair for small businesses and farmers and individuals by eliminating the death tax. Over the long haul, tax relief will encourage work and innovation. It will allow American workers to save more on their pension plan or individual retirement accounts.

Tax relief expands individual freedom. The money we return, or don't take in the first place, can be saved for a child's education, spent on family needs, invested in a home or in a business or a mutual fund or used to reduce personal debt.

The message we send today: It's up to the American people; it's the American people's choice. We recognize, loud and clear, the surplus is not the Government's money. The surplus is the people's money, and we ought to trust them with their own money.

This tax relief plan is principled. We cut taxes for every income-tax payer. We target nobody in; we target nobody out. And tax relief is now on the way.

Today is a great day for America. It is the first major achievement of a new era, an era of steady cooperation. And more achievements are ahead. I thank the Members of Congress in both parties who made today possible. Together, we will lead our country to new progress and new possibilities.

It is now my honor to sign the first broad tax relief in a generation.

ESSAYS

Essay 13–1 is "Why Has the Budget Shifted from Deficit to Surplus?" which is a section from *Achieving Growth and Prosperity through Freedom: A Compilation of 1999–2000 Joint Economic Committee Reports*, issued in December 2000. In this report Senate Republicans dispute President Clinton's interpretation of the expansion of the 1990s. They point out that his claim that the 1993 tax increase eventually contributed to lower interest rates is factually incorrect. They cite the rising interest rates of 1994. They provide their own explanation for the '90s boom, including Reagan defense policies in the '80s, the tax receipts that began to flow into the Treasury as a result of the Individual Retirement Accounts enacted in 1982, and favorable demographics. The next two essays both come from *American Economic Policy in the 1990s*, edited by Jeffrey Frankel and Peter Orszag, and published in 2002. This volume is an exhaustive study of the economy of the 1990s. It is made up of fifteen papers with comments by panelists on various aspects of '90s policy written by leading scholars. Essay 13–2 is by Robert Rubin, who chaired President Clinton's National Economic Council and then served as Secretary of the Treasury from 1995 to 1999. In his "Comments on Fiscal Policy in the 1990s," Rubin notes that Bill Clinton consistently followed his strategy of deficit reduction throughout his presidency, and that it had a favorable effect on confidence both here and abroad. This reassured markets that the United States would not try to solve its debt problems by either inflation or large tax increases. Rubin laments the reaction of Clinton's critics who were so sure his plan would fail and still work to "deny credit to the policies they had …reviled." Essay 13–3 is excerpts from N. Gregory Mankiw's "U.S. Monetary Policy During the 1990s." Mankiw, an economics professor at Harvard and a successful textbook author, chaired the Bush Council of Economic Advisers from 2003 to 2005. His view of the '90s is that a combination of good luck and inspired monetary policy produced the great expansion.

13–1. *ACHIEVING GROWTH AND PROSPERITY THROUGH FREEDOM: A COMPILATION OF 1999–2000 JOINT ECONOMIC COMMITTEE REPORTS:* "WHY HAS THE BUDGET SHIFTED FROM DEFICIT TO SURPLUS?"

From 1987–89, the federal budget deficit was approximately $150 billion each fiscal year. The deficit rose during the contraction of 1990–91 and fell as the economy began to recover. The Clinton Administration claims that its 1993 tax increase reduced the budget deficit and led to lower interest rates that propelled the expansion of the 1990s. The facts are inconsistent with this view. Interest rates, which had fallen steadily throughout 1992 and the first half of 1993, began rising almost immediately following the Clinton tax increase and passage of the 1993 budget. By July of 1994, the interest rate on 30-year Treasury bonds had risen to 7.6 percent, up from 5.9 percent in October of 1993. Other rates followed a similar path. President Clinton's scenario that his 1993 tax and budgetary policies lowered interest rates and unleashed the current expansion is simply mythology.

If the Clinton tax and budgetary policy had little to do with the transformation of the federal budget, what accounts for the turn around? Aside from the cyclical effects of the expansion, a variety of other factors caused the federal budget to turn from deficits to projections of large and growing surpluses.

Higher defense spending in the 1980s enabled spending to be lower in the 1990s

Higher real defense spending in the 1980s proved to be an excellent investment. It led to victory in the Cold War. Following the collapse of the Soviet Union, however, real defense spending declined as the American people asked for a "peace dividend." As the Clinton Administration often highlights, the unemployment rate remained high in 1991 and 1992, the last years of President George Bush's administration, even though the economy was expanding. The transitional movement of resources out of defense and into non-defense industries was a major factor underlying the unusually high unemployment of the period. The United States was able to shift more than 2 million jobs out of defense-related industries between 1989 and 1993. In the short run, this was a major contraction of an important sector, resulting in sluggish growth and upward pressure on the unemployment rate. However, our free market economy created new jobs to use the talents of the displaced defense workers. This exerted a positive impact on the long-run health of the economy.

Favorable demographics

During the 1990s, prime-age workers grew rapidly as a share of the work force, while the elderly population grew much more slowly. The rapid growth of the prime-age workers propelled federal revenues, while the slow growth of the elderly population restrained spending.

Flow of funds into and out of tax-favored savings accounts

Tax legislation during the 1980s encouraged individuals and families to channel funds into tax-free Individual Retirement Accounts (IRAs) and 401(k) accounts. As funds flowed into these accounts in the 1980s, federal revenues were reduced. Funds began to flow out of these accounts in the late 1990s because federal law requires people to start withdrawing from them by age 70½ or face penalties. The withdrawals are taxable. In early 1999, the Congressional Budget Office estimated that withdrawals from taxable IRAs would rise from $93 billion in 1999 to $195 billion by 2008. Currently, 401(k) assets are about 60 percent as large as IRA assets, indicating that withdrawals from them will also generate significant tax revenue in the coming years.

Can the Great Expansion continue?

When analyzing the factors underlying the Great Expansion, one thing is clear: a major paradigm shift occurred between the 1970s and 1980s. In the 1970s, economists and policy makers alike believed that inflationary policies would reduce unemployment. The policy makers of the 1980s rejected this view and redirected economic policy toward price stability and long-term goals regarding taxation and spending. In the 1970s, it was widely believed that stop-go monetary and fiscal policy could smooth the ups and downs of the business cycle. Only the demand-side effects of fiscal policy were recognized; the supply-side incentive effects were ignored until the 1980s. These were fundamental changes in economic thought that shifted economic policy toward an environment more conducive to economic growth. Can the Great Expansion continue? It is unlikely that the business cycle has been repealed. Surprise shocks will no doubt occur in the future and they will exert a destabilizing influence on the economy. In this regard, the recent dramatic rise in the price of crude oil is a source of concern. When oil prices rise, oil-importing nations like the U.S. have to give up more of other things for each barrel of oil imported. This adversely affects their potential output and short-term growth. Energy consumption, however, is now a smaller portion of the U.S. economy than was true two decades ago. In 1981, energy expenditures comprised 14 percent of GDP; today the comparable figure is 7 percent. Petroleum expenditures were over 8 percent of GDP in 1980; today they are just 3 percent. Sustained high oil prices may cause the U.S. economy to slow, but given its current strength, they are unlikely to throw it into a recession.

The most important lesson of the Great Expansion is a positive one: monetary and price stability, free trade, small government, and low taxes provide the prescription for stability and prosperity. The Federal Reserve has kept its focus on achieving price stability during the Great Expansion. This should continue to be its focus in the future. Lower trade barriers will enhance the growth of an economy for years to come. The U.S. economy can expect to reap gains from NAFTA for at least another decade, and additional gains can be achieved from further reducing trade barriers. Favorable demographics—the large share of the work force in the prime-age category—will continue for another decade. However, around 2010 the demographic trend will become less favorable. This will not only slow growth; it will also tend to expand the size of government unless Social Security and Medicare are reformed.

The lesson of the last two decades is clear: a continuation of the strong and steady growth experienced during the last 18 years is achievable if we follow sound policies. Now we turn to the steps that need to be taken to provide prosperity for the next generation of Americans.

13–2. ROBERT RUBIN, "COMMENTS ON FISCAL POLICY AND SOCIAL SECURITY POLICY DURING THE 1990s" IN *AMERICAN ECONOMIC POLICY IN THE 1990s*

Before getting to the specifics of our panel's topic, let me make a general comment that in my view, at least, is essential in thinking about the Clinton years. From the very beginning of this administration, the president had a comprehensive and consistent concept of his economic strategy, and he followed that strategy consistently throughout the administration. During the 6½ years that I was in this administration, the president faced many difficult and controversial topics, and there was often a lot of speculation as to where he would come out on these issues. I used to say in response that on the big issues I had no doubt as to where he would come out. And that was because his decisions were not ad hoc responses to circumstances or to different sources of advice, but rather grounded in his consistent strategy.

In contrast, he was often seen as wavering and as responding to influences of the moment. I once mentioned that perception to him, and he said that he had given a great deal of thought to that contrast, and he had concluded that he often discussed his thinking in public, together with his weighing and balancing of competing considerations, and what people wanted instead was a man on a white horse with a simple answer. In fact, one of the difficulties the administration had in conveying to the American people the president's economic strategy was precisely that it was not simple but broad based and had an intellectual complication commensurate with the complexity of the world which it addressed. That complexity, in my view, was a virtue with respect to setting policy, but clearly was a problem with respect to communication. Thus, for example, in the trade arena, the president consistently supported trade liberalization measures, but he also recognized the dislocations that change—whether from trade or technology—could bring, and he acknowledged those dislocations and advocated a parallel agenda of education, health care insurance, and the like to deal with those dislocations.

I lived on a daily basis through the development of the globalization of capital markets and integration of trade and capital flows across national boundaries. President Clinton had an exceedingly good understanding of the new landscape of the global economy, and that understanding of the greatly altered landscape created by globalization, spread of market-based economics, the new technologies, the growth in developing countries, and so much else informed the president's strategy and decisions.

Turning now to the subject of our panel's discussion, I thought that the paper by Douglas Elmendorf, Jeffrey Leibman, and David Wilcox captured the actions and debate in the administration around fiscal and Social Security problems very well, with a couple of limited exceptions.

In my view, the single most important moment in this administration's life with respect to the economic issues was the transition meeting on January 7, 1993, which has been much reported but not always with great accuracy.

The new economic team had put together a set of options with respect to fiscal policy, viewed as the central decision that the president needed to make. When we arrived for the six-hour meeting in Little Rock, one of his political advisers told me that we could not possibly expect the president to make a decision on substantial deficit reduction at this first meeting, especially since that meant sacrificing or deferring so much else that he wanted to do.

As I recollect, very early in the meeting, the president-elect looked at us and said that deficit reduction was the threshold issue, that the economy, in his judgment, could not be put on a track of sustained recovery without deficit reduction, that he was elected to restore economic health, and that he was going to put in place a significant deficit reduction program even though it meant considerable curtailment of other programs he advocated. It is also important to remember that all of this took place after a late December 1992 substantial increase in the projected deficit by the outgoing administration.

The discussion was then conducted in the context of that remark, and the debate centered around varying possibilities with respect to how powerful a substantial deficit reduction program should be, but all against the backdrop there would be a deficit reduction program. Laura Tyson, Alan Blinder, and Lawrence Summers made a key presentation discussing the trade-off between the contractionary impact of deficit reduction and the potential expansionary impact of the lower interest rates that would hopefully flow from deficit reduction. Only later did we realize that even more important would be the effect on confidence. That discussion, as well as many subsequent discussions and decisions over the ensuing months, was conducted predominately in the context of the effects on the bond market, though the effect on the Federal Reserve Board also entered into the discussion. That statement is contrary to one reported view, which is totally at odds with all this evidence of these many months of meetings and is, in my view, simply wrong, that there had been a deal between the president and the chairman of the Federal Reserve Board.

I remember the economic malaise of the early 1990s very well, and one of the central features was loss of confidence in our country—both here and abroad—that in some fair measure was created by our fiscal mess, in part because our fiscal position was taken to symbolize a larger inability on the part of our country to manage its economic life effectively and with discipline. The consequence of the deficit reduction program of 1993, once the market actually believed that it was real, was not only lower interest rates, but also—in my view, probably much more importantly—a great increase in confidence both here and abroad, both for the intangible symbolic reasons I just mentioned and because the restoration of fiscal discipline reduced or eliminated the possibility that continued fiscal morass would eventually lead either to an effort to inflate our way out of debt problems or to higher taxes to pay debt service. And that increase in confidence affected business decisions about investment, expansion, and hiring, as well as consumer decisions, and produced a greater flow of foreign capital into our savings deficient nation to finance investment here, thus lowering our cost of capital. I have no doubt that the 1993 program and the eight years of a policy of fiscal discipline were key and indispensable in a virtuous cycle of deficit reduction promoting growth which further reduced the deficit, which then in turn further increased growth, and so on back and forth, and that this policy was thus key and indispensable in generating the economic and fiscal developments of the Clinton years. It may well be that the tools of economic analysis won't capture this, for three reasons: (1) the beneficial effect on interest rates was real but masked because demand for funds was increasing during an economic recovery; (2) more importantly, the increase in confidence and the effects of increased confidence are hard to capture but were key to this whole period; and (3) the mutual feedback between fiscal policy and economic growth may make meaningful deconstruction difficult or impossible. The fact is that there was a remarkable eight years that coincided with a dramatic shift in fiscal policy, and from the very beginning of the new policy, the many critics of the policy predicted large increases in unemployment, even recession, and reduced tax revenues. Instead, the opposite occurred. This created eight years of frustration for the critics, who then strenuously worked throughout this period to find ways that would deny credit to the policies they had so vigorously criticized or even reviled for the prosperity that they had predicted would not happen. And that process is still going on.

Throughout the eight years of the Clinton administration, there was great tension between the administration's espousal of fiscal discipline and the espousal by the Republicans in Congress of lower taxes, and that tension produced many of most important political conflicts of this period—for example, the struggle over the 1993 deficit reduction program, the 1995 government shutdown and the difficulties over the debt ceiling, the 1996 presidential campaign, and the 1998 decision (so very well described in the paper) by the administration to save Social Security first. I think a lasting legacy of this administration will be the successful experiment of promoting economic recovery and sustained growth through fiscal discipline rather than through fiscal expansion, and, as discussed in the paper, the redefinition at the end of the administration of budget balance to focus on the non-Social Security budget—or perhaps even the nonentitlement budget—as opposed to the unified budget. I do believe that the tax cut enacted in 2001 by the new administration—based on ten-year projections universally acknowledged as unreliable and numbers on discretionary spending and extension of expiring tax benefits that neutral budget experts view as unrealistically low, and involving a much higher running rate in later years and substantial additional debt service cost—creates a high likelihood of deficits on the nonentitlement side of the budget and was most unwise.

Let me now use my remaining few minutes to comment on a few separate items I wish to discuss.

I entered the administration knowing virtually nothing about the exceedingly complex rules and practices with respect to the federal budget, but developed a fascination with the budget. My own experience left me with a view that there is relatively little understanding of federal budget matters, not only in the public, but even among many members of Congress, and that there is also relatively little appetite for accepting the real trade-offs, including present constraint for future good, that are involved in fiscal matters or Social Security. Both make meaningful public debate and optimal decision-making in the political system far more difficult.

At the beginning of the Social Security discussion in 1997, I had the feeling that there might be some chance to seriously consider—and then accept or reject—some real changes in the Social Security system, for example, perhaps some change in the retirement age effective many years in the future or realistic adjustments to the CPI. However, once a greatly increased surplus was projected that created the far easier path for Social Security reform of focusing on using the surpluses for funding. The other political easy path was to substitute equities for debt, and then take credit for greatly increased expected rates of return. While higher expected returns might accurately reflect history, this is a far more complex subject than a simple extrapolation from the past would suggest and the risks in equities and the vast range of possible outcomes for the market overall or for individual portfolios, though considered in the debate, was not appropriately weighed in the decision-making, in my view, by many of those involved. Clearly the discussion of equities was heavily influenced by the atmosphere of rapidly increasing equity prices during that period. Moreover, having spent close to 28 years on Wall Street, I think that many people are not equipped, in terms of understanding securities valuation and in terms of discipline and thoughtfulness, to invest effectively in equity markets for the long term. In addition, if there were to be untoward results in equity markets over a substantial period, or if there were periods during which large numbers of people were adversely affected in their individual portfolios, there is a substantial probability that the political pressure to make good on those losses from the federal budget would be enormous, and doing so would increase the cost of funding future retirement. Once these politically easier paths became apparent, the politics of reform of the program itself went from difficult to impossible. Unlike a report I saw in today's press, carve-out private accounts, after careful examination, were rejected on the merits, and were not supported by any senior members of the president's economic team, as opposed to accounts outside of Social Security, which had strong support.

One matter not touched on in the paper, except slightly, was the intense focus the administration had on allocating resources within the context of deficit reduction. As the paper said, in 1993, even though the budget was directed predominately toward deficit reduction, the earned income tax credit was greatly increased, and throughout the 6½ years that I was there, there was always a strong effort to increase the portion of the budget used for the public investment areas that the president advocated so strongly.

For me, perhaps the moment of greatest surprise during my entire 6½ years in government was the assertion by some in Congress—even a few on Wall Street—that default by the federal government through refusal to raise the debt ceiling was a price worth paying to pressure the president into signing the congressional majorities' budget proposal in 1995. I believe that default by this country, as a political act, could have done untold damage, by undermining the concept of the sanctity of debt obligations in the global financial system. We avoided this result though unprecedented use of various mechanisms over a period of seven to eight months. Fortunately, as time went on, the concept of default lost its political appeal, and thus this problem was solved. I don't believe that the future Congress will be tempted to resort to this mechanism, though I do believe that the debt ceiling should be eliminated.

Let me end with two points. First, while budget rules can be useful, there are many ways to evade them through various mechanisms or the assumptions being used. Thus, I believe the real key—as the paper suggests—is the political environment and attitude with respect to fiscal discipline. Second, market reaction to economic policy—whatever it may be—is critical, and in 1993 one of our great concerns was whether the markets would believe in the validity of our deficit reduction program, given the markets' well-grounded skepticism about the political system's willingness to deal with the deficit. In that instance, the program gained market credibility very quickly. I believed then, and still believe, that the key reason was that our assumptions and numbers were real. Another reason was the inclusion of a small energy tax, because that was taken as evidence of seriousness of purpose and thus had disproportionate symbolic purpose.

Let me conclude that in my view, because of the great economic changes at work in the 1990s and because the Clinton administration was intently focused on implementing a strategy geared to that greatly changed environment, what this administration thought and did—whether you agree or disagree with that—is worth intensive focus, in providing input to future policy-making. Thus I think this conference is a very useful undertaking, to try to create a record of what happened and why, while it is still relatively fresh in people's minds. I would guess that five or ten years from now, with the distance of time, another level of analysis and judgment will be possible about the experience of this period, and I think the record created so soon after the fact can be very useful for those efforts. I greatly appreciate being invited to join with you in this undertaking. Thank you.

13–3. N. GREGORY MANKIW, IN *AMERICAN ECONOMIC POLICY IN THE 1990s*: CHAPTER I—U.S. MONETARY POLICY DURING THE 1990s

...No aspect of U.S. policy in the 1990s is more widely hailed as a success than monetary policy...Fed Chairman Alan Greenspan is often viewed as a miracle worker...Greenspan's tenure at the Fed has had its share of historic events, impinging on (as well as being affected by) the stance of monetary policy. On October 19, 1987, two months after Greenspan took office, the stock market fell 22 percent—a one-day plunge larger than anything seen before or since. The Fed reacted by flooding the economy with liquidity, lowering interest rates and averting a recession. But soon inflation became the more pressing concern, and the Fed started raising interest rates. The federal funds rate rose from 6.7 percent in November 1987 to 9.8 percent in May 1989. This Fed tightening, together with other factors, pushed the economy into a recession the following year. More than any other single event, the recession set the stage for the economic policies of the 1990s: it helped Bill Clinton, a little-known governor from Arkansas, defeat George Bush, an incumbent president who, only a short time earlier, had enjoyed overwhelming popularity following the Gulf War.

The Clinton years brought their own challenges to monetary policy-makers. International financial crises in Mexico in 1994–95 and in Asia in 1997–98, as well as the infamous failure of the hedge fund Long-Term Capital Management in 1998, put the world financial system in jeopardy and the Fed at center stage. At the same time, the push for fiscal discipline, which turned the U.S. government budget from deficit to surplus, made the Fed's job easier. So did the acceleration of productivity growth, which most analysts attribute to the advances in information technology associated with the so-called new economy. Another (perhaps related) development was a gradual decline in the U.S. unemployment rate, without the inflationary pressures that normally accompany such a change. Explaining this happy but surprising shift, as well as deciding how to respond to it, remains a topic of debate among students and practitioners of monetary policy.

The purpose of this paper is to look back at these events. My goal is not to tell the story of U.S. monetary policy during the 1990s: Bob Woodward's widely read book *Maestro* already does that. Instead, I offer an analytic review of monetary policy during this period, which should complement more narrative treatments of the topic....

I begin by comparing the performance of the economy during the 1990s with other recent decades. I concentrate on three standard time series: inflation, unemployment, and real growth. Economists, policy-makers, and pundits watch these measures of the economy's performance more than any others. They do so for good reason: If a nation enjoys low and stable inflation, low and stable unemployment, and high and stable growth, the fundamentals are in place to permit prosperity for most of its citizens.

Inflation is the first piece of data to look at, in part because a central banker's first job is to keep inflation in check. There is no doubt that central bankers also influence unemployment and real growth and that they do (and should) keep an eye on these variables as well. But according to standard theories of monetary policy, central-bank actions have only a transitory effect on unemployment and real growth. By contrast, the effects of monetary policy on inflation continue in the long run—and indeed are strongest in the long run. So, if monetary policy-makers take a long view of their actions, inflation is their first order of concern....

As judged by the average inflation rate, the 1990s were not exceptional. Inflation was lower in the 1950s and 1960s than it was in the 1990s. For those with shorter memories, however, the 1990s can be viewed as a low-inflation decade. There was substantially less inflation in the 1990s than there was in the 1980s and especially the 1970s.

This decline in inflation is largely the result of the tough disinflationary policies that Paul Volcker put into place in the early 1980s: inflation fell from a peak of 14.8 percent in March 1980 to 3.6 percent three years later. As is almost always the case, this large and persistent decline in inflation was associated with temporarily declining production and rising unemployment. By most measures, the recession of the early 1980s was the most severe economic downturn since the Great Depression of the 1930s.

The 1990s look more exceptional once we look at the standard deviation of inflation... Inflation was far more stable during the 1990s than during any other recent decade. The differences are substantial in magnitude. Inflation was only one-third as volatile during the 1990s as it was during the 1980s. It was 24 percent less volatile during the 1990s than it was during the 1960s, the second-best decade as ranked by inflation volatility. There is no doubt that by historical standards the 1990s were a decade of remarkably stable inflation.

Another way to look at the data is to examine how bad inflation was at its worst... Inflation was lowest in the 1960s and 1990s. But there is an important difference between these two periods. In the 1960s, the highest inflation rate occurred at the end of the decade, representing the beginning of a problem that would persist into the 1970s. By contrast, in the 1990s, inflation peaked at the beginning of the decade and thereafter became tame. After January 1992, inflation remained in a remarkably narrow range from 1.34 percent to 3.32 percent.

These comparisons of inflation over the past five decades bring up a classic question of economic theory: What costs does inflation impose on a society? Or, to focus the issue for the purposes at hand, is it more important for the central bank to produce low inflation or stable inflation? If low average inflation is the goal, then the monetary policy-makers of the 1990s can be given only an average grade. But if stable inflation is the goal, then they go to the top of the class.

Textbook discussions of the costs of inflation emphasize both the level and stability of inflation. A high level of inflation is costly for several reasons: (1) Because inflation raises the costs of holding money, it diverts people's time and attention toward conserving their money holdings and away from more productive uses. (2) Inflation induces firms to incur more "menu costs"—the costs associated with changing prices and distributing the new prices to salesmen and customers. (3) Because price adjustment is staggered, inflation induces spurious volatility in the prices of some firms relative to others, which impedes the price system's ability to allocate resources efficiently. (4) Because the tax laws are not indexed, inflation raises the effective tax on capital income and thereby discourages capital accumulation and economic growth. (5) Inflation makes economic calculation more difficult, because the currency is less reliable as a yardstick for measuring value....

The other key aspect of macroeconomic performance beyond inflation is the real economy, which is most often monitored by unemployment and growth in real GDP. Keep in mind that monetary policy is not the most important determinant of these economic variables. Indeed, according to standard theory, the Fed has no ability at all to influence unemployment and real growth in the long run.

Yet monetary policy influences unemployment and growth in the short run. What the "short run" means is a subject of some dispute, but most economists agree that the central-bank actions influence these variables over a period of at least two or three years. Therefore, the central bank can potentially help stabilize the economy. (And if policy is badly run, it can destabilize it—the Great Depression of the 1930s being a prominent example.) In the jargon of economics, monetary policy is neutral in the long run, but not in the short run. The practical implications of this textbook theory are the following: The average levels of unemployment and growth over long periods are beyond the central bank's powers, but the volatility of these series from year to year is something it can influence.

...The average level of unemployment during the 1990s was lower than it was during the previous two decades (although still higher than during the 1950s and 1960s). There is no consensus among economists on the reasons for this decline in the normal level of unemployment. It could, for instance, be related to the aging of the workforce, as the baby boom reaches middle age. Older workers tend to have more stable jobs than younger workers, so it is natural to expect declining unemployment as the workforce ages. Alternatively, as I discuss later, the decline in normal unemployment during the 1990s could be related to the acceleration in productivity growth resulting from advances in information technology. But whatever the cause for the long-run decline in unemployment, few economists would credit monetary policy.

Data on real economic growth show that average growth during the 1990s was similar to that experienced during the 1980s and substantially lower than that experienced during the 1950s and 1960s. This fact might seem surprising in light of the great hoopla surrounding the so-called new economy. The explanation is that the acceleration of economic growth occurred in the middle of the decade. Once the rapid growth in the second half of the decade is averaged with the recession and slow growth in the first half, overall growth during the 1990s is no longer impressive.

What's important for evaluating monetary policy, however, are not the averages...but the standard deviations. Here the numbers tell a striking story: Unemployment and economic growth were more stable during the 1990s than during any recent decade. The change in the volatility of GDP growth is large. The economy's production was 27 percent less volatile during the 1990s than it was during the 1960s, the second most stable decade.

These statistics suggest amazing success by monetary policy-makers during the 1990s. As we saw earlier, the economy enjoyed low volatility in inflation. One might wonder whether this success came at a cost. That is, did the Fed achieve stable inflation by giving less weight to the goals of stable employment and growth? The answer appears to be no: the economy became more stable in every dimension.

Of course, improvement in economic stabilization does not necessarily mean that policy-makers are doing a better job. Perhaps they were just lucky.

The Fed's job is to respond to shocks to the economy in order to stabilize output, employment, and inflation. Standard analyses of economic fluctuations divide shocks into two types. Demand shocks are those that alter the overall demand for goods and services. Supply shocks are those that alter the prices at which firms are willing and able to supply goods and services.

Demand shocks are the easier type for the Fed to handle because, like monetary policy, they push output, employment, and inflation in the same direction. A stock market crash, for instance, reduces aggregate demand, putting downward pressure on output, employment, and inflation. The standard response is for the Fed to lower interest rates by increasing the money supply. If well timed, such an action can restore aggregate demand and offset the effects of the shock on both inflation and the real economy.

Supply shocks pose a more difficult problem. An increase in the world price of oil, for instance, raises firms' costs and the prices they charge. These increases tend to raise inflation and, for given aggregate demand, push the economy toward recession. The Fed then has a choice between contracting policy to fight inflation and expanding policy to fight recession. In the face of supply shocks, the Fed cannot stabilize inflation and the real economy simultaneously. Supply shocks force upon the Fed a trade-off between inflation stability and employment stability.

Yet during the 1990s the U.S. economy enjoyed stability of both kinds. One possible reason is dumb luck. Perhaps the economy just did not experience the supply shocks that caused so much turmoil in earlier decades.

The most significant supply shocks in recent U.S. history are the food and energy shocks of the 1970s. These shocks are often blamed as one proximate cause of the rise in inflation that occurred during this decade not only in the United States but also around the world. So a natural place to start looking for supply shocks is in the prices of food and energy....

The 1990s were a lucky time...Large supply shocks were not common. Moreover,... good shocks were more common than bad shocks.

Not surprisingly, the worst shock in the entire period was in the 1970s: because of adverse shocks to food and energy, CPI inflation rose 4.65 percentage points more than core inflation during the 12 months ending February 1974. By contrast, the worst shock of the 1990s...occurred in 1990 as a result of the Gulf War. For the rest of the decade, there was no adverse food and energy shock as large....

Given these data, it is hard to escape the conclusion that the macroeconomic success of the 1990s was in part due to luck. Food and energy prices were unusually well behaved, and the economy reaped the benefit of this stability.

Another potential source of supply shocks is the rate of technological advance. This is a natural hypothesis to explain the good macroeconomic performance of the 1990s. During these years there was much discussion of the "new economy" and the increasing role of information technology.

What is more anomalous is the low volatility of productivity growth...To the extent that productivity reflects technological progress, the 1990s were a decade of smooth advances in technology. It is possible that this fact might explain the low volatility in other macroeconomic variables. Yet it is also possible that the tame business cycle led to low volatility in productivity, rather than the other way around.

The productivity data suggest an intriguing observation: The 1990s were in many ways the opposite of the 1970s. The 1970s saw a large increase in the price of a major intermediate good—oil. At the same time, productivity growth decelerated, while unemployment and inflation rose. The 1990s saw a large decrease in the price of a major intermediate good—computer chips. At the same time, productivity growth accelerated, while unemployment and inflation fell.

Economists do not fully understand the links among productivity, unemployment, and inflation, but one hypothesis may help explain the 1990s. If workers' wage demands lag behind news about productivity, accelerating productivity may tend to lower the natural rate of unemployment until workers' aspirations catch up. If the central bank is unaware of the falling natural rate of unemployment, it may leave more slack in the economy than it realizes, putting downward pressure on inflation. Thus, even if the average rate of productivity growth was not exceptional during the 1990s, the surprising acceleration from the poor productivity growth of the 1970s and 1980s may have acted like a lucky shock to aggregate supply.

It would be an oversight in any discussion of luck in the 1990s to neglect the stock market. For investors in the stock market, this decade was extraordinarily lucky.

...The 1990s were exceptional. Returns were high, and volatility was low. There was never a better time to be in the market.

To a large extent, the performance of the stock market is just a reflection of the macroeconomic events we...[see] in other statistics. Low volatility in the stock market reflects low volatility in the overall economy. The high return reflects the surprising acceleration in productivity growth, which helped fuel growth in corporate profits. If the stock market is merely a mirror being held up to the economy, then it has little independent role in the conduct or analysis of monetary policy.

There are, however, two reasons why the stock market may have a role to play. The first is that the stock market may be an indicator of things to come. According to the "efficient markets" theory, stock-market investors are rationally looking ahead to future economic conditions and constantly processing all relevant information. Thus, news about the economy might show up first in the stock market. The 1990s are a case in point. The bull market preceded the acceleration in productivity growth by several years, suggesting the possibility that Wall Street knew about the "new economy" long before it showed up in standard macroeconomic statistics.

A second reason why the stock market may be relevant to monetary policy is that it can be a driving force of the business cycle. John Maynard Keynes suggested that movements in the market are driven by the "animal spirits" of investors. Alan Greenspan reprised this idea during the 1990s when he questioned whether investors were suffering from "irrational exuberance." Such exuberance could push stock prices higher than their fundamental value and make households feel richer than they truly are.

Under either theory, monetary policy-makers might react to a rise in the stock market by setting interest rates higher than they otherwise would. This is the other side of the coin to the Fed's policy in October 1987, when it responded to a stock market crash by increasing liquidity and cutting interest rates. Regardless of whether the movements in the stock market are rational, they alter the aggregate demand for goods and services, and as a result they are of interest to monetary policy-makers. Indeed, the decline in the personal saving rate during the 1990s was mostly due to the booming stock market, for the "wealth effect" was a potent stimulus to consumer spending.

Of course, saying that monetary policy might react to the stock market is different from saying that it did. As I will discuss in the next section, there is scant evidence that the booming stock market of the 1990s played a large, independent role in monetary policy during this period.

Let's now turn to looking directly at policy to see how, if at all, it was different in the 1990s than in earlier decades. I look at two standard gauges of monetary policy—the money supply and interest rates....

As a first approximation, the central bank's only policy lever is the supply of high-powered money (currency plus bank reserves), which it controls through open-market operations and, to a lesser extent, lending at its discount window. It can use this single lever to target a broad monetary aggregate, such as M1 or M2, an interest rate, an exchange rate, or the price of bananas. But once it chooses one intermediate target, the game is over: the central bank has used up its power over economic conditions.

There once was a time when critics of Fed policy thought the key to good monetary policy was stable growth in the money supply. If the Fed would only keep M1 or M2 growing at a low, stable rate, the argument went, the economy would avoid high inflations, painful deflations, and the major booms and busts of the business cycle. Milton Friedman was the most prominent proponent of this so-called "monetarist" view.

It is easy to see how such a viewpoint arose. The two most painful macroeconomic events of the 20th century were the Great Depression of the 1930s and the Great Inflation of the 1970s. Both calamities would likely have been avoided if the Fed had been following the Friedman prescription of low, stable money growth.

In the early 1930s, high-powered money continued to grow at a moderate rate, but the collapse of the banking system caused broader measures of the money supply to plunge. Worries about bank solvency caused households to hold more money in the form of currency rather than demand deposits and banks to hold more deposits in the form of reserves rather than bank loans. Both actions reduced the amount of bank lending; the creation of inside money by the banking system went in reverse. As measured by currency plus demand deposits, the quantity of money fell by 25 percent from 1929 to 1933. If the Fed had been committed to stable growth in the broader monetary aggregates, it would have pursued a more expansionary policy than it did, and the Great Depression would have been less severe.

Generals are said to often make the mistake of fighting the last war, and the same may be true of central bankers. Perhaps because of the memory of its insufficient expansion during the 1930s, the Fed was too expansionary during the 1970s. The proximate cause of the Great Inflation was not monetary policy: the fiscal expansion resulting from the Vietnam War in the late 1960s and the OPEC oil shocks of 1973–74 and 1979–81 deserve much of the blame. But monetary policy accommodated these shocks to a degree that ensured persistent high inflation. The money supply grew rapidly throughout the 1970s, and inflation reached some of its highest levels on record. How best to handle supply shocks is a topic about which economists disagree. But there is no doubt that if the Fed had kept money growth to a slower rate during the 1970s, it would have better contained the inflationary pressures.

With these two formative episodes as the historical background, one might have expected subsequent improvements in monetary policy to be associated with increased concern at the Fed to maintain low, stable money growth. Indeed, increased reliance on target ranges for the monetary aggregates was allegedly part of Paul Volcker's 1979 change in the direction of monetary policy, which helped set the stage for the 1990s. If the improved macroeconomic performance of the 1990s went hand in hand with greater stability in the money supply, monetarists could have claimed intellectual victory.

Alas, it was not to be....

[T]he data give no support for the monetarist view that stability in the monetary aggregates is a prerequisite for economic stability. The standard deviation of M2 growth was not unusually low during the 1990s, and the standard deviation of M1 growth was the highest of the past four decades. In other words, while the nation was enjoying macroeconomic tranquility, the money supply was exhibiting high volatility.

From the standpoint of economic theory, this result is not a puzzle. The money supply is one determinant of the overall demand for goods and services in the economy, but there are many others, such as consumer confidence, investor psychology, and the health of the banking system. The view that monetary stability is the only ingredient needed for economic stability is based on a narrow view of what causes the ups and downs of the business cycle. In the end, it's a view that is hard to reconcile with the data.

This lesson was not lost on monetary policy-makers during the 1990s. In February 1993, Fed chairman Alan Greenspan announced that the Fed would pay less attention to the monetary aggregates than it had in the past. The aggregates, he said, "do not appear to be giving reliable indecations of economic developments..." It's easy to see why he might have reached this conclusion when he did. Over the previous 12 months, M1 had grown at an extremely high 12 percent rate, while M2 had grown at an extremely low 0.5 percent rate.

Depending on how much weight was given to each of these two measures, monetary policy was either very loose, very tight, or somewhere in between.

Henceforth, the Fed would conduct policy by setting a target for the federal funds rate, the short-term interest rate at which banks make loans to one another. It would adjust the target interest rate in response to changing economic conditions, but it would permit the money supply to do whatever necessary to keep the interest rate on target. If the subsequent performance of the economy is any guide, this policy of ignoring data on the monetary aggregates has proven a remarkably effective operating procedure.

Choosing the short-term interest rate as an intermediate target for Fed policy is only the first step in conducting monetary policy. The next, more difficult step is to decide what the target rate should be and how the target should respond to changing economic conditions....

...A central bank should raise its interest-rate target in response to any inflationary pressure by enough to choke off that pressure. How much is enough? Economic theory suggests a natural benchmark: if the central bank responds to a one-percentage-point increase in inflation by raising the nominal interest rate by more than one percentage point, then the real interest rate will rise, cooling off the economy. In other words, it is not sufficient that the central bank raise nominal interest rates in response to higher inflation; it is crucial that the response be greater than one-for-one.

These theoretical insights go a long way to explaining the success of monetary policy in the 1990s, as well as its failures in previous decades.

The responsiveness of interest rates to inflation has been rising over time. In earlier decades, the response was less than one-for-one. In the 1960s, for instance, when inflation rose by 1 percentage point, the federal funds rate rose by only 0.69 of a percentage point. The theory of spiraling inflation may be the right explanation for the Great Inflation of the 1970s. In other words, this episode was the result of the inadequate response of interest-rate policy to the inflationary pressures arising first from the Vietnam war and later from the OPEC oil shocks.

The situation was just the opposite during the 1990s. Each rise in the inflation rate was met by an even larger rise in the nominal interest rate. When inflation rose by 1 percentage point, the federal funds rate typically rose by 1.39 percentage points. This substantial response prevented any incipient inflation from getting out of control.

Although the 1990s saw high responsiveness of interest rates to inflation, it was not a decade of volatile interest rates. The...federal funds rate, in fact, exhibited low volatility by historical standards. High responsiveness and low volatility may seem a paradoxical combination, but they are easy to reconcile: the more the Fed responds to inflationary pressures when they arise, the less of a problem inflation becomes, and the less it has to respond to later.

Overall, the U.S. experience with monetary policy during the 1990s teaches a simple lesson. To maintain stable inflation and stable interest rates in the long run, a central bank should raise interest rates substantially in the short run in response to any inflationary threat....

...The interest-rate during the 1990s can be viewed as largely a response to the contemporaneous levels of inflation and unemployment.

A corollary to this...is that the many other issues that dominated public debate over monetary policy during the 1990s must be of secondary importance. The media spent much time discussing the Fed chairman's broad interests, including the stance of fiscal policy, the "irrational exuberance" of the stock market, the productivity gains of the "new economy," the financial crises in Mexico and Asia, and sundry obscure economic data. Apparently, these did not exert a great influence over interest rates...

...[While] the Greenspan Fed of the 1990s would likely have averted the Great Inflation of the 1970s,...[the] Fed policy-makers of the 1990s responded more to rising inflation than did their predecessors.

...The Greenspan Fed would have been much more expansionary in the early 1980s. As the economy experienced the deepest recession since the Great Depression, the Fed would have cut interest rates much more aggressively. The disinflation would have been less rapid, but some of the very high unemployment would have been averted.

So far, this paper has said little about the Clinton administration. In some ways, this absence is to be expected: Monetary policy is made by the Federal Reserve, which is independent of the executive branch. But the administration did influence monetary policy in several important ways.

The most obvious is the reappointment of Alan Greenspan. In retrospect, this decision may seem like a no-brainer, but at the time it was less obvious. When Greenspan came up for reappointment during Clinton's first term, his reputation was not as solid as it would become: Some observers (including some members of the administration of the elder George Bush) blamed Greenspan for the recession of 1990–91. Moreover, Greenspan was a conservative Republican. It would have been natural for Clinton to want to put a more Democratic stamp on the nation's central bank. That he chose not to do so is notable. To the extent that Greenspan's Fed has been a success, the Clinton administration deserves some of the credit.

The Clinton administration also influenced monetary policy with its other appointments to the Board of Governors. These included Alan Blinder, Ned Gramlich, Laurence Meyer, Alice Rivlin, and Janet Yellen. Compared to the typical appointment to the Fed by other presidents, the Clinton appointees were more prominent within the community of academic economists. Some observers may applaud Clinton for drawing top talent into public service (while others may decry the brain drain from academia). Whether this had any effect on policy is hard to say.

In addition to appointments, the administration also made a significant policy decision: Throughout its eight years, it avoided making public comments about Federal Reserve policy. Given the great influence the Fed has on the economy and the great influence the economy has on presidential popularity, presidents and their subordinates usually have a tough time remaining silent about monetary policy. Yet the Clinton administration avoided this temptation.

A large academic literature indicates that more-independent central banks produce lower and more stable inflation without greater volatility in output or employment. One contributor to this literature was Lawrence Summers, who would later spend eight years as a high Treasury official in the Clinton administration, culminating in the position of Treasury secretary. Thus it is hardly an accident that the Clinton administration was unusually respectful of the Fed's independence. What effect this attitude had on policy is hard to gauge. Perhaps the administration's restraint made it easier for the Fed to raise interest rates when needed without instigating political opposition. It may also have made it easier for the Fed to cut interest rates when needed without sacrificing credibility in the fight against inflation. In this way, the administration's respect for Fed independence may have contributed to the increased responsiveness of interest rates to inflation. If so, the White House again deserves some credit for the Fed's success.

In May 1964 the *Journal of Finance* published a short paper by a young economist named Alan Greenspan. It was called "Liquidity as a Determinant of Industrial Prices and Interest Rates." Greenspan began his summary of the paper as follows: "I have endeavored to integrate several theoretical approaches to the forecasting of prices, with special emphasis on its relation to interest rates."

The paper was a sign of things to come in several ways. First, and most obviously, it showed Greenspan's early interest in liquidity, inflation, and interest rates—topics that are the essence of monetary policy. Second, the paper demonstrated his interest in looking intensely at the data to try to divine upcoming macroeconomic events. According to all staff reports, this has also been a hallmark of his time at the Fed.

Third, the desire to integrate various points of view shows a lack of dogma and nimbleness of mind. Without doubt, these traits have served Greenspan well in his role as Fed chairman. They have made it easier to get along with both Republican and Democratic administrations and to forge a consensus among open-market committee members with their differing theoretical perspectives. They have also made it easier for him to respond to economic circumstances that are changing, unpredictable, and sometimes inexplicable even after the fact.

But there may also be a fourth, less favorable way in which Greenspan's paper presaged the author's later career: It left no legacy. According to the online Social Science Citation Index, the paper was cited in the subsequent literature exactly zero times. This observation raises the question of whether the monetary policy of the 1990s faces a similar fate. Will Greenspan's tenure as Fed chairman leave a legacy for future monetary policy-makers, or will the successful policy of the Greenspan era leave office with the man himself?

Imagine that Greenspan's successor decides to continue the monetary policy of the Greenspan era. How would he do it? The policy has never been fully explained. Quite the contrary: the Fed chairman is famous for being opaque. If a successor tries to emulate the Greenspan Fed, he won't have any idea how. The only consistent policy seems to be: study all the data carefully, and then set interest rates at the right level. Beyond that, there are no clearly stated guidelines.

There is a great irony here. Conservative economists like Milton Friedman have long argued that discretionary monetary policy leads to trouble. They claim that it is too uncertain, too political, and too inflationary. They conclude that monetary policy-makers need to be bound by some sort of monetary-policy rule. This argument is the economic counterpart to John Adams' famous aphorism that "we are a nation of laws, not of men."

These views, together with the great inflation of the 1970s, have influenced central banks around the world. Although no country has yet replaced its central bankers with computers programmed to an automatic monetary rule, as the most extreme critics suggest, there has been movement away from giving central bankers unconstrained discretion. During the 1990s, many nations adopted some form of inflation targeting. In essence, inflation targeting is a commitment to keep inflation at some level or within some narrow range. It can be viewed as a kind of soft rule, or perhaps a way of constraining discretion.

Despite this environment, as well as the fact that a prominent conservative headed the U.S. central bank, the Fed during the 1990s avoided any type of commitment to a policy rule. Conservative economists are skeptical about policies that rely heavily on the judgments of any one man. But that is how monetary policy was made over this decade, and it was hailed as a success by liberals and conservatives alike.

As a practical matter, Fed policy of the 1990s might well be described as "covert inflation targeting" at a rate of about 3 percent. That is, if the Fed had adopted an explicit inflation target at the beginning of the 1990s, the rest of the decade might not have been any different. The virtue of eschewing such a policy framework is that it kept options open—as unconstrained discretion always does. The downside is that it makes it harder for subsequent Fed chairmen to build on the legacy of the 1990s, because it is hard to know what that legacy is.

This paper has covered a lot of ground. So I finish by summarizing four key lessons for students of monetary policy.

1. The macroeconomic performance of the 1990s was exceptional. Although the average levels of inflation, unemployment, and real growth were similar to those that were experienced in some previous decades, the stability of these measures is unparalleled in U.S. economic history.

2. A large share of the impressive performance of the 1990s was due to good luck. The economy experienced no severe shocks to food or energy prices during this period. Accelerating productivity growth resulting from advances in information technology may also have helped lower unemployment and inflation.

3. Compared to previous eras, monetary policy during the 1990s adjusted interest rates more aggressively in response to changes in core inflation. This approach prevented spiraling inflation. Increased stability in monetary aggregates played no role in the improved macroeconomic performance of this era.

4. The low inflation and economic stability of the 1990s shows that discretionary monetary policy can work well. Yet it leaves only a limited *legacy* for future policy-makers. U.S. monetary policy-makers during the 1990s may well have been engaged in "covert inflation targeting" at a rate of about 3 percent, but they never made that policy explicit.

ADDITIONAL READINGS

Krugman, Paul, *The Age of Diminished Expectations: U.S. Economic Policy in the 1990s* (1990).

Krugman, Paul, *The Great Unraveling: Losing Our Way in the New Century* (2003).

Leduc, Sylvain, "Deficit-Financed Tax Cuts and Interest Rates," *Business Review* (Second Quarter 2004) 30–37.

Madrick, Jeffrey, *The End of Affluence: The Causes and Consequences of America's Economic Dilemma* (1995).

Rubin, Robert, with Jacob Weisberg, *In an Uncertain World: Tough Choices from Wall Street to Washington* (2003).

Samuelson, Robert J., *The Good Life and Its Discontents: The American Dream in the Age of Entitlement 1945–1995* (1995).

Stiglitz, Joseph, *Globalization and Its Discontents* (2002).

Stiglitz, Joseph, "The Roaring Nineties," *The Atlantic Monthly* (October 2002) 76–89.

Stiglitz, Joseph, *The Roaring Nineties: A New History of the World's Most Prosperous Decade* (2003).

Woodward, Bob, *The Agenda: Inside the Clinton White House* (1994).

Woodward, Bob, *Maestro: Greenspan's Fed and the American Boom* (2000).

Conflict and Consensus Among Economic Historians

As the readings in this volume indicate the study of American economic history does not involve the mastery of dry facts and statistics, but rather requires careful and creative analytical thinking. In their effort to understand the past, economic historians interpret the available evidence to provide what seems to them the most logical and most likely explanation to such questions as: was the colonial economy hurt by British mercantilism, was American slavery a profitable labor system, what caused the Great Depression? But each economic historian confronts the past with a unique perspective shaped by his/her experience, values, attitudes, and the times in which he/she lives. Differing perspectives, in turn, sometimes lead them to emphasize different pieces of the available evidence in their effort to understand the past. As a result, interpretative disagreements over what is the most likely explanation for such questions often arise. As many of the readings in this volume emphasize, each generation of economic historians revises and reinterprets the past. Thus, the definition of history as "a search for a usable past" Henry Steele Commager provided many years ago is no less true for economic history.

But lest readers of this volume come away with a view of economic history as a nihilistic intellectual free-for-all where one interpretation is as good as another, we conclude with a 1995 essay by Robert Whaples, Professor of Economics at Wake Forest University. In it Professor Whaples analyzed a survey made of the views of 178 members of the Economic History Association on 40 important questions on American economic history. The survey indicated that there continued to be significant areas of conflict among economic historians but that there was also substantial consensus on a number of issues. Along with Professor Whaples, we hope that students will use the survey results to get a clearer sense of the current state of the economic history profession and as a guide to shape their own research agenda.

E–1. ROBERT WHAPLES, "WHERE IS THERE CONSENSUS AMONG ECONOMIC HISTORIANS?"

Is there a consensus among American economic historians on the critical issues at the heart of the discipline? Although assertions of consensus are frequently made, they are usually only conjectures. We do not systematically observe the final product of the intellectual production process—the beliefs held by the large, often silent, body of scholars after the evidence in support of competing views has been weighed. This article disturbs the silence. It examines where consensus does and does not exist among American economic historians by analyzing the results of a questionnaire mailed to 178 randomly selected members of the Economic History Association....

Table E.1 contains the questionnaire and compares the responses of economists and historians, performing Chi-square and f-tests for differences in responses between the two groups. The questions address many of the important debates in American economic history. The answers show consensus on a number of the issues, but substantial disagreement in many areas. They also expose areas of disagreement between EHA members in history departments and members in economics departments.

Table E.1 RESPONSES TO QUESTIONNAIRE ON AMERICAN ECONOMIC HISTORY

The top row of numbers next to each question gives the percentage distribution of responses by economists. The second row gives the percentage distribution of responses by historians.

E = economists
H = historians
A = generally agree
P = agree,—but with provisos
D = generally disagree
Pr = confidence level with which one can reject the equality of the distribution of the two groups' answers, using the Likelihood Ratio Chi-square statistic, followed by the confidence level with which one can reject the equality of the percent who disagree with the proposition, using a pooled variance *t*-test.
% = percent of economists who answered the question, followed by percent of historians who answered.

Colonial Economy

	A	P	D	
	A	P	D	1. The economic standard of living of white Americans on the eve of the Revolution was among the highest in the world.
E	83	12	5	
H	81	16	3	
Pr	22/36			
%	91/95			
	A	P	D	2. Indentured servitude was an institutional response to a capital market imperfection. It enabled prospective migrants to borrow against their future earnings in order to pay the high cost of passage to America.
E	82	11	7	
H	67	21	13	
Pr	74/65			
%	98/100			
	A	P	D	3. Eighteenth-century rural farmers in the North were isolated from the market.
E	6	33	61	
H	9	20	71	
Pr	57/63			
%	78/90			

Economic Causes of the Revolution and Constitution Making

	A	P	D	
	A	P	D	4. The debts owed by colonists to British merchants and other private citizens constituted one of the most powerful causes leading to the Revolution.
E	0	8	92	
H	12	15	74	
Pr	97/95			
%	78/87			
	A	P	D	5. One of the primary causes of the American Revolution was the behavior of British and Scottish merchants in the 1760s and 1770s, which threatened the abilities of American merchants to engage in new or even traditional economic pursuits.
E	10	31	59	
H	12	15	73	
Pr	62/73			
%	63/67			

	A	P	D	6. The costs imposed on the colonists by the trade restrictions of the Navigation Acts were small.
E	60	29	12	
H	65	24	11	
Pr	11/12			
%	91/95			

	A	P	D	7. The economic burden of British policies was the spark to the American Revolution.
E	21	26	53	
H	13	29	58	
Pr	35/30			
%	94/97			

	A	P	D	8. The personal economic interests of delegates to the Constitutional Convention generally had a significant effect on their voting behavior.
E	27	43	30	
H	25	22	53	
Pr	91/95			
%	80/92			

Antebellum Period

	A	P	D	9. During the early national and antebellum period, export trade, particularly in cotton, was of prime importance as a stimulant to the economy.
E	36	33	31	
H	56	28	17	
Pr	83/85			
%	91/93			

	A	P	D	10. Antebellum tariffs harmed the southern states and benefited the northern states.
E	49	44	7	
H	34	37	29	
Pr	96/98			
%	89/90			

	A	P	D	11. Nineteenth-century land policy, which attempted to give away free land, probably represented a net drain on the productive capacity of the country.
E	16	14	70	
H	3	13	84	
Pr	84/83			
%	80/82			

	A	P	D	12. The lower female-to-male earnings ratio in the Northeast was one of the reasons it industrialized before the South.
E	17	34	49	
H	23	20	57	
Pr	58/48			
%	76/77			

	A	P	D	13. Before 1833, the U.S. cotton textile industry was almost entirely dependent on the protection of the tariff.
E	30	36	33	
H	9	36	55	
Pr	94/92			
%	72/85			

Slavery

	A	P	D	14. Slavery was a system irrationally kept in existence by plantation owners who failed to perceive or were indifferent to their best economic interests.
E	2	4	98	
H	3	8	90	
Pr	20/46			
%	100/100			

	A	P	D	
E	0	2	98	15. The slave system was economically moribund on the eve of the Civil War.
H	3	3	95	
Pr	54/52			
%	98/92			

	A	P	D	
E	48	24	28	16. Slave agriculture was efficient compared with free agriculture. Economies of scale, effective management, and intensive utilization of labor and capital made southern slave agriculture considerably more efficient than nonslave southern farming.
H	30	35	35	
Pr	67/49			
%	100/95			

	A	P	D	
E	23	35	42	17. The material (rather than psychological) conditions of the lives of slaves compared favorably with those of free industrial workers in the decades before the Civil War.
H	22	19	58	
Pr	75/85			
%	94/92			

Populism

	A	P	D	
E	30	41	30	18. The agrarian protest movement in the Middle West from 1870 to 1900 was a reaction to the commercialization of agriculture.
H	38	32	30	
Pr	33/2			
%	96/95			

	A	P	D	
E	19	47	35	19. The agrarian protest movement in the Middle West from 1870 to 1900 was a reaction to the movements in prices.
H	49	46	5	
Pr	99/99			
%	94/95			

	A	P	D	
E	22	24	54	20. The agrarian protest movement in the Middle West from 1870 to 1900 was a reaction to the deteriorating economic status of farmers.
H	34	37	29	
Pr	92/97			
%	89/97			

Southern Economy Since the Civil War

	A	P	D	
E	27	24	49	21. The monopoly power of the merchant in the postbellum rural cotton South was used to exploit many farmers and to force them into excessive production of cotton by refusing credit to those who sought to diversify production.
H	36	42	21	
Pr	96/96			
%	89/85			

	A	P	D	
E	26	14	60	22. The crop mix chosen by most farmers in the postbellum cotton South was economically inefficient and therefore southern agriculture was less productive that it might have been.
H	31	25	44	
Pr	65/82			
%	91/82			

	A	P	D	
E	26	21	52	23. The system of sharecropping impeded economic growth in the postbellum South.
H	47	20	33	
Pr	83/89			
%	91/77			

	A	P	D	
E	47	26	26	24. American blacks achieved substantial economic gains during the half-century after 1865.
H	27	27	46	
Pr	85/91			
%	83/85			

	A	P	D	
E	26	40	34	25. In the postbellum South economic competition among whites played an important part in protecting blacks from racial coercion.
H	0	22	78	
Pr	99/99			
%	76/69			

	A	P	D	
E	38	24	38	26. The modern period of the South's economic convergence to the level of the North only began in earnest when the institutional foundations of the southern regional labor market were undermined, largely by federal farm and labor legislation dating from the 1930s.
H	50	23	27	
Pr	45/64			
%	80/78			

Banking and Capital Markets

	A	P	D	
E	72	15	13	27. The inflation and financial crisis of the 1830s had its origin in events beyond President Jackson's control and would have taken place whether or not he had acted as he did vis-à-vis the Second Bank of the U.S.
H	69	28	3	
Pr	83/85			
%	85/82			

	A	P	D	
E	0	2	98	28. "Free banking" during the antebellum era hurt the economy.
H	17	17	67	
Pr	99/99			
%	87/77			

	A	P	D	
E	12	24	63	29. During the late nineteenth and early twentieth centuries, the Gold Standard was effective in stabilizing prices and moderating business-cycle fluctuations.
H	12	21	67	
Pr	5/22			
%	89/85			

Railroads

	A	P	D	
E	9	2	89	30. Without the building of railroads, the American economy would have grown very little during the nineteenth century.
H	13	21	66	
Pr	99/99			
%	98/97			

Labor Markets

	A	P	D	31. The increased participation of American women over the long run has resulted more from economic developments, such as the decrease in the hours of work, the rise of white-collar work, and increased real wages, than from shifts in social norms and attitudes.
E	26	53	21	
H	66	19	14	
Pr	99/58			
%	83/93			

	A	P	D	32. The reduction in the length of the workweek in American manufacturing before the Great Depression was primarily due to economic growth and the increased wages it brought.
E	54	28	18	
H	63	19	19	
Pr	36/7			
%	85/82			

	A	P	D	33. The reduction in the length of the workweek in American manufacturing before the Great Depression was primarily due to the efforts of labor unions.
E	5	24	71	
H	6	32	62	
Pr	29/58			
%	89/87			

Great Depression and Business Cycles

	A	P	D	34. Monetary forces were the primary causes of the Great Depression.
E	14	33	52	
H	17	17	66	
Pr	74/75			
%	91/90			

	A	P	D	35. The demand for money was falling more rapidly than the supply of money during 1930 and the first three-quarters of 1931.
E	48	12	40	
H	46	23	31	
Pr	46/50			
%	54/67			

	A	P	D	36. Throughout the contractionary period of the Great Depression, the Federal Reserve had ample powers to cut short the process of monetary deflation and banking collapse. Proper action would have eased the severity of the contraction and very likely would have brought it to an end at a much earlier date.
E	32	43	25	
H	31	47	22	
Pr	7/24			
%	96/82			

	A	P	D	37. A fall in autonomous spending, particularly investment, is the primary explanation for the onset of the Great Depression.
E	18	44	39	
H	23	29	49	
Pr	55/59			
%	85/79			

	A	P	D	38. The passage of the Smoot–Hawley Tariff exacerbated the Great Depression.
E	60	26	14	
H	64	21	15	
Pr	11/12			
%	94/85			

	A	P	D	
E	27	22	51	39. Taken as a whole, government policies during the
H	6	21	74	New Deal served to lengthen and deepen the Great
Pr	97/95			Depression.
%	89/87			
	A	P	D	
E	54	24	22	40. The cyclical volatility of GNP and unemployment
H	73	23	3	was greater before the Great Depression than it has been
Pr	95/97			since the end of World War Two.
%	89/77			

Colonial Economy

Three disparate questions deal with the colonial economy. There is an overwhelming consensus that Americans' economic standard of living on the eve of the Revolution was among the highest in the world. Likewise, a vast majority accept the view that indentured servitude was an economic arrangement designed to iron out imperfections in the capital market. Neither of the statements has generated heated discussion recently in light of the well-known works by Alice Hanson Jones and David Galenson.

The third colonial era topic has been the subject of much argument. New Left historians, such as James Henretta, have laid out the case that many eighteenth-century farmers in the northern colonies were "isolated" from the market. Winifred Rothenberg has spent considerable effort attempting to refute this idea and seems to have succeeded. 61 percent of economists and 71 percent of historians in the sample disagree with the characterization of these farmers as "isolated from the market." Among those who agree, only a handful do so wholeheartedly—most would add provisos to the statement.

Economic Causes of the Revolution and Constitution Making

Four of the questions deal with the causes of the American Revolution. There is a consensus on some of the narrower propositions: that debts owed by colonists and the practices of British merchants were not primary causes of the revolution; and that the costs of the Navigation Acts' trade restrictions were small. Nonetheless, almost half of the economic historians believe that the economic burden of the British policies was "the spark" to the American Revolution. Most who favor this position, however, do so with provisos. The bottom line is that there is no consensus on whether or not the economic burdens of British policies sparked the colonists' bid for independence.

At the beginning of the century, Charles Beard laid out the case for an economic interpretation of the making of the U.S. Constitution. Among other things, he argued that the *personal* economic interests of delegates to the Constitutional Convention had a significant effect on their actions in writing the Constitution. Although historians are divided on the question, the consensus among economists in the EHA is that this proposition is correct. (Of course, this does not necessarily imply an agreement with Beard's more particular claims about which personal interests mattered and how they mattered.)

Antebellum Period

Consensus exists on the two propositions concerning antebellum trade. Most agree with Douglass North's position that during the early national and antebellum period, export trade, particularly in cotton, was of prime importance as a stimulant to the economy. Likewise, most agree that antebellum tariffs harmed the southern states and benefited the northern states. In both cases, however, a considerable number would add provisos to these statements.

There is substantial disagreement with the proposition that nineteenth-century U.S. land policy probably represented a net drain on the productive capacity of the country. Terry Anderson and Peter Hill have recently restated this proposition, pointing out that the opportunity cost of squatting... is high because it removes productive resources from their most valuable use. Evidently, those surveyed do not buy (or are unaware of) this logic.

There is divided opinion on the two questions concerning industrialization. Roughly half those surveyed agree with the proposition put forth by Claudia Goldin and Kenneth Sokoloff that the lower female-to-male earnings ratio in the Northeast was one of the reasons it industrialized before the South. The other half disagree. There is also a split on the proposition that before 1833, the U.S. cotton textile industry was almost entirely dependent on the protection of the tariff. More than half the historians disagree, whereas the economists tend to accept the recent quantitative arguments of Mark Bils and Knick Harley that an unprotected American cotton textile industry could not have competed.

Slavery

Perhaps the most exciting time in the history of the profession was the period in which the issue of slavery dominated the agenda. Publication of Robert Fogel and Stanley Engerman's *Time on the Cross* generated a cottage industry of refutations and rebuttals. Now that most of the dust has settled, whose arguments have won the day?

The survey's four propositions about slavery come straight out of *Time on the Cross*. Two of them prove to be noncontroversial and were probably already widely accepted when Fogel and Engerman restated them. There is near unanimity that slavery was *not* a system irrationally kept in existence by plantation owners and that the slave system was *not* economically moribund on the eve of the Civil War.

One of the most contested issues in the debate has been Fogel and Engerman's proposition that slave agriculture was efficient compared with free agriculture. Economies of scale, effective management, and intensive utilization of labor and capital made southern slave agriculture considerably more efficient than nonslave southern farming. Apparently Fogel, Engerman, and others have convinced most of the profession that this proposition is correct. Almost half the economists generally agree with the idea, another quarter agree if provisos are added to the statement. Historians are almost as supportive of the proposition. Only 28 percent of the economists and 35 percent of the historians generally disagree with the assertion that slave agriculture was efficient compared with free agriculture.

On the last slavery question, opinion is sharply divided. More than half of the historians and almost half of the economists disagree with Fogel and Engerman's proposition that the material (not psychological) conditions of the lives of slaves compared favorably with those of free industrial workers in the decades before the Civil War. Among the half that concur with the statement, most do so with some reservations.

Populism

Three of the survey's questions consider the "puzzle" of Midwestern agrarian discontent in the late 1800s. The three "explanations" of populist protest are not mutually exclusive. First, there is a consensus in support of Anne Mayhew's proposition that the protest was a reaction to the commercialization of agriculture. However, most support Mayhew's proposition only if some provisos are added. A near consensus holds that the protest was a reaction to "movements in prices." On this question economists are much more likely to dissent than historians. Finally, there is considerable disagreement over the third proposition, which blames the protest on "the deteriorating economic status of farmers." A slight majority of the economists disagree with the idea, probably citing quantitative evidence on relative prices and absolute incomes. However, many, especially the bulk of the historians, agree with the proposition that "deteriorating economic status" inflamed agrarian discontent.

Southern Economy Since the Civil War

As the debate over slavery cooled down, disagreement about the aftermath of emancipation intensified. Occupying center stage in this second debate was Roger Ransom and Richard Sutch's *One Kind of Freedom*. Three of their propositions are addressed in the survey. On none of the three do economists and historians see eye to eye. Historians are much more likely to embrace the positions of Ransom and Sutch.

Economists are almost evenly divided on the proposition that the monopoly power of the merchant in the postbellum rural cotton South was used to exploit many farmers and to force them into excessive production of cotton by refusing credit to those who sought to diversify production. The vast majority of historians support this position. Three out of five economists reject the argument that the crop mix chosen by most farmers in the postbellum cotton South was economically inefficient and therefore southern agriculture was less productive than it might have been. Yet, a little over half of the historians accept the argument. Finally, a slim majority of economists reject the suggestion that the system of sharecropping impeded economic growth in the postbellum South. However, only one-third of historians reject the proposition. Thus, on the issues of monopoly merchant power, crop mix, and sharecropping there is no consensus among EHA members and considerable differences among economists and historians.

On two of the other questions about post-Civil War southern economic history there are also divisions between historians and economists. The consensus opinion among the economists is that "American blacks achieved substantial economic gains during the half century after 1865." Nearly half of the historians do not concur with this interpretation. Differing standards of "substantial" may be at the center of this disagreement. Robert Higgs's proposition that in the postbellum South economic competition among whites played an important part in protecting blacks from racial coercion yields the most dramatic difference of opinion found in the survey. Economists and historians have reached the opposite conclusions. Two-thirds of the economists support Higgs's statement, only 22 percent of historians do. These responses highlight a recurring difference dividing historians and economists. The economists have more faith in the power of the competitive market. For example, they see the competitive market as protecting disenfranchised blacks and are less likely to accept the idea that there was exploitation by merchant monopolists.

The final question on the southern economy tests Gavin Wright's argument that the modern period of the South's economic convergence to the level of the North only began in earnest when the institutional foundations of the southern regional labor market were undermined, largely by federal farm and labor legislation dating from the 1930s. Most of the respondents accept Wright's position.

Money and Banking

Economic historians have reached a consensus on all of the survey's questions regarding money and banking. The vast majority agree with Peter Temin's conclusion that the inflation and financial crisis of the 1830s had their origin in events largely beyond President Jackson's control and would have taken place whether or not he had acted as he did vis-á-vis the Second Bank of the U.S.

The economists are nearly unanimous in their rejection of the idea that "free banking" (free entry into the banking business, rather than freedom to conduct business without regulation) harmed the economy during the antebellum era. Although most historians have reached the same conclusion, as many as one-third accept the proposition that free banking hurt the economy. This difference is another indication that economists have greater confidence in the power of a competitive market.

Finally, about two-thirds of both groups reject the idea that the Gold Standard was effective in stabilizing prices and moderating business-cycle fluctuations during the nineteenth century.

Railroads

Before he turned to slavery, Fogel's estimates of the social savings of the railroads ignited a fervent debate. The survey indicates that Fogel's ideas have carried the day in this dispute. Almost 90 percent of economists and two-thirds of historians now reject the "axiom of indispensability."

Labor Markets

Goldin has argued that the increased labor force participation of American women over the long run has resulted more from economic developments, such as the decrease in hours of work, the rise of white-collar work, and increased real wages than from shifts in social norms and attitudes. The vast majority of those surveyed agree.

Two of the labor market questions concern the forces responsible for the decline in the length of the American workweek in the period before the Great Depression. The consensus here is that economic growth and increased wages were mainly responsible. Most economic historians reject a primary role for labor unions.

Great Depression and Business Cycles

Four of the questionnaire's propositions are taken from Temin's *Did Monetary Forces Cause the Great Depression?* and Milton Friedman and Anna Schwartz's *The Great Contraction*. The answers reveal a lack of consensus on the causes of the Great Depression.

The first proposition restates the Friedman and Schwartz position that "monetary forces were the primary cause of the Great Depression." Economists are almost evenly split on this question, whereas about two-thirds of the historians reject the monetarist proposition.

The second question of this section is much narrower. It must be treated with caution because it has the lowest response rate of the survey, with two in five of the sample members declining to respond. Sixty percent of the economists and nearly 70 percent of the historians agree with Temin that the "demand for money was falling more rapidly than the supply during 1930 and the first three-quarters of 1931."

Although the traditional Keynesian explanation holds the edge in the first two questions, there is a consensus among both groups that "throughout the contractionary period of the Great Depression, the Federal Reserve had ample powers to cut short the process of monetary deflation and banking collapse. Proper action would have eased the severity of the contraction and very likely would have brought it to an end at a much earlier date." However, most supporters of this position require that unnamed provisos be added before the contention is fully accepted.

Finally, economic historians are sharply divided over the traditional Keynesian alternative explanation of the depression that a fall in autonomous spending, particularly investment, is the primary explanation for the onset of the Great Depression. About 40 percent of economists and 50 percent of historians disagree with the hypothesis: only about one-fifth accept it without provisos.

Do these results indicate a belief among economic historians that both monetarist and Keynesian explanations have some merit? Or is this a message of irreconcilable differences? Despite considerable innovative and painstaking subsequent research about the causes and nature of the Great Depression, this may be a debate from which no consensus will ever emerge.

Although the central causes of the depression are still hotly contested, there is a consensus that the "passage of the Smoot-Hawley Tariff exacerbated the Great Depression...."

On top of the profession's lack of agreement about the genesis of the Great Depression, there is a disagreement about the effect of the New Deal. In fact, the economists in the sample are almost evenly divided on the question of whether or not when taken "as a whole, government policies of the New Deal served to lengthen and deepen the Great Depression." The consensus among historians is that the new Deal did *not* lengthen and deepen the depression.

The final debate addressed in the survey concerns the cyclical volatility of the economy before and after the Great Depression. Christina Romer has argued that earlier studies overstated the pre-Great Depression volatility of the economy. Her findings generated a flurry of research and rethinking on the issue. The current consensus is that the volatility of GNP and unemployment were greater before the Great Depression than they have been since the end of World War II.

Conclusions

The results of the survey can be very useful in the classroom. The findings go farther than textbooks in helping students get a sense of the collective wisdom of economic historians and emphasize that economic history like both its parents, economics and history, is full of unsettled debates.

The results can also guide the research agenda of economic historians. Some scholars will find that their beliefs run against the prevailing consensus. This need not mean that their beliefs are incorrect. Each one of us probably disagrees with one or more of the consensuses shown in Table E.1. Those holding minority views may wish to re-evaluate their position or to redouble their efforts to convince their colleagues by restating their case or pursuing additional research.

PERMISSIONS AND CITATION INFORMATION

Every effort has been made to cite completely the original source material for each document and article used in this collection. In the event that something has inadvertently been used or cited incorrectly, every effort will be made in subsequent editions to rectify the error

Documents

1-1 Navigation Act of 1660, in Danby Pickering, ed., *The Statutes at Large from the Magna Charta*, 46 vols. Cambridge: J. Bertham, 1762–1807, vol. 7, pp. 452ff.]

1-2 Charter of Carolina, in William L. Saunders, ed., *The Colonial Records of North Carolina* , Vol. I—1662 to 1712. Raleigh: P. M. Hale, 1886, pp. 20–33.

1-3 Thomas Whately, *The Regulations Lately Made Concerning the Colonies, and the Taxes Imposed Upon Them, Considered.* London: J. Willkie, 1775.

1-4 Adam Smith, *An Enquiry Into the Nature and Causes of the Wealth of Nations*, London: Routledge, 1880

2-1 Constitution of the United States, 1787.

2-2 Alexander Hamilton, Report of the Secretary of the Treasury, With His Plan for Supporting Public Credit, January 9, 1790; *Annals of Congress*, 1st Congress, Appendix, pp. 2041–2074

2-3 Alexander Hamilton, Report on Manufactures, December 5, 1791; *Annals of Congress*, 2nd Congress, 1st Session, pp. 971–1034.

2-4 Henry Clay, In Defense of the American System, February 2, 3, and 6, 1832; Gales & Seaton's *Register of Debates*, 22nd Congress, 1st Session, pp. 257–295.

2-5 Andrew Jackson, Message from the President of the United States Returning the Bank Bill to the Senate with his Objections, July 10, 1832; Gales & Seaton's *Register of Debates*, 22nd Congress, 1st Session, Appendix, pp. 73–79.

2-6 John Finch, "Notes of Travel in the United States", *New Moral World*, January–April, 1844; reprinted in John R. Commons, *et al.*, eds, *A Documentary History of American Industrial Society*, Cleveland: Arthur H. Clark Co., 1910, vol. VII, pp. 47–71.

2-7 Thomas Mooney, *Nine Years in America*, 1850; reprinted in John R. Commons, *et al.*, eds, *A Documentary History of American Industrial Society*, Cleveland: Arthur H. Clark Co., 1910, vol. VII, pp. 71–80.

3-1 "The Railroad System," *The North American Review*, (CIV) April, 1867, pp. 476–511.

3-2 James Dabney McCabe, *The History of the Grange Movement, or The Farmer's War Against Monopolies*, Philadelphia: National Publishing Company, 1873, pp. 236–251.

4-1 Frederick Law Olmsted, *The Cotton Kingdom: Observations on Cotton and Slavery in the American Slave States*, New York: Mason Brothers, 1862.

4-2 Frances Anne Kemble, *Journal of a Residence on a Georgian Plantation in 1838–1839*, New York: Harper & Brothers, 1863.

4-3 Author identified as "A Mississippi Planter," "Management of Negroes Upon Southern Estates," *DeBow's Review*, X (June 1851), pp.621–627.

5-1 "Forty Dollars Reward," Philadelphia *National Gazette*, October 13, 1830; reprinted in John R. Commons, *et al.*, eds, *A Documentary History of American Industrial Society*, Cleveland: Arthur H. Clark Co., 1910, vol. V, p. 69.

5-2 "One Cent Reward," *Mechanics' Free Press*, February 6, 1830; reprinted in John R. Commons, *et al.*, eds, *A Documentary History of American Industrial Society*, Cleveland: Arthur H. Clark Co., 1910, vol. V, pp. 69–70.

5-3 "Report of Committee on Education," *Free Enquirer*, June 14, 1832; reprinted in John R. Commons, *et al.*, eds, *A Documentary History of American Industrial Society*, Cleveland: Arthur H. Clark Co., 1910, vol. V, pp. 195–199.

5-4 "Strike of the Journeymen Bakers," New York *Evening Post*, June 10, 1834; reprinted in John R. Commons, *et al.*, eds, *A Documentary History of American Industrial Society*, Cleveland: Arthur H. Clark Co., 1910, vol. V, pp. 304–305.

5-5 "The Working People of Manayunk to the Public," *Pennsylvanian*, August 28, 1833; reprinted in John R. Commons, *et al.*, eds, *A Documentary History of American Industrial Society*, Cleveland: Arthur H. Clark Co., 1910, vol. V, pp. 330–334.

5-6 "The Cost of Living," New York *Daily Tribune*, May 27, 1851; reprinted in John R. Commons, *et al.*, eds, *A Documentary History of American Industrial Society*, Cleveland: Arthur H. Clark Co., 1910, vol. VIII, pp. 314–315.

5-7 "The Factory System," *The Harbinger*, November 14, 1846; reprinted in John R. Commons, *et al*, eds., *A Documentary History of American Industrial Society*, Cleveland: Arthur H. Clark Co., 1910, vol. VII, pp. 132–135.

5-8 "Obtaining Operatives," *Voice of Industry*, January 2, 1846; reprinted in John R. Commons, *et al.*, eds, *A Documentary History of American Industrial Society*, Cleveland: Arthur H. Clark Co., 1910, vol. VII, p. 141.

6-1 Ida M. Tarbell, *The History of the Standard Oil Company*, New York: Macmillan, 1904.

6-2 Russell Sage, "A Grave Danger to the Community," *North American Review*, DXXXIV (May, 1901), pp. 641–646.

6-3 James J. Hill, "Industrial and Railroad Consolidations: Their Advantages to the Community," *North American Review*, DXXXIV(May, 1901), pp. 646–655.

6-4 Charles R. Flint, "Industrial Consolidations: What They Have Accomplished for Capital and Labor," *North American Review*, DXXXIV(May, 1901), pp. 664–677.

6-5 F. B Thurber "Industrial Consolidations: The Influence of 'Trusts' Upon Prices," *North American Review*, DXXXIV(May, 1901), pp. 677–686.

7-1 Bruce Barton, "His Method," in *The Man Nobody Knows*, Indianapolis: Bobbs-Merrill Company, 1925, pp. 89–123.

7-2 Samuel Crowther, "Everybody Ought to be Rich: An Interview with John J. Raskob," *Ladies Home Journal*, 46 (August, 1929), pp. 9 ff.

7-3 Frederick Lewis Allen, "Coolidge Prosperity," in *Only Yesterday: An Informal History of the Nineteen-Twenties*, New York: Harper & Brothers, 1931, pp. 159–185. Reprinted with permission.

8-1 Carl Snyder, "The World-Wide Depression of 1930," *American Economic Review*, 21(March 1931) supplement, pp. 172–178.

8-2 Irving Fisher, "The Debt-Deflation Theory of the Great Depression," *Econometrica* 1 (October 1933), pp. 337–357.

8-3 Herbert Hoover, "Address at Madison Square Garden in New York City, October 31, 1932," in *Public Papers of the Presidents of the United States: Herbert Hoover, 1932–1933*, Washington, D.C.: United States Government Printing Office, 1977, pp. 656–680.

8-4 Franklin D. Roosevelt, "'New Conditions Impose New Requirements upon Government and Those Who Conduct Government,' Campaign Address on Progressive Government at the Commonwealth Club,' San Francisco, Calif., September 23, 1932," in Samuel I. Rosenman, ed., *The Public Papers and Addresses of Franklin D. Roosevelt, Volume I, The Genesis of the New Deal, 1928–1932*, New York: Random House, 1938, pp. 742–756.

9-1 Rexford G. Tugwell, "The Economics of the Recovery Plan," in *The Battle for Democracy*, New York: Columbia University Press, 1935, pp. 78–96.

9-2 Franklin D. Roosevelt, "Second 'Fireside Chat' of 1934—'We Are Moving Forward to Greater Freedom, to Greater Security of the Average Man,' September 30, 1934," in Samuel I. Rosenman, ed., *The Public Papers and Addresses of Franklin D. Roosevelt, Volume III, The Advance of Recovery and Reform*, New York: Random House, 1938, pp. 413–422.

9-3 John Maynard Keynes, "Can America Spend Its Way Into Recovery?," *Redbook Magazine*, New York, 64 (Dec. 1934), pp. 24 and 76.

9-4 Harry L. Hopkins, "Twenty-Seventh Annual Report of the Secretary of Commerce 1939," Washington, D.C.: United States Government Printing Office, 1939, pp. v–xxxiv.

9-5 Alvin H. Hansen, "Fiscal Policy in the Recovery," in *Fiscal Policy and Business Cycles*, New York: W.W. Norton, 1941, pp. 83–95.

9-6 Beardsley Ruml, "Financing Post War Prosperity: Controlling Booms and Depressions," *Vital Speeches of the Day*, 10 (November 15, 1943), pp. 95–96.

9-7 Franklin D. Roosevelt, "'Unless There Is Security Here at Home, There Cannot Be Lasting Peace in the World'—Message to the Congress on the State of the Union, January 11, 1944." in Samuel I. Rosenman, ed., *The Public Papers and Addresses of Franklin D. Roosevelt, 1944–45: Victory and the Threshold of Peace*, New York: Harper & Brothers, 1950, pp. 32–44.

10-1 Alvin H. Hansen, *After the War—Full Employment*, a publication of the National Resources Planning Board, Washington, D.C.: United States Government Printing Office, 1943.

10.2 Harry S. Truman, "Special Message to the Congress: The President's Economic Report, January 7, 1949," in *Public Papers of the Presidents of the United States: Harry S Truman, 1949*, Washington, D.C.: United States Government Printing Office, 1964, pp. 13–26.

10-3 John F. Kennedy, "Commencement Address at Yale University, June 11, 1962," in *Public Papers of the Presidents of the United States: John F. Kennedy, 1962*, Washington, D.C.: United States Government Printing Office, 1963, pp. 470–475.

10-4 Lyndon B. Johnson, "The Economic Report of the President, January 28, 1965," in *Public Papers of the Presidents of the United States: Lyndon B. Johnson, Volume I, 1965*, Washington, D.C.: United States Government Printing Office, 1966, pp. 103–117.

10-5 Richard M. Nixon, "Annual Budget Message to the Congress, Fiscal Year 1972, January 29, 1971," in *Public Papers of the Presidents of the United States: Richard M. Nixon, 1972*, Washington, D.C.: United States Government Printing Office, 1972, pp. 80–95.

11-1 Gerald R. Ford, "Annual Message to the Congress: The Economic Report of the President, January 26, 1976," in *Public Papers of the Presidents of the United States:*

Gerald R. Ford, 1976, Volume I, Washington, D.C.: United States Government Printing Office, 1979, pp. 85–91.

11-2 Walter W. Heller, "Statement of Walter W. Heller, Regents' Professor of Economics, University of Minnesota," *Hearings Before the Joint Economic Committee, Congress of the United States*, 94th Congress, 2nd Session, Part 2, Washington, D.C., United States Government Printing Office, 1976, pp. 280–286.

11-3 The Full Employment and Balanced Growth Act of 1978, Public Law 95–523, 95th Congress, 2nd Session, October 27, 1978. *United States Statutes At Large*, 95th Congress, volume 2, Washington, D.C., United States Government Printing Office, pp. 92 STAT. 1887– 92 STAT. 1908.

11-4 Milton Friedman, "Humphrey–Hawkins," *Newsweek*, August 2, 1976, p.55. Reprinted with permission.

11-5 Jimmy Carter, "Economic Renewal Plan, August 28, 1980," in *Public Papers of the Presidents of the United States: Jimmy Carter, 1980–81, Volume II*, Washington, D.C.: United States Government Printing Office, 1982, pp. 1585–1591.

12-1 Arthur B. Laffer, "Prepared Statement of Arthur B. Laffer—The Roth–Kemp Bill," *Hearings Before the Joint Economic Committee of the United States*, 95th Congress, 2nd Session, Part I, pp. 130–133, Washington, D.C., United States Government Printing Office, 1978.

12-2 Walter W. Heller, "Prepared Statement of Walter W. Heller—Tax Cuts, the Kemp–Roth Bill, and the Laffer Curve," *Hearings Before the Joint Economic Committee of the United States*, 95th Congress, 2nd Session, Part I, pp. 22–25, Washington, D.C., United States Government Printing Office, 1978.

12-3 Ronald Reagan, "Program for Economic Recovery, February 18, 1981," in *Public Papers of the Presidents of the United States: Ronald Reagan,1981*, Washington, D.C.: United States Government Printing Office, 1982, pp. 116–132.

13-1 William J. Clinton, "Address Before a Joint Session of Congress on Administration Goals, February 17, 1993," in *Public Papers of the Presidents of the United States: William J. Clinton, 1993, Volume I*, Washington, D.C.: United States Government Printing Office, 1994, pp. 113–122.

13-2 "Preamble" and "Objectives—Chapter One," *North American Free Trade Agreement, 1992*. Washington, D.C.: United States Government Printing Office, 1992, pp. iii, 1–1—1–3.

13-3 William J. Clinton, *Economic Report of the President, February, 1999*, Washington, D.C.: United States Government Printing Office, 1999, pp. 3–7.

13-4 George W. Bush, "Remarks on Signing the Economic Growth and Tax Relief Reconciliation Act of 2001, June 7, 2001," in *Public Papers of the Presidents of the United States: George W. Bush, 2001, Volume I*, Washington, D.C.: United States Government Printing Office, 2003, pp. 621–622.

Essays

1-1 Robert Paul Thomas, "A Quantitative Approach to the Study of the Effects of British Imperial Policy Upon Colonial Welfare," *The Journal of Economic History*, 25 (December, 1965): pp. 615–638. Reprinted with permission of Cambridge University Press.

1-2 Larry Sawers, "The Navigation Acts Revisited," *The Economic History Review*, 45:2 (1992) pp. 262–280.

2-1 George Rogers Taylor, *The Transportation Revolution, 1815–1860*, New York, Harper & Row, 1968, pp. 3, 5–6, 10, 13, 17–18, 26–27, 32, 34–37, 52, 56–58, 69–70, 72,

74, 102–103, 132–138, 153, 155–167, 169–170, 175, 396–398; originally published by Holt, Rinehart and Winston, 1951.

2-2 Douglass C. North, *Economic Growth of the United States 1790–1860*, 1st Edition, © 1961. Reprinted by permission of Pearson Education, Inc., Upper Saddle River, NJ.

3-1 Leland H. Jenks, "Railroads as an Economic Force in American Development," *The Journal of Economic History*, 4 (May, 1944). Reprinted with permission of Cambridge University Press.

3-2 Robert William Fogel, "A Quantitative Approach to the Study of Railroads in American Economic Growth," *The Journal of Economic History*, 22 (June, 1962). Reprinted with permission of Cambridge University Press.

4-1 Robert William Fogel and Stanley L. Engerman, *Time on the Cross: The Economics of American Negro Slavery*. Copyright © 1974 by Robert William Fogel and Stanley L. Engerman. Used by permission of W. W. Norton & Company, Inc.

4-2 Fred Bateman and Thomas Weiss, "Profitability of Antebellum Southern Manufacturing and the Investment Response," *A Deplorable Scarcity: The Failure of Industrialization in the Slave Economy* by Fred Bateman and Thomas Weiss. Copyright © 1981 by the University of North Carolina Press. Used by permission of the publisher. www.uncpress.unc.edu

5-1 Excerpts from Jeffrey G. Williamson and Peter H. Lindert, *American Inequality: A Macroeconomic History*, pp. 3–5; 67–73; 75; 281–282; 285–287. Copyright © 1980 by the Board of Regents of the University of Wisconsin System on behalf of the Institute for Research on Poverty. Reprinted with permission.

5-2 Robert A. Margo and Georgia C. Villaflor, "The Growth of Wages in Antebellum America: New Evidence," *The Journal of Economic History*, 47, (December 1987). Reprinted with permission of Cambridge University Press.

6-1 Selections from Jonathan Huges, *The Vital Few: The Entrpreneur and American Economic Progress* (1986). Reprinted by permission of Oxford University Press, Inc.

6-2 Selections from Glenn Porter and Harold C. Livesay, *Merchants and Manufacturers: Studies in the Changing Structure of 19th Century Marketing*, pp. 1–4, 10–12, 154–155, 158, 168–173, 192–198, 203–205, 211–213, 228–231. © 1971 The Johns Hopkins University Press. Reprinted with permission of the Johns Hopkins University Press.

7-1 John Kenneth Galbraith, "Cause and Consequence," excerpted from *The Great Crash 1929*, Boston: Houghton Mifflin, 1988, pp. 168–194. © 1954, 1955, 1961, 1972, 1979, 1988, 1997 by John Kenneth Galbraith. Reprinted by Permission of Houghton Mifflin Company. All Rights Reserved.

7-2 W. Elliot Brownlee, "The 1920s: A Glimpse of Modernity," in *The Dynamics of Ascent: A History of the American Economy*, New York: Alfred Knopf, 1974, pp. 264–284.

7-3 Eugene N. White, "The Stock Market Book and Crash of 1929 Revisited," *Journal of Economic Perspectives*, Vol. 4, No. 2 (Spring 1990), pp. 67–83.

8-1 Milton and Rose D. Friedman, "The Anatomy of Crisis…and the Failure of Policy," *Journal of Portfolio Management* 6 (Fall 1979): 15–21. Reprinted with permission.

8-2 Christina Romer, "The Nation in Depression," *Journal of Economic Perspectives* 7 (Spring 1993): 19–39. Reprinted by permission of the author.

9-1 E. Cary Brown, "Fiscal Policy in the 'Thirties: A Reappraisal," *American Economic Review*, 46 (December, 1956), pp. 857–879. Reprinted with permission.

9-2 Adapted from Robert Lekachman, "The General Theory," in *The Age of Keynes*, New York: Random House, 1966, pp. 78–111. © 1966 by Robert Lekachman. Reprinted by permission of Random House, Inc.. Reprinted in the U.K. by permission of Penguin Books.

9-3 Herbert Stein, "Lessons of World War II," in *The Fiscal Revolution in America*, Chicago: University of Chicago Press, 1969, pp. 169–196. Reprinted by permission of University of Chicago Press.

10-1 Jacob L. Mosak, "National Budgets and National Policy," *American Economic Review*, 36 (March, 1946), pp. 20–43. Reprinted by permission of the University of Chicago Press.

10-2 Excerpt from Arthur Okun, *The Political Economy of Prosperity* (Chapter Two). Reprinted by permission of the Brookings Institution Press.

10-3 William S Salant "The Spread of Keynesian Doctrines and Practices in the United States" in Peter A. Hall (ed.), *The Political Power of Economic Ideas*. © 1989 Princeton University Press. Reprinted by permission of Princeton University Press.

10-4 Walter W. Heller, "Is Monetary Policy Being Oversold?" in Milton Freidman and Walter W. Heller, *Monetary vs. Fiscal Policy*, New York: W.W. Norton, 1969, pp. 13–42. Used by permission of W.W. Norton & Company, Inc.

10-5 Milton Friedman, "Has Fiscal Policy Been Oversold?" in Milton Freidman and Walter W. Heller, *Monetary vs. Fiscal Policy*, New York: W.W. Norton, 1969, pp.43–62. Used by permission of W.W. Norton & Company, Inc.

11-1 Milton Friedman, "The Role of Monetary Policy," *American Economic Review*, 58 (March, 1968), pp. 1–17. Reprinted with permission.

11-2 Mark H. Willes, "'Rational Expectations' as a Counterrevolution," in Daniel Bell and Irving Kristol, eds, *The Crisis in Economic Theory*, New York: Basic Books, 1981, pp. 81–96. Reprinted with permission.

11-3 Paul Craig Roberts, "The Breakdown of the Keynesian Model," *Hearings Before the Joint Economic Committee of the United States*, 95th Congress, 2nd Session, Part 1, pp. 143–156, Washington, D.C., 1978. Reprinted with permission.

12-1 Uwe E. Reinhardt, "Reganomics, R.I.P.," *New Republic*, April 20, 1987, pp. 24–27. Reprinted with permission of the author.

12-2 Martin Feldstein, "Supply-side Economics: Old truths and New Claims," *The American Economic Review*, Vol. 76:2 May 1986. Reprinted with permission.

13-1 Joint Economic Committee of the United States, "Why Has the Budget Shifted from Deficit to Surplus?" from *Achieving Growth and Prosperity Through Freedom: A Compilation of 1999–2000 Joint Economic Committee Reports*, 106th Congress, 2nd Session, December 2000, Washington, D.C., 2001, pp. 78–81.

13-2 Robert Rubin, "Comments on Fiscal Policy in the 1990s" in Jeffrey Frankel and Peter Orszag, eds, *American Economic Policy in the 1990s*, Cambridge, MA, MIT Press, 2002, pp. 130–135. © 2002 Massachusetts Institute of Technology, by permission of The MIT Press.

13-3 N. Gregory Mankiw, "U.S. Monetary Policy During the 1990s" in Jeffrey Frankel and Peter Orszag, eds., *American Economic Policy in the 1990s*. Cambridge, MA, MIT Press, 2002, pp. 19–43. © 2002 Massachusetts Institute of Technology, by permission of The MIT Press.

E-1 Robert Whaples, "Where Is There Consensus Among American Economic Historians? The Results of a Survey on Forty Propositions," *The Journal of Economic History*, Vol. 55, No. 1 (Mar., 1995), pp. 139–154. Reprinted by permission of the author.

INDEX

An Economic History of the United States
From 1607 to the Present

Ronald E. Seavoy

With crisp prose and handy headers, *An Economic History of the United States* not only renders the complex simple to understand, but is a captivating read—no small feat for a survey half the length of the heavy textbook tomes on the market. It will prove an asset to college students and advanced scholars alike.

> *Jonathan J. Bean, Professor of History, Southern Illinois*

Nothing like Seavoy's work has been produced for several decades. Anyone interested in how and why the U.S. economy was propelled to world leadership in a short time will find this work of value.

> *David O. Whitten, Professor of Economics, Auburn University*

Covering more than 400 years, from the founding of Jamestown to the global business economy of today, *An Economic History of the United States* provides an accessible and informative survey that illustrates how the American economy has transformed the nation from its humble beginnings as a British colony into one of the world's foremost superpowers.

Beginning with the commercialization of agriculture in the pre-colonial era, through the development of banks and industrialization in the nineteenth century, and ending with the globalization that has come to characterize today's business economy, Ronald E. Seavoy offers a comprehensive overview of the history of the American nation and the complex sociopolitical and economic forces that have shaped it since its inception.

Some of the themes covered include

* The colonial political economy and indentured servitude
* The growth of the North Atlantic commercial empire
* The rise of railroads and western expansion
* The grange movement, Populism, and agrarian discontent
* How the mobilization of capital accelerated industrialization
* The emergence of new commercial institutions after World War II
* The creation of consumer culture
* The role of cooperative institutions in creating the global economy

Ronald E. Seavoy is Professor Emeritus of History at Bowling Green State University in Bowling Green, Ohio. He is the author of *The Origins and Growth of the Global Economy, Subsistence and Economic Development, The American Peasantry, Famine in Peasant Societies, Famine in East Africa,* and *The Origins of the American Business Corporation, 1784-1855.*

ISBN 13: 978-0-415-97981-8 (pbk)   ISBN 10: 0-415-97981-1 (pbk)
ISBN 13: 978-0-415-97980-1 (hbk)   ISBN 10: 0-415-97980-3 (hbk)

Consumerism in World History
2nd Edition

Peter N. Stearns

Reviews of the first edition:

'This is a clever book.' — *Business History*

The desire to acquire luxury goods and leisure services is a basic force in modern life. *Consumerism in World History* explores both the historical origins and world-wide appeal of this relatively modern phenomenon. By relating consumerism to other issues in world history, this book forces reassessment of our understanding of both consumerism and global history.

This second edition of *Consumerism in World History* draws on recent research of the consumer experience in the West and Japan, while also examining societies less renowned for consumerism, such as Africa. Every chapter has been updated and new features include:

- a new chapter on Latin America
- Russian and Chinese developments since the 1990s
- the changes involved in trying to bolster consumerism as a response to recent international threats
- examples of consumerist syncretism, as in efforts to blend beauty contests with traditional culture in Kerala.

With updated suggested reading, the second edition of *Consumerism in World History* is essential reading for all students of world history.

ISBN13 978-0-415-39586-1 (hbk)   ISBN10 0-415-39586-0 (hbk)
ISBN13 978-0-415-39587-8 (pbk)   ISBN10 0-415-39587-9 (pbk)

Hagley Perspectives on Business and Culture

Hagley Perspectives on Business and Culture presents new outlooks from leading scholars in the emerging fields of business and consumer history. Accessible and engaging for students and scholars, each book presents ten to fifteen original essays, with introductions from the volume editors, on topics ranging from food studies to gender, technology, and consumerism.

The Hagley Series is edited by **Philip Scranton** and **Roger Horowitz** in conjunction with the prestigious Hagley Center for the History of Business, Technology, and Society in Wilmington, Delaware.

Beauty and Business: Commerce, Gender, and Culture in Modern America
Beauty and Business leading historians set out to provide an important cultural context for the commodification of beauty. With topics ranging from the social role of the African American hair salon, the sexual dynamics of bathing suits and shirt-collars, and the deeper meanings of corsets, to what the Avon lady tells us about changing American values, these essays force us to reckon with the ways that beauty has been made, bought, and sold in modern America.

Boys and Their Toys?: Masculinity, Technology, and Class in America
Boys and Their Toys is a collection of essays that places masculinity and work at the core of class formation. Negotiating the divide between *respectable manhood* and *rough manhood* this book explores masculinity at work and at play through provocative essays on labor unions, railroads, vocational training programs, and NASCAR racing. This groundbreaking collection begins new insights into the complexities of masculinity, and its relationship to class and society.

Industrializing Organisms: Introducing Evolutionary History
Everyone knows Darwin's theory of natural selection, but what about his idea of artificial selection—how humans, not nature, rework natural organisms to meet our needs? *Industrializing Organisms* brings us to the threshold of the new field of evolutionary history—from the mobilization of war horses in the 19th century to today's engineered plants and manipulated animals.

Technological Fix: Visions, Trials, and Solutions
The term "technological fix" should mean a fix provided by technology—a solution for all of our problems. Instead, technological fix has come to mean a cheap, quick fix using inappropriate technology that usually creates more problems than it solves. This collection sets out the distinction between a technological fix and a true technological solution, addressing such "fixes" as artificial hearts, industrial agriculture and climate engineering. These essays examine our need to turn to technology for solutions to all of our problems.

Commodifying Everything: Relationships of the Market
"Commodification" refers most explicitly to the activities of turning things into commodities and of commercializing that which is not commercial in essence. *Commodifying Everything* is a fascinating take on creating consumer products and consumer identities when what's for sale goes well beyond the thing itself. It will be a course-in-a-box for instructors who want to teach their students about commodification.

Available at all good bookshops
For ordering and further information please visit:
www.routledge.com